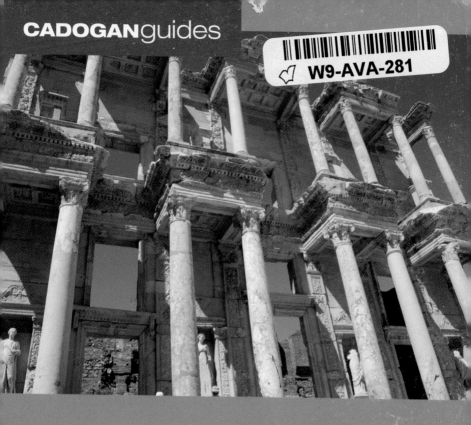

TURKEY

*'a rich, comfortable place, living on the crest
of the wave of Classical civilization.'*

Michael Pauls

About the Guide

The full-colour introduction gives the authors' overview of the country, together with suggested itineraries and a regional 'where to go' map and feature to help you plan your trip.

Illuminating and entertaining cultural chapters on local history, culture, food, drink and everyday life give you a rich flavour of the country.

Planning Your Trip starts with the basics of when to go, getting there and getting around, coupled with other useful information, including a section for disabled travellers. The Practical A–Z deals with all the essential information and contact details that you may need while you are away.

The regional chapters are arranged in a loose touring order, with plenty of public transport and driving information. The author's top 'Don't Miss' ✪ sights are highlighted at the start of each chapter.

A language and pronunciation guide, a glossary of cultural terms, ideas for further reading and a comprehensive index can be found at the end of the book.

Although everything we list in this guide is personally recommended, our authors inevitably have their own favourite places to eat and stay. Whenever you see this Author's Choice ★ icon beside a listing, you will know that it is a little bit out of the ordinary.

Hotel Price Guide (see also p.75)

Luxury	€€€€€	€240 and above	480 YTL and above
Very Expensive	€€€€	€100–240	200–480 YTL
Expensive	€€€	€60–100	120–200 YTL
Moderate	€€	€25–60	50–120 YTL
Inexpensive	€	under €25	under 50 YTL

Restaurant Price Guide (see also p.80)

Very Expensive	€€€€	€35 and above	70 YTL and above
Expensive	€€€€	€20–35	40–70 YTL
Moderate	€€	€10–20	20–40 YTL
Inexpensive	€	under €10	under 20 YTL

About the Authors

Dana Facaros and Michael Pauls have written over 30 books for Cadogan Guides. They have lived all over Europe with their son and daughter and are currently ensconced in a old farmhouse in southwestern France.

5th Edition published 2009

01 INTRODUCING TURKEY

I n our travels from the Aegean coast to the Armenian border, we have met every sort of traveller – carefree young backpackers and chic sophisticates, beachcombers and folklore scholars, Canadians, Iranians, and people from every country in between. Some are regular visitors to Turkey, and almost all of the first-timers say they'll be back as soon as they can. Don't be surprised if you find yourself among them. Turkey's coastal resorts, dramatic landscapes and hospitable people make the country attractive to every holidaymaker, but there is more to it than broad beaches and a touch of the exotic conjured up in a puff of smoke from a traditional water pipe. Turkey has more classical ruins than Greece and more Islamic monuments than Arabia. Its attractions range from the huge, decapitated stone kings of Mount Nemrut, to the exquisite and refined tile work in the imperial mosques of Istanbul. You can ski in an Alpine-style winter resort or bathe in the Mediterranean sea in November; watch the dervishes whirl in December and greased wrestlers tussle in the spring. You can take in the renowned biblical sites, from the Harran of Abraham to the Ephesus of St Paul, or go on a gourmet tour, sampling ingenious dishes first prepared for the Ottoman sultans.

Whatever you have heard about Turkey, behind the enigmatic face it turns to the outside world there is a land and a people whose unaffected charm and surprising hospitality will make your travels easy and pleasant. For all its exoticism, Turkey is a country where visitors usually find themselves feeling entirely at home. The land that gave the world the cherry and the tulip is a land of many small delights. You'll probably bring home souvenirs – everyone

Previous page: Library of Celsus, Ephesus, p.258

Above, from top: Sumela Monastery, p.374; tea glasses

Above: Pots, Çavuşin, Cappadocia, p.447

who sets foot inside a Turkish bazaar does – and the low prices may make you stay longer than you intended. The best part of Turkey, though, is free – landscapes untouched by industry, goatherds and their charges wandering through the olive groves and ruined temples, women gossiping around the neighbourhood well, banana-shaped dwellings carved from the rocks of Cappadocia, an amiable mystic demonstrating the 99 names of God inscribed on the human palm, hundreds of giggling, well-scrubbed schoolchildren in their blue smocks snaking single file through a museum at a breathless pace, only pausing to ask you in earnest English, 'Is Turkey beautiful?'.

It is indeed.

A Little Geography

Turkey is more or less a rectangle, 400 miles wide (north to south) and almost 1,000 miles long (east to west), at once in Europe and Asia and the Middle East. The variety of its topography tends to surprising and dramatic extremes; Turkey is a country of verdant forests and of vast, empty plains, of rivers and lakes and scorched desert wastes. Wherever you go, you are never far from **mountains**; 89 have peaks that climb to 10,000ft and above, and both the Mediterranean and Black Sea coasts are bordered by tall ranges. The great Anatolian plateau is an extension of the Himalaya-Alpine range that rises gradually as you head east to culminate at majestic Mount Ararat (Ağrı Dağ), 16,786ft high. The Taurus mountains stretching along the southern coast are the largest chain in the country, sweeping upwards in an arch towards Malatya where they become the Anti-Taurus mountains, the roof of Turkey.

With so many heights, Turkey cannot help but be a land of **lakes**; the most famous is soapy Lake Van, far out in the east, but there is an entire district of big lakes around Isparta in the southwest, an interesting corner of Turkey not yet much bothered with tourism. There are **rivers** too, many flowing down from the Anti-Taurus mountains; the Tigris (Dicle), the Euphrates (Fırat), the Halys (Kızılırmak) and the Yeşilırmak. Another river famous in antiquity, the Maeander (Menderes), flows from the Taurus mountains to the Aegean, its annual floods creating the country's most fertile valley.

Geography has a lot to teach us about Anatolia's history. The west has big rivers that flow all year, but none of them is navigable. The coasts are also ringed with mountains. Because of these two factors, Anatolia's coasts have always had different destinies from the interior – as in ancient times, when the coast was populated by Greeks, facing an interior under Persian rule; the two had little to do with one other. Greeks continued to populate much of the coasts until 1923. Until the modern Turkish republic, there has never been a state with an inland capital that also controlled the coasts.

Above: wheat fields, near Antalya, p.322

Below: Cappadocian valley, near Göreme, p.440

Where to Go

This guide starts with incomparable **Istanbul**, the main attraction for most visitors to Turkey. After that, there is a brief foray into **Thrace**, the three per cent of Turkey on the European continent, which includes Edirne and the battlefields of Gallipoli as well as Bursa with its magnificent mosques, and the **Marmara**.

Turkey's coasts, separated from the interior by difficult mountains, are a world unto themselves, and we have grouped them together, beginning with the **Aegean coast**, with its famous resorts and Greek ruins, as well as ancient Troy and modern İzmir. The **southern coast** divides neatly into four distinct regions: lovely Lycia, with its spectacular coastline; the flat Pamphylian coast, jam-packed with ancient ruined cities; the pine-scented, largely undiscovered Cilician coast; and finally the Hatay, the hinterlands of ancient Antioch, bordering on Syria. The cooler, less touristed **Black Sea coast**, where tea, hazelnuts and cherries grow, is considered next.

We have quartered **Anatolia**, the interior: first the **northwest**, with the archaeological sites of the Phrygians and Hittites, Ankara, Turkey's thoroughly up-to-date capital, and the pretty Yeşilırmak valley. The **southwest** offers the little-visited lake district around Eğirdir, Konya, the city of the whirling dervishes, and the well-known natural wonderland of Cappadocia. In the **northeast**, wide open spaces are the rule, and lots of snow in winter; the star attractions are the ruined city of Ani and Mount Ararat. And the **southeast**, hot and dry and formidably exotic, with fascinating cities like Şanlıurfa and Diyarbakır, the bizarre mountaintop shrine of Nemrut Dağ, and the most memorable scenery of all, around Lake Van.

Opposite page:
Ballooning in
Cappadocia, p.441

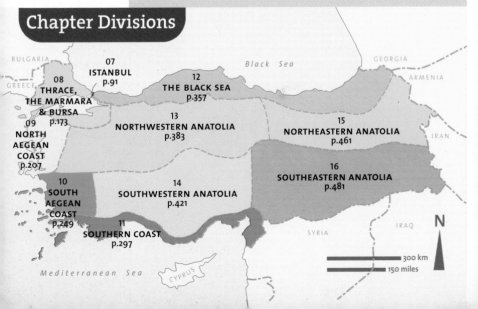

Chapter Divisions

BULGARIA

GREECE

07 ISTANBUL p.91

08 THRACE, THE MARMARA & BURSA p.173

09 NORTH AEGEAN COAST p.207

10 SOUTH AEGEAN COAST p.249

11 SOUTHERN COAST p.297

12 THE BLACK SEA p.357

13 NORTHWESTERN ANATOLIA p.383

14 SOUTHWESTERN ANATOLIA p.421

15 NORTHEASTERN ANATOLIA p.461

16 SOUTHEASTERN ANATOLIA p.481

Black Sea

GEORGIA

ARMENIA

IRAN

SYRIA

IRAQ

CYPRUS

Mediterranean Sea

N

300 km

150 miles

Istanbul

The fabulous capital of two great empires in its long history, Istanbul is now a city of twelve million people. Between Ottoman minarets and modern glass skyscrapers there's a lot to see , and a sparkling urban life to enjoy. And the view over the Golden Horn in the morning light is something few places on earth can match.

Above, clockwise from top left: Blue Mosque, p.107; Bosphorus Bridge, p.154; Topkapı Palace, p.112; bed of Atatürk, Dolmabahçe Palace, p.150

Itinerary 1: A Week in Istanbul

Above: Frescoes, Kariye, p.140

Below: Ortaköy Camii, p.155

Day 1 Join the crowds and do the inevitable: the **Aya Sofya**, the **Blue Mosque**. Take a walk around the **Divan Yolu** and the **Sultanahmet** district to get to know the city.

Day 2 A hard day's slog through the endless attractions and museums of the **Topkapı Palace**: the Harem and the Sultan's pavilions, the Museum of Archaeology and the Çinili Kiosk.

Day 3 Shopping day! Spend the morning in the **Covered Bazaar**, then explore the back lanes of the market district and have a look at Mimar Sinan's great **Süleymaniye Mosque**.

Day 4 Head over to **Beyoğlu**, the old 'European' quarter. Start at the lively Galata Bridge and work your way up through the back streets, the Tünel and the İstiklâl tramway; lunch and entertainment are provided in the colourful fish market, the **Balık Pazarı**.

Day 5 Ride some minibuses, and get to know the newer quarters of the city beyond Beyoğlu. Have a look at the **Dolmabahçe Palace**, the wonderful **Soldiers' Museum** or the pavilions of **Yıldız Park**.

Day 6 Devote a day to relaxation: take the **cruise** up the Bosphorus on the regular ferry service, looking out for sights like the great **bridge** and the **Ortaköy Camii**; and stop at one of the villages along the way for a seafood lunch.

Day 7 Spend a day exploring the fascinating back streets of old **Stamboul**. Among the many venerable Byzantine churches in this area, don't miss the frescoes of the **Kariye**. Take some time to inspect the greatest urban fortifications ever built, the **Theodosian walls**.

Above, left:
Safranbolu, pp.361–2

Above right, from top:
village house; Orhan Gazi
mosque, Bursa, pp.192

Turkey's Other Exotic Cities

Half Europe and half Asia, modern Turkey's other towns and cities offer as many dramatic contrasts as its past. Turks are open about their culture and their religion, and you can go in as deep as you like; savour the peace sitting in a thousand year-old mosque, admire the stonework of a caravanserai, or simply enjoy smoking a *narghile* in the cafés.

- Bursa, the first Ottoman capital, pp.189–201
- Konya, home of the Selçuk sultans, and the Mevlâna, pp.430–9
- Şanlıurfa, holy city since the time of Abraham, p.487–91
- Edirne, with Mimar Sinan's masterpiece mosque, pp.175–9
- Sivas, a medieval oasis of culture, pp.414–15
- Diyarbakır, capital of the Kurds, with a medieval style all its own, pp.504–10
- Safranbolu, the most Turkish of small towns, pp.361–2

Above: Green Mosque, Bursa, p.194

Right, from left: Whirling dervish, Konya, p.435; caravanserai stonework

Natural Wonders

At 301,400 square miles, Turkey is over three times the size of the UK, and twice as big as California. Within that wide land is a tremendous diversity of landscapes and climates: in a day you can travel from the fringes of the Syrian desert to balmy Mediterranean beach resorts, from the fertile sesame fields and green hills of the centre to places on the high Anatolian plateau that get 40 feet of snow a year.

Above: Fairy chimneys, near Göreme, p.445

Below: Sesame fields; Pamukkale, p.277; forest house, Black Sea coast, pp.358–82

- The dramatic, deeply forested Lycian and Black Sea coasts
- The geological wonders of Cappadocia, pp.440–60
- Ararat, the 'roof of the world' of the ancient Middle East, p.479
- Lake Van, ringed with mountains and wild flowers, pp.513–22
- Unique limestone forms at Pamukkale, the 'Cotton Castle', p.277
- The lake district of the southwest, pp.423–40

Above: Göcek, near Fethiye, Southern Coast, p.302

Five Thousand Miles of Coastline

Turkey's seas are the seas over which the Greek heroes sailed for Troy, where the Argonauts searched for the Golden Fleece. They've been messing about in boats ever since, and, for many, a trip to Turkey means a spell on the water: sailing on a 'Blue Cruise', beachcombing, water sports, riding the ferry up the Bosphorus or diving for a look at archaeological treasures beneath the sea.

Low prices, dreamy seasides and good food make this country one of the best bets for Mediterranean beach lounging.

- Behramkale/Assos: arty and idyllic, pp.216–18
- Ayvalık: low-key and laid-back, pp.220–23
- Eski Foça: small bays and crystal waters, pp.232–3
- The Çeşme Peninsula: golden coves and urbane nightlife, pp.244–8
- The Bodrum Peninsula: beaches tucked under boutique hotels and villas, pp.289–92
- Dalyan: delicious shady sands, p.300
- Patara: wide beaches, with an ancient city to explore, pp.307–308
- Antalya: cosmopolitan beach life in a stunning setting, pp.318–21
- Alanya: lovely, historic town with 22km of non-stop beach, pp.334–8
- Kızkalesi: sands opposite a castle floating in the sea, pp.343–6

Above: Lycian tomb

The Presence of the Past

With the recent discoveries of monumental 13,000-year-old ruins at Göbekli Tepe, Turkey now holds the title of 'the birthplace of civilization'. No country on earth has a bigger or more diverse collection of archaeological remains. The Greeks left nearly as much here as in Greece itself, and before them this land gave birth to the Hittite Empire, the Phrygian Empire, the Lydians of old King Croesus, the Lycians, Carians, Urartians and more.

- Göbekli Tepe, history's 'new beginning', p.491
- Hattusas, metropolis of the Hittite Empire, pp.406–11
- Phrygian temples at 'Midas City', pp.390–92
- The underground cities of Cappadocia, pp.449–51
- Mountaintop colossi on Nemrut Dağı, p.498–500
- The rock-cut tombs and temples of Lycia, pp.300–318
- The cliff tombs of Myra, near Demre, p.315
- The acropolis of ancient Pergamon, pp.226–8
- The Temple of Athena at Assos, p.218
- The ruins of Roman Ephesus, pp.255–60
- Ankara's Museum of Anatolian Civilizations, pp.401–402
- The sunken city of Kekova, pp.313–14
- Roman mosaics at Antakya and Gaziantep, p.354 and p.486
- The Byzantine monuments of Istanbul, pp.94–172

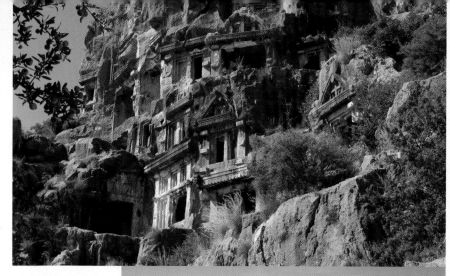

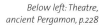

*Above: Rock-cut tombs,
Myra, p.315*

Right: Assos, p.218

*Below left: Theatre,
ancient Pergamon, p.228*

*Below right: Kekova
sunken city, pp.313–14*

01 Introduction | The Presence of the Past

Itinerary 2: Beaches and Lost Cities: Along the Mediterranean Coasts

This trip can be done by car or on the local buses. No one's ever in a hurry on this coast, so take this itinerary as a brief outline only, and stay a while at whatever place catches your fancy.

Day 1 Start at the top of the Aegean coast at Çanakkale (p.213), with the most storied ruins of them all, at Troy (p.209).

Day 2 Pretty beaches and islets along the beautiful **Gulf of Edremit** (p.218), with a look at the ruins of **Assos** (pp.216–18).

Days 3–4 Proceed to the laid-back resort of **Ayvalık** (pp.220–3), where you won't mind spending a day, and then take in the ruins of one of the most cultured Hellenistic cities, **Pergamon** (Bergama, pp.224–9).

Days 5–6 Next comes a stop at another friendly resort, **Eski Foça** (pp.232–3), on the way to **İzmir** (pp.234–40). The one big ancient city (Smyrna) that was never abandoned has attractions and a lively urban scene; you can also use it as a base for a trip to the ruins of Sardis, capital of old King Croesus and the Lydians.

Day 7 South of İzmir, lost cities line the coast thickly: **Colophon**, **Notium**, **Claros** (all p.251). End up at **Selçuk** (p.252) or **Kuşadası** (p.261), for a tour of the grandest ruins of all, at **Ephesus** (p.255).

Days 8–9 Two of the ancient towns most worth visiting are little, well-preserved **Priene** (p.264) and **Didyma** (p.269). In the same area are the beach at **Altınkum** and lovely **Lake Bafa** (p.270).

Day 10 There are long distances to cover today, on scenic roads. You might wish to take a detour and an extra day to experience the frenetic resort life of **Bodrum** (p.284) or **Marmaris** (p.292); otherwise continue on to **Fethiye** (p.302) and the Lycian coast.

Day 11 Visit two ancient Lycian cities: **Xanthos** (p.304), the capital of this enigmatic nation, and **Patara** (p.307), which also has a lovely beach at hand. Finish at **Kalkan** (p.308).

Day 12 The charming resort town of **Kaş** (p.311) is worth at least a day, with time to look at Lycian tombs, the submerged city of Aperlae, and the rock-cut temples of **Myra** (p.315).

Day 13 Continue eastwards through **Finike** (p.315), see the ruins of **Phaselis** (p.317) and if it's dark you might see the Chimaera, the natural flame on **Mt Olympos** (p.316) before you get to Antalya.

Day 14 Antalya (p.318) has a beach, a fine archaeological museum and many other delights, and if you have more time you can continue on to the towns of the Pamphylian coast with their exceptional Greek and Roman ruins: **Perge** (p.324), **Aspendos** (p.327), and its great theatre, and **Side** (p.329), where a pleasant holiday town has grown up right in the middle of the ruins.

Above: Traditional gulet

Below, from top: Beach, Patara, pp.307–308; stone carving, Demre, pp.314–15

CONTENTS

History

02

Turkey's present inhabitants are relative latecomers, and the millennia of history before their arrival witnessed an incredible pageant of peoples and cultures. If we learned in school that early history belonged almost entirely to Egypt and the Fertile Crescent, it is only because chance led the archaeologists there first. With two recent remarkable archaeological finds, the beginnings of history have been pushed way back, and the mountains and plains of Anatolia can now also stake their claim as one of the birthplaces of civilization.

Ancient History to 2500 BC

Discoveries in the Karain Cave and other sites around Antalya take habitation in Turkey back as far as Neanderthal man, but the really exciting event has been the recent (1994) excavation of an advanced Neolithic culture 11,000 years old, with complex architecture and art, at Göbekli Tepe, near Şanliurfa. Before that, the big news came from **Çatal Höyük** near Konya, where an accomplished and artistic

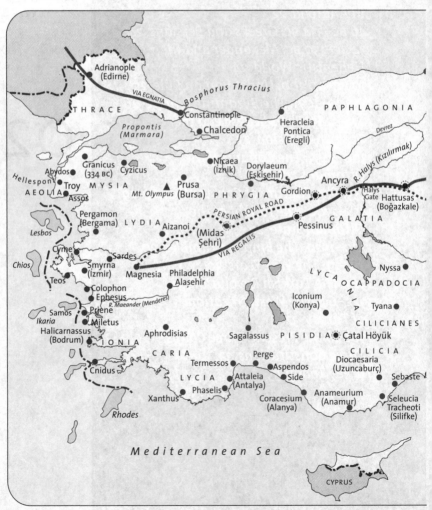

culture 9,000 years old was uncovered. This was a peaceful, matriarchal town that lived on agriculture and the obsidian trade. It grew into a city of some 32 acres, the oldest truly urban culture yet discovered. Its chubby goddesses and bull-horn shrines, along with the rest of its artworks, are in the Ankara Museum. The latest levels of the excavations show evidence of fire and strife, and we can take Çatal Höyük's end, *c.* 5500 BC, as the beginning of the first dark age. The Neolithic cultures that replaced it, as at **Mersin** and **Hacılar**, were not nearly as sophisticated.

2500 BC–1180 BC: The Bronze Age

After its great beginnings Anatolian civilization entered a period of little interest, falling behind Egypt and Mesopotamia. Revival came with the **Hattian culture**, another recent discovery, about which little is yet known. The Hatti people flourished in central Anatolia *c.* 2500–2000 BC, caused their neighbours little trouble, and created some of the finest works of art of their age. At this time,

Ancient Sites

a separate Bronze Age culture began to develop around **Troy**, more closely related to the peoples of the Aegean than to those of Anatolia.

Around 2000 BC, a new nation arrived from the Balkans, the **Hittites**, a warrior aristocracy who imposed themselves on the Hatti and founded a great capital at **Hattuşaş**, east of Ankara. They introduced writing to Asia Minor by learning the Assyrian cuneiform and later developing their own hieroglyphics to fit their Indo-European tongue. They also gave Anatolia its first empire, a Bronze Age superpower that contended with Egypt for the mastery of the Middle East. Throughout this era, Hittite control over the coastal areas was tenuous at best. Their records show constant problems with the Kingdom of Arzawa, in the southwest of the peninsula, the 'Lukka Lands' (Lycia) and a people called the **Ahhiyawa** (probably the Mycenaean Greeks, the Achaeans of Homer). Besides Greece proper, the Ahhiyawans ruled a bit of the Anatolian coast, with a capital there called Millewanda, probably Miletus. About 1180, their empire came to a sudden end at the hands of unknown invaders from the west (possibly the Phrygians). The slender evidence available suggests a period of warfare, migrations and famines all through the 12th century. A mixed multitude, called the 'Sea Peoples' in Egyptian records, seem to have ranged over Anatolia and the Levant, briefly threatening even Egypt; the Achaeans were one of the nations listed among them (the other tribes later spread across the Mediterranean, including the Sicels of Sicily, the Sards, the Etruscans, the Phrygians and the Philistines). This period of catastrophes, which also witnessed the fall of Troy, sent Asia Minor into another dark age.

1180 BC–546 BC: New Nations in Anatolia

Political and cultural unity in Anatolia died with the fall of the Hittites, and for centuries to come the region was divided among a number of new peoples, many of whom had migrated into the region only after the Hittite collapse.

Urartians

During the Hittite empire, a confederation of two peoples, forming the 'Hurri-Mitanni state', lived precariously as a buffer between the Hittites and Assyria. Successors to the Hurrians, a related people, the Urartians appeared in the region around Lake Van in the 12th century BC. They called themselves the Biainili, but as the Urartians (the name by which they are known in the Assyrian chronicles) they gave their name to Mount Ararat. An Urartian state gradually coalesced, reaching its greatest extent under King Sarduri II, c. 750 BC. Assyrian King Tiglath-Pileser III soon cut them down to size, and the Scythians finished them off in 609 BC.

Late Hittite Kingdoms

These survived all over southeastern Anatolia, usually as Assyrian dependencies such as Malatya, Maraş and Carchemish. **Kizzuwadna**, roughly all of what would later be called Cilicia, was throughout the period ruled by relatives of the Hittite kings. Though politically powerless, they carried on the traditions of Hittite art.

Phrygians

This people, talented in music and art, took the place of the Hittites in much of west central Anatolia; their real name was the Mushki, or Moschians. A little empire, ruled by kings alternately named Midas and Gordius, flourished until about 695 BC, when it was wrecked by an invasion of Cimmerians. The Lydians picked up the pieces in 650, and replaced Phrygia as the dominant power. The Phrygian capital was Gordium, west of Ankara. After the conquest, a Phrygian state lived on in the hills south of Eskişehir. A pastoral people, the Phrygians exported wool to the Greeks and diverted themselves with their orgiastic cult of Cybele and their music. They claimed to have invented the pan-pipes; Marsyas, the mythological flautist who had the bad judgement to enter a contest against Apollo, was a Phrygian.

Greeks

Recent finds around İzmir suggest that Greeks began expanding into Anatolia's coasts as early as the 11th century. The colonization was not a unified movement, but undertaken individually by Greek cities, and colonies long retained the tribal characters of their founders: the Aeolians in the north, around Troy and Assos; Ionians in the centre; and the latecomers, the Dorians, in the south. Pamphylia, the 'land of all tribes' on the southern coast, may also have been colonized early.

The cities of Asia Minor never worried much about political unity. The self-sufficient city-state was the model, and the greatest of these was **Miletus**, which by the 8th century was probably the leading commercial and sea power of the Aegean. After c. 700 BC, the Greek city-states found themselves blocked by the power of Lydia, and unable to expand their territories further inland. Instead, they moved into sparsely populated coastal areas further north. Miletus took the lead, founding **Abydus** (Çanakkale) and other towns on the Marmara and Black Sea, while the Megarans founded a number of colonies including **Byzantium**.

Lydians

The wealthy and commercially minded Lydians lived to the east of İzmir, but in their heyday in the 6th century BC they controlled an empire that included a vast area of western Anatolia. Under kings like the famous Croesus, the Lydians were a contented, blissfully decadent people who exported perfumes and other luxury goods around the Mediterranean. Ancient writers credit them with the invention of money. Before 546 BC, when the Persians under Cyrus put a brutally sudden end to Lydia as an independent power, its kings held sway over all the Greek coastal cities.

Carians

One of the more obscure nations, the Carians, or Lelegians, were related to the Lydians and originally occupied the area from Miletus to Lake Köyceğiz; they are mentioned in Homer as allies of the Trojans. Though the Carians may once have been an important sea power, the Greeks pushed them from the coast at an early date. The interior (roughly between modern Aydın and Muğla) remained Carian throughout antiquity, though subject to ever-increasing Greek cultural influence.

Lycians

On the southwest coast of Anatolia, the Lycians, like the Phrygians and Lydians, were a native people speaking an Indo-European language who were later Hellenized by the Greeks. Their origins are lost in time, though opinion in antiquity had them coming from Minoan Crete and founding Miletus before migrating to the southern coast. Although they were mentioned by Homer, their relative inaccessibility and reputation for fierceness kept them out of the mainstream of history; their most remarkable accomplishments were the lovely rock tombs they carved into cliffs all over Turkey's southwestern coasts.

None of these states was destined to last long. The aggressive and brutal **Assyrian Empire** (860–612 BC) kept Anatolia in constant turmoil. Even worse, tribes of mounted warriors from across the Caucasian mountains were constantly marauding through Anatolia. The Cimmerians learned cavalry tactics from the Scythians; in the 7th century BC, they occupied most of the eastern half of Anatolia. The **Medes** (c. 620–549 BC), who founded the first great Persian empire, destroyed the Assyrians and the Cimmerians, and succeeded to both their domains.

546 BC–334 BC: Greeks and Persians

The Achaemenid kings of Persia, who replaced the Medes in 549 BC, created an empire for themselves within two generations. After Cyrus's conquest of Lydia had given them undisputed control of the whole of Anatolia, the Persians sent their general Harpagus on a campaign through Ionia to enforce the submission of the Greek cities. **Satraps**, or governors, were appointed over the various provinces, and, although Persian rule was on the whole just, unoppressive and enlightened, the Greeks, accustomed to governing themselves, found it hard to take. An Ionian revolt in 499 BC, supported by Athens, was brutally crushed by the Persians, and resulted in the burning of Miletus. Persian military power was now embroiled with Greece at the height of its Classical age, and a confrontation was inevitable. Under King Xerxes, the Persians invaded Greece in 490 and were defeated at Marathon. The second attempt, ten years later, again resulted in defeats at the battles of Salamis and Plataea. In the aftermath, the Greek cities liberated themselves and joined the Athenian-led alliance called the **Delian Confederacy**. Athenian ambition and arrogance, however, led to this league of equals gradually becoming more of an Athenian empire – the cause of the long, bloody **Peloponnesian War**, in which Athens and her allies were finally defeated by the **Spartans** (404 BC). Even though the Asian cities had generally managed to avoid the fighting, their fate was no longer theirs to decide. The exhausted Spartans could not maintain control, and by the King's Peace of 387 BC they reverted to Persian rule.

From the beginning, these cities were more than colonies. An integral part of the Greek world, they contributed more than their share to the culture of Greece's golden age, despite usually being under foreign rule. Homer, who lived in the 8th or early 7th century BC, was probably born at Smyrna. In the 6th century, the Ionian cities, notably Miletus, produced the first Western philosophers: Anaximander, Thales, Xenophanes and Heraclitus. Art and architecture also flourished. The first temples were only built in the 8th century, but by the 6th century Ephesus and Samos were contending with the wealthy Greek cities of Sicily to build the biggest temples in the world.

334–150 BC: Alexander and the Hellenistic World

The Persian army, meanwhile, had not been keeping up with battle tactics. The Greek **hoplite**, or armoured infantryman, was the ultimate weapon of the day, and it only needed one Greek state to afford enough of them to really make a splash.

Thanks to a chance find of gold, that state was **Macedonia**, and Philip of Macedon recruited his forces with the announced purpose of a crusade against the Persians. After his assassination, the job was left to his son **Alexander the Great**. With 40,000 men, he crossed the Hellespont in the spring of 334 BC, and almost immediately defeated a large Persian army. Within a year, Alexander had conquered all of Anatolia, opening up the way to turning the Persian Empire into his own.

Soon after Alexander's untimely death in 323, his generals carved up the newly created empire for themselves. Anatolia fell to Antigonus, but his attempts at reunifying the empire led the others to combine against him, and his cause died at the Battle of Ipsus in 301 BC. Another general, Lysimachus, seized Anatolia, and was in turn beaten by Selucus in 280 BC; the **Seleucid Kingdom** the latter founded stretched from the Aegean to India, and was to last over a century. Meanwhile, **Cappadocia** had become a virtually independent kingdom, and another former general, Philetarus, who had grabbed Alexander's treasure after his death, used the booty to found the city state of **Pergamon**, which grew in power and influence for another century and came to control much of western Anatolia by c. 150 BC.

Meanwhile, Anatolia was becoming thoroughly Hellenized. Trade and commerce boomed; vast and wealthy new cities appeared, such as Pergamon and Antioch, while older ones, particularly Smyrna and Ephesus, grew to metropolitan size. Greece proper was beginning its long economic decline, partly thanks to the emigration to Asia sponsored by the Seleucids and other rulers, and Anatolia's new wealth and power gradually made it the centre of the Greek world. Most of the ruins you will see in Turkey date from this time, if not from the centuries of Roman rule; Anatolia had another 800 years of calm and prosperity ahead of it.

One unusual event of the time was the invasion in 275 BC of the **Galatians**, Celts really, who installed themselves in the centre of the peninsula. Though eventually defeated by the Pergamenes, the Celts stayed, and their red-haired and freckled descendants can still be seen in Ankara and in many other Turkish towns today.

150 BC–AD 300: Under Roman Rule

Roman control came gradually and irresistibly, a province at a time. With Pergamon and Rhodes as close allies, the Romans carefully watched their influence grow through the 3rd century, while they were busy with their struggle to the death against Carthage. An ambitious Seleucid king, **Antiochus III** (223–187 BC), conquered Syria and Palestine and forged an alliance with Macedon against Rome. The legions marched in and bloodied them both. By AD 146, Greece was under direct Roman rule, and the Seleucid kingdom a mere fragment. In 133 the last king of Pergamon saw the writing on the wall and willed his kingdom to Rome.

Outside their Pergamene windfall, the Romans never ruled much of Anatolia directly; there were client kings, as in Armenia and Cappadocia, and many of the Greek cities maintained control over their internal affairs, and the right to mint their own coins. The Romans were happy to soak the wealthy cities with taxes that were as high as the cities could bear, plus occasionally pillaging art treasures. A trip east with the legions, with its promise of loot and fame, was the perfect stepping-stone to power in Rome. Sulla used his victory over the last independent Anatolian state, the Pontic kingdom of Mithradates, to become dictator of Rome in 82 BC, and a decade later Pompey's successful campaign against Cilician pirates allowed him to become Sulla's successor. After that, Anatolia was disturbed only by the civil wars after Julius Caesar's assassination in 44 BC. Brutus passed through, grabbing all the men and money he could, and sacking cities that resisted. After him came Antony, demanding ten years' taxes in one, and dallying with Cleopatra at Alanya and Tarsus.

After all that, Anatolia deserved a rest, and the new empire founded by **Augustus** laid the foundations for over two centuries of peace and prosperity, in which the region reached its peak of wealth and ease, climaxing perhaps in the reign of **Hadrian** (117 BC–AD 38), a Grecophile and great benefactor of the cities. Commerce and the arts flourished, and cities like Ephesus, Smyrna (İzmir) and Antioch (Antakya) each counted over 500,000 inhabitants. Throughout this time, the opulence of life and loss of independence and responsibility was working a slow change on the Greeks. It can be seen in the art of the Imperial centuries, wilder, more emotional and intense, and above all in the growing obsession with religion and the 'salvation of the soul'. The old mystery cults of the Anatolian goddesses, especially **Cybele**, attained new popularity, while newcomers like **Mithraism**, a Persian import, gained many adepts. In the cities were large and prosperous **Jewish** communities established after the diaspora; their religion too found many converts. More importantly though, these communities provided the basis for the surprisingly rapid spread of **Christianity**. **St Paul** began his travels around Anatolia, as recorded in the *Acts of the Apostles*, in AD 43.

AD 300–1071: The Byzantine Empire

The founding of **Constantinople** in the 4th century AD and the division of the Roman empire into halves seemed to confirm Asia Minor in its central role. As the West receded into anarchy, successful Eastern emperors like Theodosius the Great (379–95), Justinian (527–65) and Heraclius (610–41) effected the transition of the state into the theocratically Christian, Greek-speaking **Byzantine Empire**, while keeping Avars, Alans, Persians and Slavs at bay.

Unfortunately, the diseases that had sapped the strength of the old empire were built into the new one from its birth: a gigantic bureaucratic state, with crushing taxes to support itself along with the army and the Imperial court. Christianity, while providing a new basis of unity, wiped out what remained of free thought and learning. Meanwhile the gap between rich and poor continued to increase. For most of Anatolia, this period witnessed a gradual but irreversible decline, as Byzantine misgovernment slowly strangled the economies of the cities and the great landowners pushed the majority of the country people into serfdom. Think what you learned in school about the Dark Ages, and then consider that most parts of western Europe managed better under barbarian rule and constant war than Asia Minor did under the successors of the Roman empire. Beginning in the 7th century, mutually destructive warfare with the Persians and a new menace, the armies of the Muslim Arabs, added the finishing touches. Trade died, and the coastal cities withered and disappeared; the once-fertile farmlands reverted to malarial plains. After a millennium and a half of civilized life, Asia Minor had been destroyed.

Throughout the 8th century, the Byzantines had been preoccupied with the **Iconoclastic** struggles, in which disputes over the desirability of painted icons masked a tremendous confusion of religious, economic and political conflicts (the example of rising Islam made the Greeks' love of divine images seem pure idolatry to many minds, but behind that stood a deeper discontent with the power of the monks and the Church hierarchy). The prohibition of icons began with a Church council of 754, and lasted until 843. Attacks from the surrounding Arabs, Avars, Serbs, Bulgarians and Petchinegs brought the Byzantines to their senses, and under emperors Basil I (867–86), Basil II, 'the Bulgar-slayer' (976–1025), and Nicephorus Phocas, the 'Pale Death of the Saracen' (963–9), Byzantium achieved a cultural revival and a level of political stability. This was little relief to devastated Anatolia; such culture as survived existed only in Constantinople.

1071–1243: The Selcuks Lead the Turkish Invasion

In the emptiest of Asia's empty spaces, north of Manchuria, Chinese chroniclers note a 'hill shaped like a helmet', the ancestral home of the 'Tu-kueh' – the **Turks**; they first appear in history c. 500 BC, making trouble for the Chinese emperors. In about AD 800, a confederation of tribes called the **Oğuz** was gradually heading towards Europe. By AD 900, many of the tribes had become Muslim, warrior clans that helped the central Asian states as they infiltrated them, just as the various 'barbarians' had done in Rome. Though not the first Turks to find their way into the desolated bear-pit of Asia Minor, the **Selcuks**, under their chief Alp Arslan, were the first to do it in style, gobbling up the Armenians and ending Byzantine rule over much of Anatolia once and for all with a resounding victory at Manzikert, north of Lake Van, in 1071. They called their state, centred at Konya, the **Sultanate of Rum** – to the peoples of distant Asia, Rome was still a magic name. As soon as they settled down, the Selcuks transformed themselves with amazing speed into gifted rulers and patrons of the arts. At the height of their power, under the early 13th-century sultan Alâeddin Keykubad, they were the strongest and most civilized state of the eastern Mediterranean, one considerably influenced by the culture of Persia, then under the rule of a separate Selcuk clan; Selcuk architecture, seen in the schools and mosques of Konya and so many other Anatolian cities, marks not only the beginning of Turkish art but one of its greatest achievements.

The Selcuks were only the first wave of a huge migration from central Asia. As well as the other Turkish tribes who set up petty emirates across the Middle East, the **Mongols** came, ending the Sultanate of Rum at the **Battle of Kösedağ** in 1243 and once more returning Turkey – we may now call it that – to anarchy. The most important result of their invasion was to push other Turkish tribes westwards, into the wastelands still nominally ruled by Constantinople. The first Turks to settle the Aegean coast, the **Menteşe**, founded a little emirate around Milas and Bodrum in the 1260s. By 1300 the situation had stabilized with the **Karamanlı emirate** ruling central Anatolia, the 'six emirates', including the Menteşe, Hamitoğulları and Germaniyids, in the southwest, and a number of tribes in the northeast.

Even before 1243, the Selcuks had been beset on all sides, not only by Turks, but also by the **Crusader states** founded by the Franks in the 12th century. The greatest of these in Anatolia, the County of Edessa (Harran and Şanlıurfa), survived for over a century, and orders such as the **Knights of St John** controlled much of the southern coast throughout the Middle Ages. The Crusaders soon learned to leave the Selcuks alone, and, not wishing to tackle the other Muslim nations either, decided to go after the heretics in Constantinople. A new Crusade in 1204, serving the ends of Venice and the Pope, took advantage of the absent Byzantine army to storm and sack Constantinople for the first time, humbling its pride, violating most of the women, and carrying off nearly every bit of its 900 years of accumulated treasure. The Byzantine empire ends here. Although a government in exile was set up at İznik (Nicaea), from which emperor Michael Paleologos chased out the Italians and reclaimed the city in 1261, it was an impoverished, enfeebled Constantinople that survived until 1453 behind its impregnable walls. In 1359, emperor John Paleologos gave in and became a tribute-paying vassal to his son-in-law, Sultan Orhan, leader of a new and growing Turkish tribe, the Osmanlı, or Ottomans.

1300–1453: The Coming of the Ottomans

According to legend, these Turks were riding across Anatolia when they chanced upon a battle being fought on the plain beneath them. Under their chief, Ertuğrul, they chivalrously decided to join the losing side, and soon turned their defeat into victory. The lucky victors were the Selcuks, who rewarded their new allies with lands in western Anatolia. About 1300, Sultan Osman laid the foundations of the state and dynasty that was to bear his name. Equally talented in war and government and virtuous to an extreme, Osman made his state a power in the region. All his successors were girded with his sword in place of a coronation, and the cry that went up was not 'Long live the Sultan' but 'May he be as good as Osman!'

Orhan (1324–59), his son, conquered Bursa in 1326 and made it his capital. His marriage to a Byzantine princess was not a rare case; by the 14th century Greeks and Turks had come to know each other very well. Anatolia's gradual process of 'turning Turk' had begun with the Selcuks. Gradually, many of the Greeks had converted to Islam, often entire towns at a time; most of the rest, considering their alternatives, saw the tolerant Turkish Muslims as a lesser evil than the schismatics of Europe and their hated pope. (The average Turk of today probably has far more Greek and native Anatolian blood in him than Turkish.) Orhan, an able and liberal ruler, increased the Ottomans' prestige as he widened their boundaries. Early in his reign, a group of adventurers called the Catalan Grand Company, paid to defend Constantinople, had ferried Orhan's army across the Bosphorus to help. The Ottomans took one look at Europe and decided they wanted to keep it; Orhan conquered Thrace, and his son Murat I (1359–89) added Serbia, Bulgaria and Macedonia.

The Turks, changing from nomadic warriors to an imperial aristocracy, suffered from a shortage of women and, consequently, a shortage of Turks for a state with such big ambitions. They solved this problem with the devşirme, a harvest of five per cent of the infant boys from captured Christian provinces (first-born sons were excluded). All were educated and brought up as Muslims; the best became the sultan's generals and vezirs (ministers), while the rougher were enrolled in the Janissaries (yeniçeri, 'new troops'), a corps of highly trained soldiers that were to be the terror of Europe. The Janissaries were kept under the control of the Bektaşi dervishes, from whom they inherited an unusual tradition of rituals and titles based on soup. To show their displeasure with a sultan, for example, they would turn their large kettle upside down and refuse to eat. In later years, as the

Janissaries became a law unto themselves, they did this whenever they felt like deposing a sultan. As long as discipline was maintained, though, they were the finest fighting force in the world. For **Beyazıt I**, 'Thunderbolt' (1389–1403), they destroyed the flower of French chivalry at Nicopolis in 1396, finally damping the crusading urge. Beyazıt, a young hothead, addicted to battle even more than to wine, met his destiny in the person of **Tamerlane** in 1403. The invincible Mongol destroyed the Ottoman force at Ankara and took Beyazıt prisoner, and then mysteriously turned around and went back east. **Mehmet I** (1413–21) and **Murat II** (1421–51) picked up the pieces and carefully rebuilt, finding time in 1444 to win undisputed control of the Balkans at the Battle of Varna, after which the head of King Ladislas of Poland and Hungary ended up on the top of a pike in Bursa.

1453: The Capture of Constantinople

Almost from the beginning, this was the Ottoman goal. Earlier attempts against the city had failed, and it was left to **Mehmet II** (1451–81) to take the prize. Mehmet, perhaps the most remarkable sultan, was a poet and scholar who had mastered six languages and, unthinkable for a Muslim, had his portrait painted, by Gentile Bellini. He saw himself as a man of destiny, sent to fulfil Mohammed's prophecy about the capture of the city, and went about the task methodically. By 1453, he had an enormous army, the biggest cannons in the world and a brand-new fleet. Inside the city, whose population had dwindled from over a million to under fifty thousand, an Italian *condottiere* named **Giustiniani** led 8,000 Greeks and mercenaries for the defence. Against the odds, they held out for two months. The tide turned with Mehmet's brilliant trick of dragging his ships over land, around the famous chain across the Golden Horn, to the exposed side of the city. On 23 May Giustiniani died, and the disheartened mercenaries fled. The few Greeks remaining beat back a furious attack, but in their excitement left open a postern gate; some Turks found it, and the empire breathed its last. Mehmet ordered that the usual three days' pillage should spare all the buildings; he walked in awe through the Aya Sofya and the abandoned palaces, and remembered a bit of Persian poetry:

> The spider weaves the curtain in the Palace of the Caesars,
> The night-owl keeps the watch in the Tower of Afrasiyab.

To the Turks, Mehmet is *Fatih*, the Conqueror. He knew what the city meant, and rebuilt it as fast as resources allowed. In 1461 he added the Empire of Trebizond to his conquests, the last free Greek state, founded by refugee noblemen after the sack of 1204.

1454–1700: The Height of the Ottoman State

Mehmet's son, **Beyazıt II**, 'the Mystic' (1481–1512), seldom disrupted his reading for further conquests, but **Selim I** (1512–20) made up for him by swallowing up Egypt (thus gaining the Caliphate) and much of Mesopotamia. *Yavuz* Selim, as the Turks call him, is an honorific meaning 'the Formidable', but historians like to call him Selim the Grim for his frequent massacres of Shiite heretics (he was the first Ottoman to trouble himself about religious orthodoxy), and his habit of beheading his grand vezirs at an average of one a year. His son, **Süleyman the Magnificent** (1520–66), presided over the glorious noonday of the Ottoman state; under him the empire reached its greatest extent with the conquest of Hungary and North Africa. His title comes courtesy of his close allies, the French; to his own people he was 'the Lawgiver' for his thorough reforms of the legal code and commercial regulations. Unfortunately, he also began the empire's slow decline. The trading concessions he granted to François Ier were the first step in the Ottomans' loss of control of their own economy. From his weakness for his scheming harem-favourite Roxelana, he brought the harem into the palace and inaugurated the period of palace intrigue that was eventually to ruin the state. The sultans that followed show clearly how far the decay had already penetrated. Selim the Sot (1566–74) and İbrahim the Mad (1640–8) lead the parade of wastrels, drunkards, sex perverts and imbeciles that decorated the latter-day Ottoman throne. Directly upon Süleyman's death the real power had passed to the Janissaries, the eunuchs and the ladies in the endlessly changing factions in the harem. **Osman II** (1618–22), who wanted reform, was murdered; his successors until 1832 were virtual prisoners of the Janissary guard.

In the *Divan* (cabinet), meanwhile, a remarkable dynasty of grand vezirs of Albanian descent, the **Köprülü** family, did their best to hold the leaderless state together throughout the 17th century. By the 18th, decadence had progressed so far that the European powers had to keep the Ottoman corpse propped on its throne to keep the Russians from occupying the straits.

1700–1910: The Empire Crumbles

For three centuries, the Russians kept the pressure on with 43 declared wars, while, in the 19th century, some of the empire's captive nations, the Greeks, Serbians, Bulgarians and Egyptians, successfully gained their independence. Attempts to reform were too few and too late. Under **Mahmut II** (1808–39), the Janissaries were massacred in what the Turks call the 'Auspicious Event', but the empire was too far behind the Europeans militarily and technologically for it to make much difference. Mahmut's successors, **Abdülmecit I** (1839–61) and **Abdülaziz** (1861–76), proved too stupid and indifferent to keep his reforms going, and the paranoid **Abdülhamid** (1876–1909) sold his nation to European economic interests while ruthlessly stamping out any progressive thinking at home.

Despite his efforts, underground attempts to bring Turkey out of its political nightmare continued, especially among circles in the army. In Salonika, now Greek Thessaloniki, a group of discontented army officers formed the Committee for Union and Progress, known in the west as the **Young Turks**, led by **Enver Paşa**. Their manœuvrings within the upper echelons of the Ottomans led in 1909 to the fall of the hated Abdülhamid and the creation that same year of a constitutional monarchy, governed by an elected parliament.

1911–19: The War Years

During this period, the 'Sick Man of Europe' finally expired. The Italians started the final collapse when in 1911 they invaded the Turkish colony of Tripoli (Libya) and took it with ease. Encouraged by this, Montenegro, Serbia, Bulgaria and Greece joined forces to drive the Ottomans out of Europe in the **First Balkan War** (1913). A truce was negotiated by Istanbul before too much territory was lost, but Enver Paşa and the Young Turks seized power in a *coup d'état* and restarted the war. More defeats followed. Crete was lost; so too were the Dodecanese, and by 1913 Turkish domains in Europe consisted of just Istanbul and half of Thrace, the latter only because Bulgaria and Greece could not agree who should have it.

All of this should have put Enver Paşa off wars for good. It did not. When the Great War exploded in 1914, the Ottomans threw their fez in with the Germans, whom the Paşa hoped would help him realize his pan-Turkish dream of an empire extending to the shores of the Caspian Sea. Immediately, the Turks found themselves fighting on two fronts, at Gelibolu (Gallipoli) in the west and against the Russians in the east, while their empire fell apart, country by country. Sultan **Mehmet V** announced a *jihad* against the Triple Entente, hoping that all Islam would rise in his support, but the Ottomans had done the Arabs no favours when ruling them and now all blithely turned a deaf ear. A state of near revolt among the Armenian minority on the Russian front led to the genocide of 1915–16, in which the Young Turk leaders organized the massacre or death through inhuman deportation of over one million Armenians.

The Turks won at Gallipoli, but every other front became a disaster. By autumn 1918 Enver Paşa and others of the Young Turk *junta* had fled the country in disgrace, smuggled out on a German destroyer. By November of that year, British warships were at anchor in Istanbul. In May 1920 the Triple Entente handed down their judgement on the old Ottomans, in the form of the **Treaty of Sèvres**. It carved up the country: Istanbul and a few surrounding areas were retained, but İzmir fell to Greek jurisdiction, an independent Armenia and an autonomous Kurdistan were to be set up in the east and the remaining areas of Anatolia handed out to France and Italy as spheres of economic influence. The Greeks saw their opportunity to put their long-dreamed-of *Megalo Idee* ('Great Idea') into practice – the recapture of Constantinople and the recreation of the Byzantine empire. Encouraged by the British, the Greek army advanced from İzmir into Anatolia. Old, silly **Mehmet VI**, the last of the sultans, sat in his palace and wondered what would happen next.

1919: The Turkish Revolution

What happened was astounding. Throughout the Ottoman empire, as under the Byzantines, Anatolia had been a neglected backwater of the empire, which saw its heartland more as Thrace and the Balkans. To be called a 'Turk' was something of an insult among the aristocratic Ottomans; the patient Turkish peasants and townsmen of Anatolia put up with as much scorn and as little help as any minority of the empire. Now, for the first time, Anatolia made a stand. Opposition to the Sèvres treaty centred around a brilliant, difficult general, **Mustafa Kemal**, with a military reputation from Gallipoli and a head full of nationalist ideas. He escaped from the intrigues of Istanbul on 19 May 1919, and landed at Samsun with the force of a Napoleon returning from Elba. Nationalist congresses were soon held at Sivas and Erzurum, and a provisional government set up for the deliverance of the nation.

Somehow a new army was created. Under Kemal the Turks chased out the French and Russians and decisively defeated the Greeks at the two **battles of İnönü** in January–March 1921. The Greeks burnt and pillaged their way back to the coast; by September 1922, the country was clear of all foreign troops. A republic was declared one year later, with Mustafa Kemal as its first president and Ankara, right in the middle of Anatolia, as its capital. A new treaty was negotiated at Lausanne to replace the redundant Treaty of Sèvres; it included the ghoulish 'Exchange of Populations', by which some two million Greeks were forced out of Anatolia, where Greeks had lived for nearly 3,000 years, in return for pushing a few hundred thousand Turks out of Greece. In retrospect, it seems a historical turning point. Neither Mustafa Kemal nor the Greeks probably had any idea of the evil they were loosing on the world. It was the beginning of the tribal politics and 'ethnic cleansing' we know today, the insistence that people must not be allowed to get on together if politicians and propagandists find it inconvenient. In all the bloody 20th century, few greater crimes were committed – yet, at the time, the whole world believed they were doing the right thing.

1922–60: The Westernization of Turkey

Few nations have ever had the will or unity to effect as many reforms as the Turks did in the 1920s and '30s, trying to make up for so many centuries of lost time. Mustafa Kemal's republic was to be thoroughly secular: the Caliphate was abolished, education and marriage secularized, the wearing of the fez banned. Turkey adopted the Christian calendar and made Sunday the day of rest. The language was also reformed. Arabic and Persian words were rooted out, and the Roman alphabet replaced the Arabic. As the simplest way of westernizing its laws, Turkey simply adopted the entire Swiss Legal Code, almost word for word. Women acquired equal rights. International time and measures were adopted, and the government worked to improve industry and communications. To crown it all, the president decreed that every Turk should have a Western-style surname. Mustafa Kemal's was chosen for him by the nation – **Atatürk**, 'Father of the Turks'.

It was only his moral authority as the nation's hero that enabled the changes to be accepted with so much enthusiasm and so little resistance. In politics, Atatürk began what has become a modern Turkish tradition by establishing a dictatorship to make reforms, while constantly and sincerely telling his people that their first aspiration must be democracy. After his death in 1938, his right-hand man from the War of Independence, General **İsmet İnönü**, took over with a pledge to bring democracy. The **Second World War**, in which the Turks remained neutral, postponed the experiment, but free elections in 1949 resulted in the victory of the new opposition Democratic Party and its charismatic leader **Adnan Menderes**. For the coastal areas, the most important event in over a millennium was something few histories even bother to mention – the anti-malaria campaign of 1948, made possible by the invention of DDT and American aid. DDT may be murder on birds (that's why it's outlawed in most countries now), but by cutting down drastically the number of anopheles mosquitoes, it made possible the resettlement of places that had been wastelands since Byzantine times. Without it, much of Turkey's coastline would still be empty today.

DDT was just one part of a revolution that Menderes brought to Turkey. Rapid modernization of agriculture and industry changed the lives of millions. But it nearly bankrupted Turkey. The Democrats' corruption, mishandling of the economy and attempt to create a one-party dictatorship brought increasing chaos. To distract attention from their failures, elements within the government organized the riots of 1955 in Istanbul, in which thousands of Greek businesses, churches and homes were sacked; in the aftermath nearly all of the city's surviving Greek community, over 100,000 people, chose to leave. Democratic misrule led to an **army coup** in 1960, and the installation of the unwilling army leader, the genial and democratically minded General **Cemal Gürsel** as president. Menderes was executed after a sensational trial; the story goes that Gürsel was ready to pardon him but his underlings cut the phone lines to the prison. The memory of this complex character is still alive in his political stronghold, the farming lands of western Anatolia. In the last two decades nearly every town has named a street after him, something that would have been unthinkable earlier. Every Turkish populist party in the decades since has been more or less the Democrats under a different name, continuing the same pro-Western, pro-Islam and pro-free market policies.

1960 to the Present: Three Coups, Three Constitutions

Democracy was restored the following year, under an extremely liberal constitution proposed by Gürsel, and a new coalition government bumbled along under the watchful eye of the army. In 1965 the **Justice Party** (the old Democrats), led by **Süleyman Demirel**, achieved a working majority but his government was beset by the Cyprus crisis; domestic issues, including a rapidly worsening economy, took second place. By 1970 the mild civil unrest that marked the preceding years had exploded into bloody riots and once again the army stepped in.

It was not until 1973 that a new civilian government took office, led by **Bülent Ecevit** of the **Democratic Left Party**, but it was to fare no better than its predecessor, the war in Cyprus and the OPEC oil-price hike dominating its attention. Amidst the economic troubles, political violence between left and right threatened to turn into civil war. In 1980, after a year of over 3,000 political murders, the army stepped in once more, with a coup orchestrated by a real martinet, General **Kenan Evren**. All opposition to the new regime was stamped on, firmly. Political leaders from both sides, including Demirel and Ecevit, were jailed, sharing their cells with journalists, student leaders and trade unionists. In 1982, Evren proposed a new **constitution**, providing for a strong presidency. A referendum was passed – with the support of the vast majority of the country – which included an election for the new office of president with only one candidate, Evren. He was to hold the post until 1988.

Parliamentary elections the next year were won by the new **Motherland Party (ANAP)**, led by **Turgut Özal**, an economist from Malatya. A typically Turkish paradox, Özal was a modern, Western-trained technocrat, a believer in democracy, and a devout Muslim – the first prime minister of the republic to have made the pilgrimage to Mecca. His skill in mastering the moribund Turkish economy and his diplomatic treatment of the army started Turkey on the longest period of freely elected government it has yet enjoyed – 25 years, so far. In 1988 he stepped into Evren's presidential shoes and lasted until his death in 1993, popular abroad for his support of the United Nations during the Gulf War and at home among those who can remember the condition their country was in before he gained office. Support for Özal, however, was not transferred to the Motherland Party in the 1991 elections, when that old stager Süleyman Demirel gained a working parliamentary majority for his centre-right **True Path Party (DYP)**, in coalition with the mildly leftist **SHP**.

After Özal's death Demirel became president and the economics minister, **Tansu Çiller**, became Turkey's first female prime minister. A friend of Margaret Thatcher, she sought to bring similar free-market policies to Turkey. Although she was fêted by some business leaders for her efforts to privatise Turkey's state enterprises, her government's currency manipulations contributed much to runaway **inflation**, and revelations of gross governmental corruption filled the press. In late 1995, disillusioned Turks gave vent to their indignation and frustration at the ballot box, with the Islamic **Refah (Welfare) Party**, led by **Necmettin Erbakan**, gaining the largest share of the vote. In a desperate bid to prevent Refah from forming a government, ANAP and DYP pieced together a shaky minority governing **coalition**. This was brought down in the summer of 1996, and Turkey, an avowedly secular republic, witnessed Erbakan, a veteran Islamist, becoming prime minister. By embarking on a series of visits to Libya and Iran, he hardly endeared himself to the **National Security Council**, Turkey's all-powerful guardian of secularism, made up of the military top brass and President Demirel. After just 11 months, the council let its displeasure be known. Erbakan was forced to resign in what was termed a 'soft coup', and Refah was dissolved on the dubious grounds that it was mixing religion with politics. Refah party members soon reconstituted themselves into **Fazilet**, the **Virtue Party**, which was in turn banned by the courts in 2001. The Islamist movement then split into two; the hardcore **Saadet (Felicity) Party** and the younger, more moderate **Justice and Development Party (AKP)**.

The AKP made history when it won a majority in 2002 elections, and its leader **Recep Tayyip Erdoğan** brought in Turkey's first single-party government in decades. Erdoğan, who grew up selling *simits* on the streets of Beyoğlu, and spent years working for the city bus line and playing semi-pro soccer before working his way up to the Istanbul mayor's chair, is a phenomenon, a man who combines a sincere faith with a thoroughly Western attitude to politics and the economy. Keen to appease fears over his party's Islamic roots, he has kept close ties with the USA and Israel, and launched an aggressive European Union drive which resulted in Brussels agreeing to restart accession talks. The AKP's foreign-investment-friendly, liberal economic policies have resulted in a booming economy, growing at an average eight per cent per year since they took power. Turkey's 'Kemalist' (secularist) establishment, though, is still deeply suspicious of the AKP; in 2007, thousands of Kemalists took to the streets, backed by the powerful generals, to prevent AKP founder **Abdullah Gul** from becoming president, because his wife wears a head-scarf. (She is the first Turkish first lady to do so.) That bid backfired, however, resulting in early elections which the AKP won with 47 per cent of the vote.

The two camps have come to loggerheads over a number of issues, most recently a government drive to lift a ban on female students wearing headscarves at universities. Secularists argue that the AKP has a secret Islamic agenda and that lifting the ban paves the way for other Islam-based moves, but the AKP says those fears are unfounded. Turkey faces a turbulent but ultimately hopeful future if it can learn to strengthen its democratic institutions and public debate and to resolve differences without resorting to another military intervention. Until both sides start speaking the same language, however, the volatile nature of Turkish politics is unlikely to calm down in the near future.

Turkey Today

Modern Turkey stands between the developed and developing countries. Any statistics relating to economic development are affected by millions of Anatolian farmers, only just now working their way out of poverty. Many of them migrate to the cities; Istanbul, with a population estimated as high as 12 million, has become the second largest city in Europe, and one of the most economically dynamic. Many others find their way to western Europe (they joke that Berlin has become the 68th Turkish province). Their fertility is startling: the 70 million Turks today have one of the highest rates of **population growth** in the world. The population is one of the world's youngest, with more than 26 per cent under the age of 14.

Turkey continues with its eternal, and eternally frustrating, accession talks with the **European Union**, and many Turks are beginning to suspect it's all just a joke. Some European opponents, such as France's President Sarkozy, scarcely bother concealing their bigotry any more, while the double standard Europe employs on the Cyprus question leaves Turks increasingly exasperated. While most Turks remain committed to Europe, some worry that as an EU member their country might once more be the sick man of Europe, bossed around and buoyed up by grants. There is a new temptation for the government to look to the east, to the new states of Azerbaijan, Uzbekistan, Turkmenistan and Kazakhstan, all Turkic-speaking, all with predominantly Muslim populations, who see Turkey as an economically successful, capitalist, modern Muslim role model. Let us form a Near-East Community, say some politicians; better to be king of your own castle than doorkeeper to another's in the West. Others disagree: why tie the nation to a pack of impoverished, dysfunctional dictatorships in a dangerous neighbourhood?

Relations with the old nemesis **Greece** make a more encouraging story. Since the 1980s, public figures on both sides have been working quietly to find common ground, and build confidence and understanding. A surprising and delightful turning point came with the great 1999 İzmit earthquake, when Greek rescue teams were among the first to appear on the scene. Since then co-operation has proceeded on many fronts. Recently a group of Greek and Turkish historians has come together to investigate the 1922 fall of Smyrna and other contentious events.

Events in the **Kurdish conflict** in the southeast have been less encouraging. Some 20 per cent of the population are Kurds, spread across the whole country, but concentrated in the southeast. They are a proud people with their own distinct language, culture and history who have never had their own state (though Saladin, who turfed the Crusaders out of the Holy Land, was Kurdish). In Turkey, the Kurds have always seen themselves as second-class citizens, and with some justification. For decades their aspirations to autonomy and to the practice of their culture and language were suppressed, sometimes with horrible violence, as in the rebellions of 1925 and 1939; speaking Kurdish was not decriminalized until 1991.

There was little the Kurds could do about this while Turkey was under military or semi-military rule, but as the nation emerged into democracy they made their voice heard, most sinisterly in the form of the terrorist Kurdish Workers Party, the **PKK**. At first financed and trained by a rogues' gallery of Turkey's enemies – Syria, the Palestinians and the Soviets – the PKK thrived by extortion and racketeering, killing everyone it could who disagreed with it, occasionally entire villages at a time. The skirmishes between the PKK and the army turned into full-scale warfare in the late 1980s. The government's response was witless and nearly as destructive as the guerrillas: hundreds of villages in unsafe zones were forcibly evacuated, and Turkey's already hard-pressed cities filled with Kurdish refugees. A lot of the people who work in Turkish hotels and restaurants are Kurds; ask them about it and you'll get an earful.

The fighting died down in the aftermath of the 1999 capture of PKK leader **Abdullah Ocalan**, now serving a life sentence on an island jail in western Turkey. Right now, though, things seem to be heating up again. The US invasion of Iraq resulted in an autonomous Kurdish region in north Iraq which looks increasingly like a mini-state, with its own flag, parliament and language. The shake-up allowed the PKK to regroup and relaunch its campaign; small-scale attacks on Turkish soldiers in the southeast have been making the news almost on a weekly basis, while bomb attacks in Istanbul and other cities have become increasingly frequent.

In fact the PKK may be only a shadow of what it was in the 1980s and '90s, but its continued presence only underlines the necessity for Turkey to deal with its restive minority. Europe and the USA have made it clear they want a political solution. The AKP government has improved cultural rights and shown a willingness to address the problem, but rising Turkish nationalism has made dialogue difficult.

Behind all the political troubles is a booming but unstable economic situation. Twenty years of rapid modernization have greatly widened the gap between Turkey's rich and poor, and the southeast, underdeveloped and still in parts mired in feudalism, remains vastly poorer than the wealthy west. Ankara hasn't been sitting still. Its answer to the southeast's problems is the **GAP**, the Southeast Anatolia Project, one of the biggest stories in the Middle East today. GAP (*see* p.494) isn't just about giant dams, irrigation and electricity. Like its model, the Tennessee Valley Authority in Franklin Roosevelt's New Deal, the project works on many fronts to lift an entire region out of poverty, and now that it is nearing completion its benefits to the largely Kurdish population are becoming clear.

The discontent of Turkey's poor did much to put votes in the column of the AKP, and the government's subsequent economic success did much to win it a second round in power. Since then, the three-way friction between moderate Islamists, campaigners for greater democracy and old-line Kemalists has sharpened considerably. While the government nudges Turkey towards a greater role for religion, the more Westernized Turks are in the streets demonstrating for greater freedoms, tolerance for minorities and a more democratic constitution, a movement that has accelerated considerably since the dramatic assassination (possibly with connivance from the security forces) of the ethnic Armenian journalist and human rights campaigner Hrant Dink in 2007. In the summer of 2008 political tensions reached new heights. One court heard a prosecutor's demand that the AKP be banned (this was rejected by one vote) and that Prime Minister Erdoğan and other leaders be barred from politics. Meanwhile, a second court was beginning to deal with 86 political, military and intellectual figures, apparently members of a shadowy extreme nationalist group called **Ergenekon**, charged with plotting to overthrow the government. At this point it is unclear whether the next battle over the soul of the nation will be fought out in the courts and the newspapers, or in the streets. Stay tuned.

Topics

03

The Turkish People

Othello didn't like the Turks very much:

In Aleppo once / Where a malignant and a turbaned Turk / Beat a Venetian and traduced the state / I took by the throat the circumcised dog / And smote him thus.

History has been unkind to the Turkish people, especially history written from a European point of view. To writers and commentators of the past they were slothful, lazy, dirty, backward and devious, yet to be fair to those bigoted scribes, most Ottoman sultans did run their country in a manner that did little to dispel such prejudices. Of course, all of the adjectives above are utter nonsense; in fact, it's hard to meet a people nicer than the Turks.

The word for guest in Turkish is *misafir*, and to the Turks it is almost sacred. Wherever you go, you'll be offered a glass of tea; for many people, Turkish hospitality is almost overwhelming. Yet one never has the feeling that it derives from a sense of religious obligation, rather from a warm and spontaneous friendliness and concern for their fellow man. Coupled with this, especially in the small villages, is a keen curiosity about the foreigner. In eastern Anatolia the good farmer may just stop and stare at you; it's a bit unnerving but he means no harm. Anyone who knows a few phrases of English, especially the school children, will want to try them out on you. The country women are shyer. If they're in a group (you'll see them coming and going from the fields in large trailers pulled by jaunty tractors), they may smile. Otherwise, they probably won't address you, unless you're a woman on your own. Then they open up and are even more friendly than the men. Turks dote on children and if you take them with you, they'll spoil them horribly. '*Maşallah, maşallah!*' they'll say, patting them on the head and giving them more sweets and fruit than they could eat in a year. '*Maşallah*' means 'May God preserve [him or her from evil]'; children are too precious to receive any direct compliments that might incur divine jealousy.

As well as warmth and hospitality, the other central characteristic of the Turks is their intense nationalism and pride. This is the heritage of the Great Atatürk. When Turkey was still referred to as 'The Sick Man of Europe', he boosted his countrymen's morale with slogans that you still see everywhere, even inscribed on hillsides in giant white letters: '*NE MUTLU TÜRKÜM DİYENE*' ('How lucky for a man to call himself a Turk!') and '*BİZ BİZE BENZERİZ*' ('We resemble ourselves'). Speak disparagingly of Turkey at your own risk, although you'll find plenty of sympathy on many subjects, from telephones to traffic conditions in Istanbul. Atatürk himself is the one really taboo subject, unless you want to pay his memory a compliment. It's also bad form to say 'Constantinople' instead of Istanbul, or to imply that Turkey is not a member of the Western community.

Atatürk

People in the West who are unacquainted with Turkish history have probably never heard of him, but in Turkey his face is everywhere: in statues, in the portraits that adorn all public places and most businesses, on coins and banknotes, on banners and even in neon lights. The best ones try to emphasize his sharp features to make him into a kind of mythological hero; instead he comes out looking like the Wizard of Oz.

At first he was just Mustafa, a sullen, red-haired, blue-eyed boy from Salonika (no doubt with a lot of Celtic blood, like so many Turks). His house there still stands, next to the Turkish consulate. A teacher who recognized his abilities gave him the name Kemal, meaning 'perfection'; by the time he and his crack 57th Division were helping whip the British at Gallipoli, he had become **General Mustafa Kemal Paşa**, a leader with a reputation for putting himself in the thick of the battle – a habit that got him wounded at Gallipoli. Emerging from the disastrous war as the only general with a record of victory, Mustafa Kemal was the man of the hour, at a time when the Ottoman empire had collapsed and the Turkish lands were descending into total anarchy. The Allies, particularly Lloyd George, had decided on a cynical rape of Anatolia, meaning to parcel it out among themselves and the Greeks. No novice to political affairs – he had led one of the units that occupied Istanbul in the Young Turk coup of 1909 – the general found himself in the same position as de Gaulle in 1940, and he made the most of it. Even more than de Gaulle, Mustafa Kemal was able to lead his hastily rebuilt army to victory against the Greeks, defy the will of the Allied powers, and force the British, French and Italians to leave.

With that accomplished, there was still the task of dragging a proud but woefully backward and disorganized nation into the 20th century. Make no mistake, without him not a tenth part of it would have been accomplished as quickly or as success-fully. All the important initiatives of Turkey's unique cultural revolution came from Mustafa Kemal: a republic, a Westernized legal system, women's rights, language reforms, economic modernization, educational reforms and the divorce of religion from politics. Nowhere in history is there a comparable example of such rapid, radical change in a nation's life and institutions – only the reign of Peter the Great in Russia comes remotely close. **Atatürk**, or 'Father of the Turks', was the surname he assumed by general acclaim during his campaign to westernize Turkish names in the 1930s. Cults of personality were all too common in those days, and we might easily dismiss Atatürk as just another strongman. On the contrary, he has earned a place among the very few great statesmen this century has produced. One of the famous photos of Atatürk shows him in European formal attire, demonstrating Roman letters to a crowd of his earnest but probably bewildered countrymen. It wasn't just what a modern politician would call a 'photo opportunity'; he did it many times all over Turkey. He took his job seriously, and, after so many centuries of decay, the job couldn't have been done any other way. Atatürk thoroughly deserves all the statues and tributes, but they are more than just a memorial to a leader. Though he died in 1938, they stand as a symbol of the revolution he began, and of the modern, secular nation that is still the aspiration of most Turks today.

The Evil Eye

You'll notice them everywhere: hanging from necklaces, on babies' cradles, dangling from the rear-view mirror of a dolmuş, over the front door of a home, wherever there is anything of value and importance. The *boncuk* ('bead', sometimes called a *göz boncuğu*, or 'eye bead') is easily recognizable; big or small but always a circle or oval of blue, centred with two other circles to represent an eye. They are worn to guard against that unseen, most nefarious of forces, the evil eye. Folklore dictates that some people, either knowingly or otherwise, have in their eyes an evil spirit that can do untold harm. The blue 'eye' medallion reflects this wicked spirit back to the originator, so that he or she who displays one has nothing to fear. The medallion can be made from any substance – usually glass, but sometimes stone, bone, shell, even silver and gold – the important thing is that it's there. One newspaper prints a *boncuk* in colour in the top corner of the front page, perhaps to protect readers against all the malevolent influences emanating from the news.

Most of Turkey's evil-eye medallions are manufactured near İzmir, at the villages of Karabağler, Karşıyaka and Kadifekale. This is perhaps suprising, for this region is one of the most prosperous and developed in the country. But it is also a region that was Greek, not so long ago, and the *boncuk* is really Greek in origin. In ancient times, the Greeks feared the mysterious influence of the eye, particularly the eyes of serpents or snakes, which they believed had the power of hypnotizing their prey. They called this power βασκανια, a word that passed through Latin into modern languages as *fascination*. Some people have it too; you'll know *you* do if you go to Greece, and old women cross the street when they see you coming. Something very similar to the snake's eye, surprisingly, is flattery. Any unsuspecting person can be the bearer of the evil eye in this manner. Compliments of any sort induce pride, and so invite Nemesis – especially where children are concerned.

Not only in folk customs, but in music, cuisine and nearly everything else, much of what you see in Turkey comes from the Greeks (the average inhabitant of western Anatolia has as much Greek blood as Turkish). The influence works both ways, of course; you'll still hear old men in Greece greet each other with *selam aleyküm – aleyküm selam* (peace be with you – with you be peace), as any good Muslims would. The two peoples lived together so long, and have so much that is similar – from worry-beads to coffee – that it is often hard to disentangle them and puzzle out who influenced whom the most. In fact, the more time you spend in this part of the world, the more you'll think that Greeks and Turks are really the same people, divided only by language and religion. Maybe that is why they love each other so dearly. It's fortunate at least that both have their blue beads. With politicians on both sides still making the evil eye at each other, both peoples need them.

East and West

William Butler Yeats, in his murky meditation *A Vision*, wrote of east and west eternally contending. He saw them as alternately fertilizing each other with new cultures in successive ages. However you choose to interpret this aspect of the world's secret history, it undoubtedly exists, and Turkey is its battleground. The Aegean coast, in fact, has usually been the front line ever since the rise of the ancient Greeks. It may go back even further, to Mycenaean times, when early Greek people occupied the Aegean islands and part of the coasts. The Greeks do get credit for inventing Western civilization, of course, and looking back beyond them means looking into a glass that is very dark indeed. But, remembering that both the

Hittites and the Phrygians probably invaded Anatolia from Europe, it just might be possible that this old quarrel goes back even earlier.

As far as we know, however, it begins with the **Trojan War**. The next round, some 700 years later, was what the Greeks knew as the **Persian Wars**, an attempt by the greatest empire of its day to squash a minor but troublesome nuisance on its far western border. It was the Greeks' finest hour, and in victory they began to grow conscious of their strength. A century and a half after that, **Alexander the Great** carried Greek culture and philosophy triumphantly eastwards through Anatolia, and pushed the boundaries of the west as far as India – for a short time. His successors brought back roses, astrology and, among a hundred other things, the Persian concept of the divine ruler, without which the cult of the deified Roman emperors could not have been.

Christianity began its drive westwards in Asia Minor, in a score of towns and churches mentioned in the New Testament; from the Sufi poets, the Crusaders adopted the cult of chivalry; the troubadours, alchemy and many themes found in medieval literature owe their beginnings to Islamic culture. Today, the Republic of Atatürk heads the incursion of our secular, mercantile culture into the Middle East.

Somehow, Homer's epic had the power of summing up all this to-and-fro, and evocations of Homer fill the pages of Turkey's history. Like Alexander, Mehmet the Conqueror took time to visit Troy. In 1453, he declared that by taking Constantinople he had avenged the 'peoples of Asia' on the arrogant Greeks. On his entry into the city after the conquest, Mehmet, according to tradition, knocked off with his sword one of the serpent heads of the old bronze column that stood in the Hippodrome. This monument had been brought to the city by Constantine the Great, who had looted it from Delphi. There is probably no way Mehmet could have known that it commemorated the victory of the Greeks over the Persians at Plataea in 479 BC – almost 2,000 years before.

Eleven Days at the Pera Palace

Some time in late 2009, after its lengthy restoration is completed, one will once more have a chance to sip tea in the splendiferous lounge of the grand old Pera Palace Hotel in Istanbul. If they've done the job right, you should feel time-warped, rushed back to the days when Europe's élite carved up the crumbling Ottoman Empire on paper and stroked their moustaches as a grand piano tinkled gently.

The Pera Palace was founded in 1892, to provide travellers on the Orient Express with suitable accommodation in Istanbul after their trying journey: chandeliers, antique carpets, an elaborate electric-powered lift, a piano. Few hotels had a better pedigree or were richer in charm. Atatürk stayed here often, as did Edward VIII, the last Shah of Iran, Mata Hari, Greta Garbo, Tito and Jackie Onassis. Agatha Christie wrote *Murder on the Orient Express* here. In fact, there is an unusual tale concerning Agatha Christie and the Pera Palace. Christie 'lost' eleven days in her life. Neither she nor anyone else could account for her whereabouts during this time. In their film of her life, Warner Brothers accounted for the missing days as best they could. Their best wasn't good enough and the film was savaged by the critics. Affronted, Warner Brothers took the rather bizarre step of consulting a medium, Miss Tamara

Rand, requesting her to call up the soul of Agatha Christie and solve the puzzle once and for all. Which is what happened – well, almost. Agatha Christie told Miss Rand that the key to the mystery could be found in room 411 of the Pera Palace Hotel, Istanbul. On 7 March 1979, with the world's press gawking, a search of room 411 was made, aided by a telephone connection to Miss Rand in the States who gave the searchers long-distance directions after consulting Agatha Christie. Eventually, they found the key – literally. Under a wooden panel near the door was a large, rusty key. Warner Brothers' representatives were ecstatic; they grabbed telephones to babble the good news to their bosses stateside. As they did so, Hasan Süzer, chairman of the Pera Palace, quietly pocketed the key. Later, at a press conference, Süzer announced that he would give the key to Warner Brothers in return for $2,000,000, to be spent on sorely needed refurbishments to the hotel.

Warner Brothers decided to go back to Miss Rand, who called up Agatha Christie and told her their woes. She told Miss Rand that if the medium were to hold that key in her hand, she would be told the location of the long-missing and long-sought-after diary of Agatha Christie, in which would be the secret of the missing days. Warner Brothers hot-footed it back to Istanbul and begged the loan of the key. Negotiations were held. Eventually it was agreed that Tamara Rand would come to the Pera Palace on 20 August 1979, to hold the key and to reveal the site of the diary.

Unfortunately, on 30 June that year, staff at the Pera Palace began a year-long strike and the visit had to be postponed. During that year further negotiations collapsed and the two sides decided that they disliked each other enough not to care about unlocking the past. So it is that the key to the eleven missing days in the life of Agatha Christie now lies in a safety deposit box in a bank in Istanbul.

The Fatal Glass of Beer

After another hot day tracking down Phrygian ruins or Selcuk medreses in a small Turkish town far from the tourist trails, you might think a glass of beer would be a good idea. Depending on the town, you may unfortunately expire before you find one. These days, the influence of the Islamic equivalents of the bluenoses and prohibitionists that often plague America is having an effect. As in some rural county in Kentucky or Tennessee, there will be plenty of alcohol all around you, but you may have to ask a man with a red nose if you want to find any. Bars tend to be tucked away behind curtained windows, or upstairs, or in hotels; look for the blue and yellow *Efes Pilsen* sign. Most small towns also have at least one outdoor beer garden on an obscure side street. In any case, the availability of beer will always provide a convenient index of the mood and morals of the place you're in. The fundamentalists may wish to get rid of bars altogether, but in the secular Turkish Republic they must be content trying to keep them out of sight, so that innocent lads who never yet tasted beer need not suffer constant temptation.

Ever since Plato recommended mixing wine with three parts water, alcohol has been an issue in this part of the world. Ironically, though, this recurring monster of Temperance exists in a land that has developed a great drinking culture. In the cities' cafés and restaurants, you'll see parties of men at their *rakı* sessions, with a bottle of the 'lion's milk' in the centre of the table. It goes down very slowly, interspersed with plates of *mezes* or snacks and plenty of lively conversation. Such an evening is a Turkish ritual, an art, and getting too drunk would be very bad form. The best place to do it is in an old-fashioned *meyhane*, or tavern, a smoky den that stays open late; you'll know you've found the right joint if someone produces a lute or other instrument and begins some impromptu music.

It is entirely possible that great ages of creative drinking go hand in hand with great periods of art. Certainly the Ottoman empire was at its best during the 'Tulip Period' of the early 1600s. Encouraged by the example of the decadent sultans, Istanbul at that time was quite a swinging place. Turkish traveller and writer Evliya Çelebi wrote with amazement of the hundreds of *meyhaneler* in the cosmopolitan quarter of Pera. Though these were largely patronized by infidels, notably sailors, Turks began to catch on. They had just introduced coffee to Europe, and the Europeans were returning the favour with beer and gin. There was already plenty of wine and *rakı*. The Greeks never stopped making it, and they ran most of the bars.

All things considered, the current trend for prohibitionism, or closed-curtainism, should only be taken as one more example of the tenacious continuity of history. All through the Ottoman centuries, it seems that periods of serious public tippling alternated with waves of reaction. Whenever a serious-minded sultan, prodded on by the imams, decided to clean up the Empire, the curtains would appear for a while, or the *meyhaneler* would be driven upstairs. The Turkish Republic so far has been a golden age for drinkers. Partially inspired by the example of Atatürk himself, who died of cirrhosis of the liver, drinking was respectable – also Western, and therefore a sign of modernity (not to mention the fact that the state monopoly was bringing in bushels of lire from its alcoholic products, in a country where more direct sorts of taxation have always proved problematical). There's a story that Atatürk once heard that one of his provincial governors went out drinking every night with his cronies, behind curtains in a hotel. 'Pull them down!' he ordered. 'With curtains up they'll think you have girls dancing on the tables too!'

The Green Man

The vast spaces of the Anatolian interior pull at the heartstrings. Almost all of it is wonderfully lonely and wonderfully beautiful, with a hint of Paradise and a hint of *The Waste Land*, sometimes side by side. So much time and history: the Turks often seem innocents to it, relative newcomers who've been in the neighbourhood a mere 800 years.

Somewhere, dozing off by a bus window driving through these endless land-scapes, you may catch a fleeting glimpse of a man in green, riding a grey horse. **Khidr** (the 'green one') is a character of pre-Islamic mythology, though his origins remain unknown. There seems to be a mention of him in the story of Utnapishtim in the Sumerian *Book of Gilgamesh*, the world's oldest written epic. As Khizr, he is mentioned in the Koran as the 'unknown'; some old legends say he was vezir to a Persian king in the 6th century BC, who was blessed by God with eternal youth. Muslim Sufi mystics mention him often; his sudden and unpredictable appear-ances are a symbol for the inspiration or enlightenment that comes without warning. In a way, Khidr is a kind of patron saint for the Sufis, and he made his way into Europe along with so many other tales and legends in the early Middle Ages, the time of the Crusades and the troubadours, when the influence of the more civilized Muslim world was extremely strong, much stronger than you will ever read in conventional Eurocentric histories.

Christian stories taken from Islamic sources sometimes transform him into the prophet Elijah, or St George. Reminders of this mysterious character turn up in unexpected places, in the 'Green George' of Gypsy and Slavic spring festivals and, some scholars contend, the 'Green Man' of so many English pub signs. We might see Khidr also in that greatest of medieval allegorical poems, *Sir Gawain and the Green Knight*, a profoundly mystical work whose meanings have never been completely explored. And there is little in Professor Tolkien's *Lord of the Rings* that doesn't strike an echo from somebody's mythology; we shouldn't be surprised to find the Green Man turn up here too, in the person of Tom Bombadil. Khidr has been with the Turks since they first rode off the far Asian steppe into Anatolia. He is mentioned in the *Legends of Dede Korkut*, the collection of epic tales from the Oğuz Turks' nomadic days that was first written down in the 1400s. In the *Tale of Boğaç Khan*, he appears out of nowhere to save the life of the wounded hero; miraculous cures, often involving the 'water of life', are often attributed to him.

The Turks of today, besides being wonderfully meticulous farmers and gardeners, must also be among the most manic tree-planters on the globe. The first thing you'll notice in Istanbul is the trees – a few hundred thousand of them, in a belt of new parks that line the Marmara shore and the Golden Horn. Someone comes out to water the younger ones nearly every day, and they all look green and thriving. In many parts of the interior, the Orman Genel Müdürlüğü, the national forestry service, has done wonders with scant resources in preserving forests and reclaiming land wasted by millennia of deforestation. We have an entirely unconfirmable suspicion that Khidr spends a lot of his time in Anatolia. Travelling west from Beyşehir to Konya, through some of the bleakest and emptiest spaces Turkey has to offer, your eyes will fall on a vision: tiny young pines planted over the hillsides for miles and miles, stretching belief as they stretch on and on. This is the Atatürk Centennial Forest, a wonderfully quixotic and uneconomic attempt at creating a huge forest on what was previously barren land. In all there must be several million trees already planted. Look closely; you might catch sight of him there.

Music

Music is an important part of the Turks' cultural heritage and still one of the things they do best. Western travellers unsympathetic to it have given Turkish music a bad name, calling it monotonous; even if you don't go out of your way to find it, you'll hear enough of it on radios and in buses to get accustomed to it and make up your own mind. What you hear most of, unfortunately, is something called **oryantal** ('oriental') or arabesk, a noxious Arab-influenced pop style. Irritating as it is, the vocal strength and feeling of the performers, especially the women, makes Western popular music sound like a nursery school pageant.

Western classical music came into fashion with Atatürk, although the last sultans had cultivated opera and kept large dance orchestras. Today it is quite popular, and several Turkish singers and musicians have made names for themselves abroad. The Turks have their own classical tradition, however, and you hear what they call *sanat müziği*, 'art music', anywhere, even in night clubs. At first, this was heavily influenced by the Mevlevi dervishes; its main instrument is the lute (our word comes from the Arabic *al ud*). The lutes hanging in Turkish music shop windows differ in no respect from those in medieval tapestries and illuminations; the Crusaders brought them back from Anatolia. To this the Mevlevis add the *ney*, a ghostly, reedy flute. Both types of music are ruled by modes (*makamlar*), like ancient Greek music. Their subtleties will require all your attention and goodwill.

The real treat, however, is Turkish **folk music**, which Béla Bartók said was the richest he had ever experienced. The *âşıklar*, rural troubadours who improvise to a stringed instrument called the *saz*, similar to the lute, can still be found (there may be one seated next to you on a bus) and folk music and dancing are still practised widely (the Black Sea and Aegean coasts, Konya, Kars and Silifke are especially known for them). Wild dances for men, like the Aegean *zeybek* and the *horon* of the northeast, are its most spectacular manifestation, along with popular, mainly improvised dances like the *çiftetelli*, traditionally performed at weddings. Besides the *saz* and lute, other instruments are the clarinet and accordion, a two-headed drum called the *davul*, the *kanun* (a 78-stringed dulcimer related to the Hungarian cimbalom), the *kaval* (shepherd's pipes), the *kemençe* (a tiny violin played like a cello) and the *cura* (a sort of zither that has been traced back to the Hittites).

Finally, there's the **Mehter** music played by the Janissaries under the walls of Vienna and a thousand other towns to dishearten the defenders. With the aid of enormous drums carted around in their own wagons, the 66-piece Mehter bands made grand and gloriously noisy music (you can hear a Mehter concert Wed–Sun afternoons, at the Soldiers' Museum in Istanbul). Though its art and melodiousness were probably lost on the besieged garrisons, Mehter is the ancestor of all our military music and marching bands; it has also found its way into Western classical music through the Turkish bagatelles of Mozart, Beethoven and Weber.

Perusing the *Polis*

There are certainly plenty of other things to do on Turkey's coasts, but as far as sightseeing goes one item stands out above all – ruins. No place around the Mediterranean, possibly no place in the world, has so many once-thriving cities that simply became abandoned and disappeared. Thanks to the earthquakes that regularly shake down all the products of human vanity in this part of the world, not too much of these cities is left standing. To get anything at all from your visit requires a little imagination, and a little knowledge. Here is a very brief primer on Greek cities, so you'll know your way around when you visit one.

A Greek city was more than just a convenient place for people to live and work. It was the sacred *polis*, from which we get words like *politics* and *politeness* (the Romans carried on the idea in their *civitas*; to be 'civilized' was to live in a city). The Greek *polis* was a noble creation, unlike anything the world had known. These little walled towns, self-governing and self-sufficient communities of free citizens, were the seeds from which Western culture grew. As its living heart, each had its **agora**, much more than just a central square. At first only an open stretch of ground at the centre, with a platform for speakers at the citizens' assemblies, the agora also served as a marketplace, and there were also religious shrines or images, and many statues of civic benefactors, soldiers and athletes (and later, the reigning Roman emperor; often they'd just knock off the head and stick on a new one for a new emperor). Greeks did not compartmentalize the various aspects of their public life the way we do: the political, the sacred, civic monuments and day-to-day business shared the same space, a symbol of how life in the *polis* was a seamless whole.

To define the agora, the Greeks came up with an invention perfectly suited to their climate and their way of life: the **stoa**, a long, colonnaded portico, usually closed by wings at the ends. The 'Stoic' philosophers took their name from the stoa, because that is where they liked to gather – along with the rest of the population. At all hours of the day, the stoa gave citizens an attractive place to spend their idle time and talk about the weather or argue about politics. Greek stoas were infinitely adaptable; some excavated examples show stone tables for meat and fish stands. The same ones might have been used at other times by bankers and merchants, or by the city's courts. You'll have to go to Athens to see the reconstruction of a stoa, but they were always mentioned as among a city's major architectural works, often with famous frescoes on the inner wall; Pergamon, always the flashiest of cities, had some that were two storeys tall.

The two important public buildings of the *polis* will also be found around the agora: the **bouleuterion**, or council house, usually in the form of a small, enclosed theatre; and the **prytaneion**, the city's 'common house'. Here a perpetual fire was kept on the sacred hearth, as a symbol of its communal life of the city; a separate room served as a dining hall, in which the city could offer hospitality to visitors, ambassadors, or citizens who brought home victories from war or the games.

In Hellenistic times, planners began to think symmetrically, and when there was a chance for rebuilding they started making perfectly rectangular 'peristyle' agoras surrounded on all sides by stoas (there is a good example at Ephesus; the same idea was used in the Imperial Forums of Rome). Originally stoas would also be built that closed off one side of the agora, and continued from there down one of the main streets – a pretty trick of town design to make a gradual transition from the private spaces of the residential districts to the public space of the agora. In the opulent conditions of the 1st and 2nd centuries AD, this idea grew into the **colonnaded street**, the main status embellishment of any town of the Roman Empire. These often extended as far as the town gates. Towns that had two or more of them, such as Antioch, Side, Perge or Ephesus, were really doing well. Whenever you're exploring a ruined city in Turkey, it should be remembered that most of what you see dates from this period, when the economy of Asia Minor reached its height; it was then that the most impressive public buildings, the basilicas and the gymnasia were built. Only towns like Priene that did not flourish in Roman times give the full effect of what a classical Greek or Hellenistic city was like.

The greatest **temples**, however, were raised in the 5th–3rd centuries BC. Before Roman rule, when the ethos of the Greek city-state was at its height, towns competed to build the most impressive temples, as the towns of medieval France vied to build the biggest cathedrals, or American cities the tallest skyscrapers. A

Greek temple did not have to be in the centre of town: its site was usually determined by tradition, some place that had been holy for centuries or even millennia. The temple itself was a relatively late idea, and never the centre of religious observance, the way a church or a mosque is. It housed a cult image (usually a statue), as well as ex votos and other gifts to the sanctuary; architecturally it served as a kind of stage backdrop for the sacrifice and other rites. In the sophisticated, secular age of the empire, temples were little more than glorified art museums.

The important business of Greek religion was the sacrifice, and this took place in the open air. The **temenos**, or sanctuary, dedicated to a god, is the holy ground where sacrifices were performed, and it could be in or near the agora, or anywhere else, even out alone in the countryside. The temenos would usually be walled off, and it would contain the altar for sacrifices, with the temple façade behind it to the east, as well as a home for the priests or priestesses, and often a sacred grove; important sanctuaries might be entered by a monumental gateway, a **propylaea** or **propylon**. Originally the altar itself was just a simple slab or even a heap of stones – every passer-by would add another to the pile. But by Hellenistic times these sometimes grew into magnificent buildings, such as the Altar of Zeus at Pergamon.

Of the Greeks' homes, you will see almost nothing. It would be surprising how simply they provided for themselves, did we not know how all-important was their communal life. There were neither sharply defined wealthy districts nor slums. The Greeks never minded rubbing elbows with their fellow citizens, of whatever condition; and their houses differed little in outward appearance or in any other way besides size. Few details of Greek houses are well known, only that the fancier ones were built around courtyards. In Roman times these often developed into impressive peristyle courts, with a fountain or pool at the centre.

Where the outlines of streets survive, as at Priene, you'll notice they usually run straight as arrows. The first town planner whose name survived is Hippodamus, an Ionian who redesigned the port city of Piraeus in a grid-iron plan for the Athenians in the 5th century. Hippodamus brought this sort of plan back from his home city of Miletus, which had recently been rebuilt on a grid plan after its sacking by the Persians. Rectilinear street plans came naturally to the geometrically minded Greeks; in the colonies of Asia Minor, this form was the easiest way to lay streets, measure land and get a new town started, just as it was in 19th-century America.

The Greek ideal of *paideia*, intellectual and physical education, treated as one, is symbolized in the **gymnasion**, usually a large complex of buildings that included an enclosed **palaestra**, or exercise ground, but also classrooms and lecture halls (Plato's Academy was a gymnasion). If space permitted, there would also be plane trees for shade (any kind of greenery was very rare in a Greek city), a spring or fountain, and often a temple, perhaps dedicated to Hercules or Hermes. In Roman times the gymnasion grew much more luxurious; palaestrae became monumental colonnaded courtyards, and often a bath complex was added on – Pergamon, as usual, gives the most lavish examples. Occasionally, where there was room for it, there would be a **stadion** too, a course for footraces so called from the measure of length (about 200 yards). Classical stadia were simple open spaces with an earthen bank on one side for spectators; real stadia, with marble seats, colonnades and elaborate entrance gates, did not arrive until Roman times.

The first Greek theatre was the agora itself; in archaic Greece the open space of an agora was often called the **orchestra**, a word that meant a 'dancing place'; it is a reminder of how classical theatre grew up out of the rites and dances that attended the cult of Dionysos. To accommodate growing populations, cities began to build proper theatres wherever there was a natural slope, with a banked, semicircular area for spectators called the **theatron** (or **cavea**), sited wherever possible with a grand panoramic view for a background to the play. When the classical plays were first performed, the orchestra (generally circular or trapezoidal, and unpaved) was still the centre of the action. Only in later centuries was a **skene**, or stage, built; this logical and adaptable feature served much the same functions as the simple, two-level stages we usually use for productions of Shakespeare. Again, only in Roman times did impressive columned stage buildings appear, and they were never universally popular in Greek towns. Neither were the Romans' barbaric gladiatorial games, which explains the lack of amphitheatres in Greek cities – though in many places you can see the Greeks slipping, and building walls around the orchestra of a theatre to protect spectators at such games. It's a sad sight: theatres meant for the works of Euripides and Aeschylus being transformed into arenas for butchery. Nothing could illustrate more clearly the decay at the heart of that opulent age.

Religion

In the *hadis*, the collection of traditions and stories from the days of Mohammed that serves as a commentary on the Koran, it is recorded that the Angel Gabriel, disguised as a Bedouin, confronted the Prophet one day and demanded to know the practices of the true belief. Mohammed's five answers satisfied the angel, and, as the **'five pillars of Islam'**, they continue to guide Muslims today, a solid foundation for the simplest of the world's great religions.

One of the pillars is the professing of the simple formula 'There is no god but Allah and Mohammed is his prophet.' This is painted or inscribed in elegant Arabic calligraphy over all the mosques of Turkey. Another pillar is the pilgrimage to Mecca, for all who are able. Giving alms to the poor is a third; in Turkey, however, begging is frowned upon and the mendicant dervishes and *kalenders* have been outlawed since 1925, so this duty is performed discreetly.

Muslims are also expected to keep a total fast during the daylight hours of Ramazan, the holy month of the Muslim calendar. In public, at least, the fast is well observed. During Ramazan a mood of peaceful contemplation occupies the faithful. Much of radio and television airtime is given over to religious programmes, and every evening at sunset in many towns a cannon booms out the signal that the fast has ended. Mosques are often gaily decorated with coloured lights, nowhere more so than in Istanbul where Koranic messages are spelled out in strings of lights between the minarets of the great imperial mosques.

The most conspicuous of the five pillars is the obligation of saying prayers five times a day, at hours proclaimed by the muezzins from the minarets (often now via loudspeakers attached to the minarets). It is permitted to perform these anywhere, and, although Muslims usually go to the mosques for the midday Friday prayers, there is no Mass or ritual in the Christian sense. In the main, Islam avoids ritual and ceremony. The *imam* (priest) is present merely to lead the prayers; the formulaic discourse he declaims afterwards is hardly a sermon.

Mosque architecture illustrates the simplicity of Islam. Most are large halls furnished only with the *mimber* (pulpit), and the *mihrab* (the niche in the wall facing Mecca), which concentrates the thoughts and prayers of the faithful like a lens. Non-believers are allowed inside Turkish mosques, except during prayer time. Leave your shoes at the door, dress sensibly (no shorts, short skirts, or bare arms and shoulders) and don't make a nuisance of yourself, but don't feel unwelcome either. Muslims themselves enjoy coming to the mosque for meditation and quiet, and they are pleased to share them with you. To miss the interiors of the Ottoman mosques of Bursa and Istanbul and the Selcuk 'Great Mosques' of the cities of Anatolia would be to miss much of the finest in Turkish art and architecture.

One Islamic ceremony you may encounter accompanies the rite of circumcision: a small parade with a bravely smiling nine-year-old in a costume, crown and cape. Most weddings in Turkey are civil, and the ballyhoo and decorated cars differ little from those in other lands; the busy marriage chapel next to Istanbul's city hall is a good place to watch them.

Most Turkish Muslims are Sunnis, the majority, orthodox creed, but all around the country you'll find a substantial minority of Alawis (or Alevis), a fascinating sect who have no mosques. They do have a relaxed and tolerant attitude about religious matters, combined with a practice of equality of the sexes and often radical political beliefs. Alawis include groups around the Black Sea, the Bektaşi dervishes (*see* p.444) and entire villages inhabited by the nonconformist Tahtacılar in the southern mountains. They are also strong among Turkish intellectuals.

According to the last census, 99.04 per cent of Turkey's population are Muslim, but there are no figures on how many practise their religion seriously. During the 1930s, when Turkey was hell-bent on reform and secularism, religion became unfashionable, at least in the cities. Today, the nation has been experiencing an Islamic revival that could not help spilling over into politics. In many towns, mosques that were once almost empty for Friday prayers are now almost full. Big money pouring in from Saudi Arabia and elsewhere finances not only fundament-alist politics, but scores of rabble-rousing preachers and tract publishing houses; you'll notice the stands they set up on weekends outside the main mosques. Much like what is happening now in the United States, a strange and shadowy battle is currently under way in Turkey for the hearts and minds of the people. The funda-mentalist forces, well organized and well financed, have so far been able to gain success portraying all political issues as a struggle between good and evil. Those who support the secular republic of Atatürk seem confused and divided among themselves. They have yielded ground for many years, but there seems now to be a stalemate. No one knows how this struggle will end, but the spectre of the radical side of fundamentalism should not blind the visitor from the diversity – and beauty – of Islam in this country. Religion's moderate voices here have interesting points to make, and they show a sincere concern for Turkey's future. More than in most Muslim countries, a more tolerant side of Islam has always flourished in Turkey, a long tradition best symbolized by the figure of **Celâleddin Rumi**, the Mevlâna.

The Sultan of Scholars

Islam has no saints, but Celâleddin Rumi, poet and Sufi mystic of Konya, approaches as nearly to that exalted state as is allowed. For Westerners who have never been able to take Islam seriously, he is the man to know.

Born on 30 September 1207 in Balkh, Afghanistan, Celâleddin and his family – his father Bahaeddin Veled was a renowned scholar – fled before the Mongol invasions to Anatolia, where they took refuge in the Selcuk capital, then in its heyday under Sultan Alâeddin Keykubad. Here he remained as a teacher in the city's mosques, withdrawing more and more into his meditations and his poetry until his death on 17 December 1273. The Mevlevi order of dervishes – the 'whirling dervishes' – he founded was tremendously influential throughout the Middle East, and the hereditary line of its sheikhs, descended from the Mevlâna (literally 'our master'), even intermarried with the Ottoman dynasty during the reign of Beyazıt I.

Few poets in the world have been more prolific. His greatest work, a subtly arranged medley of lyric poetry, mysticism and anecdotes called the *Mesnevi* (or *Mathnavi*), runs to some 25,000 couplets (longer than *The Faerie Queene*, the longest poem in English), and there are 44,000 more couplets in the anthology called the *Divan of Shems-i Tabriz*. The title of a third work, *Fihi-Ma-Fih*, 'in it what's in it', clearly expresses the Sufi informality and disdain of dogmas and church establishments. All were written in Persian, the language of court and culture in Selcuk times (good translations of selections exist, notably by Professors Nicholson and Arberry).

The Mevlâna's poetry has been described as an ocean: vast and boundless, encompassing all the systems and creeds of lesser men within it. In truth there is no readily discernible philosophy in his work that does not state the obvious; the Mevlâna wanted it to appeal to all men at all levels. The unity of God and of creation is a recurring theme, consistent with Islam and the teaching of the Sufis. It is the revelation of divine love that sets his work apart, and the spiritual allegory of the 'lover' and the 'beloved', the soul and its dissolution into the infinite, is the core of his thought. On this rarefied plane of understanding, the claims of the various religions seem mere games of language, and issues such as predestination or free will simply cease to be relevant.

As for the whirling dervishes, the Mevlâna and his followers believed as much in music and dance as forms of spiritual expression as they did in poetry. The *sema*, the ritual dance still performed annually in Konya on the anniversary of the Mevlâna's death, 17 December, is his teaching of the abandonment of the self set into motion. The dervishes' tall hats represent their own gravestones, the jackets, which they shed, their graves. As the dancers spin around the floor, symbolically reflecting at once the movements of the cosmos and the soul's search for God, the dancers themselves attain a controlled mystic communion. With one hand raised and the other extended towards the ground, they '...take from God and give to man, keeping nothing for themselves...'

Food
and Drink

04

The Turks themselves are fond of saying that there are three great cuisines in the world – Chinese, French and Turkish. Whether or not you agree, eating is one of the main pleasures of visiting Turkey; there is a wide variety of dishes, the freshest ingredients are common, and, on the whole, the diet of the Turk is a healthy one, based on fresh fruits and vegetables, grilled fish and meat, with many kinds of salad and yoghurt dishes. Have a close look at any Turkish market. Without too many of the chemical tricks used in Western countries, the Turks manage to grow fruits and vegetables that not only taste better than at home, but are much more colourful: tomatoes redder and more luscious than anywhere, and aubergines perfect in form and of a heartbreaking shade of violet (not to mention some exotica like the little purplish carrots of a type that originated in Afghanistan, the ancestors of all the carrots in the world). Western Anatolia has the perfect climate, and some of the most fertile land in the world. Give credit also to the Anatolian farmer, one of the most careful and loving tillers of the soil you'll ever see.

Turkey is one of the few nations to be self-sufficient in agriculture. From tea along the Black Sea coast to bananas along the Mediterranean, everything a Turk could desire grows well somewhere in the country – everything except coffee. Fruit is abundant and wonderful, especially the cherries, strawberries and peaches from around Bursa. The Turks have been exporting fruit for centuries, and even today in Egypt a lemon is called *adaliya*, after Antalya on the southern coast. Pistachios, almonds, walnuts, chestnuts and hazelnuts are often used, plain or in a number of exotic dishes; dried fruits and jams are excellent and plentiful.

Cheeses are also very good, made from the milk of cows, sheep, or goats. Popular varieties include *tulum* (made in a skin), *beyaz* (soft, white, salted), *mihaliç* (rich, unsalted, made from sheep's milk) and *kaşar* (hard, yellow).

Turkish Specialities

A typical menu will offer hot or cold **mezes** (*hors-d'œuvres*, of which Turks often eat several instead of a main course) and soups (*çorbalar*) for starters. Cold *mezes* (*soğuk mezeler*) will commonly include stuffed vine leaves, various kinds of beans in sauces, mushrooms, cooked aubergine salad, spicy tomato salsa, *hummuz* and *cacık* (garlic yogurt with mint and cucumber). Of hot *mezes* (*sıcak mezeler*), the one you'll see most often is *börek*, pastries stuffed with cheese or meat, but here is the chance for a good cook to be creative (and these can really run up the bill if you aren't careful). Seafood restaurants often have prawns, *calamari* (squid) or shellfish. Almost always, you can point and pick out what looks good from the cooler or have the waiter bring you a mixed plate with a little of everything, Of the common **soups** on offer – chicken, yogurt, tomato, tripe or noodle – by far the most popular is *mercimek çorbası*, red lentil soup served with a squeeze of lemon.

For the **main course**, there'll be the ubiquitous kebabs (*see* below) or a mixed grill of various kinds of kebab served on flat bread (*pide*), along with steaks (*bonfile* or a cheaper *biftek*), barbecued chicken, grilled meatballs (*köfte*), roast lamb or grilled lamb chops (*pirzola*). Another popular dish is *saç kavurma*, a stir-fry of lamb and vegetables. If it's seafood, some consultation with the waiter is in order. You should get a chance to pick out your fish; always ask the price beforehand, since fish is the only really expensive food in Turkey. Along with the main course comes normal bread and/or *pide* bread. The bread is delicious and plentiful: while we look at bread as an accompaniment to meals, Turks look at their meals as something to go with their bread. There may also be chips or *pilaf* if you want, and almost always a typical Turkish salad of tomatoes, cucumber, onion, peppers (often these will be hot peppers) and parsley, occasionally with olives, lettuce, rocket and other ingredients. After this comes dessert (hardly ever as elaborate as what you can get in pastry shops), and a coffee or glass of tea. In many restaurants you can top off your meal with a seasonal fruit platter of plums, grapes, apricots, medlars, cherries, strawberries, and every Turk's favourite, *karpuz* (watermelon).

At the less expensive restaurants, usually called a *lokanta*, ready-cooked dishes are displayed on a steam table, and you point at what looks good: there will usually be a nice choice of stewed chicken and lamb dishes, plenty of beans and *patlıcan* (aubergine) cooked in various ways, stuffed peppers or tomatoes, rice *pilaf* and *bulgur* (cracked wheat, a favourite out in the east). Portions are usually small, so don't be shy about choosing several. Many of these places do kebabs too, as well as salads and sometimes barbecued chicken. Such places, where working Turks dine, are breathtakingly cheap, especially those with self-service (*kafeterya*), but they almost never offer wine or beer. An *ocakbaşı* is a kind of Eastern barbecue, where you sit around a charcoal grill while the chef cooks your food – also very good value.

As well as the *lokanta* and *restoran*, there are several types of restaurants that specialize in particular dishes. **Kebap** salons are popular: *kebap* can really mean almost any kind of grilled, roasted or barbecued meat in small pieces, from favourites like *şiş kebap* and *döner kebap* (a herbed lamb roll that cooks slowly as it rotates, served in slivers with sauce, often as a sandwich on pitta bread) to specialities like *kağıt kebap* (lamb and vegetables cooked in foil), *taş kebap* (stewed lamb, sometimes with vegetables), *çöp kebap* (literally 'rubbish kebab', small pieces of lamb or beef on wooden spits cooked over charcoal), *fırın kebap* (a roast lamb dish popular in Konya and on the southern coast), or *İskender kebap* (a mixed platter with a tomato-based sauce and drenched in spicy melted butter). This is the speciality of Bursa; a good one can be divine, while a bad one will lurch in your stomach for hours. *Piliç* (chicken) *döner* is a more recent fad: white chicken layered up on a vertical spit and shaved off like a lamb *döner* (it can be a little dry without the right sauce). Look out for places that advertise 'Gaziantep style' or have names like 'Kahramanmaraş' or 'Şanlıurfa' – these three cities out in the southeast are all famous for their kebabs, and cooks from there have spread all over Turkey. Adana has a reputation too, and *Adana kebap* is a special treat for anyone who likes it hot.

Pide salons are the Turkish approximation of pizza parlours; *pide* is a delicious flat bread, served with various toppings cooked in a wood-fired oven. *Lahmacun* has ground meat, tomatoes and onions, the delight of the Anatolian peasants. *Ramazan pide*, eaten during the holy month of fasting in lieu of bread, is plain with sesame seeds. Perhaps the best is the Black Sea variety (*Karadeniz pidesi*) with cheese, sausage, and so on. The Turks claim tripe soup is the best cure for a hangover, which in part accounts for the popularity of the **İşkembeci**, establishments specialising in tripe, sweetbreads, brains, etc. **Börekçi** specialize in *börekler*, flaky pastries filled with cheese and herbs, or meat. **Muhallebici** concentrate on milk puddings, yoghurts, sweets and chicken soup. Most **meyhaneler** (*meze* bars) also do food, either just simple snacks or chips.

Pastry shops and some restaurants specialize in **sweets**, some with evocative names like *Hanım Göbeği* (Lady's Navel) and *Dilber Dudağı* (Beautiful Woman's Lips), both served in syrup, as is the better-known baklava and shredded *kadayıf*. Turkish pastry chefs produce a number of excellent cakes (often with chestnuts and hazelnuts), a wide variety of *helva*, good ice cream (*dondurma*) and of course Turkish delight (*lokum*), flavoured with rose, pistachio or mastic.

Eating Out

Some tips on restaurants: every tourist resort has lots of them, usually around the harbour. Most of these are open in summer only, and scrape by with temporary staff. You'll do better trying to find one that stays open year-round. Hotel restaurants are usually better left alone. Asking a local is a good idea, but not so much taxi drivers or hotel staff, who all have cousins with a restaurant around the corner. If you're in a provincial, non-touristy town and can't find a decent place, head for the town park; if there's only one restaurant in town, that's where it will be.

On the coasts, near highways and around beaches, look out for small **outdoor seafood restaurants**, usually a house with a few tables and no sign. Here the owner goes out with his boat before dawn, and what he catches will be in the refrigerator for you to choose. Another kind of 'informal' restaurant (they don't really exist, you see, and pay no taxes) can be found at picnic spots or any other place in the country where people from towns come for an outing. Someone comes and sets up a grill and tables, and there you are. Some of these can be amazingly elaborate, with *mezes*, salads, chips and desserts. Both these kinds of places are fun and cheap, and the food can be a real treat, but you'll only find them by accident, or by asking.

Snacks and Street Food

Street food, no matter where you go, will be as varied and pleasing as the restaurants. Every street corner seems to have its **büfe**, a small stand that makes sandwiches or plates of *döner*, *köfte* or other kebabs; many have a few tables in the shade for you to sit down. Vendors on the street sell sandwiches, *lahmacun*, *pide*, *börek*, mussels and other things (watch out for the carts where something that looks like a very long roast is being barbecued – it's really wound-up *kokoreç*, sheep's gut; in fact it's not too bad). Any of these will do you for a light lunch (or breakfast), and any time of day you will also have your choice of a dizzying array of snacks. Vendors will sell you a *simit* (a bread ring covered with sesame seeds), peeled cucumbers, fruit in season, fruit juice (sometimes from elaborate, jingling brass dispensers borne on the back), pumpkin seeds, chickpeas, dried fruit and nuts. Look out for *çiğköfte*, literally raw meatballs, a speciality of southeastern Turkey. This delicious, highly spiced patty is made from bulgur, tomato paste, fresh herbs and lean ground meat. The mixture is kneaded until the friction and spices actually 'cook' the meat. It is often eaten wrapped inside a lettuce leaf and washed down with an *ayran* (*see* below) to cool the palate.

Kahramanmaraş out east is an inferno in summer but every Turk knows it as the capital of **ice cream** (*dondurma*). So when you see a fellow out on the street dressed in a sort of Hollywood-*Arabian Nights* costume, manipulating what seems to be a gigantic wad of bubble gum with two sticks, he's making Kahramanmaraş-style home-made ice cream. For another summer treat, look for kiosks with coolers of *vişne* – fresh black cherry juice, which is tart and delicious and makes being out in the sun worthwhile (at least when it hasn't been sitting in the cooler too long).

Drink

Turkish **wine** is quite good, but due to heavy government taxation it has become surprisingly expensive, especially in restaurants. It is produced all over the country, especially in Thrace, Cappadocia and scattered parts of western Anatolia. Two good varieties are Buzbağ, a red (*kırmızı*) from out east around Elazığ, and Turasan, a Cappadocian white (*beyaz*). The most popular labels in restaurants are Kavaklıdere, and Villa Doluca, which come in both red and white.

Thirty years ago, Turkey was the world's sixth-largest wine producer, but wine has been in steady retreat with competition from **beer**, the most popular drink in Turkey. Everywhere, you'll find Efes Pilsen, made by the state alcohol and tobacco monopoly TEKEL, under licence from Pilsener Urquell. It's pretty good, but you may prefer an imported beer; most likely this will be Tuborg, Troy, Miller or Carlsberg.

Rakı, the favourite strong drink (50% proof), is distilled from raisins and flavoured with aniseed; it's the same as Greek ouzo, really, and always cut with water. The secret, as every Turk knows, is a long drawn-out meal or a constant supply of snacks to go with it. The rakı you'll see most often is Yeni Rakı, previously corrosive, now more refined as a response to competition from newer brands like Tekirdağ. Kulüp is much rarer (Turkish folklore says the two tipplers on the label are Atatürk and İsmet İnönü), as is Altınbaş. All are made by the state monopoly, as are most of the **spirits** on offer; imports are much more expensive. In most places, alcohol can be purchased only at TEKEL outlets; there's one in the centre of any town.

Soft drinks are mediocre, though in the generally beerless *lokantas* and kebab stands you'll see Coca-Cola and a decent orange soda called Yedigün. Fizzy bottled mineral water (ask for *soda* or *maden suyu*) is readily available, and good for you, as the red crescent on the label testifies. Fresh, bottled or canned **fruit juices** may be found at snack stands (*büfe*) in all but the smallest villages. The white, milk-like drink you see everywhere is *ayran*: yoghurt, a little salt and water.

Turkish coffee – very sweet (*şekerli*), with a little sugar (*orta şekerli*) or without sugar (*şekersiz* or *sade*) – is good and thick. **Tea**, however, is far more common. It is grown on the Black Sea coast and sold by the state monopoly, and all Turks can afford it. As a guest, you will constantly be offered tea (or even apple tea) – as soon as you arrive almost anywhere, someone will appear with a tray and several glasses. Ubiquitous as tea is, however, the old-fashioned tea salons are increasingly hard to find, with their beautiful gleaming samovars and *nargileler*. But in towns you will never be more than a short walk away from a *çay bahçesi* (tea garden). Every park and square has one or several, and in the town centres there will usually be a whole collection of them, packed in the evening.

Turkish Menu Reader

kahvaltı	kah-vahl-tuh	breakfast
öğle yemeği	er-leh yeh-meh-ee	lunch
akşam yemeği	ahk-shahm yeh-meh-ee	dinner
yemek listesi	yeh-mek lihs-teh-sih	menu
hesap	he-sahp	bill
ekmek / poğaça	ek-mek / poh-ah-juh	bread / bun
simit	see-meet	bread ring with sesame seeds
tereyağ	te-re-yay	butter
reçel / bal	reh-chel / bahl	jam / honey
yumurta (haşlama)	yoo-moor-tah (hahsh-lah-mah)	eggs (boiled/poached)
omlet	ohm-let	omelette
menemen	meh-neh-mehn	scrambled eggs with tomatoes, cheese and peppers
kaymak	kahy-mak	cream
peynir	pay-nihr	cheese
tuz	tooz	salt
şeker	shek-ehr	sugar
sirke	sihr-keh	vinegar
zeytinyağ	zay-tin-ya	olive oil
turşu	toor-shoo	pickles
salça	sahl-cha	sauce

Meze	Meh-zeh	Hors-d'Œuvres
Arnavut ciğeri	ahr-nah-voot jee-ehr-ih	'Albanian' liver (cold, spicy, fried)
cacık	jah-juhk	cucumber, garlic and yoghurt
fasulye	fah-sool-yeh	green beans (in olive oil)
gözleme	gurz-leh-meh	Turkish pancakes
kısır	kuh-suhr	bulgar with onions, pepper, parsley
mantı	mahn-tuh	ravioli
pastırma	pahs-tuhr-mah	very spicy pastrami, with garlic
sigara böreği	sih-gah-rah ber-ay-ee	flaky pastry filled with cheese
sucuk	soo-jook	Turkish spicy sausage
yalancı dolma	yahl-ahn-juh dohl-mah	stuffed vine leaves

Çorba	Chor-bah	Soup
düğün çorbası	dooh-oon chor-bah-suh	'wedding soup' – lamb soup with eggs and lemon
et suyu	et soo-yoo	consommé ('meat water')
ezo gelin çorbası	e-zoh geh-lin chor-bah-suh	tomato, lentil, mint, lemon soup
İşkembe çorbası	ish-kem-beh chor-bah-suh	tripe soup with egg sauce
mercimek çorbası	mehr-jih-mek chor-bah-suh	red lentil soup
paça çorbası	pah-chah chor-bah-suh	sheep's trotters soup
şehriye çorbası	shehr-ee-yeh chor-bah-suh	chicken noodle soup
yayla çorbası	yiy-lah chor-bah-suh	rice, yoghurt, egg yolks in broth

Salata	Sah-lah-tah	Salads
beyin salatası	bey-ihn sah-lah-tah-suh	sheep's brain salad
çoban salatası	cho-bahn sah-lah-tah-suh	mixed vegetable salad
patlıcan salatası	paht-luh-jan sah-lah-tah-suh	pureed aubergine (eggplant)
tarama salatası	tah-rah-mah sah-lah-tah-suh	roe with olive oil and lemon juice
tarator salatası	tah-rah-tohr sah-lah-tah-suh	sesame syrup, walnuts and garlic

Et	Et	Meat
bamya etli	bahm-yah et-lih	okra stew with beef
biftek	bihf-tehk	beef steak
ciğer	jee-ehr	liver
cizbiz	jiz-biz	grilled meatballs

dana	dah-nah	veal
et saç kavurma	et sahtch ka-voor-ma	thin slices of lamb, tomatoes and peppers sautéed at the table
haşlama	hahsh-lah-mah	leg of lamb with carrots and celery
hindi	hin-dih	turkey
İşkembe nohutlu	ish-kehm-beh noh-hoot-lu	tripe (with chickpeas)
kıyma	kee-mah	minced meat
köfte	kerf-teh	meatballs
kadın budu köfte	kah-duhn boo-doo kerf-teh	'ladies' thighs' meatballs (minced lamb and rice)
kuzu	koo-zoo	lamb
kuzu incik patlıcanlı	koo-zoo in-jik paht-luh-jahn-luh	lamb shank with eggplant
kuzu kapaması	koo-zoo kah-pah-mah-suh	lamb stew with vegetables
papazyahnisi	pah-pahz-yah-nih-sih	mutton stew
sığır	suh-uhr	beef
tavuk	tah-vook	chicken
beğendili tavuk	beh-en-dih-lih tah-vook	chicken with mashed aubergine (eggplant), milk and cheese

Balık	**Bah-luhk**	**Fish**
barbunya (kağıtta)	bahr-boon-yah (kah-uht-ta)	red mullet (in foil)
dil balığı	dihl bah-luh-uh	sole
iskorpit	ihs-kor-piht	rock fish, stone bass
istavrit	is-tahv-riht	mackerel
istiridye	ihs-tihr-ihd-yeh	oyster
kalamar	kah-lah-mahr	squid
kalkan	kahl-kahn	turbot
kamsi	kahm-sih	anchovy
karagöz	kahr-ah-gerz	sargus
karides	kah-ree-des	prawn
kefal	keh-fahl	grey mullet
kılıç balığı	kuhl-uch bah-luh-uh	swordfish
kılıç şiş	kuhl-uch shish	skewered swordfish kebabs
lüfer	leu-fehr	blue fish
mercan	mehr-jahn	pandora
midye	mihd-yeh	mussels
palamut	pahl-ah-moot	bonito
pavurya, yengeç	pah-voor-yah, yen-getch	crab
pisi balığı	pih-sih bah-luh-uh	brill

Sebze	**Seh-bze**	**Vegetables**
biber	bee-behr	green pepper
domates	doh-mah-tes	tomatoes
kabak	kah-bahk	courgette (zucchini), squash
lahana	lah-han-ah	cabbage
patlıcan	paht-luh-jan	aubergine (eggplant)
yaprak	yahp-rahk	vine leaves

(any of the above can be *dolması* (dohl-mah-suh): stuffed with rice and meat)

bamya	bahm-yah	okra
bezelye	beh-zehl-yeh	peas
enginar	en-gee-nahr	artichokes
fasulye / fava	fah-sool-yeh / fah-vah	beans / broad beans
havuç	hah-vooch	carrots
ıspanak	uhs-pahn-ahk	spinach
kuşkonmaz	koosh-kahn-mahz	asparagus
mantar	mahn-tahr	mushrooms
marul	mahr-ool	lettuce
nohut	no-hoot	chickpeas
patates	pah-tah-tes	potatoes

pilav	pihl-ahv	rice
soğan	so-ahn	onion
zeytin	zay-tihn	olives
imam bayıldı	ih-mahm bay-yuhl-duh	aubergine stuffed with onions and garlic in olive oil
iç pilav	itch pihl-ahv	rice with chopped liver, raisins and pine nuts
bulgur pilavı	bool-goor pihl-ah-vih	bulgar with onions and tomatoes
fırında makarna	fuh-ruhn-dah mah-kahr-nah	baked macaroni, a bit like lasagne

Meyva — May-vah — Fruit

ahududu	ah-hoo-doo-doo	raspberries
armut	ahr-moot	pear
badem	bah-dem	almond
ceviz	jee-veez	walnut
çilek	chih-lek	strawberry
elma	el-mah	apple
erik	eh-rihk	plum
incir	in-jeer	figs
karpuz	kahr-pooz	watermelon
kavun	kah-voon	melon
kayısı	kiy-uh-suh	apricot
kiraz	kih-rahz	cherry
muz	mooz	banana
portakal	por-tah-kahl	orange
şam fıstığı	shahm fis-tuh-yuh	pistachios
şeftalı	shef-tah-luh	peach
vişne	vish-neh	cherry

Tatlı — Taht-luh — Desserts/Sweets

aşure	ah-shur-eh	pudding with beans, cereals, nuts and raisins
çikolata	chik-o-lah-tah	chocolate
dondurma	don-duhr-mah	ice cream
ekmek kadayıf	ek-mek kah-dah-yuhf	bread in syrup
kabak tatlısı	kah-bak taht-luh-suh	slices of pumpkin in syrup
lokma	lohk-mah	round doughnuts in syrup
lokum	lohk-uhrm	Turkish delight
muhallebi	mu-hal-le-bih	milk pudding
pasta	pah-stah	cake
sütlaç	seut-lahtch	rice pudding
tavuk göğsü	tah-vook ger-seu	milk pudding with chicken breasts
tel kadayıf	tel kah-dah-yuhf	shredded wheat in syrup
un helvası	oon hel-vah-suh	halva made of flour and butter
zerde	zehr-deh	sweet rice with saffron

Drinks

su / maden suyu	soo / ma-dehn soo-yoo	water / mineral water
süt	seut	milk
çay	chiy	tea
ada/ elma çayı	ah-dah/ el-mah chiy-uh	sage /apple tea
kahve / Neskafe	kah-veh / nes-kah-veh	coffee / instant coffee
suyu / meyva suyu	soo-yoo / may-va soo-yoo	juice (literally 'juice of') / fruit juice
oralet	or-a-let	orange-flavoured hot drink
salep	sah-lep	a winter hot drink: milk, sugar and salep (powdered orchid tuber)
bira	bih-ra	beer
beyaz / kırmızı şarap	beh-yaz / kuhr-muh-zuh shar-ahp	white / red wine
buz	booz	ice

Planning Your Trip

05

When to Go

For a few days' sightseeing in Istanbul, any time is a good time, although you should take a thick coat and waterproof shoes in winter. To see the Turkish countryside at its most colourful and flower-filled, go in **April** or **May**. Those intent on the archaeological sites on the Aegean and Mediterranean shores should avoid **July** and **August**, when the sun can be uncomfortably intense. For a guarantee of near-perfect weather, however, these are the months to go, especially if you intend to visit the Black Sea. In **May**, **June** and **September** it will still be deliciously warm on the coasts and also less crowded. Eastern Anatolia should only be visited between the months of June and September, even though that is when the south of the region is at its most tinderbox-hot. At other times of the year, many towns are either impassable or unreachable due to snow or landslides.

Climate

Turkey is large enough for each region to have its own meteorological tendencies. The south Aegean and Mediterranean coastlines get the best of the weather, with a bathing season that extends from early April to the end of October. It rains in winter but is rarely desperately miserable – unlike in Istanbul, the Marmara and Thrace, where from November to February you can expect snow and long, gloomy spells. The Black Sea is the wettest and most humid region, where only in July and August can the weather safely be forecast as warm and dry. Central Anatolia and Cappadocia can be bitingly cold in winter, but not as cold as in northeastern Anatolia, where the mercury will dip to well below freezing for months on end. South-eastern Anatolia is the driest region; here

Turkey touches the Middle East and in summer the sun is so hot so that even stepping out of the shade can make you feel burnt to a cinder.

Packing

Those who intend to visit Turkey in the height of summer should pack a few items to guard against the sun's more malevolent effects: a hat, for example, which should always be worn. A large (at least one-litre) water bottle is essential, particularly if you plan to do some hiking. Sunscreen should be at least factor 15 and preferably factor 25.

A torch can be useful for exploring dark nooks and crannies (and for when your cheap hotel suffers a power cut), and a sink plug is also worth packing.

Toilet paper is often unavailable in public lavatories, so unless you're prepared to use your left hand, bring some.

Women may want to pack a headscarf and a long skirt for visiting mosques and for travelling in Turkey's more conservative regions.

Festivals

The two major national festivals in Turkey follow **Ramazan** (*see* pp.48–9), and thus the time changes from year to year. The first, **Şeker Bayramı** or Ramazan feast, lasts for 3½ days and comes directly after the month-long fast. Shops are stocked with sweets for children; the general mood is light and carefree.

More important is the 4½-day **Kurban Bayramı** or Feast of the Holy Sacrifice, about a month after Ramazan. It is a time of visiting, giving gifts to children, and feasting. Traditionally, a sheep or lamb is bought and sacrificed on the day the festivities culminate, in imitation of Abraham's sacrifice of Ishmael, who takes the place of Isaac in the Mohammedan version. Both are bad times to travel; buses, trains, and aeroplanes are crowded with people going to visit relatives.

Other annual festivities are listed in the box opposite. If you're in the vicinity, it would be a shame to miss one; the Turks will probably go out of their way to treat you as a special guest. Indeed, the summer festivals in the major tourist centres along the coast are put on to entertain visitors with displays of folklore, music and dancing.

Average Daily Temperatures in °C/°F

	15 Jan	15 April	15 July	15 Oct
Istanbul	5/41	12/54	23/73	16/61
Izmir	9/48	16/61	28/82	16/61
Antalya	11/52	16/61	28/82	20/68
Ankara	7/45	12/54	23/73	16/61
Trabzon	0/32	11/52	23/73	13/56
Erzurum	−9/16	5/41	19/66	9/48

Calendar of Events

January
First week Sarayköy camel fights, Denizli, Aydın (Sultanhısar) and Selçuk

February
6 Camel wrestling, Yenipazar, Aydın

Second week Camel wrestling, Nazilli, Aydın; Istanbul film festival

March
13–18 Anniversary of the 1915 Sea Victory, Çanakkale

April
14–16 Tulip Festival, Istanbul

19–23 Traditional Mesir Festival, Manisa

29–30 Sultan Hisar Nyssa Arts Festival, Aydın

May
First week International Ephesus Festival, Selçuk; Spring festivities, Iznik and Bursa; Kirkağaç Pine Festivities, Manisa

6–10 Yunus Emre Culture and Arts Week, Eskişehir

Second week Regatta, Marmaris

Mid-month Music and Folklore Festival, Silifke; Tulip Festival, Sincan, Ankara

18 May–3 June Istanbul Theatre Festival

20–23 Black Sea Aksu Festival, Giresun

Last week Marmaris Festival; Pergamon Festival, Bergama; Mesir Festival, Manisa; Şuhut Karadıllı Wrestling Festival, near Afyon

June
First week Nasrettin Hoca Festivities, Eskişehir; Strawberry Festival, Bartin

1–10 International Bandırma Bird Paradise Festival, Balıkesir

Second week International Mediterranean Festival, İzmir

11 Isparta Cherry Festival; Kırkpınar Festival and Greased Wrestling, Edirne

Second week Enez Fish Festival, Thrace; Golden Hazelnut Festival, Ordu; Keles Kocayayla Festivities, Bursa; Kafkasör Culture and Art Festival, near Artvin; Tea and Tourism Festival, Rize

16–24 International Hittite Festival, Çorum

Third week Tekirdağ Cherry Festival

Mid-June–mid-July International Istanbul Music Festival; Aspendos Opera and Ballet Festival; International Bursa Festival; International İzmir Festival; Istanbul Biennial (every two years– 2007, 2011, etc.)

July
First week Yarımca Sports and Folklore Festival, near İzmir; Uluborlu Greased Wrestling; Sea Festival and International Song Contest, Çeşme; İhlara Tourism and Culture Festival, Aksaray; İskenderun Culture and Tourism Festival, Hatay

Second week Golden Karagöz (Black Eyes) Folk Dance Competition, Bursa; Nasreddin Hoca Festival, Aksehir; Traditional Circumcision Feast, Kütahya

Mid-month Şarkıkaraağaç Halvah Festivities, Isparta

Third week Dereli Yayla (Plateau) Kümbet Festival, Giresun; Antakya Tourism, Culture and Art Festival

Last week Datça Knidos Festival; Dereçıne Black Cherry Festival and Sultandağı Black Cherry Festival, both near Afyon; Avanos Handicrafts and Tourism Festival; Abana Sea Festival, Kastamonu

August
First week Veli Baba Memorial Day, Isparta

Second week Babaeski Agriculture Festival, near Kırklareli

10–18 Çanakkale Troy Festival

15 Assumption of the Virgin, Selçuk

16–18 Hacı Bektaş Remembrance Day and Ceremonies, Nevşehir; Burdur İnsuyu Festival

Early–mid-Sept İzmir International Fair

September
First week Elmalı Yeşilyayla Wrestling Matches, near Antalya; Taşköprü Garlic and Hemp Cultural Festival, Kastamonu; Grape Harvest Festival, Manisa

10–12 Söğüt Ertuğrul Gazi Commemoration Ceremonies, Bilecik

Mid-month Cappadocia Wine Harvest Festival, in Ürgüp and Göreme; Ayvalık Tourism Festival

Third week Çal Wine Harvest Festival, near Denizli

20–22 Kızılcahamam Soğuksu Festival

Weekends Mahmudiye Horse Races

October
First week Seben Apple Festival; Antalya Film Festival and 'Golden Orange' Film Competition

Second week Kırşehir Ahı Evran Crafts and Folklore Festival, Kırşehir

December
All month St Nicholas festival, Demre, near Antalya

10–17 Mevlâna Remembrance Day and Ceremonies, Konya

Tourist Information

Turkish Tourist Offices Abroad

UK: 4th Floor, 29–30 St James's Street, London SW1A 1HB, t (020) 7839 7778, *www.gototurkey.co.uk.*

USA: 821 United Nations Plaza, New York, NY 10017, t (212) 687 2194, *http://www.tourismturkey.org*; 2525 Massachusetts Ave, Washington, DC 20008, t (202) 612 6800, *dc@tourismturkey.org*; 5055 Wilshire Boulevard Suite 850, Los Angeles, CA 90036, t (323) 937 8066, *la@tourismturkey.org.*

Canada: Constitution Square, 360 Albert St, Suite 801, Ottawa, Ontario K1R 7X7, t (613) 230 86 54, *info@turkishtourism.ca.*

Australia: Room 17, Level 3, 428 George St, Sydney NSW 2000, t (02) 92 23 30 55, *turkishtourism@bigpond.com.*

Embassies and Consulates

Turkish Embassies, etc. Abroad

UK: (embassy) 43 Belgrave Square, London SW1X 8PA, t (020) 7393 0202, *http://turkishembassylondon.org*; (consulate) Rutland Lodge, Rutland Gdns, Knightsbridge, London SW7 1BW, t (020) 7591 6900, *www.turkishconsulate.org.uk.*

Ireland: 11 Clyde Road, Ballsbridge, Dublin 4, t 0668 5240, *turkemb@iol.ie.*

USA: 2525 Massachusetts Ave, Washington, DC 20008, t (202) 612 6700, *www.turkishembassy.org*, *www.turkey.org*; 821 United Nations Plaza, New York, NY 10017, t (212) 949 0160 (4); 6300 Wilshire Blvd, Suite 2010, Los Angeles, CA 90048, t (323) 937 0118, *www.trconsulate.org*, *www.e-konsolosluk.net.*

Canada: 197 Wurtemburg Street, Ottawa ON, K1N 8L9, t (613) 789 4044, *www.turkishembassy.com.*

Australia: 60 Mugga Way, Red Hill, Canberra A.C.T. 2603, t (06) 295 02 27.

Foreign Embassies, etc. in Turkey

Adana

US Consulate: Girne Bulvarı No 212 Guzelevler Mah. Yüregir, t 0322 346 6262, *http://adana.usconsulate.gov.*

Ankara

British Embassy: Şehit Ersan Caddesi 46/A, Çankaya, t 0312 455 3344, *www.britishembassy.org.tr.*

US Embassy: Atatürk Bulvarı 110, Kavaklıdere, t 0312 455 5555, *http://turkey.usembassy.gov.*

Canadian Embassy: Cinnah Caddesi No 58, Cankaya, t 0312 409 2700, *http://geo.international.gc.ca/canada-europa/turkey.*

Australian Embassy: Ugur Mumcu Caddesi No 88, 7th Floor, Gaziosmanpaşa, t 0312 459 9500, *www.turkey.embassy.gov.au.*

New Zealand Embassy: Iran Caddesi No 13 K:4, Kavaklidere, t 0312 467 9054, *www.nzembassy.com.*

Antalya

British Vice-Consulate: 1314 Sokak 6/8, Genclik Mahallesi, t 0242 244 5313.

Bodrum

British Consulate (honorary): Kibris Sehitleri Cad, Konacik Mevkii No 401/B, t 0252 316 0093.

İstanbul

British Consulate-General: Meşrutiyet Cad. 34, Tepebaşı, Beyoğlu, t 0212 334 6400.

US Consulate: Kaplıcalar Mevkii Sokak No 2, İstinye, t 0212 335 9000, *http://istanbul.usconsulate.gov.*

Canadian Consulate (honorary): Istiklal Caddesi, 189/5, Beyoğlu, t 0212 251 9838.

Australian Consulate-General: Asker Ocagı Cad. No.15, Elmadağ, Sisli, t 0212 243 1333.

New Zealand Consulate-General: Inonu Caddesi No.92/3, Taksim, t 0212 244 0272, *www.nzembassy.com.*

İzmir

British Consulate: 1442 Sokak 49, Alsançak, t 0232 463 5151.

US Consulate: 1387 Sokak No 1/8, Alsançak, t 0232 464 8755.

Entry Formalities

Visas

Citizens of many Western nations require a visa for Turkey. They are no trouble to obtain and can be purchased upon entry. Visas for

British visitors cost £10. US and Australian citizens must pay US$20 for a single entry visa valid for three months. Canadians, however, have to fork out $60. Nationals of Austria, Belgium, the Netherlands, Portugal, Spain, Hungary, Poland and Italy have to buy visas; citizens of most other countries, including New Zealand, do not.

Those intending to travel on to either Armenia or Georgia from Turkey should contact the relevant embassy in their home country before leaving, as border formalities concerning these countries are in a state of flux. If there is no embassy, speak to the Russians. Iranian visas must be purchased before leaving home, a lengthy process that can take up to three months. They are impossible to obtain at the border. You can't get a visa at the Syrian border either, although you can get one quite quickly at home. You may be able to purchase a visa at the Syrian Embassy in Ankara, depending on your nationality (less chance if you're British or American) and on the mood of the official. Remember that 'no' may mean 'not unless you can convince me otherwise'. The border with Iraq is, at present, closed.

Customs

Turkish customs officials generally don't look in the luggage of tourists entering the country. You are allowed to bring in 200 cigarettes and 1 litre of alcohol. Customs controls are tight on leaving the country. Keep the receipts of large purchases, and see p.83.

Currency

There are no restrictions on the amount of Turkish liras or foreign currency that travellers can bring into Turkey. No more than $5,000-worth of Turkish lira (YTL) may be taken out of the country. Currency exchange receipts should always be retained: they help prove to customs the cost of large purchases. On your last few days in Turkey, keep close track of the amount of YTL you have; you'll find it's difficult to get rid of back home.

Disabled Travellers

Turkey is not the easiest of countries for the disabled traveller. There's no easy way onto a bus, or around an archaeological site, and

Disability Organizations

UK

Access Travel, 6 The Hillock, Astley, Lancashire M29 7GW, t (01942) 888844, www.access-travel.co.uk. Travel agent for disabled people.

Holiday Care Information Unit, Tourism for All, Hawkins Suite, Enham Place, Enham Alamein, Andover, Hants SP11 6JS, t 0845 124 9971, www.holidaycare.org.uk.

RADAR (Royal Association for Disability and Rehabilitation), Unit 12, City Forum, 250 City Road, London EC1V 8AF, t (020) 7250 3222, www.radar.org.uk. Open Mon–Fri 10–4.

RNIB (Royal National Institute for the Blind), 105 Judd Street, London WC1H 9NE, t 0845 766 9999, www.rnib.org.uk.

USA

Alternative Leisure Co., 165 Middlesex Turnpike, Suite 206, Bedford, MA 01730, USA t (718) 275 0023, www.alctrips.com. Organizes vacations abroad for disabled people.

American Foundation for the Blind, 11 Penn Plaza, Suite 300, New York, NY 10001, t (212) 502 7600, or t 800 232 5463, www.afb.org.

Mobility International USA, 132 Broadway, Suite 343, Eugene, OR 97440, t (541) 343 1284, www.miusa.org. Provides information on international educational exchange programmes and volunteer service overseas for the disabled.

SATH (Society for Accessible Travel and Hospitality), 347 5th Ave, Suite 610, New York, NY 10016, t (212) 447 7284, www.sath.org. Travel and access information.

Emerging Horizons, www.emerginghorizons.com. International online travel newsletter for people with disabilities.

pavements are usually in an atrocious condition, full of holes and with kerbs knee-high in places (Istanbul, especially, has bottomless abysses in its pavements, with no rails). Worse, the Turkish tourist industry seems to have no concept of the needs of the disabled. Yet this is not to say that a holiday in Turkey is impossible. Turks are waking up to this poor state of affairs and recently the tourist office has begun to publish hotel lists that include information on which hotels have facilities for the disabled. It's not much but at least it's a start. They do not publish lists of tour operators that provide facilities for the disabled in their holiday packages; however, local and national organizations for the disabled should be able to help out here.

Insurance and Health

No **inoculations** are required for Turkey. However, a **tetanus** booster and a **typhoid** jab are wise precautions for travellers heading east of Ankara. A **gamma globulin** vaccination will protect against **hepatitis A** and is advisable if you intend to travel in eastern Turkey, which is less developed than the rest of the country. If you plan to visit the Cilician plains east of Mersin, or any place in south-eastern Turkey for any length of time, you should consult a doctor about taking **malaria** tablets. While on this subject, we can't help mentioning the **mosquitoes** (*sivrisinek*). Especially on the Aegean and southern coasts, these are lusty, magnificent beasts; they take long drinks. Mosquito coils, available anywhere, are a sound investment; nothing else seems to work.

Rabies does exist in Turkey, as in most countries, although cases are extremely rare. Nevertheless, you should avoid any contact with any animal. If this worries you (and it should no more than if you were going to, say, France), ask your doctor about immunization shots. If camping, particularly amongst rocks, be aware that Turkey has several species of poisonous snakes and scorpions.

Turkey has **no reciprocal health agreement** with any Western country and you must pay for all treatment received. Costs are lower than in Europe and the United States but even so can still be expensive. The best medical **insurance** policy is one that will fly you home in an emergency. Be sure to read the small print concerning 'activities' before you sign (scuba-diving, for example, may be viewed as a 'dangerous activity' by some companies). Some policies require you to pay on the spot and then to reclaim the cost (in which case keep all bills and documentation), while others simply require that the doctor or hospital concerned send the bill directly to the insurance company. Policy premiums begin at around £35 a week and usually also include cover against theft.

Maps

The free map distributed by the Turkish Tourism Office is quite good and up to date; for minor roads, the Auto Club (TTOK) map is good. Beware the Turkish habit of putting all provincial capitals in large type; sometimes these have only a few thousand inhabitants (like Bilecik), while an insignificant-looking dot may have a population of 100,000 (like Tarsus). Maps sold in your home country are often out of date or inaccurate.

See also 'Orientation and Addresses', p.68.

NB: there are no definitive spellings of the names of Turkish towns, and you will find different versions in almost any source. We have used the *Ana Yazım Kılavuzu* (Master Spelling Manual, produced under the auspices of the Old Turkish Language Foundation) as a source wherever possible to achieve consistency. Also, Turkish towns and streets undergo frequent changes of name and in some cases (Adapazarı/Sakarya, Eski Foça/Foça) two or more versions may be in use. We have attempted to make this clear.

Money and Banks

Fifteen years ago, it was 2,000 liras to the pound, and tourists joked about using 10 lira notes as toilet paper in bus station toilets. By the end of 2004 the lira had reached an incredible 2,700,000 liras to the pound. On larger sums, an eye-popping amount of zeros were even having an effect on international money markets. In 2004 an average car of £15,000 might have cost you 40,500,000,000 lira. Imagine what a deal worth several million dollars might look like on your spreadsheet! On 1 January 2005, travellers and Turks alike breathed a huge sigh of relief when Turkey shaved six zeros from its currency and introduced the **New Turkish Lira** or **YTL**. At writing the **exchange rate** is approximately 2.35 YTL to the pound, or 1.2 YTL to the dollar, with the currency strong and relatively stable (check latest rates on *www.xe.com/ucc*). During your travels you may still hear people quoting prices in millions; the older generation in particular are still adjusting to the change. If you hear '1 milyon', it simply means 1 lira.

Numbers in Turkish are listed in the **Language** chapter on pp.526–7; study this well, because you're going to need it a dozen times a day. In tourist spots it is quite common to hear prices quoted in dollars or euros.

Learn the colour and design of the current **banknotes** as soon as you can. At present, currency ranges from the impressive 100 lira note to the shiny new, bimetallic, European-style 1 lira coin. Smaller denominations are called *kuruş*. The Turks don't like bills of large denominations much, because they are a struggle to change. It is wise to make sure you have smaller notes on you when boarding taxis as the drivers often don't.

Changing money will be a major source of entertainment. Cash, travellers' cheques and Eurocheques are easily changed in any bank, and sometimes in main post offices too. Rates and commissions differ from bank to bank, and from day to day. Most banks will have rates posted outside, but this is less important than the rate of commission, which you should always find out before handing over any money. Major banks like HSBC, Garanti, Denizbank, Akbank and T.C. Ziraat Bankası will usually give you a fair shake. Many banks across Turkey are equipped with **ATMs**, some of which accept foreign cards (especially Visa), particularly in areas where tourism is big business, but don't count on finding one when you need it. Many bank offices will give you some cash against a major card; as anywhere, though, fees can be high and this is best left as a last resort. Banks also run exchanges at airports and many border crossings, and you'll get as good a rate there as in their main offices. It is best to get your lira in Turkey rather than before you leave home, as you will certainly get better rates.

If you're carrying cash – fat wads of dollars like every Turkish businessman does – you'll want to change it in a *döviz*, a private exchange. These invariably have up-to-the-minute rates displayed on illuminated, computer-controlled screens. These rates can be slightly better than a bank, but commission may be charged. Most of these accept any convertible currency, but very few of them, unfortunately, take travellers' cheques. Ask at any *döviz bürosu* in a large town and they can probably send you to one that does.

Banking hours in Turkey are 8.30–12 and 1.30–5, Monday–Friday. Some banks, like Garanti Bankasi, are open on Saturdays.

Major international **credit cards** are still only honoured in major towns and tourist centres, but bring them along anyhow, as they can be very handy for getting cash in a pinch, for airline flights and for car rentals.

Getting There

By Air

Istanbul has two airports. The main one is the tastefully modernized **Atatürk International Airport** (code IST), *www.dhmiata.gov.tr*, around 20km from the city centre. The smaller **Sabiha Gökçen Airport** (code SAW), *www.sgairport.com*, is around 50km from the city centre on the Asian shore, and services mainly low-cost European airlines such as easyJet.

Turkish Airlines (THY) and the relevant national carriers, such as British Airways, Austrian Airways, Alitalia and Lufthansa, fly to Istanbul daily from most European capitals, including British Airways from London. The flight from the UK to the Turkish coast or the capital takes 5–6hrs. Flights from Germany are the most frequent due to the high concentration of Turks working there; daily services operate from Munich, Frankfurt and Berlin. Some smaller carriers also operate from Germany with bargain fares (*www.germanwings.com*), as they do from London. From southern Europe, Olympic Airways and THY connect Athens with Istanbul at a cost of around £140 including tax.

There are other international airports in İzmir, Antalya, Dalaman and Bodrum, so if you are going to the coast you do not need to fly through the capital.

From the **USA**, Turkish Airlines flies non-stop daily from New York (JFK) to Istanbul. Prices start from around $1,252 return in low season, although cheaper promotional fares are sometimes offered. There are no other direct flights, but several European airlines, for example British Airways, American, Delta, Continental, United Airlines and Virgin, have daily flights from the States to London or other European cities with onward connections to Istanbul, which may well work out cheaper as well as more convenient.

As yet, there are no direct flights between **Canada** and Turkey. A connecting flight is the only option, with an airline such as Alitalia or THY from Toronto, Vancouver or Montreal.

Airline Carriers

From the UK

British Airways (BA), t 0870 850 9850, *www.ba. com*. London Heathrow to Istanbul three times a day, prices from £175 return. Also, London Gatwick to İzmir twice a week, and Gatwick to Antalya and Dalaman in summer.

Turkish Airlines (THY), t (020) 7766 9300, *www.thy.com*. Daily flights to Istanbul and Ankara from London Heathrow with prices starting from £166. There are also departures from Manchester and London Stansted on select days.

easyJet (EZY), *www.easyjet.com*, have a daily flight to Istanbul with prices from £39–79 one-way, if you book well in advance. Flights depart London Luton and fly to Istanbul's Sabiha Gökçen airport. You can also fly from London Gatwick to Dalaman.

For direct flights to the coast:
Cyprus Turkish Airlines, t (020) 7930 4851, *www.kthy.net*. Direct flights to İzmir, Dalaman, Adana and Antalya, then on to northern Cyprus, with fares varying from £200 to £380 according to season; flights leave from London Heathrow, London Stansted, Manchester and Birmingham on various days of the week.

Thomson Holidays, t 0870 165 0079, *www.thomsonfly.com*. Good-value flights from late May–October to Dalaman, Antalya and Bodrum from London Gatwick, Manchester and a variety of regional airports. Fares vary from £140 to £300 according to season.

First Choice, t 0871 200 7799, *www.firstchoice. co.uk*. Summer flights to Bodrum, Antalya and Dalaman, plus a limited service in winter. Fares vary from £140 to £300 according to season.

Websites
www.avro.co.uk
www.charterflights.co.uk
www.cosmos.co.uk
www.pegasusair.com
www.skybargains.co.uk
www.sunexpress.com.tr
www.thomascook.com
www.whichbudget.com

From the USA and Canada

Turkish Airlines (THY), 437 Madison Avenue, New York, NY 10022, **t** (212) 339 9650, *www.thy.com*. Non-stop daily from New York (JFK) to Istanbul.

For flights to London:
Air Canada, t 1-888 247 2262, *www.aircanada.ca*.
American Airlines, t 1-800 433 7300, *www.aa.com*.
British Airways, t 1-800 247 9297, *www.ba.com*.
Continental Airlines, t 1-800 231 0856, *www.continental.com*.
Delta, t 1-800 221 1212, *www.delta.com*.
Northwest Airlines, t 800 225 2525, **t** 800 328 2298 (hearing impaired), *www.nwa.com*.
United Airlines, t 1-800 864 8331, *www.united.com*.
Virgin Atlantic, t 1 800 821 5438, *www.virgin-atlantic.com*.

Websites
www.eurovacations.com
www.expedia.com
www.flights.com
www.orbitz.com
www.smartertravel.com
www.traveldiscounts.com
www.travelocity.com

Airline Offices in Istanbul

British Airways, Buyukdere Cad. No. 20 Tekfen Tower 17th Floor 4, Levent, **t** 0212 317 6600.
Cyprus Turkish Airlines, Büyük Dere Caddesi No. 56/B Mecidiyeköy, **t** 0212 274 6932.
Turkish Airlines, Taksim, **t** 0212 252 1106; Atatürk Airport, Yeşilköy, **t** 0212 463 6363.

By Train

From the UK and Northern Europe

Although direct rail routes from London to Istanbul no longer operate, it is still possible to travel from London to Istanbul by train, via Hungary, Romania and Bulgaria, although this involves changing trains at Paris, Vienna and Budapest or Belgrade.

For Paris, **Eurostar** trains leave from London St Pancras, Ashford and a new station in north Kent, Ebbsfleet International (near Dartford), travelling via the Channel Tunnel to Paris Gare du Nord (2hrs 15mins).

Even with the discounts that are on offer to pensioners, children and those under 26, going by rail is still more expensive than flying. However, both one-way and return tickets are valid for two months and you can break the journey and restart it at any of several points within that time; the train offers a good opportunity to see a little of Europe en route to Asia.

For detailed information on available trains and routes visit the award-winning website The Man in Seat Sixty One, *www.seat61.com*. Note that the German railways website *www.deutsche-bahn.co.uk* has a useful English-language journey planner and ticket-booking service for all of Europe, though it will only get you as far east as Istanbul.

Eurostar, t 08705 186 186, *www.eurostar.com*.

Rail Europe (UK), 178 Piccadilly, London W1, t 08708 371 371, *www.raileurope.co.uk*.

Rail Europe (USA and Canada), t 877 257 2887 (US), or t 800 361 RAIL (Canada), *www.raileurope.com*.

InterRail and Eurail

Anyone travelling InterRail (€599 / £430 full price, discounts available for under-26s), which offers unlimited travel on all European railways for one month, can use their ticket to travel to and within Turkey. However, since rail travel in Turkey is so slow and so cheap, it's far better to use up the month's travel on the more expensive lines in northern Europe before heading south. InterRail is available to all EU citizens who have been resident for six months in the country where they buy their ticket. It can be bought from any British Rail main line station or from some travel agents.

North Americans can travel to and within Turkey on a Eurailpass ticket, but, like Inter-Rail, it is not really cost- or time-effective.

See the **Rail Europe** websites for full details.

From Greece

A train leaves Athens daily for Istanbul via Thessaloniki. The journey time will be an excruciating 36 hours, taking into account the likely long delays at the border. There are no first-class seats. Fly, sail or take the bus!

By Bus

This is no longer the cheapest way to get to Turkey, as it was in the 1970s and '80s, and there is no longer any direct service from London. Still, with some effort and planning true masochists may enjoy the pleasure of bumping across Europe's highways on the three-day slog to Istanbul, with changes in Paris, Munich or Budapest and perhaps elsewhere. For further information and to reserve the initial parts of the journey, contact Eurolines or any National Express agent.

A bus runs daily between Athens and Istanbul, taking about 24 hours. Travel agents in the Plaka and Omonia Square areas of Athens sell tickets. Turkish bus companies like **Ulusoy**, *www.ulusoy.com.tr/eng*, have comfortable coaches that run daily between Istanbul and Athens via Thessaloniki.

Eurolines: t 08705 80 80 80 (7.91p/min), *www.eurolines.co.uk*.

By Car

From London, it's a good four-day 1,900-mile (3,000km) drive to Istanbul.

The fastest way of crossing the English Channel is to take the **Eurotunnel** (t 08705 353535, *www.eurotunnel.com*). It takes only 35mins to get through the tunnel from Folkestone to Calais. Fares start from around £125 for a standard return in low season, rising in summer and high seasons. The price for all tickets is per car less than 6.5m in length and 1.85m high, plus the driver and all passengers.

If you prefer to go by sea, for ferry fares and times to France and Belgium go to *www.ferrybooker.com*.

Motorists have a choice of four **points of entry** from Europe: İpsala and Kastanea-Pazarkule on the Greek border, or Kapikule and Aziziye on the Bulgarian frontier.

The quickest **route** – through Belgium (Ostend), Germany (Munich), Austria (Salzburg), Slovenia (Ljubljana), Serbia (Belgrade) and Bulgaria (Sofia) – cannot be recommended, because of the instability of former Yugoslavia. Possible alternatives are to detour east, via Hungary (Budapest), Romania (Bucharest) then Bulgaria (Sofia), or drive further south through France and Italy, and take a car ferry from Italy to Greece then on by road, or take the ferry direct from Italy to the Turkish port of Çeşme near İzmir on the Aegean coast. **Marmara Lines**, *www.marmaralines.com*, sail once a week from Ancona and Brindisi in Italy to Çeşme. It's a 56-hour crossing so be sure to have a good thick book with you. Departures are from early March to November. Prices for passengers with car start from 1,200 YTL/£500 per person, and increase depending on the class.

Car ferries also operate from Haifa, Alexandria, Cyprus and Odessa, and, year-

Drivers' Clubs

For more information on driving abroad, contact the AA, RAC or, in the USA, the AAA:

AA, general enquiries, **t** 0870 600 0371, *www.theaa.com.*

RAC, general enquiries, **t** 0870 572 2722, *www.rac.co.uk.*

AAA (USA), **t** 800 222 4357, *www.aaa.com.*

round, between the **Greek islands** and their nearest Turkish port. Crossings are daily in summer but can drop to only one or two a week in winter. Boats cross between Rhodes and Marmaris, Mytilini (Lesbos) and Ayvalık, Kos and Bodrum, Samos and Kuşadası, and Chios and Çeşme (the last two have some room for cars). Both Greeks and Turks levy capricious 'port taxes' on these short runs, which are all very overpriced as it is. See *www. ferries.gr.*

For more information and reservations for ferries contact **Alternative Travel & Holidays**, *www.alternativeturkey.com.*

Driving Regulations

To bring your car into Turkey you'll need an international driver's licence, vehicle registration papers and insurance that covers both European and Asian Turkey; a Turkish policy may be purchased at the border. The vehicle is noted in your passport, allowing it to enter for a maximum of six months in any one year. It must be taken with you when you leave, or else be placed in the care of customs until you return to Turkey. Motorists must carry a fire extinguisher, a first-aid kit and two warning triangles.

The driver's best friend in Turkey is the **Turkish Automobile Club** (Türkiye Turing ve Otomobil Kurumu or TTOK, *www.turing. org.tr/eng*) which gives information on all aspects of driving in Turkey, as well as a repair service (free if you belong to a home automobile club, see box above) and excellent maps; for TTOK addresses in Turkey, *see* p.72.

Getting Around

Orientation and Addresses

Most Turkish cities are compact and easy to explore **on foot**. Many larger cities, such as Bursa, have grown up on a linear plan, with all the main points of interest spread out along one or two main routes, served by dolmuşes (*see* p.73). You'll know you're in the centre of town if you can see the Atatürk monument.

One major problem in towns of all sizes is the lack of **street signs**, but almost every local tourist office can provide you with a **map**. City tourist offices almost always provide acceptable maps; those for Istanbul and İzmir are as good as any you pay for. For maps of the country as a whole, do not expect to find anything with the detail available in maps of western European countries; nothing like the Ordnance Survey or US Geodetic Survey is on offer. The familiar 'Tourist Map' of all Turkey, given out by any tourist office, is surprisingly accurate and helpful within its limits. Commercial maps are no better; their road networks will usually be far out of date.

Addresses can be a minor nightmare. İzmir is the worst town, with its bizarre habit of numbering streets randomly, up to four digits – imagine trying to ask someone the way to the corner of 1348 and 655 Streets in Turkish. Antalya and other cities do this too. Often an address includes the city district, or *mahalle* (abbreviated *mah.*), with the street name after it. Often, too, instead of or in addition to a district name there will be the name of a main street; so if your hotel is at Gazi Mah. Atatürk Cad. Zeytin Sokak, you're looking for a side street called Zeytin, just off Atatürk Caddesi, in the Gazi neighbourhood. *Caddesi* means avenue; *Sokak*, street; *Bulvar*, boulevard; *Meydan*, square. In smaller towns, you'll find addresses like *Hasan Postaci Evi* – 'by the house of Hasan the postman'.

Most **historical sites** are near villages, and can be visited without recourse to a taxi, by taking a minibus from your base to the village and walking (a place that was convenient for a town in 500 BC is often just as convenient in 2000 AD – they're rarely more than a mile or two apart). However, be sure you have transport back! If it's a very small village, the minibus that brought you will often not return until noon the next day, and there may not be anything resembling food or lodging. If you do get stuck, hitching a ride back is your best bet. Buses will almost always stop for you anywhere along the road, if there's room.

By Air

Turkey's air network has grown rapidly over the last 10 years. You can easily fly from Istanbul to İzmir, Antalya or Ankara. Besides these, there are also frequent services from Istanbul to Dalaman (between Fethiye and Marmaris), Kayseri (for Cappadocia), Adana (the nearest airport to the eastern Cilician coast) and Bodrum, as well as to Denizli (Pamukkale).

The main two domestic airlines competing with **THY** (Turkish Airlines, the national airline), are **Onur Air** and **Atlasjet**, both making connections from Istanbul to İzmir, Antalya, Dalaman, Bodrum, Adana, Erzurum, Kayseri, Trabzon and Van.

The airlines change schedules and prices from season to season. In general, the longest internal flights cost around £90/$180 for a single ticket. Fares are generally slightly higher on THY than on their competitors. Children aged between 2 and 12 get a 50 per cent discount on THY flights, and infants of 2 years and under get 90 per cent.

Istanbul–İzmir and Istanbul–Antalya flights run daily at least, even in winter. THY runs a daily service to Konya in summer, weekly in winter. It is best to book your ticket a few days in advance as seats can be in demand.

For any flight, make sure you're at the airport two hours in advance. Security at Turkish airports is admirably tight, or annoyingly tight, depending on your point of view. Passengers are frisked and their baggage X-rayed when they enter the airport. Istanbul's domestic terminal is about half a mile from the international terminal; a bus service connects the two. For details on Istanbul's airports, and getting in and out of the others, see 'Getting around' sections for each town.

Turkish Airlines (THY), *www.thy.com.*

Onur Air, *www.onurair.com.tr.*

Atlasjet, *www.atlasjet.com/en.*

By Sea

The iconic old Bosphorus ferries diligently shuttle people between Istanbul's European and Asian shores throughout the day; they are a joy to behold and to ride.

Istanbul Deniz Otobüsleri or **İDO** (Istanbul Ferries) operates fast catamaran car and passenger services with routes across the Sea of Marmara. These connect Istanbul's Yenikapıport to Bursa, Bandırma and Yalova. A ferry runs between Istanbul and İzmir in the summer operated by the recently formed **Denizline**. Car ferries cross the Dardanelles between Gallipoli and Çanakkale. There are also regular ferries between Girne on the southeast coast and Taşucu in The Turkish Republic of Northern Cyprus.

Istanbul Deniz Otobüsleri, *www.ido.com.tr.*

Denizline, *www.denizline.com.tr.*

By Train

Turkish State Railways (TCDD) has a rail network 5,127 miles long. However, for the most part the trains are old and slow; buses are much faster, much more convenient, and almost always cost less. Lack of speed is the big drawback. Turkey built its railway network a century ago on the cheap; there are few bridges and tunnels, and tracks meander all over the countryside instead of taking the most direct route. If you have the time and money, however, it's fun to take the train, especially overnight, where you can get an inexpensive *küşet* (couchette). For a change from riding buses, a comfortable, air-conditioned first-class seat is nice; and, compared to anything in the world except a Turkish bus, the fare is still a bargain. A reduction of up to a third is available on return tickets; students get 10 per cent off on top.

In **Istanbul**, the starting point for routes to Europe and the west is **Sirkeci Station, t** 0212 527 5051; all trains to Anatolia depart from **Haydarpaşa Station** on the Asian side, **t** 0216 336 4470. Highly popular are the night express trains between Ankara and Istanbul (the **Yataklı Ekspres** and the **Fatih Ekspres**) and the **Ankara–İzmir express**, all with sleeping cars. The country's 'old faithful', however, is the **Doğu Ekspresi**, which leaves Haydarpaşa daily at 11.55pm to wheeze its way for nearly two days across Anatolia to Kars, calling in at İzmit, Bilecik, Eskişehir, Ankara, Kayseri, Sivas, Erzincan and Erzurum.

Note that there are no trains at all on the southern coast: the mountains foiled the engineers completely, and they never got further than Aydın. You can get to little Eğirdir on the lakes by train, but not to the major city of Antalya. The Turkish State Railway has a major new project in development for a high-speed rail link between Istanbul and Ankara that will reduce the 6½hr journey to just 2hrs 30mins.

Turkish State Railway, *www.tcdd.gov.tr*.

By Bus

Forget the trains; you are most likely going to spend a fair piece of your holiday riding the praiseworthy Turkish bus, with white-shirted businessmen and penniless army recruits, housewives and laughing children, students and scholars. The Turkish bus is a great democratic institution, and one of the most pleasant ways of getting around ever invented, an essential part of the Turkish experience. The coach companies are private, highly efficient and incredibly cheap. Fares are proportionate to time and distance: as a guideline, each hour on the bus costs around 4 YTL. Most buses are Mercedes-Benz, air-conditioned and quite comfortable.

You can buy **tickets** in advance from bus company offices in the city centres, but between cities this is hardly ever necessary. All you do is show up and, before you know it, a bus agent will have you on a vehicle to your destination; occasionally you'll have to wait an hour or two, but usually you'll be on your way within 15 minutes. It's worth shopping around in the station ticket hall, though: another company may have an earlier, faster or more direct bus. Prices are supposedly controlled, but some companies may offer a slightly better deal.

Since almost all of the **bus stations** (*otogar*, a corruption of the French *autogare*) are on the outskirts of towns, some of the bigger companies have **shuttle buses** (*servis arabası*) in and out of the centre; remember to ask if you buy your ticket in advance. Usually, you'll have to take a city bus, taxi or dolmuş to and from the *otogar*, which is no problem. Some are close enough to walk to from the centre with a bag; details for each town are in the 'Getting around' sections.

Some of the companies are growing quite large and monopolistic in their areas, which may reflect itself in better service, swanky double-decker buses and tea and biscuits; **Istanbul Seyahat**, *www.istanbulseyahat.com*

(in Turkish); **Varan**, *www.varan.com.tr*; **Ulusoy**, *www.ulusoy.com.tr*, and **Kamil Koç**, *www.kamilkoc.com.tr* (in Turkish) are dependable.

Almost every bus (and train) station has an *emanet*, a **left-luggage** facility. Always remember to find out when they close.

A few small companies, as a point of honour, seat foreigners in the front. On steep mountainous routes, this is a dubious privilege. Stops for tea and snacks are frequent, usually lasting about 20 minutes, and on long journeys there will be a stop for lunch or dinner in a roadside inn, where meals will be simple and very cheap. Most buses carry cold bottled water, free on request from the conductor. They also have another of the sweet courtesies that surprise first-time visitors to Turkey: every hour or so, the conductor will appear with a bottle of lemon cologne to splash into your cupped hands. Rub the cologne over your face, neck and arms: it will both refresh you and mitigate the more malodorous effects of a bus crowded with 52 sweaty passengers on a roasting day. Smoking is prohibited on most public buses.

By Car

Apart from in Istanbul, where traffic is a law unto itself, driving can be the best way to see the country, especially its many archaeological sites. Many of these cannot be reached by any public transport. And there are always unspoiled beauty spots along the coast or up in the mountains only half an hour away from you – if only there were a way to get to them.

Most of the main **routes** along the coasts have been improved and widened, and traffic is still usually light. The busiest stretches of road are on the motorway between Edirne and Istanbul, from Istanbul to Ankara, and on the highway east of Adana (auto club repair trucks are available to those in need). Almost all signs have been converted to conform with the **international highway code**, and towns are clearly **signposted** (blue), as are most archaeological sites (yellow).

Law enforcement on the roads is in the shaky hands of the *Trafik Polisi*. They either clear up traffic jams or create them in the cities, and molest bus and truck drivers at rural intersections to make sure papers are in order and the weight limits observed. They may stop you too, and give your car the once-over, looking for mechanical faults. They do not seem to be much nuisance to tourists. Some of their behaviour can be alarming, though – they may zoom up behind you in heavy traffic and screech something over their loudspeakers, which may mean 'pull over', but is actually more likely to mean 'hurry up!' Occasionally, in Istanbul, they will block a busy street and send everyone up the side streets, or even dead-end alleys; apparently the plan is to prevent big blockages down the road by breaking them up into smaller ones everywhere else.

Be careful: Turkey's **accident** rate is disproportionately high. Night driving is best avoided, simply because you can't see many of the hazards, such as sharp, winding roads, cattle and sheep crossings, drag-racing tractors with no rear lights, slow buses with no rear lights, or oil trucks careering to petrol stations that close at 10pm – with no rear lights. In fact, in some parts of the country, you would be forgiven for thinking that it is perhaps illegal to use lights at night, especially on tractors, motorbikes and old lorries. This is not the case of course. In rural areas, many Turks seem to use lights to *see*, but don't seem too bothered about *being seen*.

Getting involved in an **accident** can be a major problem. Find someone to call the *Trafik Polisi*, and wait at the scene to make a police report (no matter how long it takes). Do not move the vehicles. You may be asked to take a breath test; if it's a serious accident there will be a court hearing, which can be the same day, to determine the cause.

According to the highway code, passing is on the left, but in practice you will be **overtaken** on either side (or both at the same time). The basic principle of driving, as in most other Mediterranean countries, is that wherever a car can go, sooner or later it will; Turkish Fiats seem to be specially adapted for driving up and down stairways, and creating third and fourth lanes on two-lane roads.

The **speed limit**, unless otherwise marked, is 90kph in the country and 50kph in villages and towns. Traffic lights are scarce even in Istanbul and rarely heeded; street signs are also rare.

Street Signs

Signs conform to the international standard, and there are only a few cases where you're likely to be confused:

dikkat caution
dur stop
girilmez no entry
park yapılmaz no parking
şehir merkezi city centre
tehlike danger
tek istikamet one way
yavaş slow
yasak bölge / askeri bölge forbidden area or military zone (no photographs)

In the cities, especially Istanbul, **parking** can be a real headache (*Park Yapılmaz* means 'No Parking'). If Turks are parking on the pavements, they probably have special permits to do so. If your car has foreign plates, you may park anywhere as the police won't ticket you. They may, however, haul your beast away, something that is increasingly common in cities and even in some resorts, such as Bodrum, where parking problems are as bad as in cities. Fines are not high, but the inconvenience can be considerable. The Trafik Polisi often do drivers the courtesy of announcing a sweep, cruising down the avenue with a siren that sounds like an eagle with haemorrhoids, bellowing the tag numbers of illegally parked cars over a loudspeaker, a warning before they haul them away. If you hear any such noise (outside electoral campaign periods), go out and check.

If you have a **breakdown** or need a repair, every town has a street or quarter on the outskirts called the *oto sanayi*, given over to mechanics, each specializing in a certain type of repair. In Istanbul, the closest to the centre is in the Dolapdere neighbourhood in the centre of Beyoğlu; in other cities, there are little car-repair compounds that hardly ever close on the outskirts. Spare parts are likely to be your chief problem (though not for most Renault or Fiat cars, which have Turkish-made counterparts), especially outside the big cities. Bring a kit with you if you can. Turkish mechanics, however, are very experienced: if they can't fix the problem, they can probably get your car going so that you can get to the next big city.

Most of the **filling stations** are along the main highways: you'll find BP, Mobil and Shell and the Turkish company, Petrol Ofisi, at the sign of the wolf, and Türkpetrol at the sign of the tipped cap. The price of petrol varies from one place to another, depending on how far the fuel has to be transported. LPG and unleaded fuel are available at most stations.

Car Hire

Credit cards can be used for car rental in the major centres. Plastic money should not be relied upon in the outlying provinces, and in general the further east you go, the more decrepit your Renault or Fiat-Murat will be. Local car hire companies can charge as little as half as much as the big international firms, but usually charge extra if you need to drop the car off at another point. The large firms usually don't charge for this. Unfortunately, hiring a car is the only really expensive thing you can do in Turkey; rates are currently as high as in any European country.

You can arrange your car rental in advance, either through your travel agent, or direct with companies like Avis (UK, *www.avis.co.uk*, USA, *www.avis.com*); or Hertz (UK, *www.hertz.co.uk*, USA, *www.hertz.com*). A valid UK or EU **driver's licence** is acceptable for up to 90 days as long as it is the photocard-type; if not, it must be accompanied by an international driving permit, which North Americans will also need. Most cars in Turkey have manual gearboxes, not automatic.

Turkish Automobile Club

The Türkiye Turing ve Otomobil Kurumu or TTOK, *www.turing.org.tr/eng*, is one of the nation's most remarkable institutions. They do the things an auto club is supposed to do – help with breakdowns, insurance and so on – but even if you aren't driving you will cross their path many times. Under its long-time director, the late Çelik Gülersoy, a legend in his own time, the TTOK became the country's major force in promoting tourism, and also in historical preservation. Especially in Istanbul, you will be enjoying the lovely parks and drinking in the cafés they have refurbished. They have even started hotels in some of the wooden Ottoman houses they restored, around the Aya Sofya and Kariye especially. Many of the park benches and street signs you'll see are their work too.

TTOK Offices

Ankara: Gazi Mustafa Kemal Bulvarı, Kültür Sk. No 11 – Tandogan, **t** 0312 229 3806.
Antalya: Kışla Mah. 47 Sok. Köken Apt No 5/4, **t** 0242 247 0699.
Istanbul: 1 Oto Sanayi Sitesi Yanı, Levent, **t** 0212 282 8140.
İzmir: Ali Cetinkaya Bulvarı, Akkaya Apt No.31/2 – Alsancak, **t** 0232 421 7149.
Samsun: Liman İşletmeleri Müdürlügü, **t** 0362 445 0676.
Taşucu: Abdi İpekçi Caddesi 27b, **t** 0324 741 4463.
Border posts: **Kapıkule** (Bulgaria), **t** 0284 238 2327), **Gürbulak** (Iran), near Doğubayazıt, **t** 0472 321 2036, and **İpsala** (Greece), **t** 0284 616 1574.

The TTOK has mobile repair units along many of the main highways. They have reciprocal agreements with the British AA and RAC (*see* p.68), though not the American AAA. They have offices in many towns.

By Taxi

The Turkish driver can coax movement out of a car that would remain dead to any other driver. He can also drive a car containing singularly few of the more generally accepted essentials, such as windscreen, mudguards, brakes. As long as the engine can turn over, a Turkish driver will somehow manage to take his car across open country and to the tops of mountains.
H.V. Morton, *In the Steps of St Paul*

Morton wrote this back in 1936, but some day, out in the wilds looking for an obscure ruin, you may find it's still true. Taxis are ubiquitous and by European standards very cheap. Almost everywhere, they are equipped with meters, and within towns there's no nonsense about them – no bargaining, no surprise, and only rarely a surcharge (for airport runs, night driving – when the meter says *gece*, ''night-time', rather than the usual *gündüz*, 'daytime', etc.). Turkish taxi drivers are usually honest, and almost always (except in Istanbul and İzmir, where folks have taken on big-city manners) taxis provide another object lesson in the amiable differences of Turkish life. If you care to, sit in front – you aren't a *paşa* being chauffeured, but a companion, at least for the duration of the trip. Often, the driver will offer you a cigarette (if you don't offer him one first). And when you reach your destination this gentleman may well refuse a tip. Of course, if you're on your way to the bus station, he may offer to drive you to wherever you're bound instead. He'll bargain the rate ferociously even if he knows you have no intention of taking a taxi to Erzurum; it passes the time. In Istanbul the driving can be hair-raising at times.

If you haven't a car, taxis are the only alternative for seeing many of the outlying archaeological sites; in many places, the drivers do it regularly and have set prices, for a half or a whole day or for individual excursions. To cut costs, you can often share the taxi fare with other travellers. In many places the tourist office will arrange a trip for you.

By Dolmuş or Minibus

Dolmuş ('stuffed' or shared) taxis run in and between cities and towns. You can tell them by the little sign in the corner of the windscreen stating the destination. You just wait for a suitable one, and pile in. You can get off wherever you like along the route. Once the car would probably have been a shiny old American bathtub with tons of chrome, left behind in their thousands by the US military in the 1950s. Today, the dolmuş is more likely to be a purpose-built minibus ('dolmuş' and 'minibus' are used interchangeably in this book, as they commonly are by the Turks). Your fellow passengers – a woman with a giant potted geranium, a man with a chicken on his lap – will welcome you aboard in the grand spirit of dolmuş conviviality. They are an excellent way to meet the locals .

In cities, regular city buses are gradually replacing dolmuş lines, but there are still some around. The red dolmuş stop signs are rare, but anywhere on the main streets of a town you can wait and flag one down; usually though, it is more convenient to go to one of the dolmuş terminals (in the centre of most cities; Istanbul has many) and find one that goes near your destination. They're very cheap, and the driver will make change while he's waiting for a green light; no need to hurry to pay as you go in.

Dolmuşes just like Turkey's were very popular in US cities 80 years ago. They were called jitneys then, from a Yiddish slang word for a nickel, the usual fare; tram lines used their influence with city governments to force them out of business after 1920.

Between towns, on long-distance routes, you get a proper bus (see p.70); for towns close together, or between a provincial capital and outlying villages, there'll be a dolmuş or minibus. In some places, they leave from a central minibus otogar; in others, they start from the main otogar, or at least make a stop there. In some small towns there's no terminus at all, but only a stop along the main street (see 'Getting around' sections throughout the guide). These work just like the city dolmuşes and usually run frequently.

Where to Stay

The quality of accommodation on offer in Turkey varies from luxury five-star chain hotels and all-inclusive 'themed' resorts to basic *pensions* and charming family-run guesthouses. Turkish **holiday villages** (*tatil köyü*) are a good option for families. The large resorts along the coast cater more to package holidays. There is also a healthy boom in the **boutique hotel** sector. These smaller establishments often have more charisma than the large four- or five-star hotels and can be more rewarding.

Hotels and *Pansiyonlar*

Four- and five-star hotels are the same as everywhere else in the world. The staff will speak English, and there will be restaurants and bars, usually a disco and often a hamam. Some luxury hotels are housed in converted Ottoman mansions or caravanserais (many of these are in this book), though most are very modern and surprisingly sharp-looking, well-designed and well-equipped; the best are as good as those of anywhere in Europe. If you can afford to splurge, these can be great bargains, especially out of the high season. Rates are often negotiable (try a little *pazarlık – see* p.85 – over the phone).

Two- and three-star hotels will also be much as you would expect, although in the tourist areas they can be hastily flung together and consequently very functional and soulless, the kind of places built specifically for package tours. In the **one-star**

category, you may struggle to find a member of staff who speaks English, although the rooms will be clean and often have private showers and toilets.

The **staff** in Turkish hotels, like the Turks in general, are extremely friendly and helpful. They are willing to handle almost any difficulty that may arise: giving directions, finding taxis, making reservations and handling laundry (*çamaşır*). If you get a room that is dirty, or the lock or lights don't work, don't hesitate to complain or demand another one.

Breakfast, on offer in all hotels with stars and many of the *pansiyonlar*, is usually a simple Mediterranean affair with bread and jam or honey, cheese, olives and tea or coffee, though in fancier establishments it will often be an elaborate buffet. Hotel restaurants, even in Turkey, the land of wonderful cuisine, are, in general, overpriced and dull, although we've found several exceptions.

The sort of *pansiyon* (*pension*) you are most likely to encounter in the coastal resorts will usually be quite pleasant: a modern concrete building which your hosts may have all to themselves, or share with other apartments. The rooms are generally bright and airy, and there may be a roof terrace for breakfast (part of the deal in some but not all establishments; you'll almost always have a choice of whether to take it or not). Most of them also have heating; you'll notice a lack of blankets, though if you ask for some they will be supplied. Unless the hotel has 'continuous hot water', take your shower early in the morning or in the evening when the hot water's turned on. In smaller hotels and *pansiyonlar* you may have to ask at the desk for it to be turned on. If the hot water is solar-heated, then shower in the late afternoon.

There may well be a younger member of the family in your *pansiyon* who speaks some English – but you may already have met him, at the bus station. You don't have to work to find a *pansiyon* in any Turkish town where tourists come; they'll find you. When you're getting off the bus, or even walking down the street carrying a bag, someone will probably materialize from a doorway and start on about the lovely place run by his mom or brother or cousin, where the hot water is ever so dependable. Surprisingly, if you can't find a room in one of the places mentioned in this book, you'll find that just giving in and following him gives you the same odds as hunting up a place yourself. Just because a hotel has to go out looking for trade, it does not necessarily mean it's a dive. It's just as likely that the family that runs the *pansiyon* is working hard to succeed, and will give you the same attention during your stay.

Some tips for playing this game. Find out whether the tout is a family member or just someone on commission; a little casual chat will usually tell you a lot about the person you're dealing with. Ask the price straight off; don't wait until you get to the place. Then, if you care to, tell them you're looking for some place a third cheaper. Get clear answers about the place's location, facilities, etc. If there are lots of touts around, look helpless and talk to them all, then enjoy watching them bid the price down among themselves.

Rock-bottom Accommodation

Even today, it is possible to find a room in non-touristy areas of western Turkey for as little as 30–40 YTL if you look hard. Hotels and *pansiyonlar* at the very bottom of the scale provide little more than a bed and plastic slippers; you have to supply your own towel, soap and toilet paper. Like almost all of the *pansiyonlar*, these unclassified hotels are regulated, not by the Tourism Ministry, but by the municipal authorities (*belediye*), who fix their prices and will listen to any complaints; the chances of being ripped off are very slight. Some are grungy and depressing, others quite tolerable; many proprietors of cheap hotels in outlandish places go to great lengths to provide pleasant accommodation. These places see mostly Turks – migrant workers, TIR drivers and such – who turn in early and snore loudly. Usually, you will find them in provincial towns and villages, inland where few tourists go.

Holiday Villages, Hotel Chains and Ski Resorts

At the opposite end of the scale are the big international **chain hotels** in Ankara, Istanbul, İzmir and Antalya (Hilton, Sheraton, Ramada, Rixos, etc.). There are several Turkish chains, almost all along the west coast and Antalya region: **Turban** (which also operates several yacht marinas and campsites – get their latest booklet from the Tourism Office); **Tusan** (mainly motels on the outskirts of the most popular towns); **Etap** (in Ankara and Istanbul – usually expensive); the luxury **Dedeman** chain of hotels; and **Merit**, with sites in many Turkish cities. Chain hotels are never bargains – they get too many businessmen on expense accounts – and there will always be comparable places nearby with much more character. In winter, however, large **resorts** along the south coast may offer incredibly cheap **all-inclusive package deals**. Keep an eye on the national press where the hotels advertise these offers. It must be said that in Turkish cities the chain hotels are the social centres for the city's élite, with the most lavish (and by far the most expensive) restaurants, gyms and sports facilities (usually open to the public) and nightclubs.

Mainly on the coasts, there are several **holiday villages** (*tatil köyü*) that are quite nice and very good for families; in listings they are rated **TK1** or **TK2** – but you'll probably always get a better price on these as part of a package deal arranged at home. In Turkey's rapidly growing winter sport centres, there are a number of alpine-style chalets.

Prices

We wish we could tell you! In the true homeland of *pazarlık* (bargaining), there is simply no such thing as a fixed price. All hotels are supposed to post their prices near the desk; some actually do. It's standard procedure to walk in, scrutinize the price list and then ask the man at the desk the *real* price of a room (*'Son fiyatı ne kadar?'*). Some hotels may be willing to reduce their officially listed price, especially in the off-season.

Note that at some establishments, usually in the higher categories, there is an additional **tax**, up to 18 per cent of the total bill.

Apart from star ratings there are other ratings: **S** means a special licence, often for a historic (or at least old) building that has been remodelled, as in Antalya's old town or Istanbul's Sultanahmet; prices for these can be the same as a one- or a four-star hotel. A motel, **M**, is usually on a highway, and costs the same as the higher-class *pansiyonlar*. Holiday villages are **TK1** and **TK2**, roughly corresponding to two- and three-star hotels

Hotel Price Categories

Note that prices listed here and elsewhere in this book are for a double room in high season.

Hotels often quote prices in **euros**; at time of writing, 1 YTL = €0.54 / €1 = 1.85 YTL. For the current exchange rate, see *www.xe.com/ucc*.

luxury	€€€€€	480 + YTL
very expensive	€€€€	200–480 YTL
expensive	€€€	120–200 YTL
moderate	€€	50–120 YTL
inexpensive	€	– 50 YTL

(though some can be a lot more). And **O** is an *oberj* (*auberge*, or inn).

Because of the myriad classification systems and the variations in price between hotels with similar ratings, we have simply divided this book's hotel listings up by price into categories; *see* box, above. The prices in the ranges are for double rooms, and are the highest price you can expect to pay, except perhaps in July or August in a place that's really crowded. All categories cover a wide range; of the extremes, the higher are usually in Ankara and Istanbul, the lower in the eastern provincial cities. You may take the middles of these ranges as typical of prices.

Youth Hostels

Youth hostels are rare. In Istanbul there are several unofficial along with the official ones; you need a **Hostelling International (HI)** card.

UK: HI International Youth Hostel Federation, **t** (01707) 324 170, *www.hihostels.com*. Also **YHA**, **t** 0870 770 8868, *www.yha.org.uk*.

USA: Hostelling International USA, **t** (301) 495 1240, *www.hiayh.org*.

Canada: Hostelling International Canada, **t** (613) 235 2595, *www.hihostels.ca*.

Camping

There will be no problem finding a campsite around any of the coastal resort towns. There are even campsites in Istanbul, near the airport. Don't think of camping here as a way to save money. Prices are complex – separate charges for each person, tent, trailer and so on – but at the average site the total ends up much the same as a *pansiyon*. A detailed brochure (*Turkey: Camping*), listing over a hundred of the better-equipped places, is available at any local tourist office.

Tour Operators, Self-catering and Special-interest Holidays

Over a hundred companies offer holidays and travel to Turkey; make sure the one you choose has an ATOL licence and/or is a member of ABTA, AITO or other relevant industry-recognized bond.

Mainstream operators with large pro-grammes and flights from a variety of UK regional airports include **Cosmos**, t (020) 8464 3444, www.cosmos.co.uk; **Intra Travel**, t (020) 7619 6700; **Metak Holidays**, t (020) 8290 9292, www.metakholidays.co.uk; **Mosaic Holidays**, t (020) 8574 4000, www.mosaicholidays.co.uk; **New President Holidays**, t (020) 8406 4440, www.newpersidentholidays.com; and **Thomson Holidays**, t 0870 165 0079, www.thomson.co.uk.

Tour operators are becoming more sophisti-cated in Turkey. 'Seven days' yachting, seven days 'on land' holidays are growing in popular-ity, as is fly-drive. Also, together with the stan-dard, attractively priced two-week-plus-beach package, more off-beat options are available.

In Turkey

Geo Tourism, t 0212 232 3290, www.geotourism-tr.com. Upmarket tours, corporate events and city breaks.

Senkron Tours, t 0212 638 83 40, www.senkrontours.com. Istanbul and Turkey tours.

In the UK

Creative Turkey, t (020) 7385 5200, www.creativetraveller.com. Family villas and boutique hotels.

Exclusive Escapes, t (020) 8605 3500, www.exclusiveescapes.co.uk. Upmarket villas and hotels.

Exodus, t 0845 863 9600, www.exodus.co.uk. Adventure, trekking and multi-activity trips.

Fez Travel Turkey, t 0871 855 2927, www.fezbus.co.uk. Backpacker holidays and ANZAC tours.

Holt's Battlefield Tours, t (01304) 612248, www.holts.co.uk. Specialist Gallipoli tour.

IAH Holidays, t 0871 855 2925, http://iah-holidays.co.uk. North Cyprus and Turkey specialist.

Journey Anatolia, t (020) 8761 5605, www.journey-anatolia.co.uk. Small-group cultural and photography tours, hot-air ballooning and boutique beach hotels.

Naturetrek, t (01962) 733 051, www.naturetrek.co.uk. Birdwatching tours.

Peter Sommer Tours, t (01600) 888 220, www.petersommer.com. Specialist archaeological tours and *gulet* cruises.

Responsible Travel, t (01273) 600030, www.responsibletravel.com. A selection of trips from various operators with a focus on responsible tourism.

Sherpa Expeditions, t (020) 8577 2717, www.sherpa-walking-holidays.co.uk. Trekking and mountaineering.

Tapestry Holidays, t (020) 8995 7787, www.thetapestrycollection.com. Private villas and boutique hotels.

Westminster Classic Tours, t (020) 8286 7842, www.westminsterclassictours.com. Cultural and historical tours.

Worldwide Christian Travel, t 0870 844 2742, www.christian-travel.com. Biblical tours.

In the USA and Canada

Apollo Tours, t 800 228 4367, www.apollotours.com. Classic Turkey tours.

Blue Odyssey, t (415) 332 3811, www.blueodyssey.com. Adventure tours and cookery.

Classic Journeys, t 800 200 3887, www.classicjourneys.com. Cultural, culinary and walking tours.

Country Walkers, t 800 464 9255, www.countrywalkers.com. Walking tours and sailing holidays.

CTC Turkey, t 888 711 4500, www.ctcturkey.com. A wide variety of tours and Mediterranean cruises.

Cultural Folk Tours, t 1-800 935 8875/t (714) 252 9072, www.boraozkok.com. Silk route and folklore-focused tours.

Elder Treks, t (416) 588 5000, www.eldertreks.com. Sailing and walking tour.

Grand Circle Travel, t (800) 959-0405, www.gct.com. US operator with various tours.

Geographic Expeditions, t (415) 922 0448, www.geoex.com. Customized trips and *gulet* cruises.

Glory Tours, t (800) 768 6986, www.glory-tours.com. Religious tours and pilgrimages.

Heritage Tours, t (800) 378 4555, www.heritagetoursonline.com. A variety of well-researched tours and custom itineraries.

Homeric Tours Inc., t (212) 753 1100, www.homerictours.com. In Turkey and Greece: archaeological sites, history, etc.

OTI, t 800 817 0544, www.oti.travel. Canadian specialist with a variety of tours.

R&H Voyages Inc., t 800 862 2476, www.rhvoyages.com. A selection of set tours.

Tangents, t 415 584 4367, www.tangents.com. Small-group music tours.

Practical A–Z

06

Imperial–Metric Conversions

Length (multiply by)
Inches to centimetres: 2.54
Centimetres to inches: 0.39
Feet to metres: 0.3
Metres to feet: 3.28
Yards to metres: 0.91
Metres to yards: 1.1
Miles to kilometres: 1.61
Kilometres to miles: 0.62

Area (multiply by)
Inches square to centimetres square: 6.45
Centimetres square to inches square: 0.15
Feet square to metres square: 0.09
Metres square to feet square: 10.76
Miles square to kilometres square: 2.59
Kilometres square to miles square: 0.39
Acres to hectares: 0.40
Hectares to acres: 2.47

Weight (multiply by)
Ounces to grams: 28.35
Grams to ounces: 0.035
Pounds to kilograms: 0.45
Kilograms to pounds: 2.2
Stones to kilograms: 6.35
Kilograms to stones: 0.16
Tons (UK) to kilograms: 1,016
Kilograms to tons (UK): 0.0009
1 UK ton (2,240lbs) = 1.12 US tonnes (2,000lbs)

°C	°F
40	104
35	95
30	86
25	77
20	68
15	59
10	50
5	41
-0	32
-5	23
-10	14
-15	5

Volume (multiply by)
Pints (UK) to litres: 0.57
Litres to pints (UK): 1.76
Quarts (UK) to litres: 1.13
Litres to quarts (UK): 0.88
Gallons (UK) to litres: 4.55
Litres to gallons (UK): 0.22
1 UK pint/quart/gallon =
   1.2 US pints/quarts/
   gallons

Temperature
Celsius to Fahrenheit:
multiply by 1.8 then
add 32

Fahrenheit to Celsius:
subtract 32 then multiply
by 0.55

Turkey Information

Time Differences
Turkey: + 2hrs GMT; + 7hrs EST
Daylight saving from early April to end of
October (dates change annually)

Dialling Codes
*Note: to dial within Turkey from one province to
another, include the area code (0XXX).*
Turkey country code 90
To Turkey from: UK, Ireland, New Zealand 00 /
USA, Canada 011 / Australia 0011; then dial 90
and the number without the initial zero
From Turkey to: UK 00 44; Ireland 00 353; USA,
Canada 001; Australia 00 61; New Zealand 00
64; then the number without the initial zero
Directory enquiries: 118

Emergency Numbers
Police: 155
Ambulance: 112
Fire: 110

Embassy Numbers in Turkey
UK: 0312 455 3344 (Ankara); **USA:** 0312 455 5555
(Ankara); **Canada:** 0312 409 2700 (Ankara);
Australia: 0312 459 9500 (Ankara); **New
Zealand** 0312 467 9054 (Ankara)
See p.62 for consulates in other cities.

Shoe Sizes
Europe	UK	USA
35	2½ / 3	4
36	3 / 3½	4½ / 5
37	4	5½ / 6
38	5	6½
39	5½ / 6	7 / 7½
40	6 / 6½	8 / 8½
41	7	9 / 9½
42	8	9½ / 10
43	9	10½
44	9½ / 10	11
45	10½	12

Women's Clothing
Europe	UK	USA
34	6	2
36	8	4
38	10	6
40	12	8
42	14	10
44	16	12

Crime and the Police

Crime in Turkey is still rare, except perhaps for pickpocketing in the larger cities, especially in the marketplaces. There are almost no robberies.

Turkey is certainly a well-policed country, and cops come in all shapes and sizes. The **regular police** wear blue uniforms with golf caps, designed to make them look less threatening. It hasn't really worked, but foreigners will usually find them courteous and helpful. Related to these are the *Trafik Polisi* (*see* pp.70–71), who are assigned traffic duties.

In towns, there is a special branch of the police that oversees trade and business matters, the *zabıta*. They control weights and measures in the markets, watch over the bus and dolmuş services, and investigate complaints from consumers.

Istanbul and Bursa have their own **tourist police**; they always have someone around who speaks English or some other Western language. In remote country districts (mostly out in the east), the peace is kept by the *jandarma*, part of the armed forces, much like the famous Mexican *federales*; dressed in green fatigues and often carrying rifles.

Drugs

You may have thought *Midnight Express* a fine film, or you may have dismissed it as racist trash, but its basic message was spot on: don't do drugs in Turkey. Even a conviction for possession will almost certainly result in a prison sentence. How long depends on the amount in question.

Terrorists

All through the 1990s, the Kurdish terrorist group **PKK** waged war against the Turkish state in the Kurdish mountains, while occasionally setting off bombs in tourist areas and even resorting to kidnapping. With the arrest of the PKK leader **Abdullah Ocalan** in 1999 (*see* 'History', p.36), the threat of terrorism diminished; from his prison cell, Ocalan declared a ceasefire and ordered his fighters to leave Turkey. Now, unfortunately, the conflict may be heating up again. The US invasion of Iraq, with the subsequent appearance of a de facto autonomous Kurdistan, gave the PKK a chance to regroup and

rebuild, and today skirmishes with Turkish troops in the southeast, and army incursions into Iraq to attack PKK bases, have become regular occurrences. The story took a new turn in July 2008 when the PKK kidnapped three German climbers on Mount Ararat, an event widely considered as a reprisal for the German government's crackdown on PKK activities in their country. The Germans were unexpectedly released after two weeks, but how things will go from here is anybody's guess. The PKK were also behind a serious bombing in Istanbul in the same month. Keep an eye on the news, especially if you are planning to visit the area around Ararat or anywhere in the southeast.

Earthquakes

As the ruins of countless ancient cities destroyed by earthquakes indicate, Turkey has a long history of seismic activity. The earthquakes of 1999, causing thousands of deaths and traumatizing the entire country, came as a violent reminder that Turkey lies on a tectonic plate boundary. Many of the buildings to collapse were shoddily constructed apartment blocks in the *gecekondu* districts; an incensed public has demanded tighter building regulations for new buildings ever since. Experts are divided over whether the devastating earthquakes of 1999 will be followed by further violent seismic activity in the near future. Some Turks keep a torch and a small supply of food and drink by their bedside just in case; you may want to do the same. If you find yourself indoors during an earthquake, head for a doorway or supporting pillar; failing that, small rooms such as bathrooms or walk-in cupboards usually offer greater protection than large rooms. Desks or tables can protect you from falling debris.

Eating Out

By western European or American standards, prices are very low; if you're on a limited budget, you can eat well for five or six dollars a night. See **Food and Drink** chapter (p.51), for more on types of eating establishment and local specialities.

Restaurant Price Categories

very expensive	€€€€	over 70 YTL
expensive	€€€	40–70 YTL
moderate	€€	20–40 YTL
inexpensive	€	under 20 YTL

Wherever you eat, the service will be somewhere between very good and wonderful. Service is usually included, but it's good form to leave a tip, 10% or so, on the table.

Restaurants in this guide are divided into four categories based on a meal for one person without wine; *see* box, above. The 'bill' is *hesap. See* also 'Smoking', p.86.

Electricity

Electricity is 220 volts. Some outlets have two prongs, some three, so come with adapters and converters.

Health and Emergencies

Police **t** 155
Ambulance **t** 112
Fire service **t** 110

'And how was your stomach?', people will ask on your return from Turkey. Chances are you'll be able to say it was fine. Problems with **food poisoning** in Turkey are vastly exaggerated and in many restaurants, particularly in the west of the country, standards of hygiene in food preparation are the same as you would expect in Europe. If you are worried, though, the things to watch out for are raw, unpeeled fruits and vegetables, restaurants with steam tables where things have been sitting around, the tap water, and certain kinds of street foods (mussels, for one obvious example) in hot weather.

If afflicted with **diarrhoea** or food poisoning, rest yourself and your digestive system for a day or so, sticking to water and dry bread. It's better to let your body fight the infection first, strengthening your own immunity, before taking codeine or anti-diarrhoea tablets. If you resort to tablets and the symptoms persist after 36–48 hours, see a doctor. Diarrhoea dehydrates the body very fast and can leave you feverish; if suffering, it is important to drink lots of (bottled) water, even if that doesn't seem like a very good idea at the time.

Rabies does exist in Turkey, as in most countries, although cases are extremely rare. Nevertheless, you should avoid any contact with any animal. If camping rough, particularly amongst rocks, be aware that Turkey has several species of poisonous **snakes** and **scorpions**.

Tap water is not always safe to drink (and never in Istanbul). This is especially true in summer, when a combination of the high temperatures and water sitting in pipes for prolonged periods provides an ideal breeding ground for potentially harmful bacteria. Bottled water, however, is inexpensive, and you may want to stick to it rather than have the discomfort of new bacteria in your system.

Most towns have at least one **doctor** who speaks English; in the tourist areas they may advertise their bilingual proficiency on the doors of their surgeries. The quality of care is usually good, although as a rule it is better in private hospitals (a **hospital** is a *hastane*) than the state-run hospitals and clinics. For minor problems – if you can make yourself understood – consult a **chemist** (*eczane*). Every town has a night pharmacy, or *nöbetçi*, open by turns; most pharmacies have the schedule posted in their window.

See also 'Insurance and Health', p.64, for information on inoculations.

Foreign Hospitals in Turkey

Istanbul

Italian Hospital (İtalyan Hastanesi), Tophane Defterdar Yokuşu 37, **t** 0212 249 9751.

German Hospital (Alman Hastanesi), Sıraselviler Caddesi 119, Taksim, **t** 0212 293 2150.

International Hospital, Istanbul Caddesi, Çınar Oteli Yanı 82, Yeşilköy, **t** 0212 663 3000.

American Hospital (Amerikan Hastanesi), Güzelbahçe Sokak, Nişantaşı, **t** 0212 311 2000.

The American and German hospitals have emergency services.

İzmir

American Hospital (Amerikan Hastanesi), 1375 Sokak, **t** 0232 484 5360.

Gaziantep

American Hospital (Amerikan Hastanesi), Tepebaşı Mahallesi Yüksek Sokak No 3/a, 27010 Şahinbey, **t** 0342 220 0211.

The Turks are quite fond of **herbal remedies**, and in the towns you will see special shops for these.

The Internet

Turkey is pretty much wired up for the web. Internet cafes can be found in most towns of any size, particularly in tourist areas. Try to use ones with emergency power back-up in case the mains supply fails, which happens frequently in Turkey's overburdened towns and cities.

Some hotels accept reservations by email. As you'll notice when you first let your fingers loose on a Turkish keyboard, the Turkish ı and i are two separate keys and can cause confusion, since the ı key is usually located where the i key should be, but shows up on emails as a **y**. At least it makes for quaynt readyng to your fryends back home.

Media

Turks love reading **newspapers**, and they are big business, with most of the large dailies being distributed nationally. As in Britain, the press has two levels. *Cumhuriyet*, a highbrow daily with a small readership, is the most respected paper. *Hurriyet*, *Milliyet* and *Sabah* are three more of the better dailies; they bring politics out into the open and scramble for circulation as best they can. For the tourist, there's the *Turkish Daily News*, in English, printed in Ankara, an invaluable source of education on Turkish life and politics – though the lessons are often unintentional, from the cryptic, roundabout and very Turkish way this paper goes about discussing difficult subjects (it's online in English at *www.todayszaman.com*, along with a bright newcomer, *Zaman*). Freedom of the press in Turkey does suffer somewhat from state repression, though in contrast to previous decades such matters are now much more open for debate.

The *Turkish Daily News* is available in the big cities and resorts and occasionally turns up elsewhere. Foreign papers and magazines can be found in Istanbul and the popular resorts. You should be able to find a good selection of British and American dailies.

If you have a **radio**, the Third Programme of the state-run TRT (Turkish Radio and Television) gives very limited news in English, French and German at 9 and 12, and 2, 5, 7 and 10pm, in various places on the FM band (try 88.2, 94 or 99MHz). Turkish radio can be entertaining, with a mixture of Turkish and Western classical music and wild music-hall entertainments that are funny even if you can't make out a word. In all, there is more good music on Turkish radio than most of its European counterparts, though Western ear candy and Turkish pop are making increasing inroads.

Over the last ten years, Turkish **television** has undergone a major revolution. Most of the familiar international channels are now also operating in Turkey. These include the Turkish franchises of CNN, Fox, Eurosport, Discovery, MTV and National Geographic Channel to name just a few. They are broadcast mainly from Turkey's largest satellite TV company, Digiturk. Home-grown channels tend to show garish variety spectaculars, obscure old films, heaps of game shows, football, and Turkish soap operas, which have become phenomenally popular in recent years, even leading to feature film spin-offs. If you tune in late, though, you may hear a concert of Turkish classical music.

More important, is the role news programmes are assuming in discussing political affairs, even those previously taboo, such as the Kurdish question.

National Public and Religious Holidays

Banks and post offices are closed during the festival of **Kurban Bayramı** (*see* overleaf) and on the following official holidays:

1 January New Year's Day

23 April National Independence and Children's Day

19 May Atatürk Commemoration and Youth and Sports Day

30 August Victory Day (victory over the Greeks, that is, in 1922)

29 October Republic Day (anniversary of the declaration of the Republic)

There are plenty of other holidays, but the only ones likely to interfere with your travelling or shopping are the two important religious holidays, **Şeker Bayramı** ('sugar festival'), a 3½-day period at the end of **Ramazan**, and **Kurban Bayramı**, which lasts 4½ days, in commemoration of Abraham's sacrifice. Trains, buses and resort hotels (in resorts frequented by Turks) will be crowded, and banks and shops will mostly be closed. Both of these holidays are determined by the Islamic lunar calendar, so their dates slide backwards about 11 days each year.

Ramazan in 2009 begins on 21st August. Şeker Bayramı is 18–21 September 2009, and Kurban Bayramı on 27 November–1 December 2009. People do tend to extend holidays to take in weekends.

Whenever it falls, Ramazan should cause the non-Muslim traveller in Turkey little inconvenience. In resorts and big cities you might not even notice it, and elsewhere you'll be able to find restaurants open for lunch (though they may put curtains over the windows in conservative areas; in these places, such as Konya, you should be discreet about eating or smoking in public). By Islamic tradition, travellers are exempt from fasting anyhow. You might also consider keeping the holiday; it is a peculiar sensation, a kind of sense of community, knowing that almost everyone around you is doing the same. You'll find yourself sitting in the restaurant in the evening with a big crowd of hungry Turks, waiting for the cannon to boom from the local castle to mark sunset – or, more likely, watching the television to see their town's name appear at the bottom of the screen. Dinner appears in an instant, and always tastes wonderfully good.

Opening Hours and Museums

Most **museums** in Turkey date from the early years of the Republic. To Atatürk, recreating an interest and pride in Turkey's great civilizations of the past was an important part of nation-building, and his government fostered the creation of archaeological collections and the restoration of old buildings throughout the country. Today,

besides the great museums of Istanbul and Ankara, almost every town of any size has its own. Don't assume they aren't worth visiting; even the most obscure often have surprises even for the jaded culture tourist. Almost all are government-owned. Hours vary slightly, but most are closed for an hour or so at noon, and almost all are closed on Mondays.

Note that almost all the ruins and castles of Turkey, in fact all the **outdoor sites** of any archaeological or antiquarian interest, are maintained by the government as 'open-air museums' to which the same closing times apply. There may or may not be an admission charge, and the person on duty or caretaker may or may not feel like collecting it. Very few of the smaller sites are enclosed in any way, so if you can reach them (most of the ruined ancient cities are far from public transport; those that are accessible will be noted in the text), don't worry about 'opening hours'. Someone may be around to sell a ticket or give a guided tour, but you'll be pretty much on your own. If there's a gate, there will also be an easy way around it.

Access to **mosques** is usually restricted for tourists during prayer times, the most important of these being on Fridays. Exact prayer times change according to sunrise. The main prayer on Fridays is around noon.

Government offices and **tourist offices** are usually open Mon–Fri 8.30–12.30 and 1.30–5.30 (but often with longer lunch breaks). **Banks** are open Mon–Fri 8.30–12 and 1.30–5. **Shops** open Mon–Sat 8.30 or 9.30–7 or later; some open on Sundays. Shopping malls are open daily 10–10.

Photography

Turkey is wonderland for photographers, with some reservations. Look out for military or prohibited zones; the government can be touchy about them and they aren't always obvious.

At some important sites, such as Aphrodisias, and at many museums, cameras are prohibited at the request of the archaeologists. These busy scientists will make you wait until their monographs are in print before you take photographs.

Finally, don't make a nuisance of yourself by waving your camera at picturesque country people in traditional clothes; most Turks don't mind at all, but you may find some good Muslims who find the depicting of the human form offensive.

Post Offices

These are easy to find: look out for their yellow PTT signs. Larger ones have telephones (*see* p.88) and *poste restante* (general delivery) services. To make sure letters reach the central post office, have them addressed care of *Poste Restante/Merkez Postanesi*, followed by the name of the town. For telephone services only, large central post offices in the major cities are sometimes open 24 hours a day, or as late as 11.30pm. For postal business, most will close at 5 or 6pm.

The Turkish post does work, though it can be slow. Don't count on getting anything to or from Britain in less than a week, even by airmail (two weeks, sometimes). There isn't any real express post, and the only way to do it faster is the *acele* service; there is a special window for this at most post offices, but it is fantastically expensive (about 70 YTL for a mere letter), and even here speed is not guaranteed. International courier companies like DHL and UPS also have branches in Turkey. Sending packages can be time-consuming, since there are plenty of regulations and red tape. Postal rates are not much cheaper than in Europe or the US, and you might as well carry the thing home with you if there's room in your bag.

Shopping

Customs men in most countries are on to this. 'And what did *you* buy in Turkey?' they ask. There are so many pretty things, and prices are so low, that everyone goes home with something, aided in their choice by a merchant whose spiel will equal that of even the most high-powered time-share sales executive. The real masters of patter are to be found in the Covered Bazaar in Istanbul, where, after a few hours' strolling, you could be forgiven for wondering if the city's name is merely a derivation of 'instant bull'.

Almost all purchases in Turkey incur a steep **value-added tax** (**KDV**). Find out first if it's included in the price (*KDV dahil*) if you're doing any bargaining.

Antiquities

Trying to smuggle native antiquities out of Turkey could result in your getting home much later than planned, with a stripy tan gained through the bars of some Turkish jail. Unfortunately, there is no clear legal definition as to what is an antique and what is not. Use common sense: if you are contemplating a large purchase that may be antique, such as a carpet, ask the dealer to draw up a document stating that the item is not antique, and giving the purchase price. If he will not do this, you have a problem: seek advice from either the nearest tourist office or the curator of the local museum.

Carpets

Turkish carpets are famous the world over, and Turkish carpet merchants think you're only there to see them. They'll entice you into their shop, bring lots of tea and unfurl with a flourish dozens of wonderful creations, from carpets hand-woven in silk to machine-made kilims, thin, colourful cotton rugs that serve the Turks as coverings for floors, walls, beds or furniture. Remember, however, that a carpet is not a cheap buy – prices start at around 250 YTL for something decent.

If you've a notion to purchase one, it's worth talking to your local rug dealer before you go, or scouring the libraries, to get some idea of what to look out for. Turks know a great deal about carpets (it's a degree course in many Turkish universities), but for the very basics, read on.

Turkish carpets can be either hand- or machine-made. Hand-made are better: not only will they last much longer (for several generations, if cared for), but they have a greater nostalgic value; knowing that your carpet was hand-woven in an outlying Anatolian (or more likely Afghan or Turkmenistani) village is infinitely more pleasurable than knowing it came off a factory production line in downtown Istanbul. The difficulty, of course, is telling the difference. Look at the knots: if they are irregularly spaced (and thus with better binding), the carpet is probably handmade; if the knots are neat, even and tidy, the chances are it came off a machine. The carpet must be of either silk or wool; anything else, such as cotton, will not last beyond a few years. To discover whether the wool used in the carpet was hand- or machine-spun, ask the dealer to snip a length off one of the tassles and burn it: hand-spun wool will flare and exude a strong odour, machine-spun wool will not. In actuality, how the wool was spun makes little difference to the quality of the carpet, but following this ritual may fool the dealer into thinking that you know a little more than you do.

The quality of the dye used to colour the yarn should also be ascertained. Most carpets these days are chemically dyed, and, while most are OK, inferior dyes will run and smudge when wet. To check, rub a damp white cloth over the carpet; if colour comes off onto the cloth, imagine the effect of a pot of tea spilt onto it. Investigate the carpet's origins: which outlying village of which town it is from, what the design signifies, whether that design is exclusive to that village, and so on. If the dealer can't tell you, there's something fishy about him. Besides, it's nice to know.

Although the traders there will do their best to convince you otherwise, Istanbul is not necessarily the place to buy a new carpet, and neither are the main coastal resorts. The quality of the carpets will still be good, but prices will almost certainly be higher. This is not because the dealer is trying to rip you off (not necessarily, anyhow), but because he will have had to buy in his carpets from wholesalers in the carpet-making regions, around towns such as Ayvacık, Kayseri and Konya. Try to buy your carpet in a 'carpet town' and cut out the middle man.

Always insist on, and keep, an official receipt – customs men sometimes like to see proof of purchase – and never, but never, purchase an antique carpet unless you have no intention of taking it out of the country. If you are caught trying to smuggle an antique carpet out of Turkey you will almost certainly be jailed. If you are unsure of the age of a particular carpet, consult the curator of the local museum. If he or she then declares it not to be antique (60 years or less should be OK), ask for an official letter confirming this before handing over your money.

Jewellery

Jewellers are everywhere, particularly in Istanbul's Covered Bazaar where whole streets and *bedestenler* are devoted to their wares. The gold is normally of fair quality but be careful about buying silver, unless you know what you're doing. Fakes abound. In general, Turkish jewellery tends towards the heavy and showy, but in recent years the jewellers have learned to adapt a little to the tastes of visitors.

Leather

After carpets, leather is the next big buy, and here again, time spent shopping around is time well spent. Jackets, in particular, can be of very variable quality. Have a look at the stitching, especially on the inner lining, and at the buttons: if buttons are shoddily sewn on, it doesn't say much for how the rest of the jacket was put together. Leather jackets are cheaper in Turkey than elsewhere in Europe, although not substantially so; for anything of decent quality, expect to pay around 120 YTL.

Handbags, holdalls and briefcases are also popular buys (check the stitching; it's a good sign if the flaps have been turned twice and double-stitched).

Other Buys

Ceramic plates and tiles range from tourist trinkets to works of a very high quality; many are beautifully hand-painted in traditional designs from the 17th and 18th centuries. The widest choice is in Istanbul, where prices range from 40–900 YTL, but you can get a better deal in their town of origin, Kütahya, the ceramics centre of Turkey, where almost every street is lined with workshops and showrooms. Similar work, though on the whole not as good, is done in İznik, the town that was once synonymous with fine ceramics.

On a more practical basis, **clothes** are very good and very cheap; a trip to Turkey may be your opportunity to outfit your children for the next ten years. It isn't just cheap stuff any more, though. In Istanbul's modern districts and malls, you will be introduced to the world of Turkish *haute couture* – sharp designer fashions at very attractive prices (*see* the shopping section in 'Istanbul', pp.158–61). Many well-known western European and American concerns, such as Levi's and Benetton, have much of their clothing made in Turkey, and it is available here for much less than you'll see it at home.

The back streets of Anatolian bazaars are full of surprises. Ask a tailor to make you up a pair of *şalvar*, the traditional baggy trousers for women or men: he'll do it in an afternoon for about 15 YTL, and you'll be a fashion sensation back home.

The speciality of Bursa is **linens and embroideries**, on display everywhere in that city's Covered Bazaar. These are one of Turkey's real shopping joys, everything from simple towels and cloths to spectacular embroidered silk bedclothes.

Copper is also a popular purchase; the best and the cheapest is found out east, in places like the bazaar of Urfa, where you can buy direct from the manufacturer, in a street full of old men and their much put-upon apprentices who beat out designs on trays and plates with careful precision. They've been there for centuries. In the west you'll see them occasionally at big markets. Antique metalwork of all kinds is popular, as in the flea markets of Istanbul; just make sure that what you're buying is not a genuine antique that may not be taken out of the country.

Traditional **musical instruments**, from a simple *ney* to a hand-made, medieval-style lute, can be tremendous bargains; *see* the shopping section in 'Istanbul', p.160.

Pipe-smokers may want to invest in a **meerschaum pipe**. They can be found across the country but all originate in Eskişehir; the best are beautifully carved with a wealth of intricate detail. **Water pipes**, **daggers**, **belly-dance costumes**, mother-of-pearl inlaid **hamam slippers**, **Karagöz puppets** and other such oriental paraphernalia can be bought in all major towns, and in plenty of smaller villages near the tourist centres.

Bargaining

Bargaining (*pazarlık*) is an accepted form of doing business for large purchases and is,

except in Western-style shops, entirely expected. 'Tell me what you will pay,' shopkeepers urge. Bargaining is not a game, however, and merchants will be extremely displeased if you waste their time haggling over an item of small price, or one you have no intention of buying. It's a good idea not to disclose immediately the item you're interested in, but to enquire about it last when the merchant is giving up hope of making a sale. As a bargaining guideline, offer a price of about half to two-thirds of what the dealer asks, and go on from there (if you're knowledgeable at all about the wares, offer two-thirds of what you think it's worth). You cannot drop your price to below that of your first offer. If you plan to buy a number of items, get your best price for just one first, and then ask if there might possibly be a discount for buying in quantity.

If you allow yourself to be guided into a shop by a friendly chap with a 'brother/cousin/friend who sells carpets/jewellery/leather', and then buy something from that shop, you will have paid over the odds. Charming though that chap may be, he will expect a cut of the profit that the shopkeeper makes on your purchase. The shopkeeper will add the cost of the commission to the 'best price' he will offer you.

Don't be intimidated by *pazarlık*. Our Western, fixed-price way of doing things is a triumph of banality over humanity from the Turkish point of view, an aberration that could only have been invented in a society where people basically dislike and mistrust each other. You may look at the glass of tea you are offered as a trick, something that makes you feel obliged to buy – or you may see it as an elementary courtesy, which it is. You may consider bargaining as a grim battle of wits, in which someone is going to get handled, while the other party is making a sinful extra penny he doesn't really deserve. But how is it any different from the sort of deals Western businessmen make with each other every day? Many Westerners fear paying over the odds, but, as a Turkish shopkeeper pointed out to us, just by putting price tags on their goods, shops in the West can get away with charging more than ten times cost price for an item. The point of bargaining is to allow two people to come to an agreement that both will be happy with. No shopkeeper will sell his goods for cost price (a fact that many customers forget in the heat of bargaining), but if business is slow he may let you walk away with a real bargain.

Buying something in the **bazaars** of big tourist colonies such as Bodrum, though, you may often find the procedure somewhat lacking in grace. Many merchants have become a bit jaded by too many tourists that are either easy marks, or at the opposite extreme are full of suspicions and none too polite. It is also true that the situation encourages some merchants (and their commission minions) to be so persistent that they make nuisances of themselves. To these, just say goodbye.

As shopkeepers are quick to remind you, 'looking is free'. And if just looking is what you intend, say so clearly at the beginning; most shopkeepers, if they have the time, won't mind showing off their wares and teaching you a little something about them. A promise to consider, and perhaps return later on, is something no honest merchant could object to. Never, ever, buy something you don't want, or for a price you aren't happy with. Why should you? Also, don't be put off if, whatever you happen to say, about the weather or whatever, he constantly steers the conversation back to those carpets. In most cases, he isn't really being pushy. Many merchants, if they know English at all, have a deceptively good commercial vocabulary in it but are hard pressed to say much on any other subject. It isn't an easy part of their job – they may have to do the same in German, French and Arabic too, and some of the more enterprising ones are polishing up their Japanese. Bargaining can be pleasant enough if you know what you want, know what you care to spend for it, and go about in a cool and courteous manner. Use Turkey as a chance to match wits with the experts; it's good practice for the next time you buy a car.

Smoking

Sublime tobacco! which from east to west
Cheers the tar's labour or the Turkman's rest.
Byron, *The Island*

More than almost anything, Turks love to smoke, and they do so at all times of the day and night, on buses, in hospitals, in gas works, anywhere you can think of. There is very little you can do about this, particularly in restaurants where the situation is worsened by the Turks' dread of draughts, which makes them close windows on anything but the hottest of days.

Where smoking is forbidden, however, the ban is generally adhered to – on some local buses and in ferry lounges; shocking though it may seem, the TCDD (Turkish State Railways) and inter-city bus lines currently have non-smoking sections. Furthermore, the unthinkable has happened! The Turkish parliament recently voted to introduce a **full smoking ban** in public places, in line with those already in place in most of Europe. The full ban including restaurants and bars is expected to come into force by July 2009.

If you want to smoke like a Turk, the proper way to do it is with a *nargile*, or hookah, the glass contraption that the English used to call a 'hubble-bubble'. They seem to be making a comeback, and you'll find plenty of humble *kıraathaneler* (old-fashioned working men's coffee houses) and boulevard cafés where you can have one brought over, along with a sinister-looking wad of rough-cut *tömbeki* tobacco that smells like a camel's bum even before it's lit. You'll catch Turkey's only legal buzz, and watching you try to keep it going will entertain the locals royally.

In between cafés, you'll have to settle for cigarettes. Western imports are prohibitively taxed, but Turkish smokes are better anyhow, with excellent tobacco from the lovely green valley of the Yeşilırmak, near the Black Sea.

Sports and Activities

Water Sports

Water sports are widely available in the resorts along the south Aegean and Mediterranean coasts. **Yachting** (*see* below) is extremely popular, and opportunities for **windsurfing** and **snorkelling** abound. For **scuba divers**, there are schools in Çeşme, Kuşadası, Bodrum, Kaş and several of the other more obvious resorts; rates are relatively cheap when compared to, say, Greece.

Sea pollution is only a problem near the main shipping harbours, around Istanbul,

İzmir, Mersin, İskenderun and several of the ports on the Black Sea coast. In July and August the Aegean coast is often plagued by the *meltemi* wind, making rough seas.

Yachting

Chartering a yacht or sailing your own along the Turkish coast has been popular for decades. One of the most memorable ways of spending a holiday in Turkey is to float along the delightful pine-forested coast, in and out of a hundred picturesque coves dotted with the remains of ancient cities, dining in the evenings off the day's catch or in tiny restaurants in hidden bays accessible only by boat. Prices are still quite reasonable when compared to other Mediterranean countries: the tourist office has lists of agents and charter companies with whom you can reserve a boat (bare or with crew) in advance; outside July and August you can usually get a boat on the spot in the major resorts – Antalya, Marmaris, Bodrum, Göcek or Kuşadası.

Sailing along the southwest coast between Kuşadası and Antalya is known as a **Blue Cruise**. Where you go is up to you, but opting for the full cruise takes you to the following: Kuşadası, Didyma, Güllük, Bodrum, Gökova Bay, Knidos, Datça, Turunç, Marmaris, Dalyan, Göcek, Fethiye, Kalkan, Kaş, Kekova, Demre, Finike, Phaselis and Antalya. You may want to stop off at a few of the Greek Aegean islands en route; nearest to this length of coastline are Samos, Patmos, Lipsi, Kalymnos, Kos, Nissyros, Sými, Rhodes and Kastellorizo. Basic information on some of these is supplied in the text; for more, refer to Cadogan's *Greek Islands* guide.

Since a full Blue Cruise would take at least one month, most prospective sailors have to opt for a shorter voyage that can be fitted within the given length of their charter. As a guideline, in one week you could travel from Kuşadası to Bodrum, from Bodrum around Gökova Bay and back again, or from Bodrum to Marmaris. Two weeks could take you from Kuşadası to Marmaris (via a few Greek islands), or from Marmaris to Antalya.

For companions, you can either get your own group together (between 7 and 12 persons) or take a 'cabin charter', whereby specific berths are set aside for individual

passengers. The boats themselves are likely to be *guletler*, pine-built with a rounded aft and a pointed fore, with double berths (bunk beds) measuring two metres long by two metres wide. Luxury yachts can also be chartered. The cost will be between 100 YTL and 200 YTL per day, per person, not including food, depending upon the season, the size of the boat and the facilities on offer. April, May, September and October are the cheaper months. The tourist office publishes an annual list of tour operators offering yachting holidays; alternatively, you can talk to owners of the boats that crowd every resort harbour and probably make a better deal if the time is right.

If you have your own yacht, official **ports of entry** include: Çanakkale, Bandırma, Istanbul, Akçay, Ayvalık, Dikili, İzmir, Çeşme, Kuşadası, Güllük, Bodrum, Datça, Marmaris, Fethiye, Kaş, Fınıke, Kemer, Antalya, Alanya, Anamur, Taşucu, Mersin, İskenderun, Samsun, Silifke, Trabzon, Adana, Didyma, Derince, Tekirdağ, Zonguldak and Ordu. On arriving in Turkey the captain must fill out a transit log. If you leave Turkish waters for seven days or less, you can leave the transit log with port authorities and reuse it on your return. Foreign yachts may remain in Turkey for up to two years for maintenance and winter berthing.

Mountains, Rafts and Caves

Mountain-climbing is another fair-weather sport; due to the dangers involved, it is strictly controlled. Foreign mountaineering groups need special permission before setting off; apply to the Ministry of Foreign Affairs in Ankara. Those wishing to climb the steepest peaks – those only for experienced mountaineers – should contact the tourist office, who can supply names of travel agencies who will arrange all documentation, guides, provisions and so on.

White-water rafting enthusiasts have sent out rave reviews about the Barhal river near Yusufeli in the northeast, as well as the River Göksu on the southern coast.

The tourist office can help out with information on excursions to Turkey's numerous and often dazzling **caves**. The greatest collection of these is found in the mountains north of Antalya.

Skiing

The best-known and most developed ski resort is **Uludağ**, located in a national park near Bursa with 25 runs of varying difficulty and a view of the Sea of Marmara. The season here lasts from November to March, although those not enamoured by the patter of tiny skis should avoid Uludağ in late January/early February when the pistes become packed with Turkish schoolchildren. At other times the slopes should be blissfully uncluttered.

The resorts with the best snow and most challenging runs are in eastern Turkey, notably at **Palandöken** near Erzurum, where the 2,200–3,170m-high slopes are emptier and the snow more consistently powdery than elsewhere.

Just north of Antalya, in the Beydağı mountains at **Saklıkent**, in the months of March and April you can ski in the morning and swim in the Mediterranean in the afternoon.

Fishing and Hunting

Fishing for sport requires no licence; hunters, however, can only go out in organized groups with a licensed travel agent. **Wild boar hunts** in the autumn are organized in Muğla province (Marmaris), in the Taurus mountains and on Mount İda, near Akçay.

Email the **Association of Turkish Travel Agencies**, *tursab@tursab.org.tr*, for a list of agents.

National Sports and Recreation

If you're in the right place at the right time (see 'Festivals', pp.60–61), you may be able to see three of the Turks' home-grown sports. Although **football** has more of a following, **wrestling** is still considered the national sport, and contests take place throughout the summer. Edirne is the **greased wrestling** capital of Turkey and hosts the most famous tournament. **Camel wrestling** (*Deve Güreşi*) pits camel against camel in a slow, clumsy-elegant ritual in which one beast eventually establishes dominance; they are separated before doing each other any harm. This is most common along the Aegean coast in December and January, especially in Selçuk.

To see *Cirit* ('javelins'), a rather dangerous but exhilarating sport featuring galloping horsemen hurling blunted wooden javelins at each other, you'll usually have to head out east to Erzurum where it's still popular. There are exhibitions in Konya in September.

Less strenuous activities include lounging around a **spa** (there are famous ones in Bursa, Yalova and Gönen, all easily accessible by sea from Istanbul; also at Ilica near Çeşme, Pamukkale and Hüdayı, in Afyon province), playing *tavla* (backgammon) in the coffee houses and, of course, taking a Turkish bath or hamam.

Almost every town has a **hamam**, either with separate facilities for men and women, or open to men and women on alternate days. The Turkish bath is a direct descendant of the Roman bath, adopted by the Byzantines and then the Ottomans; it is a wonderfully sensuous ritual, especially if you have a chance to luxuriate in one of the historic hamams in Istanbul: the 16th-century **Çemberlitaş Hamamı**, Vezirhan Caddesi 8, near the Burnt Column; the 17th-century **Çağaloğlu Hamamı**, on Yerebatan Caddesi near the Aya Sofya; the 16th-century **Galatasaray Hamamı**, at Turnacıbaşı Sokak 24 in Beyoğlu; or the 19th-century **Pangaltı Hamamı**, on Dolapdere Caddesi 224 in Pangaltı. In Edirne, there's the beautiful 16th-century **Sokullu Mehmet Paşa Hamamı**.

The *halvet* is the hot room where you perspire; the *göbektaşı* is the hot marble slab on which the bath attendant rubs you down. This they tend to do with great enthusiasm, either with a glove that removes dead skin or even by walking across your back; if it hurts, you can always call out '*yavaş, yavaş*' ('slowly, slowly'). Be sure to tip the bath attendant when you leave.

Telephones

Public Phones

The national network, **PTT**, has phone booths throughout Turkey. **Phone cards** are particularly useful for short long-distance and international calls. The cards come in units of 30, 50 and 100. A 100-unit card should give you an international call long enough to have somebody at home ring you back at the phone box. You can buy cards at post offices, high street phone centres, some general stores and street kiosks. Once in the booth you can choose the language for the instructions. Pick up the receiver and place the card into the slot. When a beeping sound is heard, dial the number. More beeping is a signal that you are about to be cut off, but then a 'change card' message appears on the display to remind you to put in a new card or else the call will end. Press 'change card' and change it when the machine says so. You do not need to insert a card to dial an emergency number.

Occasionally you will find phones where you use a **token** (*jeton*), although these are rapidly disappearing. Pick up the receiver and place the appropriate token into the slot. Dial when you hear beeps and a red light goes off. When you are about to run out of time, the beeping cuts in again until you insert additional tokens. If you dial an emergency number from a phone that takes tokens, you need to insert a token, which is returned to you after the call.

'Smart cards' can be also used in pay phones and are sold in units of either 100 or 350. There are also different telephone cards for different telephone boxes, sold in units of 50, and a growing number of credit-card-operated phones in major cities. The Türk Telekom Global Card is valid for making domestic and international calls in Turkey and to call anywhere in the world. Both types of cards are sold at a range of places including Türk Telekom shops, small vendors and news-stands near phone booths, and Bakkal or Büfe convenience shops (look for signs in the shop windows).

Making long-distance calls from your **hotel** is as bad an idea as in any other country; hotels always take a substantial mark-up.

The other practical way to do it is from a **call centre** or **post office**, where there is usually a separate room for telephone services. Some offices have metered booths, though at others, they'll simply hand you a telephone over the counter when your call goes through, and you can talk to your sweetie back home from the middle of a crowd of amused Turks.

Area Codes and the Operator

When making **domestic calls** to anywhere in Turkey with a different area code, dial 0, then the 3-digit area code, then the 7-digit number. Istanbul, true to its position spanning two continents, has two different area codes: 212 for the European side and 216 for the Asian side. If you are calling from one side to the other, you need to prefix this code with 0. This is counted as a 'within the city' (*şehiriçi*) call.

For **international calls from Turkey**: dial 00 + country code (Britain 44, USA and Canada 1, Ireland 353, Australia 61) + area code (omit the initial 0) + number. For calls **from the UK to Turkey**: dial 00 + 90 + area code (omit the initial 0) + 7-digit number.

To be connected with an **operator** to give instructions about the number you wish to call, and if you need to reverse the charges, call 115 for international calls and 131 for domestic calls. Operators generally speak Turkish only.

Directory enquiries is 118.

Mobile Phones

Over the last few years there has been an explosion in mobile phone usage in Turkey, with almost everyone from young school children to remote farmers owning one. It has become big business; high street phone retailers are as common as kebab restaurants and all the latest handsets are available.

If you plan to use your mobile phone, note that Turkey uses the **GSM** (Global System for Mobile Communications) network. Most phones are compatible with this, but some North American brands may not work. Be sure to activate your **international roaming** facility with your home network before leaving, and also, find out the rates; roaming in Turkey is not cheap and differs from network to network.

If staying a few weeks or longer, it may be more cost-effective to buy a Turkish **SIM card**. This would mean receiving international calls is free and you pay local rates when making calls. If you don't have your own 'unlocked' GSM phone, buying a second-hand cheapie or renting a phone is simple enough. A recent law states that your phone must be registered with the mobile network you subscribe to; if it isn't, you may find you are cut off after a period of two weeks. Registering a phone or buying a prepaid SIM package can be done at most retailers; just ensure you have your passport with you for identification.

The most popular networks are Turkcell (*www.turkcell.com.tr/en*), Avea (*www.avea. com.tr*) and Vodafone. All have branches in towns and cities, and, in keeping with traditional Turkish hospitality their customer services normally have an English-language option too.

Time

Throughout most of the year Turkey is two hours ahead of Greenwich Mean Time and seven hours ahead of Eastern Standard Time (New York), ten hours ahead of California. At times this may vary by an hour either way, depending on when **daylight saving** hours are introduced.

Toilets

Conveniences in varying states of decomposition will be found in petrol stations, bus depots, etc. – just ask for the *tuvalet* or WC (pronounced 'veh-veh-jeh'); attendants collect a nominal fee. French-style holes in the floor await you in many of the cheaper hotels, but never in the government-listed establishments. The use of toilet paper is not a universally accepted custom (that's what the little taps are for); seasoned travellers carry their own. Turkish loos that flush with

enthusiasm are rare. Please put toilet paper in the little bins provided; if no bin is provided, it is more hygienic to start a small pile of paper in a corner than to cause a blockage in the plumbing.

Women

While travelling with children in Turkey poses no special problem (except that disposable nappies and baby foods are hard to come by in many places, and many children dislike the milk served in the cafés), a woman travelling on her own, or with a girlfriend, may have to contend with stares, personal questions and some typical Mediterranean male annoyances. The Turks, especially off the well-travelled tourist routes, are simply not used to seeing women on their own. Don't be afraid to use the word '*ayıp!*' ('shame') loudly if harassment reaches uncomfortable levels; this may elicit the help of passers-by. Face-slapping is stupid and potentially very dangerous. But don't be afraid to go. It is rare for a man to try to force you into something you don't want. Turks may make the women sit in the back of the mosque, but they have a respect for their rights and dignity that could be an example to many men elsewhere. They are also quite modest and conservative socially; wearing your bikini in the village, topless sunbathing and becoming noisy and drunk are provocative. Have respect for their ways and you should find that respect reciprocated.

Istanbul

Istanbul will not disappoint. It is inexhaustible, pleasant to walk around, full of surprises. You could take your old aunt here on holiday or have a Bohemian dream vacation; live like a tycoon or like a tramp. For those who have already been to Istanbul, if your last visit was more than a few years ago it's time to have another look – you'll hardly know the place today. Istanbul is booming, perhaps blossoming, a mildly schizophrenic metropolis of skyscrapers and street vendors, where some women wear veils and others the latest in Italian designs. All the energies of the nation seem concentrated in it now, as the millennary city transforms itself, while doing its best to drag the rest of Turkey with it into the 21st century.

07

Don't miss

⭐ **The House of Divine Wisdom**
Aya Sofya **p.103**

⭐ **The Palace of the Sultans**
Topkapı **p.112**

⭐ **The treasure-house of an empire**
Imperial Museums **p.119**

⭐ **The height of Ottoman architecture**
Süleymaniye **p.130**

⭐ **Exotic back streets and markets**
Beyoğlu **p.144**

See map overleaf

Selimiye

YAVUZ SELIM CAD.

Cistern of Aspar

HALIÇ CADDESİ

G o l d e n

YOLCUZAD

Church of Christ Pantepoptes

ABDÜLEZEL PAŞA CADDESİ

BOSTAN HAMAMI S.

CİBALİ CADDESİ

Jewish Museum

Atatürk Bridge

TERSANE C

Fatih Camii

HAYDAR CADDESİ

Pantocrator Church

UNKAPANI EMİNÖNÜ

ATLAMATASI CAD.

H o r n

FATİH

Amcazade Külliye

FATİH TÜRBESİ S.

İTFAİYE CADDESİ

B U L V A R I

HACIKADIN CAD.

Vefa Kilise Camii

VEFA CAD.

Süleymaniye Camii

SİYAVUŞPAŞA SOK.

Rüstem Paşa Camii

Eminö Squa

EM

FEVZI PAŞA CAD.

Municipal Museum

CEMAL YENER

KİRAZ LİMESCİT S.

SÜLEYMANIYE C.

HASIRCILAR CAD.

HA

Spice Market

MACAR KARDESLER CAD.

Aqueduct of Valens

TOSYALI CAD.

Istanbul University

ÇARŞI CADDESİ

FIRINCILAR

YOKUŞU

Marcian's Column

HORHOR CADDESİ

Şehzade Camii

ŞEHZADEBAŞI CADDESİ

Burmalı Minare

Kalenderhane Camii

DARÜLFUN

FUATPAŞA CAD.

UZUN

Beyazit Tower

MAHMUT PAŞA

Mehmet Paş Camii

BEZCI

AKSARAY

Valide Camii

ATATÜRK

GENÇTÜRK CADDESİ

Lâleli Cami

LÂLELİ

CAD.

Beyazit Camii

Covered Bazaar

Nuruosr Camii

CAĞ

ORDU CADDESİ

VEZNECİLER CAD.

Çorlulu Ali Paşa Medrese

Çember

PEHLIYAN

VAHYAPASA

Beyazit Square

Merzifonlu Karamustafa Medrese

Atik Ali Paşa Camii

Mirelaon Convent

KOCA RAGIP CAD.

Museum of Calligraphy

SOKAĞI

PİVERLOTI CAD.

MUSTAFA KEMAL CADDESİ

KÜÇÜK LANGA CAD.

KURBAN SOKAĞI

KUMKAPI

Mehmet Paşa Camii

TÜLCU SOK.

Binbirdi Cister

Yenikapı Station

KADIRGA CADDESİ

Havas Airport Bus

FLORYA SAHİL YOLU

Kumkapı Station

S. KÜÇÜK

Küç Aya S

500 metres
500 yards

1 Gate of Salutations (Bab-üs Selâm)
2 Harem
3 Gate of Felicity (Bab-üs-Saade)
4 Audience Chamber and Library
5 Wardrobe and Treasury

N

to Balık Pazari & Pera Museum

Sishane Square

BEYOĞLU

YOLCUZADE CAD. Tünel

OKUMUSA CAD.

GALIPDEDE CAD.

AIRZIYA PAŞA CAD.

KUMBARACI YOKUŞU

BOGAZ KESEN CAD.

Museum of Divan Literature

Tophane Square

to Nüsretiye Cami

St Benoit Church

KEMERALTI CADDESİ

NECATIBEY CADDESİ

GALATA MUMHANE

Kiliç Ali Paşa Camii

Jewish Museum

Galata Tower

Arap Cami

VOYVODA CAD.

MUKSEKKALDIRAM

TERSANE CADDESİ

Tünel

Karaköy Square

Yeraltı Camii

Bosphorus

To Üsküdar

Galata Bridge

Eminönü Square

Paşa

Ferry Docks

EMINÖNÜ

Yeni Camii

Seraglio Point

Atatürk Monument

Spice Market

SIRKECI

HAMIDIYE CADDESİ

YENI POSTANE CAD.

CADDESİ

KENNEDY   CADDESİ

Sirkeci Station

Goths' Column

YOKUŞU

MAHMUT PAŞA

Main Post Office

M. HÜDAVENDIGAR

ANKARA

EBUSSUUT CAD.

HATUN CAD.

Imperial Museums

6
4
2   5
3
1

Topkapı Sarayı

Mehmet Paşa Camii

TÜRKOCAGI CAD.

BEZCILER SOK.

Vilâyet

Cağaloğlu Baths

YEREBATAN C.

Nuruosmaniye Camii

NURUOSMANIYE CAD.

Sublime Porte

Gülhane Park

Aya İrene

Ali

Çemberlitaş

CAĞALOĞLU

BABIALI CAD.

SULTANAHMET

Kaiser Wilhelm II Fountain

Yerebatan Sarayı

Bab-i Humayun

PIYERLOTI CAD.

FARER

KLOT

DIVAN YOLU

Firuz Ağa Camii

Sultanahmet Sq.

Aya Sofya

SOĞUK ÇEŞME SOK.

Fountain of Ahmed III

Museum of Turkish and Islamic Arts

MIMAR MEHMET AĞA CAD.

Aya Sofya Baths

ŞAKIRPAŞA CAD.

Binbirdirek Cistern

Blue Mosque

Hippodrome

TERZIHANE SOK.

TAVUKHANE

KABASAKAL CAD.

Küçük Aya Sofya

ÜK

AYASOFYA CAD.

MUSTAFAPAŞA S.

CANKURTARAN CAD.

Mosaic Museum

Bucoleon Palace

SAHIL   YOLU

Sea   of   Marmara

Getting to and away from Istanbul

By Air

See **Planning Your Trip**, pp.65–6.

There are various cost-effective options available for getting to and from **Atatürk International Airport**, **t** 0212 465 3000, *www.dhmiata.gov.tr*. The **LRT** (Light Rail Transit) runs between the airport and Aksaray. To reach Sultanahmet, change at Zeytinburnu for the **tram**. The total journey is approximately 50mins and costs around 2 YTL. The Havaş **bus** company run a half hourly service to and from Taksim Square, in front of McDonald's, from 6am with an extra bus at 5am. This is a more pleasant 45mins ride via the Marmara coast and costs 10 YTL. The bus also stops on Mustafa Kemal Caddesi in Aksaray – and if you ask the driver he'll probably let you get off anywhere else you like along the way. An **airport taxi** is your other option, costing around 30 YTL to Sultanahmet.

Sabiha Gökçen International Airport, **t** 0216 585 5000, *www.sgairport.com*, is 50km east of Taksim on the Asian side of the city and a ride into the centre will take the best part of an hour. Havaş and other city **buses** depart regularly for Kadıköy where you can board a **ferry** to the European shore, and Levent 4th, where you can take the **metro** to Taksim. There are also buses to Bostancı with its seabus connections to Eminönü and Beşiktaş. A **taxi** to the centre of town will cost you in the region of 85 YTL. Alternatively, check with your airline to see if they provide a transfer service to Taksim or Sultanahmet.

By Train

The days of the Orient Express are long gone, but just in case you should be riding the Turkish rails, know that European destinations are served from **Sirkeci Station**, **t** 0212 527 0050, at the tip of Stamboul's peninsula; besides international arrivals, the main event here is the daily train to and from Edirne, which departs from Sirkeci at 3.50pm.

Trains for Ankara and everything else on the Asian side (also to Russia) begin at **Haydarpaşa Station**, in Kadıköy (**t** 0216 336 4470). The express-runs to Ankara (the Fatih Ekspres and the overnight Yataklı Ekspres) have the most comfortable cars and best services in the country, and are the only train-runs in Turkey that come close to competing with the buses in speed and price.

The only way to get from one station to the other, besides a ludicrously long taxi ride over the Bosphorus Bridge, is to take the **ferry** from outside Haydarpaşa to Karaköy, by the Galata Bridge, and then walk or take a taxi to nearby Sirkeci. The ferry and taxi combination is also the quickest and cheapest way to get from Haydarpaşa to the touristic heart of Istanbul in Sultanahmet.

By Coach

Every traveller will agree that the new **International Bus Terminal** (Uluslararası Istanbul Otogarı), **t** 0212 658 0505, at Esenler, out in the far western suburbs, is one of the most gratifying of the city's many recent improvements. It is a completely modern facility, a bizarre, space-age architectural apparition among the grim concrete suburbs. Every bus that comes to Istanbul uses it. If you're heading for any big town there will be no need for a reservation; just turn up and you'll probably be on a bus within ten minutes.

Getting there is no problem. The new **tram/metro** from Aksaray pulls right into the middle of the station (about a half-hour trip), or else you can take a **taxi** for about 20 YTL from Sultanahmet. If you're arriving in Istanbul from anywhere in Asian Turkey, your bus is likely to stop at the Harem Otogarı in Asian Istanbul before continuing to the main coach station. The quickest way to Sultanahmet is to get off at Harem and catch the ferry across to Sirkeci, from where it is a short taxi ride to Sultanahmet.

Perhaps still traumatised by its loss to the Ottomans in 1453, the Greeks still insist on calling it Constantinople, and print it that way on all their maps. The Ottomans never really meant to change the name; they thought of themselves as the successors of the Romans, just as the Byzantines had, and they did their best to keep Constantine's column in good repair. But, through centuries of trade and diplomacy with the Greeks, they had often heard this fabulous remnant of antiquity referred to as *stin poli* or 'in the city'. Turkish has no prepositions, and to their ears it must have sounded like one word.

The name stuck, and what could be better for such a place than to be called, simply, 'The City'? To the Turks, the Mongols and other peoples of distant Asia this was a kind of half-mythical land of dreams, known more through poets than historians or travellers, just as Cathay and the Indies were for medieval Europeans. All these Asian peoples migrated west to the 'Land of Rome' and its golden capital, and one day made it their own.

For sixteen centuries, Istanbul was the metropolis of the eastern Mediterranean. The Byzantines had a word for their legitimate heirs to the throne, those sons of emperors born in the famous Purple Chamber of the palace: Porphyrogenitus, or 'born to the purple'. This we can take as a title for the city itself, whose location astride both the land and sea routes between east and west guaranteed its long rule. There is a sinister aspect to this. Istanbul, under both the Byzantines and the Ottomans, was the most predatory city the world has ever known save Rome itself, sucking the economic lifeblood out of hundreds of provinces, even entire nations. For a long time, its matchless fortifications protected, even encouraged the kind of decadence that nature and history usually root out of societies. Only now is the city just waking up from the terrible Ottoman hangover; it can take its place as a modern commercial emporium, realizing what a blessing it is to have the burden of governance lifted from its shoulders.

Its new burden, and one it gladly accepts, is carrying the Turkish economy; one-third of the nation's factories are here, and more than two-thirds of Istanbul's population of over 13 million are recent migrants from Anatolia, come to try their luck in the second-largest city in Europe (Moscow is first). The old diversity of peoples remains, even increases; added to the long-established Greeks, Armenians and Jews are vast numbers of new arrivals from Eastern Europe, the Middle East and Turkophone Central Asia.

History

Byzantion was already a sizeable town when the decision was made to transform it into an imperial capital. Set on the Bosphorus, bridging Europe and Asia, it was certainly the logical site for one, and it's surprising that no one took better advantage of its strategic position before Constantine the Great. The town's acropolis stood roughly where the Topkapı Palace is now, and archaeologists have uncovered fragments going back to Mycenaean times. The Greeks had a legend, though, that the city was founded by a certain Byzas of Megara in the 7th century, the great age of Greek expansion and colonization.

By the 3rd century AD, decadent Rome had already been largely abandoned by the emperors. Concerned above all with the two key strategic fronts, the Danube and the Euphrates, many of them kept their court at Milan, or at places like Sirmium and Serdica (Sofia) in the Balkans. The Balkan region, in fact, was one of the most important of the late Empire. Most of the army and its generals came from there, and more than a few emperors, including Constantine himself. As soon as he had consolidated his hold on the empire, Constantine began work on his new capital, in AD 328.

Like Rome, the new city was said to have seven hills (*see* box, below). It was given its own lavish dole, a racetrack, a forum and its own senate. The fleets of ships that had brought Egypt's bounty of grain to fatten Rome were now re-routed to Constantinople. Constantine meant the new capital not only as a base to defend the two hot edges of his realm and as a monument to himself, but for a third purpose too: creating a specifically Christian city as the capital for his new Christian Empire. No pagan temples were allowed. Facing the new forum, the Augusteion, rose one of Constantine's great basilicas, later rebuilt as the Aya Sofya. Constantinopolis's official date of birth was 11 May 330, the day the city was consecrated by Christian priests.

With rich imperial subsidies and building programmes, Constantinople rapidly became the metropolis of the eastern empire, drawing population and economic life from the older cities of Greece and Asia Minor and beginning their fatal declines. A second wave of growth and embellishment came with the reign of Justinian (527–65). As the booty rolled in from Byzantine conquests around the Mediterranean, Justinian found the money to rebuild the Aya Sofya, the imperial palace and much else. The beginning of his reign, however, saw the most serious outbreak of civil strife in the city's history: the Nike Riots of 532, really a full-fledged popular revolt against the emperor's oppressive rule, crushed by the army with tens of thousands of deaths.

After Justinian's bloody but glorious reign, Constantinople hung on for almost a thousand years as the capital of a venerable, declining, somehow unsinkable empire. By the 12th century, appearances were still kept up but both empire and capital were mere shadows of their former selves. The new quarter of Galata

The Seven Hills

Constantine very consciously meant to make his foundation the New Rome; that was its name at first, until the emperor's vanity overcame him. Like the old Rome, it had a golden milestone, a Senate House and a forum; to govern it, Constantine divided it up into fourteen wards, just as Rome had been divided, and, most importantly for imperial continuity, he declared that it had seven hills.

Finding some of these requires an effort of the imagination. Only three reach any height: the First Hill, where the Topkapı Palace and Aya Sofya stand; the Fifth Hill along the Golden Horn with the Fener and the Selimiye Cami; and the Third Hill, crowned by the Süleymaniye. None of the others will strain your legs: the Second Hill, roughly north of the Burnt Column; the Fourth Hill, around the Fatih Mosque; the Sixth Hill, at the Topkapı Gate, the centre of the land walls; and the Seventh Hill, in the southwest corner of the city.

was growing up across the Golden Horn, largely inhabited by the Italian merchants – Genoese, Pisans, Amalfitani and above all Venetians – who had seized control of the empire's economy. So resented were the predatory Italians that in 1180 a Greek mob massacred those they could catch; the state exiled the rest soon after. In 1203, the Venetian fleet ferried the largely French troops of the Third Crusade down to Constantinople on their way to the Holy Land. The Crusaders couldn't pay their passage, and so the Venetians arranged the Italian revenge. Alexius, the rightful heir to the Byzantine throne whose father had been deposed in a coup, agreed to pay the bill if only the Crusaders would get him back his throne. That was easily done, but the empire was broke and Alexius could not come up with the money. Another coup drove Alexius out, and in February 1204 the Crusaders and Venetians decided to take the undermanned city. After a siege of two months, they smashed their way in, the first time anyone had done so in 900 years. The sack that followed may well have been the richest in all history. The Westerners methodically looted everything, nailed down or not; the Venetians, who had masterminded the whole affair, got the lion's share – including the famous bronze horses of St Mark's, which originally stood in the Hippodrome.

Constantinople would never be the same. For the next forty years, the city endured life as capital of a French-run 'Empire of Romania', and when the Greeks retook the city in 1246 under Emperor Michael Paleologos they had neither the cash nor the energy to restore it. Constantinople's last two centuries were a sad affair, with much of the city centre in ruins; even the court deserted the old palace for the Blachernae Palace out by the Theodosian walls. It was those incomparable walls, besieged so often by Bulgars, Avars, Arabs and Turks, that kept the dilapidated capital and the pathetic empire in business for another two centuries, while the Ottoman Turks were gradually grabbing all Anatolia and the Balkans and eventually even building castles on the Bosphorus.

The end finally came in 1453, with the determined Sultan Mehmet, along with his matchless army, modern fleet and the most advanced artillery in the world. Largely empty, and defended by a handful of Greeks and Venetians, Constantinople fell after a siege of two months. Getting the city back on its feet again proved to be a much greater task than capturing it, but Mehmet proved as capable a ruler as he was a conqueror. The presence of the court itself helped in the economic revival, but Mehmet also moved quickly to re-establish the Covered Bazaar, the cornerstone of the city's economy, while pumping in lots of money for public works: fixing up the walls, streets and water supply, and building the Topkapı Palace and scores of mosques. Incentives were given to get people to move back into the city and improve property. His

Getting around Istanbul

Public transport in all forms is refreshingly inexpensive. If you are staying in Istanbul for more than just a few days, you may consider buying an **Akbil tab** (a small plastic keyring with a magnetic button in the end) which gives you discounted travel on all İETT buses, trams, subway trains, ferries and seabuses, and more importantly saves you the trouble of buying tickets or tokens each time you need to get somewhere. These can be bought for 6 YTL at kiosks with the sign *'Akbil satışı'* and can be topped up with credit at booths with the sign *'Akbil satılır'*. For more information about Akbil see the İETT website: *www.iett.gov.tr*.

By Bus

Although it's a little cumbersome to use, the Istanbul transit system (İETT) website, *www.iett.gov.tr*, has useful information in English on bus routes and timetables. Alternatively, the best thing is to walk over to the nearest main station, as all lines begin and end at one of these: Beyazıt Square; Eminönü, in front of the Spice Bazaar by the Galata Bridge; Karaköy, on the Beyoğlu side of the Galata Bridge; Sirkeci Station; Taksim Square; Beşiktaş; and on the Asian side Harem, near Haydarpaşa Station and Kadiköy near each ferry quay.

The word for **bus stop** is *durak* or *otobüs durağı*; signs are usually painted orange.

Unless you have an Akbil tab, you'll need to buy **tickets** beforehand. You can buy books of them at the unmarked orange kiosks at these stations. Buses are efficient and cheap, but they will usually be indecently crowded. Tickets, at time of writing, sell for 1.30 YTL.

By Tram, Metro and Train

Istanbul has the beginnings of a modern rapid transit system. There is already an **underground** system from Taksim to Levent 4th, but digging in this great old city, with all the world's archaeologists looking over the workmen's shoulders, is not an easy task.

There are two inexpensive above-ground **tram** lines, which run underground where they can. One, the **Çağdaş line**, or **metro**, starts from Aksaray Meydanı underground, then surfaces and heads out to the coach station in the distant suburbs on the European side. The other line, the **Hızlı** ('speedy'), is an above-ground tram that starts at Eminönü near the Yeni Cami, runs to Sultanahmet Square and then down the Divan Yolu, Stamboul's main street, ending up at Zeytinburnu, past the Topkapı Gate. (A third line runs from Sirkeci Station around the tip of the peninsula and along the Marmara shore, but it isn't much use to visitors.) The tram/metro lines use different (equally cheap) **tickets** from the buses; every stop has a booth that sells them but they aren't always open: carry a few around or use an Akbil.

Istanbul's most entertaining public transport is on the Beyoğlu side. If you're travelling from Galata Bridge to Taksim, you'll first meet the **Tünel**, the world's shortest underground (and one of the oldest) with the world's smallest tokens, sold in booths at either end. The Tünel is really an inclined railway, which gets you from the bridge up the steep hill to the bottom end of İstiklâl Caddesi. From there, you can take the delightfully named **Nostaljik Tramvay** up İstiklâl to Taksim Square – real turn-of-the-century streetcars, carefully restored, with conductors in costumes to match. You need to buy tickets at the Tünel or Taksim station before you get on.

By Taxi

All the taxis are yellow, all have meters, and you'll have no trouble finding one on any major street. In the day, the meter should read *gündüz* (daytime). After midnight fares go up, and the sign reads *gece* (night). Drivers often stick to the main thoroughfares to avoid traffic jams, even if this seems to go out of your way. Taxis are still relatively inexpensive – 10–20 YTL for an average trip in the city – and invaluable when you get hopelessly lost. If you're staying in a small hotel or in an out-of-the-way street, be sure to write the name down, as well as any nearby main streets or landmarks, as the drivers often don't know the city as well as they might – especially when you try to pronounce your destination in Turkish. Whilst most drivers are friendly and do an honest day's work, the odd rogue may drive you in circles to up the fare a little. Still, try to have fun and enjoy the ride; it should not cost too much more and avoids argument. Better still, have your hotel call a reputable taxi for you. One strange custom here – if you cross over one of the Bosphorus bridges, you'll be expected to cough up the toll.

By Dolmuş

The dolmuş is a communal taxi. The bad news for anyone who loves Istanbul is that dolmuşes seem to be on their way out. The other means of transport – minibuses, İETT buses and trams – work well enough that it is becoming hard for the individual dolmuş driver to make a living. Nevertheless there are still a few operating around the centre, especially around Taksim. Getting into a dolmuş is easy; just wait near one of the red, white and black dolmuş signs, or hail one from anywhere on the street, see if the destination sign on the roof or front window of the car is anywhere near your own, and pile in. In some outlying parts of the town, they're simpler to use than the buses, and equally inexpensive.

By Minibus

These work much like the dolmuşes, and operate mostly from the city walls, going down the main streets of Istanbul; few penetrate further in than Beyazıt Square. Above all they'll be helpful if you mean to do some exploring around the Theodosian walls and the outlying quarters of old Stamboul. Like the dolmuş, they have destination signs. Don't mistake Topkapı Gate for Topkapı Palace.

By Boat

Outside Venice, there's no city in Europe better for messing about in boats. For many Stamboullu, a ferry ride with this remarkable cityscape for background is just a part of the daily commute.

Ferries for all points depart either from docks on either side of the Galata Bridge, or the Kabataş landing near Dolmabahçe Palace or Beşiktas. **Cruises** up the Bosphorus (Boğaziçi) depart from the Stamboul side of the bridge (pier 3, just to the right of the bridge), usually twice a day; you can get off where you please, or stop for lunch and catch the boat on the return trip, from any of its stops along the straits.

Ferries to the Asian side go up to four times an hour from Eminönü (the docks nearest Sirkeci Station; departing from pier 1 to Üsküdar, or from pier 2 for Kadıköy and Bostancı), and from Kabataş or Beşiktas to Üsküdar. Other boats for Kadıköy–Haydarpaşa Station leave from Karaköy landing, on the Beyoğlu side of the bridge. **Istanbul Ferries (IDO)**, information t 0212 444 4 436, www.ido.com.tr.

For the **Princes' Islands**, several boats a day (more in the summer and at weekends) leave from both Galata (pier 5, behind Sirkeci station) and Kabataş landings. Some are express, getting to Büyükada in about an hour; others call at all four islands and several Asian ports as well. Note that you only pay for the trip to the islands – the return fare is included in the price. The shortest trip to the islands is from Bostancı landing on the Asian side.

Another, less frequent, boat from pier 5 goes to **Yalova**, across the Marmara; there are also boats from Kabataş to Yalova. From the pier to the left of the Galata Bridge on the Stamboul side (pier 6), a boat leaves every half-hour to go up the Golden Horn (Haliç) to **Eyüp** and beyond.

Other boats leave from the docks near Tophane Square (Sorayburnu) for **Marmara Island** (five hours) and **Avşa Island** (six hours) in the Marmara, and the port of Bursa.

Ticket booths are clearly marked; in some cases you cannot buy tickets in advance, but most lines run on tokens that can be used any time.

Car Hire

If you're willing to risk the Istanbul traffic, and ridiculously high rates, the major car hire chains are here, including **Avis**, t 0212 444 2847, www.avis.com.tr/english; and **Europcar**, www.europcar.com. The tourist office has a list of cheaper local firms. At a pinch, try **Decar**, t 0212 288 4243, www.decar.com.tr.

For anyone driving in Istanbul, some explanation is in order. Driving is a hassle, but the traffic is nowhere near as insane as many would have it; from end to end of the town, it hardly ever moves fast enough to let the Turkish driver express himself. Parking is the real problem. Don't worry so much about parking tickets – but if you leave your beast in a really dumb place it could well be towed away.

---

successor, Beyazıt II, resettled thousands of Jewish refugees thrown out of Spain in 1492, starting the city off on its new career as a polyglot place where Turks, Greeks, Armenians, Jews, Arabs, Slavs and Albanians lived side by side. Beginning with Mehmet, each sultan in turn embellished the city with new mosques, pavilions and religious foundations. 'The City' was back in business.

From the 17th century to the First World War, The City did not share fully in the Ottoman decay; it monopolized whatever art and architecture, modernity and economic progress there was. Non-Turks, particularly Greeks, dominated both business and culture, and the Greeks' Phanar (Fener) quarter grew into a city within the city. Istanbul really opened to the West after 1839, the year of the

Orientation

Istanbul's medieval street plan isn't really so bad; as in most old cities, remember that the streets are laid out to make sense to your eyes, more than to be read on a map. After walking for a while through old Istanbul, you'll learn to spot the major landmarks. A brief orientation will help in sorting out the complexities of the layout. Note that there are three parts. On the European side, the triangular peninsula south of the estuary of the Golden Horn is **Stamboul**, the old town (formerly Constantinople and Byzantium) which rises like Rome on seven hills, surrounded by the largely intact Byzantine walls; most of the sights – the Aya Sofya, Topkapı Palace, the Covered Bazaar, Süleymaniye Camii and the Blue Mosque – are concentrated within the square mile of its tip. We mention this only because you may not notice. Whether you're on foot or in a cab, the impenetrable maze of meandering streets makes them seem to be in different parts of the city. Study the map before you set out.

Two bridges span the lower end of the Golden Horn: the Atatürk and the famous, newly rebuilt Galata, connecting old Istanbul with **Beyoğlu**, the 'European quarter' ever since Italian merchants colonized it in the latter days of Byzantium. Its outer fringes have been fashionable for two centuries now. Galata Bridge, and the Eminönü Square behind it in the old town, are the nearest thing Istanbul has to a centre; the busy comings and goings here were a feature of Istanbul life before there was a bridge, going back to the days of the Byzantines.

Ferryboats from Galata Bridge go to the districts of the Asian shore: **Kadıköy**, **Haydarpaşa** and others. Up the **Bosphorus**, Istanbul's metropolitan area has absorbed the picturesque villages on both sides, almost as far as the Black Sea.

Tanzimat reforms. Foreign businessmen poured in to take advantage of the empire's weakness, and Beyoğlu, or 'Pera', transformed itself into a proper European city where French was more commonly heard in the streets than Turkish.

All this was a mixed blessing. The reign of Abdülhamid II especially (1876–1909) proved a disaster for Istanbul, as it was for the rest of the empire. With the state desperately in need of foreign investment and technology, the city was completely at the mercy of the foreign interests Abdülhamid's vezirs invited in. The beautiful shore of the Golden Horn was degraded into an industrial nightmare, while the new railway line to Sirkeci Station devastated the equally scenic Marmara side.

In 1919, British and French troops occupied Istanbul. The British government hoped to prop the gormless Mehmet V on the Ottoman throne as a puppet, while gaining de facto control of the straits for itself, plans that came to naught with the victory of Atatürk's nationalists. Much of the Greek population fled, although, like Mehmet, Atatürk took pains to reassure those who stayed behind. Though no longer a capital, Istanbul remained the economic heart of Turkey and its window to the West. One of the saddest and least remembered events in Istanbul's recent history was the anti-Greek pogrom of September 1955, during the beginnings of the conflict over Cyprus. Elements of the Menderes government bussed in mobs from the provinces to trash Greek businesses, homes and churches. Only thirteen were killed, but, after it was over, Istanbul's Greek population quickly dropped from an estimated 150,000 to about 2,000.

Istanbul Today

Over the last two decades, the big story has been the tremendous surge of migration into the city. Mostly rural folk, some 400,000 a year from every corner of Turkey, come to try their luck. Istanbul is where the jobs are. The newcomers have been a tremendous burden on the city's resources; water and public health head a long list of urban problems. Even so, the immigrants are contributing their hopes and hard work to a city that is changing faster than at any time since Mehmet the Conqueror – a city alive, exploding with energy.

The Streets of Istanbul

You may come to this city for the monuments and museums, to see the sultan's jewels or the gold of the Byzantine mosaics, or simply to watch the sunset over the skyline of minarets and domes. The fantasies you entertain may be out of the *Arabian Nights* or an Eric Ambler spy thriller of the 1930s. Whatever your particular purpose, take care that you keep your eyes and ears open to the life in the streets. This is the real Istanbul, for which the mosques and palaces are merely decoration, and the people of the city have had centuries to cultivate this life of Istanbul into an art form.

Especially in the small things, Istanbul has sacrificed little to modernity. If your hotel is in one of the older residential districts, like Aksaray or Sultanahmet, you are likely to be awakened to the cry, '*Nefis...simit, simit...*' – 'exquisite *simitler*' – and the man who carries these sesame-encrusted circles of bread, on a stick or in a glass box, may differ only in dress from those in 16th-century prints. If you were a Stamboullu, you might drop down a basket on a long rope for one. After the *simit* man comes the tinker's rattling empty cart, and his long unintelligible cries seem less a plea for trade than an eternal rambling monologue on God's unfairness to tinkers.

Of course there are street markets: some of the old quarters are named after the day of the week on which they would occur. In Istanbul, though, in the Middle Eastern manner, every street is an actual or potential market. Some have permanent sites: by Galata Bridge each morning housewives and stray cats circle around tired fishermen, angling for their share of the day's catch, while, opposite, in the narrow maze of streets climbing to the Covered Bazaar, the metal doors bang open to reveal thousands of tiny shops, segregated into streets according to their trade: an avenue of baby clothes, a street of copper pots, a cul-de-sac of used Korans. More money probably changes hands on the bridge itself than in a large department store. On Galata Bridge, on any given day you may spend a few lira on socks, wind-up monkeys, copies of the Turkish Highway Code, contraband blue jeans, clothes hangers, pastel knickers, aubergines, spanner sets (Imperial or metric), bicycle mirrors, hamsters, or portraits of Mehmet the Conqueror.

To all these, add the shoeshine boys: young apprentices with cheap wooden boxes and old paint tins to sit on, and dignified professionals with dozens of cut-glass bottles in gold-plated cases, embellished with scenes of Mecca and autographed pictures of overripe *chanteuses*. Sellers of sherbet, *ayran*, unidentifiable pastries and even water abound. You can try your hand at shooting with the young men who have invested their capital in an air rifle and target, or patronize the poorest of all, those whose business consists of a single rusted set of bathroom scales, waiting to weigh all comers.

As background, add the beggars, military policemen, hosts of shabby-genteel cats and pigeons, tourists from Iran and Indiana, seven hills, 1,300 minarets, gypsies, ferryboats, Roman cisterns, and the strangest Art Nouveau buildings east of Palma de Mallorca.

The older neighbourhoods have no monopoly on all this; it is the everyday ambience the Stamboullu takes for granted, varying in degree from the venerable precincts of Eminönü and Sultanahmet to the newer streets around Taksim Square and those on the Asian side, but never especially dirty or dilapidated. The old town is the real surprise. Following Turkish rather than European ideas of town planning, there are lots of trees, and the houses are as spread out as land values permit. Many of the outlying districts are really suburbs within the Theodosian walls, or better, aggregations of villages.

You'll see the new Istanbul clearly if you arrive from the east; after the car passes over the Bosphorus Bridge you're on the ring motorway, the Çevre Yolu; for miles you'll look down on vast new neighbourhoods, full of attractive modern flats. Amidst these are shopping malls as modern as anything in California, and over it all rises a new crown of skyscrapers. There's a modern new metro, new tramways, a second suspension bridge over the Bosphorus and a tunnel in construction. New suburbs have gobbled up almost all the countryside along the Bosphorus, and for sixty miles down the Asian shore. In the 1980s major infrastructure and slum clearance programmes were begun under mayors Bedrettin Dalan and Nurettin Sözen. Much of the impetus for all this came from Istanbul's as yet unsuccessful bids to host the Olympics. Because of that, a large part of the effort has been devoted to cosmetics – most spectacularly, the ambitious plan to reclaim all of old Stamboul's waterfront. Already over half the Golden Horn and Marmara shores have been cleared and turned into parkland.

Old Istanbul (Stamboul)

Sultanahmet Square

Most visitors begin their tours of the old city in Sultanahmet Square, the lovely garden of fountains and flowers between Aya Sofya and the Blue Mosque, and in season it can be a real tourist inferno, full of carpet salesmen and every other sort of tout. A pavilion housing a very helpful tourist information centre is here, near the **Kaiser Wilhelm II Fountain**, a small gift from Sultan Abdülhamid's big brother in Berlin, in the days when Germany was the declining Ottoman Empire's greatest ally. The low buildings along the southern edge, the **Aya Sofya Baths**, are among the few that survived the modern reconstruction of the square, when acres of Ottoman buildings were cleared (*see* p.107).

If you could have stood here in Byzantine times, however, you would have been in the city's grand ceremonial square, the enclosed, colonnaded Augusteion. Just to the left of Aya Sofya, the main street of the city passed through the Bronze Gate. A tall column bearing a golden statue of Justinian stood in front of the church, and near it was the golden milestone from which all distances in the empire were measured. The Baths of Zeuxippos, a domed structure probably not unlike the modern Turkish hamams, occupied the western edge of the square, and, next to this, the bulk of the Hippodrome could be seen behind the towers of St Stephen's. The south edge fronted the Senate House, where the last remnant of the Roman Republic survived as a rubber-stamp council almost until the end of Byzantium. The emperors could be seen in this square at their accessions, and on the feast days of the Church. After the sack of 1204, when the Crusaders looted the square of its gold and ornaments, the area drifted gradually into ruin. Already the emperors had moved to the Blachernae Palace in the suburbs, and the restored empire after 1261 lacked the resources to keep up the church. One 14th-century traveller wrote of finding the great church eerily empty, its doors lying on the ground. You may feel the same, and may hear the ghostly echo of Justinian's 'Solomon, I have surpassed thee!', as you walk under the dome of the denuded church, once glowing with a golden altar and iconostasis, chandeliers and acres of mosaics.

Aya Sofya

⭐ Aya Sofya
open summer
Tues–Sun 9–7.30; winter
Tues–Sun 9–5; adm

Since 1933, the Aya Sofya has been a museum, and lacks even the prayer rugs and mihrab to relieve the tremendous desolation. Even so, in its present state the lack of ornamentation perhaps makes the beauty and audacity of the architecture easier to appreciate. Undoubtedly this is the greatest dome in Christendom, though St Peter's in Rome and St Paul's in London are larger. In the 6th century, nothing like the Aya Sofya had ever been built, or even imagined, and even today the impression that it makes cannot be experienced anywhere else.

Building Aya Sofya

The original Aya Sofya, which the Byzantines called simply the Great Church, was built by Theodosius II in 415, on the site of an even earlier church built under Constantine the Great. Theodosius's Aya Sofya burned during the street battles of the Nike Revolt at the beginning of Justinian's reign (*see* p.109). To provide a symbol for his dreams of imperial grandeur, and to a certain extent to justify them, Justinian determined to rebuild as quickly and on as large a scale as possible. The cornerstone of his new church was laid exactly 40 days after the suppression of the revolt.

The two men chosen to design the church were not really architects. Not long before, the emperor had decreed an end to the Athenian Academy, the centre of learning of the classical world, and the last stronghold of philosophy untainted by the Gospels. In doing so, he put two of the greatest mathematicians of the age, Anthemius of Tralles (modern Aydın) and Isidore of Miletus, out of work. Between them, they accepted the job, and got it built in only five years. The imperial treasury had been strained to the limit, but the new Great Church was consecrated in solemn ceremony on 26 December 537, St Stephen's Day.

The difficulties in the construction were manifold; no architect alive had experience of a task of such magnitude. Improvisation was a daily necessity. The four massive piers on which the entire structure is hung have stones held together not with mortar, but with molten lead. The distinctive shape of Aya Sofya's capitals is no mere design conceit, such as those of the classical Greeks; it is absolutely necessary to the structure. The 'impost capital', as it is called, had already been invented to give proper support to arches and vaults, but here it was perfected. One of the problems was reconciling the strengths and weaknesses of so many different types of stone. Just as the emperor spared no expense in getting in the best architects and workmen, every variety of stone in the empire is represented here: green marble from the Peloponnese, yellow from Libya, rose from Phrygia and Lydia, great slabs of porphyry that were floated down the Nile from upper Egypt. Ancient buildings were looted for tall columns; of those in the galleries, the red are from the Temple of the Sun in Baalbek, the green probably from the Artemision of Ephesus.

One enters the church just as a Byzantine commoner would, through side gates in the outer porch (the exonarthex). The centre gate was for the emperor alone, and it continues through a long thin hall to the **narthex**. Here, where the emperor passed into the church itself, one of the surviving gold mosaics portrays Emperor Leo IV kneeling before a seated Christ. Below, on the brass lintel, the Holy Spirit descends with a book, open to the words, 'The Lord said, "I am the door of the sheep: By me if any man enter in...he shall find pasture."' An empty throne stands concealed behind.

You can walk right in. The central gate opens at the rear of the great **nave**. As you pass through, turn and look up at the best-preserved mosaic of the church, the Virgin Mary cradling the infant Jesus. To her right, Constantine offers her the city of Constantinople; to her left, Justinian proffers the Aya Sofya. More mosaics, mostly geometric and floral patterns, cover the rest of the narthex roof. Though many of these have not yet been restored, they will give you some idea of how the decoration of the church's interior must have looked. One of the first things Atatürk did after converting Aya Sofya to a museum was to arrange for the restoration of the mosaics. The work was done over the next two decades by the Byzantine Institute, a private organization in Boston. Justinian's church had no mosaics: those that remain – of the original estimated four acres – date mostly from the 9th century or later, after the defeat of the Iconoclasts.

As you approach the centre of the church, you realize the particular architectural problem Anthemius and Isidore faced, and their brilliant solution. For reasons of grace and symmetry, with a little bit of geometric mysticism mixed in as well, the emperor wanted a central plan, symmetrical on two axes. The forms of Byzantine ritual, however, required a basilica-plan church with a long nave. To accomplish this, Anthemius flanked his **dome** with two semi-domes along the axis of the nave and enclosed the space under the lateral arches with solid walls full of windows. Underneath these, the mass is distributed down to the ground through a network of smaller **semi-domes** (exedrae), **vaults** and **columns**, thus opening to the light a space six times the area of the dome. This conquest of gravity is the magic of Aya Sofya. The 6th-century chroniclers tell of visitors and citizens afraid to enter lest all collapse, or becoming dizzy trying to look at the top of the dome, 181ft above the floor. The Byzantines always spoke of this dome as being suspended from heaven by a golden chain.

Artistic details in the interior are few; little survived the Iconoclasts, the Crusaders and the Muslims. The bronze doors of the narthex are original, and the monograms of Justinian and Theodora can be seen on many of the capitals. The largest mosaic, on the apse above the place where the altar stood, is a portrait of the Virgin Mary with the infant Jesus; below it, figures of the Archangels Michael and Gabriel can be made out. In place of the altar and iconostasis, only the Muslim mihrab and mimber fill the void, along with the raised loge built for the prayers of the sultans, with İznik tiles and carved wood details. The four huge medallions on the columns, painted calligraphically with the names of Allah, Mohammed and the early caliphs, were removed by Atatürk but have recently been replaced as a gesture to the Muslim fundamentalists (also, they now broadcast the call to prayer from Aya Sofya's minarets). Above the medallions, four sinister-looking Byzantine seraphs stare down from the pendentives.

The Muslims, like the Greeks, segregated their women, putting them upstairs in the spacious galleries around the nave, making them climb about 50ft of ramps to get there. It's worth the walk, for the view and for the best of the remaining mosaics. In the centre of the galleries, at the far end of the church, two green columns from Ephesus mark the place where the empresses worshipped. The ladies, in fact, had only the North Gallery; the **South Gallery** was reserved for the rest of the imperial family – the Turks gave the lovely screen that partitioned it the fanciful title of 'Gates of Heaven and Hell'. A celebrated series of the 13th-century mosaics, one of the last improvements to the church under the Byzantines, can be seen around the gallery: Emperor John Comnenus and his family, Empress Zoe and her third husband (his face painted over that of number two) and Jesus with Mary and John the Baptist. On the floor near this last one is a slab inscribed with the name Henrico Dandolo, the aged, bitter Duke of Venice who led the Sack of 1204. Surprisingly, the Greeks never disinterred him when they recaptured the city; the Turks did, within weeks of Mehmet's conquest. This South Gallery often served for the transaction of church business; two General Church Councils, the second and the sixth, were held in it. High on a wall of the adjacent gallery is a faded mosaic of the Emperor Alexander, who ruled only from 912 to 913. The inscription above his diademed head reads: 'Lord help thy servant, the orthodox and faithful Emperor Alexander.' Lord help him indeed. He was a habitual drunkard who died of apoplexy after a particularly heavy session.

You may be disconcerted to see that very few of the columns of the galleries are actually in plumb. Some list at alarming angles, many are cracked and bound with iron rings, and the impression of a house of cards is inescapable. Even before Atatürk, the Turks kept a constant vigil over this fabulous patient, on and off the critical list for 14 centuries. Anthemius and Isidore, for all their skill, could not make their church perfect. The dome, shallow enough now, was originally 20ft lower, and had to be reconstructed when a 40-day series of earthquakes toppled it in 558. In the 10th century, the next thorough restoration kept the church closed for 10 years. Again in the 14th century, a collapse seemed imminent; the emperors scraped the bottom of the treasury to construct the four colossal buttresses that so mar the exterior. No more money could be found to complete the repairs, and by the time of the Conquest, the church was no longer in use. Mehmet added more buttresses and the first minaret, and Mimar Sinan himself tore down much of the ruined old imperial quarter to get stone for further strengthening. Seven thorough restorations since have accomplished the preservation of the mosaics and the reinforcement of the dome with steel; specialists are still on guard for any further signs of weakness. The galleries, they say, are in no danger now.

The theology of the Muslims would, on the whole, have seemed almost acceptable to a man like Justinian, and, as fate would have it, the Muslims were to be the vehicle for preserving his symbol and his dream over the centuries. Justinian must surely have thought the building of his church would mark the advent of a new world age. His choice of men from the Academy to put it up was as much symbolic as practical. Here, the entire harvest of classical science and philosophy was to serve the ends of the Christian God. The Muslims, who already had taken their own deep draughts of Greek thought, felt entirely at home after 1453. More than any other place in the Christian or Islamic worlds, this is the great house of monotheism, the place where human understanding and accomplishment were recognized as the Divine Wisdom, the Hagia Sofia both faiths believed it to be.

Around Aya Sofya

Just outside the main entrance, excavations have uncovered the foundations of the portico of Theodosius's church; an architect's reconstruction posted by the door shows an elegant classical building, architecturally a bit old-fashioned. Some bits of the columns and the cornice have survived, with reliefs of the Lamb of God. The Muslims had more of a sense of humour than the Christians. In the **mausoleums** they built around Aya Sofya's garden were interred nearly all the worst of the worst Ottoman sultans: Mustafa I, an imbecile and tool of the Janissaries, İbrahim the Mad, the ultimate libertine who picked off his subjects from the Topkapı walls for target practice, and Selim the Sot, whose honorific tells us all we need to know. His mausoleum, decorated with fine İznik tiles, is a work of Mimar Sinan. Facing the row of mausoleums is the pretty, covered **Fountain of Mehmet II**, and a primary school built by the same sultan in 1742.

Behind the Aya Sofya, adjoining the walls of the Topkapı Palace, the indefatigable restorationists of the Turkish Automobile Club have rebuilt an entire street of characteristic Ottoman wooden houses, **Soğukçeşme Sokak** ('Cool Fountain Street'), many of which are now in use as guest houses. This is only one part of their plan for beautifying the centre of old Stamboul. South of the Blue Mosque, they have a complex including shops in a restored medrese and the lovely wooden **Yeşil Ev Hotel**, one of the best-restored examples of Ottoman vernacular architecture in Istanbul.

Also behind the church, a famous monument of the Tulip Period (*see* p.116) can be seen as introduction to another aspect of Turkish architecture. The **Fountain of Ahmed III**, built in 1729, really a small pavilion, is covered with a wealth of green and blue tiles painted in floral motifs, and with verses of the sultan who built it. Yet another beneficiary of cosmetic surgery, its tiles and gilt trim shine with their original splendour, highlighting one of the finest works of the Ottoman 18th century, one that captures perfectly the super-refined and delicate sensibility of the 'Tulip Period'. There is much more of this behind the walls of Topkapı; the outer gate, the Bab-i-Humayun, stands only a few yards away.

Between the Aya Sofya and the Blue Mosque, the **Aya Sofya Baths** have become the Turkish Handwoven Carpet Sales Centre. Don't let the name put you off. Once Sultanahmet's most elegant, most regal hamam, this was built by Sinan in 1556 on the orders of Süleyman the Magnificent to honour his favourite wife, the cunning and perfidious Roxelana. The first room is domed, and adorned with 16 lovely arched stained-glass windows. The baths lead on through three rooms into the central steam room, with numerous cubicles secreted away around it for more personal bathing, and continue onwards for its full length. This was a double, mixed-sex hamam, men bathing at one end, women at the other. Ignore the carpets draped everywhere and picture the place as it once was, a haven of refreshment for the empire's most illustrious. Or, if you're crazy for carpets, compare what is on offer here with the fine antique works in the **Museum of Turkish Carpets and Kilims** (Halı ve Kilim Müzesi), just around the corner on Mimar Mehmet Ağa Caddesi, in Sultanahmet Comii.

Museum of Turkish Carpets and Kilims
open Tues–Sat 9–4; adm

The Blue Mosque (Sultanahmet Camii)

Blue Mosque
open Tues–Sat 9–4; access restricted during prayer times

Across the square from Aya Sofya, Sultan Ahmet in 1619 constructed the Sultanahmet or Blue Mosque, like a matching bookend – not so much to compete with the old church, but because all the other available sites already had big mosques on them. Even then, he had to knock down the palaces of several of his ministers to make space. None of the city's other monuments has occasioned more argument; some critics claim it is the finest work of architecture in the city, while others say it is overdone and uninspired. Certainly there are no new departures in the plan, just another copy of the Aya Sofya, only more rigidly symmetrical than

07 **Istanbul** | Old Istanbul (Stamboul): Sultanahmet Square

the others. Like Mimar Sinan's mosques, the plan is an almost perfect square. The main attraction here is the interior with its 21,043 blue İznik tiles, painted with the blue arabesques that give the mosque its familiar name. Each one of these tiles set Ahmet back 18 *akçeler* – twice the daily wage of a teacher in the palace school. The great dome, 70ft across, stands on four semi-domes, each of these on three exedrae and each of the exedrae on two arches. At any time, two-thirds of the mosque will be given over to Muslims at prayer and a rail watched by a mosque official separates the faithful from the flummoxed. The imperial loge is a lattice of pure marble, and the window shutters are of exquisite design, inlaid with ivory, mother-of-pearl and tortoiseshell.

Ahmet was sure he was building for the ages, and with an arrogance possible only from a Commander of the Faithful he had his architect, Mehmet Ağa, build six minarets instead of the two or four customary in Ottoman imperial mosques. (Don't forget this; knowing that the Blue Mosque is the one with six minarets may come in handy some time when you're good and lost in old Stambol.) Previously, only the shrine of the Ka'aba in Mecca had been allowed six, and, after a shrill chorus of protests from the divines of Islam, Ahmet was forced to send Mehmet Ağa down to Mecca to build a seventh. Also unusual in this mosque are the rows of great doors around the lovely courtyard – 36 of them, all leading nowhere. Ahmet died at 27 and was buried near his creation; his *türbe* stands in the square between the mosque and the Aya Sofya. Buried with him are his wife and his sons, two of whom, Osman II and Murat IV, went on to the sultanate themselves.

Yerebatan Sarayı

Yerebatan Sarayı
*open Tues–Sat
9–5.30; adm*

Also across from the Aya Sofya stands the unprepossessing entrance to the Yerebatan Sarayı. No one has yet proposed old Constantinople's water supply for associate membership in the Wonders of the Ancient World, but this perhaps is only because this network of cisterns is so little known. The 'Underground Palace', as the Turks call it, is a great hall 230ft by 460ft, supported by ranks of columns and vaults. Though the largest, it's only one of several in the city. Two more have recently been discovered near the Aya İrene, and it is possible that some others remain unknown. By the 16th century, although the old aqueducts were still in use, these reservoirs had been quite forgotten. A French antiquarian named Petrus Gyllius spent weeks looking for this one in 1545, until he had the good fortune to find a resident of the quarter who had a trap door in his house. Down in the cistern, this gentleman kept a boat and used it daily to catch fish, which he sold to his puzzled neighbours. No one suspected the cistern existed, even though the wells of their houses led directly into it.

Each of the 40ft columns – there are over 300 of them – has a capital to bear the arches, and some of these are carved as if they had been part of a church, instead of a reservoir. Justinian, who was responsible for most of these works, was forced to demolish an old basilica that stood above the cistern, and just reused the capitals.

The Hippodrome

In Byzantine times, the site of the Blue Mosque held the Golden Hall, the outermost building of Justinian's Topkapı Palace where the throne was kept and the affairs of government transacted. A private corridor connected this part of the palace with the **Kathisma**, or imperial box of the Hippodrome, which once stood just to the west. This arrangement copied the tunnel between Rome's Palatine and the Circus Maximus, and, as at Rome, the Hippodrome played an important role in its city's public life. Much more went on here than just chariot races and athletic events. Emperors celebrated their victories, and executed their enemies. Even the games should not be taken as simple entertainment; during the Roman period they had evolved into a strange sort of mystic communion between the emperor, who of course picked up the bill, and his people. Everything about the games became a symbol, reflecting some aspect of the politics of the day.

Blues, Greens and Purple

Construction of the Hippodrome began in 203, the same year Septimus Severus was building the Circus Maximus in Rome, but it remained unfinished until the reign of Constantine. Subsequent emperors improved and enlarged it, and by the time of Justinian it was nearly a third of a mile long, with seats for 100,000.

Much has been made of the Hippodrome factions, the Blues and Greens, that caused so much trouble in Constantinople in the 6th century. It would, however, be giving the Byzantines more credit for decadence than even they deserved to suppose that the course of the empire was governed by militant sports fans. Originally, there were four factions, the Reds and Whites later merging into the others. They were nothing less than the organized *demes*, or tribes, traditional in any Greek city. (Rome had the same four colours and factions, though it is likely that the Romans adapted the idea from the Greeks or the Etruscans.) They had both military and civilian functions; it was they who built the city walls, and their leaders received salaries as officers of the state. Gradually they came to identify with socio-economic divisions within the city; exactly how the historians can't tell, though it seems the Greens were somewhat more proletarian and politically radical. But when the Blues and Greens joined forces in the Nike Revolt they were fighting for the city's liberty, and their own, against imperial absolutism and all its aggression abroad, its cops and spies, and its unbearable taxes.

Nike means Victory, the battle cry of the rebels; the revolt began in 532, five years after Justinian's accession to the throne. The rebels soon gained control of the city: chroniclers paint a picture of the young emperor staring helplessly from the palace balcony, too amazed and terrified to act. The story goes that Theodora, the low-born dancing girl who had so captivated Justinian that he made her an empress, finally snapped him out of it and put a little steel in her man's soul. When he proposed to flee the city, she refused, insisting that he should stay and fight, telling him, 'The purple [the imperial colour] is the noblest winding-sheet.' The rebels were defeated when the great General Belisarius, at the head of an army of Goths and Alans – the Greeks could not be trusted – surrounded the rebels in the Hippodrome and massacred them all: 60,000 of them if contemporary sources are to be believed.

The Crusaders in 1204 thoroughly laid waste the Hippodrome and, as the restored empire had no money to spend on games, the great **stadium** gradually fell into ruin. Under the Turks, most of its stones found their way into new building projects, but the sultans always left the surviving monuments alone, and kept the ground clear for practising their game of *cirit*, a form of polo. From this, the square where the Hippodrome once stood came to be known as the **At Meydanı**, Horse Square, and this name is still sometimes heard. In the late 1960s the square became something of a hippy encampment, until Turkish patience finally ran out.

The Monuments of the Hippodrome

The present square, though it follows the contours of the Hippodrome's field, is less than half as big. Its centre line can be traced through the three surviving columns. This line was the *spina*; the Byzantines liked to call it the 'Axis of the Empire'. Originally its two ends were marked by golden columns representing the sun and the moon – the symbolism of the games was astronomical as well as political. These were the pylons around which the charioteers raced; between the two columns, the *spina* boasted an almost unbroken line of monuments. The Crusaders carried away or wrecked most of these when they sacked the city, most famously stealing the bronze horses of Lysippus that now adorn St Mark's in Venice. The three that remain were too heavy to move.

In the case of the first, the **Column of Constantine Porphyrogenitus**, the Crusaders had to settle for melting down the bronze plates that covered it. The second monument, the **Serpentine Column**, a twisted stump of bronze, retains little of beauty or interest to remind us of its fascinating history; from faint inscriptions on its base it has been determined that this column was the monument dedicated by the united Greek cities to celebrate their victory over the Persians at Plataea in 479 BC. After transporting the column in joyous ceremonies through all the towns that shared in the victory, it was erected at the Temple of Apollo at Delphi, where it stood until Constantine the Great stole it to embellish his capital. Before it toppled, some time around 1700, the column had the form of three intertwined serpents, their heads supporting the legs of a golden tripod dedicated to Apollo.

The third monument, the **Obelisk of Theodosius**, was acquired by that emperor in 390 especially for the Hippodrome; an obelisk was something no stadium could be without. This one came from Heliopolis, and the hieroglyphic inscriptions on its sides record the victories of the mighty Pharaoh Thutmose III. Like most of the Egyptian obelisks that have found their way to the world's capitals, this one is in surprisingly good shape for its 3,400 years; all the hieroglyphs still stand out clearly. The marble base on which the obelisk was raised has been called one of the finest works of 4th-century sculpture; its reliefs portray Theodosius and his family in the Kathisma, viewing the games, the emperor with a wreath in his hand ready to crown the victor. Another relief shows the transporting of the obelisk; the inscriptions on the sides, in both Greek and Latin verse, recall the difficulties of erecting the heavy stone and the praise due to Proclus the prefect for accomplishing it. The wells in which these monuments are sunk gives you an idea how much the land has risen since the Hippodrome was last in use. A group of British officers on leave excavated the bases of the three monuments during the Crimean War.

Around the Hippdrome

North of the Hippodrome, back near Kaiser Wilhelm's Fountain, stands a small mosque that is one of the oldest in Istanbul. The **Firuz Ağa Camii**, built in 1491, has nothing of the grandeur of later imperial mosques, but its architecture definitely points towards them, in a transition from the old, plain Ottoman style, the masterpieces of which you can see in Bursa. Five times a day, a real muezzin climbs up the short minaret to give the call to prayer. The big mosques usually have only loudspeakers, but with the renaissance of Muslim piety in Turkey, many mosques have gone back to the old-fashioned way.

Just across the street from the monuments of the Hippodrome, the palace of İbrahim Paşa, a grand vezir first favoured then executed by Süleyman the Magnificent, has recently been restored to house the **Museum of Turkish and Islamic Arts** (Türk ve İslam Eserleri Müzesi), with a well-arranged collection of ceramic and brass works, carpets and carved lecterns, some dating from the first centuries of Islam.

Over the last decade this museum has grown into one of the best planned and presented in Turkey, as well as one of the most comprehensive collections of its kind anywhere. Objects on display go back to the earliest times: peculiar mosaics from the Abbasid Caliphate, along with acanthus-leaf capitals that show a Greek influence. There are some fine Selcuk ceramics, with figurative representations of people and animals. Beyond these there are Persian miniatures, lovely geometrically carved doors and window shutters, and early Korans. Ottoman works, not surprisingly, make up the best parts of the collection: 16th- and 17th-century silver and brass work, İznik tiles, tulip art, inlaid wood chests and Koran stands. There is a 'magic shirt' that belonged to Beyazıt I (it didn't help him against Tamerlane) and several examples of the *mülkname*, state decrees in exquisite calligraphy, adorned with the Sultan's personal *tuğra*. On many old Ottoman buildings, such as the Sublime Porte (*see* p.111), you will have noticed this unusual

Museum of Turkish and Islamic Arts
open Tues–Sun 9–5; closed Mon; adm

07 Istanbul | Old Istanbul (Stamboul): Sultanahmet Square

symbol, made of Arabic characters in a scroll of concentric loops. The *tuğra* was the mark of the Ottoman Empire from the early days. It originated with Murat I, who, like his predecessors, was illiterate and signed documents with his thumbprint.

It's easy to overlook the the museum's basement, entered by a small door off the courtyard. This section is devoted to traditional Turkish life, and the star exhibit is a complete *toprak ev*, or yurt, the sort of tent used by the Turks' nomadic ancestors, along with some fascinating displays on the natural dyes and other crafts that went into making it. There is also a 'black tent' of goat hair (the *yörükler*, nomads of eastern Turkey, still use these today), and tableaux of an Anatolian village house and 19th-century homes, complete with authentic costumes and furnishings.

All of the area west of the Hippodrome is built over another of Justinian's underground cisterns, though the entrance is difficult to find. From Divan Yolu, the main street of the city, head three blocks south on Klotfarer Caddesi to a playground where bits of a large retaining wall are visible. Here you'll find the entrance to the **Binbirdirek Cistern** – the 'thousand and one columns', the name a familiar Turkish hyperbole. This one, though smaller than the Yerebatan Sarayı, is dry, and you can explore its entire extent. In Byzantine records it was known as the Cistern of Philoxenes.

Binbirdirek Cistern
open daily 9–4; adm

Topkapı Palace (Topkapı Sarayı)

⭐ Topkapı Palace
buildings and museums open April–Oct Wed–Mon 9–7; Nov–May Wed–Mon 9–5; closed Tues; adm; separate adm for the Harem buildings, with guided tours hourly in various languages – check ahead for times of tours in English; a few rooms in the palace complex are usually closed for restoration at any given time

Immediately after the Conquest, Mehmet Fatih built his first palace on the hill north of Beyazıt Square. In 1468, he began a summer palace on the beautiful and largely unoccupied hill at the tip of the peninsula, where the Golden Horn joins the Bosphorus. Later sultans favoured the site, and Süleyman the Magnificent was the first to move here permanently. Most of the present buildings are from the 18th century; by then the sultans had made themselves captives in this lovely soap-bubble of a world. Some of them spent more of their revenues here than in all the rest of the empire. Even though much of the Topkapı's treasure was sold off in the 19th century, when the empire was constantly facing bankruptcy, the hoard that survives is incredible, including the richest collections of porcelain and emeralds in the world. There's hardly enough space to display all the trinkets the sultans squirreled away here – the curators say they can only show about three per cent of it at a time.

The hill had been the acropolis of ancient Byzantium, with two theatres overlooking the Bosphorus, temples, a stadium, and an arsenal and drill field called the Strategion. Just inside the Bab-i Humayun stood the little city's main square, the Tetrastoon. Not a trace of any of this remains, and we know surprisingly little of the use the quarter was put to after Constantine.

First Courtyard

The **Bab-i Humayun**, a simple stone gate, looks to have been more for defence than decoration, and it was. The many revolts and skirmishes of the empire's decadent years put it to the test. Mahmud II hid here from his bloodthirsty Janissaries. Whatever the outcome, the gate would usually be adorned with the heads of the losers. Through it, one enters the First Courtyard, a large park. Two centuries ago, it was full of the palace outbuildings: the imperial mint and, most importantly, the barracks of the Janissaries. From here this praetorian guard was able to keep a constant watch on its sultans, standing between them and any hope of aid from the outside world. Mahmud demolished their buildings soon after their demise in the Auspicious Event.

In the same year Aya Sofya was completed, Justinian and Theodora dedicated a smaller church, **Aya İrene**, just behind it. The two churches shared a common sanctuary, but were cut off from each other when the Turks enclosed Aya İrene in the First Courtyard. The site may have originally been occupied by a temple of Aphrodite; like the Aya Sofya, the church you see now replaced a work of Theodosius burned down in the Nike Riots. Aya İrene, the Divine Peace, was never used as a mosque: its keys were given to the Janissaries who, following the precepts of the Bektaşi order of dervishes, were never allowed to enter a mosque. Instead, they used it as their arsenal, and kept it in good shape over the centuries. The church is a basilica in form, but with a small dome and transepts, a very unusual plan for a Byzantine work. On the apse where the altar stood, a simple black and gold mosaic of a cross is believed to be original. For a while under the republic, Aya İrene was kept open as a military museum, making use of the curiosities accumulated over the years by the Janissaries. The church is now closed to the public, but occasionally used for concerts during the Istanbul festival and for exhibitions during the Istanbul Biennial.

Bab-üs Selâm

At the end of the First Courtyard stands another wall and the **Bab-üs Selâm** or Gate of Salutations, the entrance to the official part of the Saray (for which permission was required to enter); now it's where you buy your ticket. The medieval air of this gate, with its conical spires, is no accident. Süleyman was so taken with the castles and churches of Hungary when he campaigned there that he brought back Hungarian architects to build it for him. One of the customs of this gate was that no one except the sultan and his mother might pass through it on horseback. The head gardener of the Saray had his office here; this is a good example of the Turkish fancy for euphemism, for the 'gardeners' were really armed guards who shared fully in the palace intrigues, and the 'head gardener' was none other than the sultan's chief executioner. The block, and the fountain in which he washed his blade, can be seen near this gate, along with the 'warning stone' on which severed heads would be displayed *pour encourager les autres*.

Second Courtyard: Court of the Divan and Harem

The next courtyard, the **Court of the Divan**, was divided between the highest council chamber of government and the palace kitchens; this arrangement would never seem silly to an Ottoman, for whom all real government was embodied in the person of the sultan. For Divan, understand the sultan's cabinet; the vezirs met once a week in the Divan hall, under its tower on the left-hand side of the courtyard. The earlier sultans would have been present at these meetings, where the affairs of the government were discussed. Süleyman introduced the screen to keep his vezirs honest; they could never know if he was behind it listening or not. His successors hardly went to the Divan at all.

Unfortunately, most of the Divan chambers are usually closed, but they may let you in to see the lovely, thoroughly restored 16th-century council chamber. Other rooms house a collection of arms and armour, including the swords of many of the sultans. From a distance, the landmark of the entire palace complex is the **Divan's tower**, built in 1825 by Mahmut II as a watchtower, and strangely reminiscent of a New England church steeple.

The Divan is attached to the **harem**, a group of buildings and courtyards that cover one-sixth of the total area of the Saray. Süleyman began its construction when his favourite wife Roxelana convinced him he could not live without her; as power devolved upon the ladies and their eunuchs, later sultans expanded it into the labyrinthine complex we see today. After Abdülmecit moved to the Dolmabahçe Palace in 1853, the surviving favourites of his predecessors lived on here, lonely and forgotten, some well into the 20th century. If you wish to visit the harem – after the big jewels, it's the most popular attraction in the palace – make sure you stop beforehand at the booth by the harem gate to buy a ticket and check the times for English-language tours, usually every half hour. Just inside the gate are the apartments of the eunuchs, including the **Court of the Black Eunuch**, all rebuilt after a fire in the 1660s. From here the **Altın Yol**, the 'Golden Road', the corridor down which the harem women would walk to meet their rendezvous with destiny when a sultan called, leads to the rest of the harem, beginning with the **Courtyard of the Sultan Valide** (the Sultan's mother), adjacent to the eunuchs' quarter. Considering the bizarre

Birds in a Gilded Cage

Harems are good business, as the Turkish Culture Ministry well knows; not only do they make a fair amount of the money needed for the palace's upkeep from harem tours, but nearly every summer, as part of the Istanbul Festival, they put on a production of Mozart's *Entführung aus dem Serail* in the harem courtyard. Tickets sell out fast. *Harem* is really an Arabic word; the Turks called this place the *Darissade* (and, as you may have guessed, *seraglio* is a corruption of the Turkish *saray*, or palace). It isn't a barbarous oriental innovation; Turks and Arabs both learned the joys of confining women from the Greeks, who from their beginnings right up to the end of Byzantium were possibly the champion male chauvinists of all time.

Ottoman sultans led normal private lives up to the time of Yıldırım Beyazıt. When he and his family were captured by Tamerlane, the sultan's wife was forced to serve dinner naked to the conqueror and his generals. After this ultimate humiliation, no sultan ever legally married again – save only Süleyman the Magnificent, besotted with his Roxelana. The others had their collections of concubines, though they were only shut up in a harem after the conquest of Constantinople. When Roxelana brought the harem inside the palace, she intended only getting closer to Süleyman and increasing her influence over affairs of state, but over the next two centuries the harem became established, gradually building up its famous institutions and peculiarities. The cast of characters included the girls, or '**odalisques**', as many as 800 of them, who lived in drab dormitories. The '**Favourites**', including the '**First Four Women**' (the first to give birth to sons) merited luxurious apartments. To watch over the girls, and more often after themselves, there were the **Black Eunuchs**. These ugly creatures (the sultan's slavemaster picked out the ugliest, to avoid any chance of arousing the girls) were usually given names like 'Hyacinth' or 'Daisy'. With the silver tubes that assisted them in trips to the WC perched nattily in their tall turbans, the Black Eunuchs became, in the latter days, a power unto themselves. Their chief, the **Kızlar Ağası** or 'Lord of the Girls', was, after the Ağa of the Janissaries, the most useful ally any scheming lady could have. (The **White Eunuchs**, by contrast, looked after the Selamlık, the sultan's quarters, and the education of the pages brought in by the *devşirme*, or 'boy tribute'.) The only other men allowed in the harem were the '**Tressed Halberdiers**', whose job was to bring in the firewood. They had to wear their long hair in coils, hanging over their faces so they would be less likely to catch a glimpse of the women.

Sultans prefer blondes. Many of the women were slender, fair Circassians, Slavs, Armenians or Georgians. All of them, of course, were slaves, and despite the little courtesies of harem life it is not likely that many of them ever had any illusions about their true status. The vast majority of them led wretchedly dull lives here, chaste as any nuns, except for the few who managed to catch a sultan's fancy. Even these were left only with a thank-you, a small present and the fervent hope that they might conceive a male child. It is pretty certain they did not get up to many high jinks; the eunuchs installed old women to sleep next to their beds, to keep an eye on them at night, and, as an astonished Venetian ambassador once noted in his memoirs, care was taken even to ensure that all cucumbers were sliced.

issues of harem politics – the steering of the right girls into the sultan's bed, the manipulation and sometimes murder of prospective heirs – it becomes clear how only the greatest schemers of all could attain the glorious position of Sultan Valide. Their suite was usually the vortex of all palace intrigues. The next courtyard to the west housed the women servants, again mostly black, and beyond them lay the damp, chilly, unadorned quarters of the beauties themselves.

Perhaps the greatest attraction of the harem quarters, now that you're thoroughly disillusioned, will be the rooms of the northern half of the harem, the chambers where the sultans came for their pleasures. Several of these, the **Bedroom of Murat III** and the **Library of Ahmet I**, for example, are adorned with some of the most

Tulips, Tiles and Turtles

The Great Tulip Speculation of the 17th century is one of the oddities of European history. In Germany, France and Holland, these flowers briefly became an obsession, pursued with the kind of fervour we have until so recently devoted to gold bullion and commodity futures. The bulbs of some exotic varieties actually brought more than their weight in gold; great financial houses and canny opportunists rose and fell with the fortunes of their favourite blooms, and tulip quotes filled coffee-house conversation as stock market closings do today. The Turks can take all the credit. Tulips, like cherries, pizza, parchment and angora wool, are among Anatolia's contributions to civilization.

A century later, it was the Turks' turn to get silly over tulips. What Ottoman historians call the 'Tulip Period' is generally associated with the reign of Ahmet III (1703–20). Here, a genuine artistic revival was accompanied by some genuine decadence, as the sultans and their court reached their most Chinese extreme of contrived refinement while the empire careered into decay. With their wedding-cake turbans, layers of silk and brocades, and turned-up slippers, the bizarrely decorous Ottomans made a picture that fascinated contemporary Europe. Night garden parties among the tulips were the rage, illuminated by candles on the backs of wandering turtles. Tulip art – for the sultan interested himself in little else – can best be seen in the lovely tiled chambers of the Topkapı Harem. If you want to see what started all the hubbub, there are wild tulips in the national parks around Ankara and Yozgat.

beautiful painted tiles to be found anywhere in Turkey. The **Dining Room of Ahmet II**, the most famous room of the whole Topkapı Palace, is lined with wood panelling painted with colourful flowers and fruits, the apotheosis of the gentle art of the Tulip Period. The designs may have violated Muslim taboos against images, but then few imams or members of the Ulema, the Muslim hierarchy, were ever invited in to see them. From the Dining Room, the tour guides may take you to see the **swimming pool** put in by Murat III, and the **chambers of the Favourites**, on a pretty terrace.

Some of the rooms on the upper floors are thought to have been the location of the notorious **Kafes**, or Cage, the most thoroughly perverse of all the perverse customs of the Ottoman throne. Beyazıt II, a scholarly, peaceful sultan, was plagued by his younger brother Prince Cem, a romantic adventurer who caused plenty of trouble trying to seize the throne for himself. When Beyazıt caught him, he sent him off to exile in Italy, where it seems he was eventually poisoned by his keeper, the Borgia pope Alexander VI. After that, sultans began murdering their brothers as soon as they were able. Eventually, the Cage was decided upon as a more humane solution. Younger brothers were simply locked up, with a few harem girls for company and a few deaf mute slaves for servants. They stayed there the rest of their lives unless the death of their reigning brother should make them a sultan (if any of their concubines got pregnant, they would be bundled up in a silk bag with some stone weights and dropped into the sea). A few of these unfortunates actually did make it out of the Cage and onto the throne. All of them turned out to be both insane and dangerous; the most notable of these was İbrahim the Mad, who had spent 22 years in the Cage. In his short reign it is estimated that he ordered the deaths of over 4,000 of his friends, relatives and servants.

After the harem there are two more sections of the museum you may wish to visit before passing through to the third courtyard. The **Carriage Room**, once the sultan's stables, is full of the various conveyances of the 19th-century rulers, who were as fond of fancy phaetons and landaus as modern autocrats are of shiny new cars. The **Palace Kitchens** across the courtyard, partly designed by Sinan, were ready, at the sultan's command, to whip up almost anything, from a snack for one to a dinner party for five thousand. In the 17th century some 1,200 people worked here, and the archives record as many as 22,000 sheep being turned into kebabs every week. The kitchens contain some of the largest soup pots ever constructed on this planet, and a tedious infinity of silver and china from the 19th century. The sultans accumulated these as presents from foreign rulers, in greater numbers than even a dinner for five thousand could require. The collection of Chinese porcelain is world-famous and priceless; note especially the celadon ware, a favourite of potentates everywhere, since it was reputed to change colour in the presence of poison.

Third Courtyard

This is a wonderful **park** of plane trees and poplars. Visitors are often surprised to see how open and airy old Turkish palaces are. A love of nature, the necessity of having more than a bit of green around, was something the Ottomans never lost, even in their years of decay. They copied the form of the Saray – three successive courtyards of increasingly greater isolation – from the Byzantine imperial palace that once stood nearby (curiously, the Hittite palace at Boğazkale also had the same plan). However, where the Byzantines probably had small, paved squares in the classical mode, the Turks built gardens like this, squeezing their buildings into thin quadrangles between them and the forested slopes of the Topkapı hill, for a view of trees on both sides.

To match this setting, the Turks evolved an architectural style very different from the grey mathematics of their mosques, a unique 18th-century concoction of distinctive, very oriental shapes and forms, limited perhaps to the Topkapı and the now-vanished gardens and villas that once lined the Golden Horn and the Marmara shores. One of the finest examples is in this courtyard: the **Bab-üs-Saade** or Gate of Felicity, the entrance to the **Selamlık**, the sultan's quarters. Very few outsiders were ever allowed the privilege of using this gate. On ceremonial occasions, such as a new sultan's accession to the throne, the Bayram festival or the commissioning of a new general, the sultan would meet the assemblage seated directly under it, on the same portable bejewelled throne that went with him on campaigns. The Chief White Eunuch had his rooms here in the buildings around the gate, from which he and his fellow *castrati* oversaw the smooth operation of the Selamlık.

The **Audience Chamber**, a pretty parlour just inside the gate, served for the sultan's meetings with his grand vezir and foreign ambassadors. Its ambience is thoroughly Turkish; perhaps for the sultans it recalled the tents of their nomadic ancestors. The fountain in this chamber wasn't just for decoration; its running water made it difficult for anyone to overhear the sultan's conversations. The coloured tiles and lovely hearth were added to Mehmet Fatih's original building by Ahmet III, but the Baroque ceiling came much later. Ahmet also built the **Library** just behind it, a marvellous small pavilion with lots of glass and window seats, to be envied by all serious readers. Before a 17th-century fire that damaged much of the Selamlık, this space was occupied by the Great Hall, a building that housed the Enderun, the school for pages where the Christian children collected in the *devşirme* round-up were converted into the ministers and generals of the empire. Before the decline, it had a reputation as the finest school in Europe, counting all the great Turkish poets and scholars among its instructors. The Enderun was the special preserve of the Chief White Eunuch, and any of these fortunate enough to serve under a sultan who liked boys better than girls would find himself, and not the Chief Black Eunuch, top dog around the palace.

Most of the fabulous treasures of the sultans, the gold and jewels and the holy relics, are exhibited in the halls around the third courtyard. The spirit of the Topkapı was never to throw anything away, and one result is that extraordinarily well-preserved costumes of every sultan after Mehmet Fatih can be seen in the **Wardrobe**, from the gaily coloured flower-printed robes of Mehmet to the dreary European monkey-suit of Abdülhamid. Osman II, most tragic of the sultans, is represented by the blood-splattered caftan in which he was murdered. These costumes bring the sultans to life more than any other exhibit, and provide a few surprises along the way: the bright pink caftan covered in huge yellow polka dots is garish enough to put most jockeys to shame.

It may prove difficult to get excited over the riches of the **Treasury** next door, simply because it's hard to convince oneself that they're all real. The four rooms of bejewelled vessels and weapons, coffee sets and cabinets, as well as famous gems like the 86-carat Spoon Diamond, make up the richest hoard in the world, particularly if you include the additional warehouseful they haven't room to display. Other stars of the collection include the Emerald Dagger, made famous by the film *Topkapi*, and a golden casket supposedly containing the head of John the Baptist.

At the far end of the courtyard, the **collection of miniatures** displays examples of another very Turkish art form; it seems the first portraitists of Islam felt guilty about breaking the law, and so made their paintings very, very small. One two-volume set of these, the *Hünername* or *Book of Talents*, ranks among the greatest works of Turkish painting and calligraphy. The celebrated **clock collection** occupies the next room. Byzantine historians often wrote of their emperors' love of mechanical contraptions, like the famous golden tree full of singing birds, and like them, the Ottoman sultans were always pleased by gifts of clocks and music boxes.

When Selim I conquered Egypt, whose ruler at the time was the Caliph, the head of all Islam, that title fell to him and his successors. The later emperors' oriental inapproachability had not a little to do with the fact that now they were Commander of the Faithful and the Shadow of God on Earth. In token of this great office, the Sherif of Mecca sent Selim the keys to the Ka'aba, and here at Topkapı they remain in the **Hırka-i Saadet**, the hall of holy relics to which Muslims make pilgrimages, near the clock collection. Under a great silver dome added by Murat IV are Mohammed's sword, bow and standard, and the cloak he once bestowed on a poet who converted to Islam. Other relics include the Prophet's seal, a broken tooth, a cast of his footprint, hairs from his beard and a bullying letter he sent with an embassy to the Copts of Egypt. The sword of Osman, symbol of the Ottoman state, is also kept here.

Next to this chamber, a fourth and final gate leads to the **residence of the sultan**, a group of individual pavilions, or 'kiosks' (from the Turkish word for pavilion, *köşk*) around a courtyard, all with the best views of the Bosphorus and the Golden Horn. Two of these, the **Revan Köşkü** and the **Bağdad Köşkü**, must be accounted among the very greatest works of Turkish architecture for the simple magnificence of their form and decoration. Murat IV built them both, to commemorate his conquests of Erevan (now capital of Armenia) and Baghdad, and here he drank himself to death in the increasing revels of the last years of his reign. Among the marble terraces and roses of the Revan Köşkü is a marble fountain of three basins that approaches perfection more nearly than any other work of art in all the halls of the Saray.

To leave Topkapı, retrace your steps to the First Courtyard; from here instead of returning through the Bab-i Humayun, you can take the other route, around Aya İrene and down a shady cobbled lane towards the **Gülhane Park** and the imperial museums.

The Imperial Museums

Osman Hamdi Bey, by the standards of the late 19th century, was one very unusual Turk. A painter by trade, his knowledge of the ancient Greeks got him a job under Sultan Abdülhamid looking after the empire's antiquities. So well did he perform his duties, and with such panache, that he revolutionized the affairs of

⊕ Imperial Museums

all three museums open Tues–Sun 9–5.30; adm; a board at the entrance shows which of the nine departments are open on a particular day; due to staff shortages, up to a third of the exhibitions may be closed archaeology and museum-keeping, not only in Turkey but in the rest of Europe. Personally responsible for the first law anywhere governing the export of antiquities, he also made patriots of all the nations under Ottoman control work hard to keep their own archaeological discoveries from being shanghaied to the new Archaeology Museum that he had talked Abdülhamid into building. More often than not, they failed. Among the many excavations he oversaw was the one that uncovered the famous Alexander sarcophagus in Sidon. During the lengthy process of transporting this block of several tons to Istanbul, Hamdi Bey literally bound himself to it to impress upon the sailors that they had better take good care of it. On one later occasion, the sultan proposed presenting the sarcophagus to the visiting Kaiser Wilhelm II. Hamdi Bey had the effrontery to inform the sultan that this would only be accomplished by dragging it over his dead body, and the Kaiser went home empty-handed.

Archaeology Museum (Arkeoloji Müzesi)

The collection Hamdi Bey and his successors piled up in this tasteful, eclectic building – the very image of what his generation thought a museum should look like – is one of the greatest in Europe. Sarcophagi were his speciality, and there's not enough room for them all; many more line the square in front of the museum. The Alexander sarcophagus, not actually that of Alexander but decorated with scenes from his conquests, is perhaps more bombast than art, but it's considered one of the finest examples of late Roman sculpture. Two other sarcophagi, one Hamdi Bey called 'Des Pleureuses', and the other a barn-roofed Lycian model, are in the same room, along with a bust of Alexander.

The museum's other attractions include bronze pedestals that once supported statues in the Hippodrome, carved with scenes from the games; coats of arms of various states; Egyptian works; Greek and Roman bronzes; the famous statue of a young man called the Ephebos of Tralles; a mosaic of Orpheus and the wild animals; and a remarkable 12ft statue of the Phoenician god Bes – the Greeks know him as the 'Cypriot Hercules' – toying with a lion.

Museum of the Ancient Orient (Eski Şark Eserleri Müzesi)

Across from the Archaeology Museum, the government more recently created the Museum of the Ancient Orient, an equally impressive cache of pre-classical finds from Turkey and the Middle East. Some of its best works are from Babylon: the city's Ishtar Gate is largely reconstructed here with its glazed reliefs. In the Assyrian Room are reliefs from the palace of Assurbanipal; nearby, two 3,600-year-old copulating Kassites (from Northern Mesopotamia) may well be the world's oldest erotic art.

Also in the Assyrian room, the museum has assembled a collection of 'interesting documents' from ancient civilizations, with translations: love poems and tables of astronomical events in Assyrian cuneiform, laws and penalties for various crimes ('two-thirds of a mina of silver for cutting off someone's nose with a copper knife'), and the king of Lagash describing his struggles against his own government bureaucracy. The Treaty of Kadesh is here, an agreement of 1269 BC between the Pharaoh and the Hittite King Hattusilis which was found in the state archives at Boğazkale; it's the oldest treaty ever discovered.

Museum of Turkish Ceramics (Çinili Köşk)

The third building in the square is the Çinili Köşk, an exquisite small palace built by Mehmet Fatih in 1472 as part of the original Topkapı Sarayı. Its painted tiles show the lingering influence of the Selcuks in their design. Fittingly, the pavilion now houses a museum of Turkish ceramics from Selcuk times up to the present.

Sublime Porte and Gülhane Park

Head down from the Çinili Köşkü towards Gülhane Park for the north gate of the palace, the **'Sublime Porte'** that became the metaphor for the Ottoman government during the 19th century. Built into the walls here is the **Alay Köşkü**, the Saray's window on the outside world, where the sultan would review his troops and be seen by the people – on very rare occasions. **Gülhane Park**, a part of the Saray, was converted to a public garden in 1913. This lovely oasis, with a pond and woebegone zoo, stretches all the way to Sarayburnu, **Seraglio Point**. Here Istanbul keeps its **Atatürk Monument**, perhaps the only one in Turkey not on a main square. Across the road, just under the walls of the sultan's quarters of the Saray, you can see the stump of a granite column that is the oldest monument in the city: the **Goths' Column**, commemorating the victory of the Romans over the invading Goths in AD 269.

Sultanahmet District

In Istanbul, the Blue Mosque is more commonly referred to as the Sultanahmet Camii, after its builder, and in this form the mosque has given its name to the quarter west and south of it, one of the most interesting old residential neighbourhoods of the city. The lower parts of Sultanahmet are charmingly schizophrenic these days, with half the Ottoman houses restored as hotels in pretty pastel colours and the other half falling to pieces; poor children playing football share the narrow streets with bewildered-looking young tourists.

The plumbing was probably better when this part of the town was the **Palace of the Byzantine Emperors**. Since no excavations have ever been made, it's impossible to tell much about the layout. The palace began to decay already in the 12th century, when Alexius Comnenus abandoned it for Blachernae out by the city walls. From contemporary accounts we can expect there were plenty of golden domes and towers, and that its three divisions, the Chalce, the Daphne and the 'Sacred Palace', covered an area not much smaller than the Topkapı Sarayı.

Mosaic Museum
open Tues–Sun 9–5;
closed Mon; adm

The **Arasta Bazaar**, a restored shopping arcade opened in 1985, is southeast of the Blue Mosque. It was built by Sultan Ahmet to provide revenues for his mosque and lies on top of remains of the Byzantine palace (*see* 'Shopping', p.160). Among the shops can be found the **Mosaic Museum** (Büyüksaray Mozaikleri Müzesi), opened in 1987, housing 6th-century floor mosaics from the large peristyle court of the palace. These mosaics, including charming scenes of children and animals, are largely in situ. Otherwise, all that is left of the palace is a small court, believed to have been part of the stables, that housed another mosaic museum before its removal to the Aya İrene, and a section of the sea walls to the west where Justinian built his Bucoleon, the seaside pavilion. The area between the Blue Mosque and the Marmara, apparently, was devoted to the imperial polo grounds. Throughout the history of the empire, polo was the top snob sport, and most of the emperors, if not too debilitated by their lifestyles, indulged in it.

Küçük Aya Sofya

If you follow the twisting side streets south of the Hippodrome, where you can see the stone walls that supported the closed end of the stadium above the slope, with luck you will find the Küçük ('little') Aya Sofya, the name the Turks give to the 6th-century church of St Sergius and St Bacchus. Emperor Justinian's first major building project in his capital, modelled after the famous church of S. Vitale in Ravenna, begun the year before, can be seen as an experiment on the way to the big Aya Sofya, with its semi-domes, exedrae and two levels of arcades around the central space. This church, like S. Vitale, is square with an octagon of piers and columns inside it, supporting a dome just small enough to avoid the need for pendentives. The building has been used as a mosque for centuries, and a complete restoration was finished in 2007. The interior is a calm and delicate Ottoman Baroque, though you can still see the finely carved capitals, with the monograms of Justinian and Theodora. Some vine motifs can be seen in playful allusion to Bacchus, who with his comrade Sergius was the first Christian soldier in the Roman legions to suffer martyrdom. Sergius and Bacchus were the patrons of soldiers, and especially meaningful to Justinian, preoccupied in the early years of his reign with one war after another. As an adjunct of the imperial palace, Küçük Aya Sofya was given the role of occasional Catholic church, where embassies from the pope were allowed to say Mass according to their own usages. Pope Gregory the Great, before his election, was long the papal legate to Byzantium, and he must have prayed here often.

The Divan Yolu and Cağaloğlu

On your way back to the Divan Yolu, try to find Kadırga Sokak and the **Mehmet Paşa Camii**, built in 1571 for one of the Sokollu grand vezirs. This small mosque, along with its courtyard, porticoes and school complex, is one of the most beautiful of all the works of Sinan, though few people trouble to see it in its out-of-the-way location. The **Divan Yolu** was and is the main street of Istanbul. Though now it changes its name every few blocks – to Yeniçeriler Caddesi, and then to Vezneciler Caddesi after Beyazıt Square – in Byzantine days, the whole stretch as far as the Adrianople Gate was known as the Mese (the Middle), and lined with arcades. Today it carries old Stamboul's swanky new tram line, running out to the Topkapı Gate and Zeytinburnu.

Cağaloğlu, the area north of Divan Yolu, takes its name from the **Cağaloğlu Baths** on Kazim İsmail Gürkan Cad., built in the 18th century and still popular. This is one of the prettier parts of old Stamboul, where mostly 19th-century buildings are interspersed with fine mosques and institutions endowed by the sultans and their courtiers. It is also the home of most of the national newspapers and book publishers – in the years of political troubles its streets were often a battleground. The **Press Museum**, or Basın Müzesi, is on the Divan Yolu here.

Cağaloğlu Baths
open daily 8am–8pm

Çemberlitaş

Çemberlitaş, the 'bound monument' further up Divan Yolu, commemorates the very beginnings of the Byzantine Empire. The Column of Constantine, as it was called, was the first monument erected by that emperor on his refounding of the city; with the modesty for which his house was so renowned, Constantine had a golden statue of himself bolted on top. The Forum of Constantine, of which the small square you see today is the only remnant, was the business centre of the city, and the monument served as the site for many public festivals. A storm in the 11th century brought the old emperor down to earth, and the golden cross with which Manuel Comnenus replaced it did not survive long under the Turks. The sultans left the column standing, however, contributing the bronze bands that have held it together since a fire in the 18th century; it took its name from these. The fire gave rise to the scorched monument's other popular name, the Burnt Column.

Immediately before the Burnt Column, on the same side of the road, is the **Türbe of Sultan Mahmud II**, a dull and ugly building set behind high steel railings within an Ottoman cemetery. Beneath the outrageous glass chandelier rests Mahmud II, with his son, Sultan Abdülaziz, and his grandson, Sultan Abdülhamid, plus family members of each and their favoured ministers. Across the road is the **Köprülü Kütüphanesi** (library), built in 1661 by members of the distinguished Köprülü family of Albania, which contributed five grand vezirs in the 17th century. Next to the Burnt Column itself is the 17th-century **Çemberlitaş Hamamı**, commissioned by the wife of Selim II and still open for bathers.

Just past the Burnt Column, still on Divan Yolu, is the **Atik Ali Paşa Camii**, built for that gentleman in 1497 by Beyazıt II in honour of services rendered as grand vezir. It is a peaceful mosque, plain and simple, set in a lovely garden with lots of Christmas-tree firs. The larger mosque behind it, the **Nuruosmaniye Camii**, the 'light of Osman', is one of the more restrained examples of Turkish Baroque. The mosque's tout-patrolled courtyard leads directly to the main entrance to the Covered Bazaar. Near the Nuruosmaniye, the **Mehmet Paşa Camii** is the oldest in Istanbul, built just 10 years after the Ottoman conquest. Nuruosmaniye Caddesi, leading from here back towards Aya Sofya, has recently been given a complete facelift; lined with graceful plane trees, it is the fashionable shopping street of old Stamboul.

Back on the Divan Yolu, the **Külliye of Koca Sinan Paşa**, grand vezir under Murat III and Mahmud III, stands just beyond the Atik Ali Paşa Camii. The complex was erected by Davut Ağa, who had the unenviable task of succeeding Sinan as chief architect to the sultan. Nearby is the **Çorlulu Ali Paşa Medrese**, built in 1711. Across the road to the left, the **Merzifonlu Karamustafa Medrese** was built in 1690 in honour of the Grand Vezir Karamustafa by Mehmet IV. It has an octagonal plan, unusual in a mosque. Now it is a research institute named for the 20th-century Turkish writer Yaşar Kemal. Here the Divan Yolu becomes Yeniçeriler Caddesi, lined with buildings from the 1960s breeze-block-and-cement school.

Sirkeci and Eminönü

Crossing Nuruosmaniye Caddesi, one of the main thoroughfares of Cağaloğlu is **Babıâli Caddesi**; if you follow it north to where it becomes Ankara Caddesi, passing the most conspicuous of Istanbul's consulates – the Iranian – and the provincial government house, the **Vilâyet**, you'll end up in the **Sirkeci quarter**, a zone of hotels and small businesses around the ornate Victorian **Sirkeci**

Station (1885). Foreign companies built the first railway into Istanbul, and they and Sultan Abdülhamid were responsible for the greatest act of municipal vandalism in the city since the Sack of 1204: for the tracks, they destroyed the entire Marmara shore and many of the gardens and woods of the Topkapı hill.

Eminönü, the area just west of Sirkeci along the Golden Horn, was in the last century the business district of old Stamboul, as opposed to the European-dominated Beyoğlu across the Golden Horn. Its streets are still lively and if you must pass through to visit the monumental **Main Post Office**, take time to admire this and the many other outlandish works of *c*. 1910 eclectic architecture. Two of the best Art Nouveau works, grimy fantasies with cast-iron flowers on their balconies and pseudo-Ottoman painted tiles, are the small business block on the square opposite the post office and the **Büyük Vakıf Han**, an enormous landmark just two blocks away, in the direction of Eminönü Square, old Stamboul's window on the Golden Horn. From the square, the famous Galata Bridge crosses over to Beyoğlu, carrying the life of the city back and forth.

Galata Bridge

Just after the Conquest, Mehmet's army engineers built the first bridge here, of boats lashed together and covered with planks. One of the succeeding sultans, the Turks say, invited Leonardo da Vinci to design a permanent structure, but he declined, and none was constructed until 1845. The present, like its companion the Atatürk Bridge further up the Golden Horn, is a floating metal drawbridge. Caissons could only have been planted into the mud bottom with great difficulty, and so this unusual method was adopted. German engineers built it in 1912 but the Turks had to reconstruct it almost from scratch after a fire in 1992. Both bridges are opened only in the early morning hours, when long lines of ships pass in and out. In the days of the sultans, they were also opened at the least sign of trouble in the city, in order to prevent riots from spreading. The 1992 fire began in one of the little fish restaurants housed on the bridge's lower level. For the rebuilding, there was much talk of making a proper modern bridge, instead of the incredible floating café and jumble sale the old one always was. In the end, custom and sentiment won out – the new bridge looks exactly like the old one, with plenty of room on the pavements for the fishermen that line its edges angling for whatever the Bosphorus brings their way, the hawkers to sell their wind-up turtles and polyester negligées, and of course spaces underneath for the restaurants.

The docks on either side, from which you can catch ferry boats to Asia, the Bosphorus or the Princes' Islands, once were the busiest part of the commercial waterfront. Old travellers always remarked how close the city's life was to the life of the sea; any trip through town was likely to involve elbowing your way past deck hands and stevedores, and staring into the cannons of the ships-of-the-line. Today, besides the creaky ferries, the maritime experience is limited to the informal fish market on the Beyoğlu side, and the cafés on the lower deck of the bridge, where you can sit and sample the notorious aromas of the Golden Horn. All this lies in the shadow of one of the great imperial mosques, the Yeni Cami.

Yeni Cami and Spice Market (Mısır Çarşısı)

Spice Market
open Mon–Sat

The **Yeni Cami** mosque, a landmark more for its location than for any special virtue of its architecture, was begun by a Sultan Valide (mother) named Safiye, a wife of Murat III, in 1597. Three different architects had a hand in the work, only finished in 1663. Of the original *külliye* of foundations, only two fountains and the Sultan Valide's *türbe* remain, along with the **Spice Market**, whose rents still go to the upkeep of the mosque. Most of the locals call this market the Mısır Çarşısı, the 'Egyptian market', since most of the herbs and concoctions traditionally sold here came from the banks of the Nile. Today, in the long, L-shaped hall, a smaller version of the Covered Bazaar, you may purchase anything from jewellery to electric tin-openers to caviar, but at a few of the old stands it's still fun to guess just what the hundreds of items displayed in barrels, bags and jars could possibly be. 'Spices' to the Turks, as to the rest of Europe, once meant not simply herbs for cooking, but drugs, dyes, preservatives, cosmetics and any other useful substance that grows. One of the biggest sellers today is *kına*, or henna dye. But this is also the place to head for herbal teas, nuts, honey, cheeses, sweets, Turkish delights, pastramis, essential oils, lotions, eccentric perfumes, all kinds of potions and aphrodisiacs claiming wonders for your love life, and last but not least, the dried figs stuffed with nuts advertised as Turkish Viagra!

Eminönü Market, a green and crowded yard between the Spice Market and the Yeni Cami where caged birds, seeds, bulbs and garden tools are sold, was also the traditional home of the city's scribes, the placid gentlemen with typewriters on little stands, who composed letters for the unlettered and filled in government forms for the bewildered. Perhaps it is a sign of progress – on our most recent visit we didn't see a single one.

Rüstem Paşa Camii

As seen from the bridge or from Beyoğlu, the Yeni Cami stands in the shadow of the great Süleymaniye, on the heights to the southwest. Between the two, the little mosque called Rüstem Paşa Camii is hardly even noticed. A closer look will reveal one of Sinan's most elegant works, built in 1550 for Süleyman's grand vezir. The real surprise, though, is within; the mosque is almost entirely covered with the very best İznik tiles, in a spectacular variety of colours and patterns. For all these Ottoman creations, it will never do to ask where the funds came from. Rüstem Paşa was a son-in-law of Süleyman the Magnificent and Roxelana, and the sultan's favourite, in her endless intrigues, determined to make him grand vezir. To accomplish it, all she had to do was to persuade Süleyman to have his old friend the Vezir İbrahim murdered. She had little trouble; İbrahim was soon strangled by the palace mutes, and Rüstem distinguished himself by starting the practice of putting government offices up for sale, an Ottoman tradition ever after.

The Covered Bazaar (Kapalı Çarşı)

Covered Bazaar
open Mon–Sat
8.30–6.30

It seems likely that Constantinople had some kind of market on this spot; over one of the arches of this vast, rambling structure, a Byzantine eagle can be made out clearly. Long before the days of shopping malls, covered markets like this were an Eastern tradition, not only for convenience but to discourage burglars. No one disputes Istanbul's claim that theirs is the largest in the world.

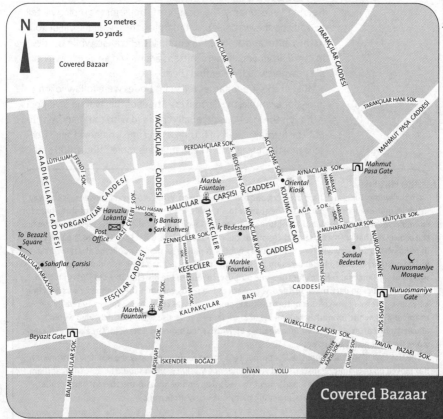

Covered Bazaar

07 Istanbul | Old Istanbul (Stamboul): The Covered Bazaar

Since Mehmet Fatih built the two *bedestenler*, or stronghouses, in the 1460s, street after street of shops, covered with simple barrel vaults and skylights, have grown up around them, always well maintained and promptly rebuilt after such disasters as the earthquake of 1896 or the fire of 1954. Today, the Kapalı Çarşı, as it is called, is a city unto itself, with over four thousand shops, a mosque, a school, even its own post office and police station.

It isn't just for tourists – far from it. Though you'll see plenty of trinkets and little signs proclaiming the owner's proficiency in English or German, the Covered Bazaar has its more prosaic side, as the purveyor of all manner of goods to the Stamboullu, from diamonds to dustpans; note that Mehmet built it before embarking on either his mosque or his Topkapı Palace – the market was the key to bringing the half-abandoned city back to life. Even today, despite the advent of industrialism and high finance in Turkey, what goes on here, and in the seemingly endless maze of wholesalers, warehouses and workshops to the north of it, still carries some weight in the nation's economy.

This mighty citadel of the independent businessman also stands ready to give any perceptive visitor some advanced lessons in a free-market economy. The location of shops, for example, will tell you all about everyone's profit margins; the jewellers will be found in the centre and around the entrances, of course, while the dealers in raw leather or children's mittens are tucked away in low-rent alleys where you'll never find them.

Most of the street names tell what trades were followed long ago – for example, the Fezmakers' Street or the Avenue of Slippers – though the locations gradually changed with the years. Atatürk put the fezmakers out of business long ago, and now their street sells mostly blue jeans. Other names are more colourful, like the

If the Hat Fits...

On the whole, Turks are sharp dressers, and always have been. What is unusual, however, is the way in which matters of dress manage so frequently to insinuate themselves into matters of state: hats, for example. Most of us have heard of Atatürk's famous Hat Law of 1925, outlawing the wearing of the fez, the conical felt hat with a tassel that Egyptians call a *tarboosh*. Here, what the Father of the Turks had in mind was to do away with one conspicuous symbol of pious reaction; in public, he always wore a fedora or smart cloth cap to set an example. Ironically, the fez itself had been introduced during the 19th-century Tanzimat reforms for the same purpose: to replace the disreputable old Turkish turban.

Hats in politics go back much further. As far back as the 1460s, Mehmet the Conqueror was enacting a hat law, governing the colours of turbans that could be worn at court: green for vezirs, red for chamberlains, white for muftis, red, yellow or black for everyone else except infidels, who weren't allowed a turban at all. Mehmet followed this up with a shoe ordinance: black for Greeks, blue for Jews, violet for Armenians, and so on.

The Hat Law of 1925 accomplished its purpose in a roundabout way. Today the hot new controversy has moved on to Islamic headscarfs and whether or not Muslim women should be able to wear them in universities. In February 2008, parliament passed an amendment to lift the 20-year ban despite serious protests by the secularists, including many university professors.

Louse Bazaar. You may wander its broad avenues and dim cul-de-sacs, recently renovated and cleared of their ugly thicket of electric signs, and look for bargains to your heart's content. Don't miss the **İç Bedesten** at the centre, devoted to copper and rare antiques; they glitter in Mehmet's dim hall like the treasure in the Cave of the Forty Thieves.

Stamboul's market district really stretches as far as the Golden Horn, and the Kapalı Çarşı is only its glamorous retail end. Many of the surrounding streets, like those inside, have a particular function. One of the most interesting is the **Sahaflar Çarşısı**, the old Booksellers' Market, just outside the Beyazıt Square entrance to the Covered Bazaar. This lovely courtyard full of tiny shops, with its fountain and large population of cats, is believed to have been around in one form or another since Byzantine times – it's the best place in Istanbul for books and souvenirs. North of the Covered Market, around **Uzunçarşı Caddesi**, are a number of old *hanlar*, no longer performing their old functions as merchant hotels, but still buzzing with porters and handcarts, the whirr of old machinery, and decorous transactions made over tea.

Beyazıt Square and Beyazıt Camii

An old story relates that when Beyazıt II was building the mosque that bears his name (the oldest of the Ottoman imperial mosques still standing), a pious old woman offered a pair of pigeons – Turks are fond of pigeons – for the courtyard and gardens. Their descendants rule **Beyazıt Square** today, and you'll earn yourself some credit in Allah's bank of grace for spending a few liras on them; someone will always be there to sell you a plate of seeds. The square, entirely redone several years ago, has become an outstanding piece of modern urban design with few admirers apart from the pigeons, who seem happier than ever even if there are fewer trees. This is what the critics would call an architectural square, a vast expanse of grey granite blocks on different levels; it is a veritable symphony in grey, between the pavement, the pigeons and the subtle variety of grey tones in the **Beyazıt Camii**, the grand and beautiful mosque that the square was designed to show off.

Whether or not this was the mosque that set the pattern for later imperial foundations we have no way to tell. The mosque of Beyazıt's father Mehmet, the original Fatih Camii, was destroyed in an earthquake. Its architect was a Greek named Christodoulos; the Beyazıt Camii, completed in 1504, is the work of his sons. They built their mosque after the plan of the Aya Sofya, only without the upper gallery, and endowed it with a fine courtyard and fountain.

Museum of Calligraphy
open Tues–Sat 9–4.30; adm

Also on the square is what is claimed to be the world's only **Museum of Calligraphy**, the Beyazıt Hat Sanatları Müzesi, concentrating on the art of the Ottoman era.

Istanbul University

Across the square, the monumental gateway in some sort of
Persian rococo is the entrance to Istanbul University. The date over
the arch, the Roman numerals for 1453, is a sorry deception. That
was the year of the Conquest, but the university was not founded
until 1845, as part of the reforms of Abdülmecit. Since Atatürk, the
university has expanded greatly, taking over the buildings of the
old Seraskeriat, the War Ministry, in the large park behind the gate.
If you want to meet the students, the wonderful, tree-shaded
open-air café behind the Beyazıt Camii, at the entrance to the
Sahaflar Çarşışı, is full of them.

Mehmet II built the 200ft **Beyazıt Tower** on the campus in 1823 as
a watchtower for fires (or insurrections); it is the tallest structure in
old Stamboul. Along Yeniçeriler Caddesi, on the south side of the
square, the recently excavated ruins lying about belong to the
Forum of Theodosius – Beyazıt Square's ancestor on this site.

Süleymaniye Camii

⭐ Süleymaniye
Camii

Mimar Sinan, in the last years of his life, is supposed to have said
that the Selimiye in Edirne was his favourite among all his scores of
mosques; the great architect chose to live, however, near his
Süleymaniye (1557), and nearby also is his tomb. If you have the
chance to visit only one of the imperial mosques, your time would
be best spent here. No features of the construction are unique or
original; the same elements of the classic design will be found in
the same places. The building's only excuse for existing is
perfection. The outstanding features are subtle: the excellent stone
porticoes on either side, the courtyard and the smooth plain
hierarchy of domes, to which we could add the surviving stained
glass, the work of a legendary artist called İbrahim the Drunkard.

No mosque in Istanbul, and certainly not the Aya Sofya, has such
a feeling of openness within. For a moment, it's easy to forget the
reality of columns, arches and vaults and imagine the Süleymaniye
as a great stone tent, hung on the four square solid piers at the
corners of the dome. Just as Süleyman's reign marked the high
noon of the Ottoman state, so does this mosque that Sinan built
for him declare the zenith of his nation's art. Time would show that
neither had much more to give.

Almost alone among the imperial mosques, the Süleymaniye
retains almost all of its *külliye* (complex of religious and educational institutions). This is the grandest *külliye* ever built by the
Ottomans, an integral part of Sinan's composition, and no one has
dared to tamper with it. The eight low buildings, with over 200
domes between them, have all recently been restored, and several
are creatively reused, one as a library and another as a clinic, to

The Master Builder

Not all Christian boys pressed into the Janissary corps ended up as soldiers. One young Greek, born about 1489, worked his way up through the military engineering branch to become the head architect of the Ottoman state. At the age of 59, Sinan built his first mosque, the Şehzade in Istanbul, for Sultan Süleyman the Magnificent. It was the beginning of a brilliant collaboration that created scores of mosques, schools, bridges and fortifications – the launching of the Ottoman imperial style, as well as its greatest achievements. For the Turks, his profession became a title; they call him Mimar Sinan: Sinan the Architect.

It would have been impossible for one man to have accomplished the tremendous output with which Sinan is credited – several hundred buildings in all. Like the Renaissance artists who attached their names to everything that came out of the workshop, even if all the details had been handled by students, Sinan must really be thought of as head of a huge public works collective. All these works (most are in Istanbul) are distinctive and gracefully proportioned, but those that most clearly bear the stamp of the master are the Selimiye in Edirne, the little Sokollu Mehmet Paşa Mosque and the Süleymaniye.

benefit the people of the neighbourhood, just as their builders intended. In the courtyard of the mosque, you can see the separate *türbeler* of Süleyman and Roxelana, both done in fine İznik tiles. A smaller tomb, at the narrow angle of a street in the northernmost corner of the complex, is that of Sinan himself.

Just west of the Süleymaniye, in a small courtyard off Kirazlı Mescit Sokak, stands the small **Vefa Kilise Camii**, formerly the church of St Theodoros; although much was rebuilt in the 12th century, the foundation and much of the structure are from the 5th, making this the oldest religious structure in Istanbul.

Around Atatürk Bulvarı: Şehzade and the Aqueduct

Returning to Beyazıt Square, and continuing west along Vezneciler Caddesi, still following the route of the old Mese, we pass reminders of the Ottoman or Byzantine eras on almost every block. The **Kalenderhane Camii**, at the corner of the Büyük Reşit Paşa Caddesi, where six streets meet, was originally the church of the Akataleptos Monastery; 13th-century frescoes and a mosaic were recently discovered inside, but they have now been removed to the Archaeological Museum. The *kalenders* were members of a dervish order, and it appears that the function of this and many other monasteries changed little after the Conquest.

Şehzade Camii

Many consider the Şehzade Camii (1548), two blocks further east, to be one of the finest of the Ottoman mosques, but its lofty dome conceals a great crime – also, perhaps, the secret of the decline of the Ottoman Empire. Süleyman the Magnificent had a son named

Mustafa by one of his concubines, an intelligent and virtuous young man who gave every promise of being an excellent soldier and ruler. All that stood between him and a brilliant reign was the unfortunate matter of his mother's name not being Roxelana. The sultan's favourite had sons of her own, younger than Mustafa, and she was determined to do anything to see them on the throne. She had already driven Süleyman to murder once, in the case of the Grand Vezir İbrahim, and now, on the evidence of forged letters that suggested that Mustafa was planning to stage a revolt, she persuaded the sultan to do him in.

Mustafa, called back from the province he was governing, went unsuspectingly to his doom; it is said Süleyman watched from behind a curtain while the mutes and the bowstring went to work – spilling royal blood was an unthinkable crime, and garrotting with a bowstring was the custom for such necessities. Roxelana, ironically, never lived to enjoy the power of a Sultan Valide, but her son Selim II, called the Sot, was to reign for eight years as the first dissolute Ottoman before succumbing to cirrhosis. It is said Süleyman built the Şehzade Camii, the 'Prince's Mosque', out of remorse. Sinan used the opportunity to experiment, bestowing upon his mosque one of the most unusual exteriors to be seen in Istanbul, with Persian and Moorish-inspired detail on the minarets, domes and windows. Later Turkish architects were to draw on these, but Sinan himself returned to his accustomed austerity just in time to design the Süleymaniye.

Just behind the Şehzade, a small mosque called the **Burmalı Minare** was built by an Egyptian paşa two years after its larger neighbour. The name refers to the 'spiral' minaret, unique in the city. All this area around the intersection of the Mese – called Şehzadebaşı along this stretch – and Atatürk Bulvarı was developed into a park as part of Istanbul's first planning scheme in the 1940s.

Across the street, the steel and glass **City Hall** was its centrepiece, and broad **Atatürk Bulvarı**, designed for cars, its major improvement. Amazingly, in 1,600 years this was the first ever street laid out to form a direct connection between the Marmara and the Golden Horn. The park was opened up partly to expose the **Aqueduct of Valens**, supported by an arcade over half a mile in length between the Third and Fourth Hills, and nearly 60ft tall where it passes over Atatürk Bulvarı. The 4th-century Emperor Valens really only expanded and repaired an older aqueduct, but the popular name credits it to him even though most of what you see was constructed by, of course, Mimar Sinan. The aqueduct was in use well into the 20th century; today you can follow its crumbled end into a street of car mechanics in the Fatih district.

Church of the Pantocrator

A walk a few blocks north along Atatürk Bulvarı will take you past the **Zeyrek Kilise Camii**, once the **church/monastery of the Pantocrator**, built in 1124, its history intertwined with that of the empire in its last centuries. John Comnenus, 'Good John', who presided over the last spell of peace and prosperity for Byzantium, built it, and was buried here along with his Hungarian wife Irene, a great patroness of the arts. During the occupation of the Crusaders it became a Catholic church, the seat of the Venetian Bishop Morosini; ironically, later it was to be the church of Gennadius, the prelate who worked so fervently in the 1440s to avert the proposed union of the churches, Constantinople's last hope for aid from the West against the Ottomans. Mehmet rewarded Gennadius after the Conquest by making him the first patriarch under the new dispensation. The monastery of which this church was a part has completely disappeared; the retaining walls of the huge cistern that served it and the neighbourhood are all that is left. In the southernmost of the three adjoining churches, if you ask very nicely they might turn over some of the carpet to show you the fine stone intarsia floor of human and animal figures that is underneath.

After passing Atatürk Bulvarı, the old Mese changes its name one last time, to Fevzi Paşa Caddesi. The *külliye* here, a fine example of Turkish architecture, is the 1698 **Amcazade Külliye**, built by one of the grand vezirs of the Köprülü family. Two blocks south of Fevzi Paşa, the most complete surviving Roman monument in Istanbul stands on a quiet street of apartment blocks: the **Column of Marcian**, built *c.* AD 450. The tall granite shaft, surmounted by a Corinthian column and a much-effaced winged symbol, once bore a colossal statue of this vain emperor. If you want to see it, you'll have to go to Barletta in southern Italy, where it washed ashore from a shipwreck after the Venetians stole it in 1204.

Lâleli District and Aksaray

East of Marcian's column, the quarter around Atatürk Bulvarı south of the Mese is called **Lâleli**, named after the **Lâleli** (tulip) **Cami**, on busy Ordu Caddesi, a famous work of the Turkish Baroque built under Mustafa III in 1760. The high stone platform on which the mosque stands now contains a little bazaar of shops added in the 1950s. Long ago, before the mosque was even built, this substructure was the central hashish and opium den, a distinction it seems also to have had under the Byzantines. Murat IV, a tremendous drunkard, closed it down for the good of the nation.

Across Ordu Caddesi, **Aksaray** is a bustling, thoroughly modern district packed with hotels and foreigners. A decade ago there was a large Arab and Persian influence; now in a transition that native Stamboullu find amazing and amusing, the quarter has become home to thousands of Russians, Poles and other East Europeans. Many of them are in the textile and fashion trades, and their boutiques can be seen along every street. Aksaray and Lâleli have become the most frenetic corner of the city, a raucous street scene, day and night, that includes wall-to-wall street vendors, *hamallar* (porters) struggling under enormous burdens, Slavic prostitutes (Turks call them 'natashas') and suspicious-looking folk from all over the world. It explodes into total confusion several times a day when lorries packed with cloth pull in from the docks, or from Adana, centre of the cotton country of the southeast. Brokers and shopkeepers descend on them like locusts, and impromptu auctions start in the middle of the street. Here too, tucked away on Mesihpaşa Caddesi, is the heavily restored but nonetheless charming **Bodrum Camii**, originally the church of the **Mirelaion Convent**, built in the 10th century over a huge circular cistern.

The Lâleli Cami may be the place where Turkish Baroque went over the edge, but the indescribable **Valide Camii**, on Aksaray Square, must be the supreme example of Ottoman preciosity; the Turks were as eclectic as anyone in 1870, and the idea here was to invent Turkish neo-Gothic.

Fatih District

North of Lâleli, Fatih, the enormous quarter named after Mehmet the Conqueror and the great complex of religious buildings he erected at its centre, is home to over 100,000 of Stamboul's working people; plain and honest, it has survived both urban decay and creeping modernity. At present, it has a reputation as the stronghold of the fundamentalists in the city. When Mehmet built his **Fatih Camii** here in 1463, this Fourth Hill was one of the choicer districts of the city. Here stood the church of the Holy Apostles, the church second in size and importance only to Aya Sofya. Mehmet demolished it, one of the few instances of wanton destruction of Christian buildings. Eighteen of its columns can be seen in the mosque's courtyard. It should not be too hard to imagine how the Holy Apostles looked; St Mark's in Venice was modelled on it. The church is also said to have had a unique conical dome; underneath it for a time lay the remains of the city's founder and 'thirteenth apostle', Constantine.

Mehmet's mosque, which we know had two equal domes in the fashion of the earlier Ottoman mosques of Bursa, was shaken down by an earthquake in 1766. The reigning Sultan Mustafa III had it rebuilt even bigger in the classical style, but the result is just another uninspired copy from the same mould. The *külliye*, an enormous complex elevated on a platform that turns a vast blank face towards Fevzi Paşa Caddesi, is even larger than that of the Süleymaniye; its institutions and foundations still provide important services for the people of the Fatih.

Another small, inconspicuous Byzantine building can be seen a few blocks to the north on Küçük Mektep Sokak, the 11th-century **church of Christ Pantepoptes** built by Alexis I Comnenus. Now it's the **Eski İmaret Camii**, though much of its attractive exterior survives, decorated with patterns of tiles and bricks.

Outlying Areas to the West

The Exokionion

On the map (*see* pp.136–7), you can follow a line of avenues – Haliç Caddesi, Akdeniz Caddesi and Kızıl Elma Caddesi among others – starting at the Golden Horn and winding an irregular course behind the Fatih complex and across the peninsula. These generally follow the line of the original long-vanished walls of Constantinople, paced off by Constantine himself after a vision showed him how best to defend the city. Even after the Theodosian walls were built further west, this area beyond the older line had the legal status of an extramural district, and during the various conflicts over Church dogma heretics were allowed to hold religious services here. The Greeks called this wide swath of land between Constantine's and Theodosius's walls the **Exokionion**. Today it is home to hundreds of thousands of Stamboul's poorer residents, in a disorganized conglomeration of villages and market gardens with some dense concentrations of flats, all up and down the Fifth, Sixth and Seventh Hills.

With the help of the dolmuş and minibus, those with a real interest in tracking down the wealth of Ottoman and Byzantine monuments here can start their expeditions. Doing it properly will require some walking, and some climbing – around the Fifth Hill in particular, the only one of the seven that truly deserves the name. Your troubles will be rewarded by an endless supply of curiosities past and present, as well as insights into the working life of the more prosaic corners of the fantastical city.

The neighbourhood directly north of the Fatih, along Darüşşafaka Caddesi, gets the travelling market on Wednesday (**Çarşamba** in Turkish), which has given the quarter its name. From here Yavuz

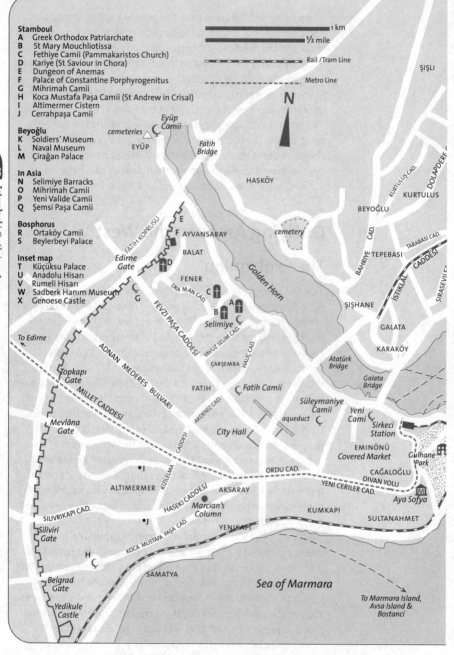

Stamboul
A Greek Orthodox Patriarchate
B St Mary Mouchliotissa
C Fethiye Camii (Pammakaristos Church)
D Kariye (St Saviour in Chora)
E Dungeon of Anemas
F Palace of Constantine Porphyrogenitus
G Mihrimah Camii
H Koca Mustafa Paşa Camii (St Andrew in Crisal)
I Altimermer Cistern
J Cerrahpaşa Camii

Beyoğlu
K Soldiers' Museum
L Naval Museum
M Çirağan Palace

In Asia
N Selimiye Barracks
O Mihrimah Camii
P Yeni Valide Camii
Q Şemsi Paşa Camii

Bosphorus
R Ortaköy Camii
S Beylerbeyi Palace

Inset map
T Küçüksu Palace
U Anadolu Hisarı
V Rumeli Hisarı
W Sadberk Hanım Museum
X Genoese Castle

1 km
½ mile
Rail /Tram Line
Metro Line

Selim Caddesi ascends the Fifth Hill to the **Sultan Selim Camii** or **Selimiye**, begun by the conqueror of Egypt but not completed until 1522, in the reign of his son Süleyman. Selim built his *türbe* in the garden behind this austere and beautiful mosque. From here, you

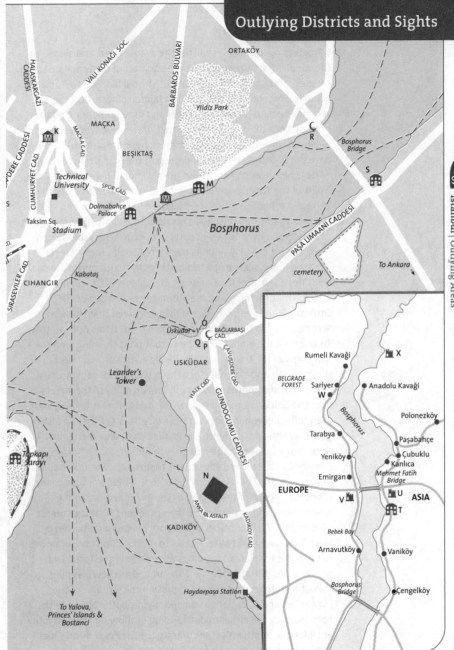

can look out over the rooftops of one of Stamboul's oddest neighbourhoods, a pretty sunken village built around crags of antique masonry at the bottom of the **Cistern of Aspar**, a 5th-century addition to Constantinople's water supply.

Fener Quarter

Progressing any further will require a stout heart and shoes, for the streets that introduce you to the quarter of the Fener are the steepest and roughest in all Istanbul. The old ladies storm up and down like mountain goats, and the children play vertical tag, but you may be hard pressed. The Fener and its neighbouring quarter of Balat, once the city's Jewish district, are a world where streets meander aimlessly, maps lie and street signs are rare, but if you have the time, the patience and the puff they can be fascinating.

The Fener takes its name from the old **Phanar** (lighthouse) **Gate**, a part of the Theodosian walls along the Golden Horn. After the Conquest it became the district allotted to the Greeks, and some live here to this day. Since 1955, however, most have either returned to Greece or moved to newer parts of the city across the Golden Horn. The Fener today, with its melancholy, half-empty streets wrapped in the silence of a tomb, stands in sharp contrast to past centuries. Even after the Conquest, the talents of the Greeks in the arts and in commerce, and the natural disinclination of the Ottoman élite to earn an honest living, ensured that the more accomplished of the infidels would find many doors open to them. Throughout the empire, the Greeks controlled shipping, finance and many of the trades, and provided the sultans with most of their officials and tax collectors. The capital of this conspicuous and favoured community was here, and on many of the streets near the Golden Horn you will see the ruins of great houses, and even some fashionable late 19th-century blocks of flats, to testify to the wealth and influence the Phanar – as it was then called – once enjoyed. The stranglehold they maintained over the empire's economy, and thus over the sultans themselves, was notorious; the monopolies they held in many fields contributed as much to the economic decline of the empire as the incompetence of the government, and so great were their exactions from the subject peoples that 'Phanariot' became a term of opprobrium used by Slavs, Turks and Arabs alike. Thanks to various European initiatives many of these splendid buildings are now being restored and property prices in this poor neighbourhood are now creeping up.

Most historians have chosen to present the struggle of the Byzantines and Ottomans as an apocalyptic battle of two faiths, both incapable of either understanding or showing any sympathy at all for one another. On the contrary, the Greeks and Turks had known each other for so long before 1453 – four centuries of alliances, intermarriages and scholarly discussion – that, when the end came for Byzantium, the transition was accomplished with a minimum of hysteria. After the pillage Mehmet had promised his troops, life for the Greeks gradually returned to normal, and even improved, as the sultan's efforts to re-establish trade began to pay off. In the Phanar, the heirs of the imperial Byzantine families, the Paleologues, the Comneni and the rest, were reported still to be around as late as the 1900s.

One of the first acts of Mehmet after the Conquest was to co-opt the Greek church by naming Gennadius patriarch, as much a servant of the sultan as was the Sheikh ul-İslam, and meant to act as an intermediary between the Greeks and the Ottoman state. Gennadius's successors live on in the **Greek Orthodox Patriarchate [A]** on a steep hill just above the Golden Horn. Old St George's Church, where the patriarchs sat on the throne of St John Chrysostom, burned down in 1941, and the centre of the complex is now a huge tower – built in the 1880s, in Victorian Gothic, incredibly enough. The main gate of the Patriarchate has not been opened since Easter Sunday 1821. On that day the Patriarch Gregory, implicated in the Hetairist conspiracy of the Phanariot Greeks working for their nation's independence, was hanged from it. All those with business here enter from the side. The Patriarchate today has a lonely and forlorn air. The Greek school, supported by the republic as it was by the sultans, appears almost empty. Few Greeks, for that matter, seem to be left in the neighbourhood, if the faces of the inhabitants and signs in the shops are any indication. The tiny, unpretentious chapel a block away has great meaning for the remaining Greeks: **St Mary Mouchliotissa [B]**, from the 13th century, is the only surviving pre-Conquest church never to have been converted to a mosque. Its benefactress, 'Saint Mary of the Mongols', was a Byzantine princess married off for political reasons to a Khan of the İlhanlı Mongols in 1282. After his death she returned to the city and built this church as part of the great monastic complex in which, long before, the Empress Theodora had spent her last days.

Just a few blocks away, overlooking the Golden Horn, have a look at the strangest church in Istanbul, **St Stephen of the Bulgars**. When Bulgaria gained its independence from the Ottoman Empire in 1871, the Turks weren't sore losers. They allowed the Bulgarians of Istanbul to build this church in celebration of the event. A church that defies all attempts at architectural classification, St Stephen's is made entirely of cast iron. A foundry in Vienna cast it, then shipped it down the Danube and Black Sea on barges to Istanbul, where the pieces were assembled.

With luck, you'll be able to pick your way through the tortuous lanes towards the walls to see two other important Byzantine monuments. The 11th-century **Pammakaristos Church [C]**, quite near the Patriarchate, has one of the most unusual and most elaborate exteriors of any church in the city, in patterns reminiscent of those on the apse of the famous Greek-Norman cathedral of Monreale in Sicily, built at the same time. One distinctive feature is the delicately carved window mullions, unique to this church. Inside, a fine 13th-century mosaic scene of the baptism of Christ has recently been restored, along with a large number of excellent mosaic figures of saints. The Pammakaristos ('most blessed') was the seat of the Patriarchate from 1456 to 1586. If you ask for directions, try using its old name of Fethiye Camii, even though it's been a museum for some years.

Church of St Saviour in Chora (Kariye)

Church of St Saviour in Chora (Kariye)
open Tues–Sun 9–4.30; closed Mon; adm

From here, Fethiye Caddesi, changing its name to Draman Caddesi, will bring you to the church of St Saviour in Chora **[D]**, or Kariye. This is nothing less than the finest collection of Byzantine mosaics and mural painting in Turkey. You'll find the trip worth the trouble, especially since Çelik Gülersoy and his Automobile Club have transformed the surroundings – in the middle of a very shabby neighbourhood – into a small oasis with a garden café and a number of restored Ottoman houses. The art inside, like that of the Aya Sofya, was restored by the Byzantine Institute.

Originally built by Justinian, and completely rebuilt by the Comneni in the 11th century, it is always associated with the name of Theodore the Logothete, a high official in the late 14th century who fell victim to political intrigue and ended his days as a poor monk in the church he had restored and beautified. In the latter days of the empire, when the Aya Sofya was falling into decay and the emperors had moved to the Blachernae Palace nearby, the Chora became the city's fashionable church, where the imperial family usually attended services. An icon of the Virgin kept here, one of those supposedly painted by St Luke, was credited with saving Constantinople from the siege of Murat II in 1428; the Turk's final attack failed shortly after the icon was carried solemnly around the walls.

Architecturally, little in the Chora is outstanding; the major attraction is its wealth of frescoes. Byzantine painting has always been undervalued by the critics, their eyes dazzled by the gold of the less expressive, less articulate mosaics. The restoration of the frescoes in the Paraecclesion, or mortuary chapel, of the Chora, as well as those in other late Byzantine churches like the Aya Sofya in Trabzon, has already gone a long way towards correcting this. In these paintings, it is easy to see the influence and the inspiration without which the Italian Renaissance would not have been possible. Of these, the greatest perhaps is the spectacular version of the Last Judgement, in which Jesus raises the dead over a shower of broken locks and keys; Adam and Eve are shown redeemed, along with the unbaptized kings and prophets of the Old Testament. The remainder portray various Biblical scenes, the

Burning Bush and Jacob wrestling with the angel, as well as a whole catalogue of Orthodox saints and some unusual *trompe l'œil* borders. Theodore the Logothete himself appears in one of the mosaics, presenting his rebuilt church to Christ. A figure of the Christ Pantocrator and other mosaics with scenes from his life and portraits of apostles and saints cover the outer and inner narthexes; unfortunately few have survived in the nave.

The Theodosian Walls

The Theodosian Walls can be seen just a few blocks west of the Chora. In their own right, they are among the greatest monuments of Istanbul. No city has ever had better; without them, the Byzantine capital could easily have succumbed on scores of occasions to Huns, Avars, Bulgarians, Russians, Arabs, Goths or Turks; with them, even in its darkest and most decadent moments, the empire was able to maintain itself as the bulwark of Christendom and the heir of Rome.

Fully 17 miles in length, the walls stand almost intact between the Golden Horn and the Marmara, but in fragments along the shores. The inland walls, the easiest to attack, are the most impressive. Anthemius, Theodosius's prefect, made them invulnerable by doubling them, with a raised inner wall looking down over and protecting the outer, and a deep ditch in front of that. For most of their length, you can walk between them or even on them. A word of caution is in order, though: some of the areas around the walls, particularly in the Topkapı Gate area, have a reputation as being a bit dangerous, and a lot of Turkey's drug manufacturing business is said to go on here.

Where the wall meets the Golden Horn, two towers stand as remnants of the **Dungeon of Anemas [E]** where the Byzantines kept unsuccessful schemers and political prisoners. These walls are actually not part of the original work, but a long loop added around the Palace of Blachernae, the huge suburban garden palace of the late emperors. Very little of it remains; the palace encompassed all of what is now the green district called **Ayvansaray**, its houses and gardens betraying occasional traces of an old wall or a bit of carved stone. The **Palace of Constantine Porphyrogenitus [F]** adjacent to the Blachernae still stands, a stony pile, literally a shell of what it once was. The palace last served as a poorhouse before it fell into ruin in the 1600s; currently it is undergoing restoration.

Just inside the **Edirne Kapı**, the old Adrianople Gate, is another fine mosque built by Sinan for Süleyman the Magnificent, the **Mihrimah Camii [G]** (1562), named after the sultan's favourite daughter. The section of the walls to the south, in the dangerous spot depressed by the valley of the Lycus stream, saw much of the heaviest fighting during the siege of 1453. Here Mehmet's cannons pounded away relentlessly for days. Giustiniani, the Venetian commander, was wounded there, and, although the wall was not breached, his loss greatly disheartened the defenders and contributed much to the fall. The postern gate of Charisius, the one accidentally left open that caused the defeat, is just north of the Mihrimah. The tallest of the towers is at the old Rome Gate, now the **Topkapı Gate** ('cannon gate'), main entrance to the city by road.

On the Marmara shore, the **Marble Tower** at the end of the inland walls was a famous Byzantine landmark. Just to the north was the **Golden Gate** where all the emperors, on their accessions or their triumphs, entered. Most of its legendary embellishments are long gone, including the famous golden doors, but the Crusaders could not remove the marble triumphal arch at the centre of the gate, built to commemorate Theodosius's victory over the pretender Maximus in 391. To its four towers, Mehmet II added three more and an inner wall, creating the **Yedikule** ('seven towers') **Castle**, restored and open to visitors. Here Osman II was murdered by the Janissaries. Later sultans used it for incarcerating foreign ambassadors when the mood struck them; many of these, along with other prisoners, have left interesting inscriptions on the walls. Keep an eye out for the concerts and other events here in summer.

Yedikule Castle
open Tues–Sun 9.30–5; closed Mon; adm

Southwestern Istanbul

This part of the city has little to offer. Byzantine churches like those of the monastic complex at Studion and the Peribleptos Monastery have long ago been battered out of recognition by earthquakes and rebuildings. Under the Byzantines, the Studion was the centre of learning of the Greek world, the prototype of the university. All that is left of it today is one of its churches, **St John in Studion**, now the İmrahor Camii on İmrahor İlyas Bey Caddesi. Even this has little to show from its past: just a few capitals and a 12th-century patterned pavement. Another church, that of **St Andreas in Crisal** [H], is still substantially intact, just to the north at the western end of Koca Mustafa Paşa Caddesi; now it is the **Koca Mustafa Paşa Camii**. Many Armenians live in this area, and their mostly 19th-century churches are still in use, including the Armenian Patriarchate in Sarapnel Sokak near the Marmara end of the Atatürk Bulvarı. The largest of all open cisterns, the **Altımermer** [I], may be seen in the quarter of the same name, and the 1593 **Cerrahpaşa Camii** [J] is the most interesting of the area's mosques.

Rather than visiting these, take yourself to **Adnan Menderes Bulvarı**, one of the broad, empty boulevards driven through Stamboul in the 1940s, and see the ancient metropolis from the top of the **Ferris wheel** in the little amusement park there. Not long ago this street was called Vatan Caddesi; they changed it, ostensibly to commemorate the deposed prime minister of the 1950s, whose name was still taboo only a few years ago – but also perhaps because this was the lowest-rent street in the Turkish version of Monopoly (the highest is Barbaros Bulvarı in Beşiktaş).

Eyüp

Once upon a time, the Golden Horn was the most beloved of all the embellishments of Istanbul. From Eminönü Square all the way up the estuary, both banks were lined with *yalılar*, the wooden mansions of the paşas, set among gardens and groves of plane trees and cypresses. Marble quays brightened the shores, and the only boats to be seen were pleasure craft and water taxis. Then, in the 19th century, Abdülhamid the Damned – Abdülhamid II, the sultan of whom not even the Turks will speak kindly – let in the foreign syndicates and industrialists, and in no time at all the Horn became a seamy polluted waterfront, the black sewer of Istanbul.

Just beyond the inland walls at Ayvansaray, the little village of Eyüp was, before Abdülhamid, the jewel of the waterway. Set on a height, enjoying the best view of the domes and minarets of the city, Eyüp was a garden suburb of lovely modest houses, favoured by the most influential artists and public men of the Ottoman Empire. Today, surrounded by factories and *gecekondu* sprawl, Eyüp has become a poor district and somewhat bedraggled, but still tries its best to keep its head above the miasma.

Although it is believed the spot has been holy ground since ancient times, Eyüp acquired its sanctity for Muslims during the Siege of 1453, when Mehmet or one of his vezirs had a dream directing him to the unmarked grave of Eba-Eyüp el-Ensari, the standard bearer of the Prophet Mohammed, who had died here during the first Arab attack on Constantinople in the 7th century. Eyüp – the name is the Arabic form of Job – was found just where the dream had promised. Mehmet built a *türbe* and mosque, and, when an earthquake knocked it down in 1800, Sultan Selim III replaced it with the **Eyüp Camii** you see today. It was here that the sultans, upon their accessions, were girded with the sword of Osman, which served them in place of a crown as the symbol of sovereignty. All around, between the blocks of small shops selling Korans and a strange assortment of Islamic trinkets, the living village shares the space with acres of beautiful **cemeteries**, their marble headstones laid out in walled gardens with names like the Pavilion of Idris and the Valley of the Nightingale.

To get back to the present in a hurry after the ancient piety of Eyüp, take the Fatih Bridge over the Golden Horn to the seldom-visited neighbourhood of **Hasköy**, where in an old shipyard at

**Rahmi M. Koç
Museum**
*open Tues–Fri 10–5,
Sat–Sun 10–7; adm*

5 Hasköy Caddesi you'll find the new **Rahmi M. Koç Museum**. Turkey's biggest industrialist must have had a bit of Henry Ford in him, for he has spent a good chunk of his money gathering this enormous collection of all the gadgets that helped bring his country into the modern world. There are steam engines, Bosphorus tugboats, early automobiles, chronometers, zoetropes, jet fighters, locomotives, a street of reconstructed old shops, the railway carriage of the 19th-century sultans, even a Second World War submarine you can crawl around in. Bring the kids.

Beyoğlu

 Beyoğlu

In Byzantine times, there was no bridge over the Golden Horn – there was no reason to cross it. The little settlement on the opposite shore called Sycae never played much of a role in the life of the city. **Galata**, the port of Beyoğlu on the tip of the Golden Horn, began as a Genoese trading colony in the 9th century. As the Italian control of trade routes strengthened, Constantinople's economic power declined, and by the 14th century Galata was a prosperous town; such trade as passed through the Bosphorus landed here, not at the impoverished capital. Italians had long played a role in the city, not only the Genoese, but Pisans, Venetians and Amalfitani. Their capitalistic arrogance, not to mention their heretical Christianity, infuriated the Greeks, and in 1180 a mob – among whom we may guess were many of the Italians' debtors – massacred thousands. Diverting the Fourth Crusade to sack Constantinople was the Italians' way of returning the favour.

When the Greek emperors returned in 1261, Galata began to build walls against the possibility of another such debt moratorium. The restored empire, weak as it was, became entirely dependent on the Genoese. The Genoese nonchalantly declared their neutrality during the siege of 1453, and kept some of their privileges under the Turks for a while. Under Ottoman rule, Galata maintained its role as a foreign compound; the Genoese were gradually replaced by the French and others, who were granted their first commercial privileges, or 'capitulations', by Süleyman the Magnificent in 1525.

The ambassadors of the European powers soon began to construct large embassy compounds on the lovely hills of Pera (Beyoğlu) above Galata. Fashion and influence followed, and enough money flowed into the capitulations to build Galata and Pera into the real centre of the city. As the Turks and their government became increasingly impotent and irrelevant, eventually even the sultan joined the migration, building a new palace, the Dolmabahçe, on the Bosphorus in the 1850s. Most of the recent growth of the city has occurred on the Beyoğlu side of the Golden

Horn. While in many places you can still look out over open country-side from the Theodosian walls of Stamboul, new districts have spread for miles northwards from Pera; today even the villages along the Bosphorus are considered part of the metropolitan area.

These streets were once legendary throughout the world for their scenes of ostentatious wealth mixed with age-old grime and squalor, their Levantine mix of a hundred nationalities and languages, their excesses and their intrigues. The departure of the embassies, after Atatürk moved the government to Ankara, simply let all the air out of them; some 20 years ago, this neighbourhood had hit rock bottom. **İstiklâl Caddesi**, its main thoroughfare, had been thoroughly trashed in the anti-Greek riots of 1955. It was a grimy, degraded shadow of its former self, lined with sordid night spots and porno theatres; few of its buildings were occupied above the ground floor. Since then the change has been dramatic. İstiklâl has been scrubbed up and polished and closed to traffic, embellished instead with the charming (and also totally practical) **Nostaljik Tramvay**, to carry people between Tünel and Taksim Square. Businesses, in particular the media and retail sector, have moved back in, and the renewal is spreading down the side streets.

Today the area is often called the Soho of Istanbul. It buzzes with charming *meyhaneler*, funky bars and some of the best restaurants and artistic cafés in town. In the long summer season they take over the streets, creating an atmosphere that rivals Europe's best street cultures. During the day İstiklâl may teem with shoppers, but in the evening it is the domain of revellers; on a busy summer evening the atmosphere around Asmalımescit or Nevizade Sokak, lined with bustling taverns, can only be described as carnivalesque.

Karaköy

Coming across the Galata Bridge, you meet first the grey mess of warehouses, workshops and office blocks of Karaköy, 'black village', the modern name for Galata. Istanbul's oldest Catholic church and other odd relics of Galata's past are tucked away in corners where it will take you some effort to find them. Just a block east of the bridge, the **Yeraltı Camii** or 'underground mosque' originally occupied the cellar of a defence tower believed to have been built by the Romans. The more conventional mosque building over it was added in the 1750s. To the west, off Tersane Caddesi, the **Arap Camii** started as a Byzantine church, and was rebuilt as a Dominican chapel in the early 14th century; in 1492 Beyazıt II converted it into a mosque for Muslim refugees expelled from Spain.

Voyvoda Caddesi takes its name from the redoubtable 15th-century Voyvode of Wallachia and Transylvania, Vlad III Dracul, enemy of the Turk and inventor of a hundred novel ways of disposing of captives and indiscreet ambassadors. His metamorphosis into the blood-sucking Count Dracula at the hands of novelist Bram Stoker is well known. The Turks say they caught him and stuck his head on a pike; it is supposed to be buried somewhere along this street. The Romanians, and most of the historians, say his own men did him in. Come some night and look.

Galata Tower
open daily; adm

The **Galata Tower**, the most conspicuous symbol of the quarter and the centre of its skyline as seen from the Stamboul side, was built in 1350 as part of the Genoese fortifications. Under the Ottomans, it was put into service as a fire tower. Now restored, it has a restaurant on the top floor with a fine view of the city, and is also open to visitors who want to simply take in the views. The streets surrounding the Galata Tower are an enticing tangle of steep and crumbling steps and narrow walkways, flanked by old apartment blocks. Workmen's hammers clang from within dark and musty workshops and cars hoot ceaselessly as they try to squeeze their way through. This area houses a small section of Istanbul's Jewish population, and a modest **synagogue** can be found 100 yards down from the tower towards the sea on Büyük Hendek Caddesi. Called the **Neve Shalom**, it is identifiable only by the row of Stars of David above the glass doorway. It was here that Palestinian terrorists massacred 21 worshippers one terrible Shabbat in 1986. Another synagogue nearby on Kadaköy Meydani now houses the newly opened **Jewish Museum of Turkey**.

Jewish Museum of Turkey
open Mon–Thurs 10–4, Fri and Sun 10–2; adm

Museum of Divan Literature
open Tues–Sun 9.30–4.30

Nearby, on Galip Dede Caddesi, the **Museum of Divan Literature** or Divan Edebiyatı Müzesi is really the subtle Turkish republican way of preserving Istanbul's Mevlevi House, the *tekke* (lodge) of the whirling dervishes, after the order's dissolution in 1925. While the *tekke* began here as early as the 1490s, most of what you see now are the contributions of the 19th-century sultans, traditionally the friends of the Mevlevis. There are exhibits of musical instruments and other dervish paraphernalia, a smaller version of the Mevlâna Museum in Konya. This is also part of a working monastery; performances of the dervishes' dances are given on Sundays and occasionally on Saturdays. Stop in ahead for tickets if you wish to see it; they usually sell out well in advance.

Kemeraltı Caddesi and Tophane Square

As a startling counterpoint to the dervish house, Istanbul has long kept its red-light district in a compound of shabby blocks off Kemeraltı Caddesi, guarded by a policeman at the front gate to keep out unlicensed females and anyone with a camera. This is a highly organized, officially sanctioned operation. Kemeraltı continues westwards, past the 15th-century **St Benoit Church**, tucked awkwardly between two warehouses. Long the church of Pera's French community, St Benoit holds the remains of Ferenc Rakoczy, the 18th-century Hungarian patriot who fought not the

Turks, but the Habsburgs of Austria, and ended his life in exile in Turkey after the defeat of his revolutionary army.

Kemeraltı ends at **Tophane Square**; the name commemorates the first Turkish cannon foundry built here in the early 19th century by Sultan Selim III. The **Kılıç Ali Paşa Camii** here is a noteworthy late work of Sinan; the larger mosque to the east, the 1826 **Nüsretiye Cami**, was completed just as Mehmut II won his death struggle with the Janissaries – hence its name, 'Victory Mosque'. On the docks here, an old warehouse has been converted into the **Istanbul Modern Art Museum**, with a permanent collection of mostly Turkish artists, and changing exhibitions and films.

Istanbul Modern Art Museum
open Tues, Wed and Fri–Sun 10–6, Thurs 10–8; closed Mon; adm

The Tünel and the Pera Museum

No trip to Istanbul would be complete without a ride on the world's shortest underground, the **Tünel**, which will take you from the environs of Galata Bridge up the modest slope to İstiklâl Caddesi. The motives for building this little inclined railway in 1877 are unclear; some say its original purpose was to move livestock through to Istanbul avoiding the crowded streets of Pera. Affectionately known as the 'Mouse Hole', it was built by the Frenchman Henri Gavand in 1873, and if it takes longer than 90 seconds to hurtle up its 600-yard track, then it's travelling slowly. From Tünel Square, where it ends, you may start up İstiklâl or go back to **Şişhane Square**, one of the few real tragedies of Istanbul's recent redevelopment. Once a frilly, cobbled Italianate piazza with its radiating avenues and overdressed buildings, and the site of the city hall, it has been almost totally obliterated to make more room for cars. Walking up the hill from the square, along Meşrutiyet Caddesi, you will pass one of the city's great institutions, the Pera Palace Hotel (*see* p.164), and also one of its newest treats, the **Pera Museum**. Occupying the building that once was the posh old Bristol Hotel, this museum captures the spirit of the switched-on new Istanbul nicely, as it provides us affectionate snapshots from the past. The permanent collection of 'orientalia', paintings from the 18th-20th centuries, shows portraits and scenes of Istanbul life at its most irresistibly exotic. One unexpected painter represented here is Hamdi Bey, better known as Turkey's first archaeologist (*see* pp.119–20), with his charming vignette of the Tulip Period called the 'Turtle Trainer'. There is also a collection of Kütahya ceramics, and changing exhibitions of major European artists.

Pera Museum
open Tues–Sat 10–7, Sun 12–6; adm

İstiklâl Caddesi

İstiklâl Caddesi was once known as the Grande Rue de Pera, where the ambassadors rubbed elbows with the city's commercial élite. In the 19th century it became heavily built up with European-style apartment and business blocks. Many of these are glorious

Art Nouveau works from the turn of the last century, their balconies dripping cast-iron vines and flowers over the street; one of the best is at No.479 (more good ones can be seen on Kemeraltı Caddesi and other streets in Pera). Another feature of the street is the old embassies, now reduced to the status of the world's fanciest consulates. Many of the embassy compounds included churches; today you'll need to peek behind the shops into their quiet courtyards to find them: two especially fine ones, both Italian, are the church of **Santa Maria Draperis** (1783) and **San Antonio di Padua** (1725) at Nos.431 and 331 respectively.

The antique trams run every 10 minutes up İstiklâl Caddesi to Taksim Square but it is more interesting to walk, taking care that the trams – stealthy, quietly whirring contraptions – do not flatten you along the way. Starting from the Tünel entrance, the first noteworthy consulate is the **Swedish Consulate**, on the right hidden behind big gates. Two hundred years old, it exudes a lofty elegance. Just beyond it is the **Russian Consulate**, splendidly overblown, all neo-Grecian columns and carved cornices, painted a purple that is, oddly enough, quite fetching. Designed by the Fossati brothers, the Italian architects of Czar Nicolas I, it was completed in 1837. S. Maria Draperis is up from here, on the right.

İstiklâl is full of arcades (*pasajlar*), dim covered alleys or grand follies like the Avrupa Pasajı, serving many purposes. Most famous is the one devoted to beer, the narrow **Çiçek Pasajı**. Despite all the good things that have happened to this neighbourhood in recent years, we can still shed a tear for the 'Flower Arcade'. Not long ago this was the most beloved and atmospheric watering hole in Turkey, four feet wide and lined with crowded cafés and stand-up joints with sawdust on the floor. You would get a beer in a huge glass called an 'Argentine', and the barman would dump a depth charge of vodka in it if you looked like you needed it. A dancing bear might come in to entertain. All that's gone now. Well-painted and cheerful, the arcade shelters a few colourless new cafés and fish restaurants. Across the street, the school behind the big gates is the **Galatasaray Lisesi**, once the most prestigious in the empire, where instruction was carried on, naturally, in French. At the end of a side street near the school is the **Galatasaray Hamam**, built under Beyazıt II in 1481 and still the city's most opulent.

Behind the Çiçek Pasajı, Istanbul's liveliest market, the **Balık Pazarı** (fish market) covers a maze of streets; most of the *meyhaneler* (bars) chased out of the Çiçek Pasajı by restoration have taken refuge here, on Nevizade Sokak and other streets. Immediately to the right of the entrance to the market is the Armenian church of **Surp Yerrortutyun**, its doors adorned with two distinctive Armenian *katchkars*, raised crosses, in wooden relief. Inside, the church is long and arched and graceful; incense hangs in the air. The street to the left of the market leads down to Meşrutiyet Caddesi and the **British Consulate**, built by Sir Charles Barry, co-architect of the Houses of Parliament. A few strides away from the fish market is the small **Avrupa Pasajı**, the 'European Arcade', now serving as a second-hand book bazaar. The books are mostly in Turkish but some shops sell old newspapers and colourful prints from the Ottoman era and you may pick up a curio.

Continuing down İstiklâl Caddesi, you pass on the left the **Ağa Camii**, a small and peaceful mosque constructed during the reign of Mahmut II. At the low, elegant French consulate, marked by a gargantuan tricolour, a narrow street opposite leads to the Greek Orthodox **Aya Triada** church. Built in neo-Gothic style, it is set in a well-kept garden and the narthex contains a gentle mosaic of the Virgin cradling the baby Jesus.

Taksim Square

When İstiklâl finally gives out, it leaves you stranded in Taksim Square, the centre of Beyoğlu, a dull place full of cars where the romantic airs of Pera fade into the well-painted concrete of the newer areas. The *taksim* itself, a reservoir housed in a squat building with a pointed roof, is at the very end of İstiklâl Caddesi. Istanbul's fresh water was once piped here direct from the Belgrade Forest. The **Atatürk Cultural Centre**, a bland block of glass and stone, was completed in 1962 as the home for the Opera and a showpiece of the city's cultural life. Grand opera has had a home in Istanbul since Donizetti Paşa, brother of the famous composer, conducted the Palace Symphony in the 1840s. Taksim can be a little dodgy at night, and many of the bars around it are outrageous (and dangerous) clip joints; don't let yourself get invited in.

Soldiers' Museum (Askeri Müzesi)

Soldiers' Museum
open Wed–Sun 9–5;
closed Mon and
Tues; adm

The modern neighbourhoods beyond, Harbiye, Şişli and Maçka, are bright and busy, with little to see. One attraction definitely worth a detour is the Soldiers' Museum **[K]**, housed in the old Ottoman imperial military academy in the hillside park near the Hilton Hotel a half-mile north of Taksim. The Janissaries, like the sultans, never threw anything away, and the vast hoard of souvenirs and curiosities they piled up on their tours of Europe and Asia and stored in the Aya İrene church armoury made this natural museum collection: Crusaders' swords, Byzantine battle flags, Tamerlane's coat of mail, flags of the '16 historical Turkish Empires' (including Tamerlane's and Attila the Hun's), the famous chain the Byzantines used to close off the Golden Horn, and a whole hall of wax dummies of the sultans and Janissaries – the whole crazy hierarchy from the Ağas through the Makers of Soup and Water Carriers down to the dwarfs, the *soytarılar*, who, as their card explains, 'do funny things for sultan'. There's a table-and-chair set made entirely out of rifles, a tasteful gift from Kaiser Wilhelm. If you come at 3 or 4pm, you'll be treated to one of the best shows in Istanbul, a performance of the Mehter band in all its glorious cacophony. The Selcuk and Ottoman armies marched to this music, which inspired the Turkish fantasies of Mozart and Beethoven and became the precursor of all band music in Europe.

Dolmabahçe Palace

Dolmabahçe Palace
open Tues, Wed and Fri–Sun 9–3, closed Mon and Thurs; adm; to book tickets call t *0212 236 9000*

At the end of the park, where it descends towards the Bosphorus, your view of the water will be blocked by the Dolmabahçe Palace (1852). No better monument to the spirit of the later Ottomans could be imagined. Abdülmecit, the reforming sultan of the Crimean War, was acutely aware of, and sensitive to, the growing backwardness of his nation, compared to the rest of Europe. To restore Turkey to its place in the sun, he emptied his treasury – literally putting the Ottoman Empire into receivership – not on armies, or railroads, or factories, but on this preposterous Versailles of marble. Ahmet Fethi Paşa, the Ottoman ambassador to France, scoured the luxury workshops of Europe to furnish the place, and persuaded the stage designer of the Paris Opera to come and put it all together. Here Abdülmecit could receive ambassadors in a proper frock coat, hold grand balls, even indulging in a waltz or two himself, or treat his guests to a private performance of Donizetti Paşa's orchestra. The empire was now officially up to date.

The real tragedy is that, to make room for this pile, Abdülmecit tore down a lovely expanse of gardens and pavilions that probably included some of the finest works of Tulip Period architecture, wood and tile pavilions like those at Topkapı and Yıldız Park. Eighteenth-century sultans such as Ahmet II and Mahmut III spent much of their time here. Anyhow, take the tour; you've never seen anything like it before. More bad taste is concentrated in this one building than in Napoleon's Tomb, the Great Hall of the Soviets and the Vittorio Emanuele Memorial all combined, with still enough left over to balance all the funeral homes in Los Angeles. All the gold and silk and crystal are real, of course, and there's plenty of Czech and Baccarat crystal, Venetian glass, Sèvres vases and Belgian (not Turkish!) carpets. No particular style predominates; it probably occurred to the architects and decorators early on that the sultan only desired that they should lay it on thick.

Czar Nicholas sent polar-bear rugs, and a present of elephant tusks came from the governor of the Hejaz. The British, though, knew what the Ottomans really liked; Queen Victoria sent him the biggest chandelier in the world.

The Dolmabahçe has lots of clocks, all of which have been stopped at the same time, 9.05am, the hour that Atatürk died here on 10 November 1938. To his credit, the Turkish leader occupied only a small room on his visits here; he converted the rest into a conference centre and exhibition hall. Today, the city uses it to put up whatever kings, sheikhs and presidents happen to visit. In addition to the main palace you may also want to join the guided tours for the **Selamlık** (ceremonial quarters) and the **Harem** (women's quarters), which have separate admission fees.

Beşiktaş and Yıldız Parkı

Beşiktaş, the neighbourhood northeast of the palace, further up the Bosphorus, begins the fashionable quarters of the modern city. Where its main street, Barbaros Bulvarı, meets the Bosphorus, Turkey's **Naval Museum [L]** contains not only ship models, elaborately carved figureheads and other relics, but entire ships: pretty things like the 1876 gilded barge used by Abdülaziz's harem for outings, and a 144-oar naval galley from the 18th century. The point is to remind you that the Ottoman state was, in the early 16th century, the leading sea power of Europe. The **Tomb of Barbarossa**, just outside, honours the brutal Greek-born corsair who, in the service of Süleyman the Magnificent, made that pre-eminence possible. In 1863, 11 years after Abdülmecit built Dolmabahçe, his successor Abdülaziz grew tired of it and built a new one half a mile up the Bosphorus. **Çırağan Palace [M]** is only a third as large; presumably that was all the great powers and their Ottoman Debt Commission would allow. A fire in 1910 left only the four enormous exterior walls standing, and Çırağan was for years a ghostly shell before being converted into a luxury hotel.

In another 13 years, Abdülaziz was gone – deposed for his reckless extravagance – and his successor Abdülhamid, finding the treasury even emptier, still managed to build the extensive **pavilions** in **Yıldız Park**. These were left to rot after the deposition of the sultans, but recently the Automobile Club has restored both the buildings and the grounds to their original appearance, adding open-air cafés and terraces with a view over the Bosphorus. Altogether the park is one of the most beautiful in Turkey, and the restoration of the **Malta Köşkü** has won an architectural award. Another pavilion, the **Şale Köşkü**, was a residence for guests of the sultans, and is now open for visits, while another houses Istanbul's **Municipal Museum**. The collection includes maps and views of the city, expropriated relics from the dervish orders, imperial *firmans* directed to the city, portraits, Karagöz puppets and bric-a-brac.

After all this you may think you have seen Istanbul, but there's still another world to it. Up Büyükdere Caddesi from Beşiktaş lie the huge, shiny new districts where most of the well-off and middle classes live, full of motorways, malls, construction cranes, chain stores and suburban villas. There aren't a lot of reasons to

Naval Museum
open Wed–Sun 9–5; closed Mon and Tues; adm

Şale Köşkü
open Tues, Wed and Fri–Sun 9.30–5; closed Mon and Thurs; adm

Municipal Museum
open Fri–Wed 9–4.30; closed Thurs; adm

07 Istanbul | Beyoğlu

come up here because everything is so new, but you may enjoy a day experiencing the jarring contrast of an Istanbul on the cutting edge of modernity. **Levent** is the new business centre, with its American-style skyline on what was dairy farms only 40 years ago. Currently there are plans for a pair of 100-storey office blocks here, financed from Dubai. Incredibly, not far away is another, separate skyline, almost as impressive, in the **Maslak** district. Nearby **Etiler** is the prime residential area, with the **Akmerkez shopping mall**, which any Turk will tell you is the finest in the world.

Istanbul in Asia

In truth, the Asian side is older. The Delphic oracle had told Byzas the navigator to settle 'opposite the land of the blind'; when his Argive expedition arrived at the Golden Horn, they found a colony of Megarans already established near what is today the suburbs of Kadıköy. Byzas knew who the blind were; the advantages of the European side for building a city were plain. In the Roman and Byzantine eras, Kadıköy was the sizeable town of **Chalcedon**, the site of many councils of the early Church. The emperors never favoured Chalcedon; on the contrary, they sealed its fate when they took most of the stone from its walls to rebuild their own aqueducts after various sieges. Chalcedon dwindled to nothing in the last days of the empire, and the Turks took the rest of its stones for their own projects; columns from its famous Church of St Euphemia can be seen in the courtyard of the Süleymaniye.

On the ferry from Eminönü or Karaköy, you pass **Leander's Tower**, a Bosphorus landmark since Byzantine times, with its lighthouse and customs house. You can also see the two king-sized landmarks of Asian Istanbul, Haydarpaşa Station and the Selimiye Barracks.

Kadıköy and Üsküdar

The Stamboullu claim that the Asian side of the city is very different from the European side. It's calmer, they say; so much more relaxed. They're right, and you'll notice the change the minute you alight from the ferry, probably at **Kadıköy** (the destination of most boats from Europe), to set foot in another continent. It's the space that does it; ahead is a wide, uncluttered square with only a statue of a benevolent Atatürk stretching out his hand to Turkish youth. The extravagant blue building across the square (Buckingham Palace meets the Blue Mosque) is another 19th-century disaster of Ottoman architecture, now housing the local **government offices**. The mosque near the dock is the 1761 **Sultan Mustafa III Camii**, simple and appealing. In the streets around Kadıköy there are snazzy clothes shops, while at the port at least a dozen boot-blacks line up in a row, semi-pornographic pictures pasted to their elaborate gold-painted foot rests. A five-minute walk along the dock leads to the most elegant railway station in Turkey, **Haydarpaşa Station**. Sirkeçi is nice but this is quite remarkable. Built in 1908 by Sultan Abdülhamid's friends, the Germans, it is named after an old general of Selim III. The ceiling is vertiginously high and twistingly ornate, the windows colourfully stained and the waiting room a revelation: wood-panelled, with chandeliers and a huge rubber plant. There is a police station, a restaurant of considerable repute, a barber shop and a post office; you can catch a train as well.

Further along, up a gentle hill on the road to Üsküdar, is the **Selimiye Barracks [N]**. Built as part of the military reforms of Selim III, this was the home of the new model army the reformers hoped would replace the Janissaries – until the Janissaries ordered it to be disbanded. During the Crimean War (1854–6), when Britain was allied with Turkey against Russia, it served as a hospital and it was here that Florence Nightingale made her name. Her work room and personal quarters have been converted into a small and simple museum by the Turkish Nursing Association (she is as big a heroine in Turkey as she is in the UK). The Selimiye Barracks are now the headquarters of the Turkish First Army, charged with the defence of Thrace and the Dardanelles. At their entrance is the **Selimiye Camii**, built by Selim III for the spiritual health of his ill-fated army and set in a charming garden. At the top of the street, over the road, is the immense, haunting **Karaca Ahmet**, the largest cemetery in Istanbul, prettified with shady cypress trees.

Selimiye Barracks Museum
open daily 9–5 but best to phone ahead to check, t 0216 343 7310

From here **Üsküdar** is a five-minute dolmuş ride away. Like Kadıköy, it is a bustling yet relaxing neighbourhood. To the Byzantines it was Chrysopolis, 'city of gold'; today it is more a 'suburb of food' with a lively fish, fruit and vegetable market held daily and lots of good, inexpensive restaurants where the menus are in Turkish, not English. No one takes much notice of tourists here and you can stroll amongst the noisy shoppers and traders enjoying an anonymity impossible to achieve in Sultanahmet.

Two large and beautiful mosques decorate the open space around Üsküdar landing. Sinan was responsible for the **Mihrimah Camii [O]** (1547), which, like the other Mihrimah, was built in honour of Süleyman's favourite daughter. Standing opposite it is the 18th-century **Yeni Valide Camii [P]**, built by Ahmet III. Up the hill from the dock is another work of Sinan, the **Şemsi Paşa Camii [Q]**.

Up the Bosphorus (Boğaziçi)

Even if you have only a little time in Istanbul, you will probably want to invest some of it on a trip up this lovely waterway. Roads

It's Only a Shanty in Old Shantytown...

It's no surprise that the inventor of quick-setting cement was a Turk. Under Turkish law, the authorities may not remove any squatter's shack if the roof can be raised in one night. As country people flocked to Istanbul and Ankara in the last 30 years, in search of modern life and good jobs, the outskirts of these and other cities filled with *gecekondu* ('put-up overnight') neighbourhoods. They are the outward manifestation of Turkey's continuing social revolution. Most of them, as you will see if you travel out into the vast suburbs beyond the Theodosian walls or on the Asian side, by now have grown into real neighbourhoods with real houses, as their hard-working inhabitants gradually make their way into urban society. Turkish planners once looked upon them as their greatest problem, and their populations are still a tremendous strain on the city's budget; but by the curious and immutable laws of urban economics, it seems their resourceful, upwardly mobile people may be one of the nation's great resources. Big cities in western Europe and America went through stages like this in the 19th century, and it was just as rough for them.

In Istanbul, though, the poor aren't the only ones who can enjoy the delights of the *gecekondu*. Largely because of the ludicrous bureaucracy involved in getting a building permit, some 70 per cent of all construction in the city is illegal, a figure probably much higher than even Naples. About 200 new buildings get started every night. Istanbul's boom involves not only penniless migrants, but an exploding class of *nouveaux riches*; they need houses too. More money is flowing around Istanbul these days than at any time since the days of Süleyman the Magnificent, and a sizeable proportion of it is being invested in real estate. The ultimate status symbol in Istanbul today is a villa with a balcony overlooking the straits. Nearly all of them are *gecekondu* – even if they're worth a million dollars.

A new class of building speculators has rapidly become the richest and most powerful interest in the city. Often tied to organized crime (and to high government circles) it has its ways of corrupting local governments and muscling common people off desirable plots of land they own. Nothing – not the best efforts of the few, underpaid city building inspectors, nor the outcries of Turkey's small environmental preservation groups – has been able to stop the tidal wave of villas and flats that has irrevocably ruined the Bosphorus shores. There is simply too much money at stake.

follow both the European (Rumeli) and Asian (Anadolu) sides, but the best way to see the Bosphorus is by boat. Regular ferries from Galata Bridge traverse its length, most taking a zigzag course up and down the straits and giving you the chance of a fine fish dinner in one of the villages before your return. In the last three decades, however, almost all of the wide open spaces along the Bosphorus shore have been swallowed up by the relentless growth of the city. On both sides of the straits, as far as Rumeli Kavağı and Anadolu Kavağı, villas and blocks of flats have been built on every square inch where the slope isn't too steep.

The Bosphorus Bridge

Just as you leave the built-up areas of the city, you will pass the Bosphorus Bridge, a new symbol of Istanbul often seen on souvenirs and brochures these days. It's the fifth largest suspension bridge in the world, the longest in Europe and the only one to link two continents. It was completed in time for the 50th anniversary of the republic, and the Turks like to think of it as an emblem of the great progress they have made. The tolls on this bridge have already paid for the construction of another, the Mehmet Fatih Bridge, positioned further up the Bosphorus at the point where the waterway was first spanned, in 512 BC by King Darius of the Persians, using a bridge of boats. The Mehmet Fatih Bridge was opened in 1988, exactly 2,500 years after Darius first made the connection.

Two symbols of the bad old days are underneath the Bosphorus bridge: the 1854 **Ortaköy Camii [R]**, on the European side, a mosque with Corinthian columns, looks even more like a 1920s American movie-palace than the others of its ilk. On the Asian side Sultan Abdülaziz found the money for yet another marble pile, the

Beylerbeyi Palace
open summer Tues, Wed and Fri–Sun 8.30–5; winter Tues, Wed and Fri–Sun 8.30–4; closed Mon and Thurs; adm

Beylerbeyi Palace [S]. Napoleon III's wife, the Empress Eugénie, spent a few weeks here in the 1860s, and she must have felt quite at home. The Beylerbeyi's other famous occupant was Sultan Abdülhamid, who was allowed to stay on at the palace by the Young Turks after they deposed him. Abdül the Damned lived out his life here in a simple room with simple furniture; he brought none of his concubines or servants with him – just his cat, the only creature he trusted. On the hills above Beylerbeyi, Turkey's tallest structure, the TRT television tower, stands atop **Çamlıca Hill**, a popular resort in the old days, with a wonderful prospect of the city and the straits. There are cafés and carriage rides, part of the recent rehabilitation and relandscaping of the hill by the TTOK.

Arnavutköy and the Rumeli Hisarı

Back on the European side, **Arnavutköy**, the 'Albanian village', was once the prettiest town along the Bosphorus, with tall, elegant 19th-century houses built up to the water's edge. A few of these are still left, but Arnavutköy has suffered more than any of the villages from creeping urbanization. A little further on, the straits open up into **Bebek** ('baby') **Bay**. The little palace across the way, a cupcake compared to the over-frosted wedding cakes down the

Küçüksu Palace
open summer Tues, Wed and Fri–Sun 9–5; winter Tues, Wed and Fri–Sun 9–4; closed Mon and Thurs; adm

straits, is the **Küçüksu Palace [T]**, built by Abdülmecit. This is often called the Palace of the Sweet Waters of Asia, for the lovely stream that flows down from Çamlıca. In Ottoman times, the rivers that led into the Golden Horn were called the 'Sweet Waters of Europe'.

Just after Bebek Bay, the straits close to their narrowest point, guarded by two Turkish castles that antedate the Conquest. Sultan Beyazıt I built the **Anadolu Hisarı [U]** in 1393 to choke off Constantinople's Black Sea trade. Across the straits, Mehmet tightened the grip with the **Rumeli Hisarı [V]** in 1452. It's difficult to believe the latter could have had any military purpose: draped languidly over the slopes, with its neat crenellations and perfect round towers, the Rumeli Hisarı is the most picturesque castle imaginable. Once it had wooden towers inside, but these have been cleared out and, instead of old cannons and dust, the castle is filled with flowers and trees; it also has an open-air theatre where plays and concerts are presented in the summer.

From Emirgan to the Two Kavağıs

Emirgan [W], on the European side, grew up around a garden-palace compound the sultans used for captured or exiled potentates in their care. The grounds and pavilions have been restored (by the Automobile Club, of course), most notably the lovely **Yellow Pavilion**, an outstanding example of the Turkish talent for fairytale architecture. An annual Tulip Festival is held here in April–May. Right on the Bosphorus, across from the Emirgan Mosque, is the **Sakip Sabancı Museum**. The Sabancı family, one of Turkey's two big industrial dynasties, has created this new museum in what was once a family villa; there are now collections of paintings (mostly Turkish), Ottoman calligraphy, archaeology and decorative arts. They've put on some important special exhibitions here recently, including of Picasso and Rodin.

Sakip Sabancı Museum
open Tues–Sun 10–6; adm

All the land west of this section of the Bosphorus is Istanbul's famous and beautiful suburban park, **Belgrade Forest** (Beograd Ormanı), originally a hunting preserve of the Ottomans. The name comes from the Serbian prisoners of war that the sultans settled here; they and their descendants formed a tight little community charged with the responsibility of keeping up Istanbul's aqueducts and reservoirs, until the paranoid Abdülhamid had them expelled for fear they would poison the water supply. Much of the city's water still comes from here, transported via a graceful aqueduct built by Mimar Sinan.

The oldest surviving wooden *yalılar* can be seen at **Kanlıca** on the Asian side, hanging gracefully out over the water. A few miles north, in the hills above **Çubuklu**, you can see a very different kind of house, the **Hıdiv Kasrı**, an Art Nouveau palace of an exiled Khedive of Egypt, now restored with a restaurant and tea salon. From nearby **Paşabahçe**, you can get to **Polonezköy**, some five miles (8km) to the east. This weekend resort, famous for food and scenery, has been, as its name implies, thoroughly Polish since 1842, when refugees from the freedom struggles against Russia settled here. The land was a present from the sultan, in return for the Poles' services in the Crimean War. Having a common enemy in the 18th and 19th centuries, the Poles and the Turks were quite close.

More towns on the European shore are **Yeniköy**, where a small Greek church overlooks the waterfront, **Tarabya**, a quite ritzy corner of the Bosphorus with a yacht harbour, and **Sarıyer**, where cafés and fishing boats crowd each other along the tree-lined waterfront. South of Sarıyer at **Büyükdere**, the **Sadberk Hanım Museum** is another effort of the Koç family, housed in two pretty villas. It contains a small but beautifully displayed collection of ancient Anatolian arts and Turkish handcrafts. The last two towns the ferry visits are **Rumeli Kavağı** and **Anadolu Kavağı**, a pair of perfect bookends on either side of the Bosphorus, both relatively

Sadberk Hanım Museum
open Thurs–Tues 10–5; closed Wed

quiet and pleasant. Beyond these, much of the land is given over to the military; it's very discreet and you'll never see them, but these straits are well guarded now, just as they always have been, as several ruined fortifications testify, including the **Genoese Castle [X]** north of Anadolu Kavağı; it's half an hour's climb up from the port, to a castle with medieval inscriptions and great views.

At the end of the straits, where the Symplegades, the clashing rocks of Greek mythology, were defeated by Jason and the Argonauts, all is quiet and still; two old lighthouses, the **Anadolu Fener** and the **Rumeli Fener**, wait to guide ships into the channel.

The Princes' Islands (Adalar)

There are nine of these in the Sea of Marmara, and ferries from the Galata Bridge, Kabataş or Bostancı call at the four largest, inhabited islands – Kınalıada, Burgazada, Heybeliada and Büyükada. The first two are inhabited mainly by Armenians who commute to jobs in Istanbul, while the last two, especially Büyükada ('Big Island'), have long been favoured as summer retreats, with their lovely pine groves, often dramatic cliffs dropping into a clean azure sea, colourful flower gardens, and lanes plied by horse-drawn carriages called *faytonlar* instead of cars. All the islands are car-free, and despite moves to 'modernize' and bring in traffic, the friends of the islands have so far been able to keep the beasts at bay.

In Byzantine times, these islands were a place of royal exile, as well as a popular spot for monasteries and, occasionally, pirates' nests. A few ruined churches and monastic buildings remain, but far more impressive, especially on Büyükada, are the grand old wooden summer houses, in all their pastel, 'gingerbread' Victorian-Gothic splendour. Another advantage of taking a trip out to the islands is the twilight return, 'sailing to Byzantium', when the great domes and minarets of the imperial mosques glow in the rosy dusk, creating one of the most poetic cityscapes in the world.

Büyükada, Prinkipo in Byzantine times, is as its name implies the largest and most populous of the islands. Sights include the **Anatolia Club**, originally built by British residents as a yacht club a century ago, and some Greek relics, churches and monasteries, on the hill above the town. Carriage-taxis offer tours up to these, or you may walk or rent a bike and have a picnic; like the other islands Büyükada is covered with pines, planted a century ago. The most interesting, but hardest to reach, is the **monastery of St George** on the southernmost hill, dating in part back to Byzantine times. There are small beaches at **Yörük Ali** and **Dil Uzantısı**.

The next-largest island, **Heybeliada**, lies just a mile or so to the west of Büyükada. The **Turkish Naval Academy** is here; on their

07 Istanbul | Up the Bosphorus: The Princes' Islands (Adalar)

grounds is the last church of the Byzantine Empire, the last one to be built before 1453, the **Kamariotissa** (you'll need permission from the naval authorities to visit). Overlooking the village from the top of the island is the **Aya Triada Monastery**, now closed but once the most important orthodox school of theology. As on Büyükada, you can easily find a *fayton* to take you around the island, and there are some decent beaches, the biggest of them at **Değirmen**, and others on the undeveloped western half of the island.

Two more islands are served by the ferries. **Kınalıada**, small and rather barren, is the closest to Istanbul, and largely inhabited by Armenians. **Burgazada** is steeper and greener, with ruins of another old monastery at its summit.

Tourist Information and Services in Istanbul

(i) **Istanbul >**
*Sultanahmet
facing the Aya Sofya,
t 0212 518 8754*

*Taksim Square
near the Hilton Hotel
on Cumhuriyet Caddesi,
t 0212 233 0592*

*Yeşilköy
Atatürk Airport,
t 0212 663 0793*

Tourist Police
*Yerebatan Caddesi 6,
near the Basilica
Cistern, t 0212 528 5369*

TTOK
*Halaskârgazi Caddesi
364, t 0212 231 4631*

Post Offices

There are branches all over town, including one in the Covered Market and one in İstiklâl Caddesi, Galatasaray, but the big one (24hrs) is near Sirkeci Station, on Yeni Postane Caddesi. This is where you should have *poste restante* mail sent: Post Restante, Büyük Postane, Yeni Postane Caddesi, Istanbul. All big offices have **telephone services**, which usually stay open until 10pm or even midnight. Local post offices close at 5pm.

Maps and Publications

All the usual rules for Turkish cities apply here: there are very few street signs, streets are known by different names to different people, and many people know nothing of the city outside their own neighbourhood. Although the map handed out by the tourist office is perfectly adequate for most needs, if you plan to do any detailed sightseeing, you'll want a better one; the best are published by the **Turkish Automobile Club** (from their offices), by **Aysa** (*Istanbul A–Z*, from bookshops) and by **Keskin Colour** (from hotels, news stands, and shops in the tourist centres).

Currently, the indispensable reference for events in the city is a monthly publication in English called *The Guide*, available from any of the bookshops below, or *Time Out*, which have an English edition once a month.

Money

Most ATMs will dispense cash for cards carrying the Maestro or Visa logo. Those needing a bank over the weekend, just to change money, will find one open, Wed–Mon 9.30–4, at the entrance to the Topkapı Sarayı. Most people change money at the little *döviz* offices that have sprung up all over the city; you'll generally get a better rate, and with some asking around you'll find one that takes travellers' cheques.

Credit card hotlines include:
American Express, t 0212 283 2201.
JCB/VISA/Mastercard/Eurocard, t 0212 225 0080.
Diners Club, t 0212 444 0555.

Good value for under-26s, a **youth discount card** can be bought from the front desk of the Interyouth Hostel on Caferiye Sokak behind the Aya Sofya. It grants cheap admission to most government-maintained museums, such as Topkapı Sarayı and Aya Sofya.

Shopping in Istanbul

You can get anything you want in Istanbul, from a 50 *kuruş boncuk* (anti-evil eye charm) to a full-size 20ft granite replica of a Hittite relief. For those born to shop, it's the best and the worst of all possible worlds: all the treasures of the Orient at your feet – but at a much higher price than out in the provinces. Those Kütahya plates seem a bargain at 20 YTL; a few hours' bus ride away in Kütahya, they can be one-third the price. The finest antique Ottoman-era jewellery is on display in the *bedestenler* of the Covered Market – but you might not be able to take it out of the country.

Clothing

Metropolis Istanbul has one sure trump card: *haute couture*, Turkish style, the logical development of a very talented nation with a very large textile industry. A few of the newer districts have concentrations of shops where you can find not only Turkish surprises but well-known designer labels at prices lower than you'll see them at home. Such fashion strips include **Rumeli Caddesi** and surrounding streets in **Nişantaşı**, **Bağdat Caddesi** in Erenköy on the Asian side, the **Galleria mall** in Ataköy, and the **Kanyon mall** in Levent, *www.kanyon.com.tr*, with its sleek, curved architecture and four levels of retail units including Apple Store, Harvey Nichols, Wagamama, and all the latest designer clothing stores. Most of the city's 12 million or so inhabitants are relative beginners with this type of shopping experience but the demographic is surely and steadily growing, as is the number of malls. New on the scene is the glass-roofed **İstinye Park**, hosting the usual luxury brands and costing an incredible 250 million US dollars to build.

İstiklâl Caddesi in Beyoğlu, since its recent facelift, is once again a fashionable shopping street and in our opinion has more character than all of Istanbul's malls put together. Sure, the international brands are muscling their way in, even a Virgin Megastore is planned, but there is still a refreshingly independent spirit here and enough alleys and side streets to keep that spirit alive. In one hour's' shopping here, you can treat yourself to a pair of Mavi jeans, the local brand making its own waves internationally, enjoy a wonderfully authentic workers lunch, duck into a side-alley antique shop and leaf through old Turkish film posters before enjoying a Turkish coffee in a non-standard, non-international coffee house.

For **silk and cashmere** there is a shop opposite the Galatasaray Lisesi on İstiklâl Caddesi called simply **İpek** ('silk'), where quality is high and the prices are low. For **leather**, a Turkish

speciality, the latest can be seen at Derishow in Nişantaşı and on Bağdat Caddesi and Desa on İstiklâl by the Beyoğlu Cinema. You can also try the various leather outlet stores along the coast at Yenikapi. For **shoes**, Beymen is good; there are also many shops in Nişantaşı, especially Hotiç, on Teşvikiye Caddesi, and Demirel, on Akkavak Sokak. For bargains on clothing and other items, try the **Olivium Shopping Mall** in Zeytinburnu with its many outlet stores of Turkish and international brands.

Jewellery

The obvious choice is the **Covered Bazaar**, where tons of it are on display, but there are other fine shops around the city: Diamond, on Teşvikiye Caddesi; Kafkas on Mim Kemal Oke Caddesi in Maçka, Artisan and Ayşe, both on İskele Caddesi in Ortaköy; Bazaar 54 and Lapis, both on tree-lined **Nuruosmaniye Caddesi** in Cağaloğlu.

Antiques and Carpets

These are big business, and there will be exotic trinkets to take home in all sizes and price ranges – just keep in mind Turkey's tough laws about exporting things of value (*see* p.83).

Istanbul doesn't exactly have flea markets. It has *bit pazarları*, literally 'louse markets'. The word came from a street in the Covered Bazaar called the Bit Pazar that now serves other purposes. Today, the biggest and most popular one sprawls around **Çukurcuma Caddesi** (east of İstiklâl, behind the Galatasaray Lisesi), a great place for every kind of Ottoman-era trinket and offbeat souvenir. Another big louse market takes place on the Asian side in **Üsküdar**, indoors in a rambling building at 30 Büyükhamam Sokak; mostly furniture. The same goes for the **Horhor Bit Pazarı**, a big indoor market on Kırık Tulumba Sokak in Aksaray. However, the address for real treasures is still the **Covered Bazaar**, particularly in the enclosed **İç Bedesten** and **Sandal Bedesten**: the choicest in antique jewellery, silver and gold work, even Byzantine icons and medieval astrolabes.

As for carpets, their buying and selling is the national pastime, and

Istanbul is not necessarily the best place to do it if you are concerned about price. Carpet shops around the Aya Sofya in Sultanahmet come as thick as flies, and some of the country's finest productions are brought to them. If you're experienced in the carpet game you may get a correct price there; otherwise, the carpet avenues of the Covered Bazaar or on the side streets off İstiklâl may be a better bet.

If time is short, the **Arasta Bazaar** behind the Blue Mosque has an arcade of select shops specializing in porcelain, Kütahya and İznik tiles, jewellery and, of course, carpets. While prices may be slightly higher than elsewhere, this is reflected in the quality of the merchandise.

Galleries

The **Istanbul Modern** in Karaköy, *www.istanbulmodern.org*, opened in 2005 (adm 7 YTL) is the first national museum of modern art and hosts the Biennial in odd years (September 2009 and 2011). For other art galleries and exhibitions, the Tünel end of **İstiklâl Caddesi** in Beyoğlu is promising. On İstiklâl Caddesi itself, the **Borusan Culture and Art Centre** has five floors of pictures executed to a variable standard as well as a wide range of art books. Opposite the St Antoine Catholic Church at No. 256 is **Elhamra Sineması**, a former cinema now housing **Karşı Sanat**, a huge art gallery. For cutting edge Turkish art by the likes of Hussein Caglayan as well as up and coming talent, **Galerist** is located in Misir Apartmani in Galatasaray. More intimate in scale is the **Asmanlımescit Art Gallery and Café** at Sofyalı Sokak 5/1, which has new exhibitions of pictures and sculpture every 3–4 weeks. Bean fiends should note that its café also serves real espresso coffee. For those who want to see beyond the canvas, visit the small gallery of **Neriman Oyman**, off Sofyalı Sokak at Asmalımescit Şehbender Sokak 8/2, **t** 0212 243 0173. There's little to indicate its presence on the street, just a small black nameplate and bell next to the front door. Neriman's work is displayed in the front gallery, and she paints in the studio at the back.

Food and Markets

If you're cooking for yourself or planning a picnic, food will prove no problem at all. The **Balıkpazarı** in Beyoğlu isn't just a fish market, you can get just about anything there, and in the delicatessens and speciality shops in surrounding streets. Polish-run **Sütte**, on Duduodalar Sokak, is one of the few places where you can get ham and other pork products. Most of the better delicatessens are out in the newer districts, such as **Abant Ciftliği**, on Valikonağı Sokak in Nişantaşı. The **Spice Market** has plenty of food stands, with fruits and vegetables outside, and there are weekly markets in all of the city's neighbourhood high streets. An especially big and popular one takes place in **Kadıköy**, Tuesdays and Fridays; also **Cihangir** (downhill from Galatasaray) on Tuesdays, and the big daily market in **Beşiktaş**. In the Spice Market, you can get the finest caviar: not from Russia any more, but from the Azerbaijani Republic.

Other Shopping

As in the quarters around the Covered Bazaar, some of the older streets in **Beyoğlu** are devoted to particular trades and kinds of shops. **Galip Dede Caddesi**, right at the top of the Tünel, is lined with **music shops** where you can find lutes, *neyler* and other traditional Turkish instruments, along with books on how to play them. For the best selection in recorded music though, look in the myriad little shops around the Stamboul side of the **Atatürk Bridge**. For **books in English**, and books in general about Turkey, the booksellers in the **Sahaflar Çarşısı**, between the Covered Bazaar and Beyazıt Square, have by far the best selection. They are also probably the best place to pick up inexpensive souvenirs: old prints and watercolours of the city, hand-painted boxes and other trinkets. Other shops offer rather less: most of these can be found along **İstiklâl Caddesi**, just north of the Tünel: **Haşet, Sander** and **ABC. Pandora**, on Büyük Parmakkapi Sok., *www.pandora.com.tr/english*, and the excellent **Robinson Crusoe**, on İstiklâl

Caddesi, have a collection of books and magazines in English. There is a **flower market** on the side streets off Taksim Square.

Sports and Activities in Istanbul

There are two nine-hole golf courses open to the public: the **Istanbul Golf Club** in suburban Maslak, **t** 0212 275 0975, and the new **Kemer Golf and Country Club**, a serious development in the beautiful Belgrade Forest. You can play golf, ride a horse, etc. with views of Mimar Sinan's aqueducts. Call **t** 0212 239 7770 for opening hours for non-members, *www.kemergroup. com*. You could also try the **Klassis Golf and Country Club** in Silivri, 1hr's drive from Atatürk Airport.

Some of the luxury hotels are pretty liberal about letting folks in to use their **tennis**, **handball** and **racketball courts**, gyms, etc.; try the **Hilton** on Taksim, **t** 0212 315 6000, or the **Swissotel**, **t** 0212 259 0101, first.

Most of the big hotels around Taksim and the Bosphorus let the public use their **pools**. There's even a place to **ice-skate**: the Galleria Mall in Ataköy, daily until 10pm.

Most of Turkey's top **football clubs** call Istanbul home, and you can watch them at **Beşiktaş** (İnönü Stadium); **Fenerbahçe** (in Kiziltoprak), and **Galatasaray** (in Mecideyeköy).

Hamams

Altogether, this is a wonderful town to take a bath. All the luxury hotels and a number of the less pretentious establishments have their own hamams. Wherever you stay, there will be one nearby. Some of them are historic landmarks, heating the water by traditional means; in the larger hamams more than thirty tons of wood and coal go up in smoke each month.

Cağaloğlu Hamamı, on Yerebatan Caddesi (*open for men and women 8am–8pm*). Perhaps the poshest and best-known is this palatial 18th-century hamam that even has its own bar. They are accustomed to tourists and, though it's expensive, this may be a good place for first-timers.

Çemberlitaş Hamamı, on Vezirhan Caddesi near the Burnt Column, *www.cemberlitas hamami.com.tr* (*open 6am–midnight*). Nearby, and slightly less expensive, is the 16th-century hamam patronized by Stambollu as well as tourists, and the massages here tend to be more thorough than in establishments catering solely to tourists.

Çinili Hamam, in a very out-of-the-way location on İtfaiye Caddesi, just off Atatürk Bulvarı north of the Aqueduct of Valens. One of the nicest, this 'tiled' hamam was built in the 1600s for pirate admiral Barbarossa, and it retains some of its original décor, with baths for both men and women. Because of its location it has avoided becoming touristy.

Galatasaray Hamamı off İstiklâl Caddesi. Another historic and very clean hamam; 4th generation owners.

Where to Stay in Istanbul

The subject is inexhaustible; besides the ones you'll find listed in the official tourist literature, there are literally hundreds of unclassified establishments – so you shouldn't have trouble finding a place even in summer. Prices naturally tend to be a bit higher than elsewhere in Turkey, but there is still plenty of room for bargaining in most categories.

The first thing is to decide *where* you want to stay. For seeing the sights, the most logical locations by far are the **Sultanahmet** and **Cağaloğlu** districts around the Aya Sofya and Blue Mosque. Sultanahmet has a dizzying array of hotels to welcome tourists. In recent years many of the ramshackle wooden buildings propping up this area's character have been restored into plush hotels. While the heart of Istanbul today beats across the Golden Horn in Beyoğlu, Sultanahmet is the beautifully made-up face that the city presents to the world at large.

Another large concentration of hotels, mostly in the moderate range, can be found in **Aksaray/Lâleli**, a noisy, modern district about a kilometre to the west, but still convenient for most of the sights. And there are still plenty of inexpensive hotels in the **Sirkeci** area around the rail station, convenient for the spice bazaar and Eminönü boat connections.

For businessmen and travelling paşas, most of the luxury hotels are on the **Beyoğlu** side, on or near the Bosphorus coast south of the bridge, and around Taksim Square. Some of the older ones, along with less expensive choices, can be found on and around Meşrutiyet Caddesi, a street that runs parallel to İstiklâl Caddesi through Beyoğlu.

For some Bosphorus waterfront luxury, the **Asian shore** is now home to several boutique hotels that have opened in recent years.

Phone codes for the European side are t 0212, for the Asian side t 0216.

Sultanahmet

Luxury

Istanbul probably has as many really posh hotels as anywhere in Europe, Paris included. Counting up all the royal and presidential suites, this city could accommodate about 120 kings and presidents at once.

(S) *****Four Seasons, Tevkifhane Sokak 1, t 0212 638 8200, *www. fourseasons.com/istanbul*. A former prison is an unlikely location for Istanbul's most exclusive hotel, and this Ottoman building must surely have been the prettiest prison in the world, painted yellow ochre and decorated with turquoise and cobalt-blue floral painted Kütahya porcelain tiles. These features were preserved during its recent conversion into a hotel, although the architects deemed it necessary to add some space-age smoked glass walkways to the façade. Many of the 65 luxurious rooms look onto the courtyard, planted with an inviting garden. Doubles cost upwards of €350 / 600 YTL, though candidates for a night in the presidential suite should have in the region of 4000 YTL in their slush fund.

(S) Yeşil Ev, Kabasakal Caddesi 5, t 0212 517 6785, *www.istanbulyesilev.com*. Another 19th-century mansion, once the home of an Ottoman paşa. This was one of the first restoration projects of the TTOK, and is a blissful bolt-hole of tranquillity between the Blue Mosque and the Aya Sofya, with a large back garden and rooms with period fittings and original brass beds. Reservations are essential.

Very Expensive

(S) Arena, Küçük Ayasofya Mah., Şehit Mehmet Paşa Yokuşu, Üçler Hamam Sokak 13–15, t 0212 458 0364, *www. arenahotel.com*. The best hotel in this price range in Sultanhamet is also the most difficult to find, tucked away on a quiet street near the Sokullu Camii. The hotel was once a grand mansion where the present owner was born. An oil portrait of her grandfather complete with a fez hangs in the reception. The Arena has an easy elegance and unforced intimacy that most hotels spend a fortune trying to manufacture.

(S) Blue House Mavi Ev, Dalbastı Sokak 14, t 0212 638 9010, *www.bluehouse. com*. Great location behind the Arasta Bazaar, with an unparalleled view of the Blue Mosque from its rooftop restaurant. Rooms are well kept, with large double beds and good ensuite bathrooms. Make the most of the big fluffy bathrobes provided.

(S) İbrahim Paşa, Terzihane Sokak 5, Adliye Yanı, just north of the Hippodrome, t 0212 518 0394, *www.ibrahimpasaotell.com*. With its air of quiet sophistication, this tastefully furnished boutique hotel makes a most refined refuge from the bustle of the city. The central staircase with its original '*cini*' floor tiles is full of character and the diner on the ground floor is very inviting. The minimum requirement for a booking here is three nights, though they may budge on that if they are not busy.

Empress Zoe, Akbıyık Cad. Adliye Sok. No.10, t 0212 518 2504, *www.emzoe. com*. Boutique hotel with a diverse selection of rooms and suites all oozing individual character, decorated with rich kilims, dark wood furnishings and wall hangings. This is the closest an Istanbul hotel gets to a Marrakesh Riad; a pretty courtyard garden completes the picture.

Hotel Spina, Utangac Sok. No.19, t 0212 638 1727, *www.hotelspina.com*. Another Ottoman restoration project with a wooden façade in a great location on one of Sultanahmet's quiet, cobbled stone back streets. Inside the intimate hotel offers clean, comfortable rooms, very helpful staff and a roof terrace restaurant that has stunning views of the Aya Sofya and Blue Mosque. Breakfast, therefore, is pleasant set against this wonderful backdrop, though don't expect much from the instant coffee – better to order Turkish.

Expensive

⭐ Poem >

(S) Poem, Akbıyık Caddesi Terbıyık Sokak 12, **t** 0212 638 9744, *www. hotelpoem.com*. Novelty in Turkish hotels often borders on the tasteless, but not at this hotel, where each small but tastefully furnished room is named after a Turkish poem, a translation of which hangs inside each bedroom door. Set in two buildings in one of Sultanahmet's quiet back streets, the hotel has the added bonus of a small garden.

Pierre Loti Hotel, Piyerloti Cd. No.5, **t** 0212 518 5700, *www.pierreloti hotel.com*. Located near Sinan's famous Çemberlitaş Hamam on the main Divan Yolu opposite the Tomb of Mahmut II. The newly refurbished, modern rooms here even have flat screen TVs. Business travellers are well catered for and there is a decent sauna and hamam in the basement. The lobby bar is a tad stuffy perhaps, resembling an old gentlemen's club, but the friendly and professional staff more than make up for it.

Alp Hotel, Akbıyık Caddesi, Adliye Sokak 4, **t 0212 517 7067, *www. alpguesthouse.com*. Small, cosy, newly refurbished and boasting a rooftop restaurant with fine views over the Bosphorus. You could easily extend breakfast into the afternoon.

Şebnem Hotel, Akbıyık Caddesi Adliye Sokak 1, **t 0212 517 6623, *www.sebnemhotel.com*. Also on the same car-free side street, with a very relaxed atmosphere and welcoming staff. Mornings get off to a good start with a big breakfast on the terrace overlooking the Bosphorus and there is a snug little library downstairs in reception of which the owner is very proud indeed.

Moderate

By comparison with the rest of Turkey, hotels at the lower end of the scale tend to be higher-priced, and proprietors do not worry themselves as much about keeping them attractive. At least there's plenty of choice. In general, the further you are from Aya Sofya, the cheaper the hotel.

Turkuaz, near the Küçük Aya Sofya at Kadırga Cinci Meydanı 36, **t** 0212 518 1897, *www.hotelturkuaz.com*. Hardened nostalgia-seekers should make a beeline for the wonderfully eccentric Turkuaz. The wooden Ottoman mansion oozes charm and has been used a location in several period dramas. Although the tacky reproduction furniture spoils the effect somewhat, all rooms have good bathroom facilities and the Sultan's room is worth the extra liras.

Side Pansiyon, Utangaç Sokak 20, **t** 0212 458 5870, *www.sidehotel.com* (doubles €40 /80 YTL with bathroom, €30 /60 YTL without). Gives you a good range of options to save some lira. Its tile-lined top floor has the best rooms, which are clean if basic and the location is convenient.

Inexpensive

Most of Istanbul's cheap hotels can be found in Sultanahmet, places with long experience of catering to student backpackers.

Sultan Hostel, Akbıyık Caddesi 21, **t** 0212 516 9260, *www.sultanhostel. com* (dorm with bathroom €12/24 YTL per person including breakfast). Friendly, well-heated and popular with backpackers for its convenient location in bar quarter.

Konya Pansiyon, Akbıyık Caddesi Terbıyık Sokak 15/2, **t** 0212 517 6509, *www.konyapansion.net.tc*. A quieter alternative, popular with Japanese travellers. Dorm beds in this basic family-run concern are €9/15 YTL per person. Doubles are €22/44 YTL, except for the one where the bath is almost as big as the bed, which costs more.

Istanbul Hostel, 35 Kutlu Sokak, **t** 0212 516 9380, *www.istanbulhostel.net*. Dorms and double. Generally well maintained and popular with backpackers. Roof terrace with good views across the Bosphorus, and a bar.

Other cheap hotels abound in Sultanahmet and you'll have no trouble finding a place to stay; if you don't find them, they'll find you.

Around Sultanahmet: Sirkeci

Sirkeci Konak, Taya Hatun Sokak No.5, t 0212 528 4344, *www.sirkecikonak.com* (€€€€). Well-appointed doubles and suites overlooking Gülhane Park. Staff are attentive and extremely friendly; there is also a very good restaurant at ground level and a complimentary Turkish bath, sauna and spa to boot. But the real deal clincher has to be the 'pillow menu'.

****Yaşmak Sultan, Ebusuud Caddesi 18–20, t 0212 528 1343, *www.hotel yasmaksultan.com* (€€€€–€€€). Large but with atmosphere – email in advance requesting a discount.

(S) Grand Seigneur Hotel, Nöbethane Caddesi 30, t 0212 512 1034, *www. grandseigneurhotel.com* (€€). An Armenian house from 1903 near the railway tracks has recently been converted into this great value hotel. The décor of this family-run place is on the fussy side, but all rooms have private bathrooms.

Gezginci Hostel, Hocapasa Mah. Serdar Sokak 5, t 0212 527 8516, *www.gezgincihostel.9f.com* (€). An exception to the usual monolingual staff and revolting rooms in Sirkeci cheapies. Rooms are very clean but basic and can be a little noisy at night; toilets and showers are communal.

Beşiktaş

(S) *****Çırağan Saray, Çırağan Caddesi 84, t 0212 258 3377, *www. ciraganpalace.com* (€€€€€ – doubles in the hotel section from 825 YTL, up to 60,000 YTL for the Grand Sultan Suite in the palace section). Near the Dolmabahçe Palace at Beşiktaş, this former palace built by Sultan Abdülaziz gives the Four Seasons in Sultanahmet a run for its money as the city's most sumptuous hotel. Everything you could possibly require from a hotel is here: rooms overlooking the Bosphorus, sauna, hamam and deluxe suites in the sultan's apartments (the furnishings are relatively modern; the palace was gutted by fire long ago).

Taksim/Beyoğlu

Lush, Sıraselviler No.12, off Taksim Square, t 0212 243 9595, *www. lushhotel.com* (€€€€€). More of a design statement than a regular hotel, with 22 different rooms each with its own uniquely designed bathroom, and a matching brasserie if you want to sample lush food and designer cakes.

****Pera Palace, Meşrutiyet Caddesi 98/100, Harbiye, t 251 4560, *www.perapalace.com* (€€€€€, see p.147). Although it's closed for restoration until 2009, it would be a crime not to include the magnificent Pera Palace, the city's most famous hotel. Convenient for the sights, and affording a lavish view over the Golden Horn, this great Edwardian pile was built by the Wagons-Lits Company for their passengers on the Orient Express.

The Anemon Galata, Büyükhendek Caddesi, Küledibi, t 0212 293 2343, *www.anemonhotels.com* (€€€€€–€€€€). A wonderful historic building located beside the Galata Tower boasting breathtaking views of the Golden Horn (especially at night) from its rooftop restaurant. With just 21 well-appointed rooms and 6 suites, this is an intimate retreat in a pretty cool neighbourhood. A fine collection of antique furniture decorates its lobby and extends into the rooms whilst the buffet breakfast is more impressive than many of its similarly priced counterparts.

****Richmond, İstiklâl Caddesi No.445, t 0212 252 5460, *www. richmondhotels.com.tr* (€€€€). A thoroughly modern establishment; the rooms are smart with air-conditioning and other amenities but location is still the main selling point here. There is also a 'business club' on the 5th and 6th floors, with fine executive room.

***Büyük Londra (*né* 'Grand Hôtel de Londres' in 1892), Meşrutiyet, t 0212 245 0670, *www.londrahotel.net* (€€€–€€). This was the second choice to the Pera Palace in the old days. Now it's a faded beauty, with rooms in dire, dire need of renovation. Still, it's a piece of history and worthwhile if you get a room with a balcony and a view over the Golden Horn. The reception and hallways are filled with old cast-iron stoves and the bar is still a favourite with funky Stamboullus.

There are any number of hotels in the middle range around Taksim Square, but most of these are purely for businessmen, and not distinguished in any way. There are also lots of cheapies.

World House Hostel, Galipdede Cad. No. 85, **t** 0212 293 5520 *www.world houseistanbul.com* (doubles €40 /80 YTL, dorm €14 /28 YTL). Clean and simple rooms in a grand old stone building perfectly located near Galata Tower, with a cosy café downstairs. The well-travelled owners are friendly and on the ball.

***Villa**, Balıkpazarı Topçekenler Sokak 10, **t** 0212 252 2637 (€). Of the many unappetizing choices near the İstiklâl Caddesi, this is better-kept than the rest, which isn't saying much. Tiny rooms with TV and private bathrooms big enough for one leg at a time.

Edirnekapı

***Hotel Kariye**, Kariye Camii Sokak 18, **t** 0212 534 8414, *www.kariyehotel. com* (€€€). By far the best choice in this part of town is another tastefully restored Ottoman mansion beside the Church of St Saviour in Chora. An additional bonus is the highly acclaimed Asitane restaurant (*see* p.167) on the lower ground floor.

The Asian Side

Ajia Hotel, Kanlica, **t** 0216 413 9300, *www.ajiahotel.com* (€€€€€). The grandeur of the building, a stunning Ottoman mansion, and its waterfront location are the key selling points here. Jaw-dropping vistas, exquisite minimalist design touches and a sense of tranquillity ensure its popularity with those seeking a city haven. The hotel will arrange boat transfers to the European shore, but don't expect to reach the major touristic sights very quickly.

Princes' Islands

One serendipitous alternative to city hotels, for anyone who doesn't mind a ferry ride commute for sightseeing, is to stay on Büyükada, the largest of the Princes' Islands.

***Splendid Palas**, 53 Nisan Caddesi, Büyükada, **t** 0216 382 6950, *www. splendidhotel.net* (€€€). This domed hotel has pretty, old-fashioned rooms with balconies, and a small pool; built in 1908, it's pleasant if a little faded.

***Merit Halkı Palas**, Heybeliada, **t** 0216 351 0025, *www.merithotels.com* (€€€). Used to belong to the Orthodox seminary; now it is a pretty, restored hotel with lovely rooms and a pool.

Eating Out in Istanbul

Eating in Istanbul is a pure delight; the city has attracted the best of the country's chefs and many places still serve old Turkish specialities, almost impossible to find elsewhere in the country. Most of the finest restaurants are now out in the newer quarters north of Taksim Square, or along the Bosphorus, but you're not likely to starve in old Stamboul or Beyoğlu.

If you're looking for something special beyond what we offer below, you'll probably have to ask somebody, because restaurants in this city – beyond simple *lokantas* – can be surprisingly hard to find, tucked away on back alleys and in second-storey rooms. Ask the desk clerk where he'd go if he were you; maybe he'll tell you.

But who needs restaurants? It is entirely possible (and if you like to eat, almost inevitable) to spend the whole day grazing out on the pavements. There are the ubiquitous *simit* vendors – and with experience you'll learn that no two *simitler* are alike; some are divine, others can be taken home as souvenir doorstops. *Büfeler* ('buffets', another French word) and street vendors decorate every street corner; they offer tasty *döner*, nuts and pumpkin seeds, bowls of lentil soup, *börekler*, puddings, cookies, baked potatoes with dressing or roast corn on the cob, not to mention an infinity of kebabs, fish sandwiches around the docks, and lots more. Between each indulgence you can sit down for a fast glass of tea. And then there are the fantastic pastry shops.

Though most places accept **credit cards**, the cheaper establishments may not; ask first. Also, be aware that due to heavy government taxation, wine is surprisingly expensive.

Around Sultanahmet

Beside Balıkcı Sabahattin, it is hard to find anything really distinguished in Sultanahmet. We have therefore broadened the area to include options in Sirkeci, Eminönü and the Bazaar.

There are several good *börek* houses near the railway station, where a plate of *börekler* and a cup of tea make a lovely mid-morning snack. The lower deck of the Galata Bridge has several inexpensive fish restaurants and cafés. And you can still find fishing boats tied up along the docks on either side, where they grill the fish right after they catch it, and sell you a very tasty and very filling sandwich for next to nothing.

(★) **Balıkcı Sabahattin >**

Balıkcı Sabahattin, Hasankuyu Sok. 2, near the Cevriağa School in Cankurtaran, t 0212 458 1824 (€€€). A true local classic, popular with tourists and Stamboullus alike and the best option for seafood in this part of town, with a delicious *meze* selection and mains that get right down to business. The old neighbourhood adds atmosphere in the garden whilst the creaky Ottoman house provides the romance inside.

Rami, Utagaç Sokak, t 0212 517 6593, *www.ramirestaurant.com* (€€€). Serves Ottoman-influenced dishes on antique platters and has wonderfully quirky period décor that can occasionally outshine the food itself. Reserve a balcony side table on the terrace for a view of the Blue Mosque.

Sarnıç, on Soğukçeşme Sokak behind the Aya Sofya, t 0212 512 4291 (€€€). A truly remarkable restaurant sited underground in what was once a Byzantine cistern. Converted by TTOK, it is furnished in a strange baronial style with much wrought-iron work and an open fire big enough to roast a Volkswagen. Such surroundings don't come cheap – but one comes here more for the setting than the cuisine.

Giritli, Keresteci Hakki Sokak, Cankurtaran, t 0212 458 2270 (€€). New on the block but already a hit, serves Mediterranean dishes, with a large selection of *meze* and fish. This is a family operation, with acclaimed branches in Ankara and Bodrum. The venue is an added bonus: an old Ottoman house with a spacious walled garden.

Borsa, next to the walkway over Reşadiye Caddesi near the Galata bridge (€€). A chain, but it works hard to present typical kebabs and other dishes, such as *lahana dolma* (stuffed cabbage), with a little more care than the usual *lokantas*; good with soups and desserts. They are becoming quite popular – and they take credit cards. Other branches are on İstiklâl Cad., in Fenerbahçe, Eminönü and in Cüfü Kirdex Congress Centre.

Dârüzziyâfe, t 0212 511 8414, housed in the Süleymaniye's *külliye* (€€). When you visit the Süleymaniye Mosque, try and plan lunch or dinner at this thoroughly modern place with very refined cooking. The speciality of the house is spicy chicken in pastry called *tavuklu kolböreği*.

Almedros, Divan Yolu Cad., Hoca Rüstem Sok. No: 7, t 0212 522 8356 (€€–€). A good little bistro that also serves salads, pasta and pizza if you are all kebabbed out!

Hamdi Et Lokantasi, Kalcin Sokak 17, Tahmis Caddesi, t 0212 528 0390 (€). A popular terrace restaurant with views across the Golden Horn. Specializes in east Anatolian kebabs and does a fine job too. One visit may not be enough; don't miss it.

Paşazade, Sirkeci İbn-I Kemal Caddesi 13, t 0212 513 3757, *www.pasazade.com* (€). The theme park décor of Ottoman house façades may not be to everyone's taste but the food here is serious, realistically priced and very good value. Their excellent website has photos of the entire menu.

Havuzlu Lokanta, in the Grand Bazaar (western side, on Gani Çelebi Sokak), next to the post office, t 0212 527 3346 (€). Has a good range of Turkish food. Havuzlu means 'with pool', for the small marble pool outside.

Pudding Shop, Divan Yolu (€). The old 1960s international rendezvous point for hippy travellers on the overland route to Asia. It's inexpensive, and you'll get a free postcard, but it's lost a lot of its character. There's a wide choice of dishes; the *sütlaç* is an absolute dream.

Çemberli Safran Sofrası, opposite the Burnt Column, Vezirhan Caddesi 18 (€). The perfect place to refuel before or after plunging into the nearby Covered Bazaar, offering a wide selection of stews and kebabs at lunchtime only.

Subaşı, Nuruosmaniye Caddesi near the market gate (€). Alternatively, try lunch here; tasty *lokanta* cooking means it's always crowded.

Cennet, on the north side of the Divan Yolu at Çemberlitaş (€). Good for a snack or light lunch after sightseeing or shopping; it's touristy but atmospheric, decorated with kilims.

Küçük Hüdadad, hidden inside the Şapçı Han directly across from the market on Kömür Bekır Sokak (€). The best value *lokanta* around the Spice Market is also the hardest to find.

Konyalı's, on Mimar Ketnalettin Cad. 5. Valuf Han No. 332, opposite the railway station (€). Long established in Istanbul and has a fine reputation for kebabs and *börekler*. There is another branch in the Topkapı Palace.

(★) Doğa Balık >>

(★) Asitane
Restaurant >

Kariye/Edirnekapı

Asitane Restaurant, attached to the Kariye Hotel, Kariye Camii Sokak 18, **t** 0212 635 7997, *www.asitane restaurant.com* (€€€–€€). With beautifully contemporary décor, real understated elegance and majestic dishes, this has to be one of the culinary gems of Istanbul. Ottoman cuisine is a term often abused by lesser restaurants claiming authenticity but using ingredients the Ottomans never even had. Asitane is the real deal, faithful to the actual ingredients that made up the core of Ottoman cuisine. The owners spent months reviving cooking techniques from original palace archives, some dating back hundreds of years. Unless you are staying in the connected hotel, getting there will involve a taxi ride, but it is well worth the trip.

Karaköy

Liman Lokanta, upstairs in the Turkish Maritime Lines' terminal building, **t** 0212 292 3992 (€€€–€€). By the cruise ship dock, this is a long-time

seafood favourite. An old-fashioned place with a marvellous view of Stamboul, it has recently been restored to its Art Deco glory.

Beyoğlu/Taksim

Galata Tower, **t** 0212 293 8183, *www. galatatower.net* (€€€€). The attraction here is the view, and the evening belly-dancing – touristy but fun.

Four Seasons (Dört Mevsim, not to be confused with the hotel of the same name in Sultanahmet), at the Tünel end of İstiklâl Caddesi, **t** 0212 293 3941 (€€€). Has charm, sophistication, French onion soup and a very English sweet trolley.

360 Istanbul, Misir Apt 311, İstiklâl Caddesi, **t** 0212 251 1042, *www. 360istanbul.com* (€€€). This is where the fashionable crowd hang out, a funky rooftop restaurant and bar with resident DJs and stunning 360-degree views of the city. In the summer be sure to drop in for a cocktail; the food itself, a fusion of Thai, Japanese and Turkish, is so so, but the venue more than makes up for that. Reserve.

Doğa Balık, Akarsu Yokuşu Caddesi No.46, **t** 0212 293 9143, *www. dogabalik.com.tr/en* (€€€). The entrance is through the lobby of Villa Zurich Hotel, where you take the elevator to this rooftop seafood gem. The fish is faultless, but the *meze* selection steals the show; including some 30 different varieties of greens made from herbs and plants you did not even know were edible.

For a moderate meal, the easiest thing is to take yourself to **Nevizade Sokak/Kalyoncukulluğu Caddesi**, behind the Balıkpazarı, where there are scores of simple restaurants with outside tables in the 20–30 YTL range, most of which specialize in seafood. **Çiçek Pasajı** (*see* p.148) is full of restaurants, their benches and tables jostling so much for the limited space under the vaults that the whole place feels like one huge bawdy refectory. The **Pavyon** on the inside corner at No.11 (€€) is the oldest establishment, now run by two of the founder's grandsons, although the food and ambience elsewhere in the *pasaj* are equally good. Check the price of your fish before you order.

Asır, Kalyoncukullğu, is one of the most authentic surviving *meyhaneler*, offering plates of *meze* and fish.

Hacı Abdullah Lokantası, near the Ağa Camii off İstiklâl Caddesi at Sakızağacı Caddesi 17, **t** 0212 293 8581, *www. haciabdullah.com.tr* (€€). This bastion of traditional Ottoman cooking, founded in 1888, has kept its prices low, with a good selection of vegetarian options to offset the meat dishes; no alcohol.

Refik Restaurant, Sofyalı Sokak 10, *www.refikrestaurant.com* (€€). On a back street towards the Tünel area, the gravel-voiced Refik Arslan has been holding court here since 1954. During his reign, the walls have been covered with sketches, notes, posters and obscure photos which you could spend all evening trying to make some kind of sense of. You're better off concentrating on the overflowing drinks and excellent dishes from the Black Sea Region.

Yakup 2, on Asmalımescit Sokak near the upper end of the Tünel (€€). A lively, fun place, a combination neighbourhood *lokanta* and *meyhane* for the artsy Beyoğlu set.

Zencefil, Kurabiye Sokak No.8, **t** 0212 244 8234 (€). One of the few dedicated vegetarian restaurants with home cooked food in a colourful rustic setting. Look out for the daily specials written on the blackboard and the home-made lemonade with mint.

Elsewhere in Istanbul, cheap eating is reduced to the simple *lokantas* that are everywhere. Beyoğlu and Taksim have plenty – one on every corner on busy streets.

Bereket Halk Döner, 20 İstiklal Caddesi, **t** 0212 243 6759 (€). For some loose change you can sink your teeth into a plate of whatever that thing grilling in the window is (a brontosaurus leg?).

Fehmi Baba, on the northern end of Meşrutiyet Caddesi, **t** 0212 293 9326 (€). Tasty *İskender kebap* and other kebabs from 12 YTL.

Up the Bosphorus: The European Side

Poseidon, Cevdet Paşa Cad., No.58, **t** 0212 263 3823, *www.poseidonfish.*

⭐ **Adem Baba** >>

com (€€€€). Popular with the big spenders, the waterfront location could not be more perfect at this seafood tavern in the trendy Bebek neighbourhood.

Park Fora, Muallim Naci Cad. 134, Kuruçeşme, **t** 0212 265 5063, *www.parkfora.com* (€€€€). A fantastic selection of seafood and appetizers to accompany the tasty Bosphorus views from its seafront terrace.

Ortaköy is a pedestrianized square on the Bosphorus shore with dozens of moderately priced restaurants on the seafront and around its cobbled stone alleys. The combination of traditional *meze* restaurants, trendy cafés, international cuisine and great street food means you are never short of choice. It gets particularly crowded on weekends when there is also a small flea market.

İlhami'nin Yeri, Osmanzade Sokak 6 (€€). Among the best of restaurants packed into the pedestrianized roads leading off from the Ortaköy Camii. The *mezes* and fish are always fresh and the chicken kebabs are amongst the most succulent you'll savour. 40 YTL for the full works including wine, less if you let your tongue loose on a *şalgam suyu* – a crimson tang of turnip juice – instead.

The House Café, Salhane Sokak 1, Ortaköy, **t** 0212 227 2699 (€€). With its effective menu and superb interior design, the success of their first venture in Nişantaşı has led to several more branches around town, of which this one, on the shores of the Bosphorus, is particularly popular in summer. Everything in their Turkish and international repertoire hits the spot.

Adem Baba, Beyazgül Caddesi No.2, **t** 0212 263 2933, *www.adembaba.com* (€). An intimate local fish specialist in Arnavutköy. The reasonably priced menu is limited to seafood and side salads, service is fast, the food is excellent and the surroundings with netting and fishing paraphernalia add real atmosphere. Their legendary fish soup (5 YTL) is only served on Sundays; if you find yourself in this part of town, don't miss it.

Up the Bosphorus: The Asian Side

There is a huge number of seafood restaurants on the coastal Sahil Yolu from Üsküdar to Kanlıca, in particular the fishing villages of Çengelköy where the waterfront is full of them.

Körfez, near the Bosphorus bridge at 78 Körfez Caddesi, Kanlıca (Asian shore), t 0216 413 4314, *www.korfez.com* (€€€€). A good view, and lovely seafood *börekler*. This place, as well as the myriad other seafront restaurants along the straits, prides itself on local favourites such as sea bass baked in salt (not too salty when it's done, don't worry); expensive as they are, they're always crowded.

★ **Kanaat** >>

Villa Bosphorus, Albay Hüsamettin Ertürk Sk. No. 13, t 0216 422 80 80, (€€€€–€€€). With views looking out across the Bosphorus bridge and the European side of the city and a good selection of seasonal catch.

★ **Çiya Sofrasi** >

Çiya Sofrasi, Güneşlibahçe Sokak No.43, Kadıköy, t 0216 418 5115, *www.ciya.com.tr* (€€€–€€). Though a local, modest-looking place, Çiya has to be of the best options in Asian Istanbul, getting deep into Anatolian regional cuisine and presenting it with real passion. The diverse menu changes with the seasons and the choice is staggering. Visit their website and you will see what we mean, but choosing a dish isn't too difficult – just point, and the staff will be happy to guide you.

Çamlıca Café (€€). If you have a car, try to make it up to the Çamlıca hill park to this great café that serves good, typical Turkish cooking with the grandest view of all views of Istanbul.

If you want to see what the other Bosphorus villages were like 20 years ago, take the ferry to the end, to **Anadolu Kavağı**, the only one that hasn't been totally swallowed up by villas yet (though by the time you read this it may be too late). All around the waterfront are small fish restaurants with outside tables where you can get a sweet and simple dinner for about 30 YTL.

Haydarpaşa railway station (€€). While in Asia, you could do a lot worse than dine at the unnamed restaurant here with its tiled and panelled walls and respectful, uniformed waiters. You may never dine at another railway station like it.

Kadife Chalet, on Kadife Sokak, t 0216 347 8596 (€€). If you're anywhere nearby, it's well worth an evening excursion to Kadıköy, the neighbourhood south of Haydarpaşa, for a dinner here. The restaurant shares space with an art and crafts gallery in an old Ottoman house.

Üsküdar and Kadıköy are both full of good chow houses.

Kanaat, Selmanıpak Caddesi 25, Üsküdar, t 0216 533 3791 (€). Has a wide selection of classics on display for you to point and choose from and since 1933 has specialized in gorgeous, sticky desserts that are worth crossing continents for.

Arabın Yeri/Huzur, 20 Salacak İskelesi, t 0216 333 3157 (€). The coastal road in Salacak just south of Üsküdar, facing the Kızkulesi (Leander's Tower), is a good place to look for restaurants. Just off it, this is a favourite neighbourhood seafood spot, with a view over the straits. *Open until midnight.*

Princes' Islands

Almost all the island restaurants are located along the main promenade where mainland ferries dock.

Milano, Büyükada, t 0216 382 6352 (€€€–€€). Try this long-established waterfront restaurant, which serves a truly delectable prawn casserole and other dishes.

Heybeli Ada Mavi Restaurant, Büyükada (€€). Serves the usual seafood standards but with a touch of added creativity. Don't miss the grilled sardine special when in season.

Birtat, 10 Gülistan Caddesi, Büyükada (€). Kebabs and some seafood at relatively cheap prices.

Alibaba, also on 10 Gülistan Caddesi, Büyükada (€). Another cheap and friendly favourite.

Kumkapı

In Byzantine times, the Kumkapı quarter was the fisherman's port of the capital. Today, just by coincidence, this busy neighbourhood on the Marmara, south of the Covered Bazaar, has become popular with the

Stamboullu for its seafood restaurants. There are dozens of them on the pedestrian streets around **Telli Odalar Sokak** and **Arapzade Ahmet Sokak** at Kumkapı's centre. None really stands out, but at most you can get a fine fish dinner for 40 YTL or under; strolling around looking for something that catches your fancy (all the seafood will be on display in glass-fronted coolers) is a pleasant way to build up your appetite.

Istanbul Restaurant, Gedik Paşa Caddesi (€€). One of the several less expensive places on this street; outside tables amidst swarming street life and convivial waiters. Pick a good fish out from the cooler, or dine for less on soup and kebabs.

⭐ Miss Pizza >>

Beyti, Orman Sokak 8. near the airport, t 0212 663 2990, *www.beyti.com* (€€). Outside town, there's always this enormous, award-winning restaurant complete with heliport, three kitchens, and the much-imitated *Beyti kebap. Open until midnight.*

Alternative Cuisines

Oriental and Fusion

Changa, Siraselviler Caddesi No.47, Taksim, t 0212 251 7064, *www.changa-istanbul.com* (€€€€). Under the supervision of renowned chef Peter Gordon, this is the real destination for modern fusion, though it doesn't come cheap. The diverse, Asian-inspired menu has received rave reviews from just about every food magazine under the sun.

Wan-na, Meşrutiyet Caddesi No.151, t 0212 243 1794 (€€€€). Specializing in Vietnamese, Thai, Chinese and Japanese cuisine in a very fashionable setting. *Open Oct–May.*

Pera Thai, Meşrutiyet Caddesi No.134, t 0212 245 5725, *www.perathai.com* (€€€). The most authentic Thai in town, with a long list of awards and recommendations.

⭐ Baylan >>

The Great Hong Kong, Dünya Sağlık Sokak 27, Gümüşsuyu, t 0212 252 4268 (€€€). Has great dishes that, they say, carry the Chinese seal of approval.

Indian

Dubb, İncili Cavuş Sokak No.10, Sultanahment, t 0212 513 7308 (€€€). Currently the best Indian restaurant

in town – so say the Indian tourists in any case.

Russian

Rejans, hidden away on Emir Nevruz Sokak, off İstiklâl Caddesi near the Panaya Isodion, t 0212 244 1610, *www.rejansrestaurant.com* (€€€). Favourite of Atatürk's, founded by White Russians in the 1920s, and once the most fashionable spot in town, Rejans has declined a bit, but the Russian cuisine, the lemon vodka and the tatty ambience keep it popular. For the fine wood-panelled interior and the pre-Great War atmosphere of hushed stealth, you pay around 40 YTL.

Italian

Miss Pizza, Havyar Sokak 7, Cihangir, t 0212 251 3279 (€€€). Great for pizza, very popular with locals and resident foreigners.

Pastry Shops

Don't forget to save a major part of your calorie budget for these, for Istanbul is one of the world's capitals of sweet indulgence. You'll never be more than a block away from a place where you can sit down with a glass of tea and a slice of baklava at almost any hour of the day. In addition, the big hotels here have always had a tradition of keeping a master pastry chef in the kitchens of their elegant cafés. But it isn't just about baklava and other Turkish treats. With its cosmopolitan tradition (and its incurable sweet tooth), this city has embraced everything that's tasty, from Central European tortes to French *pâtisserie* and chocolates or American cheesecake.

Café Lebon, in the Hotel Richmond. Locally famous for its fruit pies.

İnci, İstiklâl Caddesi No.124. Renowned for profiteroles (they claim to have invented them).

Baylan, Muvakkithane Caddesi No.19, t 0216 346 6350, *www.baylan pastanesi.com*. A Kadıköy (Asian shore) sweets classic. If you make the journey to Çiya for lunch (*see* p.169), then save your dessert stomach for Baylan; few compare.

Some of the luxury hotel cafés roll out their finest confections for a five o'clock tea: the Çırağan Palace's

Gazebo Café and the Café Marmara, in the Marmara Hotel on Taksim Square. For overwhelming cream and chocolate spectaculars with the Central European touch, there is the Café Wien located in the Reassurans Pasajı, Teşvikiye, or the Pâtisserie Gezi, on İnönü Caddesi off Taksim Square.

Entertainment and Nightlife in Istanbul

Festivals

The big cultural centres plus other spots, including historic sites like the Aya İrene church at Topkapı, host events during the **Istanbul Festival**. Although not yet in the league of Edinburgh or Salzburg, this has an impressively ambitious programme and tickets cost well under half what you'd pay for equivalent performances in London or New York. The Istanbul Festival begins in the second half of April each year with a **film festival** showing over 150 movies in two weeks. **Theatre** takes over in the second half of May, when the curtain is raised on 40 plays. **Dance** follows in June, mostly of the Western classical variety, but with some performances of Turkish dancing. A **jazz** festival rounds off the proceedings in the first half of July. As if this weren't enough, the **Istanbul Biennial** is held from mid-September to mid-November in odd years (2009, 2011), and has a growing reputation for bucking trends and showcasing new artists. The Festival and the Biennial are both run by the **Istanbul Foundation for Culture and Arts**, **t** 0212 293 3133.

The black sheep of the film festivals is **!F Istanbul** in February, *www.ifistanbul.com/en*, showcasing independent cinema from around the globe with workshops, club nights and various other live events.

Cinemas

Istanbul is well endowed with cinemas, and each district has at least one, usually with several screens; most of the film palaces are on İstiklâl or around Taksim Square. English-language films are seldom dubbed. Try to check what's showing just before setting off, lest you fall prey to the irritating habit of last-minute programme changes.

Concerts

Istanbul has a full schedule of concerts, opera and ballet; the two big venues are the **Atatürk Cultural Centre** (known to locals simply as **AKM** – Atatürk Kültür Merkezi) on Taksim Square, and the **Cemal Reşit Rey Concert Hall (CRR)** in Harbiye. Genuine Turkish traditional and classical music is a bit harder to find; you'll get some on TRT3, 88.2 FM; beyond that consult *The Guide* or the tourist office for schedules.

Nightlife

Over the last decade, nightlife has witnessed a renaissance. Other than the glamorous open air nightclubs on the Bosphorus, most venues are concentrated in the Beyoğlu area. Istanbul caters to all musical tastes. The large commercial clubs play techno trash and house music but smaller, independent venues are blossoming too, with jazz, blues, reggae and world music also making a stand. For the latest on what's on where, a copy of *Time Out Istanbul*, in English, will prove invaluable.

A word of warning for males only. In the side-streets of İstiklâl Caddesi and Taksim Square are 'nightclubs', usually called a *pavyon* or a revue, that advertise steamy belly-dance shows. Don't go into any of these clip joints, no matter how ingratiating the tout who tries to entice you may be (sometimes, it's a man who befriends you on the street and invites you for a drink). It's the old, old story; you'll be entrapped, required to buy drinks at 100 times the going rate, and you'll leave with your wallet empty. Don't imagine you can sweet-talk your way out of this; you can't.

Reina, Muallim Nacı Caddesi No.44, **t** 0212 259 5919, *www.reina-com.tr*. The most famous super-club on the Bosphorus waterfront caters to an impeccably dressed pretty crowd with bulging wallets and fancy cars. The views and setting are second to none but you need to scrub up to have any chance of getting in.

Babylon, Şehbender Sokak, No.3, **t** 0212 292 7368, *www.babylon.com.tr*. If you are serious about your music then all roads lead here, the coolest place in town for gigs from the jazzier side of the spectrum. Baba Zula and Burhan Öçal are regular performers.

Klub Karaoke, Zambak Sokak 7, Taksim, **t** 0212 293 7639, *www.klub-karaoke. com*. This intimate venue has various rooms all with chic décor and caters to a strong following of locals who love to sing. If you like what is being sung, the atmosphere is great; if you don't, then choose a song and step up to the mic.

Turkish Theme Nights

These touristy showcases can actually be a lot of fun. Most will have an all-inclusive price that includes your meal and the entertainment.

Kervansaray, Cumhuriyet Caddesi 30, **t** 0212 247 1630. The cost, with a meal, all drinks, a belly-dance show, a singer, dancing and maybe a magician, will be in the region of 100 YTL. *Open 9pm–midnight.*

Orient House, Tiyatro Caddesi near Beyazıt Square, **t** 0212 517 6163, *www. orienthouseistanbul.com*. Similar; the only cabaret on the Stamboul side.

Galata Tower, t 0212 293 8183, *www. galatatower.net*. At the top of the tower is a restaurant which puts on a floor show that includes folk dancing. The clientele is composed almost entirely of tour groups, but at least the view from the tower is good. The restaurant opens at 8pm, and the programme starts at 9.50 and finishes at midnight. The fixed, all-in price is about 80 YTL with show. Book.

Drinking Holes

Çiçek Pasajı (*see* p.148) has long been the traditional place to start an evening's revelry, and many people still turn up in the early evening before moving on to a nightclub. Just as popular are the *meyhaneler* (traditional Turkish taverns) of neighbouring **Nevizade Sokak** and **Kalyoncukulluğu Sokak**. You'll also find lots of bars, some with live rock or Turkish folk music, in the streets off **İstiklâl Caddesi**.

5. Kat (The 5th Floor), Soğancı Sokak No.7, Cihangir, **t** 0212 293 3774, *www. 5kat.com*. One of the most popular

roof bars in town. The fantastically chic décor with deep red and purple fabrics, hanging beads and old chandeliers, together with its excellent hospitality, have won this venue a lot of fans. The restaurant is also good.

Hayal Kahvesi, also just off İstiklâl on Büyük Parmakkapı Sokak, *www.hayal kahvesibeyoglu.com*. A sort of coffee house-cum-music venue with a good programme of rock and jazz groups.

Nardis Jazz Club, near the Galata Tower at Kuledibi Sokak No.14. Jazz is king; live bands five nights a week.

Kaktüs Kahvesi, İmam Adnan Sokak 4. Head here for an evening at a lower volume setting, where, as in cafés the world over, customers sip coffee and wine while poring over newspapers and magazines.

Pano's, near Çiçek Pasajı at Kalyoncu Kulluğu Caddesi 4. Wine by the barrel; it frequently resembles a *bon viveurs'* convention and is cacophonous when heaving – which is most nights.

Some of the luxury hotels around Taksim and the Bosphorus, such as the Hilton and the Marmara Istanbul, have rooftop bars with a view: **Tepe Bar**, Marmara Istanbul, is one of them and has standard lounge singers. **Lâleazar Bar** atop the Hilton offers a view and a happy hour.

Around **Sultanahmet**, options for an evening's entertainment include:

Café Meşale, near the front entrance to the Blue Mosque along the Hippodrome. On fine evenings, this outdoor spot can be enchanting. Its low chairs and tables under the trees offer a refuge for *nargile* smokers and postcard-writers alike. You'll find many Turks sipping tea and coffee (no alcohol is served around the mosque) and swaying to the live music alongside the tourists.

Yeşil Ev Hotel, Kabasakal Caddesi No.5, Sultanahmet, **t** 0212 517 6785. The courtyard of this hotel with its delightful conservatory is a great spot for a drink away from the crowds.

Sultan Pub, opposite the Hippodrome. Tries hard to create a dimly lit 'Rick's Bar'-type ambience that is spoiled by Bogart having to share the wall with James Dean and Marilyn Monroe.

Thrace, the Marmara and Bursa

Thrace, the region Turkey shares rather uncomfortably with Greece and Bulgaria, has long held a special place in Turkish dreams and aspirations. The tribes out of the East called it Rumelia, the 'land of Rome' that they had heard so much of and so ardently sought.

Although it comprises only three per cent of Turkish territory, modern Turks, from Atatürk to the current government, pin their hopes on its being an especially magnetic chunk of land, capable of pulling the rest of Turkey away from the insoluble squabbles of the Middle East into the European Union and the democratic traditions of the West.

08

Don't miss

⭐ **Great mosques and greased wrestlers**
Edirne p.175

⭐ **The 'Green City', the first Ottoman capital**
Bursa p.189

⭐ **A touch of the Alps**
Uludağ p.199

⭐ **Gardens, ruins and beautiful tiles**
İznik p.203

See map overleaf

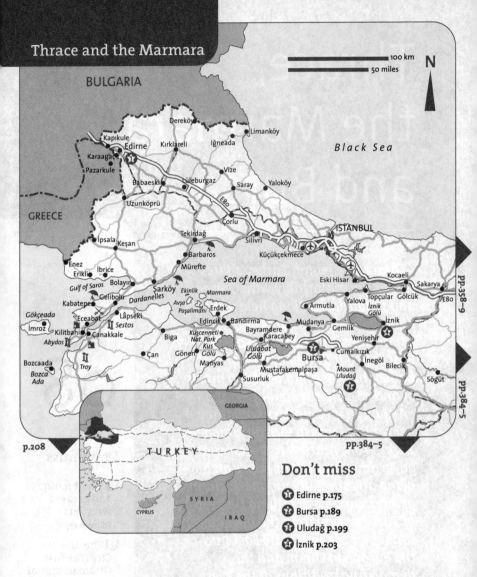

Don't miss

- ⭐ Edirne p.175
- ⭐ Bursa p.189
- ⭐ Uludağ p.199
- ⭐ İznik p.203

p.208

pp.384-5

pp.358-9

pp.384-5

Ancient Thrace was occupied by antiquity's most skilled horsemen, who had a special knack for splendid barbaric goldwork and uncouth religious practices. Unfortunately for them, Thrace was on the principal highway of conquerors bent on Europe or Asia. Xerxes and Alexander came this way, while the Romans, who went about their conquering more systematically, bisected it with a highway, the Via Egnatia (the modern Londra Asfaltı) to speed their legions to and from the eastern marches. Many towns of Thrace's three provinces began life as Roman or Ottoman garrisons, and have known other armies as well – Goths, Bulgars, Avars, Crusaders, Russians and Greeks. Battles that have changed history have taken place here, or offshore in the Dardanelles, from the days of Homer to the First World War. Until recently, much of Thrace was an off-limits military zone.

Yet Thrace is a quiet, almost lonely place, with few monuments to show for the great events that have occurred on its soil. Most of the land is a rolling plain, emerald green in spring, but hot and humid in summer, and snow-blasted in winter. As for the Marmara, it looks promising on the map, but don't expect anything like the sunny blue Aegean. In this part of the world, every corner seems to have its own climate, landscapes and moods, and the Marmara's tend to be somewhat sombre, more like the Black Sea than the Mediterranean. Nevertheless, there is some agreeable scenery in out-of-the-way places: the little-known Marmara Islands, around Lake İznik, and especially up on Mount Uludağ, where there is good skiing, just a cable-car ride away from the centre of one of Turkey's most engaging cities, the old Ottoman capital of Bursa.

Edirne

 Edirne

Thrace's one real attraction is its largest town, old Adrianople, with a population of around 120,000, four hours from Istanbul, near the Greek and Bulgarian frontiers. If you're driving from the north to Turkey, it's on the way; if you're coming from Greece, it's worth the detour from the main coastal route, for you won't find a better introduction to Turkey and its architecture – and to greased wrestling, the one thing that keeps Edirne's juices flowing these days. Although the city once served as the Ottoman capital, it has few modern industries to keep it growing and prosperous, and today looks more or less the same as it did a hundred years ago.

History

Hadrian founded Adrianople in AD 125, on the site of Thracian *Uscudama* (Hellenistic *Oresteia*). Almost exactly 200 years later, his successor Constantine the Great fought a major battle nearby, a prelude to his capture of Byzantium; a thousand years later, history repeated itself when Murat won it for the Ottomans in 1361. Since the seat of the Ottoman Empire in its early days was wherever the sultan had his divan, Edirne hosted the Ottoman court while the sultan waited for Constantinople to fall into his hands. If there was trouble in the east, the sultan stayed in Bursa; if he was interested in expanding the boundaries of Rumelia, he stayed in Edirne. Although this shuttling about ended when Mehmet the Conqueror took Constantinople, the sultans continued to bestow lavish imperial monuments on their first European capital until it reached the height of its beauty and importance in the late 16th century, before later wars and natural disasters took their toll.

Getting to and around Edirne

Edirne is linked to Istanbul by the E80 **motorway**. Several **coach** lines compete on the 2½hr Edirne–Istanbul run, and both frequency and service are excellent; this is the run on which you're most likely to get tea and cakes and television. **Radar, t** 0212 658 0970, and **Edirne Birlik, t** 0212 658 1901, are the two main coach lines.

It's rather difficult to get anywhere else from Edirne. There are two **buses** a day for Çanakkale. Bus connections to Tekirdağ are more frequent, although the onward trip by **boat** to Marmara is erratic in winter. Ring ahead to the Tekirdağ tourist office. To reach the isolated beaches at Erikli or Enez, catch a bus from Edirne or Istanbul to Keşan. Minibuses and local buses run from there to these proto-resorts.

The **rail** service from Istanbul's Sirkeci Station somehow takes 6hrs, so the bus is by far the best bet. The daily **Balkan Express** from Istanbul stops in Edirne on its way to Sofia. Edirne's rail station is out near the *otogar* to the southeast of the centre.

Both the stations are too far to walk with luggage, and you may want to take a **dolmuş** or **taxi** into the centre, although be warned that the metered taxi fares in Edirne come as a shock after Istanbul.

Edirne has Bulgarian (on Talatpaşa Caddesi) and Greek (next to the police station on Cumhuriyet Caddesi) **consulates** to help with any anticipated border difficulties. There is an hourly **dolmuş** service from the centre of Edirne to Kapıkule on the Bulgarian border. For Greece, take a **dolmuş** or city bus (both from the bus stop opposite the post office at Saraçlar Caddesi) to the small village of Karaağaç from where it is a 2½-mile (4km) taxi ride to the frontier at Pazarkule. On occasion the border may only be open 9am–noon; check with the Edirne tourist office to avoid being stranded.

Selimiye Mosque

The crowning achievement of the sultans' 16th-century building spree, itself set like a crown over Edirne, is the grand Selimiye Mosque, built by Mimar Sinan for Selim II. Sinan finished the mosque, which he considered his finest, in 1575, when he was over 80 years old. According to legend it has 999 windows and its dome is slightly larger than the Aya Sofya's; its four identical 225ft minarets, girdled with three balconies, are the tallest outside Mecca, and were supposedly aligned to appear as a single one from the distance, to deceive enemy artillery. Unlike most mosques of its stature, the Selimiye is uncluttered with a large complex of religious foundations, and those it does have are all on one side, allowing impressive views of the mosque itself from three sides.

But it was in the interior that Sinan worked his best magic. The great dome hovers at 145ft on eight massive piers over a marble fountain symbolizing the waters of a legendary source called Zem-Zem, while at floor level the eye is drawn towards the exquisitely carved marble mimber and mihrab, the latter set back in an apse with walls adorned by İznik tiles; it is perhaps the only one in Turkey with a window opening towards Mecca. An even lovelier display of İznik tiles decorates the **imperial loge**; if you weren't able to get into the harem of the Topkapı Sarayı, here's a chance to see what you missed. The **medrese**, in typical cloister style, now houses Edirne's **Museum of Turkish and Islamic Art**, with items from the local *tekke* of whirling dervishes, calligraphy and charming photographs of great greased wrestlers from Edirne's past.

An **Archaeological and Ethnographic Museum**, with a collection of costumes, kilims and carpet saddle bags, artefacts from Trakya

Museum of Turkish and Islamic Art
open Tues–Sun 8–noon and 1.30–5.30; adm

Archaeological and Ethnographic Museum
open Tues–Sun 8.30–12 and 1–5.30; adm

(Thrace) and coins, is behind the Selimiye. The arcade of shops along the west flank of the mosque, the **Kavaflar Arasta**, was built exclusively for Edirne's cobblers; as with so many other arcades, the idea was to put the rents towards the upkeep of the mosque.

More Mosques and Markets

Just below the Selimiye, off central Cumhuriyet Meydanı, are two older imperial mosques, textbook examples for studying the development of the classical Ottoman style. The **Eski Cami**, a plain square encompassing nine vaults, was begun in 1402 by the three sons of Yıldırım Beyazıt after their father's collision with Tamerlane; during the next 11 years, as the mosque was erected, the three brothers fought for control of the empire. The winner and sole survivor, Mehmet I, had the honour of dedicating the mosque. One distinct feature of the Eski Cami is the inscription in great Arabic letters painted on the outer walls, giving the mosque a curiously primitive appearance.

The second mosque, the innovative **Üç Şerefeli Cami**, was built in 1447 by Murat II; its name of 'three balconies' derives from one of its asymmetrical minarets, which at 218ft was the tallest the Ottomans ever built – until Sinan's slender rockets went up around the Selimiye. Each of the mosque's minarets is a delicately carved work, and each is different – one straight, one spiral and one in zigzag patterns. Üç Şerefeli, the last great imperial mosque built prior to the capture of Constantinople, is covered with the largest central dome the Ottomans had yet dared and a clutch of smaller domes; inside, the architect achieved a surprising airiness.

Sokullu Hamam
open daily 8am–10pm,
bath only 6 YTL,
massage and scrub
extra, women's
entrance at the rear

Although its other foundations lie derelict, the mosque's **Sokullu Hamam**, built by Sinan in the 16th century and one of Turkey's most elegant, has been restored and still serves as a bath today. Remains of the mosque's medrese can still be seen clinging to the façade of the hamam; fireplaces which once welcomed theological students after their lessons in the chilly mosque are now exposed to the windswept street. Sinan's finely restored Rüstem Paşa Kervansaray, adjoining the Eski Cami, has also regained its original function as a hotel (*see* p.180).

In the Cumhuriyet Meydanı, Atatürk has to share space with a peculiar statue of two wrestlers, each of whom has two faces, so the work has no 'back'. Also here are the two covered bazaars, the *bedesten* (1405) and Sinan's **Ali Paşa Çarşısı**, from 1569. Its mesmerising arches of brick and plasterwork stretch on for over 600ft. After a devastating fire in 1992 it was extensively restored, and now looks indecorously new. Both bazaars are fun to visit, especially if you need a plastic bucket or saucepan.

Besides these, Edirne contains literally hundreds of other Ottoman buildings in its cobbled lanes. Especially interesting (and especially in danger of collapsing) are the great wooden Ottoman houses, typically unpainted, but adorned with folk motifs carved on the gables and balconies. Edirne is one of the few places outside Istanbul where you see many of these.

If you haven't yet seen enough mosques, one of the best is up on the hills above the Selimiye, off Mimar Sinan Caddesi: the charming **Muradiye**, a landmark visible from almost everywhere in Edirne. Murat II founded the mosque in 1435 for the Mevlevi dervishes and spared no expense on its exquisite İznik tiles. Like the Green Mosque in Bursa and many others, the Muradiye is built in a T-shape; the two rooms on either side of the mosque proper were for travelling dervishes to spend the night.

Ottoman Monuments on the Tunca River

Several other imperial mosques lie on the outskirts of Edirne, mostly along the willowy banks of the Tunca, a tributary of the Meriç (the Greek Ebros), the river that forms the border between Greece and Turkey. A walk around them on a nice day is one of the most pleasant things you can do in Edirne; there are several good picnic spots around the riverbank.

Start the tour by walking to the end of Talatpaşa Caddesi. The **Gazimihal Bridge** over the Tunca, an Ottoman work on Byzantine foundations, commemorates a Greek who turned Turk and became a redoubtable general for the Ottomans; at the end of the bridge, the 1421 **Gazimihal Mosque** has a graceful portico and carved minaret. Further down the road is the 1361 **Yıldırım Camii**, but you may wish to turn right, following the riverbank; not far away stands the **İkinci Beyazıt Külliyesi**, founded by Beyazıt II in 1484 and endowed with a record number of religious foundations, now mostly empty but occupied in part by a small museum of medicine. It includes a hospital and *timarhane* (an insane asylum) considered among the most progressive and well equipped of their day, with a sumptuous therapy ward (*darüşşia*), a medical school, bakery, two hospices, and baths. Architecturally the complex is an important stepping-stone towards the grand imperial style of Istanbul: a lovely ensemble including a square mosque, decorated with simple patterns of windows, surrounded by an asymmetrical arrangement of domed buildings, set off with attractive small lanterns and chimneys. The six-arched **Beyazıt Bridge**, built at the same time, connects the complex to Edirne. Several other fine 15th-century Ottoman bridges span the Tunca and Meriç; two of them connect Edirne with the island in the Tunca called the **Sarayiçi**, just north of the Beyazıt Külliyesi. The name comes from the Edirne Sarayı, or sultan's palace, a pleasure dome built here by Murat II but blown to bits by the Turks in 1877 to keep the explosives they had stored there out of the hands of the invading Russians. Today the

The Greased Wrestlers of Edirne

The Turks call the tournament the Kırkpınar ('forty spring'); according to tradition, the bouts began in the 14th century, when Süleyman Paşa, son of the second Ottoman sultan Orhan Gazi, brought his forty heroes to campaign in Europe. In between battles, they amused themselves by wrestling. Two contestants were so equally matched, they wrestled to death and were buried by their companions. The next day a spring appeared by the tombs, which became known as the 'spring of the forty'.

The Kırkpınar (now caged up in a modern stadium) attracts thousands of competitors from around Turkey. The contestants, dressed only in their leather breeches, or *kispet*, rub their skin with olive oil and warm up to drums and a wailing oboe. Next the announcer, or *cazgır*, leads a prayer and introduces the pairs of wrestlers; part of the Turks' enjoyment of the matches is hearing the cazgır's recitation of each wrestler's claim to fame and his best tricks. The freestyle bouts last until one contestant is pinned down or simply keels over. Wrestlers compete in four categories, classed by age and prowess. A grand champion (*Baş Pehlivan*) who retains the title for three years straight is awarded the highest honour, the Golden Belt. One who won it around the turn of the century, Koca Yusuf ('Enormous Joe'), has become a legend in Edirne: he went on to challenge and defeat the greatest champions of Europe and the USA, but was drowned on his return voyage from America when his ship sank.

island is home to Edirne's biggest annual event, the Greased Wrestling Tournament (*Yağlı Güreş*), which is held in late June–early July, depending on Ramazan.

North of here, in an unmarked battlefield, Visigothic horsemen devastated Roman infantry in one of the climactic battles of history, the AD 378 Battle of Adrianople. The Visigoths had peacefully settled much of Thrace in the 4th century, and they were only rising up in revolt against the oppression and taxes of Roman rule. But the battle was a landmark in military history, demonstrating conclusively the superiority of cavalry over the Roman legions. Adrianople was the first big crack in Rome's defences, and the beginning of the end for the empire; after it, the Visigoths went on the move, raiding through Greece and the Balkans. In 410, they would sack Rome itself.

Thracian Villages and Beaches

The Thracian interior isn't holiday country – rolling, featureless farmland full of wheat and sunflowers that turns golden-brown in late July and August. The villages offer few sights, but on the whole they are happy and prosperous places. Two things you'll come across are tumuli, the preferred mode of burial of the ancient Thracians (some can be seen from the E5 around Lüleburgaz) and Ottoman-era bridges. The roads here were crucial to the 15th-century sultans, consolidating their hold on the Balkans. The most impressive of their works is in **Uzunköprü**, a village near the Greek border, the name of which means 'long bridge': a 174-arch, 4,400ft span completed in 1444 that was probably the longest in Europe at the time. South of Uzunköprü on the Gulf of Saroz are long, sandy beaches around **Erikli** and **İbrice**. Although they contain a number of simple *pansiyonlar*, these seaside villages remain undeveloped compared with resorts closer to Istanbul, such as Şarköy and Silivri. If you're really intent on getting away from it all, **Enez** on the Greek border is as good a candidate as any. A port has been on this site since the 12th century BC, and though there is a picturesque castle to keep watch, it's the beach that people come for today.

The **Yıldız Mountains** mark the boundary between Bulgaria and Turkey. Local beauty spots in the area include the frontier post of **Dereköy** and the Black Sea village of **İğneada**, both surrounded by forests. A new road has been built here, and İğneada's port, the village of **Limanköy**, has beaches and family *pansiyonlar*.

Inland, each of a triangle of small towns in central Thrace has its Ottoman ornament: **Kırklareli**, with its 1407 Hızır Bey Cami and old hamam; **Babaeski**, with its Cedit Ali Paşa Mosque, built by Sinan; and **Lüleburgaz**, ancient Arcadiopolis, with another of Sinan's works, the Mehmet Paşa Mosque and its large collection of religious foundations, including baths and a soup kitchen.

Where to Stay in and around Edirne

(i) **Edirne** >
Talatpaşa Caddesi 76a, west of the town centre,
t 0284 213 9208

Kapıkule
at the Bulgarian border,
t 0284 238 2019

İpsala
at the Greek border,
t 0284 616 1577

Edirne

Edirne not being much of a tourist destination, you can usually get a room for about €45/80 YTL in a nice hotel that would be twice as much in Istanbul or on the coast.

**Otel Şaban Açıkgöz, Çilingirler Caddesi 9, t 0284 213 0313, near the Kervansaray in the Tahmis Çarşısı (look for the yellow sign) (€€€). The best choice, with pleasant airy rooms with television (though all you can pick up is MTV).

**Sultanotel, at Talatpaşa Caddesi 170, near the tourist office, t 0284 225 1372 (€€€). Has a gloomy restaurant but comfortable en suite rooms.

**Efe, on the relatively quiet Maarif Caddesi 13, t 0284 213 6166, *www. efehotel.com* (€€€). Ask for a room on the top floor of this family-run establishment and you'll be sure to avoid any interference from the basement 'Efe English Pub'. Doubles are bright and comfortable with a private bathroom and free wi-fi.

(O) Hotel Rüstempaşa Kervansaray, in the centre on İki Kapılı Han Caddesi 57, t 0284 212 6119, *www.kervansaray hotel.net* (€€). The conversion of a historic *han* has created a hotel with service and furnishings that can't match the auspicious surroundings. Windows are on the small side and front-facing rooms can be noisy; but this is your only chance to stay in a building by Mimar Sinan. Amenities include a disco, two bars and a hamam that stays open 24 hours.

(O) Aksaray, on the corner of Maarif Caddesi and Alipaşa Ortakapı Caddesi, t 0284 212 6035 (€€ with bathroom facilities, € without). The only cheapie worth laying your hat in for a night. This 100-year-old clapboard house with a fretwork balcony looks as if it has just been vacated by the Waltons. Inside, the rooms offer further evidence of the Turks' love affair with the colour brown, but all have phones and TVs. There is a bar downstairs with a loyal local clientele.

Several **campsites** dot the area, the best of which is the **Fifi Motel Camp**, t 0284 235 7908, next to Edirne College, five miles out on the old E5 road to Istanbul. Camping facilities are available in summer only; motel rooms are open all year round.

Erikli

Simple *pansiyonlar* open in season only are the norm on this stretch of coast, such as the cheap ***Erikli Oberj**, t 0284 737 3565.

**Erikli Hotel, t 0284 737 3565, *www.erikliotel.com* (€€). With a beachfront location.

Eating Out in Edirne

As every Turk knows, Edirne is famous not only for wrestling, but for liver! The centre of town is full of *ciğer* (liver) parlours where the proprietors will be happy to initiate you – they also like liver kebabs, fried liver, and Allah only knows what liver else.

If liver is not your thing, then *köfte* and other kebabs are also widely available. Outside of that, you're not likely to find anything unforgettable in Edirne. The best restaurants are out by the Meriç River, a good 25min walk from the centre, across two narrow bridges which don't have the benefit of pavements to protect you from the local show-'em-who's-boss roadhogs. A better bet is to become one yourself (if you have your own transport) or to get a lift with one (in any dolmuş heading for Karaağaç).

Lalezar Restaurant (€€). Furthest from the road, with huge windows overlooking the river and an even bigger TV screen dominating one end of the dining room.

Villa Restaurant, next door (€€). Has a better fish selection than the Lalezar, with intriguing 'live Turkish pop and arabesque' music served up alongside the food from 8pm onwards. In summer there is also a large terrace opening out onto the river. *Open every night until 3am.*

Saray lokanta, near the main post office (€). Gets crowded at lunch time with locals filling up with ready food chosen from trays in the window.

Özge Pastanesi, next door. Does a better job with desserts.

Restaurant under the Park Hotel (€). Serves up an array of kebabs and *pide*.

Gaziantep Baklavacısı, Balıkpazarı Caddesi. Sweet teeth need not go unindulged in Edirne. This place sells a wide range of delicious southeastern-style pastries.

Roma, across from the post office on Saraçlar Caddesi. Pastry shop.

Zogo, across from the post office on Saraçlar Caddesi. More goodies.

Alcohol isn't that hard to find either, though Turkey's only entirely European city is a surprisingly conservative place. Look up: around the central squares bars are everywhere, on the first or second floors.

The Marmara Coast and Gelibolu Peninsula

The Northern Marmara Coast

Tekirdağ, ancient Bisanthe, is the largest town on Thrace's Marmara coast, and one aspiring to become a resort, with nearby beaches at Kumbağ and Değirmenaltı. Although mostly concrete and modern, Tekirdağ is spread attractively over the hills, and has two works by Sinan: the **Covered Bazaar** and **Rüstem Paşa Mosque**. On the seaside promenade stands one of the best Atatürk statues, depicting the father of his country with his famous chalkboard and pointer, teaching two earnest citizens their vowels.

A mile to the west of here lived the Hungarian patriot Prince Ferenc II Rakoczy, who spent a career leading his countrymen against the Habsburgs in the Hungarian War of Independence; in 1717, the Ottomans granted him political asylum in Tekirdağ, where he lived until his death in 1735. The song Rakoczy's troops sang in battle, the 'Rakoczy March', has roused Hungarian patriots ever

Getting around the Northern Marmara Coast and Gelibolu

Buses from Istanbul and Edirne go to Tekirdağ, and there is also a frequent service to Çanakkale via the Eceabat ferry. Tekirdağ's bus station is on the coastal road, just over a mile (about 2km) north of the centre, but for some Istanbul–Çanakkale runs you'll have to flag down the bus on the road; they don't come into the station. In summer, there are **ferries** from Tekirdağ to Marmara Island and Erdek.

Two **car ferries**, Eceabat–Çanakkale and Gelibolu–Lâpseki, cross the Dardanelles every 2hrs till midnight.

since; once, when Liszt played it as encore to a recital, it caused a riot. In 1932 the Hungarian government made the house into the **Rakoczy Museum**, on Barbaros Caddesi, containing Rakoczy's flag, documents, Hungarian weapons, and paintings from the era.

East of Tekirdağ, there's a beach at **Marmara Ereğli**; to the west, the road to the Gelibolu peninsula becomes ever rougher as it passes through vineyards to other beaches at **Barbaros**, **Mürefte** and **Şarköy**. The latter, with a fine broad, sandy beach, has grown into the biggest resort on this part of the shore; it's quite a lively place when it fills up with Istanbul families in the summer.

On the neck of the peninsula, **Bolayır** overlooks the Dardanelles and the Saros Gulf; here Süleyman Paşa, son of Orhan Gazi, and leader of the 40 heroes who captured Gelibolu fortress in 1354 – the Ottomans' first handful of Rumelia – is buried in a *türbe* at one end of the village. Next to him is the grave of the 19th-century poet Namik Kemal, a native of Tekirdağ and leader of the movement to reform the Ottoman Empire at the end of the 19th century.

The Dardanelles and the Gelibolu (Gallipoli) Peninsula

Gelibolu, the Turkish name for Gallipoli, is a pleasant fishing village, though one usually full of soldiers. Its castle has long guarded this entrance into the Dardanelles straits; the walls you see today date from the 14th century, when the Ottomans captured the town. One of the two Dardanelles ferries crosses here, to **Lâpseki**. If you're driving, the road to Çanakkale along the Asian shore is more pleasant, but the peninsula route has more tales to tell: from Protosilaus, the first casualty of the Trojan war, to battles in the Crimean War, the First World War and the Turkish War of Independence. Some nine miles (14km) south of Gelibolu, at the mouth of the stream Aegospotamos (modern İnce Liman), Lysander and his Spartans clobbered the Athenian fleet in 405 BC, in the decisive and final battle of the Peloponnesian War.

A little further south stood **Sestos**, across the strait from ancient Abydos. Nothing remains of either of these but stories. Here in 480 BC Xerxes' army, marching to invade Greece, crossed the strait on a pontoon bridge of boats while the Persian King of Kings watched from the heights of Abydos, sitting on the marble throne he had had carted along with him, and wept because none of the men labouring below would be alive in a hundred years. Here lived the famous lovers Hero, a priestess at Sestos, and Leander, a resident of Abydos, who would swim the strait every night to visit his love, guided by her lamp. One night, a storm blew the lamp out, and Leander got lost and was drowned; when his body was found the next morning, Hero flung herself into the sea. Romantic-minded travellers can make the swim as well, taking care to avoid the many steamers that ply the strait; Byron did it in 1810.

The car ferry crossing to Çanakkale departs from **Eceabat**, near a village called **Kilitbahir**, located where the Dardanelles are at their narrowest and most defensible. The trefoil castle on the shore, a striking design, was constructed by Mehmet the Conqueror to cut off Constantinople before he besieged the capital. Never one to leave matters to chance, Mehmet built another castle, across the water at Çanakkale, and slung a heavy chain between the two, sealing the straits and giving Kilitbahir its name, 'Lock of the Sea'. Kilitbahir is now empty, and can be explored.

There is a sad, melancholy loveliness to the lush and undulating Gallipoli peninsula. Over 200,000 young men lie buried in this thin pine-clad strip of land. In spring, the hills here bloom with wild flowers; appropriately, the most numerous are poppies. Although the village of Gelibolu sounds like the logical place to stay when visiting the peninsula, most visitors find it more convenient to stay across the Dardanelles at **Çanakkale** (*see* pp.213–14), which is nearer to the sights. It is impossible to see all the peninsula's monuments, museums and battlefields by public transport alone, so, unless you have a car or are prepared to hire a taxi for the best part of a day, a **guided tour** is the only real option. These are instructive, although tour operators tend to concentrate on the ANZAC-related sites.

TJs Tours
t 0286 814 3121, www. anzacgallipolitours.com; run by a Turkish/ Australian couple and offering private tours out of nearby Eceabat; they also run a hotel and pansiyon (see p.185)

Hassle Free Tours
t 0286 213 5969, www. hasslefreetours.com; operates out of nearby Çanakkale and has daily tours

The Gallipoli Campaign

It is easy to forget that behind the ill-fated Allied attack on the Dardanelles in April 1915 there existed a sound strategic rationale; had it succeeded, the Great War might well have ended that same year.

The seeds of the assault were sown only a few months after the assassination at Sarajevo in June 1914. The Allies desperately needed a way to resupply beleaguered Russia, and the only way to do it was the sea route from the south – from the Aegean through the Dardanelles and Bosphorus to the Black Sea ports on the Crimea. The route was blocked by Turkey, Germany's ally, but it was the only option open to Winston Churchill, First Lord of the Admiralty. Moreover, capturing Constantinople would enable Allied troops to drive north through the Balkans, leaving the Central Powers fighting an ultimately hopeless war on three separate fronts. In November 1914, Churchill ordered the ships of an Anglo-French fleet to charge the Dardanelles. The assault was a disaster, the naval equivalent of the Charge of the Light Brigade. The Turks had mined the straits. Three battleships were sunk, three crippled; thousands of sailors died. Later attempts to sweep the straits of mines were foiled by Turkish heavy guns positioned on the peninsula. To Churchill and his generals it was clear; the Dardanelles could not be breached by sea until the Turkish army was removed from the Gelibolu peninsula.

To achieve this, two simultaneous amphibious landings on the peninsula were planned, one at Cape Helles at the entrance to the straits, the other at Kabatepe beach eight miles north. An Anglo-French army was to conduct the former, the new combined ANZAC force (Australian and New Zealand Army Corps) the latter. The two were to drive inland, link up and together push the Turks and their heavy artillery off the peninsula. Allied troops were assembled in huge numbers on the Greek island of Limnos, and at dawn on 25 April 1915 the first landing boats hit the beaches.

By noon of that same day the Allied strategy had gone horribly awry. At Cape Helles the Anglo-French contingent had encountered massive opposition and established a beachhead only after horrific losses; the ANZAC force was hit even harder. A signals failure had directed their boats not to wide, spacious Kabatepe but to a small, narrow cove backed by sheer, towering cliffs. ANZACs died in their thousands before gaining a tentative toe-hold. More troops were landed. The push inland began. Some small advances were made. Then they were stopped.

The Gelibolu campaign was to last eight months, conducted in the steal-a-yard, lose-it-again manner of the Western Front. Much of the fighting was centered around Çonkbayırlı Hill, the peninsula's highest point, and it was here that Lieutenant-Colonel Mustafa Kemal, the commander of the Turkish 19th Division, acquired a reputation as a brilliant, tireless leader, not afraid to risk death by his men's side – a reputation that was to serve him well when Kemal metamorphosed into Atatürk.

In January 1916 the Allies pulled out. Ironically, their retreat was the most successful manœuvre of the campaign; tens of thousands of men were evacuated under the cover of night without a single loss. Czarist Russia fell first to the Germans and then to the Bolsheviks. Churchill was dismissed and was not to hold government office for another 24 years. Yet his moment was to come, as was that of his adversary, Atatürk, the man who, quite rightly, had the last words on the Gelibolu campaign:

'Those heroes that shed their blood and lost their lives, you are now lying in the soil of a friendly country, therefore rest in peace. There is no difference between the Johnnies and the Mehmets to us where they lie side by side here in this country of ours. You mothers who sent their sons from far away countries, wipe away your tears. Your sons are now lying in our bosom and are in peace. Having lost their lives on this land they have become our sons as well.'

Kabatepe museum
open daily 8.30–5; adm

With one of the finest beaches on the peninsula, **Kabatepe** is the best place to begin any tour. Here a small, spaceship-shaped museum overlooks the beach and contains a sad collection of memorabilia, from an English Tommy's last letter home to the skull of a Turkish soldier, with a bullet still embedded in the centre of his forehead. From here it is a short drive to **ANZAC Cove** where you can see just why the landings were doomed. The hills above are dotted with ANZAC cemeteries and memorials, all immaculately maintained by the Allied War Graves Commission. Trenches remain intact at **Lone Pine**, the main Australian cemetery, and on the heights of **Çonkbayırlı Hill** where five huge Turkish monoliths recount the crucial battles fought there, each stone positioned so as to represent the fingers and thumb of a man's hand, raised, pleading to God. At **Cape Helles** the British memorial towers high, in memory of the 20,761 men of the empire who have no known grave. There are six British and French cemeteries in this area and two significant Turkish monuments, the **First Martyrs Memorial** and that huge, pi-shaped structure, at once a museum and the headstone of the literally countless Turks buried on the peninsula.

**Kilia Bay
Information
Centre**
open daily 9–12 and 1–5

The **Kilia Bay Information Centre**, opened in 2005 at the main entrance to the battlefields, is a museum, library, exhibition centre and café that occasionally shows documentary films that serve as a good introduction to the history of the area.

Where to Stay on the Northern Marmara Coast and Gelibolu Peninsula

Silivri

*****Klassis, Karga Burun Mevkii, t 0212 727 4050, *www.klassisotel. com.tr* (€€€€€). On the Marmara shore, east of Tekirdağ – close enough to Istanbul to attract the city's élite. It's a striking ensemble of neo-Ottoman buildings set high over a huge, dreamy pool. They lay it on thick here: private beach, disco and every sport from squash to waterskiing. The same company has opened the **(S) Klassis Golf and Country Club**, t 0212 710 1300, 17km from Silivri, with an 18-hole golf course.

(i) Tekirdağ >
Rüstempaşa Çarşısı, 45 Atatürk Bulvarı, t 0282 261 4346

Tekirdağ and Around

***Golden Yat Hotel, Yali Caddesi 42, Tekirdağ, t 0282 261 1054, *www. goldenyat.com* (€€€). Although lacking soul, this modern addition to the seafront is probably your best bet.

Bilge, t 0282 283 6741 (€€). One of the more comfortable of the many hotels on Kumbağ beach, five miles to the east, which has its own beach.

Other *pensions* are easily found at both Tekirdağ and Kumbağ beaches.

Gelibolu

Yılmaz Otel, Liman Meydanı 8, t 0286 566 1256 (€€). Friendly hotel among the collection of inexpensive accommodation near the ferries.

Eceabat

(★) TJs Hostel >

TJs Hostel, Kemlapasa Mah. Cumhuriyet Cad. 5/A, t 0286 814 3121, *www. anzacgallipolitours.com* (€). Just 150m from the ferry port. The Turkish/Australian owners also run the **Eceabat Hotel** (€€), the largest in the centre of town, with a variety of rooms and group dorms.

Camping

There is a wide choice of campsites around the Gelibolu peninsula, including the big **Patiş Kum Motel Camp**, t 0286 814 1455, at Kum Limanı, with all the facilities, and motel rooms on hand.

Eating Out on the Northern Marmara Coast and Gelibolu Peninsula

Tekirdağ

Numerous restaurants in town and along the waterfront serve the famous *Tekirdağ köfte*, small grilled meatballs, possibly the best in Turkey, accompanied by *piyaz* (bean salad) and chilli paste. The combination with a soft drink should cost around 12 YTL. The region is also known for the production of wine and *rakı*.

İlhan Restaurant, Atatürk Bulvarı 55, t 0282 261 1507 (€€). Has a diverse menu that is reasonably priced and smart surroundings.

Rumeli Et Lokantasi, Istanbul Yolu 6, opposite the Jandarma on the main Istanbul highway, t 0282 262 8590 (€). Like most roadside restaurants in Tekirdağ, this is more of a pit stop than a fine dining experience but it serves a good *köfte* and *piyaz*.

Gelibolu

Gelibolu's eateries are mostly gathered around the harbour.

Gelibolu Cafeteria, t 0286 566 1227, *http://gelibolurestaurant.com* (€€–€). Has outside tables, and will provide dinner for 15 YTL, slightly more for fish.

Yelkenci Restaurant, t 0286 566 4600 (€€–€). A similarly priced selection of meat and fish dishes. Near the ferry port, its double terrace overlooking the straits is a relaxing place to watch maritime comings and goings.

The Southern Marmara Coast

Although the scenery along the south shore of the Sea of Marmara is quite beautiful and blessed with beaches, it doesn't feature on many foreign visitors' itineraries. As far as Biga, you'll

Getting around the Southern Marmara Coast

Towns on the south Marmara shore are easily reached by **buses** travelling between Bursa and Çanakkale, a trip of about 4hrs. From Bandırma and Erdek, minibuses serve the surrounding towns and beaches. Note that Bandırma has two *otogars*. The main one, south of town, serves Bursa–Çanakkale and other main line buses. To get from there to the waterfront station where the Erdek and Gönen buses start, you can take a taxi or die waiting, possibly, for a city bus or dolmuş.

As any local will tell you, **boat** timetables to the islands often seem to change from one week to the next. Avşa and Marmara islands are served by ferry from Istanbul, daily in the summer, and usually twice a week in the winter depending on weather conditions, *www.ido.com.tr*. Boats operate from Tekirdağ with similar frequency. Services also run from Erdek: in summer there are daily boats to Avşa and Marmara, and a twice-weekly crossing to Paşalimanı. In all the ports, look out for the fellows with boats who run informal private ferry services, or ask anyone.

see lush green countryside with muddy fields and mules, broken by little villages lost among the trees, their presence betrayed by a single minaret sticking up. Most of its ancient sites have little to show for themselves today; nothing remains of ancient Abydos or Lampsakas (modern **Lâpseki**, the second ferry crossing), although to the east two famous battles of antiquity occurred: **Biga**, where Alexander first defeated the Persians in 334 BC at the mouth of the River Granicus (Biga Çayı), and further east at **Edincik** (ancient Cyzicus), where Alcibiades and the Athenians defeated the Spartans in the Peloponnesian War. **Bandırma**, the biggest town before Bursa, is a sorry industrial settlement that was largely ruined in the war of 1922; you'll have to pass through it in order to get to Erdek and the Marmara Islands.

South of Bandırma is the **Kuşcenneti** (Bird Paradise) **National Park**, a sanctuary for migratory waterfowl, especially pelicans, grey

Alexander the Great

Before moving on to Egypt, Persia and India, Alexander polished off the Persian King Darius's satrapies in Asia Minor for practice. With some 40,000 men, including 5,000 cavalry, he crossed the Hellespont in the spring of 334 BC, sacrificing a bull to Poseidon in mid-passage. After visiting Troy and paying homage to the Homeric heroes, he and his men were immediately confronted by an army commanded by the Persian satraps of Phrygia and Ionia. At the River Granicus, they stormed across the water into the Persian lines and routed them, setting the tone for the rest of the campaign.

Then the Macedonians marched down the Aegean coast, taking Sardis, Ephesus and Miletus. In Ephesus Alexander threw out the pro-Persian aristocracy and restored democratic institutions, and by so doing made himself popular with all the Greeks of Asia Minor not in the Great King's pay. Taking auguries at Miletus, Alexander saw an eagle flying towards the shore, and took it to mean he would conquer the Persians by land, not by sea. Accordingly, he sent his Greek navy home – he couldn't afford it anyway – and marched across the Mediterranean coast to take the Persians' naval bases away. Termessos alone refused an alliance, and survived when Alexander decided it wasn't worth a siege. Perge, Aspendos and Side were brought into line, and then the Macedonian force split up, the great general Parmenion taking half the force to assault the Cilician coast while Alexander headed north to chase the Persians out of Phrygia. Here, as recorded by his chronicler Arrian, he cut with his sword the famous Gordian knot. The two forces met again at Tarsus, where the always fragile Alexander took ill from a swim in the cold River Cydnus. He recovered just in time to meet Darius, the Great King himself, at Issus near today's İskenderun. The Macedonian victory, at a disadvantage of perhaps five to one, opened the way for the conquest of Persia and Egypt.

and white herons, and cormorants, who come to nest along the willow-shaded banks of **Lake Manyas** (also known as Kuş Gölü, Bird Lake) between February and October, and then fly south to India and Africa in the winter. In all, 239 different species of birds have been spotted in the sanctuary. Just west of here, at **Gönen**, other airborne creatures – namely, tens of thousands of bats – have taken up residence in the **Dereköy Caves**. Gönen also has one of Turkey's major thermal spas for rheumatism.

Erdek and the Kapıdağı

The road into the Kapıdağı peninsula is not promising at first, passing scrapyards, gravel pits and, most impressive of all, a festering sulphuric acid plant. But persevere; it gets better. **Erdek**, the capital of the Kapıdağı, is a very modest though very agreeable resort, popular with the people of Bursa. In the lively village centre, cafés in shady gardens cluster around the shore; from here a pretty pedestrian walk leads out to the beach and the strip of modern hotels that follows it. There are less crowded beaches to the north at **Ocaklar** and **Narlı**, both with small but growing collections of cheap *pansiyonlar* and restaurants (and, for all the industry nearby, the water seems clean enough). Another beach, one of the few accessible by paved road, is north of Karacabey at **Bayramdere**.

The Marmara Islands

Before 1923, this miniature archipelago was largely inhabited by Greeks. They are nearly all gone now, and like much of the area around the Marmara the islands have a slightly rough, just-settled air to them. Lately, people from Istanbul have been buying or building houses as summer retreats, but outside of Avşa Island don't expect much of the trappings of tourism. There are a few small beaches and secluded coves, and absolutely no sights to visit. The peace and quiet is seamless when the cement mixers aren't going, and your creditors will never find you here.

Of the four inhabited islands of the Marmara, **Paşalimanı**, with its five small villages, is nearest to the mainland. There is a ferry from Erdek to its tiny capital, **Balıklı** (which means 'fishy'), and private boats make regular crossings from Narlı, which can be easier. Paşalimanı welcomes few visitors; there's really very little there, not even a beach, but at least you'll be guaranteed a peaceful stay. **Avşa**, the next nearest, is its antithesis. Loved by Turks from the cities, it is green and undulating and has some good beaches, particularly around its capital **Türkeli** (Avşa appears on many maps as Türkeli Island). Avşa has become a bit overbuilt in the last two decades – at least there'll be no problem finding a place to stay, although many of these establishments have a 'resort-that-time-forgot' feel to them. **Ekinlik**, north of Avşa, is the smallest of the islands, no more than a village, where there's even less to do than on Paşalimanı. The largest of the group is **Marmara** (Greek Elafonisos). As its name suggests, Marmara is famous for its marble, which has been quarried here since ancient times. Despite thousands of years of mining, supplies of this stone have yet to be exhausted. Today, the industry is centred around **Saraylar** on the island's northern side. It is from here that white marble softly veined with blue and grey originates – you will see and feel it all over Turkey: it is the preferred covering for the interiors of the nation's bathhouses. Despite being stonier than Avşa and lacking that island's beaches, Marmara is nevertheless well-patronized by Turks on vacation. There is a beach four miles north of Marmara village at **Çınarlı**, reachable by dolmuş or boat. Çınarlı's tea garden is protected from the sun by a gnarled monster of a tree which has been the venue for village gossip for centuries.

Where to Stay on the Southern Marmara Coast

Most accommodation in this region is open June–September only.

Erdek >
Yalı Mah., Kalyoncu Sokak 19, t 0266 835 1169

Erdek

Gül Plaj Moteli, Kumlu Yalı Caddesi 86, **t 0266 835 1053 (€€). Clean and on the beach, with half-board doubles for around 80 YTL, all with private bath. *Open June–Sept.*

Erdek's cheaper establishments are clustered around the port, most in the form of *pensions* charging around €25 /45 YTL for a double.

Ümit Hotel, **t** 0266 835 1092, on Balıkhane Sokak. One of the nicest on a quiet back street near the port.

There are also cheap choices along the beach strip.

Arseven Pansiyon, on Ocaklar beach, north of Erdek, **t** 0266 835 1464 (€€). Actually a family home that the owners rent out in summer for around 70 YTL. Still good value for money, offering spotless rooms with en suite facilities.

Avşa Island >>
a booth in summer by the docks at Türkeli

★ Camping Ant >

Camping

Camping Ant, Mangirci Mevkii, **t** 0266 855 7044, *www.campingant.com* (€). Cheap camping with private beach and great shady spots under large pine trees. Good website too.

Outside Erdek

Hotels near the thermal baths in Gönen are open all year.

****Yıldız Otel, Banyolar Caddesi, **t** 0266 762 1840, *www.gonenkaplica lari.com* (€€€). A large thermal resort where doubles costs 180 YTL, but can be negotiated if staying longer than three nights. In addition to the baths there's a sauna and hamam.

Marmara Otel, Marmara, **t** 0266 885 5476 (€). The best the island can do, though open in season only.

Avşa

**Ayberk, two miles north of Türkeli (€€€–€€). The height of luxury on Avşa, which doesn't go very high. This has light, airy rooms with balconies overlooking the beach.

Otel Temizel, **t** 0266 896 1134 (€). Pleasant, and more typical.

Eating Out on the Southern Marmara Coast

There are several small *lokantas* along the coast and on the islands, though many close in winter. In Erdek, you'll have a choice of seafood places with outdoor tables around the port:

Kafkas Restaurant will bring you out some *börek* and a fine grilled fish.

Rıhtım, on the seafront esplanade, also serves good fish.

Bursa

*All of us old
people here
dream that one
morning we will
open our eyes
and all the
factories and
cars will be gone,
and Bursa will be
as it was before.*

 Bursa

So said the elderly gentleman we met in the tourist office, lamenting the fate that has overtaken this most refined of Turkish cities. In the last few decades, prosperous, well-run Bursa has become a victim of its own success. They wanted industry, and they got it: Türk Fiat and Renault plants and scores of others. The jobs they provide have attracted vast numbers of migrants from all over Turkey, especially the Black Sea area and the northeast. The population has more than quadrupled in the last two decades, and now stands at around two million.

All these people, necessarily, have to stuff themselves into a ribbon-shaped medieval city built on the side of a mountain. Atatürk Caddesi, the only big street through it, has become a deafening motorway capable of giving anyone a headache after walking only one block. Everywhere else, crowds of people and cars make day-to-day life pretty much unbearable. The metro helps but it isn't enough; it services mainly the suburbs. Bursa is faced with the task of redesigning and rebuilding itself from the ground up, which will take time.

Not that we want to discourage you from coming. On the contrary; for all the commotion, Bursa is still an obligatory stop, with its medieval Ottoman monuments, a covered market second only to that of Istanbul, and its friendly and alert population. Bursans in many ways seem to be a step or two ahead of the rest of the Turks. Not the least of their virtues is a resolute civic pride (Bursa was the first capital of the Ottoman Empire, after all), which manifests itself in surprising ways even in difficult times. The current governor, Recep Altepe, is pushing forward cultural and historical restorations at an astonishing pace. In the last decade he has overseen the restoration of historic buildings all over the city; the **Irgandı Köprüsü**, a beautiful 15th-century Ottoman bridge lined with artisan shops, is a shining example. But the work does not stop there: new transport systems, hospitals, recycling facilities, parks, schools and sports grounds are all part of the rejuvenation plan. It is visible everywhere: monuments are extremely well kept and very clean – in the case of the old city walls, somewhat over-eagerly restored, a little too clean. Regardless, Bursa is looking to the future and the general feeling is one of optimism.

Another reason for coming is **Uludağ**, a breath of fresh air, both figuratively and literally. This 8,300ft massif is just a cable-car ride away from the centre of the city. With the snow on its peaks well into the summer, the traffic and noise seem far away. Added to this Muslim alpine setting are famous thermal baths, a huge and lovely park and plenty of trees; Bursa is the only city we have ever seen where the town council operates a flower shop. Its citizens call

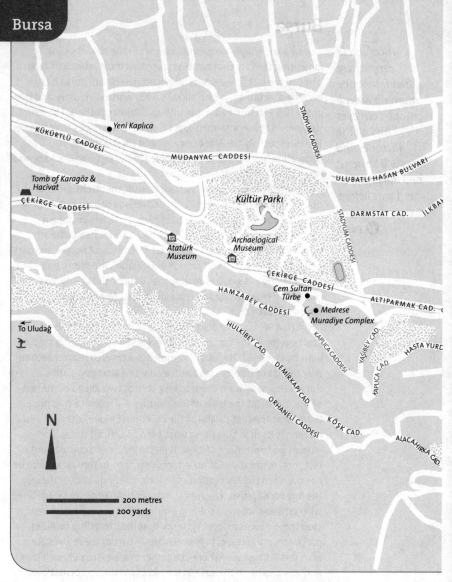

their town Yeşil Bursa, 'Green Bursa'; trees are being planted and
there is a new awareness of environmental issues.

History

King Prusias I of Bithynia founded Bursa – then *Prusa* – in the 2nd
century BC. Although today Turkey's sixth-largest city, in ancient
times Bursa was never more than a minor provincial centre. What
little is known of it comes from the letters of Pliny the Younger, the
governor under Emperor Trajan. To the Byzantines, the town was a

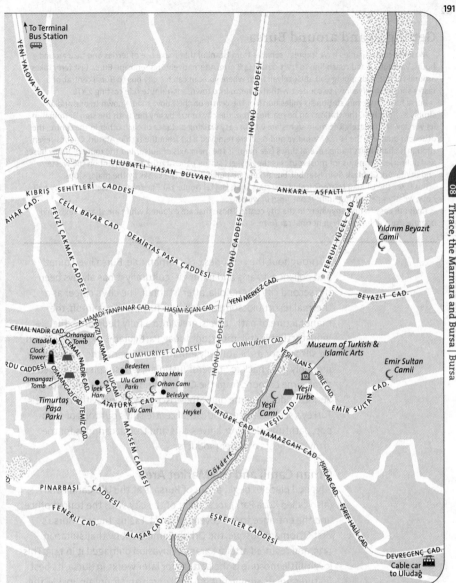

fashionable resort for its baths, but the Ottomans put Bursa on the map. Sultan Orhan captured it in 1326 and made it his capital, a position it held on and off until 1453. Here the Ottomans began to sponsor great religious architecture. Drawing on the traditions of the Selcuks and Byzantines to develop a style that would be a fit heir to the past, their architects crowned Bursa with mosques, schools and mausolea, solidly and honestly medieval, possessed of an austere but very present spirituality that earns them a place beside the more elaborate creations of Istanbul.

Getting to and around Bursa

Most **coach** companies have 'express' services from Istanbul that make use of ferries and take around 3½ hours. Varan is a good coach line to try, **t** 0212 444 8 999. Alternatively, the Yenikapi–Bursa fast **ferry** takes around 1½ hours, dropping you at Güzelyalı from where you can catch a city bus to Bursa central, or a faster shuttle bus (yellow) to connect with the metro into town, a 15-minute ride costing 2 YTL.

Bursa has a huge **bus station** six miles north of the centre on the Yalova road. Known to one and all simply as 'Terminal', the station can be reached from the city centre by any bus with the sign 'Terminal' in its window. Fortunately, the main sights are within easy **walking** distance of each other in the centre; the other old quarters, the Hisar, Muradiye and Yeşil, are removed a bit from the traffic. Atatürk Caddesi, even though it changes its name several times (*see* map), is the main axis of Bursa, and the route of many buses and dolmuşes; terminus for most routes is the Heykel ('statue'), the Atatürk monument on the western end of Atatürk Caddesi. As in Istanbul, **bus tickets** are purchased at the kiosks by the major stops.

Buses for the Uludağ *teleferik* (cable car) start from Heykel (route 3A). The *teleferik* itself runs every half-hour, weather permitting, until 10pm, 9pm in winter.

Taxis are easy to find anywhere in the city centre. Those that are coloured white are shared taxis, and operate like a dolmuş, only in normal car form.

Throughout the centuries of Ottoman rule, Bursa lived quietly and polished its arts and manners; culturally it has always been the second city of Anatolia, after Istanbul. The city's career as a thermal resort blossomed under the Turks, and a spin-off, the manufacture of bath towels, grew into a fully fledged textile industry that is still important today. Particularly, the city is known for silk and for its beautifully embroidered linens (the silk industry probably goes back to Emperor Justinian, whose spies managed to steal some cocoons from the Chinese and break their monopoly). Serious industry came only after 1950. Now, along with the towels, Turkey's second-largest industrial centre ships out tons of soda-pop, bathtubs, clothing, knives, cars and trucks, cannons for the army and hosts of other products.

Orhan Camii and the Market Area

A good place to begin a tour of Bursa is at the **Ulu Cami Parkı** (also called Koza Park), focal point of the city, with the tourist office and the entrance to the covered market. Facing these is Bursa's first Ottoman mosque, the **Orhan Camii**, built by that sultan in 1335, and restored after a Karaman invasion damaged it in 1413. This lovely little mosque is the pattern for later works in Bursa; its best features are its simple but graceful porch and fountain. Inside, the central dome is supported, not by pendentives, but by semi-domes in the corners. In some ways, this is the structural system of older buildings like the Aya Sofya turned inside out; it would not work with a larger dome. The outlandish geometry that decorates the semi-domes is just that, decoration, not part of the structure. Such polygons run amok are a recurring conceit in Bursa's mosques.

Just across the street, Bursa's **Belediye** (City Hall) is not in tourist brochures, but it's probably the largest piece of folk art in Turkey, and the prettiest city hall. Its construction of half-timber, with horizontal, vertical and diagonal beams in a seemingly haphazard manner, and bricks in between, is common in the older village homes. Here, with its painted designs of flowers and trees, and occasionally illuminated with strings of coloured lights, it's one of the unexpected delights of Bursa. Also here, on Atatürk Caddesi, is the Grand Mosque, the **Ulu Cami**, completed in 1396 by Yıldırım Beyazıt and twice restored. Here 20 domes, two minarets and the more than usual austerity of the outside give way to a virtuoso display of Arabic calligraphy and a famous carved mihrab within.

Next to the Orhan Camii on the northern side of the park are two lovely 15th-century *hanlar* that mark the entrance to the **bazaar**, the **İpek** ('silk') **Hanı** and the adjoining **Koza** ('cocoon') **Hanı** with a little *mescid* built over a fountain at the centre. Under the Ottomans Bursa was famous for silk; the trade is experiencing something of a comeback today, and each year in late June there is a big silkworm-cocoon market here. The rest of the year, this is the fancy end of the market, largely given over to leather and designer clothing shops; the jewellery and serious antiques await nearby in the *bedesten*. The rest of the market district encompasses everything north of Atatürk Caddesi, nearly a square kilometre in size. The network of covered bazaars and *hanlar* is not quite as large as Istanbul's, with less jewellery, and more bath towels and tea sets. However, it's tidier and has better bargains. You can find just about anything you want here, but the real prizes are the embroidered bed linens, bathroom sets, etc. Whether hand-embroidered on silk or done on a machine, it is some of the most beautiful work you'll see anywhere, and quite inexpensive; save some room in your suitcase. Like any good Turkish bazaar, this one is a labyrinth, a web of long arcades, with streets and *hanlar* tucked in between. Many of the arcades were destroyed in a 1955 fire, but the Bursans have rebuilt them exactly as they were. As in Istanbul, many of the surrounding streets are given over to a particular trade; Demirciler Caddesi, as its name implies, is a whole street of smiths, hammering away in ferrous harmony.

The Citadel

To the west, Atatürk Caddesi curves around the old **citadel**, an extremely strong position that had much to do with maintaining Bursa's peace and quiet over the centuries. Not much remains of the old walls built by the Ottomans, but on the slopes down to Atatürk Caddesi modern Bursa has turned the old fortress into a modern-day version of Nebuchadnezzar's hanging gardens, called **Timurtaş Paşa Parkı**; the slopes, with stairways and terraces full of trees and flowers, and bits of Byzantine arches, give ever-changing views over the old city. There are also many cafés, in which the people of Bursa practically live; wherever there's a beautiful view, common enough in the neighbourhoods on the heights, you'll find a pleasant spot to sit and reflect.

The citadel area contains the oldest houses in the city; more than other cities, Bursa has made an effort at historic preservation, noticeable in such streets as Kale Caddesi, lined with homes of the 17th to 19th centuries. Near the **clock tower**, a landmark visible from most of Bursa, are the **tombs** of the first two great Ottoman sultans, the Osmangazi Türbesi and Orhangazi Türbesi, both restored after heavy damage in the earthquake of 1855. Orhan's sarcophagus lies beside that of his wife, Nilüfer Hatun, a Byzantine princess married off for reasons of political expediency who became the first of the great ladies of the Ottoman Empire.

Two routes lead down from the citadel, one through the meandering streets west to Kaplıca Caddesi, leading eventually down to the Kültür Parkı and suburb of Çekirge (see p.198), the other going back through the hanging gardens. From here, Atatürk Caddesi continues eastwards around the market district. Just beyond Atatürk's statue, the street goes over a small bridge that crosses the narrow chasm of the **Gökdere**. Small cafés overlook the stream, with lawns and flowerbeds arranged in patterns and scrolls. Just beyond, in a little square overshadowed by an enormous plane tree, a road branches off to the left for the Yeşil ('the Green'), one of the loveliest of Bursa's neighbourhoods. This road, the Yeşil Caddesi, goes to the Green Mosque and the Green Mausoleum. Even the street signs here are green.

The Green Mosque (Yeşil Cami)

The Yeşil Cami stands among the finest mosques in Turkey, a marvel not only in the perfection of its form and decoration, but for the way these two elements, the simple structure and the lavish stonecarving and coloured tiles, are combined into a harmonious work of art. We read in the history books of the early Ottoman Turks as grim and resolute Gazi warriors, still attached in many ways to the kind of life their nomadic forefathers led out on the Asian steppe just a few generations before. Their detractors, historians like Gibbon and the Byzantine apologist Steven Runciman, paint them as semi-barbarians who could build an empire but didn't know what to do with one. Such a building as this makes us pause to reconsider. Mehmet I had the Yeşil Cami built in the second decade of the 15th century, at a time when all the Ottomans' resources must have been needed for the reconstruction of the state, so soon after Sultan Beyazıt's disaster at the hands of Tamerlane. Nevertheless, the necessary money and attention were found to construct this masterpiece.

Mehmet's architect, Hacı İvaz Paşa, attempted no radical departures here; the Ottomans had been building in this style for half a century already, in Bursa and elsewhere. Rather, this mosque represents the perfection of that style. If the Ottomans had met an early end like the Selcuks, if they had never taken Constantinople and acquired the resources to build so many copies of the Aya Sofya, the Yeşil Cami would have its page in the art histories as the greatest work of the deceased nation; we would mourn the Ottomans as we do the Selcuks, thinking, 'If only they had built more.' Decadence is a subtle disease; nations do not always reach their political and artistic peaks at the same moment.

Most visitors come down Green Avenue to the place where the Green Mosque and the Green Mausoleum face each other across the street and immediately head for the latter, their eyes caught by the masses of green tile. The very same beautiful sea-green tile from İznik is used around the windows of the mosque, though sparingly, to call attention to the excellent carved stonework. No windows like these exist in Istanbul and certainly nothing like their flowery decoration, an inheritance from the Selcuks, as is the fine gateway with its concave 'stalactite' recess.

Inside, any impression that Mehmet was being cheap with the İznik tiles is immediately dispelled. The mihrab, the ceilings, the upstairs galleries and all the walls up to six feet are covered with them, in blue and green, many with floral designs. The plan is a simple one: a central hall under two shallow domes, one slightly higher than the other, a common form for the smaller early Ottoman mosques, as in the Orhan Camii. The Islamic fascination with geometry is here on display, from the unusual 3-D shapes that support the domes to the intricate patterns, carved into the walnut doors, shutters and mimber, and the geometric medallions intertwined with Koranic calligraphy along the walls.

Some features are unusual. The ribbed interior of the domes shows a Greek influence, recalling the Istanbul Byzantine churches like the Kariye. In the dome near the entrance an oculus sends down a sunbeam at high noon over a beautiful fountain, carved from a single piece of marble. The galleries around it, with some of the best İznik tiles, were meant as private boxes for the sultan and his harem. Two *eyvanlar*, or chambers, flank the central hall, once used for the reception and repose of travelling dervishes.

The Green Mausoleum (Yeşil Türbe)

Green Mausoleum
open 8.30–12
and 1–5.30

Mehmet I, who put up the work, did not command the respect of the other early Ottoman sultans, preoccupied as he was through most of his reign with defeating the intrigues of his brothers and cousins, and with reunifying and rebuilding his shattered state. His conquests were few, but his achievements, in the worst of times, should have earned him more credit than he usually gets. The first cultured man among the Ottoman rulers, he wanted to be buried beside his great mosque, and during the reign of his son Murat II the Yeşil Türbe was built for his remains.

If the mosque had been for Allah, this was for the family. The architect was the same, Hacı İvaz Paşa, but, although he and Murat were not able to confer the same perfection of spirituality upon this tomb, at least in the best family manner they spared no expense, pouring in the rich İznik tiles in numbers exceeded only in the Blue Mosque in Istanbul. There are almost as many inside, sheathing Mehmet's immense sarcophagus, painted with sayings of the Prophet in a bold flowing calligraphy.

The Green Medrese (Yeşil Medrese)

Green Medrese/ Museum of Turkish and Islamic Arts
open Tues–Sun 8.30–12 and 1–5; closed Mon; adm

A third and equally worthy member of this complex stands just a block away on Yeşil Caddesi; the old theological school called the Green Medrese has lately been restored and converted to house Bursa's Museum of Turkish and Islamic Arts. The large ethnographic collection occupies the students' cells and the central courtyard; outside there's a pretty garden with a view over the Gökdere stream and the rest of Bursa. Inside are fine silver, carpets, and swords, İznik ceramics, Selcuk architectural decoration, books and almanacs, and some very unusual 19th-century pottery from Çanakkale, a centre of the ceramic craft after it had died out in İznik. Overhead in some of the domed ceilings around the cloister is more tile work. One speciality of the museum is figures from the old Turkish shadow play *Karagöz*. Bursa likes to claim Karagöz and Hacivat, the traditional Punch and Judy of this ancient entertainment, as its citizens; their 'tomb' is in the suburb of Çekirge. On one puppet you can see the mechanism whereby Karagöz's hat pops up when he is surprised, revealing his bald head.

Yıldırım Beyazıt Camii

Continuing beyond the Yeşil into the eastern edges of Bursa, there are two mosques of the same era, both set up on hills among the rambling cottages and stone walls of this delightful area. The **Emir Sultan Camii** (1431) stands on the street of the same name, off Yeşil Caddesi; it was built by one of the daughters of Yıldırım Beyazıt in honour of her deceased husband. From here, head northward some ten blocks to that sultan's own complex of religious buildings, the **Yıldırım Beyazıt Camii** (1395). In both of these, it's interesting to make architectural comparisons with the Green Mosque, but we can only guess at their original decorative scheme. Like the tombs of Osman and Orhan, and indeed almost everything else in Bursa, these mosques were hit hard by the 1855 earthquake; the city only had resources enough to do a complete job of restoration on the Green complex. As a result, Beyazıt's and Emir Sultan's foundations were left with plain interiors that go well with the structure's formal simplicity but are no substitute for the original.

Beyazıt's mosque may have been especially good. Its *eyvanlar* and uneven twin domes recall the Yeşil Cami, and its arched portico and single slender minaret are fine elements. Before the earthquake, this mosque was the centre of a well-endowed *külliye*, a complex that included a hospital, schools and dervish communities. Of the original eight buildings only the mosque, medrese and Beyazıt's tomb are left. This tomb, small and severe, is probably the most fitting memorial to the most ambitious and least cautious of the Ottoman sultans. Undoubtedly, it would have been grander had not Beyazıt's 14-year reign ended so ignominiously at the Battle of Ankara; here, the mercurial warrior, who expected to become the lord of Europe and Asia, instead ended up as lunch on Tamerlane's table.

Irgandı Sanat Köprüsü

The beautifully restored Irgandı bridge spans the Gökdere river in the Setbaş district. It was constructed in 1442 by architect Hajji Muslihiddin. A single stone arch supports a corridor of artisan shops and bohemian cafés which make a good pitstop on any walking tour of the city. This is one of four surviving shop-lined bridges in the world.

The Muradiye

Returning to the citadel, and beyond it to the west end of Bursa, you may visit the works of a more fortunate monarch, Mehmet II, the Conqueror, at the **Muradiye Complex**, along Kaplıca Caddesi just off the main street which, at this point, has changed its name to Çekirge Caddesi. Among the eleven buildings are a **mosque**, **tombs** and **schools**, all plain, all made of sandstone and narrow brick. There is none of the marble and fine sculptural detail of the earlier mosques here; this no doubt reflects the attitude of Mehmet, always with his eye on Constantinople. If he did not choose to embellish his *külliye*, at least he had himself buried here, next to his father, Murat II, who is interred in a simple *türbe* supported by ancient Corinthian columns with a wide oculus in the dome; Murat had requested that his tomb be open to the sky. The most elaborate tomb here, ironically, belongs to the celebrated upstart Cem Sultan, Mehmet's younger son, who rebelled and intrigued for years against Beyazıt II, his brother. Cem's career as Ottoman pretender would have been an ideal subject for a novel by Sir Walter Scott, but one with a sad end for his partisans. Beyazıt finally managed to pack him off to exile in Italy, in the care of Pope Alexander VI. Even though Beyazıt was paying huge sums for his brother's room and board, the Borgia pope eventually tired of his exotic guest, and had him poisoned. As if in compensation, the sultan brought him to this beautiful mausoleum, with its tiles and painted details in fairyland colours.

Çekirge

'Çekirge' means 'locust' in Turkish, and there are certainly enough of them in the woods that cover this slope of Uludağ. In the days of the sultans, Çekirge, with its famous therapeutic baths and lovely views, was the favoured residence of the imperial families. Today it's Bursa's wealthy suburb, with two miles of hotels and smart new apartments spreading westward from the city. The people of Bursa like to come here to play at the **Kültür Parkı**. Turks in the big cities use their parks the way Westerners would have a century ago: it's charming to see the families in their Sunday best dragging their children along and they, in turn, dragging their balloons; all coming to see and be seen, to eat ice cream and inspect flowers. There is a blue lagoon with a fountain where young couples paddle canoes, an amusement park that must have half the neon in Turkey (its two giant ferris wheels are among Bursa's landmarks), a football stadium and acres of paths. Bursa's **Archaeological Museum**, in the centre of the park, has a smattering of mainly Roman artefacts and a large jewellery and coin collection.

Archaeological Museum
open Tues–Sun 8.30–12 and 1–5; adm

In the same Victorian atmosphere are the fine homes built a century ago in the streets across Çekirge Caddesi. Most are in the typical old Bursa style, in pastel plaster with enclosed wooden balconies, but a few, like the summer houses along the Bosphorus, could easily pass for American Queen Anne-style homes of the 1880s, with more than a touch of Hansel and Gretel thrown in. The city put President Atatürk up in the best of them whenever he came to town, and it has been preserved as the **Atatürk Museum**.

If Çekirge has been the fashionable end of the town ever since Roman times, the springs and thermal baths are the reason, widely prescribed for all manner of ailments and for general well-being besides. Most of Bursa's tourist trade comes for the waters, and several hotels in the district have their own springs. Two Ottoman foundations, called locally the **Eski Kaplıca** (old spring) and the **Yeni Kaplıca** (new spring), the latter in a nice garden next to the Kültür Parkı, are open to the public and are quite popular. Even if you aren't troubled by rheumatism or gout, these are worth a visit. The Yeni Kaplıca was last rebuilt by Süleyman the Magnificent; parts of the Eski Caplıca go back to Byzantine times.

Eski Kaplıca and Yeni Kaplıca
both open all day for both men and women

Further west in Çekirge Caddesi, you pass a little monument called the **Tomb of Karagöz and Hacivat**. One story from old Bursa relates that these incorrigible clowns (the shadow-play figures) were workmen in the service of the sultan, helping to build the Birinci Murat Camii; not only did they never do their own jobs, but with continual arguing and joking, they so distracted the other workers that the sultan was eventually obliged to put them to death. In fact Karagöz and his friend could probably trace their origins back to the ancient Greeks, and they have a surprising amount in common with their 14th-century contemporaries, Harlequin and Pulcinello of the Italian *commedia dell'arte*. Just across the road, the **Karagöz Sanat Evi** (Karagöz Art House) stages shadow play performances on Wednesday and Saturday mornings. In mid-November each year, devotees from around the world gather in Bursa for the four-day **Karagöz Festival**, a puppeteering jamboree, with workshops and hilarious public performances.

At the very end of the city stands the oldest of the imperial mosques, the 1367 **Birinci Murat Camii** (Birinci means the First). At that time, Ottoman architects had not yet found their classic style; this building, good as it is, can be considered an experiment. Roughly square, the mosque occupies only the first floor, with one squat minaret in a corner. The second floor, behind a graceful loggia, was a theological school. The tomb of Murat I in the grounds has been restored too often to be of interest, though Murat himself was a great soldier and statesman who contributed much to the growth of the Ottoman state, with Balkan conquests and rationalization of the government. A Serbian prisoner stabbed Murat in the back at the Battle of Kosovo, his greatest triumph, and his son Beyazıt brought him here to this *türbe*.

Uludağ

⚡ **Uludağ**   If not for the waters, or the charms of the city itself, visitors come to Bursa to see Uludağ, literally 'great mountain' (8,300ft), the tallest peak in northwest Turkey. From Bursa, the mountain may not at first seem impressive, only a steep emerald ridge enfolding the city and stretching to no great height. Take either of the roads around it, however, towards Eskişehir or Kütahya, and you'll see the true Uludağ, standing high above the surrounding plain in the same manner as the much taller mountains of eastern Anatolia. The peak visible from Bursa is only the first of a series, stretching peak after peak into the southeast, with forests, meadows and mountain streams in between.

Uludağ is a national park, with alpine scenery, hiking trails, ski resorts with properly alpine lodges, and several hotels. Due to its proximity to Istanbul, Uludağ is one of the most popular, and expensive, resorts in Turkey, although the skiing at Palandöken near Erzurum (*see* p.463) is more varied and demanding. You can get up Uludağ either by the road off Çekirge Caddesi that runs for 20 miles (32km) almost to the highest summit, or by cable car (the *teleferik*), with a continuous service from the eastern edge of Bursa.

The ancients called Uludağ 'Mount Olympus', the Mysian Olympus, one of eight or so peaks around the Mediterranean with that name. Any mountain credited with being the home of the gods by the natives, as Uludağ was, became an 'Olympus', less a name than a category.

Where to Stay in and around Bursa

The tourist office lists two prices for the city's expensive and moderate range hotels, regular and 'reduced'. Theoretically these are for the off-season, but in many cases you can get the reduced rate any time, from a quarter to a third off the price. It doesn't hurt to try – though don't expect much from the five-star places, which get a steady business from Istanbul and from the Arab world.

(i) **Bursa** >
Orhan Gazi Parkı, Atatürk Caddesi, t 0224 220 1848; they are competent and helpful, as ever in Turkey, though the otherwise good city map they hand out pictures the city upside down; in summer a branch is open just outside the bus station

Central Bursa

(S) Safran, opposite the tombs of Osman and Orhan at Orta Pazar Caddesi Arka Sokak 4, t 0224 224 7216, safran_otel@yahoo.com (€€€). Bursa's most atmospheric hotel, in the old Tophane neighbourhood. Its wood-timbered, mustard-coloured exterior is of traditional Bursan design; inside, the en suite rooms are basic but have phones, TV, mini bar and air-conditioning. Call ahead.

***Dikmen, Maksem Caddesi 78, just north of Atatürk, t 0224 224 1840, www.dikmenotel.com (€€). A slightly cheaper alternative, away from the main drag; recommended above all because it is on a quiet side street. It has a pleasant garden terrace and rooms have TV, mini bar and balcony.

There is a dearth of cheap hotels in the centre of Bursa, a situation made worse by the closure of the city's youth hostel.

Otel Çamlıbel, İnebey Caddesi 71, t 0224 221 2565 (€€). A reasonable, pleasant option; quiet and well run with en suite rooms.

Çeşmeli, one street away, near the covered bazaar, at Gümüşçeken Caddesi 6, t 0224 224 1512 (€€). Run by a friendly Turkish lady.

The biggest collection of cheap rooms in town are near the minibus station.

Terminal, Garaj Batısı 6, t 0224 254 7220 (€€). A bit old and raggedy, but friendly enough and they do their best to keep it up; baths in most rooms, and a hamam downstairs.

Kardeş, Santral Garaj Batısı, t 0224 272 1770 (€€). Slightly more expensive, but friendly and well kept.

Çekirge

Most of the finest establishments are near the hot springs in the Çekirge suburb, a mile west of the centre. Many of these boast thermal baths.

*****Çelik Palas, Çekirge Caddesi 79, t 0224 233 3800, www.celikpalasotel.com (€€€€). The oldest and most renowned – its name, 'Steel Palace', comes from the great steel dome over the baths. It also has tennis courts, an indoor pool, a disco and nearly every other amenity.

***Termal Otel Gönlüferah, I Murat Caddesi No: 24, t 0224 233 9210, www.gonluferahhotel.com (€€€€). An old favourite that has undergone a complete facelift, and the results are most impressive. With a stunning hamam, thermal baths, spa and beautifully decorated rooms, this is most certainly Bursa's finest.

****Dilmen Oteli, I Murat Caddesi 20, t 0224 233 9500, www.hoteldilmen.com/english (€€€€; reduced rates for children and online bookings), has fewer luxuries than other four-star places. It has no main thermal bath complex, but all rooms have en suite baths with mineral water running from the taps.

***Adapalas, I Murat Caddesi 21, t 0224 233 3990, www.adapalas.com, (€€€). Has thermal baths and is good value.

Yeşilyayla, Çekirge Caddesi, Selvi Sokak 6, t 0224 239 6496 (€€). The most appealing of the few budget hotels in Çekirge. Set slightly back from the main road, the wooden building is painted green throughout; old-fashioned double doors open onto the bedrooms from the large central hallway. Although toilets are communal, guests do have use of a small hamam in the basement.

Uludağ

Most establishments on Uludağ are closed outside the winter months and full board is usually mandatory. Accommodation is mostly in chalet-style ski lodges.

****Kervansaray, 1 Gelişim Bölgesi, **t** 0224 285 2187 (€€€€–€€€). The grandest place to stay. With immediate access to the ski lifts, the hotel has any number of activities to keep you busy pre- or post-piste, from an indoor pool and squash to a disco. After all that exercise, you may not care that the bedrooms are comfortable rather than appealing.

Kar Oberj, in the national park, **t** 0224 285 2121 (midweek €€, weekends €€€ but for full board). One of the least expensive hotels.

Eating Out in and around Bursa

Bursa

İskender Kebapçı, Ünlü Caddesi 7, **t** 0224 221 4615 (€). Bursa is the home of the *İskender kebap*, a mixed grill with a tomato-based sauce served on a bed of *pide* bread, finished off with a dollop of yogurt and a drizzle of spicy melted butter. You can sample it at this restaurant that claims to have first created the dish. Founded in 1867, it's an odd-looking place, but you'll eat well for 17 YTL with a soft drink. Other *İskender kebap* places are all over town, charging an average of 9 YTL. The **Hacı Bey** chain is very good, with branches in Çekirge and on Atatürk Bulvarı, west of the post office. **Nazar Restaurant**, in the İç Koza Han in the bazaar area is a local favourite.

★ **Kalecik** >

Kalecik, Kale Sok 27, **t** 0224 225 5473, *www.kalecikcafe.com* (€€). Tucked away in a discreet *cul de sac* in the Tophane neighbourhood is the delightful Kalecik restaurant, serving a variety of tasty house inventions ranging from specially prepared steaks and kebabs to pasta, fish and vegetarian dishes. The owner, Miss Sönmez, is also a painter, and her watercolours of Bursa decorate the walls. In the evenings the Ottoman lamps are dimmed in the courtyard out back.

Sakarya Caddesi is Bursa's answer to Istanbul's Balıkpazarı, known to locals as Arap Şükrü Sokak. As you follow the main street, here called Altıparmak Caddesi, as it curves around the Hisar, Sakarya branches off to the left. This pedestrian street, lined with restaurants and bars with outside tables, is one of the two places to go in the evening. As you wander up the narrow alley, you'll see five restaurants all named after the man who put this street on the culinary map several decades ago – Arap Şükrü. Outside each establishment stands an experienced waiter casting out his rudimentary English line to the tourists drifting past. Outside dining hours there will be plenty of places open for beer and snacks.

Kültür Parkı is the other place to go, where half of Bursa comes on any given night to row boats around the lagoon and inspect the pavilions of the permanent industrial exhibition, featuring Turkish-made cars, eggbeaters and double-glazing. There are a number of agreeable outdoor restaurants, doubling as beer gardens in the off hours; the **Ocakbaşı**, near the lagoon, is one of the best-priced, with a wide choice of kebabs, delicious, thin home-made *pide* and a pretty fruit plate for dessert. At **Akarsu**, for a bit more you can enjoy the wide choice of *mezes* while overlooking the lagoon – come on a Saturday night and there may well be a wedding party in the place.

Uludağ Kebapçısı, Garaj Karşısı Şirin Sok 12, **t** 0224 254 7264. If you find yourself near the bus station, you won't do better for 10 YTL than here; serves a great *kebap*. Open until 11pm.

Akay Çiğ Borekçisi, Eski Bakırcılar Çarşısı, Dokum Sokak 5, **t** 0224 221 9924. If you need a quick pit stop in the bazaar, do not miss the bargain *çiğ borek* (stuffed savoury fritters) served at this Bursan legend. This tiny family business has been going for three generations.

North and East of Bursa

Few cities enjoy such a paradisiacal hinterland. To the south there's Uludağ and its mountain forests and lakes; any other direction takes you through landscapes so green and lush they will make you drowsy looking at them (Uludağ catches all the rain). Turkey's farmers have made good use of this land; all along the main roads they have set up stands to sell you colossal juicy peaches, perfect sour cherries or whatever else is in season.

Directly north of Bursa is **Mudanya**, a large, gloomy port that saw the signing of the armistice ending the Turkish War of Independence in 1922. Further on, past **Gemlik** and **Gemlik Bay**, you'll come to **Termal**. Emperors Constantine and Justinian enjoyed the thermal baths; you can do the same, although there's no other reason to stop. The road continues north to meet the sea at **Yalova**, from where ferries cross to Istanbul. It's a bright and breezy town, with yet another product of the Atatürk statue factory in its square; this one is more dramatic than most, depicting the Great Man in strident pose, arm upraised as if to strike. Should you wish to risk swimming in this less-than-clean stretch of the Marmara, there are beaches at **Çiftlikköy**, **Koruköy** and **Çınarcık**, all west of Yalova. The water at **Armutlu**, on the western edge of the peninsula, is clearer but the beach is nothing special.

Ancient Mysia was the province stretching from Bursa towards the east, including much of the southern shore of the Marmara and the city of **Balıkesir**, the ancient Paleokastro. Ancient geography, as is usual in Asia Minor, was never too clear about boundaries; for a while the Romans were wont to call the area around Bursa Phrygia Minor, and the city itself, along with the territory to the east, Bithynia. Today these lands along the valley of the Sakarya river, the ancient Sangarius, are in one of the more fortunate corners of Turkey, even if they no longer have a sense of being a distinct region. The countryside is green and good, and obviously cultivated with loving care; the villages, with their characteristic brick and timber dwellings, drift through the decades in a permanent state of genteel dilapidation. Bilecik would have been the most interesting, had it not been destroyed in the War of Independence. Of its early Ottoman monuments only the **Karasu Bridge**, reputed to be the work of Mimar Sinan, remains.

İnegöl, to the west, is an agricultural town famous throughout Turkey for spicy meatballs, *İnegöl köfte*, while in **Söğüt** you may visit the **tomb of Ertuğrul**, the father of Osman, founder of the Ottoman dynasty. In a way this Sakarya valley is the original Ottoman homeland, a secure and uncontested spot in the 13th century, a perfect place for an ambitious band of roving warriors to await its opportunities with patience. The Byzantines were too feeble to

Getting around North and East of Bursa

Regular **buses** from Bursa make the one-hour trip to İznik, taking the scenic route along the southern shore of the lake. If you're **driving**, consider carefully any trip from Bursa east to Yalova; traffic can be as intense as in Bursa's centre.

Mudanya has infrequent **car ferries** and summer **hydrofoils** to Istanbul, though for car and coach travellers it will usually be more convenient to take the short Güzelyalı–Yenikapı **ferry** to get to the city.

---

trouble them, and no serious enemies appeared from the east either; despite all the talent of the early Ottomans, one can perhaps attribute much of their early success to a lucky choice of locations. Maybe the spot is always lucky for the Turks; just a couple of miles south of Söğüt, the climactic battle of their War of Independence was fought at **İnönü** in 1921. A few years later, when Atatürk decided that all Turks should have Western-style surnames, he himself conferred one upon the general who had won the battle and halted the Greek offensive. İsmet Paşa now became İsmet Inönü, later the second president of the Turkish Republic.

İznik (Nicaea)

 İznik

Between the Sakarya and Gemlik Bay, an inlet of the Marmara, a circle of wooded hills isolates a large lake, **İznik Gölü**, named after the ancient city on its eastern shore. İznik, the ancient Nicaea, was founded in the 4th century BC. For a while it was the capital of the Kingdom of Bithynia, before the Romans swallowed it up, but it wasn't until the Christian era that the city achieved its fame, or perhaps its notoriety, as seat of two great church councils. First in the 4th century and again in the 8th, the querulous bishops and bureaucrats of early Christianity met here to argue, anathematize their enemies or smash them with bats, and run up uncollectible bills at the local hostelries.

> ### The Church Councils
> Constantine first summoned the church councils in 325 to decide the insoluble conflict between the Arian and Athanasian sects. His favourite, St Athanasius, came all the way from Alexandria to lead his partisans in the attack, demanding that every Christian admit both the divine and mortal natures of Christ. Arius, who has been called a 'unitarian', wanted to avoid having the godhead cluttered with extra, inessential 'essences', and got himself murdered here for his trouble, though his party won a short-lived victory. Nicaea, a beautiful resort city in a strategic location, central for the eastern half of the empire, had already been a residence of Emperor Diocletian; the Church Fathers found it a wonderfully agreeable locale for conventions and they came often, most importantly for the great council of 786, when the bishops codified rituals and beliefs into the form still observed by the Greek Church today.
>
> Empress Irene, who almost married Charlemagne but could not bear to part with the intrigues and luxury of Constantinople, may have been an outrageous tart, but she is remembered fondly by the Orthodox for calling this council to put an end finally to the Iconoclastic struggles that had so bitterly divided the empire. Convening at Nicaea's church of Aya Sofya, the bishops from as far away as Italy decided once and for all that holy images 'stimulate spectators to think of the originals', and therefore deserved an indirect sort of adoration, though not worship.

İznik Tiles

İznik tiles were made with a quality of colour and design that cannot be imitated today. Expensive though they must have been, all the early Ottoman sultans demanded them in enormous quantity for their mosques, and today they can be seen on buildings across Turkey wherever earthquakes and decay have spared them. They can be approximately dated by colour and pattern. Until 1520, all İznik ceramics were exclusively dark blue and white. About that time, turquoise was added. A kind of red, always difficult in glazing, was achieved in the 1600s. Throughout the 17th and 18th centuries, designs grew less abstract and more naturalistic; floral designs predominated in the Tulip Period and after, and even human and animal figures were appearing near the end in the early 1800s.

Nicaea's finest hour, however, came in the dark days following the Sack of Constantinople in 1204. A die-hard, Theodore Lascaris, brought the remnants of Greek resistance here and became emperor-in-exile; he and his successor, John III Vatatzes, reconstituted the empire, rebuilding its finances and army for the day when Constantinople would again be theirs.

The Selcuk Turks held the city and made it their capital for a brief period in the 11th century, and it fell again, finally, to the Ottoman leader Orhan in 1331. As a Turkish city, Nicaea, now İznik, gained fame throughout the Islamic world for its hand-painted ceramic tiles. As the finances of the empire declined, the market for these tiles disappeared, and the city with it. İznik had reached its peak of prosperity in the 17th century with 300 workshops turning out thousands of tiles a week; by the 19th century only a dismal village was left inside the old Byzantine walls, and even that remainder suffered grievous damage in the fighting of 1922.

Today, some leftover grace from its days of greatness keeps İznik free of the usual sadness that accompanies ruins. The town is simply too full of roses and children and green gardens to be melancholy. Indeed, the modest agricultural centre that İznik has become cannot nearly fill the square mile or so within its Byzantine walls, and its people wisely use the remaining space for vegetable plots and olive groves. Until recently, whatever talent was left from the long-gone ceramic industries was devoted to making cinder blocks and roof tiles. Not a jot of documentation had survived from the golden age of tilemaking: the master craftsmen of the 16th and 17th centuries had taken their secrets with them to the grave – or so they thought. The **İznik Foundation** was set up in 1993 to re-learn the lost techniques. Archaeological excavations of the İznik kiln sites had already yielded much practical information. Scientists from as far away as M.I.T. in the USA analysed the tiles, revealing that they contained up to 80 per cent quartz. Even with this knowledge, it took another two years of hit-and-miss experimentation before the foundation could come up with something approximating the original 400-year-old tile recipe. Commercial production was finally begun in 1995, but it was decided not to produce exact copies of the 16th-century designs, for fear they would be sold on to hapless tourists as originals. The foundation is situated on the lake road at Sahil Yolu, Halı Saha Arkası; the tourist office should be able to facilitate a visit. Unlike the disappointing tiles in the stack-em high, sell-em cheap shops nearby, those on display at the showroom of **Eşref Eroğlu** on the main Kılıçaslan Caddesi are masterpieces, each one signed and dated; his designs are both figurative and abstract.

Even though the foundation of the city predates the Romans, İznik has the plan of a typical Roman provincial town: two broad main streets meeting at right angles in the centre, connecting the four main gates. Nearly all of İznik's **walls** can still be seen, in various stages of decay, and along the garden paths and sheep trails you find the occasional arch or Greek inscription, towers, sally-ports and storage rooms. Two of the gates, the northern or **Istanbul Gate** and the western or **Lefke Gate**, survive, with Roman triumphal arches between their inner and outer parts, inscriptions in Greek and Latin commemorating the visit of the Emperor Hadrian, and remains of marble reliefs. The Lefke Gate is the better preserved, and near it are parts of a much-weathered decorative frieze. Also carved, inconspicuously, on the inside of the gate is something that is obviously a layout for the game of Nine Men's Morris (others can be seen on the steps of the Basilica Julia in the Roman Forum, the Basilica of St John at Selcuk and in scores of sites across the Mediterranean; this must have been the favourite game of classical antiquity). Outside the gate, the Byzantine aqueduct has suffered little from time, though it's no longer in use.

Inside the walls, little remains of ancient İznik. Near the ruined **Yenişehir Gate** at the south entrance, the half-excavated ruins of the **Roman theatre** are visible behind a fence. Amidst one of Turkey's best-kept public gardens in the centre of the town stands the derelict church of **Aya Sofya**, an 11th-century structure that replaced the earlier church from the era of Justinian that hosted the two ecumenical councils. Some fragments of mosaics and frescoes can still be seen. The conquering Ottomans added a minaret, and its stump is currently the home of one of İznik's numerous storks.

Aya Sofya
open Tues–Sun 9–12 and 1–4.30; adm

Storks, surprisingly, spend their summers in Turkey. This kind have little to do with their North European cousins, and spend their winters in eastern or southern Africa. Ruined minaret stumps make perfect bases for their nests, combining good drainage, peace and quiet, and inaccessibility to weasels. A favourite nesting place for storks is atop the ruined minaret near the Istanbul Gate, next to the **Nilüfer Hatun İmareti**, a 14th-century hospice for travelling dervishes that now serves as the **İznik Museum**. Here a selection of artefacts, from recent Turkish crafts going back to Palaeolithic tools, proves the long continuity of this site; more

İznik Museum
open Tues–Sun 8.30–12 and 1–5; adm

interesting are the grave steles and architectural fragments arranged in the garden outside. Ranging from the early Hellenistic to the late Byzantine, the steles provide a kind of glossary of symbols, a complete guide to the inexhaustible iconography of death that so long occupied the Greek world's fancy.

Not surprisingly, the most important part of the museum's small collection is devoted to ceramics, some as old as 2500 BC, as well as the best Islamic work. A city map on the wall of the museum helps in finding your way through the village to the ancient sites and around the walls. Ask at the museum about a possible excursion to the **Yeraltı Mezarı**, north of town, a 6th-century Byzantine tomb with some fine frescoes; they have the keys.

Across the street from the museum, the **Yeşil Cami**, built in the 1380s, will catch your eye with what may be the prettiest minaret in all Anatolia. The blue and green tiles that cover it are not original İznik work, however; during restorations in the last century it was necessary to replace them all.

There are no good beaches on İznik's lake shore, but people still come here, particularly from Bursa, to walk along the promenade outside the town's ruined **Lake Gate**, and to eat fresh fish in the restaurants on the water's edge. If you come on just the right day in the spring, you can ski down Uludağ in the morning and swim in Lake İznik or the Marmara in the afternoon.

(i) **Yalova** >>
Cumhuriyet Meydanı 5,
t 0226 814 2108

(i) **İznik** >
Kılıçaslan Caddesi 130,
t 0224 757 1933

Where to Stay North and East of Bursa

İznik

Çamlık Motel, t 0224 757 1631, *www.iznik-camlikmotel.com* (€€). The best available, right on the lake shore at Göl Caddesi 1. It's a friendly family motel where rooms are clean but modest; also a good restaurant.

Cem Otel, Göl Sahili Caddesi 34, **t** 0224 757 1687, *www.cemotel.com* (€€). Good value and location near the lake. *Open all year.*

Kaynarca Pansiyon, M. Günden Sokak 1, **t** 0224 757 1753, *www.kaynarca.net* (€€–€). The corridors here are a riot of colour, decked out with naïve paintings of Aya Sofya frescoes and İznik tile designs. The welcoming management tries hard to please, offering free use of the kitchen; there's also an internet café downstairs. Couples must provide proof of marriage if booking a double room.

Yalova

Otel Fatih, Cumhuriyet Caddesi 27 (€). Cheerful, comfortable and good value.

There's also a wide choice of cheap *pensions*, all near the ferries.

Eating Out North and East of Bursa

İznik and Around

In İznik fish are easy to come by in a number of restaurants along the lakeside promenade. The **Çamlık** and **Cem** hotel restaurants both have a good selection of dishes and are also popular with locals, as well as guests.

Bülbül Lokanta, on Kılıçaslan Caddesi between the tourist office and the Aya Sofya (€). Cheap, clean and friendly, serving stews and casseroles.

Konya Etli Pide, opposite the Aya Sofya (€). For meat and kebabs, with friendly staff and delicious *pide* from 6 YTL – the house special.

The North Aegean Coast

After İstanbul, Turkey's Aegean coast has long been the country's main attraction, originally for scholars and philhellenes who came to stroll through the ruins of cities renowned in antiquity, and nowadays for holidaymakers who combine a tour of the sites with the pleasures of the Aegean. The climate is pleasant, tempered by the sea in the summer and winter; olives and vineyards cover the fertile valleys and coastal plains. Mountains are never far away, nor are beaches – some in the throes of becoming major resorts, others quite deserted.

The northern part, Mysia and Lydia in ancient times, is a bit less touristy than the south – no fleshpots, but serene, laid-back resorts such as Ayvalık and Behramkale (Assos). The major attractions are archaeological: Troy, of course, and Pergamon (Bergama), one of the great cities of the Hellenistic era.

09

Don't miss

⭐ **Homeric landscapes**
Troy **p.209**

⭐ **A delightfully laid-back resort**
Ayvalık **p.220**

⭐ **The most exquisite ruins**
Ancient Pergamon **p.224**

⭐ **Turkey at its most modern**
İzmir **p.234**

See map overleaf

p.174

The North Aegean Coast

Sea of Marmara

Gelibolu

Läpseki
(Lampsakas)

Kale

Gökçeada

Eceabat

Biga

Çanakkale

Dardanelles

Bozcaada

Troy • Tevfikiye

Çan

*Bozca
Ada*

Alexandria
Troas

*Mount
Ida* ▲

Ayvacik

Attınoluk   Akçay

Assos

Küçükkuyu

Edremit

Balıkesir

*To
Kütahya*

*Gulf of
Edremit*

Ören

Alibey

Ayvalık

*Lesbos
(Mytilini)
(Greek)*

Sarımsaklı

Altınova

Soma

Bergama

Dikili

*A e g e a n
S e a*

Çandarlı   Pergamon

Akhisar

Aliağa

*Karaburun
Peninsula*

Eski Foça

*Magnesia
and Sipylum*

*Lake
Marmara*

Kuçukbahçe

*İzmir
Bay*

*Chios
(Greek)*

Erythrae

Manisa

Kemalpaşa

Sardis

To Usak

İzmir

Clazomenae

Çeşme Ilıca

Urla

Turgutlu

Teos

Siğacık

pp.384–5

100 km

50 miles

GEORGIA

T U R K E Y

p.250

SYRIA

CYPRUS

IRAQ

Don't miss

⭐ Troy p.209

⭐ Ayvalık p.220

⭐ Ancient Pergamon p.224

⭐ İzmir p.234

N

Getting to and around Troy and Çanakkale

Çanakkale is connected by **bus** to Istanbul, Bursa, İzmir and Edirne; the **ferry** crosses the Dardanelles from Eceabat hourly between 6am and midnight. The crossing takes 25 minutes and is ridiculously cheap, and it carries the very regular **dolmuş** from Kilitbahir, as well as buses to Tekirdağ and Istanbul. There are also informal ferries between Çanakkale and Kilitbahir, if you want to have a look at Mehmet II's unusual castle. These are small, usually unmarked boats that go whenever there are enough people; ask around.

From Çanakkale's *otogar*, a few streets south of the port on Atatürk Caddesi, frequent **minibuses** go to Troy and the neighbouring villages; naturally buses from across the straits stop in the centre too, on İskele Meydanı. Çanakkale is the most popular base for exploring both the Gelibolu battlefields and ancient Troy.

Troy and Çanakkale

Troy (Truva)

 Troy

From the time of Alexander the Great, travellers have come expressly to see Troy. No place is so highly charged in the Western imagination; after two and a half millennia, the wrath of Achilles, the beauty of Helen, the death of Hector, the ploy of the wooden horse, the sack of the high-walled city and the misfortunes that dogged the victors in Homer's *Iliad* and *Odyssey* have retained their poetic resonance, each character and event an evocative, ambiguous symbol deeply embedded in our culture. For the ancient Greeks, the *Iliad*'s account of the Olympian gods was the source of their religious beliefs. And who can argue with Herodotus, who saw the Trojan War as the root and mirror of all later antagonisms between East and West?

Few ancients doubted the veracity of Homer's Troy; Alexander even exchanged some of his own armour for trophies from the Trojan War still hanging in Athena's temple. But by the 6th century AD the city was abandoned, its port silted up, the Anatolian dust thickening over it until the physical Troy vanished from all memory. Outwardly the site resembled a hill, which the Turks called **Hisarlık**; scholars argued over where the city might have stood, had it really existed. Byron was one of many who visited the Troad (the region around Troy), and one of very few who left believing in more than its poetic truth. In Don Juan he wrote,

I've stood upon Achilles' tomb,
And heard Troy doubted; time will doubt of Rome.

Another believer was Heinrich Schliemann, a merchant who made a fortune from the California Gold Rush and the American Civil War. In 1868, 46 years old and tired of wheeling and dealing, he came to the Troad, where he met an Englishman named Frank Calvert who had dug a trench in Hisarlık and showed Schliemann his finds: part of a classical temple and, deeper down, signs of older civilizations, layered one on top of the other. Schliemann was hooked, and the former businessman became the greatest dilettante archaeologist of all time, one destined to unearth Troy, Mycenae and Tiryns, a series of spectacular finds that electrified the world. Subsequent archaeologists, especially Schliemann's assistant Dörpfeld and the American Carl Blegen, uncovered further proof that Hisarlık is indeed the site of ancient Troy.

Recent Theories

As Calvert had brilliantly surmised, Schliemann found layer upon layer of civilization, which he numbered from Troy I – the oldest, dating back to 3600 BC – to Troy IX, the Hellenistic city of Ilion, founded by Alexander's general Lysimachus. Although Schliemann's aim was to discover the Troy of Priam and Hector, he uncovered a fascinating chronicle of people building over and over again on the same site. Most scholars date the Trojan War to c. 1250 BC, just before the decline of the Mycenaean empire; Troy VII coincides rather neatly with that date, and it perished in a terrible conflagration. However, the city preceding it, Troy VI, was far more imposing and better fits the epithets Homer used in the *Iliad* – but it was destroyed by an earthquake.

Turkish archaeologists resolve the contradiction by seeing magnificent Troy VI as the citadel that Agamemnon's Achaeans unsuccessfully besieged for ten years; rebuilt shoddily after the earthquake, it was then easily captured. The Wooden Horse, it follows, was an offering by the Achaeans to Poseidon, the sea god and earth-shaker, whose assistance proved crucial in their sack of Troy. Others believe the *Iliad*, composed some 500 years after the traditional date of the war, recalls not one particular event but several Mycenaean raids on the Anatolian coast; or perhaps even the last great twilight expedition, recited for latter-day kings by their bards to evoke the good old days.

In any event, no definite proof has ever been discovered in Troy that the Trojan War took place, although many recent discoveries prove that the Mycenaean Greeks were in Asia Minor as early as the 15th century BC; in 1984 some of their tombs were discovered on an ancient beach at Besike Bay, one of the possible sites of Troy's long-vanished harbour.

But what has kept the debates on the Trojan War on the front burner since Schliemann is the finding of references to Troy in the dead languages of Anatolia. In the 1920s, scholars read about the Ahhiyawans – probably the Achaeans – when translating tablets from the 15th-century BC Hittite archives at Boğazkale. The archives also refer to a place called Wilusa, believed to be Ilios, Homer's other name for Troy. Then, in 1984, some very suggestive evidence turned up in Luvian – an ancient Indo-European language, possibly the language of the Trojans – referring to 'steep Wilusa' and men named Priya-muwas (Priam?) and Paris. Add the fact that linguistically some lines of the *Iliad* have been shown to be older than the traditional date of the Trojan War (1250 BC), and the problem becomes even more complicated.

The Site

The **Trojan horse** is certainly still there, or at least its modern Turkish descendant. It's the first thing you see at Troy and the only thing most tourists take pictures of. For, in all honesty, the site itself is bewildering, 'a ruin of a ruin' as some call it, a victim of 19th-century archaeology. Schliemann's original nine layers contained some 46 substrata; what you see as you walk through the excavations are fragments of a millefeuille pastry of Troys.

The tall Mycenaean **walls** of **Troy VI** are the most impressive sight and among the most beautiful of the ancient world. They fit the Homeric descriptions of 'beetling' and 'steep', and at one point in the *Iliad* (Book XVI) Homer refers to their most unusual feature – angles that divide the wall into several sections. Here, too, are the foundations of a mighty bastion, perhaps Homer's 'great tower of Ilios'. Yet, splendid as these walls still are, they are not of any great extent: this eminence was the citadel of Troy, not the city. The **Southern Gate** (Homer's Scaean gate?) facing the plain was the most important; the so-called **Pillar House** above it is the most popular candidate for Priam's Palace.

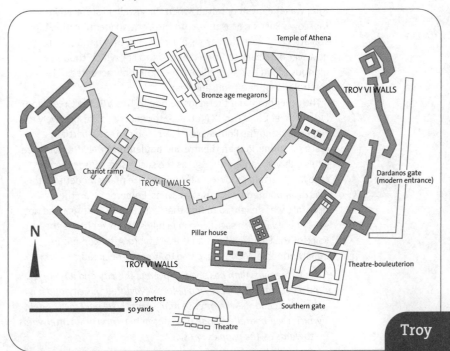

Troy

Near the entrance you can walk up a surviving section of the old **Hisarlık mound**, for a view that evokes Homer perhaps even better than the old stones. There, on a clear day, is Mount Ida to the southeast, from where Zeus watched the war. To the west, on a very clear day, you can make out Mount Fingari (Moon Mountain) on the island of Samothrace, where Poseidon sat. In the plain below wanders the Scamander River, whose god tried to drown Achilles for turning the water red with the blood of the Trojans. The two mounds near the river's mouth at Sigeion Point are by tradition the **tombs of Achilles** and his friend **Patroclus**, whose death at the hand of Hector finally roused Achilles from his sulking wrath to return to the battlefield. On most days, you are also aware of another Homeric epithet – 'windy'.

The path through the excavations leads past the ruins of the **Temple of Athena**, last rebuilt by the Romans, to the great flagged **chariot ramp**. It was near here that Schliemann unearthed the controversial 'Jewels of Helen', the one really splendid treasure found on the site. The jewellery convinced many sceptics that this was indeed the Troy of Homer, and Schliemann was so proud of his find that he couldn't resist smuggling the baubles out of Turkey to adorn his wife at Athenian parties. Finally he gave the jewellery to the Berlin Museum, from where it disappeared in 1945. Many thought it had been destroyed during the attack on Berlin, others that it had been pillaged by Soviet occupation forces. Not until 1994 was the mystery solved, when the jewellery surfaced in Moscow's Pushkin Museum, with the German identification tags still attached. Both the 'Jewels of Helen' and the chariot ramp, however, date back to Troy II (2600–2300 BC), which, though a glorious city in its day, predates the commonly accepted date of the Trojan War by a thousand years.

The other prominent remains belong to **Troy VIII**, the Greek Ilion (700–300 BC), and Troy IX (300 BC–4th century AD), respectively the Hellenistic and the Roman New Ilium. You can see a partially restored **shrine**, **Roman theatre** and **bouleuterion**. Neither of these cities was very large, although as the successors of Troy they enjoyed a certain renown. Julius Caesar, like many modern visitors, was disappointed by the meagre ruins; Emperor Julian the Apostate was delighted to find that Christianity in AD 354 had not yet done away with sacrifices on Achilles' tomb. Yet it was the voice of the East that has had the last word. After conquering Constantinople, Mehmet II came to Troy and declared:

It is to me that Allah has given to avenge this city and its people... Indeed it was the Greeks who before devastated this city, and it is their descendants who after so many years have paid me the debt which their boundless pride had contracted – and often afterwards – towards us, the peoples of Asia.

Çanakkale

Troy, or *Truva* as the Turks call it, is 27km from Çanakkale, which most visitors use as a base for visiting the excavations. On the way you can stop at **Tevfikiye**, the only oasis of tackiness Troy has produced, with its trinket shops and fake 'House of Schliemann'; actually, the whole village was built of materials quarried from Schliemann's dig. Çanakkale, at one of the Dardanelles' ferry crossings, is a pleasant, slightly faded provincial capital, the ancient Greek Abydos, successor to Troy. Its name in Turkish means 'saucer castle', 'saucer' recalling the town's old ceramics industry which once produced florid Turkish Art Nouveau – though the town lives more from tourism and tuna-fishing today. The castle, one of several built by Mehmet the Conqueror to hem in Constantinople, still guards the Hellespont, housing soldiers and a small **Military and Naval Museum** with a special display devoted to the heroics of Atatürk during the Gelibolu campaign. Outside the castle is a mock-up of the Nusrat, the Turkish minelayer that sealed the straits to Allied destroyers, thus precipitating the landings. (One bit of naval history they missed is that Çanakkale was probably the spot where the Persian King Xerxes made his famous bridge of boats in 483 BC, when his vast horde was marching to invade Greece.) The excellent **Archaeological Museum** is 2km from the centre, and stars finds from the Dardanos Tumulus. This, dating from the 4th century BC, was discovered 10km south of Çanakkale in 1959 and produced golden diadems, ivories, gold jewellery, votive statuary and the remains of a wooden harp.

The best thing about Çanakkale is its lively waterfront, where the whole town along with the visiting ANZACs come each evening for a promenade and a fish dinner. The nearest beach to Çanakkale is the thin strip of sand at **Kepez**, 6km west of town. The beach at **Dardanos**, 5km further on, is better. **Güzelyalı**, a small fishing village-cum-resort 18km southwest of Çanakkale, also has a beach.

Military and Naval Museum
open Tues, Wed and Fri–Sun 9–12 and 1.30–5; closed Mon and Thurs; adm

Archaeological Museum
open Tues–Sun 8.30–5; closed Mon; adm

Where to Stay in and around Çanakkale

ⓘ **Çanakkale >**
Next to Abdülhamid's clock tower at İskele Meydanı 67, the main square by the port, t 0286 217 1187

Çanakkale

****Akol Hotel, Kordonboyu, t 0286 217 9456, *www.hotelakol.com* (€€€). The most comfortable, and most expensive, hotel in Çanakkale; plush double rooms with air-conditioning, TV, balcony and so on.

***Otel Anafartalar, İskele Meydanı, t 0286 217 4454, *www.hotelanafartalar. com.tr* (€€). Closer to the centre and correspondingly noisier, but has

rooms with balconies that gaze across the Dardanelles to Kilitbahir.

Kervansaray, Fetvane St. No:13, t 0286 217 8192, *www.otelkervansaray.com* (€€). The most atmospheric of the hotels here, an old Ottoman house; doubles cost around €50, more during the ANZAC day memorials.

Kestanbol, just around the corner from the bus station at Hasan Mevsuf Sokak 5, t 0286 217 0857, *www. hotelkestanbol.com* (€€). Poky rooms with balconies and television.

Çanakkale can seem like a 1960s time capsule in summer, loaded with bright-eyed, clean-cut backpackers. The vast majority, as you will soon discover, hail from the Antipodes, and there are plenty of places that specialize in accommodating them.

(★) **Hotel Efes >**

Hotel Efes, on Aralık Sokak 5, t 0286 217 3256, *www.efeshotelcanakkale.com* (€). Çanakkale's best choice by far, with a peaceful garden complete with gurgling fountain. It is quieter than most, too, set back from the main street, with its own parking spaces. Run single-handedly by the house-proud and delightfully chirpy Mrs Yetimoğlu; good-value spotless doubles with private shower.

Anzac House Hostel, Cumhuriyet Bulvarı, t 0286 217 1392, *www. anzachouse.com* (€). Rooms can be a bit musty and almost half of them don't have windows; shower and toilet facilites are shared. The friendly and very helpful staff serve up beer and Vegemite sandwiches (would we lie?) and show battle documentaries on video; everyone has a good time. Like many other Çanakkale hotels, they arrange tours of the battlefield.

There is certainly no shortage of **campgrounds** around Çanakkale, from the large and well-equipped **Truva Mocamp** at Güzelyalı, t 0286 232 8025, which has a restaurant/canteen, to the simpler **Paradise Camping**, t 0286 263 6178, near the beach at Dardanos.

Güzelyalı and Tevfikiye

Güzelyalı, 18km from Çanakkale, has several comparatively swanky hotels, popular with holidaying Turks. Güzelyalı also has a handful of *pansiyonlar* and there are campsites at Kepez and Dardanos.

If you are mainly interested in Troy, as an alternative to Çanakkale you might stay in Tevfikiye, though it has only a few very modest *pansiyonlar*, plus a *lokanta*.

★★★★**İris Oteli**, Mola Caddesi 48, t 0286 232 8628, *www.irisotel.com* (€€€). The best of Güzelyalı's options; the town's only disco, as well as its own stretch of beach, and water sports.

★★★★**Tusan Oteli**, t 0286 232 8747, *www.tusanhotel.com* (€€€). In a pretty setting in the woods, new and bright and slightly less expensive, also with a private beach, windsurfing and water-skiing, etc.

Eating Out in Çanakkale

Çanakkale is a great place for a fish dinner: there are a number of good restaurants competing for your trade, all in a row near the castle, and all with outside tables on the harbour.

Yalova Liman Restaurant, t 0286 217 1045, *www.yalovarest.com* (€€). The institution where most locals and any passing politicians prefer to splurge, with its breezy rooftop terrace. You can snack on the excellent seafood mezes for 6 YTL per plate, or splash out on a full fish meal for upwards of 20 YTL.

Rıhtım, Eski Balıkhane Sokak 7–9, t 0286 212 5367, next door (€€). Very similar, and also good.

Ömur Köfte Salonu, on the waterfront near the Hotel Bakır (€). A less expensive choice; you can get tasty kebabs and *köfte*, and sometimes grilled fish.

Aussie and Kiwi Restaurant, around the corner on Yalı Caddesi (€). Recommended by readers both for the food and the proprietor.

Turkey's Aegean Islands

Gökçeada and Bozcaada are Turkey's sole possessions amongst the Aegean islands, both of them wrested from the defeated Greeks in 1923. Strategically they are important, guarding the mouth of the Dardanelles, and both are heavily militarized, staring across the sea at the equally well-defended Greek islands of Samothraki and Limnos. Historically and ethnically, the islands are more Greek than Turkish and were exempted from the population

Getting to the Aegean Islands

Kabatepe, on the Gelibolu peninsula, is the port for Gökçeada, though in summer there are also services from Çanakkale. **Boats** for Bozcaada depart from Odun İskelesi south of Çanakkale; it's a trip of less than half an hour, but first you need to get to Odun İskelesi, an hour's **minibus** ride from Çanakkale. Services to both Aegean islands can be infrequent, particularly in the winter.

exchange. Since the Cyprus conflict, many of the indigenous Greeks have left, driven out by years of nagging Turkish oppression (mirrored by the treatment of ethnic Turks in Greek Thrace).

Gökçeada (the Imbros of the Greeks and Imbroz of Homer) is a green, lumpy island whose few visitors tend to head straight for Kale in the north where there are beaches, *pensions* and restaurants. The island is the birthplace of Bartholomeos, the current Greek Patriarch in Istanbul (patriarchs are required by law to be Turkish citizens). Above the village is a ruined Ottoman castle, built by Süleyman the Magnificent. There's not much else, save for a prison and some pleasant walks. The old Aegean character of the island was somewhat tainted by a planned migration policy put in effect after 1923; migrants from the east of Turkey settled here to bolster the Turkish population, bringing with them different architectural techniques.

By contrast, **Bozcaada** is flatter and smaller, fringed with beaches and much prettier. Its one town seems very Greek, with whitewashed houses, overhanging upper storeys and narrow, serpentine streets. Its castle, vast and explorable, has been there since Byzantine days, and now guards the islanders' goats and sheep. Bozcaada (ancient Tenedos) was, according to epic tradition, the Achaean base where the Greeks hid their ships, waiting for Odysseus to emerge from the belly of the wooden horse and signal that Troy was theirs for the taking. Up until the 15th century, Greeks living on the island acted as tour guides for foreigners seeking Troy. The island is best explored with a rental car or moped.

Where to Stay on the Aegean Islands

Gökçeada

Barba Yorgo, Tepeköy, t 0286 887 3592, *www.barbayorgo.com* (€€). A simple *pension* that was formerly a Greek taverna.

There are two modest **campgrounds**.

Bozcaada

A long-time favourite of Turkish holiday makers, the island is now edging its way into international tourism and has a great selection of guest houses and boutique hotels. Most of the hotels and *pensions* on the Turkish Aegean islands are open June–September only. Outside these months, you may be able to find a room to let in a private house.

Armagrandi, Alaybey Mah. Dolapli Sokak 4–6, t 0286 697 8424, *www.armagrandi.com* (€€€€–€€€). A recent conversion from an old winery located in the main town.

Rengigul Konukevi, Atatürk Caddesi 31, t 0286 697 8171, *www.rengigul.net* (€€€). A delightful old Greek house that simply oozes charm from every room, window, hallway and creaky staircase covered with paintings, old photos, embroideries and other trinkets. The ever-creative proprietor presents an amazing breakfast spread in the courtyard. They have a farmhouse too, if there is a group of you.

Akvaryum Pansiyon >

Akvaryum Pansiyon, Alaybey Mahallesi, Mermerburun, t 0532 746 4618, *www.akvaryumbozcaada.com*

(€€–€). At the other end of the island and you will need transport. This simple family concern is the only building beside a magical bay; have the beach to yourself. If it's a retreat you are after, time to reflect and listen to the insects, then this is your place. Oh, and they don't have electricity, so you had better enjoy candlelight.

The Troad

The bulging peninsula south of Troy to Mount İda is known as the Troad, famous in ancient times for horse-breeding. Highlights include the awe-inspiring walls of ancient Assos and the sumptuous Gulf of Edremit. It's a dreamy, beautiful country, full of maples and olive trees; farmers set up stands all along the roadsides selling olives (some of Turkey's best), olive oil and home-made relishes. The best time to come is June, when the deep red blankets of poppies are an unforgettable sight.

Alexandria Troas

South of Troy lie the ruins of the city that superseded it in Hellenistic times, Alexandria Troas, a few kilometres south of the sandy beach at **Geyikli**. Many early travellers to the Troad mistook its ruins for Troy itself. The city was founded by Antigonus the One-eyed at the end of the 4th century BC, but achieved its greatest glory after another of Alexander's generals, Lysimachus, killed Antigonus in battle and renamed it in memory of his old commander. He made it the main port in the Troad and one of the richest commercial centres on the entire coast. In Hadrian's time, Herodes Atticus, the Rockefeller of his day, endowed it with a monumental bath complex and aqueduct. Its convenient position on the main sea route later brought about its demolition, as the builders of Istanbul's imperial mosques cannibalized it, block by block. Today the most impressive remains, besides the baths, are the great broken stones scattered on the beach.

Before you get to Assos, the dolmuş from Çanakkale passes through **Ayvacık**, a ramshackle village worth a stop only if you're hunting for carpets: Ayvacık is the home of DOBAG, a cooperative run by weavers dedicated to doing things the traditional way.

Assos (Behramkale)

South of Alexandria Troas, on the north shore of the lovely Gulf of Edremit, is the imposing site of ancient Assos, known to locals as Behramkale. Take the paved road from Ayvacık, crossing a charming

Getting to and around the Troad

Buses and **minibuses** between Çanakkale and İzmir serve the coast well, and there should be no difficulty getting to and from Assos or anywhere else (Assos is also known as Behramkale and minibuses always bear the latter name on their destination signs). During the day, minibuses run continuously along the northern edge of the gulf to Edremit. To reach Ören you may have to take a **dolmuş** from Edremit to Burhaniye and then a local bus to the coast. In summer, Ören is linked by boat to Ayvalık (*see* below), with four crossings a day.

Travelling between this part of the coast and the Marmara shore or points east will require a bus change in Balıkesir.

14th-century Ottoman bridge, from where you can see the town hugging the top of an extinct volcano, some 785ft over the sea. This part of Assos is known as the **Kale**. Far beneath the ruins is the **İskele** (wharf), Assos' tiny harbour, whose old stone houses and acorn warehouses have now been converted into atmospheric hotels. Several kilometres east of Assos itself is **Kadırga**, which is becoming increasingly popular – perfect (especially if you have your own transport) for a day or two on the beach and a look at the ruins; enterprising locals run day trips to Troy from here.

History

Some archaeologists believe the Hittite King Tudhaliyas IV established his colony of Ashachuva on the commanding height, in the 13th century BC, to keep an eye on the Mycenaeans troubling his western frontiers. Greek Assos was founded by Aeolians from Methymna, Lesbos, in the 1st millennium BC. The city was famous for the great Doric temple of Athena (540 BC) that once crowned the summit of the acropolis.

Assos passed through several hands – Persian and Athenian – and was once governed by a banker and once by a eunuch. The latter was Hermias, a student of Plato at the Academy, who had a chance to apply his teacher's theories of an ideal city-state to his own realm of the Troad and Lesbos. He invited other students of Plato to found a branch of the Academy in Assos, and for three years Plato's greatest student, Aristotle, lived here, founding the sciences of biology and botany, and marrying Hermias' niece. Aristotle's pupil Alexander later captured the city; after that it came under the kings of Pergamon.

In the Middle Ages, several Crusaders' battles took place nearby; the Ottomans captured Assos in 1330, and at once began to quarry the site to build a mosque and bridge over the Tuzla. The villagers of Behramkale took up the stones when the Ottomans left off; one Turkish writer describes Behramkale as 'a rusty dagger piercing the walls of Assos'. Perhaps because of this, Assos is one of the more dishevelled gardens of weeds along the coast; be prepared to scramble through the prickles to see the remains.

The Walls of Assos

Most remarkable, especially in light of the quarrying on the site, are the walls, among the best preserved in the whole eastern Greek world. Stretching some three kilometres (two miles), they stand 46ft high in places; they include some excellently preserved gates, each done in a different style. They date back to the mid-4th century BC, perhaps built under the rule of Hermias. Inner walls surround the acropolis and the **Temple of Athena**. Of this once magnificent structure little remains but its platform and a few decorative elements; its Doric friezes are scattered in museums in Paris, Boston and Istanbul. In keeping with the current vogue for the tarting up of Turkey's architectural treasures, the temple's fallen columns are in the process of being re-erected. Where the original fluted stones are missing, hollow concrete replacements have been inserted: just tap to prove it. The bird's-eye view of Lesbos and the Gulf of Edremit on one side and the valley of the Satnioeis on the other makes the climb worthwhile.

Other Hellenistic remains, all in the lower town, include two stoas (3rd century BC), an agora temple, a bouleuterion, theatre and gymnasium. Architecturally, they resemble the Pergamon style – note the location of the temple in relation to the agora, and the unusual mix of Doric and Ionic orders in the decorative scheme. Outside the main gate in the Hellenistic-Roman necropolis are numerous broken sarcophagi; Assos exported similar ones throughout the ancient world. If you're energetic you can hike down to the fine white pebble beach for a swim and a look at the remains of the ancient breakwater.

The Gulf of Edremit

The Gulf of Edremit is one of the loveliest places in the whole of Turkey, with fine sandy beaches, writhing olive groves, dark pine forests and sparkling white seaside villages. To the east looms Mount İda (Kaz Dağ) and in the gulf the emerald Alibey islets float in a crystal sea, with the shapely green outline of Lesbos as a backdrop. Unfortunately the beach resorts that line the gulf have grown so much in recent years that in many places they have now joined up together into a single ribbon of concrete. The first, **Küçükkuyu**, looks idyllic from afar, its harbour filled with bobbing fishing smacks, but closer inspection reveals a grubby, ramshackle little town with little to boast of save a small beach to the west. **Altınoluk**, 10km east, is a slight improvement. Cleaner and brighter, it has a nice, if small, beach. Halfway between Altınoluk and the next resort, Akçay, the village of **Güre** soothes your aches away in warm, mineral-filled waters, for a small fee.

Above Akçay is **Mount İda**, venue of the world's first beauty contest, where the judge, Paris, chose Aphrodite as the fairest of the goddesses after she bribed him with the promise of Helen, an ill-fated selection that led ultimately to the Trojan War. **Akçay** itself is another Altınoluk, open and breezy with a welcoming aura, a resort that, whilst it has certainly been 'discovered', has so far refrained from the mass, crass commercialism that so bedevils **Ören**, 25km south at the gulf's epiglottis. The reason for Ören's overdevelopment is quite simple: the beach is the best along the gulf, huge and wide and sandy, backed by a grassy verge that billows with flowers in spring.

Inland between Akçay and Ören, the humble town of **Edremit** can at least pride itself on its antiquity. This was ancient Adramyttium, sacked by Achilles in one of his raids along the coast. It was in Adramyttium that Achilles captured Chryseis, daughter of the priest of Apollo, and gave her as a prize to Agamemnon. The *Iliad* begins with Agamemnon's refusal to accept the father's ransom for the girl. The main road east from here will take you to **Balıkesir**, the equally humble provincial capital of all this area, a city with a grumpy air that seems to be wondering why it is stuck out in the middle of the pine-wooded mountains while all the other towns in the province are having fun on the beach. Balıkesir was the ancient Greek Paleokastron, though most of its monuments are Ottoman mosques and tombs from the 14th and 15th centuries.

Where to Stay around Assos and the Gulf of Edremit

(i) **Akçay**
Edremit Caddesi, Karabudak Apt 20,
t 0266 384 1113

(i) **Ören**
town centre,
t 0266 416 3500

Base yourself in either Assos or Ayvalık (*see* next section); when it comes to accommodation, there is little to capture the imagination in Edremit, Ören or Akçay.

Assos Harbour and Surroundings

With no more space to build on, the hotels along Assos's tiny harbour, all converted from old stone houses, cash in on their stunning location.

★★★**Nazlıhan**, t 0286 721 7385, *www. assosedengroup.com* (€€€). At the western end of the harbour, in two converted old stone houses; its rates are steep, but the rooms are tasteful.

★★★**Kervansaray**, t 0286 721 7093, *www. assoskervansaray.com* (€€€). Perhaps the best, with air-conditioning and an outdoor pool, and stone fireplaces and a winter sauna; half-board.

Lila Motel, Kücükkuyu Sahil Yolu 67, t 0286 764 0085, *http://lilamotel.com* (€€). Tastefully decorated rooms and wooden bungalows on the beach-front. The garden is well kept and the restaurant serves up decent fodder; included in the room price of around €48 per person.

Plaj Pansiyon, at the eastern end of the harbour, t 0286 721 7193 (€€). About as low-priced as you'll get, with frontier-like rooms for €30 or more.

There are plenty of **campsites** along **Kadırga** sea front as you head out of Assos towards Edremit and the main İzmir highway.

Behramkale/Kale

Up by the ruins, this is also a wonderful place to stop and offers a glimpse into local village life. The women on the roadside as you approach the ruins, selling dried oregano and hand-woven socks, are incredibly persistent; if you are not interested in their knitwear do not casually utter: 'maybe later', because when 'later' comes they will remember, and may even chase you down the street, waving socks!

Biber Evi (Pepper House), t 0286 721 7410, *www.biberevi.com* (€€€€). A beautifully restored stone cottage with a quirky pepper theme throughout. The wonderful hosts are also food fans and serve up real treats in the restaurant. A garden room will cost you €115 in season.

Dolunay Pansiyon, t 0286 721 7172 (€€). In the village centre, just near the old café, with just six basic rooms that surround a courtyard.

⭐ Timur
Pansiyon >

⭐ Assos Manti
ve Borek Evi >>

Timur Pansiyon, a few metres from the entrance to the Athena Temple, **t** 0286 721 7449 (€€). Some parts of this unpretentious, welcoming place are over 200 years old, with walls over 3ft thick. The terrace is perfectly placed for panoramic sunsets: the two owners – a brother-and-sister team – have never seen the sun set in the same way twice. Be warned: the breakfasts are truly special, different each day and using local ingredients such as village butter. With only five rooms, booking is recommended.

Eris Pansiyon, t 0286 721 7080 (€€). Another haven nearby. While it lacks views of the sea, it is one of the calmest lodgings you'll find, overlooking craggy hills of bushes, rocks and poplars. From the terrace you can hear the tinkling bells of the sheep grazing in the walled pasture below.

Küçükkuyu

Just east of Küçükkuyu is a strip of campsites, including the shady and quite inexpensive **Truva Camping**, **t** 0286 752 5206.

Eating Out in Assos

Assos Manti ve Borek Evi, t 0286 721 7050, in Assos village centre (€€€). A modest yet brilliant restaurant run by the charming Ali Dündar. Passionate about using only fresh produce grown in his garden, Ali does not serve what he himself didn't pick. This freshness comes through in every mouthful and it's tempting to order everything on the menu: the various *böreks*, the *mantı*, the *dolma*, the lamb, the stuffed courgette flowers. It's 40 YTL for a full feast with wine, if you are good, you might even get a pressie!

Ayvalık

⊘ Ayvakık

The southernmost of the gulf resorts, Ayvalık tends to be largely bypassed by visitors from overseas – inexplicably so. The charming town has excellent beaches close at hand, several local curiosities to view and the loveliest setting on the gulf, surrounded by an entourage of 25 islands and islets, all but one uninhabited, all verdant, all rising from the sea like lost cities of antiquity. Beyond them, its pine-draped cliffs bristling on the horizon, looms the Greek island of Lesbos.

Ayvalık, formerly called Kydonies, was predominantly Greek before 1923 and still retains a faintly Hellenic aura, particularly in its churches, even though most have since been converted into mosques. Unlike most of the other resorts on this stretch of coast, it is an old and sizeable town, with a charming centre of narrow streets of brightly painted houses, and little squares with plane trees. Most of the tourist activity is confined to the port area, lined with cafés, restaurants and excursion boats; from here you can see the long peninsula of Sarımsaklı to the left, where the best beaches are, and to the right the conical island of Alibey, Greek Lesbos and, on a reasonably clear day, Mount İda.

Getting to and around Ayvalık

Ayvalık's **bus station**, 1km outside the centre, opposite the new harbour on the road to Edremit, has services to most major towns in western Turkey. Most minibuses to local destinations, however, start from the central square by the old port. In season there are also very frequent minibuses to the beaches around Sarımsaklı.

The rather expensive **boat** service to Greek Lesbos operates three times a week in summer but only sporadically in winter.

Two of the churches are worth a glance, if only to see what a neo-Gothic church looks like with a minaret attached: the **Çınarlı Cami** (once Agios Ioannis) and the **Saatli Camii** (Agios Georgios). The latter is the 'clock mosque', named for the large timepiece that adorns its exterior. Another church, the **Taksiyarhis** (1844), contains a unique collection of icons painted on dried fish skins although, since its doors are permanently locked, there seems to be little hope of ever seeing them. If you pester the tourist office, they might arrange a visit. Ayvalık does have an organization dedicated to the preservation of its old quarter and the churches, and Turks from Istanbul have begun to fix up old houses and establish cultural institutions; one old church outside town has become a library, and the town has summer schools in art and music.

Try to be in Ayvalık on Thursday, for one of the busiest and most colourful **markets** on the Aegean coast – few tourist trinkets, but dozens of back streets lined with gorgeous produce; all the country folk for miles around come in to see and be seen.

Around Ayvalık

A dozen or so cruise boats permanently haunt Ayvalık's harbour, waiting to carry tourists and trippers off to the dozen or so islands and a number of good beaches. These boats can offer very good value, with all-day trips including a lunch of fish, salad and fruit for 12 YTL. If you're lucky, live music may also be thrown into the bargain. One of the prime attractions is **Alibey Island** (also called Cunda Island by the locals), the largest of the island group (for this you really don't need a boat; the island is also connected to the mainland by a causeway). Opposite Ayvalık, it curves around from the north in the shape of a badly drawn treble clef. It furnishes the town with a perfect sheltered harbour and is a popular spot with day-trippers. You can see the island's old Greek houses, now in a desperate state of repair, but most people come for the beaches.

Three km south of Ayvalık, the leafy suburb of **Çamlık** is also blessed with a beach but the first prize for sea and sand epiphanies goes to **Sarımsaklı**, 5km beyond Çamlık. Sarımsaklı (Garlic Beach) may not be to everyone's taste – lots of breezeblock hotels and overpriced restaurants – but its beach is monster-sized and utterly enticing. Yet another huge beach is at **Altınova**, a

09 The North Aegean Coast | The Troad: Ayvalık

further 8km to the south. You'll notice the olive trees around Ayvalık – about two million of them, producing what is reputed to be Turkey's best olive oil.

A short dolmuş ride from Ayvalık or Sarımsaklı, a couple of geological oddities lie in wait: the **Devil's Dinner Table** (Şeytan Sofrası), a large, flat, round rock on a promontory protruding into the Aegean, and, on the hill adjacent, another flat rock from which two slender outcrops rise vertically to a height of 13ft. They look like rabbit's ears, hence their name. Inland from Ayvalık, on the road to Bergama, you'll be skirting the truly imposing massif of the **Madra Dağı**, a beautiful and totally unspoiled area (if you have a car that can take it, consider continuing to Bergama via the bad, partly unpaved mountain road through it instead of the coastal route).

Lesbos

Greece's third-largest island, Lesbos is also commonly called Mytilini after its capital, the destination of the little ferries from Ayvalık. The island has its charms, but it isn't really the place to go for a day trip unless you simply want a taste of Greece – it's fine for that, being one of the less touristy islands; Lesbos is more concerned with its olive trees, of which there are about eleven million. **Mytilini**, under its Byzantine-Genoese castle, is an attractive town, with antique shops, a Hellenistic theatre and a number of interesting museums, including one dedicated to the works of Theophilos, Lesbos's famous naïve artist. Most visitors to Lesbos stay a few days and tour the quiet rural parts, where sights include ruins of a Roman aqueduct, several beaches, yet another Mount Olympos, a few Byzantine churches and monasteries and, of all things, a petrified forest, at **Sigri** in the north of the island.

Shopping in Ayvalık

Ceylan Bookshop, in the Süner Pasajı on Talatpaşa Caddesi. Has English books and books about the area.

White Knight Tourist Bazaar. A tiny shop behind Atatürk's statue, that sells a wide range of English newspapers and magazines.

Where to Stay in and around Ayvalık

Ayvalık

Kidonia 1887, Sakarya Mah., Cumhuriyet Cad. 118, **t** 0266 312 8324, www.kidonia1887.com (€€€). Possibly one of Ayvalık's oldest buildings, this delightful hotel has been restored with utmost good taste, both celebrating its Greek architectural heritage and boasting a rich yet understated Turkish décor; the six rooms with their wooden ceilings, artworks and attractive antiques are a real treat. A night in this little treasure will cost upwards of €65 – a bargain, really.

*Kaptan, Balıkhane Sokak 7, near the harbour, **t** 0266 312 8834 (€€). The best of the mid-range hotels, with a patio butting right up against the Aegean. Private parking, views of Alibey Island; the friendly proprietor speaks English. Ring ahead to reserve one of the three rooms with a sea view, and look out for the wonderful photo of local bigwigs in the 1920s posing in front of a flying boat in Ayvalık harbour.

ⓘ **Ayvalık** >
booth by the harbour,
t 0266 312 2122

★ **Kidonia 1887** >

Almost all the cheap accommodation is found in the centre of Ayvalık, where you are spoilt for choice.

Yalı Pansiyon, near the harbour, **t** 0266 312 2423 (€). A charming, family-run establishment. Housed in an old Greek mansion, with a garden leading out to the sea, a grandiose staircase and delicate ornamentation, its cavernous rooms go for 30 YTL per person. There are only eight of them, however, so it's best to phone ahead. Bathroom facilities here are shared.

In the back streets leading up the hill from the seafront are three *pensions* that are so atmospheric you'll be tempted to spend a night in each one. All have shared bathrooms and cost about 30 YTL per person.

Taksiyarhis, next to the church of the same name at Mareşal Çakmak Caddesi 71, **t** 0266 312 1494, *www.taksiyarhispension.com* (€). Run by an Austrian-Turkish couple. It is really three old stone houses knocked into one, creating a warren of old wooden staircases and secluded rooms, popular with backpackers and families.

Chez Beliz, also on Mareşal Çakmak Caddesi, **t** 0266 312 4897, *www.chezbeliz.web.tr* (€). A grand old house with its top floor jutting out into the street. Run by Beliz, an ex-actress with a passion for cooking, it's an experience not to be missed.

Bonjour, Mareşal Çakmak Caddesi, 5.ci Sokak, **t** 0266 312 8085, *www.bonjourpansiyon.com* (€). This imposing building has a genuine reason for indulging in French nomenclature: it was the 19th-century home of a French priest who did a bit of work on the side as French ambassador to the Sublime Porte. It was lovingly restored into a *pension* in the mid-1990s, and its courtyard is so relaxing that you may find that breakfast drifts into lunch, followed by an afternoon pick-me-up.

Alibey Island/Cunda

Zehra Teyze'nin Evi, Namık Kemal Mah., 7, beside the Taksiyarhis church, **t** 0266 327 2285, *www.cundaevi.com* (€€€). An old Greek house run by the lovely Auntie Zehra. Rooms are basic but the age and history of the house supply plenty of atmosphere. In keeping with the proprietor's roots, Cretan dishes are served in the garden restaurant.

Ortunç, **t** 0266 327 1120 (€€). A simple place hidden away in spacious grounds between a pine forest and a quiet beach on the far side of the island. Also has a campground.

Günay Motel, by the port, **t** 0266 327 1048 (€). One of a number of *pansiyonlar*; also has a nice, simple restaurant.

Ada Camping, **t** 0266 327 1211. In a peaceful, isolated setting on the far end of the island, with shade, a restaurant and a beach.

Eating Out in and around Ayvalık

Ayvalık

The area is known for its Cretan-influenced dishes, olive oil-based *mezeler* and *lokma*, a sort of doughnut. Seafood, of course, is a major draw and there are good restaurants clustered around the **Atatürk statue**, at the angle of the port.

Leading inland from the main street 50m north of the Atatürk statue is **Tenekeciler Sokağı**, 'tinmakers' street', now heaving with *meyhaneler* and cheap *lokantas*. Dining here can be a smoky, raucous experience, especially when the soccer's on.

Şehir Club, **t** 0266 312 1088 (€€€). The best of the harbour seafood places: a private establishment on the tip of the harbour which is nevertheless open to foreigners. With a clientele of demanding local businessmen, the Şehir always has an impressive range of *mezes*, as well as meat dishes and fish charged by the kilo (agree on the price before you order it).

Deniz Kestanesi (Sea Urchin), Karantina Sokak 9/A, **t** 0266 312 3262 (€€). Also good for seafood; the terrace over the sea and regular evening entertainment ensure its popularity with locals and tourists.

Martı Restaurant, Gazinolar Aralığı No: 19, **t** 0266 312 68 99 (€€). Serves traditional and modern Turkish cuisine, the *mezeler* drenched in the glorious local olive oil.

Alibey Island

The causeway between the mainland and Alibey Island is one long row of bright fish restaurants.

⭐ Bay Nihat >

Bay Nihat, Sahil Boyu 21, **t** 0266 327 1777, *www.baynihat.com.tr* (€€€). Highly acclaimed, with an imaginative selection of seafood including fish pastrami and fish sausage. Booking is essential.

Nesos, **t** 0266 327 1748 (€€€). Another seafood hotspot but also good for vegetarians with dozens of veggie dishes with a Mytilene influence.

Papalina, **t** 0266 327 1041, on the old road into Alibey from Ayvalık (€€). Very popular with locals and holidaying Turks, set in an atmospheric wooden building with fish nets hanging up outside and in.

Aeolia

The Aeolian Greeks came from Thessaly or Boeotia, perhaps as early as the 12th century BC, and until the Persian conquest Aeolia survived as a quiet little league of city-states, with its federal capital at Mytilini on Lesbos. Aeolia was famed in antiquity for the fertility of its soil; it seems the early Greek colonists spent all their labours tilling it, with little time left for the intellectual pursuits and adventures that preoccupied the Ionians to the south. But it is here in Aeolia that we find Bergama, ancient Pergamon, a city that rivalled Athens and Alexandria as a cultural centre in its day.

Pergamon (Bergama)

In the last two centuries BC, Pergamon may well have been the most beautiful and sophisticated city in the Mediterranean world. It was not an original Aeolian foundation, but rather a Hellenistic city state, a creation of Alexander's heirs. Although inhabited before Alexander, the site never amounted to much – a minor Greek-Persian satrapy, first mentioned in 399 BC in Xenophon's Anabasis. Doubtless, had it been nearer the sea, it would have thrived much earlier, for few cities could boast such a splendid defensible site, a citadel 1,300ft above the surrounding plain, with streams flowing below on two sides. When Alexander's general Lysimachus came into a fabulous fortune – 9,000 talents, the spoils of war in the Troad – Pergamon seemed the perfect place to safeguard the treasure. Lysimachus died without an heir in 281 BC, and the man he set to watch over the loot, a certain Philetairos, simply kept it, using the money to wine and dine friends and build monuments in Pergamon. His adopted son **Eumenes** is the first of the famous kings of Pergamon; Eumenes' adopted son **Attalus** (ruled 241–197 BC) gave the rulers their dynastic title, the **Attalids**.

The Site

🏛 Pergamon
*open daily 8.30 until
sunset; adm*

The average visitor is attracted first to Ephesus, where the ruins are more substantial, or Troy, where there's a story everyone knows. But use your eyes and your imagination a bit, and you may find

Getting to and around Bergama

Bergama is the **minibus** transport hub of the area, although, if you go there on any bus that doesn't end its run there, you'll be left on the highway 7km from town and have to catch a minibus in, which can be a problem. If you mean to come here on a day trip, arrange your transport back in advance, or you may be stranded in the evening.

Pergamon the most totally captivating site of all classical cities. The key to everything is the tremendously high acropolis. Try to catch sight of it from wherever you are in the town or on the plain, and imagine it as it was under Eumenes or Attalus, crowned with spectacular marble temples, and with a plume of smoke continually rising from the Altar of Zeus.

At its height, Pergamon had a population of well over 100,000. It spilled down the precipitous slope, making nearly every building visible from the valley and creating the impression of a single work

The Attalids

Attalus I spent much of his reign at Pergamon fighting for more territory; most notably, he stood up to the bellicose Gauls of Galatia, who were running a sort of protection racket in Anatolia. Upon his refusal to pay they came to collect, a fierce crew, outnumbering the Pergamene defenders, who were reluctant to fight against the odds. However, Attalus ordered a sacrifice to the gods, and miracle! – plainly written on the victim's lungs was the word 'Victory'. Inspired, the Pergamenes soundly thrashed the Gauls. Only later was it discovered that the priest offering the sacrifice, or more probably Attalus himself, had written the word backwards in ink on his hand and pressed it on the entrails when no one was looking. But even if the augury was a cheat, Attalus had freed western Anatolia from a serious threat, and in honour of the victory his successor, Eumenes II, erected the famous Altar of Zeus.

Eumenes II ruled Pergamon at the height of its power and influence. But, just as the city owed its initial prosperity to the luck of a treasure deposit, it owed its great rise in prestige to a second lucky break. Attalus had kindly sent the superstitious Romans the meteorite-cult statue of Cybele, the Great Mother Goddess of Asia (the Romans hoarded cult statues of their conquests, to keep the gods of conquered provinces in line), and in return the Romans, upon defeating Antiochus the Great at Magnesia (190 BC), gave Pergamon Antiochus' provinces of Asia Minor, stretching from the coast to Konya. Relations between Rome and its new client state became even closer as Eumenes assisted Rome against its enemies, including the most worrying, Hannibal, who ended up in nearby Bithynia after his defeat at Zama and, according to tradition, died and was buried in İznik. Eumenes' brother, **Attalus II**, continued his policy, helping Rome in the subjugation of Greece.

Eumenes' nephew, **Attalus III**, recognized the inevitable and amazed the classical world by willing Pergamon to Rome when he died in 133 BC. Some accounted it a Roman trick, and, perhaps as a result, a body of stories has grown up attesting to Attalus III's eccentricities: that he loved his mother so well that he took the title 'Philomater', that he was obsessed with poisonous plants, which he fed to condemned criminals to try out his antidotes, and that he never went out in public except to tend to his mother's tomb, where one day, in the heat, he fainted and died, only five years into his reign. Rome had no problem in accepting Attalus' bequest, and according to the terms of the will left Pergamon a free city. This state of affairs lasted until 88 BC, when **Mithridates of Pontus** came to 'liberate' the Greek states from Rome and ordered all Romans massacred, an order the Pergamenes carried out with zeal.

When Rome, in return, defeated Mithridates, Pergamon lost all its rights; 40 years later it even lost its greatest treasure, its library, when Antony looted its 200,000 volumes and gave them to Cleopatra, ending once and for all the rivalry between the libraries of Alexandria and Pergamon. Pergamon gradually dwindled under Roman rule: up on the acropolis, any walls of cheap mixed brick and stone you see probably date from Byzantine or Selcuk times.

of architecture. The city was blessed not only with its natural setting, but also with unreasonable portions of wealth and talent. Its architects and sculptors were among the finest in the Hellenistic world. To see the best of their creations you have to go to the Pergamon Museum in Berlin (where much was damaged in the last war), but the assiduous Germans left enough behind for us at least to conjure up an image of this fantastical city of dreams.

To see the ruins of Pergamon in a day without a car, you'll probably have to invest in four taxi trips: to the acropolis and back (it's a stiff 3km climb), and to the Asklepeion and back. If you only have one day, the best thing to do with it is to take a taxi up to the acropolis, then walk back down along the ancient main street. It isn't easy finding the path, but it's worth the attempt.

The Acropolis

The majestic acropolis looms behind the modern town, from where there is a paved road to the top. Since 1878, when a German railway engineer and amateur archaeologist named Karl Humann began digging here, the Germans have completed four major excavations in Pergamon, and currently a fifth is under way. One project in progress is the reconstruction of the columns of the **Temple of Trajan**, at the highest level of the acropolis; it is the only structure dating wholly from Roman times. Both Trajan and his son Hadrian were remembered here; their two huge marble heads, found in the temple, are now in Berlin. Hadrian, one of the most cultured of the emperors and a great friend of Pergamon, built the temple as centrepiece of an important complex, modelled after the great Forum of Hadrian in Rome. It may have included a library, as in Rome – perhaps intended as recompense for the Roman theft of the original. The pseudo-Egyptian capitals around the *stoa* are an unusual touch.

Directly behind the temple stood the Hellenistic **barracks** and **tower**, which were perfectly located for the view over the plain. Adjoining the barracks to the south were the two **palaces**, peristyle mansions of the kings of Pergamon, of which not much remains except walls and cisterns. Up on the acropolis, you'll notice one telling piece of evidence of Pergamon's decline: the tops of the walls, built under Roman rule, use plenty of recycled marble from earlier Greek buildings.

West of the palaces stood the renowned two-storey **library** begun by Attalus II, which at its height had some 200,000 volumes. Eumenes II in particular was obsessed with acquiring books, and had a naughty habit of borrowing and not returning. For books by Aristotle and Theophrastus he is said to have paid their weight in gold. The Pergamene library became so great that it

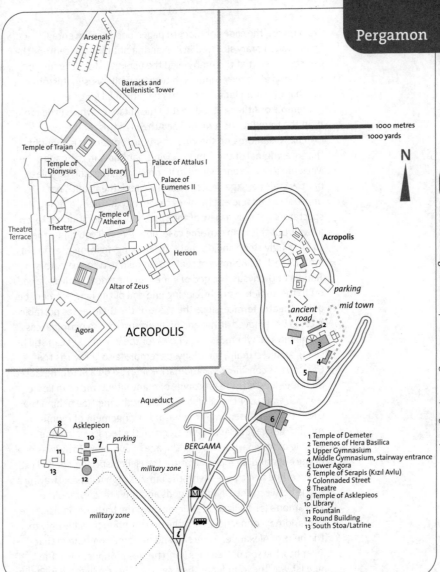

1000 metres
1000 yards

N

Arsenals

Barracks and
Hellenistic Tower

Temple of Trajan

Temple of
Dionysus   Library

Palace of Attalus I

Palace of
Eumenes II

Temple of
Athena

Theatre
Terrace   Theatre

Heroon

Altar of Zeus

Agora   **ACROPOLIS**

Acropolis

parking

ancient   mid town
road

2
1
3
4
5

Aqueduct

6

BERGAMA

8
Asklepieon
10
7   parking
11
9
13
12

military zone

military zone

M

1 Temple of Demeter
2 Temenos of Hera Basilica
3 Upper Gymnasium
4 Middle Gymnasium, stairway entrance
5 Lower Agora
6 Temple of Serapis (Kızıl Avlu)
7 Colonnaded Street
8 Theatre
9 Temple of Asklepieos
10 Library
11 Fountain
12 Round Building
13 South Stoa/Latrine

excited the jealousy of the Ptolemies in Egypt, whose library at
Alexandria was its only serious rival. As a result Egypt banned the
export of papyrus. All books at the time were written on long
scrolls of this brittle stuff; but Eumenes, undeterred, offered a large
reward to anyone who could come up with a replacement. A
certain Crates of Smyrna recalled the old Ionian custom of writing
on sheepskins treated with lime and dried. This 'Pergamon paper'
became known as parchment and, as it was too thick to roll up

like papyrus, the codex or modern paged book was invented. Pergamon's library survived in Alexandria until the 7th century; the Christians tell that the Arabs used the books to stoke the fires in their baths after they conquered the city, while Muslim historians say that Christian fanatics had torched them all long before.

A **Temple of Athena** stood next to the library, of which little more than the foundations remain. The Athena of this temple was Athena Nikephoros, or 'she who grants victory', and it is thought that the original of the famous 'Dying Gaul' now in the Capitoline Museum in Rome once stood in its precincts. From the temple a narrow stair-passage descends to the **Greek theatre**. It's not unusual to find ancient theatres carved into hillsides, offering spectators not only a view of the stage but a panoramic backdrop as well, but this is an extreme case; nowhere will you find a theatre so dizzyingly steep and dramatic, resembling an immense fan cut into the rock. Its 80 rows of seats could hold 10,000 spectators. A **Temple of Dionysus**, the god of wine and theatrical festivals, stood off to the audience's right, closing one end of the long promenade of the **theatre terrace**; since the stage of the theatre was portable, it could be removed at the end of a performance to permit access to the terrace (where the post holes for the wooden set can still be seen). Architecturally, the Dionysus temple (also known as the Caracalla) is considered a landmark – set high on a platform, closed on three sides, it is the prototype of many later temples in Rome.

As you walk over the acropolis, consider the method behind the Greek planners' seemingly haphazard arrangement of monuments. The great **Altar of Zeus** stood on the terrace below the Temple of Athena. Built during the age of Eumenes II, this was one of the outstanding monuments of the Hellenistic age, shaped like a horseshoe and covered with the famous high reliefs portraying a battle between the Olympian gods and the Titans, symbolic of Pergamon's (or civilization's) victory over the barbaric Gauls. There was another connection. With the presumption possible only to the heirs of Alexander, Eumenes and his family pretended that Telephos, the son of Hercules (who figures prominently in the reliefs), was the founder of their dynasty. These reliefs are in Berlin; all that remains on the acropolis are the altar's foundations. The Turkish government and the city of Bergama have been trying to get them back for decades. To the south of the altar, on a lower terrace, are the remains of the **Upper Agora** and its temple, in a mixture of Ionic and Doric orders, a common trait of Pergamene buildings that spread throughout the Mediterranean world. The Altar of Zeus was Karl Humann's greatest discovery (he found it incorporated into a Byzantine wall); a life-size reconstruction, along with those reliefs, is the star attraction in the Berlin museum. Humann is buried here, just below the Upper Agora.

Mid-town Pergamon

Much of the **ancient road**, connecting upper Pergamon to the mid-town area, has been cleared. While the acropolis was reserved for the kings, nobility and officers, regular citizens lived in the mid-town, which also has several important public buildings. Excavations in 1973 uncovered the **Odeion** and a '**Marble Hall**' that have both been reconstructed – a fascinating sight few visitors to Pergamon ever see. Further on, mysteries (initiations) similar to those at Eleusis in Greece took place in the enormous **Temple of Demeter**, erected by Philetairos and later enlarged by the wife of Attalus II, Apollonia. The temple – with its pit for the blood of sacrifices, fountain, and rows of seats for spectators of the mysteries – has unusual archaic palm leaf capitals. Near here are three terraces, each with a gymnasium. Young men trained and studied in the huge **upper gymnasium**, which doubled as an auditorium for ceremonial occasions with its small theatre; Attalus II created it, though what you see is largely a Roman-era rebuilding. The **middle gymnasium** was reserved for adolescent boys, and the **third** served as the children's playground. The **stairway entrance** connecting the lowest level to the second is one of the finest pieces of workmanship in all Pergamon, an early and well-preserved example of vault and arch construction.

The **main street** through the mid-town was remarkably narrow, though paved with massive blocks, worn by pedestrians and scored by chariot wheels. Along it are the ruins of shops and houses. Especially interesting here is the peristyle **House of Attalus**, a fair example of how the upper classes of Pergamon lived. Beyond the house, in the **Lower Agora**, the famous head of Alexander, now in the Istanbul museum, was discovered. If you've made it this far down, you'll already see the edge of modern Bergama below. The rest of the ancient street is unexcavated and unmarked, but, steep as it is, you should be able to pick your way down, finally ending up in some woebegone, cobbled back streets near the Temple of Serapis where the children and dogs will stare at you as if you had just dropped down from Mars.

Modern Bergama

Modern Bergama has engulfed lower Pergamon, with one monumental exception. The Turks call it **Kızıl Avlu**, the Red Courtyard. This red brick mastodon originally served as a **Temple of Serapis**, or Osiris, the resurrected Egyptian god. According to legend, the thousands of bricks in the temple were relayed to the site from hand to hand in a great human chain, so they would be neither on earth nor in the sky; indeed the whole temple is built over the Selinos stream, which still runs through an ancient tunnel below. Other underground chambers and tunnels had a religious significance. One of the temple's two massive towers now contains a mosque. The whole building was converted into a basilica by the early Christians. The church of Pergamon was one of the seven churches of Asia addressed by St John in his *Apocalypse* (*Book of Revelations*), singled out as possessing the 'throne of the Devil' – interpreted as the Altar of Zeus, or more probably as the seat of Roman authority.

Modern Bergama itself is a shabby and dusty sort of town; at first glance you would guess it was built around a factory rather than a major tourist attraction. It does have a fine little **Archaeology and Ethnographic Museum**, where there is a small model of the Altar of Zeus and some finds from the site, including two statues of hermaphrodites. The courtyard is filled with reliefs and other architectural fragments; look out for a figure of Cerberus, the three-headed hound of hell, and another relief with a poppy. Inside, there are some lovely terracotta ex votos to Asklepios, god of healing – an ear or a finger to show what part the god cured – and a Roman mosaic with the head of Medusa. Also present is that staple of all Mediterranean archaeology museums, a big nude statue of Emperor Hadrian (one of the greatest and most useful of all Roman rulers; unabashedly gay, and such a tease).

Archaeology and Ethnographic Museum
open Tues–Sun 8.30–5.30; closed Mon; adm

The Asklepeion

Asklepeion
open daily 8.30–5.30, until 7pm in summer; adm

A few arches of an **aqueduct** remain in the modern town; if you walk up the maze of streets towards them you'll eventually find the short cut to ancient Pergamon's Asklepeion, the sanctuary of healing. You can drive there: take the road that branches off next to the tourist office, passing a large military base.

Pergamon had the most renowned Asklepeion in Greek Asia, and produced one of the best physicians of the ancient world, Galen (AD 131–201), personal doctor of Marcus Aurelius. Asklepios, the god of healing, was the son of Apollo, and his priests, like Galen, treated the faithful with surprisingly modern methods – diet, baths, music and exercise in a lovely environment, combined with dream interpretation and auto-suggestion. Over the entrance of the sanctuary were inscribed the words 'By order of the gods Death may not enter here'. The sanctuary predates the kings of Pergamon and reached its greatest extent in the 2nd century AD, when the hellenophile Emperor Hadrian endowed it with most of the structures you see today. The **Sacred Way**, a wide colonnaded street that led to the Asklepeion from the Roman town, leads you to the entrance gate, or propylon, of which only a few steps remain. Within an open space is the **Temple of Zeus-Asklepios**, at one time covered with a dome, modelled after the Pantheon in Rome.

Beyond lie the main grounds of the Asklepeion itself, encompassed by three long stoae; there patients could sit in the shade or be sheltered from the rain. When bored, they could use the **library**, a square building north of the temple. The sanctuary's **theatre**, off the end of the north portico, could seat 3,500 and is believed to have been used to entertain both patients and locals. A **sacred spring** flowed into the nearby **fountain** with marble steps. Such water was very important in the healing process: an analysis in the 1970s found it to be mildly radioactive. There are two other fountains: a drinking well near the entrance of the **Sacred Tunnel**, and a carved rock pool near the **west stoa**, used for the frequently prescribed mud baths. The tunnel, 266ft long, leads from the centre of the sanctuary to a mysterious two-storey brick structure, built in Roman times, and believed to be a **Temple of Telesphoros**, a divine son of Asklepios who presided as a kind of god of convalescences. Another treatment centre, the temple was added on to the original Asklepeion rather like a hospital annexe. The tunnel itself was more than a passageway: while patients walked through its shadows, the doctor-priests would whisper healing suggestions.

The **south stoa** near here had to be supported on columns to attain the level of the rest of the sanctuary, producing a crypto-porticus you can walk through; at the far end is a luxurious marble **latrine** for men, and a small, less well-appointed one for the women; both, however, had to use mussel shells in lieu of toilet paper. The central Asklepeion had shrines to the several gods of healing, Hygiea and Apollo among them, and incubation chambers where patients slept, hoping for a cure-dream from the god.

Allienoi

Another local hangout for Asklepios was **Allienoi**, 18km to the northeast of Bergama. A dam for agriculture was planned to flood this site, a nondescript hot spring called the 'Pasha's Baths' when archaeologists in the 1990s discovered it was really an ancient healing spa, with extensive ruins concealed under alluvial mud. Frantic excavations have recovered many artefacts for Bergama's museum, and an international effort was raised to preserve the ruins. At th time of writing, in the spring of 2008, the dam is about to be filled and the outcome is still unclear. The site includes the baths, a reconstructed temple and an often-rebuilt Roman bridge.

From Bergama to İzmir

Cruise ships call at **Dikili**, the port of ancient Pergamon and the nearest beach which is safe for children. Though it's a growing resort, there's not much else to Dikili, other than some mildly attractive back alleys, a simple monument erected in memory of the assassinated Swedish prime minister Ölaf Palme (who visited Dikili in 1968) and a string of waterfront bars.

Getting to Dikili and Eski Foça

From Bergama's *otogar* there are **minibuses** every half-hour to Dikili; Dikili has a weekly **ferry** to Lesbos in summer. Direct **buses** from Bergama and İzmir also serve Eski Foça but they are infrequent. You may have to take an İzmir-bound bus from Bergama: ask to be let off at the Eski Foça junction and trust to either luck or a dolmuş to carry you the remaining 26km.

Further south, the coast as far as İzmir is dotted with Aeolian cities, of which little remains beyond their names. **Pitane**, the northernmost city of the Aeolian Confederacy (modern **Çandarlı**), has a small beach and a picturesque 13th-century Venetian castle that has been so enthusiastically restored it seems a stage prop. To the south stood **Gryneion (Temasalık Burnu)**, once renowned for its temple and oracle of Apollo, of which only a mound in a field remains. Continuing south, **Myrina** was said to have been founded by the Queen of the Amazons, and beyond that, on the coast, stood the once-great **Cyme**. Both contributed too much building material to the modern town of Aliağa to be of any interest today.

Eski Foça (Foça)

In the *Odyssey*, Homer tells of the Sirens, whose beautiful songs lured sailors to their death. They would sail towards the wonderful voices and be shipwrecked on the sharp rocks on which the Sirens sat. The cunning Odysseus, who had to sail past the Sirens on his voyage home, managed to evade disaster yet still enjoy their singing by ordering his crew to bind him to the mast and then to block their own ears with beeswax. Of the many places across the Mediterranean that claim the Sirens, Eski Foça (Old Foça, often called just Foça) puts in one of the better bids with its jagged **Siren Rocks** just off the shore that whine and howl when the wind blows through them. How the sailors could have found such a banshee-like wailing so enchanting is another question entirely, but that's Eski Foça's story and they're sticking to it.

Today, tourists sunbathe on the Siren Rocks, as they do on most of the beaches near Eski Foça, for this little town, occupying a promontory between two deeply indented bays, has now become an attractive resort. The town has not been swamped, however, and still retains a workaday atmosphere, thanks to the good fishing off its shores. The fishermen are not the only ones who appreciate the rich fishing grounds off Eski Foça: it is one of the last remaining habitats of monk seals, and in 1991 the town and its sea were declared a protection zone for these lively but reclusive beasts. Eski Foça's inhabitants take this responsibility seriously, to the extent that the obligatory statue of Atatürk in the main square has been replaced by a stone seal. In spite of all their best efforts, however, fewer than a dozen monk seals remain in the area.

Eski Foça was **ancient Phocaea**, the northernmost Ionian city, and unlike its Aeolian neighbours always looked to the sea, boasting one of the best harbours in the area. The seafarers of Phocaea founded numerous colonies, most famously Marsalla (Marseille) and Elea in Italy (where Zeno wrote his nasty paradoxes). Again, almost all the stone that remained of ancient Phocaea went into the medieval castle on the shore. Still standing, oddly, is the so-called **Taş Kule**, a mysterious 8th-century BC tomb, believed to have been built by the Phrygians or Lydians. It's along the Eski road, where you just might mistake it for an Art Deco petrol station.

Yeni Foça (New Foça), little sister of Eski, is some 20km to the north, a pleasant village with pleasant beaches that attracts the likes of the Club Méditerranée.

Where to Stay in Aeolia

(i) **Bergama** >
*Hükümet Konağı,
B Blok, Zemin Kat,
t 0232 631 2851*

Bergama

Bergama has a few good hotels – but when it's crowded in summer the best way to do the sights might be as a day trip from Ayvalık. Nearly all accommodation in the town is near the main road, so there's traffic noise. Clustered on the İzmir road just out of town are a number of hotels:

***Berksoy, t 0232 633 2595, *www. berksoyhotel.com* (€€). The best in this area, with balconied rooms facing a park, pool and tennis, and satellite TV in each room.

***Asude, opposite, **t** 0232 631 5555, *www.asudehotel.com* (€€). Rooms at the back are relatively quiet, some with bathtubs. For more intensive aquatherapy, a sauna and hamam await downstairs.

Anıl, Hatuniye Caddesi 4, **t 0232 631 1830, *www.anilhotelbergama.com* (€€). Conveniently located in the centre of town in a side street opposite the museum. Opened in 1999, it has a good rooftop restaurant and very colourful rooms with air-conditioning, TV and en suite bathtubs.

Efsane, t 0232 632 6350, *http:// efsanehotelbergama.com* (€€). Next to the Berksoy and under the same management as the Anıl; its rooftop pool makes up for outdated rooms.

As with Bergama's hotels, most of its *pensions* are prey to street noise, two exceptions being the Athena and the Nike *pansiyonlar* in the old quarter. You could follow the helpful signs egging you on to them, but this may result in hours of wandering down the narrow back lanes in a fruitless search.

Athena, Barbaros Mahallesi İmam Çıkmazı 5, **t** 0232 633 3420, *www. athenapension.8m.com* (€). From the main road through the centre of town facing the Acropolis, turn left at the Sağlam 2 restaurant. When you reach the picturesque old bridge, look around until you see this place. It's well worth the effort of finding, offering good views of the Acropolis. The main building is 160 years old, with rooms full of character: one has a built-in safe by 'Les Fils de S.O. Nicolaidis, Smyrna'. Other facilities of a lesser vintage include a satellite TV and washing machine. The owners are also renovating other historic houses in the area and doing a very good job. Three rooms have en suite facilities, costing around €10/20 YTL per person; rooms without are less.

Nike, Tabak Köprü Çıkmazı, **t** 0232 633 3901, *fikretnike@yahoo.com* (€). Across the stone bridge, this 300-year-old building has recently been restored, with large rooms and a courtyard full of flowers.

Böblingen, Asklepion Caddesi 2, on the other side of town, just off the main road, **t** 0232 633 2153 (€). A friendly, modern family *pension* that serves up an excellent breakfast. The cool rooms in the annexe to the rear escape most of the road noise; private bathroom facilities.

Berksoy Hotel (*see* above) also has a well-equipped **campground**, **t** 0232 633 2595 – you get to use their pool, too. From 10 YTL per person.

Dikili

Yali Pansiyon, Bademli Road, **t** 0232 671 9922, *www.yalipansiyon.com* (€€). Simple family set-up that looks like an apartment block, but all the rooms have sea views.

***Mysia Hotel, 3km outside Dikili at Geren Mevkii, **t** 0232 671 7010, *www. mysiahotel.com* (€€). For a little more, you can do much better here; there's a pool, watersports and its own private stretch of beach.

Eski Foça

ⓘ Eski Foça ›
Atatürk Bulvarı, at the entrance to town,
t *0232 812 1222*

Eski Foça is awash with hotels, *pansiyonlar* and restaurants, although the best rooms with the sea views are often booked out in summer.

Karaçam, Sahil Caddesi 70, **t** 0232 812 1416 (€€€). Offers nice rooms in a restored old house facing the sea, with trawlers tied up out front.

Hanedan, **t 0232 812 3650, *http:// hanedanresort.net* (€€). A modern beach resort alternative with its own restaurant (half-board available).

Hotel Amphora, İsmet Paşa Mah., 208 Sokak 7, **t** 0232 812 3930, *www. hotelgrandamphora.com* (€€). If being off the busy main strip is more important than a sea view. The lobby is decorated with amphorae, and there's a small terrace and pool.

Huzur, İsmet Paşa Mah., 139 Sokak 5, **t** 0232 812 1203, *www.huzurpansiyon. com* (€€). The best of Eski Foça's lovely *pensions*, with its perfect seafront location next to a small strip of sandy beach. The basic, clean rooms have balconies on the seaward side covered in foliage. The shady breakfast terrace edges onto the sea.

Eating Out in Aeolia

Bergama

Pergamon Pansiyon, Bankalar Caddesi (the main street's name in the town centre) (€€). Just when you think you're going to starve to death here, you find one of the most gratifying dining experiences to be had in these parts, for about 20 YTL. The restaurant is in an enclosed courtyard, with two fountains and lots of cushions everywhere, Ottoman-style. The menu, in Turkish and English, enigmatically offers 'Ladies' Thighs' for a very reasonable 5 YTL. Otherwise *börekler* and other *mezes* are excellent, the kebabs are damn spicy all right, and they serve beer. All Bergama seems to come here in the evenings, and upstairs there's a primitive bar/disco in winter.

Ozan 2 (€). One of the pitifully few inexpensive *lokantas*, which are almost all just south of the bus station on İzmir Caddesi. Serves decent *pide* and soup.

Dikili

Dikili has a good selection of water-front restaurants serving fresh fish.

Eski Foça

The resort provides good fare.

Celep Restaurant, Kücükdeniz Sahil, **t** 0232 812 1495 (€€€). On the waterfront, with a good selection of fish dishes, fresh lobster and grills; well placed for watching the sun sink below the waves.

İzmir

✪ İzmir

Of all the ancient Greek cities on the coast of Asia Minor, only İzmir (old **Smyrna**) has survived as a city into modern times. Why İzmir, and not Sardis or Pergamon or Ephesus or Miletus? Partly because of a good deep harbour that can't silt up, and partly simple luck of the draw: while the city has suffered much from history and earthquakes, it has never been completely destroyed like so many others. Few cities can boast such a splendid situation, at the head of a long narrow gulf, spread out beneath the flat-

Getting to, around and from İzmir

Adnan Menderes **airport**, 25km south of the city, is served by frequent flights from Istanbul and Ankara, as well as weekly direct THY flights from London, and numerous charters from abroad. The THY office is on Gaziosmanpaşa Caddesi, and is connected by Havaş bus to the airport, taking 40mins subject to traffic.

The main **bus terminal** (İzotaş) is about 10km from the centre in Pınarbaşı. Several buses shuttle back and forth from the city centre to this shiny new satellite. While waiting you may succumb to the tempting honking of the **taxi** drivers; they charge around 12 YTL for a one-way trip. Another terminal, serving Çeşme and other nearby southern destinations such as Çıftlik, is in suburban Üçkuyular; to get there, take the 86 or 169 bus from Alsancak Station, Lozan Meydanı or Konak.

From İzmir's central **Basmane Station**, at the head of Fevzipaşa Bulvarı, there are **rail** links with Aydın, Denizli, Konya, Ankara and beyond (e.g. Adana). The overnight **Mavi Tren** special to the capital is a relatively fast and luxurious run if you're headed that way (though still not as good a deal as the bus).

İzmir's modern **metro** currently runs from Bornova to Üçyol, 10 stations, 12km long, passing Konak and Basmane. It is the fastest and cleanest way to get around. Extensions are planned that will see this grow to some 97km of track in the future.

The **Yeni Liman** (new harbour) at Alsancak, on the northern tip of the city, is the port for **ferries** and cruise ships. Boats to Istanbul leave on Sundays; boats from Istanbul to İzmir leave at 2pm on Friday. Ferries for the short ride to Karşıyaka, İzmir's suburb across the bay, leave regularly from the Konak docks (Konak İskelesi) and Alsancak İskelesi, on the Kordon.

topped hill known as Mount Pagus by the Greeks and more picturesquely as the Velvet Castle (Kadifekale) by the Turks.

Now Turkey's third city, with over four million people, İzmir is still a new, rough creature, rebuilt from the ground up after the fire and population exchange of 1922. Understandably, it is still a city in search of an identity. To get an idea of what up-to-date, hard-working İzmir thinks, ask someone there what they think of Ankara or especially Istanbul. You'll learn a new word in Turkish: *yaramaz*, or useless. '*Istanbul yaramaz!*' Similarly, ask for a *simit* on the streets of İzmir and you'll get one; but if you use the local word, *gevrek*, you'll get one with a smile.

History

Surprisingly, when the Aeolian colonists arrived in the 10th century BC, they chose not the present site of İzmir but a small peninsula at the end of the gulf, called Bayraklı. One day, while the entire city was out celebrating the Dionysia, Ionians from Colophon sneaked in and took over. According to one ancient tradition, Ionian Smyrna was the birthplace of Homer, said to have been born on the banks of the River Meles (Halkapınar Suyu). Ancient Smyrna was plagued by the Lydians and never thrived until Alexander the Great, while hunting on Mount Pagus, dreamt that Nemesis told him to found a city there. The inhabitants on the peninsula moved to the hill, and the new Smyrna prospered and was eventually welcomed into the exclusive confederacy of Ionian cities as its thirteenth member. Strabo and many other ancient authorities referred to the city's charms, and 'beautiful Smyrna' is a name that has stuck through the centuries, despite the frequent disasters.

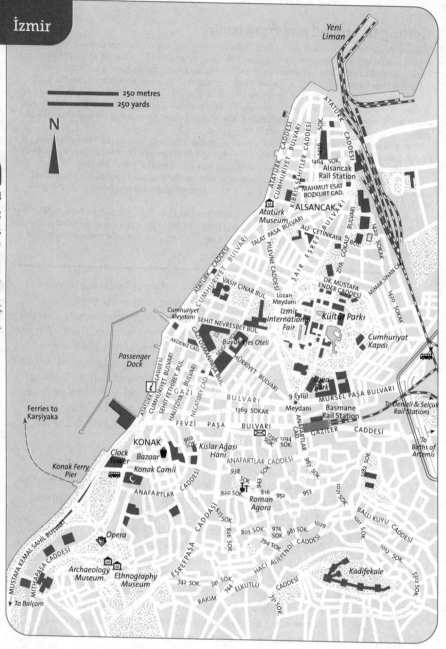

250 metres
250 yards

N

Yeni
Liman

ATATÜRK CADDESI

CUMHURIYET CADDESI

KIBRIS SEHITLER BULVARI

1445 SOK.

1404 SOK.

Alsancak
Rail Station

MAHMUT ESAT
BOZKURT CAD.

ALSANCAK

Atatürk
Museum

ATATÜRK CADDESI

ALI CETINKAYA BULVARI

1420 SOKAK

ZIYA GOKALP BUL.

SAIR ESREF BULVARI

TALAT PASA BULVARI

PILEVNE CADDESI

DR. MUSTAFA
ENDER CADDESI

MIMAR SINAN CAD.

CUMHURIYET CADDESI

VASIF CINAR BUL.

Lozan
Meydanı

İzmir
International
Fair

Kültür Parkı

1420 SOKAK

Cumhuriyet
Meydanı

SEHIT NEVRESBEY BUL.

AKDENIZ CAD.

GAZI OSMAN PAŞA BUL.

Büyük Efes Oteli

HÜRRIYET BULVARI

Cumhuriyat
Kapısı

Passenger
Dock

ATATÜRK CADDESI

CUMHURIYET CADDESI

SEHIT FETHIBEY BUL.

HALITZIYA BULVARI

NECATIBEY CAD.

GAZI BULVARI

BULVARI

Luna
Park

MURSEL PAŞA BULVARI

Ferries to
Karşiyaka

9 Eylül
Meydanı

1369 SOKAK

Basmane
Rail Station

To Denzli & Selçuk
Rail Stations

FEVZI   PAŞA   BULVARI

ANADOLU CAD.

GAZILER   CADDESI

To
Baths of
Artemis

Konak Ferry
Pier

KONAK

Clock
Tower

902
SOK.

Kislar Ağası
Hanı

1296
SOK.

1294
SOK.

961 SOK.

Bazaar

Konak Camii

ANAFARTLAR CADDESI

938

1027 SOK.

1282 SOK.

ANAFARTLAR   CADDESI

920 SOK.

648
SOK.

816

952

953

Roman
Agora

BALLI KUYU CADDESI

1071 SOK.

ESREFPAŞA CADDESI

825 SOK.

826 SOK.

803 SOK.

974
SOK.

981 SOK.

1029

1012 SOK.

MUSTAFA KEMAL SAHIL BULVARI

Opera

794 SOK.

HACI ALIEFENDI CADDESI

5312 SOK.

MITHATPAŞA CADDESI

Archaeology
Museum

Ethnography
Museum

742 SOK.

741 SOK.

744 ELKUTLU

731 SOK.

Kadifekale

RAKIM

CADDESI

To Balçom

In the late Ottoman Empire, Turks referred to the city as *gâvur
İzmir* – 'infidel Smyrna' – for its overwhelming majority of Greek
and Armenian Christians and Jews. In those days it was the
unquestioned cultural and good-time capital of the eastern
Mediterranean, full of blooming Art Nouveau buildings, buzzing

with deals being made in a score of different languages, and quite seriously looped on hashish and opium; among the city's creations was the intense, heavy style of Greek popular music called *rembetiko*, born in Smyrna's bars and drug dens. All this came to a tragic end in 1922, when Atatürk's defeat of the Greek army led to a mass exodus of Greek civilians from the city. As is traditional, the Greeks blame the Turks and the Turks blame the Greeks, but for whatever reason, while hundreds of thousands of Smyrna's citizens waited on the docks for transit to Greece, the city caught fire and over 80 per cent of its buildings burned to the ground.

Atatürk's government wasted no time in rebuilding it, in a dreary modern plan of wide, straight boulevards and traffic circles. After the last war it became the headquarters for NATO's southern command. Trade has returned, and the new all-Turkish İzmir is flourishing, the most thoroughly modern and Westernized city in Turkey, and its busiest port. Seagoing vessels are casually moored to the seafront pavement of Atatürk Caddesi, as if the captains have just left them for a minute while popping across the road for some cigarettes.

A Tour of the Town

İzmir's pride and its symbol is the **Kordon (Atatürk Caddesi)**, the shorefront boulevard where the waves of the Aegean beat almost against the doors of swank blocks of flats and cafés. At its centre, **Cumhuriyet Meydanı**, stands the big **Atatürk Monument** and the **Büyük Efes Hotel**, which thanks to a peculiarity of the 1920s plan has the role of being the focal point of the city.

To the south, especially on and around **Necatibey Bulvarı**, you can see some of the remains of old Smyrna, lovely buildings like the restored **Kizlar Ağası Hanı** on 902 Sokak, at the southern end of Necatibey. One of the few blessings the planners left İzmir is the great green expanse of the **Kültür Parkı**, İzmir's fairground. Like the similar Kültür Parkı in Bursa, this one is the place to go on weekend evenings, with outdoor restaurants, dance halls, horse-drawn carriages and a 'Luna Park' with some good rides. The İzmir International Trade Fair is held from the end of August to mid-September (when it is harder to find hotel rooms); it showcases Turkish technology both old and new, from traditional pottery to the latest machinery for pasteurising milk. Whereas in the West the public flocks to watch artisans practising dying crafts, in Turkey the opposite is true: rarely will you see such genuine enthusiasm for the most obscure apparatus – from saline pumps to gizmos for putting stoppers in olive oil jars.

Of course, no Turkish city worthy of the name would lack an **Atatürk Museum**: İzmir's is on (where else?) Atatürk Caddesi towards Alsancak and contains the usual assortment of Atatürkish knick-knacks. **Alsancak** itself, centred on **Kıbrıs Şehitler Caddesi**, is a calm pedestrianized oasis in a city notorious for its roaring traffic. With some of İzmir's more upmarket shops in the vicinity as well as dozens of restaurants with tables spilling onto the street, it makes for a pleasant stroll at any time of the day or evening.

Back on the seafront, at the southern end of the Kordon is **Konak**, the name of both a district and also its central square distinguished by its lovely **clock tower**, built in the 19th century by Sultan Abdülhamid the Damned, and the small but ornate 18th-century mosque, **Konak Camii**. From the square an underground passage leads to the shore and the ferry docks; if you have time to kill in İzmir one of the best things to do is take the ferry across the bay from here to **Karşıyaka**, not only for the views around the bay from the boat, but for the suburb's very pleasant waterfront park, full of snack stands and cafés.

Everything inland from Konak is İzmir's **bazaar district**, a maze of narrow streets and cul-de-sacs that predate the great fire. **Anafartlar Caddesi** is the main drag, and, while İzmir's market can hardly compare to Istanbul's or Bursa's, it's still worth a visit for unexpected things like the **Şunnet Çarşısı**, a pretty courtyard next to an old *han* where garden supplies are sold, or the huge glass-roofed **arcade** at 913 Sokak and Gaziosmanpaşa Bulvarı, a pre-1922 monument now come down in the world, selling cheap clothes.

Roman agora
open daily
8.30–5.30; adm

Just south of the bazaar (take 938 Sokak south of Anafartlar) are the excavations of the **Roman agora**, a rebuilding financed by Emperor Marcus Aurelius after a terrible earthquake; here you can see two rows of colonnades and three statues discovered on the site: Poseidon, Demeter and half of Artemis.

The Museums and Kadifekale

*Archaeology
Museum
open daily 8.30–12
and 1–5; adm*

South along the waterfront from the clock tower a new three-storey building houses İzmir's **Archaeology Museum**, with an extensive collection of artefacts from the region. If you're on your way to Ephesus, you should stop here first; there are models and plans of the Meryemana Kilisesi and St John's, and a number of finds from the sites. In any case, this museum is worth the trip, a treasurehouse of expressive sculpture from archaic times through the Classical and Hellenistic periods. In the latter, especially, you may appreciate the soft reflectiveness of the portraits of a *Nun of Isis* and *Aspasia*. Some of this sensibility carried on into Roman times; there's a basement full of fine Roman portrait busts, though all are larger than life and a bit Felliniesque. Some of the best works are outside in the gardens: grave steles with the common motif of death's door, friezes from Aphrodisias and a fanciful, delightful Roman frieze from Miletus, showing almost naïve hunting scenes with grinning goats, dolphins and ostriches.

Ethnography Museum
open daily 9–12 and 1–5; adm

Next door, the **Ethnography Museum** has well-thought-out displays on Ottoman life ranging from a feature on camel-wrestling to a mock-up of a Turkish boy's circumcision ceremony, complete with a mannequin of a suitably anguished adolescent.

Almost directly above the Roman agora looms Mount Pagus, or **Kadifekale**, the Velvet Castle, crowned with fortifications begun by Alexander the Great, and rebuilt in turn by the Byzantines and Ottomans. On your way up, you may see friendly gypsies or Kurdish women scrubbing their household rugs on the pavement. Once at the castle, the view of İzmir from the walls or one of the nearby cafés is vertiginous.

East of the central city, on Gaziler Caddesi, the **Halkapınar Gölü** has been identified as the ancient Baths of Artemis, where a statue of the goddess was discovered. This spring-fed pool, which lies in what are now the grounds of the İzmir water company, supplies the entire city, and is believed to be the source of the ancient River Meles. A Homeric hymn refers to a pool of Artemis in the vicinity, and, according to tradition, Homer sat on its banks and composed his iambic verse. The pool is still a charming, poetic oasis in the big city, and visitors are welcome.

Shopping in İzmir

For English books, the best bet is the **Artı Bookshop** on Cumhuriyet Bulvarı.

Where to Stay in İzmir

İzmir

Most hotels in the moderate category are drab modern places intended for travelling salesmen.

*****İzmir Hilton, at Gaziosmanpaşa Bulvarı 7, t 0232 441 6060, *www.hilton.co.uk/izmir* (€€€€€). A hideous but inescapable 500ft skyscraper, visible from almost anywhere in town. It has two presidential suites, in case two presidents happen to pass through at the same time, 24-hour room service, pool, health club, sauna, tennis and squash courts, and on and on.

*****Princess Otel, in Balçova, 8km southwest of the city centre, t 0232 238 5151, *www.izmirprincess.com.tr* (€€€€). A challenger to the title of hotel with most on offer. On top of the usual embarrassment of amenities, it also has a thermal spa which claims to have restorative effects on every ailment ranging from stomach pains to rheumatism, with dolmuş

(i) İzmir >
Ataturk Caddesi 418, Alsancak,
t 0232 422 1022

Buyuk Efes Oteli Altı, Alsancak,
t 0232 489 9278

Adnan Menderes Hava Limani, t 0232 251 5480

fatigue and archaeological overkill somewhere in between.

***Karaca Oteli, nearby, in a quiet location off Gaziosmanpaşa Bulvarı, 1379 Sokak 55, t 0232 489 1940, *www.otelkaraca.com.tr* (€€). Modern and stylish.

***İzmir Palas Oteli, Vasif Çınar Bulvarı 2, t 0232 465 0030, *www.izmirpalas.com.tr* (€€). The İzmir Palas is on the Kordon and some rooms have sea views. Prices may be lower in the off season.

**Baylan, on a quiet street a few minutes' walk from Basmane station at 1299 Sokak 8, t 0232 483 1426, *www.hotelbaylan.com* (€€). A good option for a quiet night's sleep. The staff are friendly and the rooms clean, if on the small side, but some of them can be gloomy: ask for one facing the Kadifekale. Ignore the posted prices of 80 YTL per double – you should be able to stay for half that. Drivers will be glad to know that the hotel has a private car park in which their metal beasts can take refuge from the chaotic İzmiri traffic.

Rather than pay more for one of the above, you'll do just as well in one of the perfectly acceptable inexpensive hotels on **1369 Sokak**, the traveller's best friend in İzmir. The street is located in the Basmane area near the rail station, just north of Fevzi Paşa Bulvarı, and it holds everything you will ever need (*see* 'Eating Out').

Oba, 1369 Sokak 59, t 0232 483 5474 (€€–€). The furthest hotel from the station but the first choice; clean, modern rooms with bath, some with TV, for 60 YTL (and not to be confused with the Ova nearby, an establishment that even Mae West would have considered overpowering).

Özcan Oteli, 1368 Sokak 3, t 0232 483 5052 (€€–€). Very much the same in quality and price range.

Eating Out in İzmir

The fancy places are along the waterfront on and around the **Kordon**, where seafood is the speciality.

Deniz Restaurant, Atatürk Caddesi 188B, t 0232 364 44 64 (€€€€). On the seafront one block north of Cumhuriyet Meydanı, famous for its seafood and with good reason. The service may only be lukewarm but the fish more than compensates.

Or do as the locals do and take yourself north to the trendy district of **Alsancak**, where most restaurants are. These tend to be informal places with tables out on the pavement. **Kıbrıs Şehitler Caddesi**, a pedestrian street of surviving pre-1922 houses just off the Kordon (Atatürk Caddesi), is one of the first places to look. One of its offshoots is the **Gazi Kadinlar Sokak**, lined with attractive Greek houses whose bay windows have been largely restored. Many of them now house seafood restaurants, most with simple menus of *mezes* and the day's catch.

Recis, on 1382 Sokak 31 near the Lozan Meydanı (€€). Almost every big street corner in Alsancak seems to have some sort of outdoor fast-food joint, Turkish-style. This is one step up; students are drawn by the keen prices, and their parents' generation by the healthy Turkish and European food.

Altınkapı, on a side street at the southern end of Kıbrıs Şehitler Caddesi (€€). Looks for all the world like a chain restaurant, but is a firm local favourite; kebabs and so on.

The obvious place to look for inexpensive chow is around the **Basmane rail station** and 1369 Sokak. On this pedestrian street, plenty of bars put out tables and grill kebabs outdoors (some have live music on weekends); chestnuts and mussels are on offer, and violinists and girls with roses ply the tables.

Dört Mevsim (€€–€). One of the proper table restaurants, with truly good kebabs and incredible homemade *pide* blown up like a balloon.

Grand Nazar Lokanta (€€–€). Among a score of steam-table *lokantas* on the station square; benefits from shade.

Finding something cheap and decent around **Gaziosmanpaşa Bulvarı** can be a problem.

Amazon Bar-Restoran, hidden away next to a playground behind the Hilton (€€). Seafood, pizza, roast chicken and such.

La Folie, behind the Efes hotel on Kızılay Caddesi (€€). Its globe-trotting menu has everything from curries to pizzas and Chinese sweet'n'sour dishes, but not a kebab in sight. The huge salads are a vegetarian's dream.

For the simple *lokantas*, search in the area between **Konak** and the market. Many of the city's *meyhaneler* are on or around Akdeniz Caddesi, dark dives with outside tables under a canopy, which provide some of the cheapest fare in town.

Ora, t 0232 483 36 36 (€). Serves up wooden platters of wafer-thin *lahmacun* with salad and a drink for only 3–4 YTL; a local favourite.

Plenty of street-front stands in İzmir specialize in *börekler* and other sorts of Turkish savoury pastries that everybody's mom makes, but you'll hardly ever see in restaurants. **McZeki's**, a tiny local, facetiously named, chain serves some of the best; there's one on **Fevzi Paşa Bulvarı** near the post office.

To unwind in the company of İzmir's well-heeled young set, find your way to the tree-lined **Mustafabey Caddesi** near the 9 Eylül Üniversitesi, where **Cafés Plaza** and **Biyer** nestle together under the trees. Both have Turkish and European dishes on the menu as well as a wide choice of alcohol.

Inland from İzmir

Manisa

East of İzmir is Manisa, ancient Magnesia ad Sipylum, which began its life as the westernmost outpost of the Hittites. Much later, as a Greek city, Magnesia was mentioned in Homer and in mythology – though it *isn't*, sorry, the Magnesia that gave its name to magnesium and magnets; that one is a region in Thessaly. Magnesia was, however, the birthplace of our forebear Pausanias, whose scholarly *Guide to Greece*, written in the reign of Trajan, was probably the world's first travel guide.

Manisa became an Ottoman possession in the early 14th century, and was favoured under the sultans, particularly Süleyman the Magnificent, who served as governor here before his accession to the throne. In 1922, retreating Greek troops destroyed most of the city, leaving this provincial capital modern and a bit dull, with little to show the visitor.

Manisa Museum
open Tues–Sun 8.30–12 and 1.30–5; closed Mon; adm

Finds from ancient Magnesia and Sardis can be seen in the **Manisa Museum**, among them a fine Roman statue of a young girl

Food of the Gods

Just east of Manisa, at Akpınar, there is a carved relief of the great Mother Goddess Cybele on the side of Mount Sipylus. This region is closely identified in mythology with Tantalus, his sons Pelops and Broteas, and his daughter Niobe. Broteas, the ugliest man in Greece, is credited with carving the Cybele, while Pelops, less talented, ended up on the other end of the knife and was chopped up in a soup at the banquet Tantalus prepared for the gods on top of Mount Sipylus. The gods (except for the earth goddess Demeter, who was mourning for her lost daughter Persephone and carelessly ate a bit of shoulder) recognized the meat for what it was and punished Tantalus in Hades with eternal thirst and hunger, always keeping water and fruit just out of his reach (hence 'tantalise'). Zeus put Pelops back together again (with an ivory shoulder), and he went on to conquer southern Greece and give it his name – the Peloponnese.

It's difficult to know exactly what to make of all this, but we have definitely hit a nerve: the story of Tantalus is one of the myths where the ghosts of ancient belief and ritual glare out from behind the civilized veneer laid down by the mythologizers of the classical era. A 'Feast of Tantalus' was an important midwinter holiday in western Asia Minor, celebrated by an *eranos* – a pot-luck banquet, like the one Tantalus threw for the gods. It may contain a memory of an actual human sacrifice and even cannibalism, rites suppressed in the later stage of religious evolution represented by Zeus and the Olympian gods; there are plenty of dark hints toward this in Arcadia, in Pelops's own Peloponnese. Or else the fate of Pelops may have been strictly metaphorical. We may think of him as the typical sort of sacred king, whose career, representing the sun's, begins at midwinter (the New Year's baby of popular art is a survival of this). His death and rebirth recalls the cycle of the year. Somewhere on the slopes of Mount Sipylus is a small ruin of a *tholos* tomb that the ancients called the 'Tomb of Tantalus'.

As for Tantalus' unfortunate daughter Niobe, she had seven daughters and seven sons, but was rash enough to boast that she was a better mother than Leto, who had only two children, Apollo and Artemis. These two stern archer gods avenged the insult to their mother by slaying Niobe's fourteen. Niobe's grief was so great that Zeus took pity on her and turned her to stone. A natural rock formation southwest of Manisa is believed to be the Niobe referred to by ancient writers; it lies along the road to Karaköy, near a picnic ground, one of the many scenic spots in the region.

Getting around Inland from İzmir

Both Manisa and Sardis are connected to İzmir by **rail** and **bus** (1½ hours). For Sardis, take any bus or minibus/dolmuş for Salihli or Sartmustafa.

and inscriptions from a synagogue discovered in Sardis in 1962. The museum is located in the *medrese* of the **Muradiye Cami**, a work of Mimar Sinan and noted for the tiles and goldwork in the interior. The 14th-century **Ulu Cami**, halfway up to the derelict Byzantine fortress on the ancient acropolis, has a Selcuk-style minaret, with coloured tiles and columns from an ancient temple. A third mosque, the 1522 **Sultan Camii**, built by the mother of Süleyman the Magnificent, is the most famous in Manisa, for here, at the end of May, the Mesir Festival takes place. *Mesir* is a kind of paste, a concoction of some 41 ingredients and spices, reputed to be a cure-all. It is tossed in paper wrappers from the top of the minaret. According to popular belief, it only works if you scramble for it, and hundreds of people do so every year.

Sardis (Sart)

Almost two hours' east of İzmir (take the bus for Salihli from İzmir) is the 20th-century village of Sart, built over the ruins of the ancient capital of Lydia, Sardis. Situated below the steep Mount Tmolus, dominating the fertile plain of the River Hermes (the Gediz Nehri) and located on the great Royal Road of the Persian Empire (the western part of the road may go back to Hittite times), Sardis from the 7th to the mid-6th century BC was the world's richest city. A good part of its wealth was in gold washed down from the mountain by the River Pactolus, which the Lydians collected in sheepskins spread in the shallows – perhaps the source of the legend of the Golden Fleece.

The Site

One thing the excavators have discovered is that Sardis was at its most extensive during the rule of Croesus, and it takes some walking to see it all. The **Temple of Artemis**, the most famous of ancient Sardis's monuments, is about one km up the Pactolus valley; although the sanctuary was founded in the 5th century BC, the temple wasn't begun until the 3rd. Its two Ionic capitals are among the finest anywhere; 13 others have been re-erected to give an idea of the temple's shape. In Roman times the temple was divided into two, one half dedicated to the worship of Artemis, the other half to Faustina, wife of the Roman emperor Antoninus Pius.

Along the road to the centre of Sardis, an **altar to Cybele** was discovered, as well as the workshops where the Lydians worked the gold they 'fleeced' from the river.

The Lucrative Lydians

The Greeks were fascinated by the Lydians, and their fame went as far as the Assyrians who called them the Luddi in their inscriptions. The Lydian race was a mixture of native Anatolian and Western invaders; their language used many Greek letters and was related to Phrygian and, perhaps, Etruscan (Herodotus writes that Etruria was a Lydian colony, and the mysterious Etruscans claimed to have originated in Asia Minor). Besides building giant mounds for their deceased rulers, the Lydians were also famous for condoning prostitution; it was the way a good Lydian girl earned her marriage dowry.

There were three Lydian dynasties. At the end of the second, the Heraclid, the Lydians gained ascendancy as the Hittites in the region declined. The last Heraclid king was Candaules (700 BC), who, it is said, was so proud of his wife's beauty that he contrived for his trusted minister Gyges to see her naked. The queen, however, saw the unwitting voyeur and the next day gave him a choice: either kill her husband and marry her, or die on the spot. Gyges chose the more pleasant alternative, and founded a new dynasty, the Mermnad, that brought Sardis and Lydia, literally, a golden age. By the time of Croesus (563–546 BC), Sardis controlled the whole of Asia Minor, which Croesus ruled with a very benevolent hand. Lydia had been the first nation in the world to mint coins, and Croesus the first to issue them in pure gold and pure silver. His reputation for wealth has come down to us, but did little to impress the visiting Athenian lawgiver Solon, who, after touring the fabulous treasuries, merely commented, 'No man can be reckoned happy until the end.'

A few years after Solon's visit, the Persians under King Cyrus menaced Lydia's borders. Croesus asked the Delphic oracle whether he should attack and the oracle coyly replied that if he crossed the River Halys he would 'destroy a great empire'. Encouraged, Croesus took the offensive, only to meet defeat. Cyrus chased the Lydians back to Sardis. After a two-week siege the city fell, and Croesus realized too late that he had destroyed his own empire. Condemned to be burnt at the stake, Croesus groaned 'Solon, Solon!' as the fire was lit, and Cyrus asked what he meant. Croesus told him what the Athenian had said and, moved, Cyrus ordered his life to be spared.

Cyrus made Sardis the capital of a satrapy and, as such, it was sacked when the Ionian cities revolted against the Persians in 499 BC. It recovered in the Hellenistic era, until the earthquake of AD 17 flattened it. Tiberius had it rebuilt, and it became an early centre of Christianity, one of the seven churches of Asia and an important bishopric under the Byzantines. In 1401, Tamerlane destroyed Sardis so thoroughly that it was never rebuilt; when excavations began in the early 20th century, the archaeologists had to dig down 30ft in places, so thickly had the soft rock of the acropolis silted down over the lower city.

Equally impressive are the **Roman gymnasium** and **baths** from the 2nd century AD, just off the highway; **shops** and a **synagogue** complete the complex, with the **Marble Court** in the centre. Nearby, part of the **Royal Road** has been uncovered, and, most interestingly, what appears to be a sort of prototype **bazaar** dating back to the 7th century BC, giving rise to the theory that wealthy Sardis was the first city to practise organized retail trade. Next to this, the **House of Bronzes** (6th century AD) was perhaps the residence of the bishop of Sardis.

If you're reasonably energetic you can walk up to the **acropolis**, one of the most dramatic in Asia Minor, its sheerness accentuated by the dagger-shaped rock formations around it. The walk from the valley takes less than an hour; on top the surviving fortifications are mostly Byzantine.

Ten km north of Sardis are the **Bin Tepe**, or 'Thousand Hills', actually some 100 earthworks built by the artisans, merchants and prostitutes of Sardis. The largest is the **Tomb of Alyattes**, the father of Croesus. At three-quarters of a mile in circumference and 260ft high, it's the largest mound in Turkey, perhaps in the world.

Kemalpaşa

Between Sardis and İzmir, Kemalpaşa is the ancient town of **Nymphaeum**, where Andronicus I Comnenus built the Palace of Nymphaeum in 1184, the ruins of which are just outside town.

In **Karabel**, on the main road south of Kemalpaşa, there is a second Hittite relief similar to Manisa's Cybele, this one of a large warrior. Herodotus referred to it, although, like all Greeks in the classical era, he knew nothing of the Hittites, and assumed it was Egyptian.

Incidentally, for workmanship of a more recent vintage, you could head to Kemalpaşa on a Sunday, when people come to buy and sell cars. If you're tired of riding buses, here's your chance to pick up a 1952 Chevy and do the coast in style.

The Çeşme Peninsula

The peninsula west of İzmir has several popular beach resorts and thermal spas. **İnciraltı** is the closest to İzmir and thus the most crowded; just to the south, in the modern suburb of **Balçova**, the **Baths of Agamemnon**, in use since antiquity, are noted for treating rheumatism.

Further west, near **Urla** and another beach, a causeway leads out to an islet where once stood the ancient city of **Clazomenae**. The original causeway, constructed by Alexander the Great, can be seen just below the surface of the sea; otherwise little remains of this Ionian city that produced the great philosopher Anaxagoras, precursor of Socrates, in the early 5th century BC.

Sığacık

You can go south from Urla to Seferihisar and from there to Sığacık, the prettiest village on the peninsula, its old houses clustered around an old Genoese fortress and small port. Here, by the lovely white beach of Akkum, stood **ancient Teos**, one of the wealthiest Ionian cities on the coast. Teos was the birthplace and home of the lyric love-poet Anacreon; it is also the site of a famous Hellenistic **Temple of Dionysus**, with an unusual trapezoidal enclosure. Some columns have been re-erected, to make a picturesque tableau in the olive grove. Nearby is the **theatre** which, though in poor condition, offers a fabled view from its upper seats. Better preserved is the **odeion**, with its eleven rows of seats, where concerts would have been performed.

Getting to and around the Çeşme Peninsula

There are frequent **buses** (lines 86 and 169) from İzmir's Cumhuriyet Meydanı and Konak Meydanı to Üçküyülar bus station from where buses leave regularly for Çeşme. From that town's tiny *otogar*, on the port, minibuses depart for the beaches and villages around the peninsula.

Between November and April there are usually one or two **boats** a week between Çeşme and the Greek island of Chios; in season they go every day. They can only take about five cars. If you visit Chios, you'll have to pay a small exit tax of 15 YTL. For details of ferries, contact Ertürk Travel Agency, Beyazıt Caddesi 7/8 in Çeşme, **t** 0232 712 6768, *www.erturk.com.tr*.

Çeşme is the official port for the Marmara Lines **car ferry** to and from Ancona once a week, a three-night crossing, and also as of July 2008, twice weekly to Brindisi. The website *www.marmaralines.com* has detailed information on schedules.

Çeşme

At the tip of the peninsula, opposite the Greek island of Chios, is Çeşme ('fountain'), named after its numerous hot springs. It is the westernmost town in Turkey, a distinction that has an added significance during Ramazan, when the pious Muslims of Çeşme have to wait longer than anyone else to eat supper. Çeşme makes its living as a resort, though one totally lacking in the glamour or intensity of resorts further south. It is a serene family spot to sit on the beach; that's all.

An attractive town, with red tile roofs, Çeşme is dominated by a large, sloping **Genoese castle**, captured and restored by Yıldırım Beyazıt in 1400. Beyazıt's engineers evidently discharged their duties well; the castle is in good shape and housed within the crenellated walls is a theatre, a restaurant and a small **museum** displaying the finds from ancient Erythrae.

Museum
open daily 8.30–12 and 1.30–5; adm

Two important naval battles took place off Çeşme: the decisive Roman defeat of Antiochus III in 190 BC, which gave the Romans a free hand in Asia Minor, and the destruction of the Ottoman fleet by the Russians in 1770.

Çeşme faces the Greek island of Chios, much favoured by the sultans for its breath-sweetening mastic, some of which went through the **caravanserai**, built in a U-shape by Süleyman the Magnificent in 1529; it has been restored and is now a hotel. As in all Turkish resorts, the **port** is lined with cruise ships, pretty wooden sailing craft waiting to take you away on a trip around the peninsula and its islets; the going rate for a half-day excursion with lunch is about 25 YTL.

Around Çeşme

Çeşme has a small beach but better bathing is to be had elsewhere. South of town there are beaches at nearby **Çiftlik**, much better ones at fast-developing **Altınkum** (not to be confused with the megabeach of the same name further south) and more at **Ovacık** and **Güverçinlik**.

For real seclusion head for tiny **Alaçatı**, a village 7km east of Çeşme full of old Greek houses now converted into charming hotels, and then walk south 3km to find the beach. With strong, steady winds blowing reliably all year, it's a windsurfer's paradise, and the facilities here reflect this: surf school, board rental, surf boutique, camping ground and café. At offshore Donkey Island (**Eşek Adası**), so named for its population of wild donkeys, there are several nice swimming spots; Çeşme's travel agents regularly organize day trips.

Dalyan, a fishing village north of Çeşme, is pleasant and pretty but its beach is small and poor, unlike the mammoth stretch of white sand that can be found at **Ilıca** to the east. Fronted by four large windmills, and famous for its thermal springs, Ilıca has pretensions to becoming a popular resort in its own right, with holiday homes replacing ancient vineyards, unfortunately leaving the impression that the town is just one big building site. Other beaches are at Şifne and Ildırı.

Ildırı is near **ancient Erythrae**, a member of the Ionian Confederacy, set at the foot of the rugged Karaburun peninsula. Unfortunately the site was so well quarried in the 19th century that little remains in the picturesque spot beyond some well-built walls and a ruined theatre. In ancient times Erythrae was famous for a statue of Heracles which floated on a raft from Egypt to a point between Chios and Erythrae. Both wanted it, but the raft couldn't be budged until a blind man in Erythrae dreamed that the statue could only be towed away with a rope of women's hair. The women of Erythrae refused to part with their locks, but their Thracian slaves used theirs to make the rope that did indeed pull the raft to their city. The statue restored the blind man's sight, and in the sanctuary subsequently built for it, no women were allowed except Thracians. It's now impossible to tell which of the remains was Heracles' sanctuary, but a stream that tastes bitter still flows in the walls and, according to Pliny – a notorious story-teller – it causes hair to grow all over the body.

A Trip to Chios

There's plenty to see on this Greek island if you want to cross over for a day or two. Chios (Sakız in Turkish) is famous for its rich shipping magnates and for the mastic chewing gum, made from local lentisk bushes. **Chios town**, impressively modern and prosperous, is the capital, with an excellent white sand beach just to the north at **Karfas**; or else you might take an excursion up into the mountains to **Nea Moni**, a fascinating 11th-century monastery in a beautiful setting, with Byzantine mosaics.

Chios does not see vast numbers of tourists; it's especially fun to cycle around, exploring picturesque medieval villages such as **Pirama** or **Pitios**, which like İzmir claims to be the birthplace of Homer. Around **Sklavia**, there are a number of villas and gardens from the time Chios was ruled by the Genoese.

The most memorable sight Chios has to offer is undoubtedly **Pirgi**, a village with a long-standing custom of decorating its buildings with complex, geometrical *sgraffito* façades in black and white (this was a habit in many of Anatolia's Greek villages too, before 1923, and you'll see a few forlorn examples as you travel around the coast).

Where to Stay on the Çeşme Peninsula

(i) Çeşme ›
İskele Meydanı 8, at the harbour, t 0232 712 6653

Çeşme

Hotel Cooperative has booths at the entrance to town and near the *otogar* and tourist office; they can help you find a room in summer when things are packed.

Altınyunus Tatil Köyü (the Golden Dolphin), t 0232 723 1250, *www.altinyunus.com.tr* (€€€€). The top TK1 beach resort hotel around Çeşme, with 515 bungalows and nearly every possible recreational facility, including horse riding, water-skiing and thermal baths.

Next to each other near the harbour on Cumhuriyet Meydanı are two hotels, very much alike, with private sections of beach and double rooms for about 70 YTL:

**Ertan, t 0232 712 6795 (€€). Has a roof terrace but rather soulless rooms.

**Ridvan, t 0232 712 6336 (€€). Next door, a similar set up but most rooms have balconies with sea views.

Just follow the signs for Çeşme's cheap *pensions* – there are over 100 on the peninsula. If you're looking for accommodation in this category, though, try to avoid arriving in Çeşme over the weekend in summer, when the town fills up with holidaymakers from İzmir. Most of the *pansiyonlar* are located on the hill above the port, pleasant, family-run places.

Tani, t 0232 712 6238, in a lane behind the Kervansaray (€€). Run by the delightful Mrs Tani, with a rooftop terrace overlooking the port and eight simple doubles.

Tarhan, t 0232 712 6381, next door (€€). Similarly priced and covered in bougainvillaea.

Alim Pansiyon, near the hamam, t 0232 712 1238 (€€). The top choice in the centre of Çeşme, where a sparkling-clean room with private shower awaits you for only 40 YTL.

Alaçatı

The wonderful selection of hotels, all in renovated old stone houses, do not come cheap but have terrific atmosphere. If you want to splash out a little, and are not bothered about being beachfront, then this is the best place for your money.

Taş Otel, t 0232 716 7772, *www.tasotel.com* (€€€€). Renovated from a 110-year-old Greek house, with tastefully decorated rooms, modern elegance and heaps of rustic charisma, and a nice pool in the secluded garden to boot.

Sakızlıhan, t 0232 716 6108, *www.sakizlihan.com* (€€€€). One of the famous gum trees the region is famous for dominates the garden of this stone hotel. The standard rooms are pretty basic at 210 YTL for a double.

Değirmen, t 0232 716 6714, *www.alacatidegirmen.com* (€€€). Converted from a mill, with cavernous rooms.

Lalelodge, t 0232 716 1999, *www.lalelodge.com* (€€€). For a little boutique hotel luxury, especially if you fancy having a Jacuzzi on your own balcony.

Dalyan

***Çeşme Ladin, t** 0232 724 8327, *www.ladinotel.com.tr* (€€€). A resort offering a private beach and a pool, and rooms with TV and balconies, most overlooking the sea. The emphasis is on sports, with a gym and all imaginable water pursuits.

Ilıca

***Delmar Hotel, t** 0232 723 4300 (€€€). On the beach, a large but pleasant place among the many small hotels with thermal establishments, with helpful staff and its own thermal spa and swimming pool.

There are **campsites** near the town and on the peninsula.

Vekamp, t 0232 717 2224. Campsite in a pleasant location near the beach. Rather deluxe; it also has a swimming pool fed by natural hot springs.

Eating Out on the Çeşme Peninsula

Çeşme

You can get all the kebabs and sandwiches you need, but, whether in Çeşme or anywhere else on the peninsula, anything above the tourist common denominator is hard to come by. At any rate, there will be no problem finding good seafood.

Rıhtım Restaurant, t 0232 712 74 33 (€€€). On the harbour in Çeşme; this attractive place offers *midye dolması* (stuffed mussels), and uncommon treats like octopus; the best deal among the generally overpriced harbourfront places.

İmren, t 0232 712 76 20 (€€). A nice little family affair on the main drag, serving up good examples of Aegean *meze*.

Alaçatı

Mavi Bistro, t 0232 716 04 20, *www. mavibistro.com* (€€€€). With its simple but attractive décor this is certainly worthy of your attention, though it may put a dent in your wad of lira: full meal from 50 YTL.

Dalyan

Dalyan has several good fish restaurants, although on the rest of the peninsula you'll be fortunate to find anything beyond the basic *lokanta*.

Dalyan Körfez Restaurant, t 0232 724 79 47 (€€). A rich variety of seafood and wonderful views at sunset.

Ilıca

Among the many restaurants in Ilıca, the **Altınkapı** has good kebabs, especially the speciality 'golden kebab', and, as night falls, music and dancing.

The South Aegean Coast

Once, this was fabled Ionia, where the Greeks first colonized a new land. From the beginning, there was always a little more sizzle here than in the Greece they left behind, and Ionia contributed far more than its share to the art, science and philosophy of the Classical age. Now, there's little but ruins left to tell the tale, but this region is blessed with more than past glories. Herodotus, a native of the region, wrote that the climate of Ionia is the fairest in the world, and it is endowed with a light-filled Aegean beauty.

In our day, such places can't escape a fate as holiday playgrounds, employing more waiters and diving instructors than sculptors and philosophers. Names like Kuşadası, Bodrum and Marmaris, which once sounded strange and exotic, now are counted among the noisiest fleshpots of the Med.

10

Don't miss

⭐ **An ancient metropolis come to life**
Ephesus p.255

⭐ **The perfect Classical city**
Priene p.264

⭐ **Moon-enchanted waters**
Lake Bafa p.270

⭐ **A Crusader castle and underwater archaeology**
Bodrum p.284

⭐ **Quiet beaches**
Datça Peninsula p.294

See map overleaf

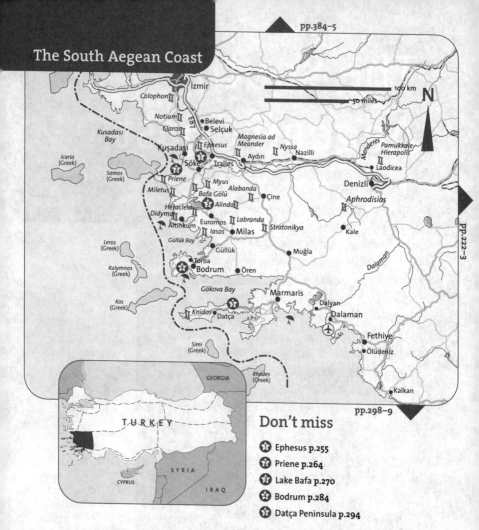

pp.384-5

pp.222-3

pp.298-9

Don't miss

- ⭐ Ephesus p.255
- ⭐ Priene p.264
- ⭐ Lake Bafa p.270
- ⭐ Bodrum p.284
- ⭐ Datça Peninsula p.294

The hard-working Turks who are pushing themselves into the middle classes and a European lifestyle in places like Aydın and Selçuk and Muğla share their little corner of paradise with sunburned package tourists, disco vampires, happy children and cultured folk poring over the lost Ionian cities. Everyone seems to get along just fine. Like the ancient Ionians, they all like to mess about in boats. While you're here, try a Greek ferry or a well-varnished little cruise boat or a harbour tour.

Kuşadası Bay

This gently curving bay, Kuşadası Körfezi, has long been one of the hot spots for tourism on the Aegean coast. Its two poles, Kuşadası and Selçuk, maintain a neatly symbiotic relationship to

Getting to and around Kuşadası Bay

Selçuk and Kuşadası can easily be reached by **bus** from anywhere, and there is also a typically slow **rail** connection to Selçuk from İzmir. Selçuk's **bus terminal** is in the town centre, on Atatürk Caddesi (the main İzmir–Muğla road). Through-buses from either direction do not usually stop in the station, but just outside it on Atatürk Caddesi facing the town park.

From Selçuk there are frequent connections to **Pamukkale** and to **Aphrodisias**; there are ten buses a day to the village closest to the latter, **Karacasu**. There is an infrequent **dolmuş** for **Belevi**.

There's no problem exploring **Ephesus** from Selçuk; you could take a dolmuş but the two-mile walk is pleasant and passes the Temple of Artemis. The only way to get to the House of the Virgin Mary, 5km from town, is by taxi. If you want a look at the ancient **Carian cities** to the south, ask at Selçuk or Kuşadası; bus arrangements change frequently and in summer there are often tours on offer.

Colophon and **Claros** are hard to reach by minibus from Selçuk or Kuşadası, but it can be done – it's better if you have your own transport and can combine the ruins with a spell on the isolated beaches.

keep all the visitors happy; together they do their best to fill the shoes of neighbouring Ephesus, one of the great metropolises of the ancient world and now one of its most evocative ruins. Kuşadası, an improbable, noisy and overbuilt resort, supplies the beaches and seafood; Selçuk, an amiable modern town, offers itself as the most convenient base for seeing Ephesus and the other classical remains in the area.

Colophon

One Ionian city splendid in its day but almost forgotten now is Colophon, on the back roads between İzmir and Kuşadası. It was the only city built very far from the sea, and the home town of Plato's courtesan Archeanassa ('Even upon her wrinkles there rests a bitter passion.'). Colophon was renowned in antiquity for its horses and mighty cavalry, and for its fierce dogs trained to fight in battle; it was also one of few places in the ancient Greek world where dogs were sacrificed (the only deity that demanded dogs was Hecate, the underworld god who may have originated in Caria). Because its land was incredibly fertile and its fleet powerful, it became so wealthy that the men wore kingly purple robes daily, drenched their hair with musk and ate 12-course meals. Lavish living made them soft, and Colophon was one of the first Greek cities to fall to the Lydians. In the Hellenistic age, it became a backwater as Ephesus stole all the trade; eventually it was destroyed by Lysimachus, and its inhabitants relocated to his newly refounded Ephesus. Today little remains except a few scanty walls.

Notium and Claros

Notium nearby was the port of Colophon and, although mainly visited these days for its sandy beach, it has some well-preserved sections of wall, the foundations of a temple and stoa and a small theatre. What really makes the trip worthwhile are the excavations at **Claros**, a 20-minute walk from Notium. Here stood the famous temple and oracle of Clarian Apollo, visited from as far away as

Britain and southern Russia. If excavation work is in progress, you may find that you have to view the ruins from behind a fence.

The valley of the temple floods every year, and over the ages the temple disappeared in the mud. In the 1960s it was rediscovered and excavated by the French, although in the winter large parts of it will be underwater. The lower chamber, to which the priest would descend to drink the sacred water and utter the oracles, is all flooded, but you can make out the purposely disconcerting maze-like corridor that led to the **adyton**, the sacred oracle chamber. The temple was built in the Doric style, surprisingly, because Doric was usually reserved for temples on heights, where it showed to better advantage. A sacred way led to the entrance from the monumental **propylaea**, or gate. Around the temple, fragments of three colossal **statues** – of Apollo, Artemis and their mother Leto – lie strewn about; Apollo's leg alone measures over 10ft. The **altar**, just east of the temple, is some 6oft long, half dedicated to Apollo, and half to Dionysus, who, as at Delphi, took over the temple during the winter months, when the sun god went to frolic with the Hyperboreans in Britain. Near the temple there's a **sundial** dedicated to Dionysus; a smaller **Ionic temple** dedicated to Apollo's twin, Artemis, lies northwest of the main temple.

Although the structures date from the Hellenistic age, Claros had been a sacred spot for hundreds of years before. The weary, pregnant Leto stopped here as she fled the relentless jealousy of Hera, before giving birth to Apollo and Artemis on the island of Delos; here also the famous Sibyl, Herophile, predicted that both Asia and Europe would be destroyed because of Helen.

Selçuk

Selçuk, the small but attractive successor to ancient Ephesus (Turkish Efes), is a happy town, grown prosperous on its proximity to some of the finest attractions of western Turkey. Ephesus is an easy walk away, bustling and overripe Kuşadası a 30-minute drive. Priene, Miletus and Didyma can all be seen by day trip. Add that to the sites and charm of Selçuk itself, and after a day or so you may not want to leave. Because of the area's religious associations – which include the home of the Virgin Mary herself – it is extremely popular among Christian tourists and groups; everybody comes here, even the pope (in 1979). Giving the Popemobile a run for its money are some of the local taxis, heavy-metal Fifties floaters that glide majestically along the streets, beaming aboard Americans in search of the heady days of youth.

Archaeology Museum
open summer daily 8.30–12 and 1–6.30; winter daily 9.30–12 and 1–5.30; adm

Selçuk has an exceptionally fine **Archaeology Museum**. Besides the two famous cult images of Ephesian Artemis (*see* box), look for a dramatic tableau of Odysseus blinding the Cyclops, some lovely

Moods of a Goddess

The star attractions of the Selçuk museum are undoubtedly the two statues of Ephesian Artemis, so covered with hanging, breast-like thingumabobs that she resembles a pine cone. No one knows what they really were intended to represent, but they certainly aren't breasts – the image of Zeus Stratius at Labranda had them too. The earliest cult images in Greek temples were weird, primitive objects dating back to remotest antiquity: conical wooden figures, shapeless stone lumps or even meteorites. The Selçuk statues, products of a very sophisticated age, nevertheless offer plenty of clues to the primeval sources; they rank among the most striking images of a deity ever produced in antiquity, and are worth looking at in detail. One Artemis wears a *polos*, a kind of crown suggesting a wall and towers that is often worn by Athena, or by the tutelary goddess of any city, which was certainly Artemis's status in Ephesus. The other has a necklace with the signs of the Zodiac, pictured just as we know them today. Astrology first came into the west in Hellenistic times, brought back from Babylon after Alexander's conquest, and it was the fascination of the age.

Note the animals, in ranks of three, that adorn much of the statues' surface, betraying this Artemis's true meaning as just a Hellenized, up-to-date name for the primeval Anatolian goddess, the mountain-top *potnia theron*, or 'mistress of the wild things'. One statue has plenty of bees on it, which to a Greek mind would be more appropriate to Aphrodite – but then this lady does not have much to do with the tenets of Classical Olympian religion. An outlandish but currently popular theory says that Artemis's 'breasts' are really testicles. Cybele, another aspect of the same Anatolian goddess, presided over an orgiastic cult whose priests offered her the ultimate ex voto: they castrated themselves. (This cult eventually spread as far west as Gaul. In the last centuries of ancient Rome it was quite popular among the city's poor.)

The consciously sanitized version of Artemis that we see in Greek mythology – the virgin huntress revelling with her nymphs – may be unpredictable and a bit dangerous, but she's never a serious threat to the reasoned order of Zeus and her brother Apollo. She is the poetic creation of a very civilized age. But as the aspect of the Great Goddess who delights in untamed nature, and rules the hunters who live from it, her origins may go back as far as the Palaeolithic. As Artemis, she first appears in a Linear B inscription from Minoan Crete. The Greek colonists in Asia Minor melded her image onto the transcendent goddess already worshipped everywhere in Anatolia. Everywhere, though, her rituals carry dark hints of a violent, half-remembered past. In many Greek cities, they included the drawing of human blood, likely a sublimation of what was once human sacrifice. More commonly, Artemis would demand a vast sacrifice of living things, hung on trees or columns and incinerated in a great bonfire. As Pausanias described one:

> ...all manner of victims, also wild boar and deer and fawns and some even bring the cubs of wolves and bears, and others full grown beasts... Then they set fire to the wood. I saw indeed a bear and other beasts struggling to escape from the first force of the flames and escaping by sheer strength. But those who threw them in drag them up again on the fire. I never heard of anyone being wounded by the wild beasts.

In any case, not a goddess to be taken lightly. You'll meet her everywhere in Anatolia, as Cybele or Artemis or Aphrodite – originally it's all the same. And in one form or another she will always be around. Currently, the people of Selçuk are so taken with their Artemis that they have reproduced her in larger-than-life marble on a fountain facing Atatürk Caddesi, just north of the town hall. That will give future archaeologists something to think about.

carved ivory furniture, erotic statuary from the brothel and a frieze from the altar of the Temple of Domitian in a style that can only be called Roman Art Deco. From Domitian's statue in the temple a weird colossal head and arm have survived, looking like lost props from a Fellini film. Note the 6th century AD statue of the city's consul Stephanos. His head is only the most recent occupant of the body; the townspeople would change it whenever a new man was elected. Out in the courtyard is more sculpture, including a memorable 2nd century BC stele with a relief of a sexy Dionysus, and a sarcophagus with the nine Muses on it.

Dominating Selçuk is the old **acropolis of Ephesus**, which Justinian crowned with the **Basilica of St John**. The Apostle John spent his last years in Ephesus writing his *Gospel*, and his burial spot is marked by a slab of marble. The church was in the form of a cross, covered by a large central dome with several smaller domes forming the arms – before the whole was shattered by earthquakes. Today the entrance is through the **Gate of Persecution**, a Christian misinterpretation of a relief of a battle scene: the baptistry and apse with some surviving 10th-century frescoes have been reconstructed. Directly above towers the **Citadel of Ayasoluk**, with its Byzantine-Turkish fortifications and grand views (closed for restoration until Judgement Day, it seems). Just below the church stands a key work of the Selçuk Turks, the **İsa Bey Mosque** (1375). İsa Bey was a prince of the Aydın Turks who briefly ruled western Anatolia, and his mosque was the first to be built with a courtyard and stalactite vaulting, anticipating the later Ottoman style. The mosque was devastated by an earthquake in the 19th century and remained an empty shell until 1975, when a new wooden roof was built. They did not add one innovation of the Ottomans, a special balcony for women's worship: this Selçuk mosque still makes do with cotton sheets strung up between pillars to segregate the sexes. Local people donated the carpets that cover the floor in a sea of colour, with crude woollen flatweaves lapping up against intricate silk masterworks.

Where to Stay in Selçuk

Accommodation in Selçuk is more than ample, though there is little that really stands out. If you really want to see the sights in style, it can be done just as conveniently from one of the resort hotels at Pamucak, on the way to Kuşadası. Although the situation has improved, some places in Selçuk exploit tourists, so be selective about letting someone lead you from the bus station.

Selçuk

(M2) Kalehan, Atatürk Caddesi 49, t 0232 892 6154, *www.kalehan.com* (€€€–€€). The pick of the bunch; a renovated, charmingly decorated stone inn with a swimming pool; for a bit more there are four luxury suites.
Naz Hanı, St John Caddesi, t 0232 892 8731, *www.nazhan.net* (€€€–€€).

One of the most atmospheric, near St John's basilica, with a pleasant courtyard, cluttered with plant pots and old brass hanging scales. Although not cheap, with only five rooms, it's often full.

There are more than 30 *pensions*, the vast majority being clean, comfortable and cheap. Most convenient for Ephesus are those in the back streets behind the museum.
Australian Pension, Prof Miltner Sokak 17, t 0232 892 6050, *www.anzguest house.com* (€€–€). Around 50 YTL for a double room with a free ride to Ephesus thrown in. It fills up fast in the summer with backpackers and can be noisy when the overland truck hits town. The Australian Pension is run by a Turk who spent 12 years down under.

(i) **Selçuk >**
in the park in the town centre, facing Atatürk Caddesi, opposite the museum, t 0232 892 6328, www.selcuk.gov.tr

Barım Pansiyon, next door, t 0232 892 1045 (€€–€). An 18th-century Greek house with a secluded courtyard and a stork on its chimney. Doubles 50 YTL, or more for rooms with showers.

Wallabies Hotel Victoria, t 0232 892 3204, *www.wallabieshostel.com* (€). An otherwise unremarkable hotel facing the aqueduct, but very popular with tourists for its rooms with views of the nesting storks along the way.

Camping choices are limited.

Garden Camping, t 0232 892 1162, out near the İsa Bey Cami. Has a pool but little else.

Eating Out in Selçuk

The pedestrian streets in the centre of Selçuk make a lively scene on summer evenings.

Tat Restoran, Cengiz Topel Caddesi (€). Run by a friendly young fellow from out East. The best of the tourist restaurants, with attractive kilims spread over the tables out on the street. Has a very good selection of *mezes*, and *saç kavurma* done at your table for 20 YTL or less.

Park Restoran, in the park at the town centre (€). One of the nicest places to dine: outside tables under the trees, and kebabs and moussaka.

Karamefle Restaurant, across the street from the Ali Bey Mosque at the edge of town (€). Despite its touristy appearance, this is also a favourite with local families. Children bring carrots to feed the pet rabbits. Rabbit is not on the menu, but you can gorge yourself on the Anatolian village staple of *gözleme* for less than 10 YTL.

Ephesus (Efes)

 Ephesus

Thanks to its proximity to the coastal resorts, more tourists come to visit Ephesus than any other site in Turkey. Yet it isn't a genuine city of classical Greece you'll see here, but a relative late bloomer, a conveniently situated city that the Romans made into the capital of their Province of Asia. That was an opulent time for Ephesus, and most of the ruins on display are the magnificent public buildings of the 1st–2nd centuries AD. Compared to the older sites, such as Priene or the Carian cities, Ephesus can seem strangely modern and familiar. Its remains are those of a rich, comfortable place, living on the crest of the wave of classical civilization, centuries after the great period of Greek cultural achievement.

History

Ephesus was first settled by the Lydians and Carians, who worshipped the great Anatolian goddess Cybele. When the Ionians arrived, around the 10th century BC, they combined the ancient cult of Cybele with their own of Artemis, a syncretism that had unusual success. From the start the cult attracted devotees from across the Mediterranean, and its temple was the one constant in the city's history, for Ephesus itself moved no fewer than four times. The early Ionian settlement was on the slopes of Mount Pion (Panayir Dağı), above the theatre, and its harbour was near Selçuk. The greatest of all the pre-Socratic philosophers, Heraclitus, was born here. Croesus, King of Lydia, conquered Ephesus in 550 BC, but refrained from destroying it when the artless Ephesians tied a rope around the town and bound it to the temple of Artemis. He did

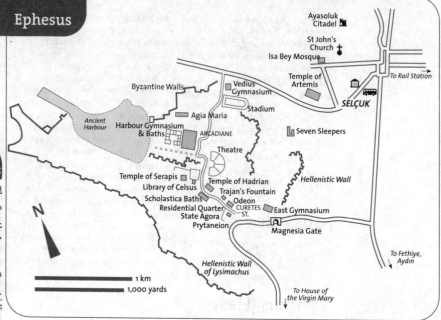

Map labels:
- Ayasoluk Citadel
- St John's Church
- Isa Bey Mosque
- Temple of Artemis
- To Rail Station
- SELÇUK
- Byzantine Walls
- Vedius Gymnasium
- Stadium
- Ancient Harbour
- Harbour Gymnasium & Baths
- Agia Maria
- ARCADIANE
- Seven Sleepers
- Theatre
- Temple of Serapis
- Library of Celsus
- Temple of Hadrian
- Trajan's Fountain
- Hellenistic Wall
- Scholastica Baths
- Residential Quarter
- Odeon
- CURETES ST.
- East Gymnasium
- State Agora
- Prytaneion
- Magnesia Gate
- To Fethiye, Aydın
- N
- 1 km
- 1,000 yards
- Hellenistic Wall of Lysimachus
- To House of the Virgin Mary

however force them to relocate to the defenceless plain near the temple. Lysimachus, Alexander's general and heir to Ionia, noticed that the River Cayster was silting up the port and induced the Ephesians to move again by building new houses downstream and flooding the old ones with tons of sewage – a convincing argument for those who had wanted to stay put.

In its new location, in the valley between Mounts Pion and Coressus, Ephesus became the boom town of Asia Minor. The population doubled when Lysimachus removed the people of Colophon and Lebedos to Ephesus. In Roman times, it became capital of the province of Asia, the banking and trade centre of the east, and, with some 500,000 inhabitants, the largest city in Anatolia. Philostratus wrote in the 1st century AD how it was devoted to dancers and pantomimes, a whole city full of pipers and effeminate rascals and noise. Or, as Heraclitus, Ephesus' native son, had earlier put it: 'May wealth never leave you, Ephesians, lest your wickedness be revealed.' Four different Roman emperors granted the Ephesians permission to construct a temple for their own worship – a great state honour. Yet Ephesus' prosperity was undermined by one constant vexation: the silting up of its harbour. Several dredgings and other solutions were attempted, with only temporary success; today the sea is more than five miles away.

Ephesus in its prime witnessed some of the events that marked the great religious conversion from the goddess Artemis to the new God of the Christians. The Apostle John converted many of the natives even before St Paul came to live in the city. After three years, his preaching had attracted so many adherents that the local silversmiths, who made cult figures of Artemis, felt their livelihoods threatened and started a riot, packing the great theatre with people shouting, 'Great is Artemis of the Ephesians!' St Paul left shortly afterwards. With the decline of Rome and the silting of its harbour, Ephesus dwindled, and in the 6th century the city was abandoned for a new site – modern Selçuk.

The Temple of Artemis

Most of what remains in Ephesus today is Roman, except for the melancholy remains of the Temple of Artemis, about half a mile from the excavations on the Kuşadası–Selçuk road. This, one of the Seven Wonders of the Ancient World, is now marked by a single column re-erected on a ruined foundation in the middle of a swamp, its tip a favourite nesting place for storks. At least three temples have stood on the site. The original, built around the 7th century BC, was replaced in the 6th with a far grander edifice (significantly bigger, for the sake of status, than the temple of Hera under construction on the nearby island of Samos). The temple measured 179 by 374ft, larger than a football field and four times the size of the Parthenon, surrounded by a forest of 129 columns. For all their sophistication, the Greek cities loved to compete in the same way cities do with their skyscrapers today. The Artemision was undoubtedly planned to be the biggest temple in the world, just a few feet longer and wider than the then-reigning champ, the 367ft Temple of Olympian Zeus in Akragas (Agrigento, Sicily). Amazingly, the whole thing was made of marble, except for the wooden roof and inner architrave. In 356 BC, on the night of Alexander the Great's birth (so they say), a mad arsonist in search of fame burned it down. It lay in ruins until Alexander himself came and offered to pay for its restoration. The Ephesians politely declined, with the excuse that one god should not build a temple to another. They then rebuilt it themselves on the same massive scale, and filled it with treasure and statues.

Gigantic as it was, by the mid-19th century, when the British railway engineer J.T. Wood tried to find the temple, not a trace remained: Justinian had quarried most of its marble for the Basilica of St John (see below) and the rest had receded into the mud. For nine years Wood searched for the temple, until 1874 when an inscription was discovered, giving directions to the Sacred Way. Wood excavated the road and followed it to the great temple.

The Main Excavations and Theatre

Ephesus
open daily; adm Excavations of Lysimachus' Ephesus were begun in 1895 by the Austrians and continue to this day. Along the road from the car

park lies the vast **Gymnasium of Vedius**, built in AD 150 by a prominent citizen, Publius Vedius Antonius; the structure includes well-preserved baths and a latrine. Next to it is a partially excavated **stadium**, much quarried by the Selcuks for their castle. Across the road are the few remains of a temple from the time of Croesus; south of this are ruined Byzantine baths and the long, narrow church of **Agia Maria**, built in the 2nd century as a bank and market. In the 3rd century it was converted into a church dedicated to the Virgin Mary – the first church anywhere consecrated to the Mother of God. In 431, the Emperor Theodosius II convened the Third Ecumenical Council here, which declared Jesus to be both the son of Mary and the Son of God.

Beyond the car park and the ticket booth are the remains of the **Harbour Gymnasium, Palaestrae and Baths**, the largest surviving structure in Ephesus, only part of which has been uncovered. It gives on to the **Arcadiane**, the street to the harbour, named for its builder, the Byzantine emperor Arcadius (d. 408). Paved with marble and lined with colonnades and stoas, this was one of the few thoroughfares in antiquity to have street lamps. At the end of the street rises the majestic **theatre** carved into the flank of Mount Pion, built in the Hellenistic era and remodelled by the Romans under Claudius and Trajan. In classic Greek theatre, all the action took place in the orchestra, but by the Hellenistic age the actors performed on a small raised stage, leaving the orchestra to the increasingly irrelevant chorus. By Roman times, fashion had moved all the drama to the stage, which reached grand operatic proportions in Ephesus – three levels with an ornate façade, adorned with statues and columns. The theatre seats 24,000, and has been restored with a heavy hand for the annual Ephesus Festival. The top seats offer a fine view of the ruined city.

Along the Marble Road

From the theatre, the Marble Road, grooved with deep cart ruts, was the main street of Ephesus. Following it will bring you to a 1st-century Doric stoa and, the most elegant of Ephesus' buildings, the **Library of Celsus**, with its lovely white marble façade, fine carvings and statues. This was built in 110 by the consul Gaius Julius Aquila as a temple-tomb for his father, Gaius Julius Celsus, whose unopened lead casket is still in its sarcophagus in the grave chamber. The reading room of the library had three floors; as in Pergamon, niches in the walls mark former shelves for the scrolls. Although the reading room was burned by the Goths in 262, the façade survived unharmed, and in the 5th century the depression around it was filled with water to make a reflecting pool. Behind the **agora** (currently being restored) stood the **Temple of Serapis**, built in the 2nd century, perhaps by the Egyptian residents of the city, although the god Serapis had a cult following among Greek and Roman alike and provided serious competition for Christianity in its early days. Like the Temple of Serapis in Pergamon, this was massive; each of its eight monolithic columns weighed 57 tons.

Street of the Curetes

At the library the street turns and becomes the Street of the Curetes. According to the Ephesians, Artemis was born nearby, at a place called Ortygia; her mother the goddess Leto, pursued by Hera, was able to deliver her here thanks to the Curetes, the young men who frightened the vindictive Hera away by banging on their shields. The Curetes had performed a similar service in Crete, at the cradle of the infant Zeus, where their banging kept his cannibalistic father Cronos from hearing Zeus' cries. 'Curetes' was also the name of an order of priests in the Artemision.

The **Baths of Scholastica** (2nd century AD) were renamed after a Christian who remodelled them in 400. Her headless statue still presides over the entrance; inscriptions indicate that the baths also served as the town brothel. Much of the stone Scholastica used for her remodelling came from the neighbouring Corinthian Temple of Hadrian, which had partially collapsed in an earthquake. Part of it has been reconstructed, and with its four reliefs (the originals are in the museum), this shrine to the good gay emperor is one of the most attractive in the city. Opposite, on the slopes of **Bülbüldağ** (Mountain of the Nightingales), a large **residential quarter** has recently been excavated, bringing to light luxurious mansions owned by Ephesian merchants, with mosaics and frescoes.

Residential
quarter
separate adm

Curetes Street continues to the **Fountain of Trajan**, or nymphaion. A colossal statue of the emperor once stood over the fountain, and what remains – his giant feet, one resting on the world – suggests a Rome already too big for its britches. The street continues past numerous small buildings, some reliefs and fountains, to Domitian Street, leading to the ruined **Temple of Domitian** (1st century AD), the first of the four temples consecrated to imperial worship. A huge statue of the sporty but paranoid Domitian stood within, enjoying a splendid view from the platform. Little survives of the **state agora** next to it. Adjoining the north stoa of the agora is the **prytaneion**, or city hall, and the **odeion**, which was probably used for government meetings rather than concerts. An eternal flame was kept burning in the prytaneion and it was here that Selçuk museum's two statues of Artemis were found, carefully buried – perhaps by a secret worshipper to hide them from the Christians.

The Seven Sleepers

The road continues past a great fountain, another bath and the **East Gymnasium** (all 2nd century AD) on its way to the ruined

10 The South Aegean Coast | Kuşadası Bay: Ephesus (Efes)

Magnesia Gate, one of the two main gates built by Emperor Vespasian *c*. AD 75. The Sacred Way to the Temple of Artemis passed through here and around Mount Pion. Following the track, you pass a large, early Christian cemetery that surrounds a church and the graves of the **Seven Sleepers**, a popular motif in Christian and Turkish folklore. In the mid-3rd century, seven young Christians of Ephesus hid in a mountain cave to escape the mandatory imperial worship. They fell asleep, the cave was sealed up, and, when they were shaken awake by an earthquake, they discovered that they had slept for 200 years and Christianity was now the state religion. When they died the Ephesians buried them here, and a church was built over their graves that became a popular pilgrimage site – an echo of the myth of Endymion (*see* below). In fact there were really eight Sleepers: one of them had his dog along.

The track continues to modern Selçuk. The other track, to the right from the Magnesia Gate, leads to the **Wall of Lysimachus**, well preserved in many places.

The House of the Virgin Mary

In a municipal park 8km southeast of Selçuk is the Panaya Kapulu, or **Meryemana**, the house where Mary, who accompanied St John to Ephesus, is said to have lived and died *c*. AD 37–45. While the site has always been associated with the Virgin, the house was unknown until a German invalid called Catherine Emmerich (1774–1824), who had never been to Ephesus, had a series of visions which enabled her to give exact directions to the house and a detailed description of its appearance. In 1891, the Lazarist order of İzmir found it exactly where and as she had described it: a brick house of the 6th century, its foundations dating back to the 1st. (The story curiously parallels Mehmet Fatih's dream discovery of the grave of Mohammed's standard-bearer Eyüp near Istanbul.) In 1967 Pope Paul IV gave the house its certificate of authenticity, and it was visited by Pope John Paul II. The Virgin's tomb, according to Catherine Emmerich, is about a mile from the house, but has never been found. The house is a busy pilgrimage site; both the Orthodox and Catholics (as well as many local people) gather here to celebrate the Assumption of the Virgin on 15 August. Mass is celebrated every Sunday, at 10.30.

Belevi

About 16 km northeast of Selçuk, on the İzmir road, the village of Belevi has two unusual monumental tombs. One, known as the **Belevi Mausoleum**, is just off the road; it stands on a massive square base carved from bedrock, topped by a chamber of marble, surrounded by columns and reliefs of the battle of Lapiths and centaurs; the sarcophagus, however, was hidden in the base in an effort to foil grave robbers (it is now in the Selçuk Archaeology Museum). Many believe the man buried here was the Seleucid King Antiochus II who died in Ephesus in 246 BC, poisoned by his wife. The other tomb, a hilltop tumulus surrounded with a wall of fine masonry, probably dates from the same century.

Kuşadası and Around

In the early 1970s, Kuşadası was still a sleepy little port town; today it's one of Turkey's slickest and most expensive resorts, where seven or eight cruise ships call each day, and luxury yachts bask in the marina. New geometric holiday homes have been gridded onto the hills surrounding the town. More than any other resort in Turkey, this town has been built by package tourism.

Kuşadası

Kuşadası means 'bird island' in Turkish; off the shore is an islet called **Pigeon Island**, the site of a Genoese castle, where cafés and gardens are dotted with pigeon houses. The town itself has grown up into a rather unlovely city, with the resort strips stretching out for miles in either direction. At the centre, the **Kale**, most of the streets have been taken over by *pansiyonlar*, souvenir shops and such; the best indication of what Kuşadası has become is the incredible thoroughfare renamed **Barlar Sokak** – Bar Street – where hordes of indistinguishable T-shirted north Europeans stumble about aimlessly until 3am in summer. The city has an entertaining and not at all touristy **market** on Friday mornings.

Ancient Anatolia had its amphitheatres; modern Turkey has aquaparks. If you are experiencing a touch of ruinitis or are accompanied by children showing symptoms of the disorder, Kuşadası offers an antidote in the form of three aquaparks, the largest of which is **Adaland**, on the hill overlooking Pamucak beach. If this doesn't do the trick, then Kuşadası's better hotels offer every imaginable type of watersport, from paragliding to windsurfing; scuba-diving costs about 60 YTL per day. Several outfits offer the five-day PADI beginners' course for around 650 YTL. The nearest beach is **Kadınlarplajı, 'Ladies' Beach'**, 3km south and backed with all the usual trappings of mass tourism. Further on is the aptly named **Long Beach** and beyond that **Silver Beach**. **Kuştur Beach** and **Pamucak Beach**, probably the best and least crowded of them all, are north of town off the road to Selçuk.

In 1985 the forests above Kuşadası and Ephesus were hit by a devastating forest fire, but beautiful **Dilek National Park** on the peninsula 32km to the south was spared. The park encompasses beautiful Mount Mycale (modern Samsundağ), 4,082ft plunging down into the strait facing Samos; it has abundant wildlife, caves,

Adaland
t 0256 618 1252, www.adaland.com; the full water works will set you back 40 YTL (28 YTL for children)

Dilek National Park
open winter daily 8–5; later in summer; adm

Getting to and around Kuşadası

To reach Kuşadası, take a direct **bus** from İzmir or a **minibus** from Söke or Selçuk.

Minibuses trundle continually up and down the coast, linking the resort to all the beaches. You'll be able to catch one on Atatürk Caddesi near the harbour for nearby Kushtur Beach. Minibuses to the other beaches, as well as Selçuk, Dilek National Park and more distant points begin from the station on Adnan Menderes Bulvarı, three short streets east of İnönü Bulvarı. The big buses, for İzmir and more distant points, use the Yeni Garaj, south of the centre on Çevre Yolu (the road for Söke).

Most of the coastal and Greek Island **cruises** stop here, and Kuşadası is also linked year-round with the Greek island of Samos. This is probably the busiest of the cross-border **ferries**; except on Sundays, there will usually always be a morning and afternoon boat. In the summer as many as five boats make the crossing each day – often tiny, cabin cruiser-type boats with room for just a few people. With the bizarre winds that frequent this part of the Aegean, this can be an exciting crossing, even in summer.

---

beaches, springs and a castle. There are campsites and picnic grounds and paths up the mountain, although visitors are advised not to go walking alone because of the bears.

The beaches on the peninsula's northern coast are quieter than those at the resort; try **Aydınlık**, **İçmeler** and **Kavaklı**, and also near the village of **Güzelçamlı**, the closest village to the park.

A Trip to Samos

Now, as in ancient times, Samos holds its place as the richest and most important Greek island after Crete. Back then, the island produced famous men such as Pythagoras and the astronomer Aristarchus; its great **Temple of Hera** was known across the Mediterranean – fittingly so, as the goddess herself was born on Samos. Lush and green compared to other islands, Samos sees plenty of tourists throughout the season, so prices can be high. In July or August there will usually be a festival in one of the villages, along with the Wine Festival in August; Samos has been known for its wines since antiquity.

Samos is also the name of the island's capital, the destination of the ferries from Kuşadası. This slick, modern town offers a museum of archaeology, and good beaches just to the south at **Possidonion** and **Psili Ammos**. **Pythagoria**, not far from Samos but on the southern shore, is the biggest draw, with ruins including Hera's temple, walls and a unique 6th century BC half-mile tunnel.

Where to Stay in Kuşadası

The really exceptional places are not in Kuşadası itself, but on the beaches to either side.

ⓘ **Kuşadası** ›
Liman Caddesi, near the quay, t 0256 614 1103

Kuşadası

There are quite literally hundreds of hotels and *pensions* in Kuşadası and finding a room is rarely a problem. However, many of the more up-market establishments tend to be block-booked by tour operators in summer, and closed in winter.

*****Ephesus Princess**, at Pamucak, 6km to the north, near Selçuk, t 0232 893 1011, www.kusadasihotels.com/ephesusprincess (€€€€). Plush air-conditioned rooms, an enormous pool, sauna and hamam and all sports facilities imaginable; in addition to the main building there are also rooms in separate bungalows and some self-catering accommodation. Full board is usual.

****(S) Club Caravanserail, t 0256 614 4115, *www.kusadasihotels.com/caravanserail* (€€€). Staying in the centre of Kuşadası isn't much fun, unless you do it at this elegant hotel, located in the centre of town in a 17th-century caravanserai, with a beautiful garden restaurant (€€€€) in the courtyard. *Closed Nov–Mar*.

The more moderate places can be an undistinguished lot: an endless supply of concrete chunks with only the names to tell them apart.

**Efe Oteli, at Güvercin Ada Caddesi 37, t 0256 614 3660, *www.hotelefe.com.tr* (€€). Your best bet in this price range. *Open all year*.

**Minay, Alitepe Sitesi at Kadınlar Beach, t 0256 614 8804, *www.otelminay.com* (€€). If you'd prefer something nearer the beach, this is a good bargain: boring but air-conditioned rooms, some with TV, a hamam and gym. *Open all year*.

As is so often the case in Turkey, most of the cheap hotels and *pensions* are clustered together in the same area; in Kuşadası this is one block south of the post office on and around Arslanlar Caddesi.

**Stella Inn, Bezirgân Sok 44, t 0256 614 1632 (€). On a hill overlooking the harbour, this has a lofty charm; very cheap, and popular with backpackers.

Bahar Pansiyon, Cephane Sok 12, in the centre of town, t 0256 614 1191 (€). Colourful, and has a restaurant on the roof; doubles are a mere 30 YTL.

Another happy hunting ground for cheap digs is in the streets behind Kadınlar Beach.

Emek Pansiyon (follow the signs from the beach road), t 0256 614 1731 (€). Good value for money – very clean and airy rooms with private shower and toilet at only 30 YTL.

Önder Camping, t 0256 618 1590. The most pleasant of the campsites around Kuşadası, out on the İzmir road, which also offers cabins (50 YTL) and a restaurant.

Eating Out in Kuşadası

Kuşadası has many expensive fish restaurants on the waterfront, but nothing particularly distinguished. Generally, the further you go from the sea, the less you will have to pay.

Kazım Usta Restaurant, at the harbour (€€€€). Has been fish-gutting since 1950, it has a tank out front from which you select your unfortunate dinner; a full meal with wine costs around 80 YTL.

Konya Pide Salonu, Kahramanlar Caddesi 65 (€€–€). A good, cheap restaurant with a more authentic Turkish ambience (a rarity in Kuşadası), where a meal of grilled meat, rice, salad and a soft drink should come to no more than 20 YTL.

Albatross, Emek Street, behind the town hall (€). Locals refuel on simple food prepared by Mrs Yucel in large pans; her doleful husband doles it out for a flat rate of 10 YTL per piled-high plate. Hearty vegetarian fare such as okra and spinach features regularly.

The Cities of Ionia

In ancient times, the heartland of this most gifted province was the valley of the Maeander (modern Menderes), the largest and most important river of western Asia Minor. Its often-changing course gave us the word 'meander'; yet, much though the river contributed to trade and the fertility of the soil through its annual Nile-like flooding, it proved as much a curse as a blessing to Priene and Miletus, the two cities at its mouth. Like Ephesus, both once stood on the coast, but the tons of silt the Maeander carried down to the sea each year filled their harbours, and caused them to be abandoned. Today both are miles from the sea.

Getting down the Coast to Lake Bafa

The village of **Söke**, with regular connections to Kuşadası, is the transport hub for the coastal area, with frequent **minibus** services to Priene and Didyma.

To reach **Lake Bafa**, take any bus from Söke to Bodrum and ask to be let off at the lake (Bafa Gölü, also called Çamiçi Gölü).

From the campgrounds, you can take a **boat** to **Heracleia**. The requisite half day's hire is expensive at 50 YTL but each boat has room for 25 people.

For seeing **Priene** and **Miletus**, transport is convenient enough (via Söke) if you use Kuşadası or Selçuk as a base. A Söke minibus goes to Yeniköy, 5km away from Miletus. Another possibility, especially if you have a **car**, is the resort at Altınkum, near Didyma.

Down the Coast to Lake Bafa (Çamiçi Gölü)

Priene

 Priene

Priene was never a large city; estimates of its greatest size range from 4,000 to 6,000 free citizens. Nor did it play much of a role in the politics of the age. In late Roman times, as its harbour gradually became unusable, the city dwindled, and after the 6th century nothing more is heard of it. Even so, you may well find its ruins more alive, more evocative of the ancient world, than any other city in Asia Minor. Despite its small size, Priene had a reputation for accomplishment. The site, largely excavated, reveals a well-built and beautiful city, especially its residential quarters. Also, Priene's very lack of prosperity under the Romans makes it, in one sense, unique. Unable to build on the scale of Ephesus, Priene changed little after the 4th century BC; scholars study it as the best example of a Hellenistic city anywhere.

Nothing remains of the first Priene, founded at the same time as the other Ionian cities. Its site on the muddy Maeander hasn't even been found. By the 4th century, the advancing coastline made a new foundation necessary, and, with the support of Athens, a new Priene was laid out on the slopes of Mount Mycale. Following the precepts of the geometer Hippodamus of Miletus, the steep and difficult site was forced into a strict gridiron plan of narrow streets, with a broad central avenue connecting the major buildings and agoras. The plan has an elegant simplicity, but it's a matter for conjecture whether the Prieneans used it for art's sake or simply to make land surveys easier.

After a fair climb up from the car park, you enter Priene through the northwest gate. Continue across the unexcavated portion of the town to one of the finest extant examples of a Classical Greek **theatre**. Unlike the theatres elsewhere in Turkey, built or remodelled under the Romans, this one is small and horseshoe-shaped, leaving ample space for the orchestra and chorus, the centre of attention in a classical Greek play. The seats around the

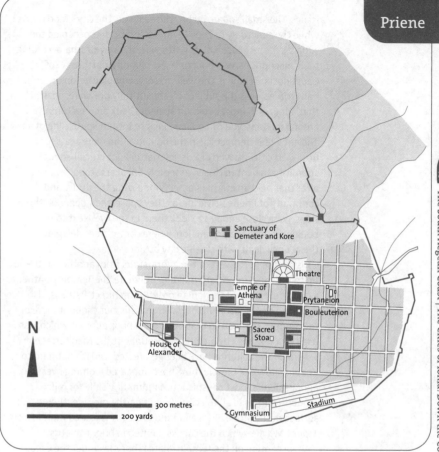

orchestra were for the nobles of the city, a kind of ancient dress circle. At the centre is an altar, dedicated to Dionysus. Also unlike later works, there is no elaborate stage building. The small colonnaded structure, the proskenion, dates from the 2nd century BC. Originally, the three doors were used for the entrance of actors, and the spaces between them covered with painted boards for scenery. The roof of the proskenion, used for the *deus ex machina*, took more and more of the action as drama evolved; eventually it came to hold the action, and the proscenium became what we know as the stage. Facing it, at the right-hand end of the first row of seats, is a square stone base that held a water clock; as Greek theatres also served for political meetings, and occasionally for trials, the water clock controlled the time allotted to each speaker.

Immediately below the theatre are the foundations of a **Byzantine church** and a **gymnasium**. Below these lie the **agora** and centre of Priene. The agora was the central square of Priene, devoted to commercial and religious affairs as well as political issues. The small square just to the east was the city's food market, while the sanctuary of Zeus Olympios, now gone, occupied the square's eastern face. On its north side, the **sacred stoa**, according to its inscriptions, was built as a gift of King Ariarthres VI of Cappadocia. Behind it, the well-preserved **bouleuterion** or council hall (200 BC) was the subject of a beautifully drawn reconstruction that appears in most books on ancient Greek architecture. Even among its ruins, you can gain an insight into the public life of an ancient Greek democracy. In the bouleuterion were seats for 600–700 citizens, who discussed matters not crucial enough to submit to the entire citizen assembly. Speakers stood next to the altar that held an eternal flame, symbolizing the purity and continuity of Priene's civic life; as they spoke, their peers, on three sides, were close enough to look them in the eye. Next to the bouleuterion is the **prytaneion**, where committees delegated by the council dealt with routine city business.

Just to the northwest of the agora, stairs from another stoa lead up to the most important building of Priene, the **Temple of Athena**, a classic example of the Ionian order. Its architect, Pytheos, also designed the Mausoleum of Halicarnassus, but thought more of this temple, so much so that he wrote a book about it which was used as a textbook by architects throughout the Mediterranean. Several of the columns have been re-erected, and it's not hard to imagine how the temple must have appeared looming over the agora, Priene's most conspicuous landmark, visible for miles around. Here, as in all the city's buildings, the grey weathered surface of the stone hides a luminous cream-coloured marble from Mount Mycale, which the Greeks painted in bright colours.

An inscription on the temple relates that Alexander the Great financed its completion. For this, and for their liberation from the Persians, the Prieneans devoted a small shrine to him, in the company of the other gods. The **House of Alexander** is near the western gate of the central avenue. Along the way, you'll pass the excavated **residential district** of Priene. Although this was laid out in a rigid grid plan, there was a remarkable individuality in the inner plans of the houses: nearly all had a central courtyard and columnar porches, and many had second floors. The finest ones are just a few squares west of the theatre.

Other sites on the north and south sides of town require some climbing. In the northern heights, not too far above the theatre, is the oldest temple in Priene, the **Sanctuary of Demeter and Kore**, where the temenos wall, benches to hold votive statues and the sacrificial pit can be seen. To the south, just below the agora at the city's walls, are the **gymnasium**, with its well-preserved washrooms where the water poured out of lion-headed spouts, and the **stadium**. Like the theatre, this is a rare example of the earlier Greek style, and was never remodelled into a Roman extravaganza. Seats are on one side only, and the course is a short and simple one-way track. Remains of the starting gate are near the entrance from the gymnasium: the Greeks started their runners as we do horses.

Miletus

Priene stood on the northern edge of the Latmian Gulf, the inlet now filled by the advancing delta of the Maeander. On the southern shore was Miletus, first among the Greek cities until the rise of Athens in the 5th century BC. Few cities have ever achieved such power and brilliance and left so little to show for it. The river again is to blame. Of the original Miletus so few traces remain that scholars still dispute its precise location. The present ruins date from the second foundation, after the original city was devastated by the Persians in 495 BC.

History

Miletus' origins are shadowy, though recent excavations have produced finds that go back to c. 1600 BC. Ancient writers claimed its founding as the work of Carians, Lycians or Cretans. The city was probably the Millewanda that appears in Hittite records of the 14th century, a thorn in the side of Hittite King Mursilis II. Millewanda was the capital of a people known as the Ahhiyawans – probably the origin of the 'Achaeans' in Homer. When the Ionians seized the town, they killed the Cretan men and married their wives. By 700 BC, Ionian Miletus began to prosper, controlling the Aegean trade routes and sending out more colonies than any other Greek city – 90 of them, from Naukratis on the Nile delta to Sinope on the Black Sea. Miletus' greatest colony, however, was the human mind. The Milesians were the first to look at the world from a detached, universal viewpoint. **Thales**, foremost among the Seven Sages and the first philosopher, suggested that water was the origin of all life; his follower **Anaximander** declared all things were infinite in substance, that the earth hung free, only one of infinite worlds; while the third great Milesian philosopher, **Anaximenes**, understood everything to be made of air, either rarefied or condensed, which encompassed the world like a human soul.

As the Persian menace grew, Ionian thinkers started moving to the growing city of Athens, keeping philosophy alive after Miletus suffered its fatal defeat in 495 BC. It broke the heart of the ancient world: when a play called *The Fall of Miletus* was performed in Athens, it caused the audience to burst into tears, for which the dramatist was fined a thousand drachmae.

Miletus was rebuilt immediately after the Persians flattened it, on a new site and on a new grid plan according to the precepts of its native son Hippodamus, the father of all urban planners. Its

Philosophy Starts Here

According to Aristotle's follower Eudemus, Thales, one of the 'seven wise men' of antiquity, brought geometry into Greece from Egypt, and showed how to use angles to find the distance from the shore to a ship in the harbour. Besides Egypt, he may also have visited Babylon, or perhaps he learned his astronomy only from contacts with the east, connections for which the cosmopolitan trading city of Miletus was well placed. His famous trick was to predict the solar eclipse of 585 BC. Though other peoples, the Chinese and the neolithic Britons, had done this long ago, it was quite a stunt for a 6th-century Greek, and it made his reputation for wisdom. 'The man's a Thales!', says a character in Aristophanes' *Birds*, written two centuries later.

Thales' successor, and possibly his student, was Anaximander, who drew the first maps among the Greeks and built the first model of the heavens and the first sundials. His student Anaximines, yet another Milesian, speculated on the cosmos and the nature of matter. From nearby Samos came Pythagoras, whose monumental contributions to mathematics are familiar enough; his brand of mathematical mysticism, in which all things could be reduced to numbers, dominates the thinking of scientifically minded people today. All of these founders of philosophy wrote in verse, and only tantalising fragments of their work remain – as with Heraclitus of Ephesus, the deepest and strangest of all, who left behind fascinating epigrams in the spirit of Zen :

This most beautiful cosmos is a pile of things poured out at random.

It is not possible to step twice into the same river... it scatters and again comes together, and approaches and recedes.

The lives of the Ionian philosophers covered only a few generations. By the 5th century the leading lights of philosophy, such as Zeno and Empedocles, were coming from the distant colonies in southern Italy and Sicily. Until the time of Plato and Aristotle, very few Greek thinkers came from Greece itself. Ionia, like Italy, was the 'new world' for the Greeks, a wide-open society of booming cities where free thinking was considerably easier than in the tradition-bound homeland.

The genuinely subversive contribution of the Ionian thinkers comes through in their attitude towards religion. As Xenophanes of Colophon put it, in one of the few surviving bits of his poetry:

Ethiopians say their gods are flat-nosed and dark,
Thracians that theirs are blue-eyed and red-haired...
If oxen and horses and lions had hands
and were able to draw with their hands and do things the same as men,
horses would draw the shapes of gods to look like horses,
and oxen to look like oxen...

Never before had anyone looked upon sacred things with such a critical eye. But the first philosophers were not trying to destroy religion, but to make faith square with what could be understood by reason. Their consensus was that God is one. Ideas make their way slowly, and the Ionians could not know they were paving the way for the acceptance of Christianity centuries later. But that, however significant, was only a small part of their achievement. The Ionian philosophers' great discovery was a perception of order at work in the world, an order comprehensible to the human mind. Their speculations marked the beginnings of philosophy and science – the start of Western civilization, no less.

arrangement of agoras and public buildings was a triumph of Greek design, but you can't see that from the ruins. If Priene is the most evocative Greek city, Miletus is the biggest archaeological disappointment of Turkey. So thoroughly has the Maeander scrubbed away and silted over its ruins that little beside the theatre remains. It is even difficult to tell where the coastline was, and the city that contributed so much to western civilization has become a creepy desolation of muck and prickly weeds. In Aristotle, we read that Anaximander believed that the water was gradually drying up from the earth – it has been suggested he got the idea from watching his city's harbour gradually silt up.

The Site

With a map from the small museum half a mile south of the ruins, you can locate a few landmarks. Miletus' great **theatre**, then as now the most conspicuous landmark, rises on a hillside above one of the city's five harbours, well preserved above the floods of the Maeander. The Roman theatre, with seats for 15,000, was built around the earlier work of the 4th century BC that seated only a third as many. The columns that marked the 'royal box' still stand. Scanty ruins of an **agora** and the **stadium** occupy the former harbour's opposite shore. From this side of Miletus, you have a good view of the island of **Lade**, now a mere lump in the Maeander Plain. Here, in 495 BC, the Persian navy destroyed the combined fleets of the Ionian cities and put an end to their rebellion. As leader of the revolt, Miletus' destruction was assured.

Climbing over the hill of the theatre will bring you to the **city centre**, a network of stoas, avenues and agoras around the narrow **Bay of Lions**. In wartime, a chain could easily be extended across this harbour to protect both the town and the fleet. Some searching among the weeds will reveal the two stone lions that stood on either side of the entrance. Inside the harbour, a large triangular base once held a monument of Augustus, commemorating his victory over Cleopatra and Mark Antony at Actium in 31 BC.

Around the harbour, the only structures of interest lie along the wide processional avenue; the first, the **Temple of Apollo Delphinius**, has the foundations of a colonnaded sanctuary with statue bases and a curious circular temple. On the same side of the avenue are the **Capito Baths**, the **gymnasium**, a **nymphaion** and a 5th-century **church**. If you follow the avenue south through the enormous **south agora**, you'll find a fine 15th-century mosque, **İlyas Bey Camii**, made of coloured marble salvaged from Miletus, belonging to the nearby village of **Yeniköy**. The low hill beyond the city's southern walls, called **Kalabak Tepe**, was the acropolis of the original Miletus founded by Crete, where a few old stones have been found.

Didyma (Didim)

If Miletus disappoints, Didyma won't. Didyma, south of Miletus and in its territory, is a temple complex and not a city. Yet few in western Asia Minor are so well preserved or as impressive.

Didyma was a holy site before the Ionians ever arrived, and was believed to be the oldest of the 19 oracles in Asia Minor. The Greeks rededicated the Anatolian cult to their own god Apollo and continued the oracle. When Croesus, the King of Lydia, was considering his invasion of Persia, he wanted the advice of an oracle, but first decided to put three of them to the test. He sent ambassadors to ask each of them, on the same day, 'What is King Croesus doing?' Only Delphi knew he was boiling a lamb and tortoise stew; Didyma failed. When the Persians sacked Miletus they burned the temple and carried off its statue. The oracle fell silent for 150 years, until it predicted Alexander the Great's victory at Issus. Then the sacred spring suddenly flowed again. A grateful Alexander sent some money, his lieutenant Antiochus brought the statue back, and the oracle declared Alexander to be the son of Zeus.

Seleucus I of Syria and the Milesians started to rebuild the temple on a massive scale, planning to make it the largest in the world. Work continued in fits and starts for some 500 years but was never completed. As with so many other things in the time of Alexander and his successors, the ambition of the original work seems to have overreached all common sense; the technical difficulties in building column-and-lintel architecture on such a scale might well have doomed it from the start. Completed, it would have surpassed even the Artemision at Ephesus. As it is, the temple provides a wonderful lesson in the transience of glory. You may never have heard of Seleucus I, but he ruled an empire that stretched from the Aegean nearly to India, building it a piece at a time with lands snatched from the other generals of Alexander, his former comrades-in-arms. Undoubtedly Seleucus' interest in the temple was in part as political propaganda, and as a monument to himself. Soon after it was begun, Seleucus moved to expand his empire westwards. He landed in Greece, and was assassinated as he stepped out of his boat.

As it was, the unfinished temple was considered by the ancients as one of their greatest works of architecture. In design it is comparable to the Artemision, encompassed by a double row of columns, some 120 in all. The cella, with its 70ft walls, was too large to be roofed over, so the cult statue of Apollo was kept in a smaller temple behind. Many columns have been re-erected by the excavators. Because the temple was never completed, some are unfluted, and many blocks still bear their masons' marks. Every five years the Didymeia – sports, drama, and music contests – was held at the sanctuary and in the **stadium** next to it; the names carved in the steps of the temple are those of spectators with reserved seats.

Lake Bafa and Heracleia (Kapıkırı)

Near Didyma are a pair of beauty spots. On the tip of Didyma's peninsula, **Altınkum** boasts fine sandy beaches, and an ambition someday to usurp Kuşadası as the coast's busiest resort. On the main north–south highway, the **lake of Bafa** was once part of the sea, but the silt-bearing Maeander dammed it off so long ago that

 Lake Bafa

its waters are more fresh than saline. In summer, the polarized blue, burnt gold and silvery green of the lake, grass and olive trees can be mesmerising. Overlooking the lake looms the jagged form of **Mount Latmos** (Beşparmak Daği in Turkish, the 'Hill of Five Fingers'), where the beautiful shepherd Endymion slept. The moon goddess Selene fell in love with him, asking her father Zeus to grant perpetual sleep to the youth. This done, she visited him every night and eventually bore him 50 children. Few places in Turkey are so hauntingly beautiful under a full moon.

Beneath the mountain stood **Heracleia**, a Carian city (the Carians, like the Lydians and Lycians, were a native people of Anatolia Hellenized by the Greeks). Heracleia was never very important, but is a must for all romantics, who, for the full effect, should sail there across the lake from the campsite on the shore. A new road also leads around the lake to the site and the modern village of **Kapıkırı**, which has basic accommodation. The ruins are impressive, especially the walls and defences built by Lysimachus in the 3rd century BC that twist and clamber up the slopes of Latmos. The setting lends the towers, gates, stairs and parapets an other-worldly air.

In the city, the cella walls of the **Temple of Athena**, high on a bluff, dominate the other monuments. The **agora** behind the temple is also mostly intact, especially its fine south wall. The theatre, nymphaeum and bouleuterion have not held up so well, but in the southern part of Heracleia is an unusual temple, the **Sanctuary of Endymion**, partially cut into the rock, rounded in the back, with a row of columns in the front. In the 7th century, Christian refugees from the Sinai built monasteries and hermitages on the lake islets and around Latmos. They converted the mythological Endymion into a Christian mystic, one who spent his life on Mount Latmos meditating on the moon, seeking the secret name of God. When he finally learned it, he died and was laid to rest here. Once a year the Christians would open up Endymion's coffin, and his bones would hum, trying to communicate the holy name.

Further south, beyond the Byzantine castle is a Carian **necropolis**: the economical Carians used natural pits in the rock and covered them with stone slabs. Some lie under the surface of the lake.

Where to Stay down the Coast to Lake Bafa

Two decades ago, the formerly malarial wastelands at the mouth of the Menderes were one of the emptiest corners of the Aegean coast. Now the growing new resort on the fine beach at Altınkum ('golden sand') has many hotels and *pansiyonlar*.

Priene and Söke

Priene Pansiyon, t 0256 547 1725, in the former Greek village of Güllübahçe, just a pleasant amble away from the ruins at Priene (€€). Set amongst a haven of pomegranate gardens and mandalin orchards. The kindly hostess offers simple, spotless rooms with wooden ceilings for 55 YTL. She also welcomes campers.

Haymanalı, near the bus station at 55 Santral Garaj Yolu, Söke, t 0256 512 0322 (€€). If you prefer hustle and bustle, this is a simple and quite comfortable hotel in town; some rooms with TV and balconies. After all the showiness of the coastal resorts, the workaday atmosphere in this warts-and-all small town may prove oddly refreshing.

(i) Altınkum >
a booth on the beach in the centre of town, open irregularly in summer

Altınkum

***Orion Hotel Didim**, t 0256 813 5550, www.letsgoaltinkum.com (€€). To do Altınkum in style, stay at this nicely flagrant piece of resort architecture right on the beach; all rooms have balcony, sea view and satellite TV. There's a pool and garden.

Altınkum's cheap *pensions* are gathered together behind the harbour: about a dozen family-run places, all charging roughly 40–60 YTL and all much the same; take your pick.

Kapıkırı

Agora, t 0252 543 5445, http://agora.pansiyon.de (€€€). The village of Kapıkırı, near the lake, is set amongst the Heracleian ruins. The best of the rudimentary *pensions* here; its 14 rooms and three separate wooden bungalows are surrounded by a garden cascading with flowers. Included is an excellent breakfast. Bathroom facilities are shared.

Lake Bafa

Club Natura Oliva, situated off the road to Milas in an olive grove sloping down to Lake Bafa, t 0252 519 1072, www.clubnatura.com (€€). This German-owned club has received a

World Wide Fund for Nature award for its sensitivity to the environment. Each of the 11 bungalows has a fireplace and terrace with stunning views over the lake. En suite doubles with wooden ceilings are priced at €53/110 YTL. The club is somewhat isolated, so venturing elsewhere for an evening meal without your own transport is difficult.

Çeri'nin Camping, t 0252 519 1086. On beautiful Lake Bafa there are several places to camp. This is the best, next to some Byzantine ruins and has a basic restaurant, as well as several rather spartan rooms for 15 YTL per person. Boat tours of Heracleia can be arranged, as well as trips to the far side of the lake, where the seldom-visited island of Ekiz is strewn with yet more Byzantine ruins. If you are on the lake in April or May, you may be treated to a migrating flamboyance of flamingos and pelicans.

Eating Out down the Coast to Lake Bafa

Şelale restaurant, right below Priene and next to the waterfall, is a wonderful oasis after clambering over the ruins in the sun, where you can eat for around 15 YTL.

There are many more restaurants and *lokantas* by Didyma, and at Altınkum – typical resort town seafood places here, none of which seems to stand out. Everywhere else, take what you can find; some informal outdoor places with lake fish open up in the summer around the shores of Lake Bafa.

Along the Maeander to Pamukkale

Myus and Magnesia ad Maeander

Up the Maeander (Menderes) from Lake Bafa's north shore are the scanty remains of one of the twelve Ionian cities, **Myus**, near the modern village of Avşar. Although it once had a harbour bristling with 200 warships, it was later best known for malaria and for having once been traded away by Philip V of Macedon in exchange for some figs given him by Myus's upriver rival, Magnesia ad Maeander. Lying between modern Söke and Ortaklar, **Magnesia ad Maeander**, like Turkey's other Magnesia (now Manisa), was

Getting along the Maeander Valley

The nearest **airport** to Pamukkale is 75km away at Çardak from where THY service buses run to Denizli. Flights are daily in summer, twice a week in winter.

Trains run frequently from İzmir and Selçuk to Aydın and Denizli; the overnight 'Pamukkale Ekspresi' connects Denizli with Istanbul. Aydın's *otogar* is south of town on the E24 highway; **buses** run regularly to İzmir, Selçuk, Denizli and Bodrum. **Minibuses** use the old station in the city centre on Gazi Bulvarı, and there is a **dolmuş** connecting service between the two.

---

founded by settlers from Greek Magnesia, who lacked imagination when it came to place names. Under the Persians, Magnesia itself had been given away to their old enemy, Themistocles, hero of the great Athenian victory over the Persians at Salamis in 480 BC. Towards the end of his career Themistocles lost the favour of the fickle Athenians and went to Persia, where King Artaxerxes had offered a reward to anyone who brought him Themistocles. The charming Themistocles claimed and received the reward himself. Artaxerxes then gave him Magnesia (for his bread), Lampsacus (for his wine) and Myus (for the rest of his dinner). When Themistocles was forced to take sides between his native Athens and Persia's ally Sparta in the Peloponnesian War, he committed suicide by drinking bull's blood during a sacrifice at the Temple of Artemis Leucophryene, the only monument of Magnesia that has survived. The temple dates from the 2nd century BC, and was erected after the goddess herself made a miraculous appearance in the city. Because of this, Magnesia was considered sacred, and therefore had no walls until Byzantine times.

Tralles (Aydın) and Nyssa

Continuing up the fertile Maeander valley, the city of **Aydın**, famous for figs and not much else, is the descendant of ancient Tralles, which lies just to the west. A military installation now occupies the site, and it can only be visited with special permission. It had two claims to fame: the 'Tralles stone', the most complete record of Greek musical notation, and its son Anthemius, mathematician and co-architect of the Aya Sofya. Aydın has a 17th-century mosque, the **Bey Cami**, and a small **museum** displaying some of the finds from Tralles, but nothing else to detain you.

Some 30km to the east, a sign points the way to **ancient Nyssa**, lost in the olives a mile from Sultanhisar. The city, in a lovely, picturesque gorge beneath Mount Messogis, was founded by Antiochus I in the 3rd century BC; most of what we know about it comes from the geographer Strabo, who studied there. He described Nyssa as a 'double city', split half the year by a torrential stream; he also wrote that the water was so greasy that the young men could dispense with oiling themselves after bathing. The imperial Roman **theatre** and the semi-circular **bouleuterion** (2nd century BC) are the best-preserved monuments in the city. Strabo

described the 350ft vaulted tunnel that helped to drain Nyssa's
spring torrents and support the city's main square and the current
car park. Two Roman bridges spanned the gorge; nearby, a pile of
stones once formed a stadium, although its seats were destroyed
by flooding – flooding that was an original feature of the building,
for the staging of *naumachiae*, or simulated sea battles.

Aphrodisias

Ancient Aphrodisias, on a lofty plateau below the slopes of
Mount Cadmos, now Babadağ ('Mount Dad'), is a 70km detour
south of the Maeander, but well worth while. Dedicated to the
goddess of love, and to art, this city is one of most exciting recent
excavations in Turkey, begun in 1961 by Dr Kenan T. Erim and
New York University, and partially financed by the National
Geographic Society.

The site was always sacred, perhaps as early as the Neolithic age;
two large hills on the site are 'tells', covering settlements that go
back at least 8,000 years. Aphrodite's predecessor may have been
the eastern goddess Enana, the equivalent of Ishtar or Astarte; the
city's original name had been Ninoe, for Enana or for the legendary
King Ninus of Assyria, founder of Nineveh, and it is believed the
Assyrians at some remote date founded a sanctuary to the
goddess here. By the Hellenistic age, the city's population was
largely Greek, and Enana had become Aphrodite.

History tells us little about classical Aphrodisias, except that
Julius Caesar, whose family claimed descent from the goddess
through Aeneas of Troy, preserved the sanctity of the great Temple
of Aphrodite. In the civil wars that followed his death, Aphrodisias
wisely chose the side of Augustus, and was rewarded with special
privileges and exemptions from imperial taxes; the first emperor
was so impressed with it that he declared, 'I choose this city from
among all those in Asia for myself...' After three centuries as a
pampered art centre, the first catastrophe to strike Aphrodisias
was the coming of Christianity; besides shutting down the market
for classical sculpture, the Christians added the indignity of
renaming the town 'Stavropolis', the City of the Cross. Then came
two major earthquakes in the 4th century, and another in the 7th.
By the 13th century it was probably abandoned. A Turkish village
named Geyre later grew up over the ruins; the village was
relocated over the last 30 years to make way for the excavations.

Though it was long known that Aphrodisias had been a centre of
scupture from Augustus' day, scholars had always believed that its
artists were mere copyists, redoing earlier Greek and Hellenistic
works. But from the quantity of excellent statuary found, made of
the fine blueish marble from Babadağ, it became clear that an
important and strikingly original school of sculptors existed here,

Getting to Aphrodisias

Getting to Aphrodisias by public transport can be a problem. If you mean to do it as a day trip, make sure you have return transportation arranged in advance. **Minibuses** provide a service to Aphrodisias from Nazilli, though most only go to the village of Karacasu, 12km away, from which you would have to take a **taxi**. In summer you might find a direct **bus** from İzmir to Geyre, or to Karacasu, with a **dolmuş** service to Geyre. Even so, the easiest way to do it without a car is to get on a **tour** from Pamukkale.

one that adorned Aphrodisias and exported works throughout the Mediterranean; signatures on statues found elsewhere are now identified with the 'Aphrodisian school'. The city's festivals featured sculptural competitions, something unique in the ancient world.

The Site

Aphrodisias
*open summer 8.30–7;
winter 9–5; adm*

Still under excavation (no photos, no dallying off the prescribed path), Aphrodisias is little more than a third uncovered. The circular tour begins with the **theatre**, with a seating capacity of 10,000, dug into the flank of a tell, or mound, in which are buried layers of earlier settlements. Built into the theatre walls are a number of inscribed stones, recording Augustus's favours to the city and decrees of later emperors. An enclosed square, the **Tetrastoon**, with a round fountain at its centre, stood here, along with a bath complex, the **'Theatre Baths'**, while to the west are the much more lavish **Baths of Hadrian**, complete with huge galleries, heated rooms and a palaestra, still retaining some tiles and mosaics. Adjacent to these baths, on the opposite side of the hill from the theatre, the **'large basilica'** was decorated with some unusual reliefs of the city's history, including figures of Ninus, his famous wife Queen Semiramis, and King Gordius of Phrygia. Also on display here is a stone carved with Emperor Diocletian's Edict of Prices of 301 AD, the economic 'reform' that fixed prices, devalued the currency and locked sons into following their fathers' professions – altogether perhaps the most catastrophic error Rome ever made, and one that probably sealed the fate of the dying empire.

The **Portico of Tiberius** and the **agora**, both impressive colonnaded quadrangles, marked the centre of the city and its marketplace, now a poplar grove. To form a grand entrance for the agora, the Julio-Claudian emperors contributed a sumptuous embellishment called the **Sebasteion**, consisting of two parallel three-storey porticos that housed shops. Some of the finest sculptural work in Aphrodisias was created to decorate it, and some has been left in situ: mythological and Homeric scenes, and imperial propaganda reliefs including Claudius subduing Britain.

To the north is the former **palace** of the Roman governor, a peristyle house converted in the 5th century into the bishop's residence. Next to it stands the **odeion**, a smaller, more intimate theatre; originally covered with a wooden roof, it was used for

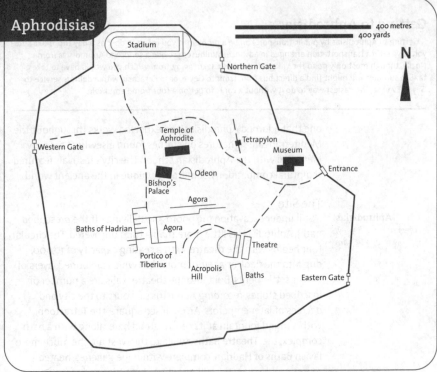

Aphrodisias

Stadium

Northern Gate

N

400 metres
400 yards

Temple of
Aphrodite

Tetrapylon

Museum

Western Gate

Odeon

Entrance

Bishop's
Palace

Agora

Baths of Hadrian

Agora

Theatre

Portico of
Tiberius

Acropolis
Hill

Baths

Eastern Gate

concerts and meetings of the town council. Behind it, the circular
platform in stone was a **heroon**, the base of a tomb or monument
to some local worthy; the surrounding area was occupied by one of
Aphrodisias's sculpture workshops.

North of the agora, the **Temple of Aphrodite** was built in the
reign of Augustus over a sanctuary at least six centuries older; 14 of
its Ionic columns have been re-erected. The Byzantines made the
whole into a basilica in the late 5th century. Hadrian added the
most remarkable building yet discovered in Aphrodisias, the
Tetrapylon, a monumental gateway that led into the **temenos**, or
sanctuary area, which in Roman times took the form of a small
park connecting the gate and the temple façade; subsidiary
buildings filled the temenos on the other three sides. Now
substantially rebuilt from the stones on the ground, the Tetrapylon
provides a great example of the 'Baroque' tendency of classical
architecture in the 2nd century AD, at the height of Roman-era
prosperity, with a tall arch boldly cut into the pediment, Corinthian
columns with spiral fluting, and sculptural trim of acanthus scrolls.

North of Aphrodite's temple is the **stadium**, perhaps the largest,
and certainly one of the best preserved ever discovered. It stretches
865ft from end to end and could seat 30,000; one side was
enclosed in late Roman or Byzantine times for use as a theatre.

The northern side of the stadium was incorporated into the walls, which may have been begun in the 5th century AD, or perhaps even as early as the 3rd, when the Goths made their great raid into Asia Minor. As a sacred city, like Magnesia, Aphrodisias had no need for defences in Hellenistic times.

A **museum** houses the marble goddesses, gods, satyrs and emperors found in the ruins of all the city's major buildings. Some of the outstanding works come from the monument of Zoilos, a wealthy benefactor of the city who had once been a favoured slave of Augustus; others were found in the theatre, including a lovely, damaged statue of Melpomene, muse of Tragedy. The cult image from the Temple of Aphrodite was never found, but another statue of the goddess uncovered here may provide some clues to its appearance: a standing figure in a gown covered with religious symbols and attributes: a crescent moon, the Three Graces, beasts of land and sea, and winged *erotes* offering a libation.

Denizli

Returning to the main highway, the E24, you'll pass **Laodicea**, chiefly remembered today as one of the Seven Churches of Asia addressed by John in Revelations and as the last residence of Cicero. At the head of the Maeander valley is the major market town of **Denizli**. Famous for its textiles and roosters, Denizli is unremarkable except for two large statues of the proud and colourful bird, one in the centre of town and one on the roundabout on the road to Pamukkale.

Pamukkale

Pamukkale ('Cotton Castle') has a lot to live up to. It features in all the tourist brochures; posters of it cover up stubborn stains on hotel walls the length and breadth of Turkey. The familiar image is of a curtain of stalagmites and stepped shallow pools, merging into one another on dozens of different levels, a fairyland of cotton-white forms and pale blue water cascading gently down. Carefree holidaymakers are shown frolicking in the warm, glistening pools, with the lovely green valley of Maeander spread out far below. But if you look closely at these pictures of people splashing about, their hairstyles may seem a little dated: the pools have been closed to bathers for several years. This UNESCO site has become a victim of its own popularity: too many hotels draining off the water in the 1980s and '90s and too many tourists tramping around the pools caused serious deterioration in the terraces. A drastic remedy was called for, and, to its credit, the Turkish government swallowed its bitter pill unflinchingly: it had the hotels crowding around the lip of the great white plateau paid off and pulled down. A team of German scientists was brought in

Getting to Pamukkale

From Denizli, frequent **minibuses** go up to Pamukkale – some wait until they have a load of passengers. Denizli city buses also make the trip, from the big square south of the *otogar*. In summer there are services direct to Pamukkale from all the nearby resorts (as many as 10 a day), and also from Selçuk.

to devise a way of restoring the damaged travertines to their former glory. Their answer has been to ensure that all the water in a particular pool has evaporated fully (leaving behind the maximum amount of calcium necessary to strengthen the pool) before diverting spring water to fill up the pool again. As a consequence of this preservation work, the pools are cordoned off and many are empty. This is undoubtedly good news for the site in the long term. Yet Pamukkale remains spectacular, rising from the valley like a glistening midsummer snowscape.

Hierapolis

The charms of Pamukkale and its thermal springs also caught the eye of Eumenes II of Pergamon, who founded the 'Holy City', or Hierapolis, on top of the plateau. Like Pergamon itself, Hierapolis was bequeathed to Rome in the will of Attalus III. An earthquake shattered it in AD 17, but it was quickly rebuilt and had its greatest prosperity in the 2nd and 3rd centuries. The Apostle Philip lived here and was martyred in the year AD 80: in the Byzantine era, the church of St Philip dominated the town.

The great **baths** near the parking area were constructed in the 2nd century and are so well preserved that they now serve as a **museum**, displaying the fine marbles unearthed by Italian archaeologists; many of the statues are now recognized to have come from the Aphrodisian school. At least three Roman emperors visited Hierapolis and bathed in the portion of the bath reserved for them. Behind the bath stands a **Temple of Apollo**, chief deity of the city, a **fountain** and a small grotto called the **Plutonium**, a sanctuary of Hades (Pluto), the god of the Underworld; a sign warns of poisonous vapours, the same that instantly killed sparrows in Strabo's day but were harmless to eunuchs.

The impressive and recently restored **theatre** dates from the 2nd century AD, and is especially interesting for the fine reliefs of Apollo's twin, Artemis. Behind the theatre and outside the Roman wall is the **Martyrium of St Philip the Apostle** of the 5th century. From the bath, the road leads to the other excavations, including, stretching on for over a mile, the **necropolis**, with a fascinating variety of tombs and sarcophagi dating up into Christian times.

Visitors can still swim in the warm and slightly effervescent water of the ancient **Sacred Pool**, although there's little sacred about it nowadays, ringed as it is by tourist stalls. Signs boast of the water's powers to heal everything from cataracts to obesity.

Where to Stay in the Maeander Valley

Aphrodisias

Aphrodisias Hotel, t 0256 448 8132, *www.aphrodisiashotel.com* (€€). Run by a Turkish owner and his French wife, and their more luxurious alternative to Chez Mestan below.

Chez Mestan, t 0256 448 8046, on the Karacasu road, near the site of Aphrodisias (€). 28 basic rooms from 30 YTL.

ⓘ **Pamukkale >**
*t 0258 272 2077,
www.pamukkale.gov.
com, above the
travertines*

Pamukkale and Around

The best hotels near Pamukkale are in **Karahayıt**, 5km west of the northern entrance to the site. ****Colossae Thermal, t** 0258 271 4156, *www.colossaehotel.com* (€€€). Most of the luxury hotels here have comfortable rooms, swimming pools and a tourist conveyor-belt atmosphere. This is an exception: an impressively stylish complex built around a courtyard with a huge pool: lavish rooms, a hamam and nightclubs and sports to keep you busy.

Pamukkale village (**Pamukkale Köyü**), bursting with mediocre hotels, is a short walk away from the calcium formations.

Turku, t 0258 272 2181, in a quiet back street off Atatürk Caddesi (€). One of the nicest, with a pleasant wooden façade and interior as well as the

obligatory small pool. Its only drawback is the cramped en suite bathrooms.

Weisse Burg, just off Menderes Caddesi, **t** 0258 272 2064 (€). This may not be the most beautiful *pansiyon* in the village, nor the best kept or situated, but it is certainly amongst the most welcoming. It is run by one of life's enthusiasts, Hacer Yiğen, and her husband. There is a swimming pool actually big enough to swim in.

Kervansaray, t 0258 272 2209 (€). English-speaking, with a swimming pool and good restaurant.

Eating Out in the Maeander Valley

Aphrodisias

Anatolia Restaurant, t 0256 448 8138, *www.anatoliaturizm.com.tr* (€€). 2km from the site and serves up various set menus at reasonable prices. It is mainly aimed at large tour groups but you can order *à la carte* too.

Pamukkale

Weisse Burg, just off Menderes Caddesi, **t** 0258 272 2064 (€). You could climb up to the rooftop for Hacer's excellent culinary creations, often including vegetarian options.

Han, on the main square (€). The usual meat dishes and fish such as speckled trout for 12 YTL, if you want to dine at a restaurant proper.

Caria

This section of the southwest coast, between Lake Bafa and Bodrum, once belonged to the Carians, yet another native people more or less Hellenized by the time history discovered them. Halicarnassus (Bodrum) was their largest city, the birthplace of Herodotus and capital of King Mausolus, who gave the world a new name for tombs.

Inland: The Carian Heartland

Even in Roman times, cultural Hellenization of Caria was largely limited to the coasts. Come up to the heights between Aydın and Muğla, to the heart of this lost nation, and you will find a remarkable little flock of stone cities, testimony to a Caria that was

Getting to and around the Carian Heartland

It won't be easy to see any of these minor sights without a car. For **Euromos**, take any bus from Söke to Bodrum and ask to be let off at **Selimiye**, the nearest village; Selimiye is also served by infrequent minibuses from Milas. For **Alinda**, take the minibus from Aydın to the village of **Karpuzlu**, within walking distance of the ruins; this will be a rather long day trip. For **Alabanda** and **Gerga**, you'll have to make a deal with a taxi if you don't have a car. **Labranda** can be reached by car or taxi on a nasty dirt road from the village of Kargıcak, north of Milas.

To reach **Güllük**, take any Milas–Bodrum bus and get off at the Güllük junction, where you can either hitch or wait for one of the very regular minibuses from Milas dolmuş terminus to pass by. In Güllük, you can get a party together and rent a boat for an inexpensive day trip to **Iasos**. **Ören** is linked by bus to Milas.

prosperous and densely populated through Roman times, and has been a desolation ever since. The architecture – the surviving ruins are substantial – and the whole feeling of the more isolated sites seems a world away from sophisticated Ephesus or Pergamon.

There are few good roads in these parts, and it's as easy to get lost in the hills as it is to become totally confused over all these sites with exasperatingly similar names. **Alinda**, near the village of Karpuzlu, about halfway between Aydın and Muğla, was once the outpost of Queen Ada, sister of King Mausolus (one that he didn't marry). She kicked up a fuss in the dynastic squabbles following Mausolus' death, and found her knight in shining armour in the person of Alexander the Great. Ada promised to support Alexander if he helped her capture Halicarnassus, and the two spent weeks plotting in Alinda. Never excavated, Alinda is one of the most attractive ruins in which to explore. The ancient town is on a dominating height. In the centre, there is a market building the size of a department store bordering its agora (two of the three floors are still intact), a theatre and a watch tower, all in a good state of preservation. From the tower it is a short climb up to the second, upper acropolis, with walls and a gate in equally good shape; oddly, this one contained no temples but only houses. If you have more time for exploring there are necropoli all around the town, and the arcade of an aqueduct, visible from the acropolis.

Less remains of **Alabanda**, 8km from modern **Çine**. This city was also briefly capital of Caria, and still has its fine wall and bouleuterion. The river Çine Çay, with its gorge, is ruggedly picturesque, especially along the road between Çine and Yatağan Göktepe. In antiquity the river was called Marsyas, after the flute-playing satyr who had the audacity to challenge Apollo and his lyre to a musical contest, with the muses as judge. When the god was proclaimed victor, Apollo, never known for his sense of humour, flayed Marsyas alive and hung his skin on a tree at Calaenae to the south, the source of the Çine Çay.

Southeast of Alabanda, on the opposite side of the Aydın–Muğla road, you can visit **Gerga**, no doubt the most bizarre ruin in western Turkey – but it won't be easy. Along the Aydın–Muğla road north of Çine, you'll see the ruined 16th-century İncekemer ('slender arches') Bridge; from here, it's a two-hour walk, not signposted, up to the village of İncekemer and from there to Gerga. The big mystery here is the endless Greek inscriptions on every monument and bit of exposed rock – 'Gergas' or 'Gergakome' (Gerga village), as if the inhabitants wanted to make absolutely sure you know where you are. Some of these are in letters three feet tall; nothing like them is recorded in any other ancient town. In fact no one knows whether this was a real town, or perhaps an important Carian religious sanctuary, or whether Gerga was its name or the name of a deity worshipped here. The major attraction is a rustic temple, almost perfectly preserved, that seems almost a parody of Greek architecture, with a stone roof carved to mimic a wooden one. Nearby is a huge fallen statue, also marked 'Gergas'. There is another fallen statue to the west, along with two oil presses and a pair of tall pyramidal monuments. Everything in Gerga most likely dates from Roman times. No ancient writers mention this town, neither has any part of it been excavated; it remains a total mystery.

Muğla, and More Carian Cities

The road to Marmaris and its peninsula begins at the provincial capital, **Muğla**, a modern and surprisingly attractive city that seems a world away from the tourist madness of the coast. Bureaucracy is Muğla's business. Like a mini-Bonn, it is full of civic pride and prosperity, though this has come mostly from the tobacco and olive fields in the surrounding countryside. There is little to go out of your way for, but you can explore the pretty, well-maintained 18th-century residential neighbourhoods reminiscent of those in Bursa, clinging to the hillsides to the north of the bazaar. Market day is Thursday. In the second week of September each year, the nearby village of **Yeşilyurt** plays host to a bull-wrestling contest. The owner of the beast who can bring the opposing animal to the ground or chase it out of the ring wins more than a government employee's average monthly salary.

Muğla is also the base for visiting the Hellenistic-Roman ruins of **Stratonikya** (Stratoniceia), 36km to the northwest, near to Eskihisar and to a lignite strip mine that has devoured the necropolis. This city began as Chrysaor, centre of the Chrysaoric Confederacy to which all Carian cities belonged. It was refounded by King Antiochus and named for his wife Stratonice, who had previously been his stepmother (a little present from his dad, Seleucus I). The city belonged off and on to Rhodes before Roman rule, and it prospered greatly until Byzantine times. At the centre of the site stands a building that is often called the 'Temple of Serapis', but may really have been the bouleuterion, bordering what was the agora. Other remains include parts of the walls and gates, a Roman gymnasium and a theatre; there's a small museum of finds. **Lagina**, north of Stratonikya near the village of **Turgut**, is the site of the **Hekateion**, an important Carian sanctuary to Hecate, the Queen of the Night. Her sacred spring can still be seen near the ruins.

Another collection of lost Carian cities can be visited south of Lake Bafa. **Euromos**, the northernmost of them, is also the easiest to find, just off the road from Lake Bafa to Milas. It is notable these days for its majestic, magnificently preserved Temple of Zeus (2nd century AD), lying tantalisingly close to the highway (Route 525). Paid for by Hadrian, it's one of the few Corinthian temples along the coast, and one of the best-preserved in Turkey; 16 of its elegant columns and their architrave still stand in place. Other ruins include a theatre and Roman-era baths.

Much more substantial is **Labranda**, a town that served as a common religious sanctuary for the Carian and Mysian cities, and was particularly honoured by the dynasty of Mausolus of Halicarnassus. Labranda's holy-of-holies was a golden double axe (a labrys, as in ancient Crete) dedicated to Zeus Labrandus. The sanctuary also had an oracle, and a pool of tame fish who, if ancient writers are to be believed, wore golden earrings and neck-laces. (The answer was favourable if the fish ate the petitioner's breadcrumbs. A similar oracle survives way out in eastern Turkey, at Şanlıurfa (*see* p.488); now it is an important Muslim pilgrimage site, but you can still feed the fish.) The remains here, excavated by a Swedish team, include the Temple of Zeus, adjacent priests' houses and well-preserved androns (palaces reserved for men-only sacred banquets). Another excavated section to the east includes a monumental stairway leading up to a Byzantine church. Behind this, a small building is thought to be the location of the oracle.

Milas

A Sacred Way ran the 16km between Labranda and the city of Milas (ancient Mylasa) in the 4th century BC. Mylasa, long the most important of the Carian cities, was the home town and first capital of Mausolus. In ancient times it had a reputation for its fine temples and public buildings, partly thanks to a nearby marble quarry. Today it's known for weaving fine carpets. Milas has been continuously occupied since ancient times, the only one of these Carian towns to survive, and consequently little remains. Bits and pieces of its ancient buildings can be seen in the town's fine collection of medieval mosques, notably the **Firuz Bey Camii**, built by the Ottomans in 1394, shortly after they captured the city. Earlier mosques, the **Orhan Bey Camii** and the **Ulu Cami**, are the work of the Turkish Menteşe emirs, who founded a little state here a century before the Ottomans. Across from the Ulu Cami is a small **archaeological museum**.

The large **Baltalı Kapı**, the Roman-era 'gate of the axe', marks the beginning of the Sacred Way, around the corner from the Orhan Bey Camii. South of here on Tabakhane Caddesi, the site of the **Temple of Zeus** is marked by a single Corinthian column, currently occupied by a stork. This is the edge of Milas's charming **bazaar district**, a pocket of narrow streets that contains a medieval *han*, the **Çöllu Hanı**, just off Cumhuriyet Caddesi. The best time to visit Milas is a Tuesday, when there is a big farmers' market. Old streets around the edge of the bazaar and on the riverbank have a number of 18th-century Ottoman mansions, in varying states of decay.

West of the centre on Gümüşkesen Caddesi, a tomb called the **Gümüşkesen** (2nd century AD) is believed to be an exact miniature of the great Mausoleum of Halicarnassus. It's ironic that Milas was the only one of these cities to survive, because it is the only one on the plain, not on a defensible hilltop. A Roman governor once remarked that 'the people who founded this city must have known no fear'. The Mylasans' citadel, now called **Beçin Kale**, lies 5km east of the city. Its castle, built by the Byzantines and remodelled by the Menteşe Turks, now contains the ruins of a later Turkish village. The Menteşe governors built a complex of buildings further up the hill, including a mosque, a *han* and the 1375 **Medrese of Ahmet Gazi**, the last governor, who is buried inside.

Iasos

Back on the coast, **Iasos** (modern Kıyıkızacık), famous in antiquity for the best fish along the coast, has recently been excavated to reveal the best-preserved Carian city, although that's not saying a great deal; most memorable here is the restored Roman-era mausoleum on the outskirts. For a while splendid mausoleums were the fad in Caria, inspired by the great model in Halicarnassus. Excavations at Iasos have turned up pottery going back to Minoan times. An ally of Athens in the Peloponnesian War, the city was destroyed by a Spartan-Persian force and thereafter refounded. Its coinage showed a boy riding a dolphin, and there was a story to go with it of a boy who had befriended one, and was brought before Alexander and made a priest of Poseidon. The scanty remains of the town itself, on a small peninsula, include a Roman-era bouleuterion, a colonnaded agora, walls and gates, a Temple of Demeter and Kore, and a Roman villa with floor mosaics. Much of the rest of Iasos was cannibalized by the Ottomans; there are good views across the coast from the **castle**, founded by the Knights of St John when their headquarters were on nearby Rhodes.

Güllük and Ören

An oasis on its own small gulf, Güllük was for years the sole preserve of locals and Germans. Now it is fast learning to live with tourism, particularly as the nearby airport has been completed.

Where to Stay and Eat in the Carian Heartland

ⓘ Güllük >>
in the Belediye on the harbour front,
t 0252 522 2776

ⓘ Muğla >
Marmaris Bulvarı 24 (a 10min walk from the roundabout which encircles a statue of Atatürk), t 0252 214 1261

Most accommodation in this area is of a modest nature, clean and comfortable but with very few frills. It's mostly in Güllük but there are a few other options.

Muğla

*****Yalçın**, facing the *otogar*, **t** 0252 214 1050 (€€). One of a few comfortable hotels here.

Ören

***Alnata Hotel**, **t** 0252 532 2813, *www.alnatahotel.com* (€€). Clean and comfortable. Facilities include two swimming pools, tennis courts and mountain bike hire.

Ören has several nice fish restaurants near the harbour and some simple *lokantas* further back.

Güllük

***İkont**, on a hill at the southern side of the bay, **t** 0252 522 2427 (€€). This friendly, unassuming place with a diminuitive pool is popular with holidaying Turks. Quiet, clean en suite rooms with balconies.

Kordon Motel, next to Güllük harbour, **t** 0252 522 2356 (€€). Rough-and-ready doubles for 70 YTL.

Kordon Restaurant, attached to the motel (€). This is typical of the eateries here; good, friendly and inexpensive, charging 20 YTL for a fish meal.

Eski Depo, a short walk away along the quayside, is also good.

This diminutive fishing village was earmarked for development, and the hulks of holiday homes fill the hills to its north. Recreation is limited to swimming off the minuscule beach or crossing the gulf to Iasos, an hour's sail away. In the evening you can fall in step with everyone else and promenade along the harbour front.

Ören, the only village on the northern coast of the gulf of Gökova, is much the better resort choice here, despite the smokestacks of several Polish-built power stations nearby. Yet it is pretty, with a good beach, and it sees relatively few foreign visitors.

Bodrum

Whitewashed and flower-bedecked Bodrum is the most sophisticated resort on the Aegean coast (even though its name means 'dungeon' in Turkish). Anchored to the southern shore of the Bodrum peninsula, it lies in a sunny region of spectacular scenery and sandy beaches; when approached by land, it makes an unforgettable impression, even at night when its great landmark, the Castle of St Peter, is bathed in a golden light.

Bodrum is big business. In the surrounding hills, dazzling white encrustations of Costa del Sol-style holiday villages and timeshares become more in evidence each passing year. Hundreds of advertising hoardings on the roads approaching Bodrum wink in the sun at passers-by. If you've booked a cruise from overseas, your voyage may well begin in Bodrum; if you'd like to initiate your own sailing holiday while in Turkey, this is a good place to do so. The diving is excellent too. What really sets Bodrum apart from the other resorts is its nightlife.

Getting to and around Bodrum

Bodrum international **airport** in Milas receives regular charter flights from across Europe as well as daily flights from Ankara and Istanbul. Bodrum is easily reached by **bus** from anywhere on the coast, though it will always be a long and roundabout trip by way of Milas or Muğla.

Minibuses serve most of the towns on the peninsula, and all of them leave from the *otogar* on the main Cevat Şakir Caddesi, a mile north of the centre. Some of the more tucked-away beaches are best visited by the boat taxis (**dolmuş motorları**) that depart from Bodrum harbour.

Boats ply between Bodrum and the island of Kos regularly from spring to autumn, less frequently in winter. In addition, the summer brings daily ferries to Rhodes, Datça and Altınkum, and at least two a week to Didyma, depending on demand. Occasionally there are even services to Patmos, Dalyan and Caunos; see any travel agent or **Bodrum Express Lines** on Kale Caddesi, **t** 0252 316 1087, *www.bodrum expresslines.com*, near the port for details. Some of these take cars, but hydrofoils are increasingly used.

History

Bodrum occupies the site of ancient **Halicarnassus**, a Carian city colonized by the Dorians from the Peloponnese *c.* 1000 BC. It belonged to the Dorian 'Hexapolis', a typical confederacy of cities that included Kos, Cnidos and the three cities of Rhodes. In the 6th century BC, the other five members gave Halicarnassus the boot: it was too ambitious, and too susceptible to Ionian free thinking. Although the city soon came under direct Persian rule, the spirit of inquiry survived to inspire Herodotus (485–420 BC), the 'father of history', the first to chronicle events (the Persian wars) without resorting to the gods for an explanation. Halicarnassus' most glorious period came late, under the Hellenophile satrap **Mausolus**, who made himself king of a powerful, independent Caria from 377 to 353 BC. He was so pleased with himself that he began the original Mausoleum, which his widow (and sister) Artemisia II finished as a tomb to beat all tombs, one of the Seven Wonders of the World. Artemisia declared herself Queen of Halicarnassus and militarily baited the Greeks so much that they put a price on her head, 'thinking it a matter of great shame for a woman to make war on Athens'. It was her younger sister, Queen Ada of Alinda, who befriended Alexander and encouraged him to attack Halicarnassus in 334 BC: for Ada's sake, Alexander spared the Mausoleum but little else.

When the Knights of St John lost their castle in Smyrna to Tamerlane in 1402, they came here; finding the Mausoleum toppled by an earthquake, they used it as material to build their Castle of St Peter. With further fortifications on the islands of Kos and Rhodes, the Knights dominated the southeastern Aegean, running a hospital for passing pilgrims and ruling the seas as privateers in their swift vessels. One of the most interesting people to reside in St Peter's Castle was the Ottoman Great Pretender, Cem Sultan, younger brother of Beyazıt II. Cem thought the Knights would assist him in his attempts to defeat and depose his brother, but the Knights, paid off handsomely by Beyazıt, had other ideas, and kept him as a hostage. They handed him over to Pope Alexander VI Borgia, who made a small fortune on the ransom before poisoning Cem. The Knights themselves were forced to move on to Malta when Süleyman the Magnificent captured Rhodes in 1523, making their outpost at Bodrum untenable.

Bodrum Babylon

The town follows the classic Turkish resort plan closely: castle in the middle, next to a harbour lined with seafood restaurants and full of attractive excursion boats waiting to take you on cruises around the peninsula. Tickets for these can be bought at the co-operative booth on the seafront. Day trips are offered to westerly beaches such as **Bağla** and **Ortakent** and the small cove known as **Akvaryum**, where the sea is so clear that you can watch fish from the boat. Boats also head for **Orak Island** and the quieter beaches to the east of Bodrum. Crewed *gülets* can also be chartered from Bodrum for two days and upwards.

The Castle of St Peter, on its tiny neck of land, neatly divides the **harbour** into two. Dreadnoughts of the wealthy tie up at the yacht marina in the West Harbour, but the action is to the east, along pedestrianized Dr Alim Bey Caddesi/Cumhuriyet Caddesi. Here the real tourist inferno begins – a rather jolly one, as tourist infernos go, with more food and carpets and jewellery lurching out at you from every shop window, cosmopolitan crowds, and a babel of signs. On Thursday afternoons and Friday mornings, there is a busy and colourful (but more than a bit touristy) market. Just north of the castle is the frenetic **bazaar district**, where mountains of gold and hecatombs of leather await the tourists. Shopkeepers keep a sharp eye on the arcades. At the centre, with some of the swankiest shops, is the restored 18th-century **Hacımolla Hanı**.

The Castle of St Peter

Castle of St Peter
open Tues–Sun 8.30–12 and 1–5; closed Mon; adm

The Knights' castle stands high on a small rocky peninsula over the original Carian settlement. Because the Knights ruled the seas, they concentrated their defences on the landward side. The first of seven **gates** to the castle is at the top of the ramp near the tourist office. This leads into the **Northern Moat**, site of the annual Bodrum Festival. Near the gate you will see the first of some 250 knightly coats of arms carved into the castle walls, as well as numerous reliefs and other architectural embellishments salvaged from the Mausoleum. A wooden bridge replaces the drawbridge leading into the outer citadel, where peacocks patrol the courtyard.

Museum of Underwater Archaeology
open Tues–Sun 8.30–12 and 1–5; closed Mon; adm

The castle now houses Bodrum's excellent **Museum of Underwater Archaeology**, showcasing the best finds from the many ancient wrecks littering the Turkish coastline. A small Gothic chapel now contains a reconstructed stern section of a Byzantine ship which sank off the island of Yassıada in 626. The subdued lighting sets the mood; when you peer into the gloomy cabin to see how the crew would have spent their last days at sea, the smell of the wooden planks wrenches you back to the 7th century more effectively than a painting or film ever could. Another penumbral room contains glass exhibits brought up carefully from the Turkish seabed. An exquisite beaker from the 11th century AD is etched on its lower half with two primitive lions eternally chasing each other's tails. But the most unusual of the beautifully lit objects is a four-inch blue glass needle from the 1st–2nd century AD.

Further chambers in the castle have been arranged to display ancient and medieval glass, coins and jewellery; best of all is the **Hall of the Carian Princess**. In 1989, a sarcophagus was discovered in Bodrum, belonging to a woman who was probably a member of the Hekatomnos dynasty, the family of King Mausolus, some time in the 4th century BC. Besides some rich jewellery and furnishings, enough of the body and clothing remained for a medical team from Manchester University to attempt a reconstruction of the poor girl in clay. They've got her standing up in a niche, wearing a ballgown and looking for all the world like Imelda Marcos.

The Knights of St John, or Knights Hospitallers, were most often the second and third sons of noblemen. They divided themselves into different *langues* (meaning nationalities), each one responsible for defending a certain area of the walls. St Peter's Castle had four *langue* towers. The **German Tower** has been restored, along with the nearby hamam, built for the prisoners when the castle was made into a state prison a century ago; the **Italian Tower** and the **French Tower**, the highest of all, offer wonderful views of the town and the harbours formed by the peninsula. The **English Tower**, on the south corner of the castle, has been done up to its medieval hilt, with tapes of medieval music and glasses of wine served by young Turks dressed as knights and ladies. On the west wall, notice the relief of a lion and the arms of Edward Plantagenet; inside on the marble windowsills are names and dates carved during many long hours of idleness. Perhaps they were relieved when England was expelled from the Order upon Henry VIII's divorce from Catherine of Aragon.

The Mausoleum

What remains of the Mausoleum of Halicarnassus is a bit outside the bustling trendy centre of Bodrum, on Turgutreis Caddesi to the west of the ancient harbour. Designed by the great Ionian architect Pytheos, only the massive foundations remain, capable of supporting a 200ft pile. Models on the site tentatively reconstruct the form of the Mausoleum, and there are a few copies of its reliefs – most of the originals were carted off to the British Museum in London. The Mausoleum was the biggest tomb ever

Hall of the Carian Princess
open for groups of 8 at a time, Tues–Fri 10–12 and 2–4; adm

Mausoleum of Halicarnassus
open Tues–Sun 8–12 and 1–5; closed Mon; adm

built by the ancient Greeks, and not just its name has come down to us: it has been imitated ever since (as in the Masonic Temple in Washington DC). The best copy, however, is in Milas (*see* p.283).

The only ancient monument of Halicarnassus to survive is the restored **amphitheatre**, with an original seating capacity of 10,000, north of the Mausoleum on Göktepe. This offers a grandstand view of the four-lane Kıbrıs Şehitler Caddesi, which snakes past just metres away from the first row of seats.

Where to Stay in Bodrum

(i) **Bodrum >**
*Kale Meydanı,
on the harbour,
t 0252 316 1091*

Bodrum

Bodrum is blanketed in hotels and *pensions*; prices are on the high side, but that doesn't keep them from filling up in the summer. Plenty of new luxury establishments have opened in recent years, but though the trend is upmarket the overwhelming majority are still resolutely middle-range. If you're the type that sleeps nights, the important thing about staying in Bodrum is to find a place not too near the nightclub strip: Dr Alim Bey Caddesi/Cumhuriyet Caddesi, in Kumbahçe, can be deafening until dawn. Most of the *pansiyonlar* are in this area, as well as more expensive places.

Half-board is required in almost all of the three- and four-star places, and in some of the two-stars.

*****Karia Princess, Canlıdere Sokak 15 near the Myndos Gate, **t** 0252 316 8971, *www.kariaprincess.com* (€€€€). There's opulence aplenty here, closer to the centre of Bodrum. Rooms have huge beds and marble bathrooms, with sufficient sports and fitness facilities to put a smile on even Arnold Schwarzenegger's face.

Antik Tiyatro, Kıbrıs Şehitler Caddesi 243, **t** 0252 316 6053, *www.antique theatrehotel.com* (€€€€). Engaging staff and one of the most elegant pools in Bodrum; a real haven from the hurly-burly. All 20 rooms have excellent views of St Peter's castle.

***Manastır, Mevkii Kumbahçe, also to the east, but closer to the town, **t** 0252 316 2854, *www.manastir bodrum.com* (€€€). With a pool, on a pretty terrace overlooking the sea, as well as a gym and tennis courts.

Su Otel, Turgutreis Cad. 1201, **t** 0252 316 6906, *www.suhotel.net* (€€€). A colourful, well-appointed little hotel with a pool and pretty garden.

Seçkin Konaklar, Neyzen Tevfik Caddesi, **t 0252 316 1351, *www. seckinkonaklar.com* (€€€). An ideal location by the West Harbour – close to the action but not too noisy. It's a low-rise complex with both rooms and apartments, and has a pool.

Ataer Pansiyon, Neyzen Tevfik Caddesi 102, **t** 0252 316 5357 (€€). A pleasant, relatively quiet place run by a pleasant family.

Bodrum Maya, Gerence Sokak, **t 0252 316 4741, *clubhedi@ superonline.com* (€€). One of the most comfortable places in town, which offers a pool and its own parking.

Most of Bodrum's *pansiyonlar* are located in Kumbahçe, what seems a whole city of them on the back streets behind the bar strip of Dr Alim Bey Caddesi; there isn't a lot of difference from one to the other.

Dönen, Türkkuyusu Caddesi 21, near the main PTT building, **t** 0252 316 4017 (€). With its own car park and set amongst eucalyptus trees this is quieter than most; rooms on the top floor are the most pleasant, with doubles costing 50 YTL with breakfast.

Kemer Pansiyon, Uslu Çıkmazı 30, **t** 0252 316 1473 (€). Rooms are basic but clean although they may be a little noisy; 30 YTL with shower.

Istanbul Pansiyon, on 1017 Sokak, **t** 0252 393 6078 (€). Welcoming place around the West Harbour area.

Eating Out in Bodrum

Like the other resorts, only more so, Bodrum has a waterfront lined with outdoor restaurants. In general, these are the last place to go – expensive, tourist-orientated places cobbled together each season with temporary staff, so check prices before you order. Still, there are plenty of places to get a good dinner.

Han, Kale Caddesi 23, t 0252 316 7951 (€€€). In an 18th-century caravanserai, this has the most original surroundings, and possibly the finest cuisine in town, with dishes like shrimp and avocado cocktail and chicken stuffed with pistachios; original desserts too, and a bar upstairs with live Turkish music.

Antik Tiyatro., Kıbrıs Şehitler Caddesi 243, t 0252 316 6053, *www.antique theatrehotel.com* (€€€). The hotel has a deservedly good reputation for its cuisine; its candlelit patio overlooking the harbour and castle makes dining here an experience for all the senses.

Buğday Vegetarian Restaurant, Türk Kuyusu Caddesi, a back street far from the tourist strip (€€). For something unexpected and memorable, head north from the town hall and seek this out. Lovely cooking, all natural ingredients, and a pretty, enclosed garden (occasional music and even art exhibitions).

Sakallı ('the Bearded') **Köfteci**, just off Kale Caddesi on Yeni Çarşi (€€). For once the portrait staring from the wall is of the restaurant's founder, not the Republic's. Bearded Sakallı Bey started the restaurant 60 years ago and seems to have been the Colonel Sanders of Bodrum. His *köfte* and onions were so good that locals used to eat them for breakfast. His successors open from lunchtime; by evening options are limited. Lentil soup, grilled aubergine and *köfte* costs 16 YTL.

Sünger Pizza, at the end of the strip near the Halikarnas disco (€). Offers a wide choice of Italian pizzas and beer for about 10 YTL. The name Sünger (sponge) derives from the family's former employment as sponge divers.

Entertainment and Nightlife in Bodrum

Almost everything is on the joyous pedestrian strip of Dr Alim Bey Caddesi/Cumhuriyet Caddesi, which becomes one long funnel of love in the evenings, directing a steady stream of revellers towards the Halikarnas nightclub at the far end. It has everything from slick discos to quiet bars with folk music, and watering holes that seem designed to attract northern lager louts. Pool halls, hippie trinket-dealers and sidewalk portrait painters decorate the streets. Prepare for sky-high drink prices.

Halikarnas, *www.halikarnas.com.tr*. The aforementioned Bodrum institution is at the top of the list. It claims to be the biggest open-air disco in Europe, with a capacity of 5,500. You can't miss it; its laser light shows bounce off the castle and around the town all night, giving the impression of an invasion from Mars. Dress up; it's 40 YTL to get in.

Marine Club Catamaran, *www. clubbodrum.com*. A former sponge warehouse on the seafront, also charging 40 YTL for entry. This may not be as big as the Halikarnas, but has outdone its rival in the novelty dance floor stakes. Moored out front is the huge catamaran, an insomniac's dream. It slips anchor at midnight filled with nautical ravers, and returns to port at dawn.

Hadigari, *www.hadigari.com.tr*. Flash disco, currently very popular.

Mavi Bar. A local classic hosting great live music and the odd celebrity. Mavi is also a platform for musicians, several house bands from the past have gone on to bigger stages.

There are some agreeable holes-in-the-wall featuring whatever live folk, jazz or blues music floats into Bodrum, such as the **Club Mani**, and the **Jazz Cafe**, near the Halikarnas.

The Bodrum Peninsula

As resorts go, Bodrum has everything – except a beach. But there are plenty of those just minutes away around the peninsula. Shaped like a badly drawn map of Africa and Asia, the Bodrum peninsula contains several burgeoning resorts, some attractive fishing villages and the ruins of ancient Myndus. It can be toured by dolmuş or by chartering your own caique.

Three km west of Bodrum, **Gümbet** is the closest and busiest beach resort, a rather characterless place with plenty of plastic hotels and evidence of more in the offing. The beach is good, however, and fitted out for every possible water sport, although windsurfers prefer **Bitez**, further west. The inland village of **Ortakent**, brooded over by the hulks of abandoned windmills above it, has a lazy charm; its beach, 6km south, is the peninsula's longest, 3,000 metres of sand and pebbles stretching westward. Even nicer are the beaches at **Bağla** and sheltered **Karaincir** to the south, with their lovely, fine sands and (usually) lack of crowds. At the southern tip of the peninsula, opposite Kos, a resort centres on fishing village of **Akyarlar**.

At the western tip, **Turgut Reis**, despite its rather inconsequential beach, is a heavily developed resort. It is named after the 16th-century Admiral Turgut (or Dragut), who was born here to Greek parents; his mentor Barbarossa, another Greek who 'turned Turk', in a moment of unusual humility declared that Dragut was ahead of him 'both in fishing and bravery'. Together the two of them terrorized the Mediterranean through much of the 16th century. Dragut led the great siege of Malta in 1565 and died there, and Süleyman's fleet and army had to return empty-handed, the first important military setback for the Ottoman Empire. Two fine beaches lie on either side of Turgut Reis: **Akyar** at a fishing hamlet, and silvery **Gümüşlük**, the site of **ancient Myndus**. Development of Gümüşlük village has been deliberately restrained due to its proximity to ancient Myndus, and the village is perhaps the peninsula's most charming. Just south of here is attractive little **Kadıkalesi**, with an abandoned Greek church on the hill above it.

The northern shore of the peninsula is blanketed with pine forests that reach the shore in many places. **Yalıkavak** is a scenic settlement, where many windmills still function, but its beach is poor, typical of those along this mostly unspoilt stretch of coastline. The villages of **Gölköy** and **Türkbükü** do their best for bathers, making the most of their narrow strips of sand.

Off the southern coast of the peninsula lies **Karaada** or Black Island, where mineral waters flow into a sea grotto, popular with bathers. The island can be reached by boat trip from Bodrum, as can **Knidos**, due south on the western tip of the Datça peninsula.

A Trip to Kos

Bodrum itself is so like a Greek island resort, it's a wonder that anyone would want to cross the border. Kos offers more of the same; its location near Rhodes has made it one of the busier

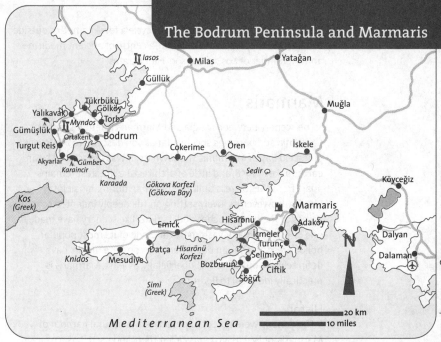

Iasos

Milas

Yatağan

Güllük

Muğla

Tükrbükü
Gölköy
Torba

Yalıkavak

Myndos

Gümüşlük

Ortakent   Bodrum

Turgut Reis

Cokerime

Ören

İskele

Akyarlar   Gümbet
Karaincir

Karaada

Sedir ♀

Köyceğiz

Kos
(Greek)

Gökova Korfezi
(Gökova Bay)

Marmaris

Emick

Hisarönü

Adaköy

Dalyan

İçmeler

Datça   Hisarönü
Korfezi

Turunç

Knidos   Mesudiye

Bozburun

Selimiye

Ciftik

Dalaman

Simi
(Greek)

Söğüt

N

Mediterranean Sea

20 km

10 miles

tourist destinations among the islands. In season, everything will be just as crowded as in Bodrum (and much more expensive). Nevertheless, Kos can invite you to some ancient attractions: another castle of the Knights of St John, a restored Roman house with mosaics, as well as other Roman-era ruins, all in **Kos town**, the

Where to Stay on the Bodrum Peninsula

Virtually every town and village on the peninsula has places to stay, although in some of the quieter villages on the northern coast there may only be basic *pensions*. Gümbet beach, 2km west of the centre, is lined with a wide selection of three-stars, good places to look for bargains when they aren't full of package tours. Gümüşlük has several very pleasing *pensions*, all charging 50–80 YTL. The main draw here is the wonderful fish restaurants that line the mini harbour.

Toloman, Bitez, **t 0252 343 1226, *www.toloman.com* (€€€). A pleasant and restful place directly on the beach. Besides the rooms there are a dozen apartments for rent.

Yıldız Motel, Ortakent beach, **t 0252 316 3195, *http://yildizotelbodrum.com*

(€€). Has a pool and spartan double rooms with bath for 80 YTL.

*Melisa, Eski Çeşme Mevkii, Gümbet, **t** 0252 316 1044 (€€). Simple rooms and a pool for about 60 YTL.

The region has a handful of campsites, of which the best equipped is **Zetaş Camping** in Gümbet, **t** 0252 326 1407, *www. zetastourism.com*. Other, more informal places, often on far nicer sites, are near the beaches nearly everywhere on the peninsula.

Eating Out on the Bodrum Peninsula

Restaurants on the peninsula range from the fancy at Gümbet and Turgut Reis to the plain at Ortakent and Yalıkavak. One highlight is the parade of fish restaurants in Gümüşlük.

island's capital. You can take a bus or cycle a few kilometres outside town to see the famous **Asklepeion**, a centre of ancient medicine and a reminder of Kos's great son, Hippocrates.

Marmaris

The scenery between Muğla and Marmaris is reminiscent of California and becomes spectacular as you descend to the lovely pine-clad Bay of Marmaris. The town itself was devastated by an earthquake in 1958, and little of architectural interest remains apart from the fortress built by Süleyman during his siege of Rhodes. However, its lovely setting on the deeply indented coast, its access to the bay's beaches and its fjord-like scenery have made it one of Turkey's major yacht ports and one of its most popular holiday resorts, though one where the concrete mixers have definitely got out of hand. Superficially, at least, Marmaris is practically identical to Bodrum.

History

The Carians were quick to appreciate the natural harbour of Marmaris, or Fyskos as it was called then, and used it as a base from which to terrorize the Phoenicians on Rhodes. After the eclipse of the Carians, the town was passed around among various powers – Egyptians (Ptolemy's empire, after Alexander), Ionians, Romans – before becoming part of the Ottoman Empire in 1425. It remained a forgotten outpost for nearly 100 years until Süleyman the Magnificent, irritated by the Knights of St John on Rhodes, who pillaged Muslim pilgrim ships and let Christians pass freely, followed the Carian example and used the town as his base to besiege the island. When the Knights finally surrendered, Süleyman was so pleased with his success that he ordered a castle to be built in the town. The result was a typically quaint Ottoman affair, almost cute, its battlements affording one of the coast's loveliest vistas. However, Süleyman didn't like it. '*Mimarı as,*' he grumbled when he saw it ('Hang the architect.').

Around the Town

Castle of St Peter
*open Tues–Sun
8.30–12 and 1–5.30;
closed Mon; adm*

The Knights' **Castle of St Peter** has since been restored and converted into an archaeological museum, with the standard collection of kilims, daggers, etc. The castle is reached through a convoluted series of back streets that offer some hints as to what Marmaris was like 50 years ago, when the town's income was derived from that most hazardous of occupations, sponge-diving. The divers would set sail every spring and return several months later, usually minus a few poor souls. The women and children would see the boats coming in and gather anxiously on the

Getting to and around Marmaris

Dalaman airport at Muğla is the closest **airport**, about a 90-minute drive from Marmaris. Buses run every hour in season to Marmaris's main *otogar*. The airport has regular domestic flights from Istanbul, İzmir and Antalya, and an increasing number of international charters, all via Istanbul.

Marmaris's *otogar* is located to the northeast of the harbour on the Mustafa Münir Elgin Bulvarı, though most **buses** also stop at the circle on Atatürk Caddesi, by the west harbour. There are frequent bus connections from Bodrum, İzmir and Fethiye.

Minibuses provide transport along the serpentine road to Datça and Knidos. Those for İçmeler and points west begin from the centre of the harbour, by the Atatürk statue (one of the new model Atatürk statues, with a top hat), as do the seasonal **boat dolmuşes** for Turunç, Bozburun, Datca and the many fine beaches and islets around the bay. Minibuses for Yalancı and Boğaz beach leave from Mustafa Münir Elgin Bulvarı, behind the marina, but you can also catch them from opposite the Tansaş shopping centre on Ulusal Egemenlik Caddesi. From May to October there is a daily **ferry** service from Bodrum to Datça. The ferry takes 1hr 30 mins or only 30mins by hydrofoil – this lands at Ovabuku.

Marmaris has one of the most reliable **ferry** services to a Greek island: Rhodes, daily, most of the year.

---

quayside. The statue of the woman and child at the **harbour** commemorates those who looked in vain. Nowadays the harbour is filled with boats offering day trips to the nearby beaches. The larger vessels can be chartered for week-long trips to Datça or Fethiye and beyond. Scuba-diving shops can also be found on the waterfront, offering a full day's diving at reefs near Marmaris for 60 YTL. Five-day PADI courses for beginners are cheaper in Marmaris than Bodrum, costing around 500 YTL.

Set back from the quayside the town's **bazaar** begins, one of the more pleasing tourist markets in Turkey. From here the town's spacious **beach** is a short walk away, to the west of town. Stalls set up at the seaside offer all manner of distractions.

East of Marmaris, over the wooden bridge, is **Günnücek Park**, a picnic spot within a grove of rare frankincense trees. You can swim off the small platform here. For better swimming, go to the islet of **Sedir** on the other side of the peninsula in Gökova Bay. The islet is only half a mile long but very popular for its unusual snow-white sand with perfectly round grains, shipped to the islet from the Red Sea some 2,000 years ago for Cleopatra. Then, a city called Cedrea stood on the islet; the ruins of walls and a theatre remain.

For yet more beaches, and for thermal springs, head south of Marmaris to **İçmeler**, a popular resort with all the adrenalin-boosting activities that this entails, from paragliding to jet-skiing.

A Trip to Rhodes

The largest and greenest of the Dodecanese is also one of Greece's most flagrant tourist playgrounds – prices will be a shock after Turkey. Rhodes has had a fascinating history: a power in its own right in Hellenistic times, home of the famous Colossus. Like Bodrum, the island was controlled by the Knights of St John for two centuries after 1306, and the Italians ruled it from 1912 until 1945. As a duty-free island, Rhodes can be a good place to shop.

The ferry from Marmaris takes just over an hour and lands at **Rhodes town**, the island's capital, where there are the castle and walls of the Knights to explore, as well as architectural contributions from ancient times up to Süleyman the Magnificent and Mussolini. The town is a major resort. From the capital the most common excursion is to **Lindos**, the island's second city, with the ruins of its magnificent acropolis. A number of villages haven't yet been too spoiled by tourism, notably **Lardos**, on the coast near Lindos; **Embona**, up in the mountains above Rhodes; and **Kamiros**, the third of the island's Doric 'three cities'. Along the west coast are a number of resorts and the famous **Valley of the Butterflies**.

Datça and Knidos

West of Marmaris, the road makes quite a dramatic ascent up to the top of mountains, before dropping down to **Datça**, one-time Doric city, now a busy Turkish resort popular with windsurfers because of its blustery location. Built around a horseshoe bay, Datça has beaches, but there are better ones further west along the **peninsula**, and local tour operators will happily sail you to them. They'll also take you to **ancient Knidos (Cnidus)**, at the very tip of the peninsula. Knidos was the headquarters of the Dorian Hexapolis (a loose confederacy of towns in Asia Minor that had been settled by Dorians). In ancient times, it was famous for a statue of Aphrodite by the great Praxiteles, modelled on the renowned courtesan Phryne (whose name means 'Toad', although she won a court case by baring her bosom before the judges). This first 3-D female nude was originally commissioned by Kos, but the islanders were too prudish to keep such a bombshell, and Knidos picked it up and made the 'Aphrodite of Knidos' the main tourist attraction of the coast, set in a temple to be viewed from all angles and tended by a lusty crew of priestess-prostitutes. The base of the statue has recently been discovered in the circular foundations of a Corinthian temple in the city. The streets of Knidos were laid out in a grid over a number of terraces; the walls and the Hellenistic theatre are the best preserved of the remains. The lovely statue of Demeter in the British Museum came from here, and although excavations are currently under way, no one has yet found the observatory of Eudoxus, a native of the city and student of Plato.

Eski (Old) **Datça** makes for a pleasant stroll and is a refreshing contrast to the modern, rather garish new town. This peaceful little hamlet with narrow cobbled stone streets has wonderfully restored, high-walled Greek houses and a few well-hidden pensions. Veer off to the right as you head in towards the town.

Hayitbuku and **Ovabuku** are both small unspoilt villages on the Datça peninsula. Before entering Datça, take the turn for Knidos and follow signs for Mesudiye Köyü.

⊕ Datça peninsula

The Hisarönü Peninsula

Taking the south branch of the Datça highway takes you to interesting pit-stops before looping back to Marmaris. One is **Orhaniye**, where a narrow, submerged sand bar extends almost halfway across the bay, giving the impression of walking on water. **Bozburun** is one of the furthest points on the peninsula and is about 18km from Marmaris, easily accessible by car and by minibuses that run frequently from Marmaris in the summer.

As the main route loops back north to Marmaris, the village of **Turunç** is situated off a small spur road and has a stunning beach and views to match. Though a tad touristy and little of historic interest to keep you there for long – a visit to the **Phosphorescent Caves**, where the water glows when disturbed, is worth the trip.

South of Turunç lies the **Rhodian Peraea**, the only mainland territory of that once-powerful island-state. The Rhodians made little use of this little peninsula, spreading between the islands of Rhodes and Kos, and there's little to see. A steep climb up from **Kumlubük**, another village with a sandy beach, leads to what remains of ancient **Amos**: fragments of some walls, and of a theatre and a temple. The ancient towns of **Saranda**, near **Söğüt** village, and **Bybassios**, have scanty remains, likely to appeal to specialists only.

Where to Stay in and around Marmaris

(i) **Marmaris >**
İskele Meydanı 2, on the west harbour, t 0252 412 1035; there is a hotel reservation booth open in season here, where you can also check information about boats to Rhodes

Marmaris

The only time of the year when it may be difficult to find a room in Marmaris is during the regatta, in the second week in May.

Iberostar Grand Azur, west of the centre of Marmaris at Kenan Evren Bulvarı 11, t 0252 417 4050, *www.hotelgrandazur.com* (€€€€–€€€). The status address on the beach front, with hamam, gym, nightclub, pools and all sorts of water sports.

Anemon Hotel, Kemal Elgin Bulvarı No:63, t 0252 413 3031, *www.anemonhotels.com* (€€€). Offers B&B as well as half board in central Marmaris.

There are plenty of moderate hotels near the beach, on Atatürk Caddesi and the back streets behind it.

*Begonya, right in the centre of the action on Hacı Mustafa Sokak, t 0252 412 4095 (€€). A family-run establishment with wooden lattice shutters and well-furnished rooms, which must be the prettiest hotel in Marmaris; the only drawback is noise from all the bars around it.

**Ünver, 112 Sokak 20, t 0252 412 2968 (€€). If you're not set on a seafront location, this family-run place is a quieter option. Set in a back street near some garden nurseries, it has a small swimming pool and clean, cool rooms with balconies. If there are no partying Danish and Dutch groups in residence, you will be guaranteed a good night's sleep.

*Ayçe Otel, 64 Sokak 11, t 0252 412 3136 (€€–€). Off the main street and therefore quieter than most.

Marmaris does not have as many *pansiyonlar* as Bodrum; it's best to arrive early in the day and check the hotel reservation booth by the tourist office. Otherwise, the best place to look is not in the old town, but in the new streets to the west behind Atatürk Caddesi.

Interyouth Hostel, near the sea front on 42 Sokak, t 0252 412 3687 (€). Not far from the PTT and slightly less expensive than the average *pension*.

It has a cafeteria, bar and laundry and is the best deal in town for 30 YTL.

Camp Amazon, t 436 9111, 39km from Marmaris in the Bordübet National Park. The nicest campsite in the region with a pool, nearby beach and every essential facility.

Datça Peninsula

Dede Pansiyon, Eski Datça, **t** 0252 712 3951 (€€). Has a pretty garden and pool in the old village; a well run and clean place to rest a while.

Olive Garden Hotel, Ovabaku, **t** 0252 728 0056, *www.olivegardenhotel.com* (€€). Highly recommended and well appointed, modern hotel with a great restaurant.

Serenity Pension, Hayitbuku, **t** 0252 728 0245, *www.serenitypansiyon.com* (€€). As the name suggests, is set in a quiet location and is ideal for a peaceful retreat.

Karaoğlu, Datça, **t** 0252 712 3079 (€). For budget accommodation in Datça, among a number of similar places on the hill overlooking the bay.

Hisarönü Peninsula

Turunç, with its long beach, has a number of adequate mid-range hotels with a special emphasis on water sports and excellent facilities.

Hotel Devamli, İçmeler, **t** 0252 455 2156, *www.hoteldevamli.com* (€€). A small, well-managed boutique hotel with 32 rooms within walking distance of the sea.

Dogan Motel, Orhaniye, **t** 0252 487 1074, *www.doganhotel.net* (€€). A family- run hotel: basic rooms with fantastic food and great hospitality. It is set within beautiful gardens with its own beach.

Eating Out in and around Marmaris

Marmaris

To escape the mainstream tourists in Marmaris, head for the Netsel Marina, where there are several restaurants set amongst the designer shops, where you can dine over-looking the marina full of boats of Turkey's rich and famous. It is situated beyond the covered bazaar.

Ney Restaurant, Kale Mah. 26 Sokak 24, in an ancient back street near the castle, **t** 0252 412 0217 (€€€). The sign outside proudly declares 'Turkish Home Cooking' and the aromas wafting out through the front door back up this claim. The irrepressible boss, Birgül Zülfikar, does all the cooking, using only fresh ingredients to create Turkish mainstays such as *börekler* and *mantı*. She has also infused this old stone house with a wonderful ambience. A *ney* (dervish flute) hangs downstairs. Wooden chairs crowd around small tables upstairs; with room for only 20 guests, booking is advisable. A full meal with wine is a reasonable 30 YTL.

Antique Restaurant, **t** 0252 413 29 55 (€€). Large selection of Turkish *mezes*.

O'Yes, on the beach promenade, **t** 0252 413 4788 (€€). Great for steaks but also has international and plenty of Turkish dishes.

Datça

Old Datça does not offer much in terms of eateries so a trip into Datca is a good idea as there is an abundance of good restaurants.

Papatya Restaurant and Bar, in the harbou. A Greek taverna style restaurant that offers some great meat and chicken dishes.

Bozburun

Orfoz Restaurant, **t** 0252 456 2209 (€€€). This is *the* place to eat and is only accessible by sea, so you need to call them to fetch you in their tiny putt-putt boat – worth the effort as the food is just divine.

Entertainment and Nightlife in Marmaris

The centre of the action is Hacı Mustafa Sokak, just behind and running parallel to the East Marina. Nightclubs and bars frequently change names and locations.

Panorama Bar, on the height next to the castle. Marmaris's best setting and view although its prices match its lofty position.

Castle Bar, even higher up the hill, but with more sensible prices.

ⓘ **Datça >**
Hükümet Binası,
t *0252 712 3546*

★ **Orfoz
Restaurant >>**

The Southern Coast

This long stretch of coast is quieter and less touristy than the Aegean side – but the choice bits are catching up fast. It comes in five distinct pieces. As most foreigners do, we'll call the first four by the names they had in ancient times: Lycia, a real Mediterranean paradise, where tourism is becoming as big as a very rugged terrain will allow; Pamphylia, a short, flat, fertile stretch that was once thickly spread with Greek cities, now populated by German children with plastic buckets playing amidst stupendous ruins; Rough Cilicia, a long, lovely and lonely expanse where the single road has sea on one side and pine-clad hills on the other; and Smooth Cilicia, a broad coastal plain with few tourists and many big industrial towns. Finally there's the Hatay, on the Syrian border, which contains ancient Antioch, a city that once rivalled Alexandria as the greatest metropolis of the eastern Mediterranean.

11

Don't miss

⭐ **A Mediterranean paradise perfected**
Kaş and the Lycian coast **p.313**

⭐ **A resort of distinction**
Alanya **p.334**

⭐ **Ruins and rural charm**
Uzuncaburç **p.342**

⭐ **Romantic castles in the sea**
Kızkalesi **p.343**

⭐ **Spectacular mosaics from antiquity**
Antakya museum **p.354**

See map overleaf

p.250

Kaunos
Köyceğiz
Ortaca Kadyanda
Dalyan Dalaman
Fethiye
Kemer
Ölü Deniz Tlos
Letoon
Patara
Xanthos
Kalkan
Myra
Kaş Üçağiz Finike
Kastellorizo Kale Demre
Kekova

Termessos
Perge Aspendos
Antalya

Selge
Karabük
Side
Manavgat
İncekum
Alanya
Seydra
Gazipağa

Kemer
Çamyuva
Tekirova

Phaselis
Olympos
Kumluca

Mediterranean Sea

N

50 km
25 miles

GEORGIA
T U R K E Y
SYRIA
CYPRUS
IRAQ

Don't miss

The Lycian Coast: Köyceğiz to Antalya

It's simply breathtaking: one mountain after another, covered in pines or maquis, sloping down to the sea and perfuming the air with wild thyme and mint. The only other place like it might be Italy's Amalfi coast. In ancient times, when the indigenous Lycian people embellished this shore with a garland of cities, the area was still something of a terra incognita for most Greeks and Romans. Even now the difficult terrain makes the interior hard to penetrate. Until the Turks finally completed the coastal road, stretching around the Lycian bulge from Fethiye to Antalya, the Lycian towns were accessible only by sea. It was the last unfinished section of the

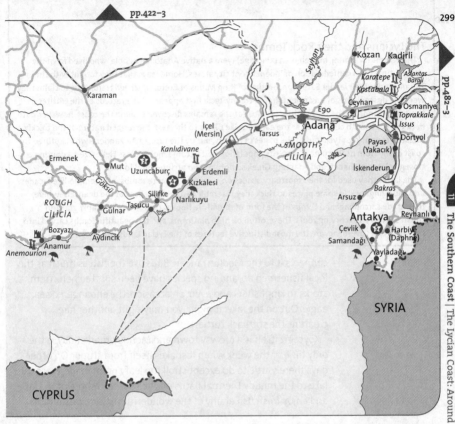

coastal highway, and its construction opened Lycia to tourism in a big way. Back in the 1980s some Saudis wanted to build a 10,000-room hotel here. They didn't get away with it, fortunately, but the Lycian coast today can be as crowded in summer as any part of the Aegean. Crowded but not overdeveloped; as on the Amalfi coast, the terrain simply doesn't permit it. Consequently, this land still retains its lazy charm, along with a transparent sea in every imaginable shade of blue and turquoise, magnificent scenery and unique archaeological sites, all in settings that would delight any romantic. In such a setting, people here tend to be convivial even by Turkish standards – friendly and talkative, and never in a hurry.

Around Lake Köyceğiz

Köyceğiz

Köyceğiz lives for the lake on whose northern shores it stands, from which it draws its name. Ringed by a phalanx of forbidding mountains, with waters transparent in the shallower stretches, this lake has supported the town for millennia, its healthy stock of fish constantly being replenished via the meandering channel that

The Lycians and their Rock Tombs

The Lycians (or Trmmi, in their own language) were a native Anatolian people, who lived from the earliest times as a confederation of independent city states. Homer says that they fought with the Trojans under their leader Sarpedon, brother of King Minos of Crete, which led Herodotus to claim they were the descendants of an ancient Cretan colony. Lycia first appears in the records of the Hittites as the 'Lukka Lands', in the 13th century BC. Most of the remains discovered along the coast, however, date back only to the 7th century BC at the earliest. Like Cilicia to the east, the rugged nature of the thickly forested terrain kept Lycia out of the pages of history, but by the time of Alexander – who captured the coast easily from its Persian satraps – its population had become more or less Hellenized, adopting a closely related alphabet, and adapting Greek sculptural and architectural forms.

The latter they used for their mortuary obsession, carving elaborate tombs with temple-like façades into the living rock, in some places so thick they resemble lost metropolises of the dead. Elsewhere, they made sarcophagi and tombs in the form of miniature houses of stone, remarkably graceful constructions with curving roofs. These, often on high platforms, and the beautiful tombs carved into the steep cliffs overhead, are the most distinctive features of the Lycian landscape.

connects it to the Mediterranean. Birds like the fish as much as the local fishermen do, and 119 species have been spotted here, from storks to kingfishers and even, on occasion, the endangered sea eagle. Out on the lake at night, you may sight another rare creature, the softback turtle.

Köyceğiz itself is a drowsy town and Monday, market day, is the only time of the week when it shakes itself from stupor. On other days there's little to do except stroll the leafy promenade, cross the lake to the muddy thermal baths on the southern shore of the lake and enjoy fresh fish at any of the wonderful lakeside restaurants.

Dalyan

This lovely village can be reached by road but it is far nicer to sail there from Köyceğiz, winding through the channel on the way to the open sea. Dalyan lies midway along this channel, a village of little more than one street, a square and a harbour, bounded to north and south by barely touched countryside. Across the water the first traces of ancient Kaunos (see below) can be seen: rock tombs built into the sheer cliff face. Over the last 10 years package tourism has increased in Dalyan owing to its proximity to Dalaman airport; in summer the area can be quite crowded. In addition, hundreds of day-trippers from the nearby resort of Marmaris come to spend the day on Dalyan's famous beach at İztuzu.

İztuzu beach, a 30-minute sail boat ride south through Dalyan's reed beds, is one of the most stunning on the Mediterranean rim, a sand-based island at the mouth of the channel. It is totally undeveloped, thanks to the presence of giant loggerhead turtles, who have used it as a laying ground since time immemorial. Tourist development very nearly killed these turtles off. The female loggerheads would lay their eggs by night in the soft sand, in clutches of about 100. By day, sunbathers would turn up to stretch out on that same sand and poke sun umbrellas into it for shade. If

Getting around Lake Köyceğiz

Köyceğiz is serviced by all **buses** travelling east or west along the coast. For Dalyan, coming from either direction, you must alight at Ortaca and take a dolmuş from there.

There are **boats** to Dalyan from Köyceğiz several times a day. Kaunos can be reached by motorboat from Dalyan or Köyceğiz; in summer you'll always be able to find someone to ferry you across.

the eggs managed to survive this treatment and hatch, the hatchlings were faced with a further problem; the bright lights from the hotels and bars on the beach would counteract the gleam from the sea that they would instinctively crawl towards. The baby turtles would set off in the wrong direction; inevitably, they died.

What was happening became common knowledge in the late 1980s and ignited a debate within Turkey that soon was to spread overseas. Influential environmentalists became involved and in 1991 the developers, who had previously been proposing that they and the turtles should have half the beach each, completely backed down. All structures on the beach were bulldozed and their foundations covered, and the entire area was ordered closed from 8pm to 8am, from May through to October, the main laying season. The beach is open during daylight hours but swimmers and sunbathers are asked to exercise special care.

Kaunos

Further down the channel from Dalyan is ancient Kaunos, a fine introduction to the southern coast's archaeological riches. This town marked the border between that sea and the Aegean, and between Caria and Lycia. Its remains show the styles of both cultures, as well as of later civilizations: there are Lycian and Carian tombs, a wall built by King Mausolus of Caria, medieval walls on the acropolis, a Roman fountain and baths (which now house a small museum) and a Byzantine basilica. The city was abandoned after its harbour silted up, a fate it shared with illustrious Ephesus.

Activities around Lake Köyceğiz

For local tours, rafting, jeep safaris, mountain biking, kayaking, scuba-diving and other fun adventures, **Kaunos Tours** in the centre of Dalyan, t 0252 284 2816, *www.kaunostours. com*, run daily trips and are very professional; they can also assist with transfers, car hire and hotels.

For serious hikers, the **Lycian Way** (*Likya Yolu*) is a newly marked route, running 500km from Fethiye to Antalya, that has been called one of the greatest hiking trails in the world; see *www.lycianway.com*.

Where to Stay around Lake Köyceğiz

In both Köyceğiz and Dalyan you can save money on hotel bills. There is nothing at the costly end of the market, although the moderately priced places and *pensions* are, as a rule, very good indeed.

Köyceğiz

Hotel Özay, Ulucami Mahalle, t 0252 262 4300, *www.ozayotel.com* (€€). Tastefully furnished rooms, a pool, and a lakeside position; the management arranges sailing, sports and boat tours, a double room will cost 50 YTL.

ⓘ **Köyceğiz** >>
Atatürk Kordonu 1, on the main square, t 0252 262 4703

Panorama Plaza, t 0252 262 3773, *www.panorama-plaza.de* (€€). At the western edge of town by the beach, and similar to the Özay.

Kordon Boyu Motel, by the lake at the other end of town, **t** 0252 262 3993 (€). Clean doubles with shower and lake-view balconies go for 30–40YTL in high season, much less if it's quieter. Near the main swimming pool, there's another, smaller, pool surrounded by high fences topped with barbed wire. Here the owner, Mr Özoğuz, keeps his pet trout, far too plump and numerous to leave unprotected and at the mercy of opportunist poachers.

Tango Pansiyon, t 0252 262 2501, *www.tangopension.com* (€). Halfway between the main square and the Panorama Plaza Hotel. Clean rooms and friendly staff.

Delta Camping, just beyond the Panorama Plaza, **t** 0252 262 1480. Wonderfully situated among the liquid amber trees.

Dalyan

Dalyan has many attractive hotels. The street leading south from the square, adjacent to the channel, is filled with small *pensions*, all charging around the same rate.

Happy Caretta, t 0252 284 2109, *www.happycaretta.com* (€€€–€€). Directly on the river, with its own boat shuttle to the beach.

Sutlanhan Apart, t 0252 284 4704, *www.dalyanotel.com* (€€€–€€). Smart rooms and a huge pool, also with a free boat service to the beach.

Dalyan Garden Pension, t 0252 284 3196, *www.dalyangardenpension.co.uk* (€€€). An attractive small hotel run by a British/Turkish couple with just eight rooms and set in a beautiful garden slightly inland from the river.

Onur, Yalı Sokak, **t** 0252 284 2107 (€). Run by a friendly family; good value, with air-conditioning but no pool.

Eating Out around Lake Köyceğiz

Köyceğiz

Thera Restaurant, t 0252 262 3514 (€€). One of the local seafood favourites, with a terrace over the waterfront. It also serves kebabs and meatballs. Bar opens only in the summer season but food is served all year round.

Mutlu Kardesler ('happy brothers'), near the main square, **t** 0252 262 2480 (€). For a real cheap eat, head to where for some loose change you can tuck into soup and kebabs.

Dalyan

There is no shortage of bars or restaurants here, and many are near the waterfront.

Sini Restaurant, t 0252 284 2497, *www.tamarisktourism.com* (€€). Serves the usual Turkish classics in a lovely garden shaded by a 90-year-old rubber tree.

Caretta Caretta, in the Maras neighbourhood, **t** 0252 284 3039, *www.carettacaretta.net* (€€). Long-established local favourite on the water's edge serving fresh fish and kebabs.

Fethiye

A modern town built over ancient Telmessos, Fethiye has Lycia's best harbour, protected by twelve islets. Telmessos meant 'Land of Light' in Lycian, and was first mentioned in the 4th century BC. Most of it lies buried under modern Fethiye (itself rebuilt after an earthquake in 1957), with the exception of the rock tombs cut into the cliff near the bus station; these, especially the grand Ionic temple **Tomb of Amyntas** of the 4th century BC, are among the finest in Lycia. Here and there throughout the modern town you see large sarcophagi. The oldest and most interesting of these is the **Lycian Sarcophagus** next to the post office, carved from a

Getting to and around Fethiye

Dalaman **airport** (50km from the town) has daily flights to Istanbul and weekly charters from abroad; there's an information office and taxis to Dalaman, from where **minibuses** run to Fethiye and everywhere else on the coast. All buses travelling this coast stop at Fethiye; the *otogar*, t 0252 614 3531, is a mile east of the centre on Süleyman Demirel Bulvarı, at the intersection of the roads for Muğla and Antalya.

Minibuses leave constantly in the summer for Çalış and Ölü Deniz from the central terminus on Çarşı Caddesi east of the castle where it intersects with Atatürk Caddesi. In season there is also a **boat-dolmuş** to Çalış, every 30mins until at least 10pm.

Getting to most of the **ancient sites** is possible without a car, though not always easy. From Fethiye, you can take a minibus to Sidyma, Araxa, Tlos, Xanthos, Pınara and the Letoon; all will require some walking once you get there. For all those close to the coastal road, you can be fairly sure of finding some minibus or even intercity bus to pick you up on your way back.

Fethiye museum
open Tues–Sun 8.30–5;
closed Mon; adm

single block of stone. The **museum** is near the school, and has exhibits from Lycia and an interesting sculpture garden.

Below the castle is the **amphitheatre**, a 6,000-seater dating from the late Hellenistic period. Abandoned in the 7th century, it remained buried under a thick layer of earth until the early 1990s; appropriately enough, the local museum director lived in a house on top of it. Only in 1992 did excavations begin on the site (once the director was ensconced in his new house). The money and manpower for the dig all came from local volunteers.

Fethiye, though modern, has a leisurely charm, and it is a good base for visiting the Lycian sites in the vicinity. After Marmaris or Bodrum, it may even look a bit down-at-heel; at least it has managed to side-step the blanket commercialism of some of the resorts on the southern coast. The leather and carpet merchants are huddled together in a relatively small area behind the **harbour**. From the harbour most of the sailboats will be offering 'twelve island tours'; some will go wherever you want.

The nearest beach is 3km away at **Çalış**, a suburb of Fethiye that is more obviously a 'resort'. It lies opposite the islet of **Şövalye** which also has a beach. **Gümlük beach**, just north of Fethiye, is in a grove of styrax (liquid amber) trees, used in perfumes and herbal medicines and once a big crop in these parts.

All these beaches, however, take second place to **Ölü Deniz**, the 'dead sea' to the south, a warm lagoon backed by pine-covered mountains. Once the haunt of pirates, this is a perfect beach, 3km long with transparent waters and fine sand; you have to pay to use the best part. The town of Ölü Deniz has been somewhat tarnished by overexposure to mass tourism, mostly British. In the mountains above Ölü Deniz the tackiness continues at **Hisarönü**, several kilometres from the beach, a small town devoted entirely to tourism. A 30-minute walk from Hisarönü is the Greek ghost town of **Karmilassos** (Kaya Köyü in Turkish), with forlorn houses and abandoned churches; as so often, when the Greeks left in the population exchange the Turks didn't move in, letting entire towns go to ruin. Recently, thanks to the efforts of private individuals, new life is slowly taking shape around this abandoned village; several *pensions* and private cottages have opened for business.

Inland from Fethiye

Inland from Fethiye you can explore – literally – three seldom-visited Lycian cities. **Kadyanda**, northeast of Fethiye near modern Yeşil Üzümlü, has a well-preserved theatre, a Doric temple, and baths, as well as other remains. **Tlos**, on the slopes of Akdağ, the White Mountain, is 48km from Fethiye, near modern Kaleasar, on the other side of the River Xanthos, the modern Koca Çay. Tlos was one of the most important members of the Lycian confederacy of the 2nd century BC and remained inhabited through the Byzantine era; in the 19th century it served as the winter headquarters of the pirate Kanlı Ali Ağa. As well as Lycian rock tombs, there are remains of Kanlı Ali Ağa's fortress on the acropolis, a Roman stadium, baths and walled necropolis, and a Byzantine church. On the other side of the modern village lies the theatre.

Pınara, another important member of the confederacy, is closer to Fethiye, on the west bank of the River Xanthus, east of Kemer – the western Kemer (there are two villages of this name, one at each end of Lycia; the name recalls those ancient invaders, the Cimmerians). Pınara is one of the more romantic sites, on a height beneath the mountains, the ruins overgrown. It is especially notable for its Lycian rock tombs; a Roman odeon and a Greek theatre are also easy to find. **Sidyma**, 14km off the coastal highway south of Pınara near Dodurga, has more rock-cut tombs.

Xanthos

Far more interesting, however, is Xanthos, the ancient capital and oldest city of Lycia, dating back to the 8th century BC and famous in antiquity for its great resistance to Cyrus' General Harpagus, who attacked in the mid-6th century BC. Although they fought courageously, the Xanthians were outnumbered. According to Herodotus, when they saw they were doomed to defeat, they retreated to their citadel, gathering together their womenfolk, children and slaves. After locking them inside, they set fire to the building and burned it to the ground. They then swore to fight to the death, and did. Indeed, when Xanthos was excavated, a heavy layer of ash was discovered over the ruins of that period.

Rebuilt by 50 families who had been away during the siege, Xanthos prospered up until the Roman period, when it once again suffered a terrible devastation, this time at the hands of Brutus in 42 BC; rebuilt yet again with the aid of Mark Antony and Emperor Vespasian, the city survived until the 12th century. Today it is one of the most revealing Lycian sites, most of it having been cleared to disclose the layout of the city and its imposing **funerary monuments**. Unfortunately they were stripped of their reliefs in 1838 but these can now be seen in the Lycian Room of the British Museum in London, along with the entire Temple of the Nereids. The Turks have replaced many of the reliefs with plaster casts.

The funerary monuments are all near the parking area, around the Roman **agora** and **theatre**; the **Tomb of the Harpies**, high on its monolith, is adorned with reliefs (plaster copies) of scenes from the Underworld. The winged female figures transporting souls, however, are not harpies but *kers*, who in true Greek religion, as opposed to the Olympian mythology, performed that function. Next to the tomb is a Lycian **tomb-sarcophagus** (4th century BC), high on its pillar. A similar tomb stands on the other side of the theatre. The **Inscribed Pillar** in the agora once supported the sarcophagus of a Lycian king; it bears writing in Lycian on all four sides, their longest inscription yet discovered, and, although this has yet to be deciphered, other evidence has led scholars to believe it was the tomb of King Kherei, who defeated the Athenians in a battle of the Peloponnesian War. The Lycian acropolis was just south of the theatre; the palace of the Xanthian kings may have stood here, on the western end overlooking the river that locals call the 'Royal Terrace', but the only ruins older than Byzantine times are those of a **Temple of Artemis**.

East of these ruins, part of a **street** can be made out, with another agora on one side and a basilica on the other; at the southern end of the street stood the **Temple of the Nereids**, which the malevolent Hyperboreans carted off to their capital a century ago as a cultural trophy. Across the path from this is an **arch** near the southern gate, donated to Xanthos by Vespasian. If you follow the street in the opposite direction, towards the northern walls, you'll come to more interesting tombs and a **Byzantine monastery**, and beyond the largely ruined walls, the city's **necropolis**.

The Letoon

Like the other ancient provinces of Asia Minor, Lycia had a federative sanctuary, a holy place shared by all the cities, the expression of their ethnic and religious unity. This was the Letoon, 4km south of the main road (the turn-off is just north of the one to Xanthos), dedicated to Leto and her children, Apollo and Artemis. Although there was a small city here, the only remains are of the temples and a small but well-preserved **theatre** on the hillside. Even though foundations of only three temples remain (the **Temple of Leto**, the largest and easternmost of the three, the **Temple of Apollo and Artemis**, and a smaller unidentified one between them), the site is one of the most pleasant along the coast. The half-sunken ruins, including a huge and elaborate semi-circular **nymphaion** and a

Apollo

Apollo, surprisingly for a god of light and reason, proves a pretty shadowy character outside Greece proper. His mother Leto – etymologically and in religion the same as Leda, Latona, Lat, or other variations in mythology – seems to have been an old Middle Eastern version of the Great Goddess. Apollo, here, must appear in his role as god of the cult of Hyperboreans ('men from beyond the North Wind') centred at Delos, and extending, if the ancient historians are to be believed, from Britain to Palestine. At Patara, the next town along the coast (*see* below), an oracle of Apollo existed that functioned only in the winter, the opposite of the oracle at Claros. In the summer, Dionysus presumably took over the temple while Apollo removed himself behind the north wind.

7th-century **monastery**, have become elegant pools for the lazy turtles and fat white ducks that abound near Leto's ancient spring, which still flows as freely as in ancient times. These share the spot with other exotic wildlife, including clouds of magenta dragonflies, and frogs straight from Aristophanes croaking '*Brekekekex coax coax!*' in the most correct classical Greek accents. On the floor of the twins' temple is a mosaic in the cella (inner sanctum) showing Artemis's bow and Apollo's lyre. Long inscriptions are everywhere; some have been removed to the nearby **museum**.

Where to Stay in and around Fethiye

(i) Fethiye >
İskele Meydanı 1,
t 0252 614 1527

Fethiye

Villa Daffodil, t 0252 614 9595, *www.villadaffodil.com* (€€). A small hotel in a beautiful spot about 1km out of Fethiye town centre. The secluded pool and well-maintained rooms have made it a local favourite.

Paradise Garden Resort, Ölüdeniz Yolu, Belcekız Mevkii, **t** 0252 617 0545, *www.paradisegardenhotel.com* (€€). A delightful boutique hotel with just 26 rooms set in 15 acres of obsessively maintained gardens and boasting a large secluded pool.

Mendos Hotel, t 0252 622 1148, *www.hotelmendos.com* (€€). Situated right on Çalış beach about 5km from Fethiye centre, a simple beach hotel with air-conditioned rooms.

Hotel Dedeoğlu, next to the tourist office, **t** 0252 614 4010 (€€–€). Air-conditioned rooms with satellite TV.

Mer Pansiyon, Dolgu Sahası Sahil Yolu 1, **t** 0252 614 1177, *www.merpansiyon.com* (€€–€). One of Turkey's best *pensions* and would put many a two-star hotel to shame. Rates for the spotless en suite rooms vary according to the view, averaging €28 per double, breakfast included.

Palmiye, t 0252 614 2140, on the shore west of the centre at Karagözler (€€–€). Breakfast served on the roof terrace. Not as good, but still nice and at a similar price.

Seketur Hotel, t 0252 622 08 90, *www.seketurhotel.com* (€). Again on Çalış beach; rooms with balconies, and a decent pool.

Anıl, Barbaros Sokak, **t** 0252 613 1711 (€). The best of the Çalış *pansiyonlar*; all rooms with bath and there's a small pool.

Ölu Deniz

Meri Oteli, directly on the beach, **t** 0252 617 0001, *www.hotelmeri.com* (€€). On a steep hillside among trees, with facilities for water sports and riding; prices from €65 for a double room all inclusive. Early reservations are essential.

There are plenty of scrappy campsites around Ölü Deniz.

Deniz Camping, t 0252 617 0045, has full facilities.

Hisarönü

Asena, t 0252 617 0154, *www.asenabeach.com* (€€€). Seven km from town at Hisarönü, and the most attractive of a number of upmarket hostelries that have opened near Fethiye in recent years. It's a lovely complex of low-rise buildings (pool, gym, hamam); riding and more on offer. Half-board available.

Eating Out in Fethiye

The open air **fish market** is a must – you buy your own fish then choose one of the surrounding restaurants to cook it for you. The cover charge is around 5 YTL including a salad, but watch out for the sting: any extras will hike up your bill.

Arena Restaurant, on the edge of Paspatur near the amphitheatre (€€). Offers modern dining with a range of European dishes. Pricier than others around but the service is good.

Meğri Restaurant (not be confused with Meğri *lokanta*, below) in Paspatur (€€). Renowned for its seafood and atmospheric setting in the centre of the courtyard.

(★) **Şömine Kebap >** **Şömine Kebap**, Mustafa Kemal Bulvarı 150, t 0252 612 0860, *www.somine kebap.com* (€€). Slightly out of town on the road to Dalaman opposite Tensaş supermarket. Find it! Prices are reasonable, the kebabs are excellent and the *pide* hits the spot, but be sure to leave space for their amazing *künefe*, a shredded wheat and cheese dessert topped with honey syrup, served warm. This dish will leave a smile on your face for weeks.

İskele Restaurant, on the main marina near the Rhodes ferry (€). Good pizza and well placed to watch the boats go by – cheap but good Turkish food.

Meğri, Çarşı Caddesi, on the far edge of the old town, Paspatur, opposite Koton (€). *Lokanta* serving mammoth collection of *mezes*, including stuffed aubergines drenched in cheese sauce.

Entertainment and Nightlife in Fethiye

The nightlife here is not frenetic; most of the few places are in the old town above the harbour. Near the harbour, Fethiye's 16th-century **hamam** on Hamam Sokak has a sign up outside inviting you to 'be a sultan for one day'. Its clientele is mostly transitory and the high prices reflect this. Be there between 7am and midnight for a 'Full Rub Down Soapy Bubbles Massage Services'.

Car Cemetery Bar. Unmistakable in the old quarter on Hamam Sokak, with the obligatory car fronts bolted above the entrance. Inside it's a dark grotto, usually heaving, in which you can get funky among the automotive parts until 4am.

Banana Night Club, in Paspatur. Offers a loud club scene for those with the energy to dance all night.

Patara and Kalkan

Patara and Kalkan both have their own loyal fan base – people who have holidayed in Turkey for donkey's years but who always end up returning to one or the other of these tiny villages. Patara is a bit shabby but comfortable, warm and welcoming. Kalkan is showier and smarter but less home-like. Either makes a good base for visiting the nearby ruins.

Patara

There are two good reasons for visiting Patara. The first is to explore the ruins of the ancient city; the second is to enjoy the 11-mile sandy beach, the longest continuous strand in Turkey and one that is, save for one café, a small colony of umbrellas and some sun loungers, completely undeveloped. As at Dalyan, giant logger-head turtles must be thanked for this. These immense amphibians have long used Patara beach as a laying spot, and it was the furore

Getting around Patara and Kalkan

The Fethiye–Patara–Kalkan–Kaş **bus and dolmuş** service is fast and regular, even out of season. In Patara, there are frequent minibuses from the village to the beach and the ancient city. Kalkan is a good place to base yourself if you are interested in archaeological sites; more than 25 can be reached within two hours by car. The new *otogar* is found at the top of the village, just down from the petrol station.

over Dalyan that raised concern in Patara as to the fate of their own turtles. Now the beach is closed off at night and daytime bathers are warned to be careful where they lay out their beach mats, lest the eggs be scrambled. Simple pleasures are the order of the day: canoes can be rented and there's a volleyball net in an egg-free zone, but otherwise it's a case of heading for the hills rising in the distance until you find a suitably deserted section of beach; you shouldn't have to go far. There is no development at ancient Patara either, in this case to protect the ruins. The village itself has remained very much the bonsai resort: whereas the growth of nearby coastal enclaves such as Olü Deniz continues virtually unchecked, Patara has been artificially stunted since 1988, when the government banned new construction. Perhaps because of this, there's little friction in Patara between the traditional and the modern: when they hear the call to prayer, barmen and waiters across the village turn down the volume of the Western music serenading their customers.

Profits from the beach café are used for the village; the primary school has recently been renovated and the roads into the village have been brick-paved. A tea garden and children's playground in the centre of the village have also been added, courtesy of the beach café and the resourceful mayor, Arif Otlu.

Ancient Patara
*open summer daily
8.30–7; winter daily
8–5.30; adm*

Between sand, sea and pines, **ancient Patara** is altogether one of the most attractive sites in Lycia. Entering the ruins, you pass some fine Lycian tombs on the right-hand side, and two apsed buildings, the Roman baths built by Vespasian and a later Christian basilica; new excavations here started in 1994. A three-gated monumental arch, stripped bare of its statues, adorned the town's main entrance, doubling up as part of the aqueduct carrying water to the baths. The theatre is in good shape, but partially covered by a tremendous sand dune, well over 100ft high. The most recent excavation on this immense sight is the **lighthouse** – thought to be one of the oldest in the world. It is now partially reconstructed, and plans are in place for its completion within one year.

Be warned: squadrons of mosquitoes patrol the site in summer.

Kalkan

The magic of its location at the mouth of a crystal bay has won Kalkan a lot of devotees, especially amongst British holidaymakers, whose steady flow has seen this old fishing village grow into an affluent little resort. Many Brits, looking for 'a place in the sun', have even taken up residence here: over the last 10 years, the hills around have become littered, for want of a better word, with new villas in all shapes and sizes. The rustic village magic that attracted travellers here in the first place is slowly fleeing away and the town risks becoming a victim of its own success. But don't be put off. Kalkan is a colourful place with a definite charm, particularly in the old town centre. It makes a nice rest stop for a day or two especially if you want to splash out on some posh nosh in the various rooftop and harbourside restaurants, and is still worlds apart from the mass tourism resort of Olü Deniz.

Kalkan has no sandy beaches; the pebbly beach near the harbour, however, serves the area well. If sand is a requirement then Patara beach is the answer to your dreams, but **Kaputaş beach**, 200 steps below a steep cliff 16km east of Kalkan, is also popular because of its great setting and can be found on the coastal road to Kaş.

Where to Stay in Patara and Kalkan

Patara

Expect to pay 35–70 YTL for a double room in peak season. The website *www.patarainfo.com* has been created by Patara villagers working as a community to raise the profile of their village. There are contact details for the various *pensions* and hotels with links to websites where relevant.

⭐ Jets Pension >>

Delfin Hotel, t 242 843 5120, *www. pataradelfinhotel.com* (€€). A recently refurbished hotel with pool and air-conditioning. Family rooms with kitchens are also available.

Patara View Point Hotel, t 0242 843 5096, *www.parataviewpoint.com* (€€). Has a scenic setting on a hillside above the village and friendly proprietors. Large pool, relaxed ottoman terrace and beach service available.

There are several cheaper hotels or *pensions* to choose from – most are family-run, simple but clean with a hearty Turkish breakfast thrown in for good measure. All have air-conditioning and Internet too.

Ferah Hotel, t 0242 843 5180, *www. ferahhotel.com* (€). Charming family-run hotel set in moderate-sized grounds with chickens roosting in tomato boxes in the trees. Good sized pool; large rooms with en suites.

Flower Pension, t 0242 8435164, *www. pataraflowerpension.com* (€). On the way into the village and a very friendly family-run *pension* that will make you feel at home straight away.

Golden Pension, t 0242 843 5162, *www.goldenpension.com* (€). One of the most established *pensions*, set in a convenient location in the village centre – run by the current mayor of the village – you will be made very welcome. Air-conditioning, shower rooms and terrace restaurant.

Jets Pension, t 0242 843 5128, *www. jetpension.com* (€). Set up on the hill on the outskirts of the village – a quiet setting with good views of the lagoon and a hearty breakfast. All rooms are newly refurbished with en suite showers. Beach service courtesy of Jets taxi (reduced rates for guests).

Istanbul Pension offers a friendly family-run camping ground which though basic does have showers and toilets attached to the main *pension* – free running water, shaded seating and a little shop selling essentials on site. Located at the entrance to the village on the right-hand side.

Kalkan

Villa Mahal, t 0242 844 3268, *www. villamahal.com* (€€€€). Recently voted the 'most romantic hotel in Europe', Mahal is pricey but worth every penny: the stunning rooms and

⭐ Coast >>

⭐ Kaptan
Restaurant >>

location mean you will have to fight to get in, so reserve well in advance. Their beach facilities are open to the public and a little boat will ferry you across from the harbour in Kalkan for around 12 YTL return, including entrance and loungers.

Hotel Pirat, **t** 0242 844 3178, *www.hotelpirat.net* (€€). By the marina, this is one of the most established hotels in Kalkan. Its former elegance is beginning to show signs of ageing but it is still clean and friendly with great barbecue evenings for guests.

Kulube Hotel, **t** 0242 844 2445, *www.kulubehotel.com* (€€). Great location close to the seafront with its own beach platforms. No children allowed.

Mediterran, **t** 0242 844 1122, *www.turkeycoastline.com* (€€). Offers a blend of self-service and hotel facilities and has a simple, modern style throughout. The well-appointed apartments have double bedrooms, sitting rooms with sofa bed, kitchenette and shower rooms. Dining in the evening in the open terrace restaurant is quite a treat too.

Caretta Caretta Pension, **t** 0242 844 3435, *www.kalkancarettapension.com* (€€). A little way from the town centre – but right on the waterfront with its own private beach platforms.

The White House, **t** 0242 844 3738, *www.kalkanwhitehouse.co.uk* (€€). In the old town area of Kalkan, with a great rooftop terrace giving views of the old town and the bay.

Eating Out in Patara and Kalkan

Patara

Gozleme houses in Patara offer tasty pancakes with a variety of sweet and savoury fillings. Try **Keziban's Pancake House** at the entrance of the village under the shade of an enormous rubber tree. **Yasemin's Pancake House** in the centre is also well worth a try.

Restaurants are concentrated around the square. Prices are far cheaper than Kalkan counterparts.

Durak Lokanta (€). Famous for its lentil soup, a cheap and cheerful *lokanta* in the village square.

Sofra Restaurant, in the centre of the village, run by the charming 'Chicken Ahmet' (€). Serves a wide selection of Turkish and European dishes, including tasty vegetarian options such as stuffed mushrooms.

Lazy Frog Restaurant, in the centre of the village (€). Run by the friendly Bayram, who will offer you great *mezes* and a choice of Turkish dishes and *pizzas*. Doubles up as a bar towards the end of the evening.

Tlos Restaurant, on the corner of the village (€). Osman can conjure up great one-off dishes but he does not serve alcohol.

Kalkan

Kalkan offers few options for the budget-conscious diner. The main draw here is the wonderful roof terrace restaurants that offer dining under the stars.

Coast, **t** 0242 844 2971, *www.kalkancoast.com* (€€€). A chic, contemporary roof terrace restaurant with a menu that takes you back to authentic Ottoman dishes and brings you back to date with Thai and Asian offerings. The delicious food and creative cocktails have built up quite a following so try to book in advance.

Zeytin ('olive'), **t** 0242 844 1395 (€€€). Another roof terrace, offering exclusively Turkish meals with setting detail to match. Great olive bread!

Kaptan Restaurant, **t** 0242 844 3166 (€€€). Located in one of the prettiest corners of Kalkan next to the old mosque and overlooking the beach and harbour. Serves a variety of Mediterranean and European dishes. Owner Ali previously worked as a waiter at the UK Houses of Parliament before realizing his dream here. The discerning easy-listening selection in the background adds a touch of elegance.

Aubergine, **t** 0242 844-3332, *www.kalkanaubergine.com* (€€€). A well-established restaurant right on the harbourside, offering big spenders a range of dishes served with a real professional edge.

Kaya, **t** 0242 844 3718 (€€). The resident magician offers fun and entertainment while you sip your beer and sample the simple, tasty menu.

Kuru's, a little out of town on the Kaş Road (€€). Past the Kelebek furniture store – on the left-hand side on the bend of the road – mind the stuffed camel! Fabulous home-made food; try the *mantı* and *çiğ börek* and, for dessert, sample the *hoşmerim* served warm with ice cream. Comfortable raised seating and sea views.

Ali Baba's, on the entrance to the main drag (€). A basic *lokanta* that offers soups and meals prepared that day, The choice is limited but, at 3–6 YTL per dish, who's complaining?

Nightlife in Kalkan

The nightlife is low-key but there are several charming bars attached to the many harbourside restaurants and some independent bars that play '*danse*' music until the early hours.

Kaş and the Lycian Coast

Kaş

Twenty years ago the delightful fishing village of Kaş, huddled shyly under the lower peaks of 9,802ft Mount Akdağ, offered perhaps the ultimate in sunny Mediterranean languor. Of course it was too good to last. Don't be put off by the hordes of summer visitors, though; it's a relaxed place, and still maintains more of its village character than most of the big resorts. Despite its small size, Kaş is one of the most cosmopolitan towns around, and it's still the best base for seeing this delicious stretch of the Lycian coast.

Arching back from the sea, Kaş ('eyebrow') was given its name for obvious reasons. Before this, it was Habessos to the Lycians and Antiphellos to the Greeks; bits and pieces from the past survive both within the town and on the cliffs behind, where several **tombs** have been cut into the almost vertical face. West of the harbour are the ruins of a **temple** and a 1st-century **theatre** of medium size, with 25 rows of seats, weathered to provide a pleasing dappled effect. The location is simply stunning, with towering mountains behind the seats and tiny islands in the open sea behind the stage. The theatre commands a quiet spot on the edge of town, the voices of the original actors almost audible in the breeze. In the centre of town stands a tomb, as tall as the two-storey buildings surrounding it, and mellowed into a warm orange-brown. Its inscriptions are in a form of Lycian that has yet to be deciphered, even though many of the letters look uncannily modern. The hole smashed in the side was made centuries before by looters, robbing the corpses of the gold and the jewellery interred with them. Another tomb is on a hill just to the west on a narrow peninsula, and another at the harbour.

All of these tombs (except the one at the harbour, which was moved by the municipality to make way for extensions), indeed all the tombs in the vicinity of Kaş, face the island of **Kastellorizo**: archaeologists and anthropologists alike are totally baffled as to why. Just a mile offshore from the town, this lonely little island (also called Megisti in Greek, or Meis in Turkish) marks the

Getting to Kaş

Kaş is easily reached by **bus** from anywhere on the coast; the *otogar* is on the northern edge of town, on the Fethiye to Antalya road (Atatürk Bulvarı). The drive from Patara to Kaş is one of the most spectacular – and stomach-churning – in Turkey. As you weave your way along the road cut into the cliff in the 1960s, islets bob invitingly out at sea, distracting you from that tortuous corner ahead. Here and there are tiny coves where you can stop off for a cool dip before pressing on to Kaş. Coming from inland, there is a good network of day and overnight buses from Istanbul, Ankara and other major cities.

easternmost boundary of the Greek republic, inherited from the Italians after the Second World War along with the rest of the Dodecanese. This quirky backwater, which once had a population of 16,000, is still recovering from 1944, when it was pillaged and burned by departing British troops in one of the more bizarre incidents of the war. The few Greeks who live there, heavily subsidized by the Greek government, come over to Kaş to do their shopping. Several boat companies make daily trips over to Kastellorizo, and in 2007 it was made a port of entry into Greece.

Around Kaş's **harbour** you'll find the usual array of cruise boats, offering day trips to Simena (Kale Köy), Uçağız and Kekova. The town's other attraction is its **farmers' market** every Friday. Though the water is crystal-clear, Kaş's two main beaches are pebbly and known respectively as **Little Pebble Beach** and **Big Pebble Beach**. The nearest sandy beach is **Kaputaş**, 16km to the west, created by the Kaputaş stream which has cut a big chasm through the rock wall. Across the bay at Limanagazı are several beach clubs, notably the excellent Don Quijote.

Inland, 19km east, are the ruins of **ancient Kyanaea**, renowned for the rows and rows of sarcophagi that dominate the site.

Kaputaş Beach
by land, accessible only via an endless flight of stone steps; you can hire a motorboat from Kaş harbour to take you there

Limanagazı
boat taxi from the harbour, around 15 YTL

Activities in Kaş

Bougainville Travel, Çukurbağlı Caddesi 10, **t** 0242 836 3737, *www.bougainville-turkey.com*. Has more on offer than most companies, from paragliding and PADI dive courses to trekking tours of some of the lesser known and more inaccessible villages, as well as sea kayaking at Kekova.

Where to Stay in Kaş

(i) **Kaş >**
Cumhuriyet Meydanı 6,
t 0242 836 1238
(faultlessly helpful)

Kaş

At the moment Kaş is rather short on luxury hotels, though one or two have been built in recent years. There are many private villas to rent.

***Hadrian, on the south coast of the peninsula, 5km from Kaş, **t** 0242 836 2856, *www.hadrianhotel.de* (€€€, half board). An oasis clinging to the rocky coast, with a seawater pool and terrace offering great views of Kastellorizo. Somewhat regimented set-up though; deckchairs, even restaurant tables, are allocated by room number! The clients are mainly Germans; that could explain it.

Gardenia, **t** 0242 836 2368, *www.gardeniahotel-kas.com* (€€€–€€). Well appointed and thoroughly modern, in the Küçük Çakıl area so walking distance from the town centre. The owner, an architect, has a keen eye for detail, and an oil painting or two; pieces collected from around the world decorate the walls.

Linda, Küçük Çakıl Mahalle, by the Little Pebble Beach, **t** 0242 836 3084, *www.kaslindahotel.com* (€€). Rooms with a view and a pool.

Çakıl Pansiyon, Little Pebble Beach, **t** 0242 836 1532, *www.cakilpension.*

com (€€). A low-priced family concern with great sea views. Lots of steps to get to the upper floors.

Kaş Otel, Hastane Caddesi, t 0242 836 1271 (€€). An enviable position on the seafront with sea platforms; walking distance from the centre. The tiny rooms are drab concrete boxes, but the saving grace: balconies are practically over the sea.

Oreo Hotel, Yaka Mah., close to the bus station, t 0242 836 2220 (€€). All rooms with air-conditioning, pool and gardens, views over the town and sea.

Kaş Kamping, t 0242 836 2637, www.kaskamping.com. On the road to Çukurbağ, and stands out among a number of campsites; it has a perfect spot right on the sea, and besides the campsite it now has several new bungalows to rent as well.

Eating Out in Kaş

The town is full of great restaurants, all reasonably priced. The little cafés around the main car park offer fresh juices and breakfast.

Chez Evy, Terzi Sokak, t 0242 836 1253 (€€€). Evy is an effervescent Frenchwoman whose personality is as delicious as her cooking. Her place has become an institution: locals and tourists alike soon get hooked on the relaxed ambience, with details such as the Camus quotation hanging in the toilet adding a dash of quirkiness. From the *calamari provençal* to the magnificent pepper steak, the food is simply superb. 60 YTL or so for a meal.

Dolphin Restaurant, Süleymen Sandikci Sokak (€€€). Amazing views over the harbour from its terrace, but you pay for it.

Sempati, Uzunçarşı Gürsoy Sokak 11, t 0242 836 2418 (€€). Run by the charming Sevim and nestled inside the nicest courtyard in Kaş, oozing Mediteranean character and offering

some great dishes too. The *mücver*, courgette fritters, is excellent, as are most of the other dishes, including a homely lentil soup and the *paçanga börek*, pastry stuffed with pastrami.

Natur-el, Uzunçarşı Gürsoy Sokak 6, t 0242 836 2834 (€€). Just across the courtyard, this also competes for the title of best home cooked food; various types of *mantı* are on offer and the *ciğborek* is also very good.

Bahçe Balik, behind the Lycian tomb on the corner of Süleymen Sandıkcı Sokak (€€). Has a romantic ambience and excellent seafood; the marinated raw seabass (*ceviche*) is just delicious.

Ikbal Restaurant, further along Süleymen Sandikci Sokak (€€). Has a creative Turkish and European menu with very tasty starters.

Çinarlar, Şube Sokak (€). Will pull a crispy pizza from their wood-fired oven for 9 YTL, providing a break from Turkish food, though the Turkish version, *pide*, is better.

Entertainment and Nightlife in Kaş

This can be at least slightly more intense than Fethiye, but nothing like Bodrum. There are some wonderfully noisy dancing spots in town.

Mavi Bar, on the waterfront, has fans from all over the country. Istanbul and Ankara folk gather here in large numbers in summer to enjoy reasonable cocktails and loud rock music.

Hideaway Café/Bar, off the main square. A real gem tucked away in a secret walled garden. Blues and light rock fans will love this one.

Hi Jazz, in a narrow alley beside Evy's. Yilmaz, the resident DJ, plays an eclectic mix of salsa, Balkan, Brazilian and other world classics, fusing them with the best of Turkish music from the 1960s and '70s. On a good night, the atmosphere is unbeatable.

Kekova Island and the Kaş Coastline

The Lycian Coast

Heavily indented and full of isolated caves and islets, this part of the coast captures in equal measure some of Lycia's most spectacular scenery and some of its most intriguing ruins, many of which lie semi-submerged in a sea as clear as any in the world. The best are at the mysterious city that once stood on **Kekova Island**, east of Kaş; along its southern shore houses, walls and kilns can be easily identified and staircases descend from the cliffs to disappear into the ocean. On a small beach a large, arched structure stands erect, once part of a boatyard. Little is known of this city, except that its name was Dolikhiste. A local theory maintains that it was inhabited by pirates who, after indulging in the pillage their occupation entailed, would then stash their loot in one of the many hidden caves. They lived here for centuries until a massive earthquake shook the city into the sea and drove the brigands away.

The village of **Üçağız**, across the water on the mainland, began life in the 4th century BC as Teimiussa. What remains of Teimiussa is spartan but striking, a plethora of rock tombs huddled together, many rising picturesquely out of the water – again, all facing west to Kastellorizo. Until 1992, Üçağız existed in a time-warp, a barely touched village of fishing and weaving that could be reached only by boat. Though now busier (restaurants line the waterfront), its setting is undeniably lovely, amidst the two bays and slender channel that give the village its name, Üçağız being a direct translation of its Greek name, Tristomo, or 'three mouths'.

Further along the mainland, clinging to the side of a hill, is **Kale**, descendant of ancient Simena, another member of the Lycian League. Its castle, built by the Lycians and renovated, so it is said, by the pirates of Kekova Island, is in good condition, its crenellations showing a variety of styles. Inside it is the **theatre of Simena**, the smallest theatre yet discovered, with only seven rows of seats – an indication of the diminutive size of Simena and also of the value placed on culture in even the tiniest Greek towns.

From Üçağız, and sometimes from Kaş, you can take a boat tour to yet another lost city, **Aperlae**. This town once prospered by rotting murex sea snails to produce the imperial purple dye (deep red, really) for the robes of kings, emperors and miscellaneous despots. A late Roman church has recently been uncovered there; not long after it was built, Aperlae succumbed to pirates.

Demre (Kale): St Nick's Home Town

Going northeast, the next modern town, Demre (which appears on many maps as Kale), stands on a little plain full of small farms, grown prosperous from citrus fruits and tomatoes. Demre is the descendant of ancient Myra, home of jolly St Nicholas, a 4th-century prelate. He was actually born in Patara, but it was in Myra that he served as bishop, sufficiently beloved for his generosity and good deeds to get himself canonized. Long before he became Father Christmas, Nicholas was a simple patron of sailors and pawnbrokers. Travel brochures have lately appeared with pictures of an American-style Santa Claus in front of the ancient ruins.

Getting around Kaş: the Lycian Coast

The easiest way to explore the Kaş coastline is by day trip from Kaş, though there's nothing to stop you hopping off the boat in Üçağız, doing some hiking or some lazing, and picking up a **boat** the following day. Each morning at 10am a **tour boat** leaves Kaş for Üçağız, returning at 6pm. To get to Aperlae, charter a boat from Üçağız. It's a short walk from where the boat docks to the site.

Also from Kaş, there are regular **dolmuşes** running in the summer for Patara, Xanthos and Kalkan. There is also a regular half-hour bus service going to Fethiye or Antalya from the bus station.

For Kyanaea, take an eastbound bus from Kaş and ask to be let off at Yavu; from there, the ruins are a hard, one-hour climb away. Be sure to get good directions as it is easy to get lost; you may want to employ someone from the village as a guide. Demre can be reached by bus from Kaş. Inexpensive tours of Kekova are arranged daily through the travel agents.

To get up to Mount Olympos without a car from Kaş, you'll have to take a bus bound for Antalya and get off at the Kemer crossroads. In 2007 a **cable car** opened from Kemer to take people up Mount Olympos at a cost of €25 each way. Most coastal minibuses will take you at least within walking distance of Phaselis, though for the sites up in the mountains, Limyra and Arykanda, you'll need to take a minibus to Finike, then another minibus to get you to the site.

St Nicholas Church
open summer daily 8–7.30; winter daily 8–5.30

Indeed, a huge sign has been erected next to the St Nicholas church advertising the 'Santa Claus Foundation', complete with a smiling Santa looking a little overdressed for a Turkish summer. Let us hope this doesn't get out of hand. Follow the 'Baba Noel' signs in Demre to find **St Nicholas Church**, a 5th-century building with extensive 11th-century additions, including a large barrel-vaulted nave and cloister. In the original structure there is fine marble inlay work and much carved stone recycled from earlier buildings. Of the later frescoes, only one unidentified saint remains.

Myra

Myra
open summer daily 7.30–7; winter daily 8–5.30

About a mile outside Demre, the ruins of Myra include an amazing collection of **tombs** cut out of the cliffs above the city, all in the form of temple façades. There are over a score of them, arranged on the cliff in an asymmetric jumble. Most are from the 4th century BC, and many contain funeral scenes in relief. Several façades have roofs carved to imitate wooden beams, suggesting that they were copied in form from wooden temples or other similar buildings that have not survived; the same is true of the Phrygian cliff-face façades west of Ankara.

Myra's other attraction is its **theatre**, a late Roman work with some uninspired sculpture. From its huge orchestra, we can guess it was used more often for games and animal shows than for classical drama. In the vicinity are a number of Byzantine structures protruding from the surrounding farms and greenhouses, and, a few kilometres to the southwest, a **Roman granary**, one of many in Lycia, decorated with a relief of Hadrian.

Around Finike

The coastal road east of Demre runs by a very long and scrubby beach, with its scattering of curious wooden holiday bungalows on huge wooden wheels. Keep on driving and you'll pass a number of small coves ideal for quick dips to break up long drives. From **Finike**, a nondescript agricultural town 30km east of Demre, you have the choice of continuing along the coast, passing by the 'Tortoise Crossing' road signs, or striking inland through the mountains. Either way will take you to Antalya, though the coastal route is considerably shorter. Travelling inland, you encounter first the ruins of **Limyra**. In the early 4th century BC, this was the most powerful city of Lycia under King Perikles, founder of the Lycian League of cities and a fighter for Lycian independence against Mausolus of Caria. The site is worth a visit for the **tombs** – if you haven't seen enough yet – spread all over the outskirts of the ancient town. Notable among them is the **Heroön of King Perikles**, in the form of an Ionic temple, although some climbing will reveal several others that rank among the best Lycian tomb architecture.

North of Limyra the road passes **Arykanda**, another ruined town. Its only distinction seems to have been a precocious and enthusiastic acceptance of Christianity, as reflected in its monuments, including remnants of an early Byzantine basilica and an even earlier temple that was converted to Christian use. The biggest ruins on the site, however, are a small **theatre**, well preserved and beautifully situated, with a view over the surrounding hills, and a **bath complex** with one of its 30ft walls still standing.

Beyond this come two lakes, **Avlan Gölü** and **Karagöl**, the 'Black Lake', its waters held back by a natural dam and overflowing through a chasm in the cliff. If you press even further inland, into the **Ak Dağlar**, you'll come to the only sizeable village in these parts, **Elmalı**, with some Selcuk remains and a tiled 17th-century mosque to match its neighbourhoods of old wood-frame houses.

Olympos and the Chimaera (Alev)

Along the coast, the road skirts the grand massif of the Bey Dağları, the 'Bey's mountains' around Cape Gelidonya, a familiar landmark to sailors. Heading northwards, **Olympos** is another ruined town in a pretty setting, though little remains of it. If you pass at night, you will see a small flame rising from the mountains above the town. All the ancient geographers mention it, and it takes its name, the Chimaera, from the myth of Bellerophon. The real Chimaera isn't at all monstrous; in the daytime it isn't even visible. Whatever combination of gases causes it has never been

Bellerophon

The Lycian king, Iobates, sent Bellerophon to kill the fire-breathing Chimaera, part lion, part goat, part serpent. With the aid of the winged horse Pegasus he succeeded, and returned, after completing other tasks set by Iobates, to Xanthos where he married the king's daughter and became heir to the Lycian throne. Carried away by his success, Bellerophon tried to ride Pegasus up to Mount Olympos. For his presumption, Zeus sent a gadfly to tickle Pegasus, who threw him to earth; Bellerophon landed in a thorn bush, which put out his eyes, and he wandered the earth, blind and lame, to the end of his days.

satisfactorily explained, but if you care to make the half-hour climb up to the spot (on a well-marked trail), you will find it can easily be extinguished, only to relight itself after a few seconds. Apparently in ancient times it put on a better show. Nearby are the ruins of a temple (to Hephaestus, of course). Bellerophon didn't have to go far to reach the home of the gods: this Lycian Olympos, one of at least three mountains of that name and fame in Asia Minor alone, is now called **Tahtalı Dağ**, the highest peak of the Bey's mountains. The dramatic summit, 2,365m, can be reached by **cable car**, an awesome 10-minute ride high above cedar and juniper forests.

Cable car
runs summer every 30mins 9–7; winter hourly 10–6; return 40 YTL

Olympos is noticeably wetter and greener than the rest of the southern coast and can provide a welcome sanctuary from the oppressive summer heat. **Çıralı Beach**, a short walk through orange groves from the ruins, is set against a dramatic backdrop of cliffs and peaks that seem more Thai than Turkish. The coarse sand beach plays host to the odd colony of wicker umbrellas and sun loungers as well as egg-laying turtles from May to September.

Phaselis and Kemer

Beneath Tahtalı Dağ on the shore are the ruins of **Phaselis**, one of the foremost cities of Lycia. Founded by Rhodes in the 7th century, Phaselis often stood apart from its neighbours, even to the extent of supporting Mausolus against the Lycian League. Phaselitians, like the people of Side, had a reputation as schemers and cut-throats; once, desperate for cash, they offered Phaselitian citizenship for sale to all comers. They met their match when a real cut-throat, the pirate Zenicertes, sacked the town and made it his headquarters, *c.* 90 BC. The ruins today are all from the rebuilt city of Roman times. Its three harbours can be seen from the shore, and there is also a theatre, an aqueduct and a number of tombs. Phaselis, though lovely, is famous for being infested with hornets.

Beyond Phaselis, the highway passes more wonderful corniche scenery through mature Mediterranean pine forests. The broad curve of the Lycian shore ends as it began, with a village called **Kemer**, its name fittingly meaning 'band' or 'arch'. From here, Antalya is just over the horizon; Kemer has grown into a big, brash resort built around a new marina – a startling contrast to the relatively unspoiled parts of the coast that precede it.

Where to Stay and Eat from Üçağiz to Kemer

Üçağiz

A small collection of lovely, ramshackle *pensions* compete for business on the waterfront. Most offer a boat shuttle service to nearby bays.

Onur Pension, t 0242 874 2071, *www.onurpension.com* (€€). A great setting by the shore, with well-kept rooms and a decent restaurant.

Üçağiz has several restaurants, none of which stands out particularly, although their waterside settings are charming. In nearby Kaleköy the **Marina** (€€) is a good bet for seafood.

Demre

İpek, on the road to Baba Noel (€). The best of the many plain *lokantas* that Demre has to offer, serving good honest Turkish fare for 15 YTL.

Finike

(S) Anadolu, Sahil Yolu, **t** 0242 855 1665 (€€–€). You wouldn't think of Finike as a prime spot for a holiday, but, if you end up there, this can provide an agreeable stay by the beach; simple rooms with bath for 50 YTL.

★ Sundance Nature Village >>

Olympos

Kadir's Tree Houses, **t** 0242 892 1250, *www.kadirstreehouses.com* (€). A legend among backpackers; basic accommodation for around 40 YTL half-board, or less in dorms.

Bayram's, **t** 0242 892 1243, *www. olymposturkey.com* (€). A tree-house resort that organizes various adventure activities.

ⓘ Kemer
Belediye Binası (city hall), **t** *0242 814 1537*

Çıralı

Güneş Pansiyon, **t** 0242 825 7161, *www.gunespansiyon.com* (€€). Run by brothers Recep and Yasin, one of the best: little detached bungalows set in an orange grove just across from the tiny bridge; 70 YTL with breakfast.

Sundance Nature Village, **t** 0242 821 4165, *www.sundancecamp.com* (€€–€). Just across the water from Phaselis and in its own private, secluded bay, Sundance offers a selection of wooden lodges, tree houses (doubles 49 YTL half- board), simple bungalows (doubles 67 YTL) and healthy food in an unblemished setting topped off with ducks, kingfishers, horses and Mount Olympos in the background. For something truly off the beaten path, the independent traveller should make a beeline for here.

Çıralı Beach, near Olympos, has a fringe of rudimentary cafés and *lokantas*, where fish is good value.

Antalya and the Pamphylian Coast

In the twilight of the Aegean Bronze Age, a time when history passes into myth, the Greeks wrote of the 'mixed multitude of peoples' set in motion by the fall of Troy; many of these found their way to the land between the mountains of Lycia and Cilicia. Historians think it likely that settlement of this region actually preceded the breakdown of civilization in the 12th century BC. The Greeks later came to call this region Pamphylia, 'land of all tribes'.

Its ancient borders are marked by the two modern towns in the area, Antalya and Alanya. Its old cities, Perge, Side and Aspendos, all prospered on the fertile plain, becoming rich and Hellenized by the time Alexander came. Although their early history was more within the Hittite-Anatolian world than the Greek, they kept stories, some from Homer, of their foundation by the seers Mopsus and Amphilochus, who had been with the Achaeans at Troy.

Antalya

The coastal plain begins at Antalya, the Lycian mountains ending abruptly to form a spectacular backdrop for the city. Ten years ago, Antalya seemed well on its way to transforming itself from a sleepy old Selcuk town to a charming Mediterranean resort city, the capital of what people back then were fond of calling the 'Turkish Riviera' or the 'Turquoise Coast'. Somewhere along the way,

Getting to and around Antalya

The city's newly extended **airport** receives daily flights from Ankara and Istanbul and charters from abroad; it is connected to the centre (Cumhuriyet Caddesi) by Havaş shuttle buses (9 YTL) *www.havas.com.tr*. A taxi will cost about 30–50 YTL.

There is no rail service in the area. **Buses** between Antalya and all points are frequent (even to Istanbul, a 13hr trip). The new *otogar* is located 4km north of the centre on Kepez Altı, the main road to Burdur.

Within the city, most sites are within easy walking distance of each other; for the museum and Konyaaltı beach, it's easy to take a **dolmuş** or the **tram** down the main street to Konyaaltı Caddesi (called Cumhuriyet Caddesi in the centre).

---

however, things got out of hand. There are plenty of palm trees, and broad, fine beaches stretching away from the city on both sides, but Antalya can hardly be called a resort any more – it's Turkey's wealthiest and fastest-growing city, with a population already over a million. Antalya can still be fun: stay in a *pansiyon* in one of the restored old houses in the old centre, and take a big city break after all those ruins and beaches.

Unlike so many of the now-abandoned coastal cities, Antalya has been continuously occupied, so very little is left to mark its history. King Attalus II of Pergamon, given this stretch of coast by the Romans for safe-keeping in 188 BC, founded the city when Side refused to acknowledge his authority. Called Attaleia, it soon surpassed Side and the other Pamphylian cities, gaining further impetus under the Romans when Augustus settled a colony here in 6 BC. When Mediterranean civilization collapsed, Attaleia showed resourcefulness, setting up a fleet to defend itself against pirates, Arabs and occasionally the Byzantine taxman, and consequently survived in a reduced state despite the contraction of seagoing trade. Recovery came with the Selcuks in the early 13th century; although various Turkish tribes had already held stretches of coastline, the Selcuks were the first to develop the area, rebuilding Attaleia and Alanya and linking them to Konya with a string of caravanserais. The sultans often spent their winters here.

The Old Town

Most of old Antalya's walls were removed long ago, but their course is followed by two modern boulevards, **Atatürk Caddesi** and **Cumhuriyet Caddesi**, separating the old and new towns. Where these streets meet, a surviving bastion of the Selcuk wall has been converted into an odd **clock tower**. To enter the old town in style, walk a few squares along Atatürk Caddesi to the restored **Hadrian's Gate**. Its three arches are decorative, but hardly a solid link in a fortification; in Hadrian's time, the *Pax Romana* was so secure that it seemed cities would never again need real walls. In many places in Asia Minor there are purely ceremonial gates like these, or their ruins. This one was constructed for Hadrian's visit in AD 130, and there would originally have been a statue of the emperor on top.

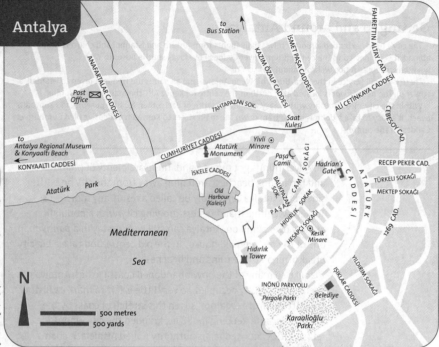

Antalya's old town is still a rather poor quarter, though many of its pretty Ottoman houses have been restored as *pansiyonlar* or restaurants, much as in Istanbul's Sultanahmet. Towards the southern end is the **Kesik Minare**, the 'broken minaret' struck by lightning long ago. The **mosque** it serves was originally a Byzantine church built in the 5th century, rebuilt and restored many times since. Heading further towards the sea, you come across a squat stone cylinder, the **Hıdırlık Tower**, believed to be the tomb of a 2nd-century Roman consul; traces of a carved fascia, symbol of the consuls' authority, can still be made out.

Surprisingly few Selcuk buildings remain in Antalya. The most important is the city's landmark, the **Yivli Minare** or 'grooved minaret', typically Selcuk in its heaviness of form. Its lobed shaft and stalactite balcony are unique. There are some surviving sections of the walls nearby, along with more lovely **Ottoman houses**. It's impossible to date the houses: the same style, with low tiled roofs, stucco or half-timber walls and second-floor balconies, continued for three centuries; some of them were actually built in the 1920s. An Ottoman mosque, the 16th-century **Paşa Camii**, is nearby, just behind the clock tower. At the eastern end of the old town, overlooking the sea, elegant **Karaalioğlu Park**, full of tea gardens, witnesses the nightly promenade of the Antalyalılar.

Another job of restoration – on a grand scale – has been performed on old Antalya's **harbour**, at the opposite side of the old town from the park. Only a few years ago this entire area (called **Kaleiçi**) was falling into ruins; the city's ambitious plan for saving it has won an international architectural award. Around the basin for yachts and other pleasure craft, roads, fountains, hotels, parks and terraced cafés have grown up; there are also streets of shops crawling with carpet salesmen, whose soft entreaties are drowned out each evening by the cacophony of hundreds of birds preparing to roost. At the top of the cliffs, on Cumhuriyet Caddesi, take a moment to admire the glory and grandeur of the most audacious, indescribable **Atatürk Monument** in all Turkey. May it stand forever.

Antalya Regional Museum

West of the old town, **Konyaaltı Caddesi** (called **Sarampol** by many locals, and on some minibus signs) heads towards the mountains, the long beach on one side, an equally long row of modern apartments on the other. About a mile out, it passes the **Antalya Regional Museum**. Of all Turkey's museums, this is the most attractive in its arrangement of exhibits, and the simplest for the visitor, with clear, multilingual explanations. It contains one of the largest and best collections in the country, with exhibits from the Stone Age remains from nearby Karain Cave, the earliest habitation yet discovered in Turkey, to a beautiful 6th-century relief of the archangel Gabriel. Greek and Roman sculptures fill several large halls. One great sarcophagus, carved in the form of a temple, portrays the labours of Hercules. Another held the remains of St Nicholas of Myra (tell the kids you've seen Santa Claus's grave). It's empty; merchants from Bari in southern Italy stole the body in 1087, and it remains there to this day, performing miracles for the faithful and oozing a mysterious holy goo that worshippers take home in tiny phials – just as it did in Byzantine times. Antique statuary in the collection includes a group of huge Olympian gods, and some equally large emperors (Hadrian, Septimus Severus and Trajan); a relief of the twelve Lycian gods; and a famous icon of the Artemis of Perge. Best of all is a remarkable, almost impressionistic scene of the underworld from a grave stele, hung behind the Hercules sarcophagus. The Byzantines are well represented in all periods. The final rooms have a very good ethnographic collection, with a special section on the Yürük nomads of Anatolia.

Antalya Regional Museum
open Tues–Sun 9–6; closed Mon; adm

Beaches

The long **Konyaaltı Beach** is a popular spot, barely visible from the street for all the restaurants, cafés and cabins. Still, there's room for all; you just need to go a little further out. Many visitors prefer the fine sand at **Lara Beach** 11km southeast of town. Here also are the **Düden Waterfalls**, plunging dramatically into the sea – when there's enough water; don't expect much of a show in summer.

Around Antalya

The northern road leads high up into the mountains from Antalya towards Burdur and Isparta. After 10km, at a crossroads, there is a choice. The right-hand route leads past a lovely forested picnic spot, **Düzler Park**, towards **Karain Cave**, where human remains some 50,000 years old were found. Beside the cave, which is a long climb up the mountain, there's a small museum.

Termessos

Up here in the mountains, we have left classical Pamphylia completely behind. Until Roman times, the influence of the Hellenized Greek cities never extended much beyond the coast; this mountainous region was known as Pisidia, the region of a fierce confederation of native Anatolian tribes who were better left alone. One of their greatest cities was Termessos, its ruins accessible on a road 26km down the left-hand fork from the crossroads.

The people of Termessos called themselves Solymians, giving the name to **Mount Solymos**, the formidable crag under whose shelter they built their city. King Iobates, as mentioned in the *Iliad*, sent Bellerophon against the Solymians and he served them just as he had the Amazons, bombing them into submission by hurling great boulders from Pegasus. Other would-be conquerors did not fare as well. The Termessians liked to brag they had defeated Alexander, who abandoned a siege here on his way to Sagalassus in 334 BC. Throughout the Hellenistic era the coastal cities were constantly at odds with the Termessians, and the Romans discreetly signed a treaty declaring the city 'friend and ally of the Roman people'. Termessos remained autonomous throughout the Roman period, not even bothering to put the emperor's picture on its coins.

The ruins, tricky to reach without a car, are well preserved but not excavated; the difficult mountainous site is an attraction in itself, altogether different from the coastal towns. Most of the ruins are from Roman times, and in no way unusual. There is a **theatre** in good condition, an **odeion** nearby, and a small indoor theatre that also served as a **bouleuterion**. Like Athens, Termessos has its **Stoa of Attalus**, in the **agora** just behind the odeion, built by the Pergamene king. The main thoroughfare, called **King Street** by the Termessians, touches the western edge of the agora on its way north, where it turned into a colonnaded street of shops, once lined with statues of prominent citizens. All these are gone, but the inscriptions tell us that many were champion wrestlers.

An outstanding feature of Termessos' remains, if you have the time to search them out among the bushes, is the large number of **tombs**, all around the slopes. Some are mere sarcophagi, others are elaborately built in the form of temples (the best are to the south). Most have inscriptions, some detailing the fines for grave robbing.

Where to Stay in Antalya

(i) **Antalya** >
Yavuz Ozcan Parkı,
t 0242 241 1747

Antalya

Antalya has some of the best hotels and *pansiyonlar* in Turkey. If you're not too fussed about being near a beach, Kaleiçi, the old citadel, is perhaps the most pleasing area: there are plenty of restaurants nearby, and many places have views of the harbour. There'll be no problem finding a reasonably priced hotel in the newer quarters or at Lara Beach.

*****Talya**, Fevzi Çakmak Caddesi 30, **t** 0242 248 6800, *www.divan.com.tr* (€€€€€). Antalya's oldest luxury hotel. Unlike many of its competitors, it feels no need to show off: instead it has a restrained elegance and wonderful ambience. It is set dramatically on a cliff top overlooking the sea just outside the old quarter of Antalya, with a pool as well as its own private beach at the base of the cliffs.

Konyaaltı and the more distant beaches have more than their share of five-star behemoths:

*****Adora Golf Hotel**, 30km east of Antalya at Belek, **t** 0242 725 4051, *www.adora.com.tr* (€€€€€). An impressive complex on a big beach with the best golf course in Turkey. There's every imaginable amenity in the rooms, many with sea view and balcony; besides golf, all sports from tennis to windsurfing are available.

(S) Marina, Mermerli Sokak 15, **t** 0242 247 5490, *www.marinaresidence.net* (€€€€). In the old quarter of Kaleiçi, this has gone to town on style. The reception area is an expanse of marble, covered with French-style furniture. There's a courtyard, with its swimming pool illuminated at night.

(S) Villa Perla, Hesapçı Sokak, **t** 0242 248 9793, *www.villaperla.com* (€€€–€€). An old house built around a pretty courtyard; it has a good restaurant too, favoured by locals.

Ninova, Hamit Efendi Sokak 9, **t** 0242 248 6114 (€€). Perhaps the best of the many excellent *pensions* in Antalya, in a quiet back street of Kaleiçi. The entrance hall of this old Ottoman house is very airy, opening on to a garden filled with free-range tortoises and trees laden with oranges, which you are welcome to pick when they ripen, in October and November. Rooms vary; all have air-conditioning.

Nearly all of the cheaper places are in the old town, and they fall into two categories: those in restored Ottoman-era houses, or modern *pansiyonlar* like those in Kaş or the other resorts, usually closer to the harbour.

Mavi and Anı Pansiyon, Tabakhane Sokak just off Hesapçı Sokak, **t** 0242 247 6373, *www.maviani.com* (€€). Among the *pansiyonlar*, readers have written in praise of this one; spotless rooms and filling breakfasts.

Özmen, Zeytin Çıkmazı 5, **t** 0242 241 6505, *www.ozmenpension.com* (€). Close to the harbour, this is one of the better modern resorts, run by friendly, helpful people: very cheap, very basic rooms with bath, and a roof terrace.

Look for campsites on the main road, between Kemer and Antalya.

Denizer Camping, **t** 0242 259 0874, at Sarısu. Fully equipped and by the sea.

Eating Out in Antalya

Kral Sofrası, down by the old harbour, **t** 0242 241 2198 (€€€). This is where Antalya's best seafood is served up at touristic prices. Despite grumpy service, locals aren't put off dining here, due to the quality of the food.

Stella's Bistro, Fevzi Çakmak Caddesi 3c, **t** 0242 243 3931 (€€). Near Atatürk Caddesi; you pay for the quality of the food and service, not the location. The menu has select dishes from around the world; Italian cuisine dominates.

Villa Perla, Hesapçı Sokak (€€). Also offers excellent food for those on a tighter budget, in an enclosed garden.

7 Mehmet Restaurant, Atatürk Kültür Parkı, **t** 0242 238 5200, *www.7mehmet. com* (€€). A large complex overlooking Konyaaltı beach; has become an institution. The *meze* dishes are varied and very well prepared.

Parlak, **t** 0242 241 6553, at the end of Kazım Özalp Caddesi, by the clock tower (€). Famous for its barbecued meats and cacophonous ambience.

Anis İşkembe Salonu, on the little pedestrian street of restaurants and cafés just across Atatürk Caddesi from the old town (Hesapçı Sokak entrance) (€). A good and cheap kebab house, extremely popular with the locals on this street for the tripe soup; also burgers and other heretical snacks.

Nightlife in Antalya

Many of the fancier hotels have chosen to be enclosed compounds, with their own clubs and discos. Visitors in town stroll around Kaleiçi and the back streets of the old town, where there are plenty of places for a quiet drink and opportunities to listen to live folk music. For club music, mainly house or eurotrash, people gather at the outdoor nightclubs, of which there a several, but take extra cash, as drinks can be very expensive. **Club Arma**, Kaleiçi Yat Limanı, t 0242 244 9710, *www.clubarma.com.tr*. Big and loud, with all the lasers you could wish for and a view over the harbour.

East from Antalya

The road east from Antalya does not follow the coast. It doesn't need to; the land is flat and there are farms, citrus groves and banana plantations on either side as far as Side. Much of this land is haunted with ruins, and it is no surprise to see an ancient column sticking up in a field or along a side road, not always easy to distinguish from the concrete aeration stacks of the irrigation systems. Except for Antalya and Side, all the ancient cities of this region were built inland, their ports being nothing more than a landing stage at the highest navigable point of the closest river.

Perge

Perge is only a mile from the highway. Claiming the Homeric figures of Mopsus and Calchas as its founders, Perge prospered throughout the Classical period and into Byzantine times. Though its ruins do not show a city of great size, its **theatre** could seat 15,000, as many as Side or Aspendos. Perge's most famous citizen, the mathematician Apollonius (3rd century BC), was a follower of Euclid who did important work with ellipses and conic sections, contributing much to Ptolemy's epicyclic theory of the universe.

The modern road to Perge passes between the **stadium**, one of the best preserved in Turkey, and the impressive **theatre**, before it reaches the car park at the main gate. The theatre retains part of its stage building, along with some of its sculpted friezes. In the stadium, the space facing the outside under the seats was rented out for shops, just as they are now in some modern Turkish stadia. Some of the runners' names and trades can still be read on the walls. The stadium seated fewer spectators than the theatre.

Perge's **main gate**, at the centre of the southern walls, is its outstanding feature – the Hellenistic inner gate, that is, which the Pergeans made into a grand ceremonial entrance. The outer gate, added in the 3rd century AD, is strictly utilitarian. Between the two, a large **courtyard** full of monuments and statues was flanked on one side by a colonnade and on the other by the propyla, a formal entrance to the baths, and the fountain or **nymphaion** that looked

Getting around East from Antalya

All the sites can be reached via the busy coastal road. If you don't have a car, **buses** and **minibuses** ply the Antalya–Side route with great frequency, so you'll never have long to wait. Side is the base for seeing the other ancient sites; its **taxi** companies make a business of such excursions, and post their rates on blackboards in town. All the turn-offs from the main road are marked with yellow signs; at some of these, such as Aspendos, taxis wait by the roadside to take in passengers descending from the minibuses. Prepare for some rough roads if you're heading for Sillyon, but there's no other way to see it than by car (a jeep would be better; currently there are not even any tours organized here on a regular basis).

Side's *otogar* is 300m from the tourist office, on the coastal highway towards the old town. The town has a unique service to get tourists in and out of town from it in summer – they load them in a wagon, pulled by a tractor; watching the bewildered, sunburned masses trundle by will make your day.

like the façade of a theatre. Many statues found here are now in Antalya's museum. To the two round towers of the gate still partly standing, the Pergeans of the 2nd century AD added another courtyard in the shape of a horseshoe, lined with statues of the city's founders. At that time, 'founder' did not necessarily mean one who had 'founded', but could be anyone who financed any great public improvement. And so, next to Mopsus and Calchas (the statues are gone but the inscriptions remain), there are such men as M. Plancius Varus and C. Plancius Varus, both identified here by their relationship to a woman – father and brother. This becomes less surprising when we get to know the lady. Plancia Magna, whose statue can also be seen in the Antalya museum, was a member of a talented family that had migrated from Italy to Perge and become wealthy through land-holdings. One of the men attained the office of Roman consul, and Plancia, as well as being a great civic benefactress, was also chief priestess of Artemis, the major cult of the city, and, for a time, even held the highest civic office in Perge, that of demiurge.

Great women in public life were not unknown in the ancient world, but for one so completely to dominate a town is exceptional. In Perge, as at Ephesus and so many other cities, the worship of Artemis, a Hellenized abstraction of the old Anatolian goddess Cybele, was far more important than that of any of the male gods. One of the archaeological puzzles here is where the Temple of Artemis, a building mentioned by many ancient writers, is located.

Compact and rectangular, Perge was cut into quadrants by two colonnaded streets and enclosed on three sides by walls, and on the north by a low hill that served as an acropolis, probably the original settlement of Perge. Little remains there now. The main streets had to be very wide, as the depressions in the centre of them between the columns were water channels, not for sewage, but probably just a unique civic embellishment.

Inside the walls most of the remains are early Byzantine, a time when Perge was still prosperous: there is the small Byzantine **basilica** next to the **agora**, adjoining the inner gateway on the

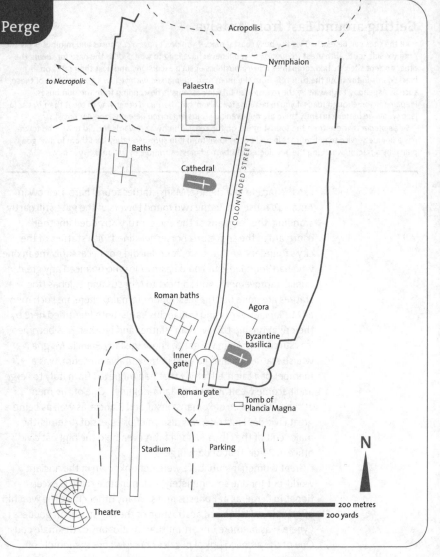

eastern side, and, further up the main street, on the left, the foundations of the **cathedral** remain; this may mark the spot where St Paul made his first converts. At the end, under the walls of the acropolis, was another **nymphaion**. Towards the west gate, the **palaestra** built during the reign of Claudius is one of the better-preserved structures.

Sillyon

Like Perge, Sillyon was first built on a low, defensible hill; you have to climb a bit to see what's left there. To reach it, take the sign-posted road to the north, 14km past Perge on the coastal road. It was never a very important town, managing to avoid most of the quarrels of its contentious neighbours, and appears in history only when Alexander passed through. The remains consist of foundations and streets and steps cut out of the rock of the hill. Some of the fortifications remain, including one complete square tower and a few well-preserved Byzantine buildings. A recent landslide swept away most of the theatre and all of the odeion.

Aspendos

The next ancient town, Aspendos, also lies north of the coast road on the banks of the Köprü Çayı, the ancient River Eurymedon. To get to the site, take a side road for 4km from the main road, passing a beautiful arched **Ottoman bridge**. In 468 BC the final battles in the long wars between the Persians and Greeks were fought here, resulting in such crushing defeat for the Great King that Persia finally abandoned its attempt to subdue the Greek world. In a single day, the boldness of the Athenian Admiral Cimon won two victories at once, on land and on sea. Both the Persian fleet and their army were concentrated at Aspendos for another assault on the Aegean. Cimon drew the fleet from its harbour in the Eurymedon, and defeated it in a day-long battle, capturing many of the Persian ships; not content with this, he dressed some of his small force of marines in Persian uniforms and sent them up the Eurymedon, where they created a diversion so that Cimon and the rest of his men, secretly landed up the coast, were able to disperse or capture the entire bewildered Persian army.

Aspendos and Side were usually the two leading cities of Pamphylia, and they never got on well with each other. After the Romans finally made them agree, Aspendos thrived until well into the Byzantine era; little is known of its eventual abandonment, although the wars and disruptions caused by the 7th-century Arabs certainly had much to do with it.

The Theatre of Aspendos

Aspendos has the best-preserved Roman theatre anywhere in the Mediterranean. This is no exaggeration; not only is the whole cavea intact, along with the arcade at the top, but the entire stage has survived. Credit is given to the Selcuks for some preservation, but no one yet knows what use they made of the building.

At the entrance, a door in the centre of the stage building, is a small **plaque** with a message from Atatürk; his government made restoration of this theatre its first major archaeological project, and the inscription records Atatürk's wish that the Turks should not 'lock it up like a museum piece', but use it for performances of classical drama – and wrestling. This is not so strange; throughout this part of Asia Minor, wrestling matches were commonly staged in the theatres. Plays are still produced for the September festival, but wrestling, as elsewhere outside Thrace, is increasingly rare. Whichever you would prefer to imagine, stepping inside the theatre magically transports you into the past, evoking the lost Graeco-Roman world in a way few ruins ever can. Not that it is a building of any great architectural distinction – no offence to Zeno, its architect (2nd century AD) – it is simply that it has survived.

All the theatres of the Pamphylian cities had stage buildings, as all of them were built in Roman times, after this innovation had come into vogue. Earlier Greek and Hellenistic theatres had been open, as at Epidauros in Greece, sited with a striking natural backdrop for the action in the skene and orchestra. Later, the plays moved up to a raised stage, or proskenion, and stage buildings were used both for manipulating the sets and props, and to shut out the outside world. Of the sculptural scheme, all that survives is a frieze of Dionysus, but on the right-hand side it's possible to make out some plaster with a red and white zigzag design. This has been identified as Byzantine work; there are similar designs in the castle towers of Alanya.

Aspendos has not been fully excavated, apart from the theatre, though there are remains of public buildings – a **stoa**, **bouleuterion** and **basilica** – around the **agora**; all the more substantial ruins are Byzantine. It's worth making the climb to see the **aqueduct**, one of the best-preserved examples anywhere, stretching from the hill of Aspendos across the plain to the distant mountains. Four long sections still stand. The two towers built into the curves of the aqueduct are a puzzle; engineers believe they contained basins that served to regulate the pressure and allow air to escape.

Back at the bottom of the hill, you may wish to visit the two **baths**, to the left of the theatre along the access road, and the half-buried **stadium**, to its right.

Selge

Another Pisidian city that can be reached from the coast, Selge was originally called by the very un-Greek name of Estlegiys; as it became Hellenized, it grew and prospered from the manufacture of storax gum, used as incense. Selge, set like Termessos in a difficult but beautiful mountain setting, has a big ruined **theatre** and **stadium**. It's out of the way, 34km north of the coast road to the village of **Beşkonak**; from there a track leads the last few kilometres up into the mountains, to the village of **Altınkaya** (locals call it Zerk). Nearby, a few kilometres north of Beşkonak, is a small, well-preserved **Roman bridge** over the Eurymedon, which serves as an introduction to the recently opened **Köprülü Kanyon National Park**, a natural wonderland of forests and waterfalls popular with whitewater rafters and hikers.

Side

All these cities, interesting as they are, must be taken only as a prelude to Side. First among the Pamphylian cities of antiquity, or so it boasted, Side now must be considered the first among Pamphylia's ruins; it was the first to be substantially excavated, and so a visit here will prove much more rewarding to the non-specialist. It also has a number of **beaches** offering every distraction, from windsurfing to paragliding.

In the 1890s, when Crete was freed from Ottoman rule, a community of Muslim fishermen came from the island to settle here. They built a village among Side's ruins, and resisted all attempts by archaeologists and the government to relocate them. The latter are still trying, but in the meantime the villagers have made the most of their opportunity, turning their town into one of Turkey's most improbable tourist traps. Its main street, full of ice-cream parlours, bars and trinket-stands, follows the route of old Side's colonnaded street, and the ancient residential quarters are filling up with hotels and *pensions*. It's pleasanter than it sounds. The beaches around Side's peninsula mainly attract Turkish and German families, the restaurants are good and the atmosphere relaxed (note that the beaches near the centre can be crowded and awful, and there's no public transport out to the good ones).

History

Cyme, the Ionian city near Smyrna, founded Side as a colony in the 7th century BC; it is thought that, despite the Greek colonists, Side remained very much the native Anatolians' city, using their own language which had been replaced everywhere else by Greek.

'*Side*' means pomegranate, and the fruit was often depicted on the city's coins, so many of which survive as to suggest great prosperity, lasting well into the 6th century AD. How they made their money is another matter. Sideans, even more than the rest of the Pamphylians, had a well-earned reputation as scoundrels, both in business dealings and in relations with other towns. In the 2nd century BC the city had an arrangement with the Cilician pirates and acted as their fence, circulating stolen goods and the pirates' captives. Until Pompey put the pirates out of business, Side ran a slave market that handled thousands of poor souls every day.

Despite this, the Sideans never fell foul of Rome. Most of the slaves ended up in Rome, and Sidean prosperity was not affected by the Roman takeover. By the 4th century AD, however, Side had so dwindled that it built a new wall near the theatre, reducing itself by half. After a revival in the 5th and 6th centuries, the depredations of the Arabs put an end to Side after a thousand years of urban life. Most of the inhabitants gradually resettled in Antalya.

Remains of the City

The modern road enters very near the ancient **main gate**, with a small semi-circular court just inside, like the one at Perge. The ruins just outside the gate belong to the **nymphaion** or fountain. Greek cities commonly had embellishments like this outside the gates, to water animals and/or to allow travellers to refresh themselves before entering the city. The long **aqueduct**, which passes through the wall's three towers to the right of the gate, carried the water to the nymphaion and from there into the city. Sections of the aqueduct in good repair can be seen for some distance north of the city, and its path inside the walls can be traced through the 'Quarter of the Great Gate', as the northernmost district by the baths and theatre is described in inscriptions.

Inside the gate, two **colonnaded streets** begin. That on the right, leading towards the theatre, was the main thoroughfare of Side, while the street on the left goes through the 'Quarter of the Great Guild', heading due south. Colonnaded streets like this were the status embellishment of Roman cities, shady arcades for business and shopping that gradually replaced the old Greek agoras as the places to see and be seen in. The two in Side, over a mile in length, testify to the great wealth of the city in Roman times; no other city in Asia Minor had as much. Most of the surviving structures in the Quarter of the Great Guild date from the Byzantine afterglow,

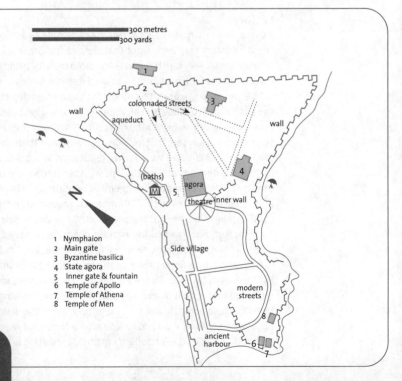

300 metres
300 yards

1
2
colonnaded streets
3
wall
aqueduct
wall
(baths)
M
5
agora
4
theatre inner wall
N
Side village
modern streets
8
ancient harbour
6
7

1 Nymphaion
2 Main gate
3 Byzantine basilica
4 State agora
5 Inner gate & fountain
6 Temple of Apollo
7 Temple of Athena
8 Temple of Men

Side

including a huge **basilica**, on the left side of the colonnaded street, a church, and an unidentified building off to the right.

Just before reaching the inner gate, the other street passes the **Roman baths** to the right and the large **agora** to the left. This was used in the 2nd century as the slave market, and it isn't difficult to imagine the crowds of woebegone captives chained to the columns. In the centre of the agora, the circular foundation and ruins belonged, quite fittingly, to the **Temple of Fortuna**. Another open square, the **state agora**, stands a few hundred feet to the east, near the old sea wall. As its name implies, it was the governmental centre of Side. Most of this part of the city is partially buried under sand dunes that have accumulated over centuries.

The baths, going back across the narrow neck of the peninsula, have been incorporated into the **Side Museum**, with an excellent collection based solely on the strength of what the archaeologists found here. There are lots of Roman statues, including some fine copies of earlier Greek works; reliefs of uniforms and weapons, found near one of the city gates, probably commemorate the spoils won in a victory over Pergamon, when King Attalus tried to conquer the Pamphylian coast. Some wonderful sarcophagi show the sentimental side of the ancient world's attitude to death.

The great arch of the **inner gate** still stands, simply because, at some later time, the citizens were compelled to wall it up, leaving a smaller entrance in the centre. It is thought that a statue of an emperor in his four-horsed chariot crowned the gate, hence the name of the neighbourhood, 'Quarter of the Quadriga'. In every Pamphylian city there is evidence of gradual impoverishment; marble façades on concrete, or sarcophagi reused and statue bases with the old inscriptions blotted out and new ones added. Here, the grand fountain to the left of the gate was originally a monument in honour of the Emperor Vespasian.

Here the **modern village** begins, built around the ruins of the old, down the colonnaded street to the end of the peninsula. The town is closed to traffic, but you may take your car if you're staying at one of the hotels. Side's well-preserved **theatre**, adjoining the inner gate and facing the agora, dominates the centre of the city. On this flat peninsula, with no natural hillside out of which to carve one, the Sideans had to erect a theatre in the air. The cavea, the largest in Pamphylia with room for 25,000 spectators, was raised on an impressive system of vaults and arches. A four-foot wall was built around the bottom row of seats in Roman times, to seal off the orchestra when combats and wild beast shows began to shove drama off the stage. The remains of two chapels, on either side of the stage building, and some inscriptions indicating seats reserved for priests, reveal that in the early Byzantine era it was used as an open-air church (note the crosses carved over entrances). The

Side Museum
open Tues–Sun 8–12 and 1–5; closed Mon; adm

Theatre
open daily 8–5; adm

11 The Southern Coast | Antalya and the Pamphylian Coast: Side

sculptural reliefs, probably scenes from the myths of Dionysus, are so completely effaced that early Christian vandalism is suspected.

Once in the modern town, you're on your own trying to find the other homes, baths and temples of old Side. The newer buildings, in and around the ruins, exasperate the archaeologist but make a picturesque setting. Unfortunately, in the last few years so much has been built inside the inner wall that it becomes increasingly difficult to trace the ruins; many have been fenced off into gardens. Some of the more important of the city's temples have been excavated at the very tip of the peninsula overlooking what was once the **harbour**. There are no natural harbours on the Pamphylian coast and Side, the foremost port city, was forced to make one out of almost nothing and dredge it continuously. 'A harbour of Side' became a figure of speech, like the labours of Sisyphus, for any unending task. Just where the water's edge once was, the platforms of the **Temple of Apollo** and the **Temple of Athena** are visible; the surrounding ruins belonged to a huge Byzantine basilica built over the temples. Part of the columns and architrave of Apollo's temple have been reconstructed. Behind these, in what must have been a square at the end of the colonnaded street, are more ruins, of a Byzantine fountain and a temple (3rd century AD) devoted to Men, an Anatolian moon god.

Attractions near Side

While in Side, avoid all proffered excursions to the **Manavgat Falls** in the mountains above Side, unless you need more souvenirs or the prospect of a three-foot waterfall excites you. Leaving the town on the way to Alanya, you pass two well-preserved caravanserais of the Selcuks: at **Şarapsahan**, 15km west of Alanya on the coast, and **Alarahan**, on the side road 9km up in the mountains. Şarapsahan is fortified, testifying to the uncertainty of the sea lanes even in the best days of the Selcuks. Near Alarahan, the **Alara Castle** is a steep climb, but gives a spectacular view over the valley. Five km before Alanya, the highway department has constructed one of its **roadside beaches**. A steep embankment had to be built for the road, 100 feet above the sea, so they simply added steps and built dressing rooms into the side. The effect is one of perfect isolation.

Where to Stay in Side

ⓘ **Side >**
on the coastal highway at the turn-off for the town, t *0242 753 1265*

Side

Side has over 25,000 beds, but the trick is to get one that is convenient for the beach, the town and the ruins while being quiet enough to allow you a peaceful night's sleep. With this in mind, follow the main street down to the harbour and bear left at the 'mosque' sign. Walk on into a bewildering array of side streets and several good, moderately priced hotels and *pensions* will present themselves.

*******Asteria Oteli**, t 0242 753 1830, *www.asteriahotels.com* (€€€€). Claimed to be the best in the town by locals. Three km out of town on the western beach, it has cavernous air-conditioned rooms with satellite TV, swimming pools, including a heated one indoors, and plenty of facilities. From €180/360 YTL full board.

****Hane, t 0242 753 2445, *www. hanehotels.com* (€€€). 6km west of town, with a good stretch of beach and a pretty park, and comfortable air-conditioned rooms; a little distant, but it has everything you'll need.

Hanımeli, Turgut Reis Sokak, t 0242 753 1789 (€€). A beautifully kept old house in a garden. A bit expensive for a *pansiyon*, but worth it.

A fair number of *pansiyonlar* are sprinkled around the village, almost all family-run places where the owners take some pride in keeping the place up (they're a bit more expensive than other towns, though, averaging about 70 YTL); those on the eastern shore boast a view of Side's Famous Sunrises, while westerners tell you about the view of Side's Famous Sunsets.

Nar Pansiyon, Nergiz Sokak, t 0242 753 1201, *www.naraparts.com* (€€–€). Basic, clean and well run in the centre.

Eating Out in Side

Moonlight Restaurant, t 0242 753 1400 (€€€). With outdoor terrace on the waterfront: for a seafood dinner without breaking the bank. The menu includes shrimp and octopus, and a full dinner can be had for around 50 YTL. But the wonderful waterside setting is the main draw here.

Orfoz Restaurant, at the end of the harbour (€€€). For whatever seafood has been netted that day – from red mullet to barbecued squid. Their specialities include king prawns. The food is good as is the atmosphere.

Agora Restaurant, Turgut Reis Caddesi (€€€–€€). Here the sea laps against the walls. It has been serving seasonal fish dishes for almost 30 years.

'Rough' Cilicia

This coastal province is ready-made for tourist brochures; the historical background is as good as even the wildest imaginings of a copywriter. Mark Antony did indeed present Cilicia to Cleopatra as a love gift – though not just for the sensuous coastal scenery or the forests and peaks of the beautiful Taurus mountains. Cleopatra, always a sharp girl, chose in this case not to see the forest for the trees. Cilicia's timber happened to be Egypt's biggest import, and the queen simply wanted to get it wholesale. Besides, these two lovers had a navy to build.

Half of Cilicia is difficult country; the ancients commonly referred to the western portion as 'rough Cilicia' and the eastern as 'smooth Cilicia', the latter a plain created by deltas of several rivers around present-day Adana. Both sections have always lacked big towns and culture; rough Cilicia because there's nothing but mountains and trees, and smooth Cilicia partly because of its location on a major medieval conqueror's highway through the Cilician Gates, and partly because of the mosquito: malaria was a problem until recent times. Few of the armies that passed through ever felt inclined to stop, and history has mostly avoided both the Cilicias.

Rough Cilicia, impenetrable and indeed almost unknown to the Greeks and Romans, enjoyed its best hour just a century before Antony and Cleopatra had their fling, as the most notorious pirate's nest in the entire Mediterranean. Following the example of Tryphon the Voluptuary, a governor of Kalonoros who turned to piracy after an unsuccessful revolt against the Seleucid King Antiochus, the Cilician pirates ruled the waves for a hundred years until the Romans decided to wipe them out; in 67 BC, they sent Pompey in with ships and money, and within six weeks the great Roman general had killed, coerced or bought off the lot of them.

Piracy made a comeback with the Arab invasions of the 7th century and Cilicia, never really prosperous at the best of times, degenerated into a beautiful wasteland. Ottoman rule did nothing to help, and until the Turkish republic Cilicia remained the poorest, most backward and disease-ridden corner of western Anatolia. In the last 40 years, the change has been dramatic. Modern Turkey's extensive water projects have turned the once-useless coast into a garden of citrus and banana groves, with cotton the major crop on the plains of Adana.

Alanya

Alanya

In Alanya, the 'pearl of the Turkish Mediterranean', not agriculture but tourism has accomplished the work of transformation. In ancient times writers sometimes included this city in Pamphylia, sometimes in Cilicia. Its great rock of a peninsula, which the Greeks called **Kalonoros** or the 'beautiful mountain', makes a natural boundary stone between the two provinces; it protrudes from the sea like a great turtle's head, the beaches to either side curving away like huge flippers and the mountains rising behind forming its carapace. Today, with some 250,000 residents and a similar number of tourists, Alanya is by far the most important town between Antalya and Mersin. It also has some of the best beaches along the southern coast, but Alanya is a town worth visiting in its own right; no brash upstart of a resort, it has memories going back to antiquity, and monuments left by the cultured Selcuk sultans.

History

Like the rest of Cilicia, ancient Coracesium only got in the news when pirates were using it as a base, as in the time of Tryphon the Voluptuary. But even in the worst times, the rock of Kalonoros continued to be inhabited. It is an almost impregnable position, as Alâeddin Keykubad discovered when he tried to take the citadel in 1220. There are various stories of how he finally got in; one has him marrying the commander's daughter and taking the whole family back to Konya, while another says that, in a final desperate move, he had his men tie torches to the horns of thousands of goats and drive them up the hill at night, tricking the defenders into thinking a great army was coming after them (one imagines they would have found the battle cry somewhat suspicious). The most plausible version has Alâeddin making a deal with the Armenian

Getting to and around Alanya

Alanya has no air or rail connection; regular **buses** travel to points along the coast and inland to Konya. **Cruise ships** call often in the summer, and there is also a **ferry** service to Girne (Kyrenia) in the Turkish Republic of Northern Cyprus, only a 3½-hour trip (no cars; the car ferry goes from Taşucu further along the coast to the east). In summer it usually runs daily, Wed–Sat, off-season only erratically, and it's becoming an increasingly popular trip for Alanya vacationers. (The Northern Cypriots will not stamp your passport, so don't worry about harassment if you pass through Greece later.) Around the harbour you'll see plenty of **boat tours** on offer, to the caves and other sights around the mountain that are inaccessible by land; the average rate is about 50 YTL per person.

As in Antalya, the coastal road is also the main thoroughfare of the town (called Atatürk Caddesi following the western beach and Keykubat Caddesi along the eastern beach); the **dolmuşes** can take you to any point along the beaches. There's a **city bu**s service from the harbour up to the citadel, with stops all along the way. Alanya's *otogar* is a mile outside town, just off Atatürk Caddesi near the western beach; there's a dolmuş service to get you there.

prince who held Kalonoros – offering him another piece of land instead, and saving them both the trouble of a siege.

Alâeddin renamed the city after himself, 'Ala'iyeh', and Atatürk, during his Westernizing campaign, changed it to the more euphonious 'Alanya'. For a while after the Selcuk decline Alanya belonged to the French Lusignan kings of Cyprus, a relic from the Crusades. With the most beautiful setting along the southern coast and endless beaches, Alanya has become a major resort, especially popular among the Germans but seeing more people from Britain every year. The lower town around the harbour and the coastal highway past the beaches on either side (those west of the citadel are less popular and less crowded) are all full of tourist clutter. The Alanyalılar take refuge, as they have done from so many other invaders, up in the lovely old neighbourhoods around the citadel.

The Red Tower (Kızılkule)

In the harbour, beside the fish restaurants, camel rides, cruises to everywhere and terraced tea gardens, you'll find the Red Tower, Alanya's landmark since Alâeddin built it in 1226. The government completely restored this octagonal 115ft bastion in 1955, and now it houses a small **ethnographic museum**.

The top floor, crenellated for cannons, offers a fine view of the city. Note how the floor is sloped with channels towards the middle – the centre of the building is one great cistern. This purely functional defensive work nonetheless ranks among the highlights of Selcuk architecture. It was constructed to protect the **Tersane** (naval dockyards) built at the same time; the two are joined by a short stretch of wall now surrounded by gardens. From the start, the Selcuks aimed to become a force at sea as well as on land, but as they never had enough time to really get under sail, the birth of Turkish seapower was deferred until the Ottomans, some two centuries later. The enclosed dockyards, connected by archways, are a cool, quiet and interesting place to visit. The other side of the

Red Tower ethnographic museum
open Tues–Sun 8–12, 1.30–5.30; closed Mon; adm

yards is protected by another tower, the **Tophane**, literally the 'cannon house' – an arsenal.

On Kalonoros

The Red Tower also guarded the approaches to the citadel. From here the modern road climbs up through the **main gate** with its Selcuk inscription (in Persian, the language of Alâeddin Keykubad's court) past old Ottoman-style houses and gardens. The grandest of these, conspicuous on the lower slopes, was restored by a former American ambassador to Turkey. Where the road passes through the second level of the fortification, traces of the original Hellenistic-era wall may be seen underlying Alâeddin's work; just to the right is a small Byzantine chapel, with the walls carefully built around it.

Further on, the road skirts the **Ehmediye**, a section of old Alanya within the walls that has survived as a charming and serene quarter, overgrown with plane trees and flowers among the stone walls and venerable cottages. At its centre are a *bedesten* and caravanserai built by the Selcuks (now a hotel), with an unusual tomb, the 1230 Aksebe Türbesi, and also the fine 16th-century **Sülemaniye Mosque**. Tourism has touched the Ehmediye only slightly. If you clamber up these ramparts in the early evening, once the tour groups have gone for the day, you can sit on the walls with the swallows wheeling around you. The first muezzin's call drifts up faintly from the city below; another starts up from the other side of town; then another. Before long the air is filled with a medley of distant voices calling the faithful to prayer.

İç Kale
*open daily
8–sunset; adm*

A few hundred yards further on and the road reaches the **İç Kale**, the inner fortress. Once reached, a quick look down suffices to explain why the citadel was never taken. Most of the buildings around the İç Kale have gone to ruin; some are certainly part of the palace or governor's residence that existed here; another building with extremely thick walls can only have been a magazine. Best preserved, surprisingly, is a **Byzantine church** that may be as early as 6th century. Inside, there are still remnants of the original frescoes on the walls. The four Evangelists must have been the theme on the pendentives, for on one a lone, fading Evangelist, his attributes gone, can still be seen poring over his book.

Most of the citadel walls have been restored. In one corner, called the **Adam Atacağı**, a platform has been erected for the view; condemned criminals were thrown off from here, according to a highly improbable local legend. The Adam Atacağı looks out over a narrow spit of land extending southwest from the rock of Alanya called **Cilyarda Burnu**, on which stand the ruins of a tower, a Byzantine monastery and chapel, and a building the Turks call the **Darphane**, or mint. There is no way of getting there on foot, but boats in the harbour take trippers to the rock and to other spots around it: the huge **Pirate's Cave** and a phosphorescent cave, among others, and of course you'll be shown the little secluded beach where Cleopatra took her dip in the ocean.

One final cave, the best of all, can be reached from near the beaches to the west of the rock. **Damlataş Cave**, with its forests of stalagmites in delicate colours, was discovered only in 1948. Most visitors come just to look, but sufferers from bronchitis and other ailments find its mixture of radioactivity and high humidity to have curative properties. Not far from the cave, the **Alanya Museum** contains local archaeological finds. **Market** day in Alanya is Friday, and it takes place on Tevfikiye Caddesi, north of Atatürk.

About 35km west, Alanya has spawned a new baby resort, around the broad sandy beach at **İncekum**. The Alanya tourist office is currently trying to promote the *yaylalar* (summer pastures), the lovely hills north of the city, as a day trip destination – if only for a picnic, as the Alanyalılar themselves are fond of doing – but there's no public transport and you'll need a car to get around. One spot that can almost be reached by dolmuş is the scenic valley of the **Dimçay**; the minibus will take you to the mouth of the stream, 6km east of town, but from there it's a trek of over 10km up to the dam, where there is swimming and restaurants. Directly north of Alanya, there are a number of picnic sites in the *yaylalar*, pine forests, and some charming villages: **Mahmut Seydi**, with an interesting Selcuk mosque, and **Türktaş Köyü**, with a little waterfall nearby.

Alanya Museum
open Tues–Sun 8–12 and 1.30–5.30; closed Mon; adm

Where to Stay in Alanya

(i) **Alanya >**
Damlataş Caddesi, across from the museum,
t 0242 513 1240

Alanya

Alanya is the land of the three–four-star package hotel; there are over a hundred. Prices are all officially about the same (about 110 YTL in season, but big discounts can often be managed) but there is a great difference in the amenities. Apart from Bedesten, you'll never be far from a beach.

*****Grand Kaptan**, Oba Göl Mevkii, 3km west of the city, **t** 0242 514 0100, *www.kaptanhotels.com* (€€€€ full board). Everything you could ask for, including a private beach, watersports, and air-conditioned rooms with a sea view and balcony.

(S) Bedesten, up on Kalonoros, **t** 0242 512 1234 (€€€). A remodelled caravanserai that has been beautifully restored. Rooms are dark and musty but, with walls several feet thick, a good night's sleep is guaranteed. There is an outdoor pool.

****Panorama Hotel**, Keykubat Caddesi 30, **t** 0242 513 1181, *www.panoramahotel.com.tr* (€€). A 10min walk east of the Atatürk statue, and right on the beach: you can stagger out of your room in the morning and plunge straight into the sea; pool, tennis and most watersports on offer.

***Yunusgücü**, Atatürk Caddesi, **t** 0242 513 3002 (€€). The archetypal Turkish resort hotel, from the little flags flying out front to the forgettable restaurant, but it's a good bargain, with air-conditioned rooms and a pool.

***Galaxy Beach Hotel**, **t** 0242 545 3801 (€€). A less expensive choice nearby; a simple place with a pool.

***İkiz**, off Atatürk Caddesi on the west beach, **t** 0242 513 3155, *www.ikizotel.com* (€€). Just fine if all you want is a quiet room with a small balcony close to the beach.

Saray Hotel, Hacı Hamidoğlu Sokak, **t** 0242 513 2811 (€). Near the west beach, simple, acceptable and cheap.

İncekum

Plenty more of the same here.

Aspendos, Avsallar Mahalle, t 0242 517 1004, *www.aspendoshotel.com* (€€€). Sleek and modern-looking, with a big pool, tennis courts and private beach; rooms are looking a little dated.

Eating Out in Alanya

Just walk down to the centre of Alanya, between Atatürk/Keykubat Caddesi and the harbour, and you'll find dozens of places to choose from, nearly all of them good, inexpensive and simple. İskele Caddesi, along the harbour, is crammed with the usual fish restaurants, averaging 50 YTL for a three-course meal.

For a country outing, take Keykubat Caddesi out nearly 6km and take the turn-off left for the valley of Dimçay; all the way up the road into the mountains are picnic spots and nice, informal restaurants under the trees that serve fresh trout and barbecue.

Gaziantep Köy Sofrası, close to the port, t 0242 513 4570 (€). Grills a nice *tavuk şiş* (chicken), among a wide choice of other kebabs. Deservedly successful, they've opened up a second and third branch around the corner; meals average 18 YTL.

İnegol Köftecisi, İzzet Azakoğlu Caddesi (the Kordon) (€). For about the same price, you can sample liver kebabs and other soul food.

Nightlife in Alanya

Like Side, Alanya is mostly a family resort, and nightlife is limited to a few discos, the occasional karaoke bar, and clubs that entertain Russians and Germans with belly-dancing displays – as '*Türkische Bauchtanzerei*' it doesn't seem quite so exotic. For intrepid disco dancers, 5km east of the centre at Dimçay Mevkii is the best area to visit for stomping sounds: **Auditorium**, *www.auditoriumclub.com*, an open-air disco, rocks until the early hours.

Alanya to Silifke

Leaving Alanya for the east, the Cilician coast road follows the beaches for some distance before the steep slopes of the Taurus, plunging directly into the sea, compel it to climb into a spectacular corniche that runs all the way to Silifke, bordered by thick pine forests that in summer exude an almost overwhelming fragrance. The Turkish forestry service takes good care of these, the most extensive forests in the country, and no knowledge of Turkish is needed to understand the signs, posted every few hundred feet, warning about forest fires: 'One tree can make a million matches, and one match can kill a million trees'. In summer, the pines will be full of cicadas, yammering away. The Turks are very fond of them; children keep them as pets, and it isn't unusual to see a grown man pick one off a tree and put it on his shoulder for company.

In this region, towns are few, but the entire coast is littered with ruins: Byzantine buildings and churches near the shore, and crumbling fortifications of different ages on the heights.

Castles along the Shore, and Anamur

All along this wonderful drive there are ruins to distract you, either a few kilometres up in the hills or directly on the shore. Few of the sites really have much to show, like **Laertes**, 11km east of Alanya, or **Seydra**, another 6km after that. The next site, **Iotape**, is

Getting around between Alanya and Silifke

If you're **driving**, avoid the coastal road at night. It twists and turns fiendishly and there are few crash barriers; one mistake and you're over the cliffs. Besides, during the day you can enjoy the scenery, some of Turkey's loveliest. The one route inland, through the Taurus Mountains to Konya, is equally picturesque, following the Göksu valley from Silifke. **Buses** travel along the coast every hour or so (6½ hours from Alanya to Silifke; pack some sandwiches).

Anamur is a sprawling town and it is difficult to see all the sites in the area without a car.

From Taşucu, the **car ferry** to Girne (Kyrenia) in northern Cyprus leaves at midnight daily in season, Monday–Friday; there are also frequent **hydrofoils**. If your passport is stamped in Girne, you may need to get a new one should you want to go to Greece. This is less of a problem these days, but just to be on the safe side, ask for a stamp on a separate sheet of paper instead.

a little better; built on a small promontory, it has substantial ruins of a bathhouse, and a good beach below the cliffs.

The best part of the drive begins at **Gazipaşa**, a fishermen's town with a beach near the ruins of an ancient town named **Selinus**. Twenty km further, at the boundary between Antalya and İçel (Mersin) provinces, another beach runs along the edge of a narrow enclosed plain full of banana fields. The village of **Kaladiran** nearby stands in the shadow of a ruined Hellenistic castle.

The first town of any size is **Anamur**, on a plateau of greenhouses. The town itself has little that is noteworthy, apart from two Turkish flags roughly the size of tennis courts fluttering high above the main road through town. There is a beach, devoid of watersports, 5km south at its suburb of **İskele**. Nearby, at the cape now called Anamur Burnu, the southernmost point of Cilicia, is what's left of **Anemourion**, a town founded in the late Hellenistic era. Its ruins seem shabby compared with the towns of Pamphylia – no marble, only the dark conglomerate that archaeologists call 'pudding stone' – but they are substantial: a church and the arcades of an aqueduct on the hillside, with a castle on top. Near the beach, there are towers and ruined tombs. Some of the mosaics unearthed at Anemourion can be seen in the small **museum** in İskele. A mile or so to the east, the 12th-century **Castle of Anamur** was built on the shore by the kings of Little Armenia, in a peaceful setting between two long beaches. The castle is almost completely intact, though not through any virtue in its construction; the Ottomans kept it in good repair after the British occupied Cyprus, and used it as a fortress in the First World War. The small mosque inside is still in use.

The coast road continues east, climbing ever higher up and down the edge of the Taurus. On the very clearest days, they say that the mountains of Cyprus, some 50km to the south, can be seen. **Softa Kalesi**, on a peak just after the holiday village of **Bozyazı**, was also built by the Armenians. 'Softa', in Turkish, means a 'student of theology', and the castle probably got its name from the chapel, still visible from the road below. On this stretch, there are several isolated beaches, but near **Ovacık** the road cuts inland for a while, up the forested **Akdere** (White Valley) and back.

When it returns to the sea, the road reaches its crescendo of scenery just before the plain of Silifke, at **Bogsak**, a pretty bay with beaches and the ruins of a medieval fort; this, and the crumbling chapel on the bay's islet, was built by the Knights of St John. While this order still occupied Rhodes and Bodrum, its fleet often gave it control of all the southern Turkish coast. **Taşucu**, an old village with a good harbour, has developed into a small and unpretentious beach resort; it's the ferry port for Girne in northern Cyprus.

Silifke

Lest we forget him, Alexander the Great left 'Alexandrias' all over three continents, and his general Seleucus I Nicator, who grabbed the lion's share of the empire after his death, founded the Seleucid Kingdom of Persia and Syria and bedevilled mapmakers with new 'Seleucias' all over the Middle East. Most have long ago fallen to ruin. One survived, and almost kept its name. Ancient **Seleucia ad Calycadnos**, once a great, thriving city, has been whittled down by the years to plain Silifke on the Göksü, a piquant and humble Turkish town. There are no signs of Seleucia apart from a single standing Corinthian column with a stork on top, and traces of a theatre south of the Göksü, but a Byzantine castle still peers down from the nearest crag, and on a slight rise near modern Silifke, in the east of the Göksü plain near the coastal highway, stand the ruins of a Byzantine religious complex the Turks call **Meryemlik**, with the once-great church of **St Thecla**. This saint was the first girl to throw over her fiancé for a life of asceticism, and later became the first female Christian martyr. Foundations of a colonnaded building that was once part of the monastery remain, as well as the apse of the large basilica. Beneath it, recent excavations have uncovered a cavern, later carved into a chapel, where early Christians hid. There are bits of mosaics and frescoes in the chapel, now a small museum for architectural sculpture from Silifke.

The Göksü, though a poor excuse for a river outside the spring floods, once changed the course of European history. The Germans like to think of their old Barbarossa, Kaiser Frederick I of the Holy Roman Empire, as asleep under his mountain, like King Arthur. By 1190 Barbarossa had made the empire a going concern, the most powerful state in Europe; he was on his way to the Holy Land to teach the Saracens a lesson when he met his match in the Göksü. According to the chroniclers, he unaccountably fell off his horse in the stream and drowned before anyone could reach him, in just six inches of water. The crusade was aborted, and German unification was postponed by 700 years. Upstream from Silifke, a small plaque marks the spot in the lovely Göksü gorge along the road to Konya.

Where to Stay between Alanya and Silifke

This area is not well travelled, and accommodation options are limited.

Melleç

Melleç restaurant, t 0324 824 2060, http://mellecpansiyon.anamuronline. com (€). Above a small deserted beach on the coastal road between Gazipaşa and Anamur, this restaurant also rents out basic bungalows and rooms.

Anamur

**Anemonia, at the easternmost edge of the beach at İskele, t 0324 814 4000 (€€). Clean, quiet. In season, turtles lay their eggs on the beach in front of the Anemonia: hence the lack of sun-loungers and streetlamps at night. The hotel's private beach is a cul-de-sac, bounded to the east by the 'Dragon River', so called because in the days before bridges many attempting a crossing were swallowed up and swept out to sea by it.

Eser, İnönü Caddesi 6, İskele, t 0324 816 4751, www.eserpansiyon.com (€). Run by two retired English teachers and their son, a very pleasant, family-friendly place right by the beach.

There are two good campsites, both with restaurants – and mosquitoes. **Yalı Mocamp**, İskele, t 0324 814 3474. On the beach, with several basic rooms (€) to let to non-campers. **Pullu Orman İçi Dinlenme Yeri**, t 0324 827 1151. 6km out of Anamur in the forests, but still near a beach.

Bozyazı

Hotel Zeysa, Ada Karşısı, t 0324 851 2051, www.hotelzeysa.com (€€). A modest family-run guest house set just a little way from a small beach.

Taşucu

*****Best Resort Hotel, t 0324 741 6300, www.bestresorthotel.com.tr (€€€€). By far the most luxurious accommodation in the area, with large, comfortable rooms overlooking the harbour. It's right on the shore; no beach, but the huge pool more than makes up for this. With a little per-suasion, the ludicrously priced rooms should drop to under 150 YTL.

Lades Motel, Atatürk Caddesi 89, t 0324 741 4008, www.ladesmotel.com (€€). Great value for money. It has a large swimming pool and rooms with fine sea views. It is also conveniently located for the Göksu Delta, a haven for birdlife; from mid-March, when migrations begin, the hotel is busy with birdwatchers from around the globe, particularly the UK.

Silifke

Hotel Göksu, Atatürk Caddesi 8, t 0324 712 1021 (€€). Although it seems stuck in a 1960s BOAC-like timewarp, the en suite rooms are very large and the service excellent. By the riverside.

Eating Out between Alanya and Silifke

Melleç

Wherever the road meets the shore on the way to Silifke, there is sure to be a fish restaurant, often no more than a few tables under the trees. Peer in the cooler and select your fish. **Melleç**, t 0324 824 2060 (€). Good and quite a bit cheaper than seafood restaurants in the resorts, with fish dishes for around 12 YTL.

Anamur

İskele has several good fish restaurants, where the prices are dependent on how good the catch was that morning. Anamur's delicious tea, ada çayı, made from sage flowers picked on the mountains, possesses innumerable healing properties. **Astor**, on the main T-junction, t 0324 814 1435 (€€). One of the best. **Ocakbaşı**, on the main highway next to the bus station (€). Mezes and good kebabs for 12 YTL per meal.

Taşucu

Babaoğulu, Atatürk Caddesi, t 0324 714 2041 (€) Across from the otogar, and much better than the dinginess downstairs would suggest. Head upstairs and you emerge into the height of provincial sophistication – a pleasant pine-clad room with ceiling fans. As well as meaty fare, there's a good selection of salads. If you get the waiters to tell you the prices, you can eat very well for under 10 YTL.

ⓘ **Silifke >>**
Göksu Mah., V. Gürten Bozbey Caddesi No.6, t 0324 714 5328

ⓘ **Anamur >**
second floor of the bus station, t 0324 814 4058

Uzuncaburç

 Uzuncaburç

Across rough Cilicia, there have been few opportunities to strike inland to look at the **Taurus Mountains**; most of the roads are unpaved and the region remains as isolated and wild as in ancient times. The Byzantines called this land Isauria, and, while its barbarous natives helped wreck the urban life of the coasts in the 5th and 6th centuries, in the process they themselves were becoming Christianized. By the 8th century they were producing Byzantine emperors, like Leo III, the famous Iconoclast.

In ancient times, the furthest Greek civilization ever penetrated into the Taurus was the mountain city of **Olbia**, founded in the 3rd century BC, known as Diocaesarea to the Romans and Uzuncaburç to the Turks. This is your chance for a mountain excursion. Not only are the ruins worth the 30km drive, but the road passes through a charming landscape of rolling, well-tended farmland, reminiscent of some corner of Italy. On the way are three **Roman tombs**, small temples in form, and almost entirely intact; two, at **Çifte Anıt**, are visible from the road, and one of these is an unusual two-level temple with an arched vestibule and Corinthian columns.

'*Uzuncaburç*' means 'tall tower', referring to the two 70ft Hellenistic towers, one in the city and another on a nearby hilltop. It's believed there were others, forming a communications system with the coast; messages were sent by flashing the sun off polished shields in a kind of Morse code. The city itself is a much more pleasant site than any on the coast in Pamphylia, a bucolic ruin shaded with walnut and fruit trees, with vineyards and goats.

Enter the city through the monumental gate, with corbels and niches for long-vanished statues, leading to the usual colonnaded street. Just outside the gate is the **theatre**, unexcavated and overgrown. The pride of the ancient city, the **Temple of Zeus Olbios** is the oldest structure yet discovered using the Corinthian order (3rd century BC). The capitals are mainly on the ground, though several columns have been re-erected; the proto-Corinthian design shows traces of the Ionic scrolls from which it evolved. An apse still stands at the east end, reminding us that the temple was later pressed into service as a church. The sculptural friezes have been gathered in the garden. Their cartoon lions, leopards, boars and bulls show a distinct decline from the best work of the Greeks, but have their own charm, reminiscent of the carvings in medieval cathedrals. From here, a crossroads of colonnaded streets will take you either to a rare, surviving arched city gate, or to the **Temple of Fortuna** (1st century BC), which, as fortune would have it, has now become a social club for goats. Outside the city, you can visit the large **necropolis** of tombs, some separate, some cut into the rock, and simple sarcophagi – many with the bones visibly still inside.

The Caves of Heaven and Hell

Back along the coast, a few km east of Silifke, feverish development has taken place at the beaches around **Susanoğlu**, **Narlıkuyu** and **Atakent**. Narlıkuyu boasts one curiosity: Turkey's smallest **national museum**, consisting only of one small room with a fountain and a famous relief of the Three Graces, Aglaia, Thalia and Euphrosyne, looking much as they do in Botticelli's painting. In the 4th century there was a Roman spa around the spring here.

The **Corycian caves**, Cennet and Cehennem, can be most easily and truthfully explained as two great holes in the ground. They're interesting enough for the Turks, who coined the names 'heaven' and 'hell' for them, and they so fascinated the ancients that an important sanctuary of unfathomable antiquity was maintained in Cennet; it may have hosted mysteries such as those in Eleusis, or perhaps an oracle – Delphi also had a 'Corycian cave'. **Cennet**, an enormous chasm difficult of entry, can be explored with the aid of a guide; at the bottom, the remains of the old sanctuary have been incorporated into a 5th-century church. The little church was never an important site for the Christians; apparently they hoped to keep the old pagan demons deep inside by building it there, like a stopper in a bottle. The chasm, turning into a cave, continues on with an underground stream, no one knows how far; many believe the stream flows to the spring of the Three Graces.

Cehennem cannot be entered at all, except by its multitude of birds; their chirping echoes weirdly through the chasm. Like its counterpart, it is enormous and bottomless. A team of alpinists went down recently, and found only the bones of the few unfortunates who had fallen in. To the Greeks, this was the lair of Typhon, the monster of monsters spawned by Mother Earth in revenge for Zeus's defeat of the Titans. Typhon actually defeated Zeus and dragged him here, from where he escaped only through the cunning of Hermes. Before succumbing to thunderbolts, however, Typhon managed to start a fine family; according to Hesiod, his offspring included the Hydra, the Chimaera and Cerberus; his grandchildren, the Sphinx and the Nemean Lion.

Kızkalesi

 Kızkalesi

In ancient days Kızkalesi was **Korykos**, never a large town, though it's remembered as the place where Cicero spent two years of his exile from Rome. In the 11th century, however, Korykos achieved prominence along with its sister settlement **Elaiussa-Sebeste** (modern **Ayas**) when the Rubenid kings of Little Armenia made it their capital.

This odd state, formed by an opportunist group of refugee nobles after the Armenian homeland was overrun by the Selcuks,

Getting to Kızkalesi

Kızkalesi is connected by frequent **bus** and **dolmuş** services to both Silifke and Mersin. The nearest airport is at Adana. Mersin has a **car ferry** service to Gazimağusa (Famagusta) in Northern Cyprus three times a week (Mon, Wed and Fri, 10hr crossing); the Taşucu–Girne **passenger ferry** is cheaper and faster.

managed to survive for three centuries by a system of alliances, first with the Crusader states, and later with the İlhanli Mongols, a remnant of the empire of Genghis Khan to which many states, both Christian and Muslim, paid tribute. By the 1200s, Little Armenia's nobles were heavily influenced by French culture, adopting feudalism and the ideals of chivalry. But life as a Christian principality surrounded by Muslims became increasingly precarious. In 1341 the state devolved through marriage to Guy de Lusignan, the French King of Cyprus. The last king of an independent Armenian state, King Leon VI, went into exile in Paris, where he was buried at St Denis in 1393.

Two decades ago, Kızkalesi was only a tiny fishing hamlet; now it has become the largest resort east of Alanya. Yet this is a resort with a difference. Foreigners are in the strict minority here and most visitors are families from the big cities of Anatolia, making Kızkalesi the most 'Turkish' of all the Turkish resorts. Those overseas visitors that do come have their chance to holiday in Turkish style, although it's worth remembering that certain Western holiday conventions – topless sunbathing for example, and excessive boozing – are simply not acceptable here. Kızkalesi has a nice beach, but there is more to the town than just sea and sand; it has two perfect Armenian castles and, within walking distance, some intriguing, barely touched historical sites.

The Armenians concentrated their military forces at the **Castles of Korykos**. These two large fortifications, which also served as their port, were begun by the Byzantine Admiral Eustachius; the Armenians enlarged and improved them, using lots of stone from nearby ancient cities, including an entire Roman gate rebuilt into the new wall. The smaller castle, called locally the Kızkalesi or **Maiden's Castle** (*see* box, right) stands romantically offshore on a small island; in the Middle Ages the Armenians joined it to the mainland with a causeway that enclosed their harbour, but today you either have to swim or hire a boat if you want to see it.

The **ruins of Korykos** begin from across the main road behind the land castle and continue for several kilometres along the coast, merging with the remains of Elaiussa-Sebeste before coming to an end in **Ayas**, where the apses of two large **basilicas** are clearly visible from the road. In some areas farmers have cultivated the land around the old stones; in other parts the landscape is wild and undeveloped and there is a ghostly pleasure in exploring the

The Castle of the Sparrowhawk

Marco Polo went all the way to China, and when he came back his neighbours in Venice didn't believe a word he said; they called him 'Mr Million', for what they thought were just a lot of wild exaggerations. He might have done better just to stay at home, following the example of one of the slipperiest travel writers of all time, the author of the medieval classic *Mandeville's Travels*. Nobody even knows who Mandeville really was – maybe an Englishman from St Albans or a Frenchman from Liège – and from all evidence he never set foot outside Europe, but merely drew on the works of real travellers and classical authors. But his book, written around 1375, was popular all over Europe and translated into many languages. When the first printing presses started up half a century later it became one of the first best-sellers. From it, many Europeans first learned about India and the Great Khan of Cathay, and that the world was round.

As a storyteller, Mandeville is hard to beat. One of the most elegant fairy-tales in his *Travels* comes from one of these castles, concerning the demise of the Kingdom of Little Armenia. In that country, he relates, there is 'an old castle that standeth upon a rock, the which is cleped the Castle of the Sparrowhawk'. He locates it near the city of Ayas, and undoubtedly means one of the Corycian castles. In the castle was a sparrowhawk on a perch, and 'a fair lady of faerie that keepith it'. To anyone who stayed there seven days alone without sleep, the lady would appear and grant a wish. A king of Armenia stood the trial, and when the lady appeared he announced he'd had enough of power and wealth, and demanded the lady herself. For such impudence she cursed him and his nation to unending strife and impoverishment, and Little Armenia withered ever after. Another knight, a Templar, stood watch with the sparrowhawk, and asked for a purse of gold that should never empty. The lady granted it, but told the knight it would mean the end of his Order, 'for the trust and the affiance of that purse, and the great pride that they should have. And so it was.' Other men fared better in the Castle of the Sparrowhawk, though Mandeville warns that any who fail and fall asleep will be forever lost.

Is the lady of this story the 'maiden' of Kızkalesi? Perhaps – though the Turks tell visitors a different, Sleeping Beauty-type story about a princess who, it was prophesied at birth, would die of a snakebite. Her father locked her up here, but the snake came out of a basket of fruit and got her anyhow.

---

ruins, identifying a house here, a cemetery there. Part of the site is given over to a huge **necropolis** dating from the 4th century AD, where there are rock tombs and ornate sarcophagi, some still with their lids, decorated with crosses, garlands and animals. In one area, some 6km north of the castles, a series of Roman-era **reliefs** is carved into the cliff – men, women, children and animals; probably this too is a funeral monument. You may chance upon these, and the necropolis, within 20 minutes of wandering, or you may search fruitlessly all day – it's that hard to find. If you're lucky, you'll meet a local who knows exactly where it is.

From Ayas, the road passes more ruins, of the ancient towns of Kanlıdivane and Soli, as the coastal plain opens outwards into the flatlands of Smooth Cilicia. **Kanlıdivane**, which means 'court of blood', is a fascinating place, built around a natural chasm that was used as a necropolis; stairs lead down, and there are fragments of tombs and reliefs at the bottom. Nearby is a well-preserved Hellenistic tower and an expanse of Byzantine-era ruins. **Soli**, originally a Greek colony, was probably happy to be re-founded by the Romans and renamed Pompeiopolis, in honour of the conqueror of the pirates. Soli had long been the butt of jokes for

Kanlıdivane
*open daily
8am–sunset; adm*

Where to Stay in Kızkalesi

****Altınorfoz**, Atakent beach, 17km from Silifke, t 0324 722 4211, *www. altinorfoz.com* (€€€; €€ out of season). The only top-class resort in the area. In a peaceful setting on a blue flag beach, it has air-conditioned rooms, a hamam and all watersports facilities.
****Kilikya**, t 0324 523 2115, *www. kilikyahotel.com* (€€ half-board). Has a large pool and boasts air-conditioned rooms with a view of the Maiden's Castle, friendly and helpful staff, and a broad stretch of beach in front.

Hotel Hantur, t 0324 523 2367, *www. hotelhantur.com* (€€). A good option if the Kilikya is full; it has what may well be the world's only stained-glass window of a snorkelling parrot.

Eating Out in Kızkalesi

Kilikya hotel restaurant (€€). The best of the many restaurants that swamp Kızkalesi. The house speciality is *tava*, a mix of meat, aubergines, spices, tomatoes and so on.
Güven Café, behind the Kilikya (€). Here you can eat for less without the sea view.

the clumsy way the inhabitants had of speaking Greek; the town gives us the word *soloikos*, or 'solecism'. The Turks call the site **Viranşehir**, or 'ruined city' – a common enough place name in this country. There is a good **beach** where people from Mersin come on weekends, and plenty of ruins; as at Side, you can trace the course of a once-impressive colonnaded street down to the harbour.

The Plains ('Smooth' Cilicia)

In the last 50 years, much to the surprise of its inhabitants, this region has made the remarkable transformation from being one of Turkey's very poorest areas to one of its richest. With the natural fertility of the soil, some intelligent planning and a double dose of DDT, the people of **Çukurova**, as the Turks call this plain, began with cotton fields and turned them into an enormous textile industry. Adana and its port Mersin, the two largest cities of the Çukurova, have grown from almost nothing to sophisticated, up-to-date cities full of palm-lined boulevards and modern office blocks.

Mersin (İcel)

Nothing in Mersin is very old or of particular interest, but the city is well built and attractive, with a lovely park running almost the entire length of its shore. Mersin has grown from nothing into a city of 650,000 over the last three decades, as the port for the busy textile industries of Adana and Tarsus. Ironically, it is one of the oldest towns in the world; remains of a 6,000-year-old culture, related to that of Çatal Höyük, have been dug from a mound called Yumuk Tepe, but from then to now, there have only been small settlements. Excavations at these have unearthed a few finds, from the Hittite to Byzantine eras; see them in the town **museum**.

Getting to and around the Plains

There are daily **flights** to Adana from Istanbul and Ankara, and the city is also connected by **rail** with those cities. The **railway station** is half a mile north of Adana city centre on Ziya Paşa Bulvarı.
Adana's and Mersin's bus stations (*otogar*) are both some way out of town and you'll need to take a taxi in. Within the cities there should be no need for transport; all are small and centralized. In Adana, you can buy intercity bus tickets in offices on the Turhan Cernal Berıker Bulvarı near the tourist office, which then entitles you to a free ride out to the *otogar*.

The most astounding sight in Mersin, though, is a 650ft luxury hotel; inexplicably thrown up in the centre of town, it stands like a visitation from outer space. Who goes there, and what do they do?

Tarsus

Tarsus lies 27km inland, to the east of Mersin. St Paul would be surprised to see his native town, an almost-abandoned ruin two centuries ago, grown into a manufacturing city of 200,000. Tarsus offers the first glimpse of the Turkey you'll see further east: more women shrouded in *chador*, more baggy trousers and cloth caps, fewer cars, more donkeys, lower standards of hygiene, more beggars and a positive dearth of English speakers.

All that survives of the ancient city is a stretch of wall and a simple, unembellished gate along the Mersin road. Antony met Cleopatra in Tarsus, so naturally the only ruin left has become **Cleopatra's Gate**. The gate's 'restoration' in 1994 caused controversy among archaeologists – so much new masonry was added that the old structure is hardly discernible. If you stay long, they'll show you the well from 'St Paul's house', too, although it's just a hole in the ground.

While levelling a site in central Tarsus to make way for a multi-storey car park, bulldozers hit upon an old **Roman road** several metres below the surface; excavations revealed a complex of **Roman shops and houses** from the first century BC.

There's more to see in Ottoman Tarsus, with the **Kırkkaşık Çarşısı**, the 'Market of the Forty Spoons', a dark, tunnel-like structure filled not with spoons but with tailors operating foot-powered Singer sewing machines. Nearby, in a 15th-century medrese, is the **town museum** whose half-dozen rooms contain a haphazard collection of relics, including a mummified arm, lying for no apparent reason across an Urartian gold diadem. More ruins can be seen at the old port of **Gözlükule**, dating from the Hittites up to Roman times.

Adana

Like Mersin, Adana has been here for a long time but only blossomed recently. As the centre of the textile industry, the town has become Turkey's fifth largest, with a population of over one million. It is a cosmopolitan place, with great bars, restaurants and world-renowned dishes, and, although places of touristic interest are limited, a stop here offers an insight into a modern, dynamic Turkish city. Unfortunately, with so much expansion and prosperity, the old town is looking increasingly shabby and neglected; even in the new districts in the north, apart from a few truly sumptuous boulevards, the city has had trouble managing its good fortune.

Old Adana grew up around the **Taşköprü**, the long Roman bridge across the Ceyhan. Built under Hadrian and restored under Justinian and many other rulers since, the bridge has acquired an oddly lopsided appearance; all its arches are different sizes.

In the **bazaar** area, just around the corner from the 19th-century **clock tower**, is the **Ulu Cami**, a very unusual 16th-century work with towers and recesses in stalactite patterns and a unique squat minaret that resembles a lighthouse.

Rising on the banks of the Seyhan next to the busy **Girne bridge** is the **Merkez Cami**, a grandiose affirmation in marble and glass of Adana's piety. Armed with six minarets and a dome as large as any in Turkey, it's also a wake-up call for distant Ankara to sit up and take note of this traditionally impoverished region's economic resurgence. Work began in 1988 using local money, but when funds ran out in 1997 the building was only half-finished. Enter Adana's most famous son, H. Ömer Sabancı, the Turkish Richard Branson, whose distinctive 'SA' logo appears across the country on everything from bottles of mineral water to tyre-fitting centres. He agreed to bail out the project in return for the mosque's being renamed Sabancı Merkez Camii. Although designed along traditional lines, the building looks heavier and squatter on the outside than Istanbul's imperial mosques. Once you cross the vast courtyard and go inside, however, the whole structure suddenly loses its ungainliness: three tiers of intricately painted domes hover high overhead; walls of hand-made İznik tiles are bathed in the light that floods through an impressive acreage of coloured glass windows. A plush fitted carpet, woven a thousand times over with a prayer rug motif, stretches across a floor with kneeling space for over 13,000 worshippers. There's room for another 15,000 more in the courtyard outside. Sabancı has invested well: by stepping in at the crucial hour, he has ensured his name will live on after he has gone. Just to be on the safe side, he built the luxurious Sabancı Hotel just opposite, and the Sabancı Cultural Centre just up the road...

Near the bus station, Adana's **archaeological museum** has mainly Roman statues and a few Hittite reliefs. The **ethnography museum** on İnönü Caddesi is livelier, with its collection of Ottoman memorabilia. Just outside the north edge of the city, **Seyhan Dam** backs up a lake that is a popular recreation area for local people.

East of Adana

With all the armies that have marched through this historical crossroads, either down from Anatolia by way of the Cilician Gates, or along the coast, it's not surprising that so much has been built on this plain, or that so little has endured. Castles sprang up here like ice-cream stands around a carnival, over 40 of them in Adana province alone, as well as remains of civilizations from the Hittites to modern times.

There is another Roman bridge at **Misis**, just east of Adana. This town's ancient name, Mopsuestia, recalls the Homeric seer Mopsus, associated with so many other Cilician towns. (Mopsus's name has recently turned up in a Hittite inscription, making him, like King Priam, a Homeric figure that is also a real historical personage.) In Islamic folklore, this was the home of the great Dr Luqman, a prototype of the physician-sorcerer of long ago.

Just before the town of **Ceyhan**, the road from Adana passes under one of the mightiest of the medieval castles, **Yılanlıkale**. The Armenians probably built it, and the emblem between two rampant lions over the gate is thought to be the arms of the Rubenid dynasty. During the Crusades, the Knights of St John occupied and extended Yılanlıkale. Its popular name, 'Castle of the Snake', may refer to the long silhouette of the walls as much as anything in its admittedly sinister aspect; the castle consists of three successive courts, each one higher and stronger than the last.

North of Ceyhan, the assiduous Armenians built two other formidable castles. **Tumlu**, from the 12th century, fell in 1375 to the Mamelukes of Egypt, traditional enemies of the Armenians as they would later be of the Ottoman Turks. **Şiş**, overlooking the village of Kozan, was the last stronghold of the Armenians, and, when a spy betrayed it to the Mamelukes in that same year, the story of Little Armenia came to its unhappy end.

Few spots in Turkey are planted as thickly with relics of the past as the environs of **Kadirli**, a little town on the Ceyhan river. The ruins of no fewer than eight castles can be seen in the vicinity, as well as Neolithic village mounds, Hittite rock reliefs, an aqueduct that served the Roman town of Flaviopolis, and at least two ruined cities. Few of these are impressive and few of the roads paved; the best bet for a detour from Ceyhan into the area would be to avoid Kadirli and head north to Karatepe. On the way, you'll pass the ruins of **Kastabala**, once known as Hierapolis, a small Roman town where there are still some temple columns and buildings.

Karatepe

From Kastabala the countryside is lovely, with well-tended farms and pine forests reaching their peak at **Lake Aslantaş**, as fair as any spot along the Turkish coasts. King Asitiwanda, who built Karatepe as his summer palace, could not have enjoyed the view as much; the lake is new, formed by the Aslantaş Dam downstream.

Karatepe is a Hittite city second only to Boğazkale (*see* p.406) in its wealth of reliefs and artefacts; here, however, on the 30 or so **reliefs** arranged under two pavilions in the open-air museum, you should expect none of the weighty religious or statist themes of the art of Yazılıkaya or Boğazkale. Perhaps by reflex, the Hittite artists added a few of their favourite fearsome lions and marble-eyed sphinxes, but most of the panels show domestic scenes – musicians with pan pipes and tambours, a mother giving suck, a merchant ship, even the king himself dining while a monkey under the table waits for hand-outs. Some reliefs are of gods, but they belong to an entirely different pantheon from those at Boğazkale; characters such as the chubby Phoenician god Bes, a bird-headed 'sun god', a centaur and an unusual 'good shepherd' figure (like the early Christian representations of Jesus) show the influence of other cultures on the tolerant and syncretic Hittites. Excavations are still under way at Karatepe.

One last castle you'll meet, whether your route takes you to the Hatay or to southeastern Anatolia, is **Toprakkale**. Its grim bulk guards the crossroads now, as it did in the Middle Ages when Crusaders and Saracens, Armenians and Mamelukes fought for its ownership. As often as it was besieged and taken, it was repaired; the key to the plain of Cilicia, Toprakkale remained in good condition for centuries.

Where to Stay in the Plains

(i) **Mersin >**
Inönü Bulvarı, near the harbour,
t *0324 237 1900*

(i) **Adana >>**
Atatürk Caddesi 13,
t *0322 363 1448*

Airport, **t** *0322 436 9214*

Mersin

*******Merit Mersin**, Kuvay Milliye Caddesi, **t** 0324 336 1010, *www. taksimotelcilik.com.tr* (€€€€). The inhabitant of the monster mentioned above. Rooms are done with little imagination but the views, as to be expected from this skyscraper, are nice. As in other Turkish cities, this luxury hotel has become the social centre of Mersin, with its restaurants, disco, health club and so on.

****Gökhan**, Soğuksu Caddesi, **t** 0324 232 4665 (€€). A solid, unspectacular city-centre hotel; it is air-conditioned, though, which can be the most important thing here in summer.

Mersinli Ahmet Caddesi is a whole street full of good, reasonably priced hotels next to the bus station, useful if you're just passing through or need to make an early start in the morning.

Akdeniz, **t** 0324 238 0187, Mersinli Ahmet Cad. Otogar Girişi Karşısı No 29, *www.akdenizhotel.net*. Rooms are large and bright at around 60 YTL. For a little extra, guests have use of the hamam and sauna.

Adana

*******Sürmeli Oteli**, Kuruköprü Özler Caddesi, **t** 0322 352 3600, *www. surmelihotels.com* (€€€€). A blissful bolthole with air-conditioning, bars and a fine restaurant. You may be able to negotiate discounts.

****Hotel Koza**, Özler Caddesi 103, **t** 0322 351 4657 (€€€€). An acceptable, if slightly impersonal establishment; cheaper when they're not busy.

Tarsus

****Tarsus Mersin Hotel**, next to the waterfall (Şelale Mevkii), **t** 0324 614 0600, *www.tarsusmersinotel.com* (€€€). Has the only really comfortable rooms in town, and is equipped with all the luxuries, including a pool, sauna and Jacuzzi.

Cihan Palas, Mersin Caddesi 40, **t** 0324 624 1623 (€€). A mediocre establishment, but at least it's been recently refurbished and has quiet rooms at the back.

Eating Out in the Plains

Adana is the home of the Adana *kebap*, hot and peppery, and every restaurant in town seems to serve it – although frankly, they cook it better in Istanbul. The secret to it lies in the flavoursome fat used from the animal's tail. Şalgam is also a popular drink in this region, a spicy pickled turnip juice, a bit of an acquired taste perhaps but a great accompaniment to the kebab.

Adana

 Yüzevler >

Yüzevler, ZiyapaÔa Bulvarı, No 25/A, **t** 0322 454 7513, *www.yuzevler.com.tr* (€€€). The Hard Rock Café of Turkish food in Adana, where the walls are covered with photographs of celebrity

guests, including the prime minister himself. And, too right, the food is outstanding, with some of the best examples of *pide*, *lahmacun*, authentic regional kebabs and *çiğ köfte* that you are likely to taste.

Gaziantep Şahinoğlu Baklava Salonu, İnönü Caddesi 149B, **t** 0322 363 2737 (€). The place for those with a sweet tooth. 4.50 YTL for succulent baklava.

Mersin

The city has a number of fine restaurants and cafés; the Tashan Galleria is a good spot to find a few, and around the waterfront there are several seafood restaurants. Mersin is the home of *tantuni* – finely chopped lamb fried in spices and wrapped in soft flat bread.

Göçtu Kebap, Žnönü Bulvarı No 190, **t** 0324 326 1287, *www.goctukebap.com* (€€). An old local favourite, which has near enough acquired cult status for its dizzying array of kebabs with reasonable prices to boot.

Alibaba Kordon, Adnan Menderes Bulvarı, Sözmen Apt. Altı 18, **t** 0324 325 06 80, *www.alibabakordon.com.tr*. Another Mersin classic, serving up the good stuff with real professionalism since 1979, often with live music at weekends.

Also, don't miss a dessert at **Tatlıcı İsmail Usta** and an ice cream at **Dondurmacı Halil**, which has even started doing mail order baklava (*www.dondurmacihalil.com.tr*)!

The Hatay

This little tongue of land, projecting into Syria to spoil Turkey's rectangularity, marks the only change in the nation's boundaries since the founding of the republic. Apart from the small chain of the Amanas Mountains, running to the sea along the Gulf of İskenderun, Hatay province is really the ancient city of Antioch, now Antakya, and its hinterlands in the lower valley of the Orontes (Asi in Turkish).

During the First World War, General Allenby's Egyptian Expeditionary Force captured the Hatay for Britain, but a League of Nations mandate gave the French the territory; they spent considerable effort and money over the next sixteen years trying to win the goodwill of the inhabitants. When the date for the

Getting to and around the Hatay

The Hatay is off the major routes, there are no rail or air connections, so your only option is a **bus**. You may wish to check with the bus lines in advance for times, and it may be bumpy, especially if you're coming from the east. From Adana the journey takes 3½ hours, and costs around 12 YTL.

St Peter's Church is within walking distance of the centre of Antakya, but for many of the other early Christian sites you'll need a **car**. Harbiye is easily reached by **dolmuş** from Antakya.

plebiscite ordered by the League finally arrived in 1939, the vote went overwhelmingly to join Turkey, and the French 'Hatay' became a historical curiosity remembered only by philatelists.

Whether you enter from the flat plain of Cilicia or the arid southeastern plateau, the contrast is striking. The fertile and well-tended countryside, its roads often lined with plane trees and oleanders, makes the Hatay one of the most civilized landscapes in Turkey. Along the coast, as soon as you have passed Toprakkale and have the Gulf of İskenderun in sight, you will be on the plain where one of the most significant battles of ancient history was fought.

Issus to İskenderun

In 333 BC, Alexander the Great began his eastern campaign by invading Asia Minor; right across the peninsula, while reducing towns and dismantling satrapies, he was seeking a final show-down with the Persian king Darius. That November, he caught him at **Issus** (**İssos**), near the Turkish town of **Dörtyol**. Ancient historians credited the Persians with some 400,000 men; nevertheless the fighting was brief and one-sided. Darius barely escaped with his life, and Alexander informed him, in the subsequent diplomatic correspondence, that any future messages to him should be addressed to 'King of All Asia'. Two years lapsed before Alexander finally entered Persepolis – there were other distractions, such as the conquest of Egypt – but the Battle of Issus had already made his title a reality.

Payas (**Yakacık**), the first town after Dörtyol, lies in the shadow of a large modern steel mill; in the 16th century, it was the major port of the region, and substantial buildings from that period remain, notably the **Selimiye complex** built by Yavuz Selim in 1574, and a harbour castle thought to have been begun by the Venetians some centuries before. Payas's harbour silted up, and since then **İskenderun** has become the port of the Hatay and one of the largest in the Mediterranean; the ships waiting for dock-space often fill the horizon, as they do in Istanbul or Piraeus. As terminal of the busiest Middle East pipeline, the port handles all Iraq's oil exports. '*İskender*' is the Arab and Turkish form of 'Alexander', and the city can trace its origins to the Macedonian foundation; other than that, İskenderun is wealthy and pleasant and remarkable only for being almost indistinguishable from Mersin.

From İskenderun the coast road can penetrate only as far as the fishing village and beach resort of **Arsuz**. South of here, ruins of a Crusader castle can be seen by boat, but a better and more accessible one lies near the route from İskenderun over the mountains, at **Bakras**, built by the Templars in the 12th century and captured soon after by Saladin himself. The castle is partially ruined, but the Gothic chapel and refectory remain.

Antakya (Antioch)

For most of the Roman era, Antioch, now Antakya, was the third-largest city of the Western world, surpassed only by Alexandria and Rome. One of Alexander's generals, Seleucus Nicator, who created his own empire by defeating most of his former comrades-in-arms, founded Antioch in 300 BC. As trade routes across the new Greek Middle East grew, so did Antioch, at a rate that astounded contemporary chroniclers. At this time, the Mediterranean world had become rich and cohesive enough to trade on a large scale with India and China; the Seleucids, in the middle, collected all the transport charges. Antioch, the metropolis of the Hellenized Syrians, renowned throughout the ancient world for their craft and subtlety in business dealings, became the first western terminal of the Great Silk Route.

Secure under the *Pax Romana*, after 64 BC Antioch's population at one time exceeded half a million. Roman client kings of the Middle East, like Herod of Judea and the Kallinikos dynasty of Commagene, brightened their images by endowing the city with great temples and public works. Learning and art were prized, even by the high standards of the time and place, and before long Antioch vied with Athens for intellectual leadership of the empire. One of the first Christian communities was started here by St Peter himself; it grew so rapidly it became the greatest stronghold of the new faith, with enough of a hold on the population, even the upper classes, to resist most of the emperor's intermittent persecutions – even though Diocletian burned down all the churches in 301.

For a time in the 4th century, Antioch competed with the city of Constantinople for pre-eminence in the East, and as the city was a bastion of the Arian heresy, the two became doctrinal enemies as well. Constantinople's rise, and the redirection of trade along the silk route, meant Antioch's decline; a tremendous earthquake in 526, one of many, hastened it along. Before the 7th century, Antioch was sacked six times by the Persians and Arabs. After a revival as a part of the Crusader kingdoms, it was sacked again, by the

Mamelukes of Egypt in 1268. That was the end; the modern city was a struggling village only a century ago.

As much of its growth took place under French rule, in the period 1920–39, Antakya has very much the aspect of a French colonial city, with a slight excess of boulevards, traffic circles and palm trees. The traffic circle on the banks of the Asi, the ancient river Orontes, was obviously planned as a kind of civic centre; but here the grandest French building is not a government headquarters or school but an Art Deco film palace. Of the ancient city, all you'll see are marble blocks built into the walls and streets of the pretty old village, across the river from the new town. **Kurtuluş Caddesi** is its main street, generally following the route of the famous colonnaded avenue of antiquity; it passes the **Habib Neccar Camii**, an exceptionally fine 17th-century mosque. On the mountains above the city, parts of the impressive ancient walls and aqueducts are well preserved, but they are difficult of access.

❸ Archaeology Museum
*open Tues–Sun
8.30–12 and 1.30–5;
closed Mon; adm*

The main reason for visiting Antakya is the collection of Roman mosaics in the **Archaeology Museum**, perhaps the finest in existence, recovered from the city and its suburb of Daphne. These mosaics, in colour and detail, and in the expressiveness of the portraiture, must be counted among the greatest works of the Roman world. A face as perfectly captured as that of the unknown lady named 'Soteria' brings that world back to life, while mythological scenes like the room-sized 'Marriage of Tethys and Oceanus', attended by all the creatures of the sea, gently reproach us for not crediting the late Roman world with enough imagination.

Around Antakya

The Hatay has been a civilized country since Neolithic times, and the plain around Antakya is littered with mounds and ruins. Just north of the city along the cliffs is what the locals claim is the oldest Christian church in the world still in use. The name **St Peter's Church (Senpiyer Kilisesi)** was natural, for St Peter himself is said to have preached here. It is a cave, with a tunnel for escape during the persecutions, a cistern and, on the floor, the remains of mosaics. The carved stone façade was added by the Crusaders. Antakya has a small Catholic community; Mass is said here and in the 19th-century church on Kurtuluş Caddesi on Sundays. Along the cliffs to the left of the cave are a number of rock tombs, and a mysterious relief of a woman, carved in the 2nd century BC.

The most renowned pleasure dome of the ancient world was **Daphne**, now **Harbiye**, a beautiful spot overlooking the Orontes with small waterfalls cascading down a series of terraces, and groves of pine and plane trees. It isn't associated with the myth of Apollo and Daphne – that all happened in Thessaly – but the Hellenized gentry of the Seleucid Kingdom thought it would have made a fine setting nevertheless. A famous temple of Apollo was erected here, and the well-to-do of Antioch surrounded it with their villas and gardens. Antony and Cleopatra courted at Daphne, and in the Roman era the Antioch games held here surpassed the old games at Olympus in popularity and importance.

Roman emperors spent time in Antioch whenever their responsibilities permitted; Julian the Apostate, having grown up here, especially favoured it. When he returned in AD 363, on his way to campaign against the Persians, and saw the Christian population wrecking the beautiful temple of Apollo at Daphne to get stone for churches, he was furious. He had it rebuilt, but the Christians immediately burned it down. Daphne shared in Antioch's misfortunes; various earthquakes knocked down what the Christians hadn't and rearranged the topography, somewhat for the worse. Today the place is known by the incongruous name of Harbiye or 'war college', but it is still a favourite resort of local people, with restaurants and picnic grounds among the waterfalls. It can be reached along the main road to the south, 6km from Antakya.

There was a dark side to Antioch's early Christianity, leading to odd extremes. In this sophisticated metropolis, instead of a blossoming of innocence and faith what happened was an outbreak of neuroses no one could have foreseen. One outstanding manifestation was the fashion for **pillar-sitting**, begun by St Simeon Stylites in the 4th century and lasting into the 5th. St Simeon spent some 25 years in the air, on a series of progressively taller columns, attracting great crowds of pilgrims and penitents and interfering in imperial politics and public morals through his pronouncements from on high. Pillar-sitting became fashionable, and at one point Church chronicles report no less than 200 copycats up in the air together. The hill where all this took place, with the ruins of the 5th-century **St Simeon Monastery**, is off the road from Antakya to the west in the direction of Samandağı. Other old monasteries in various stages of dereliction lie on the hills around **Yayladağı** near the Syrian border.

The road from Yayladağı to the coast leads to **Samandağı** and from there north to **Çevlik**, near the ruins of Antioch's old port, **Seleucia ad Pieria**. Gradually abandoned as its harbour silted up, the town has little left to see except the **Tunnel of Vespasian**, a series of great halls with 50ft ceilings carved out of the rocks near the sea, used as part of Seleucia's water supply system. Even though a smaller irrigation canal was recently built through it, you can walk through this cool and lovely spot, passing in and out of the mountain, listening to the frogs. Fine beaches line the shore all around with a beautiful backdrop of green mountains, some in Turkey, some in Syria.

Where to Stay in the Hatay

ⓘ İskenderun >
*Atatürk Bulvarı 49,
at the city pier,*
t 0326 614 1620

İskenderun

As a busy port that sees lots of businessmen, İskenderun has plenty of nice, inexpensive hotels.

Otel Altındişler, Şehit Pamir Caddesi 11, t 0326 617 1011 (€€). Basic doubles from €38/70 YTL.

Hotel Açıkalın, Şehit Pamir Caddesi 13, t 0326 617 3732 (€). The budget choice; 50 YTL for a basic room with private shower, air-conditioning and TV. There are several other cheapies dotted around the port; none looks too savoury.

ⓘ Antakya >
t 0326 214 9217

Antakya

Antakya doesn't get many tourists but, although the town is not exactly packed with places to stay, finding somewhere suitable should not be too difficult.

****Büyük Antakya Oteli, Atatürk Caddesi 8, t 0326 213 5858, *www. buyukantakyaoteli.com* (€€€). Antakya's finest; 72 air-conditioned, en suite rooms. For what you get, it's not that expensive, at around €75/150 YTL for a double with breakfast; no pool.

(S) Antik Beyazıt, Hükümet Caddesi, t 0326 216 2900, *www.antikbeyazit oteli.com* (€€€). Antakya's most atmospheric hotel, recently converted from a Hatay mansion dating back to 1903. The reception has been sympathetically restored, unlike the bedrooms, which are full of modern pine fittings; €70/140 YTL per double, though this can be reduced to as little as €50/100 YTL if they are not full and you are persuasive.

***Hotel Orontes, İstiklâl Caddesi 58, t 0326 214 5931, *www.oronteshotel. com* (€€). Has courteous and informative staff; the rooms are very nice too. Do negotiate.

Divan Oteli, İstiklâl Caddesi 62, t 0326 215 1518 (€). The first place encountered coming from the bus stop, where clean rooms with private shower and toilet go some way towards compensating for the surly, grumpy staff and noisy road.

There are *pensions* near the beaches at Samandağ and Arsuz.

Harbiye

Harbiye (Daphne) is quieter than Antakya, with cleaner air.

*Çağlayan Otel, Ürgun Caddesi 6, t 0326 231 4269, *www.caglayanotel. com.tr* (€€). Good value.

Eating Out in the Hatay

İskenderun

Saray Lokantası, Atatürk Bulvarı, t 0326 617 1383 (€). A popular spot in the centre.

Antakya

Sultan Sofrası Restaurant, İstiklâl Caddesi, t 0326 213 8759, *www. sultansofrasi.com* (€). A good meal will cost around 15 YTL here at the local favourite with a good selection of savoury dishes and desserts, some of which you may not easily find in the rest of the country.

Antakya Evi, above the aquarium shop at Silahlı Kuvvetler Caddesi 3, t 0326 214 1350 (€). Has original tiled floors and a pleasant open balcony. With reasonably priced specials.

Harbiye

Boğaziçi, Ürgen Caddesi (€€). This long-running establishment is the best here. Part of the nearby river is channelled through its outdoor dining area; red sole mature here until they're big enough for the table. The food is plentiful and delicious, the atmosphere convivial; highly recommended. Bring a car if you have one and you'll have it washed for free while you're eating.

Another enjoyable option is to head for the informal outdoor restaurants in the park – sheds or tents with picnic tables among the waterfalls and pines. At these you can get a good fish or kebab dinner at lower prices than elsewhere.

The Black Sea

Turkey's longest coast has always been the marine back door, less favoured by nature and less prominent in history than the lands along the Aegean and Mediterranean. Jason and his Argonauts may have sailed it, but the Greek merchants and colonists behind the myth founded only a few towns, none of which ever attained much status in the ancient world. Both the coast and the forest-clad mountains that rise behind it have their share of scenery, more in the western half than in the east. There are a few good beaches, but the climate lacks that Mediterranean perfection; the season is short, and rains are frequent even in summer.

12

Don't miss

⭐ **A very Turkish village**
Safranbolu **p.361**

⭐ **Cherries, hazelnuts and beaches**
Giresun **p.367**

⭐ **The last great Byzantine frescoes**
Aya Sofya, Trabzon **p.373**

⭐ **A monastery in the clouds**
Sumela **p.374**

⭐ **Georgian villages**
The Çoruh valley, Tao-Georgia, near Artvin **p.377**

See map overleaf

Don't miss

⭐ Safranbolu p.361

⭐ Giresun p.367

⭐ Aya Sofya, Trabzon p.373

⭐ Sumela p.374

⭐ Tao-Georgia, near Artvin p.377

From Jason up to the present, the only intrusion the shores of the Pontus Euxinus ever made into history was the rise of the **Pontic Kingdom** in the wake of Alexander the Great's conquest in the 4th century BC. The Pontic kings gave Rome fits for a century, but when they finally succumbed to the tenacity of the legions it put an end to Pontus as a nation forever. Since then, with the exception of the short-lived but colourful **Empire of Trebizond**, these shores have managed well enough to stay out of trouble.

Recently, the Black Sea has been just as successful in avoiding tourism. The best part of the coast begins only at Samsun; like the area around the Marmara, the coast from Istanbul eastwards has become industrialized over the last 50 years. All along the Black Sea, with the exception of a few local resorts, there is little accommodation and restaurants are scarce. Although this is gradually changing, as yet the package tours are nowhere to be seen, and, if you're not too demanding in your stretch of seaside, the Black Sea may be just the place.

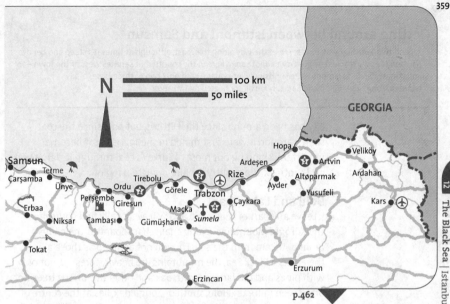

p.462

Istanbul to Samsun

East to Zonguldak

The nearest Black Sea beach resort to Istanbul is **Şile**, popular with the Stamboullu, who come here to swim and to buy the embroidered cotton shirts for which the town is renowned. Genoese merchants built the little castle here to protect their interests in the Black Sea, back in the days when they were snatching the Byzantine emperor's commerce out from under his nose. Drowsy **Ağva**, 30km on, also has a beach. After **Kandıra**, a further 50km to the east, the road leaves the coast, bypassing the promontory of **Calpe** and its islet just offshore, where a vision of Apollo appeared to the Argonauts; in classical times a Temple of Harmonia was built in commemoration of the event, but not a trace of it remains. This route leads to the provincial capital, **Adapazarı** (Sakarya), which should be bypassed in favour of the lake to its south, **Sapanca Gölü**. Well-dressed Turkish families and courting couples come here at weekends to stroll contentedly along the verdant lakeside trails.

Back on the coast, the next good beach is at **Akçakoca**, which also boasts yet another ruined Genoese castle. The town was named after a general of Sultan Orhan who captured it, the first Ottoman foothold on the coast. Akçakoca is often crowded with families from the big towns to the east: **Ereğli**, whose coastline is adorned by the Middle East's largest steel mill, and **Zonguldak**. This latter

Getting around between Istanbul and Samsun

A good two-lane **highway** runs some of the way along the coast, although at times it's steep and bendy. Samsun is easily reached by **bus** from almost anywhere in the country, but services west of the town – to Sinop, Amasra and Kastamonu – are suprisingly infrequent, with only two or three buses a day. Istanbul, Zonguldak, Sinop and Samsun are all connected by TML **ferry**.

city has been around since the Hittites, but only since the coal seams around it were first mined in the 1920s has it become important, shipping out most of Turkey's coal through its large port and centre of the country's major industrial region.

Bolu and Lake Abant

Leave any part of this coast, and you eventually find yourself in the **Köroğlu Mountains**, a long chain that separates the plains around Ankara from the sea. Though not as steep as those along the eastern Black Sea, the mountains are heavily forested, not only with pines and poplars, but with oak and other deciduous trees not often seen in Turkey. **Bolu**, south of Zonguldak, lies at the centre of the country's most popular mountain recreation area. Whenever you see '*bolu*' in the name of a Turkish town, as in 'İnebolu' and 'Safranbolu', you know it's at least as old as the Romans; it's how the Turks came to pronounce '*polis*', and this 'Bolu' was originally Claudiopolis. Nothing very old has survived, but there's a fine **Ulu Cami** built under Yıldırım Beyazıt. Bolu has a habit of building Alpine-style chalets, and a reputation for producing the best cooks in Turkey, but its citizens complain that they all go to Istanbul.

Beautiful **Lake Abant**, just to the southwest, is perhaps the best-known mountain resort. Nearly a mile above sea level, it's kept well stocked for trout fishermen. If one lake isn't enough, try the

Köroğlu, the Robin Hood of Turkey

'Köroğlu' means 'son of the blind man', and behind the name stands a personality you should get to know if you plan to spend much time here. For these mountains are Turkey's Sherwood Forest, and Köroğlu, a real bandit who flourished at the end of the 16th century, is his country's Robin Hood. The historical evidence is limited to letters from the governor of Ankara demanding Köroğlu's arrest; there are quite a few of them. The legends, still heard in rural corners here and in eastern Anatolia, start Köroğlu out in life in much the same way as his English counterpart, sworn to outlawry to avenge a wrong done by the authorities.

His father, a groom for the lord of Bolu, had been charged with the duty of selecting a gift horse from the herd of a neighbouring bey. He picked out a lean, crippled colt, so enraging his master that he had the groom's eyes put out. Köroğlu promised to avenge his father, and, with the aid of the colt, now grown into a magic grey horse called Kirat, spent a long career doing just that. With him at his mountain hideout somewhere near Gerede lived 500 warriors, some heroes in their own right, like Demircioğlu, 'son of the blacksmith', the very picture of a Turkish Little John.

Nallıhan, the tiny village south of Bolu, is a centre of the legend, and here you may see one of Kirat's horseshoes still nailed to a stone wall. Strangely, these stories were always most popular out east; another cycle of them has Köroğlu's band robbing fat merchants on the pass of Çamlibel, near Sivas.

Yedigöller National Park where there are seven, among forests of oak, elm and beech; here you may stalk the rare and elusive wild tulip. There's skiing at **Kartalkaya**, southwest of Bolu on the slopes of **Köroğlu Dağ**, the highest peak of the chain.

From Amasra to İnebolu

Returning to the coast, **Amasra** is a characterful little town made striking by the Genoese fortifications that still stand above two indented harbours. Being blessed with two ports made Amasra important long before the Genoese pitched up; it was first founded by colonists from Miletus and what has been unearthed from its past is now on show at the local archaeological museum. There is a beach here, although the cleanliness of the sea is questionable; Amasra's ports are still very much in use.

East of Amasra the coastal road begins to dip and rise and curve and occasionally cut inland. The scenery is pleasant enough but there's little to entice the visitor, aside from the quiet pebble beaches that appear every few km or so. **İnebolu** is the largest town along this stretch, boasting attractive if dilapidated traditional Ottoman houses as well as a beach. 25km further east is **Abana**, an expanding resort with a reasonable beach.

Amasra archaeological museum
open Tues–Sun 9–5.30; closed Mon; adm

Safranbolu and Kastamonu

In Roman times, the Köroğlu Mountains formed part of the province of Bithynia; one thing they have in common with the old Bithynian villages around Bursa (*see* p.202) is the style of the houses. These square, half-timber buildings, with their tile roofs and medieval overhanging second storeys, can best be seen in towns like Safranbolu, Bartın near the coast, and in the cosy little provincial capital of Kastamonu.

⭐ Safranbolu

Safranbolu was once a rich town, deriving its wealth, importance and name from its trade in saffron, the costly spice prepared from the pistils of a variety of crocus. Today the old town is isolated, hiding behind modern Safranbolu which is itself eclipsed by nearby **Karabük**, a thriving modern town situated on the railway, with an economy based on iron and steel. You will not fail to notice the steelworks – dating back to 1937, this industrial monster, oppressive and smoking from every orifice, actually has a strange beauty to it, like a kind of James Bond movie set.

Old Safranbolu has been declared a UNESCO World Heritage site and the TTOK is active in restoration and preservation. The town is a delight to wander round. In the centre, which is closed to traffic, the cobbled alleys are shaded by vines; saddle-makers sit working in open shopfronts; streets echo to the hammers of tin- and coppersmiths and shimmer with the sprays of sparks. The large half-timber houses for which the town is famous can be seen everywhere. Several of these houses have been restored and are open to the public, notably the **Kaymakamlar Evi** (Governor's House). The plan of the house is typical of its day and explains why Ottoman houses are so large: they are designed for extended families, with each room housing one nuclear family. They have a minimum of furniture: padded benches round the edges act as seats during the day and beds at night. The Kaymakam had the best room, with an adjoining chamber for his wives; his parents had the second-best. Rooms are grouped round communal areas. The large communal kitchen was used only on special occasions.

Another such house is the charming **Karaüzümler Evi**, replete with a quiet courtyard café, on Mescit Sokak. The owners are pleased to show you round (once your feet have been enveloped in shower caps to protect the floor); cupboards in several rooms open to reveal ingenious toilet facilities. As in many of these Ottoman mansions, the quality of light inside is extraordinary, with huge windows fitted wherever there's space. Another Ottoman building worth a glimpse is the wonderful stone **Cinci Hanı**, a 17th-century caravanserai that has been transformed into a plush new hotel.

A good view of the town can be had from the battlement-style walls surrounding a small Ottoman *türbe* on top of a hill. The imposing Renaissance-style mansion on another hill is the burnt-out shell of the **Hükümet Konağı** (Government House).

Safranbolu has been so well preserved that it can feel like an open-air museum; by contrast **Kastamonu**, 101km to the east, is very much more vibrant and bustling, its dilapidated old Ottoman houses cheerfully rubbing shoulders with brand new apartment blocks. The castle from which Kastamonu derives its name is, in one respect, unique in Turkey: it wasn't wrecked by Tamerlane – he built it. In modern times, the greatest thing to hit Kastamonu was Atatürk's speech here in 1925, proclaiming the Hat Reform, and the abolition of the fez. The **archaeology museum** has a good collection of Roman-era sculpture, plus recent finds from Pompeiopolis, a nearby site that was once the capital of Bithynia and Rome's old nemesis Mithradates. There is also a small **ethnography museum**, in a restored Ottoman mansion on Sakarya Caddesi.

The rugged mountains around Kastamonu offer some splendid scenery, especially in the **Mount Ilgaz National Park** south of the city, with canyons and caves to explore.

Sinop

Long ago, the sailors of the Black Sea had a saying that the only reliable opportunities for landing on the southern shore were 'June, July and Sinope'. Originally a Milesian colony like Amasra,

Of Queens and Cynics

Sinope contributed two tough customers to the lore of classical antiquity. The lady after whom the town was named was an Amazon queen whose charms attracted the attentions of Zeus. When the god came courting, he promised Sinope any gift she desired; she chose everlasting virginity, and lived happily ever after. In 413 BC, Diogenes, the original Cynic, was born here. His belief in virtue and moral freedom (far removed from latter-day cynicism) led to his decision to live the simple life of a dog, unfettered by social convention. ('Cynic' comes from the Greek word for dog.) This is the fellow Alexander the Great found one day sitting in his usual tub; the prince, always kindly disposed to cranks and philosophers, asked if Diogenes desired anything of him, and received the famous reply, 'Yes, stand out of my light.' Alexander is said to have commented, 'If I were not Alexander, I would be Diogenes.'

Sinope grew to become the pre-eminent town of Pontus during the Hellenistic era, a free trading city that maintained its liberty until King Pharnaces I annexed it to the Pontic kingdom in 183 BC. As first city and occasional capital of this kingdom, Sinope was more than compensated by the many temples and monuments the kings bestowed upon it.

As the Black Sea trade dwindled during Roman times, so did Sinop (the modern spelling), and today the only natural harbour on the coast finds itself eclipsed completely by artificial ones at Zonguldak, Samsun and even Trabzon, originally a colony of Sinope. The town still makes its living from the sea. It may be a good spot for a fish dinner along the quays, but for all its past, little is left. The **castle**, built on the foundations of Mithridates' stronghold, is Byzantine, but the most notable building is from the 13th century, the **Alâeddin Camii**, one of the last mosques built by the dying Selcuk empire. Outside town, there are good beaches at **Akliman**, an isolated spot on the bay, and at the fishing village of **Gerze**.

Samsun

Samsun, with over a millon and a half people, is the largest city on the coast and exactly the opposite of Sinop – all present and no past. The Milesians were here, too, and Samsun is just as old, but never had anything to show for itself until the 20th century. Wherever you walk in the city's nondescript grid-iron of streets, the sweet aroma of freshly cut tobacco fills the air, rising from the hug old **Tekel factory** in the middle of the town which produces most of Turkey's cigarettes. Nobody smokes like a Turk, as you will have noticed, and Samsun is doing very well. The modern, well-planned and partly pedestrianized city centre reflects this, with its shorefront boulevard lined with palms, and smooth, cleanly designed new buildings, notably the ski-jump cultural centre.

Samsun could well afford to put up the largest **Atatürk Monument** outside Ankara, but it also had good reason: the Turkish War of Independence began here, with Atatürk's escape from Istanbul on the steamer *Bandırma*. Instead of inspecting the army, as he had fooled the sultan's government into ordering him to do, he started making speeches to it and issuing manifestos to the patriots of Anatolia. Samsun welcomed him with bands and cheering crowds, and it has been a stoutly republican town ever since; ironically, it also has a reputation for being one of the most conservative Muslim cities in Turkey.

Samsun divides its busy port from the rest of the town with its **Fair**, a big park like the one in İzmir that contains the stadium, train station, public auditorium, the **Luna Park**, gardens and the **Atatürk Museum**. Old Samsun, full of market stalls and questionable restaurants, is in the city's west end; sights include the colourful **Rus Pazar**, the 'Russian Market', the 13th-century **Pazar Cami**, built by the Ilhanli Mongols, and plenty of wonderfully overdone public buildings and banks in a bastard French Second Empire style.

Where to Stay between Istanbul and Samsun

(i) **Safranbolu >>**
Arasta Çarşısı 7,
t *0372 712 3863*

(i) **Zonguldak**
Valilik building,
t *0372 253 5436*

(i) **Bolu >**
Karamanlı Mah.,
Konuralp Caddesi 11,
t *0374 212 2254*

(★) **Tabağ Ahmet Bey Konağı >>**

Most of the small coastal towns have only very limited accommodation, with cheap *pensions* the rule.

Şile

Değirmen Hotel, Plaj Yolu 24, **t 0216 711 5048 (€€€). Şile has several large beach resort hotels like this one, recently revamped with flat screen TVs and free wireless Internet.

Kurfallı Tatil Köyü, Ağva, **t** 0216 721 7243, *www.kurfalli.com.tr* (€). For something totally in contrast, try a ramshackle wooden bungalow at this beach camp in the countryside.

Bolu–Lake Abant

****Koru Hotel, Bakırlı Mevkii, **t** 0374 225 2290, *www.koruhotel.com.tr* (€€€€). In the mountains near Bolu, at Ömerler Köyü, is a lovely, large Alpine-style hotel built by the Turkish Automobile Club, with very comfortable rooms.

****Bolu Termal Otel, Karacasu Köyü, in the same region, **t** 0374 262 8472, *www.boltermalotel.com* (€€€).

***Turban Abant Hotel, also on the lake, **t** 0374 224 5033 (€€€–€€). Has a sauna and a pool. Half-board.

Amasra

Türkili Hotel, Özdemirhan Sokak 6, **t** 0378 315 3750, *www.turkili.com.tr* (€€€). Simple rooms but convenient location; breakfast is on the roof

terrace with its excellent views of the town and harbour.

Safranbolu

This beautiful little town boasts various mid-range hotels in converted Ottoman houses.

Havazlu Konak, Mescit Sokak, **t** 0370 725 2883, *www.safranbolukonak.com* (€€€). Safranbolu's plushest establishment, run by the TTOK and worth a peek even if you're staying in lesser lodgings. Spacious rooms, furnished in traditional Ottoman style and attractively carpeted, have undersized private bathrooms. Breakfast is in the sumptuous tearoom, replete with interior pool and low-lying brass tables. The restaurant, however, is nothing special.

Selvili Köşk, Çeşme Mah., Mescit Sokak, **t** 0370 712 8646 (€€). Another pleasant example on a quiet street. As well as a large and attractive first-floor salon, it has airy bedrooms with cupboards revealing ingenious bathrooms within (not for those unwilling to clamber).

Tabağ Ahmet Bey Konağı, Çarşı Çeşme Mah. Karaüzüm Sokak 3, **t** 0370 712 3319, *http://tabagahmetbeykonagi. com* (€€). A 200-year-old original timberframe classic, and one of the most atmospheric little *pensions* in town. The owner, Cengiz, may well be the warmest, most welcoming, most attentive, honest and kind-hearted host you are likely to encounter on your travels in Turkey. This is a glimpse into a type of hospitality that is becoming increasingly rare. Don't expect the trappings of a conventional hotel; it's all about the real experience here, bathrooms in the cupboard and all! The only drawback is that very little English is spoken, so take a dictionary and plunge right in.

Kastamonu

(i) Kastamonu >
Nasrullah İş Hanı,
t 0366 212 0162

*****Osmanlı Sarayi**, Belediye Caddesi 81, **t** 0366 214 8408, *www. ottomanpalace.4t.com* (€€). A late-19th-century town hall converted into a hotel. Rooms are well appointed with TVs and minibars, but it is the more historic aspects of the building that add the ambience.

(★) Toprakcılar
Konakları >

Toprakcılar Konakları, İsmail Bey Mah., Alemdar Sokak 1, **t** 0366 212 1812, *www.toprakcilar.com* (€€). Your best bet for some authentic Ottoman charm in a house similar to those in Safranbolu. The mature timberframe and wood-panelled ceilings are testament to its age, and there is a good restaurant to boot.

Selvi, Banka Sokak, **t** 0366 214 1763 (€€). On a quiet pedestrian street off the Nasrullah Meydanı, the best of a handful of cheap hotels. Some of the top-floor rooms have excellent views of the castle.

Sinop

(i) Sinop >
Valilik building,
t 0368 261 3023

****Otel Melia Kasım**, Gazi Caddesi 49, **t** 0368 261 4210, *www.hotelmelia kasim.com* (€€). The best on offer, solid but uninspiring. The pastel rooms have satellite TV and balconies with good views of the sea.

Denizci Hotel, Kurtuluş Caddesi, **t** 0368 261 0904 (€€). Characterful, with a friendly owner; clean rooms with balcony and shared bathroom.

(★) Kazan
Ocağı >>

Zinos Country Hotel, Enver Bahadır Yolu 75, **t** 0368 260 5600, *www. zinoshotel.com* (€€). A good option all round, on the seaside at Karakum.

Samsun

(i) Samsun >
Talimhane Caddesi 6,
t 0362 431 0014

*****Otel Vidinli**, Cumhuriyet Meydanı 4, **t** 0362 431 6050 (€€). Has bright and spacious bedrooms, each with a sitting area, minibar and bath. The 1960s furniture has been unusually well designed and constructed,

lending a certain utilitarian elegance to the place. There's also a top-floor restaurant which offers live music.

Otel Akça, Pazar Mah., Hastane Sokak 4, **t** 0362 431 7350, *www.otelakca.com. tr.tc* (€€). Bright front rooms decorated with vibrant bursts of scarlet and black (oddly refreshing in light of Turkish hoteliers' obsession with the colour beige).

Otel Necmi, Kale Mah., Bedesten Sokak 6, **t** 0362 432 7164 (€). Minuscule but quiet rooms which are tolerable for a one-night stay; the top floor has the (one) shower.

Eating Out between Istanbul and Samsun

Şile

Artena, Ayazma and İyot restaurants also often have live music to accompany your meal. A seafood dinner will cost around 30 YTL per person.

Bolu-Lake Abant

Chocolate Kartalkaya, **t** 0374 234 5072 (€€€–€€). An après ski lodge in the Kartalkaya ski resort; a good range of local dishes (and chocolate fondue).

Amasra

Liman, **t** 0378 315 2606 (€€€–€€). Famous for its fish, salad, and views.

Canlı Balık (Live Fish), **t** 0378 315 2606 (€€€–€€). Another local favourite.

Safranbolu

Stock up on Turkish delight; somehow it tastes better in Safranbolu. As for restaurants, they do not as yet match up to the burgeoning hotel scene, but there is still a gem or two.

Kazan Ocağı (€€). A real home-cooking affair with cheap prices to boot. The kitchen shares the same space as the 4 or 5 tables comprising the dining area. It looks modest, but do not make the mistake of not eating here! The house speciality – *peruhi*, a local pasta style with crushed walnut and melted butter sauce, is just divine, their stuffed vine leaves, *mantı*, and *imam bayıldı* are all excellent; and then, when you thought it was all over, they open the oven and pull out a tray of freshly baked baklava.

Kastamonu

Frenkşah Sultan Sofrası, t 0366 212 1905 (€€). In the 13th-century former Sultan Cemaleddin Hamamı off Nasrullah Meydanı; the most atmospheric place for lunch. The place is crammed with Ottoman curios and is an enjoyable place to sample *mantı* or, better still, the wonderful *etli ekmek* – meat-stuffed crêpes.

Uludağ Pide ve Kebap Salonu, on the corner of Belediye and Cumhuriyet Caddesi (€). A more orthodox alternative, crammed full of locals at lunchtime and in the evening and serving up its namesake dishes for 12 YTL.

Sinop

Fish restaurants line the quayside.

Saray, İskele Cad. Rıhtım Sokak 18, **t** 0368 261 1729 (€). Tables bobbing gently on the floating jetty; 12 YTL for excellent fish.

Obur Mantı, Kıbrıs Caddesi 5/A, **t** 0368 260 3810 (€). For more traditional regional Black Sea food such as *mantı* with walnut; 8 YTL.

Samsun

Fevzi'nin Yeri, Balık Hali Müdürlüğü Yanı (beside the fish market), **t** 0362 445 1575 (€€). Decorated from floor to ceiling with fishing nets, dried fish and other bits of dead sea-life. The fish they serve, however, is totally fresh and there isn't a huge selection of meze to distract you from it. Full meal 30–40 YTL.

Samsun to Trabzon

Leaving Samsun, the first town to the east is **Çarşamba**, which means Wednesday in Turkish (Perşembe, meaning Thursday, lies 110km down the coast, while Pazar, Sunday, is near the Georgian border). From Çarşamba, the road takes a short cut across the delta of the **Yeşilırmak**. This area, like most of the Black Sea region, is extremely good farmland. From Sinop to Çarşamba, and inland along the Yeşilırmak valley, Turkish tobacco has been the major crop. Now, along the roadside up to Trabzon, there are mostly hazelnut plantations; the little *fındık*, as the Turks call it, is a surprisingly important export crop.

After Trabzon, tea plantations cover most of the land. Throughout, however, one more local speciality keeps the Black Sea farmers prosperous – the best cherries anywhere. They're indigenous here; the Romans first brought cherry trees from the Black Sea into Europe, and from there they spread throughout the world.

Ünye and Ordu

The closest the Turkish Black Sea has to a seaside resort is modest, amiable **Ünye,** set on a pretty half-moon bay with beaches, restaurants and camping sites extending for several kilometres on either side of the town. Ünye itself, built around a beach and a shady promenade, retains traces of fortifications built when it was ancient Oenae. Caves along the shore near the town are one of the few Black Sea haunts of the rare, elusive monk seal. Between Ünye and Ordu the road, placid since Samsun, suddenly climbs into an exuberance of corniche turns, up and around the rugged peninsula

Getting around between Samsun and Trabzon

The **bus** and **dolmuş** services along this part of the coast are excellent and it is easy to hop from town to town. The centres of all the coastal towns are just off the main coastal road. Ask to be let off the bus there and not at the bus stations, which are sometimes inconveniently located inland. Giresun can be reached by ferry from Istanbul, Zonguldak, Sinop, Samsun and Trabzon.

the Greeks called the Promontory of Jason. Below the cliffs lie secluded fishing villages and untouched beaches; the best of these faces an islet, within easy swimming distance of the shore, where a ruin has become a home for great flocks of seagulls. Perhaps this is the 'Island of Ares', where the Argonauts were attacked by a flock of birds dropping feathered darts. A temple of Ares was said to have been founded on the island. Not long before the *Argo* was launched, according to the generally accepted order of myths, Hercules had tramped these shores on his ninth labour, securing the girdle of the Amazon Queen Hippolyta. The Amazon city Thermiscyra and its river Thermodon may have been at Terme, or near Ordu, if indeed it ever existed in the form mythographers have made for it. To the Greeks, this part of the Black Sea has always been associated with the Amazons, a confusion arising perhaps from Bronze Age Achaean merchants encountering matriarchal tribes during their exploratory voyages into Pontus.

The road to Ordu shows the Black Sea coast at its best: rugged, dramatic and verdant. Along some parts of the road, the trees are so draped in creepers and vines that the effect is almost tropical. Here too are isolated hamlets such as **Mersin** and pleasant coastal villages such as **Perşembe** which have so far been spared the concretization of the towns to the east.

Ordu, a Greek foundation named Cotyora, has grown into a city of 800,000. It keeps some reminders of the days of King Mithridates: the **Caleoğlu Castle**, 5km inland, and some cliff tombs like those in Amasya. There's a large beach east of the town, but if you're looking for something a little different, try the crater lake up in the mountains at **Cambaşı**, 70km south of Ordu, which is completely encircled by beaches. Ordu has a small museum in the centre of town, built in a restored Ottoman mansion.

Giresun and Tirebolu

 Giresun

The next town, **Giresun**, surrounds a small table-top peninsula with a Byzantine castle perched on top, a striking sight, almost a mirror image in miniature of Alanya on the Mediterranean coast. Giresun is a pleasant town, brimming with breezy charm. It is also a cherry and hazelnut centre, its streets offering glimpses into warehouses with mountains of nuts being scooped into hessian sacks and loaded onto lorries for export. As well as the castle, it has an 18th-century Greek church, now a rather uninspiring museum, and the tomb of Seyit Vakas, who won Giresun for the Ottomans in 1461. **Giresun Island**, just offshore, and another candidate for Jason's Island of Ares, is the largest of the Black Sea islands, and the only one inhabited. You sometimes hear it referred to as 'Amazon Island'; locally it's believed that the ruins belong to Ares' temple and the palace of the Amazon queens who built it.

After Giresun, the beaches never seem to end, but it is the wild mountain scenery that once more commands your attention. All along the route, those Pontic mountains have lurked close to the shore; now their wooded slopes press in closer, in a shade of green you would more expect to see in England than Turkey. From Samsun to Trabzon, there are no major roads inland across the mountains; this is one of Turkey's greatest areas of wilderness, and the difficulty of the terrain ensures it will remain so.

Further along the coast, **Tirebolu** not so long ago resembled a south Devon coastal village, with steep and partly cobbled streets and houses tumbling down towards the sea. Now the lovely old higgledy-piggledy homes have been hemmed in by their ferro-concrete descendants. Midway up the slender main street the town's new mosque overlooks the sea and the castle that stands in ruins on a rocky promontory. The next castle, at **Akçakale**, past Görele, was built by the emperors of Trebizond, serving as a reminder that you are near the borders of that lost realm.

Where to Stay between Samsun and Trabzon

ⓘ **Ünye >**
on the main coastal road next to the Ünyespar Sosyal Tesisleri, **t** *0452 323 2569*

ⓘ **Ordu >>**
Atatürk Bulvarı 116A, Belediye Binası, **t** *0452 223 1608*

ⓘ **Giresun >>**
Gazi Caddesi 72, **t** *0454 212 3190*

Ünye

Otel Kumsal, 5km west of Ünye, **t 0452 323 4490 (€€). A pleasant beach hotel with sea view doubles.

Difana Otel, Gölevi Mh. Samsun Ordu Karayolu, **t 0452 323 1602, *www.difanahotel.com* (€€). Similarly priced and on the main coastal highway, with simple but comfortable rooms, some with sea views.

Otel Hasan Bey, Devlet Sahil Yolu Gölevi Mah. 110, **t** 0452 324 1313, *www.otelhasanbey.com* (€€). One of the nicest along the coastal road, with well-appointed rooms, a good restaurant and a beachside pool.

As well as plenty of camping options 5–6km west of town such as Plaj Camping, **t** 0452 324 7368, there are a number of pleasant family-run *pensions* in Ünye:

Pınar, Devrent Mevkii 23, **t** 0452 323 3496, is a notable one. Bedecked in kilims and carpets, the rooms are very light and lead onto balconies; double from just 35 YTL.

Ordu

Turist Otel, Atatürk Bulvarı 134, **t 0452 225 3140 (€€–€). Nothing fancy, but OK for one night; spacious but characterless rooms with private bath.

Giresun

***Kit-tur Oteli, Arifbey Caddesi 2, **t** 0454 212 0245, *www.otelkittur.com* (€€). The best, with smart rooms.

***Hotel Basar, **t** 0454 212 9920 (€€). Brand new and caters ostentatiously for businessmen, all soaring lobby, glass elevators and cavernous conference rooms. Staff are friendly, however, and north-facing bedrooms look out onto the sea.

Hotel Çarıkçı, Osmanağa Caddesi 6, **t 0454 216 1026 (€€). Also has a central location and is much better value; almost comparable doubles for €40.

Eating Out between Samsun and Trabzon

Ünye

Çamlık Restoranı, set in a pine grove just off the coastal road 3km west of town (€€€). On a terrace overlooking the sea. Fish is the Çamlık's *raison d'être*, but it's also worth nibbling on some of their regional specialities such as *mısır ekmeği* (thin cornbread with butter) accompanied by *turşu kavurması* (pickles).

Ordu

Grand Mıdı, İskele Üstü No.55, t 0452 214 0340 (€€). Ordu is a good place to eat fish, as on this small pier, serving good seafood at reasonable prices.

Çotanak Restaurant, Kumbaşı Mah. Sahil Cad. 2, t 0452 212 0065 (€€). Specializes in dishes that use hazelnuts, for which the region is renowned, as an ingredient; even serves hazelnut soup!

Giresun

The little king of Black Sea coastal cuisine is a small fish called the *hamsi*, best eaten when in season. Of the 40 or so recipes for it in these parts, one speciality worth trying is the *hamsi börek*.

Hotel Basar, top-floor restaurant, t 0454 212 9920 (€€). A pricey but appetising option; the staff are very friendly and may let you sample the Black Sea specialities in the kitchens, such as sargan fish or *dible* – green beans with rice and a little oil.

Tibor, t 0454 212 3078, on the 4th and 5th floors of İncedayı Sokak 4 (€€–€). Provides a more exclusive and tasty experience. It's a private club with marble floors and wood-panelled walls and a wide selection of alcohol. Tourists are welcome; 20 YTL for an excellent meal.

Deniz, t 0454 216 1158 (€). On the main square, very large but always full.

Trabzon

Trabzon, Trebizond, Trapezus – whatever transitions the name has undergone since the merchants of Sinope founded it in the 8th century BC, it has always had an exotic ring to Western ears. When the Greeks first came, they returned with shocking tales of a people called Mosynoecians, practitioners of open-air fornication who lived in wooden castles (they may have been related to the Picts of Scotland). For centuries after the founding of the city, Trapezus was the easternmost limit of the Greek world.

In spite of the difficulty of crossing the steep coastal mountains, Trapezus somehow managed to become an important *entrepôt* for trade to the east. During the Byzantine period, after trade in the Mediterranean was disrupted by the Arab conquests, all the caravans from Persia and beyond with goods to sell to Europe found their way here. By now the name had become Trebizond, and the city had reached its balmiest days when the Crusaders sacked Constantinople in 1204. Alexis Comnenus, a member of the former dynastic family whose intrigues and corruptions had contributed to the Byzantine decline, escaped from the fallen city; in flight he raised an army of mercenaries in Asia from what he had left of the family's wealth, occupied Trebizond and proclaimed it capital of a new empire, headed by himself under the title of Grand Comnenus.

Getting to and around Trabzon

Trabzon has an **airport**, 8km out of town, with daily flights to Ankara and Istanbul. It can also be reached by **bus** or by Turkish Maritime Lines **ferries** from Istanbul.

A large new coastal **highway** now runs along most of the Black Sea shore and has made travel here a lot more comfortable, though at the expense of some small fishing communities. The roads over the mountains to the south can be an ordeal in the winter – especially the Zigana Pass south of Trabzon, where silk and spice caravans disappeared regularly in the old days.

Trabzon's sights are spread out, and the **dolmuşes** along Kahramanmaraş Caddesi, connecting the town square with Aya Sofya, can take you to most of them (look for destination signs pinned to the windscreen). To reach the old churches and monasteries of the periphery, though, it's either a long hike or a taxi ride. The main bus stops and taxi stand are in the Meydan, the central square.

Alexis had chosen well; his new city was impregnable and brought him a good income, and the Greek population was glad to have him. He and his successors of the Comnenus house brought all the oriental luxury and ceremony of Constantinople with them. Having once more the chance to indulge their fantasies, the Comnenes spread Trebizond's fame throughout the world; in the European geographies and chronicles of the day, it conjured up the same half-legendary aura as Baghdad or Samarkand. Its military fortunes rose and fell; at its greatest extent it held sway over all the Black Sea coast, but near its end its domains had dwindled to just the city itself. The Comnenes kept their state afloat less by military prowess than by craft, making good use of diplomacy, and ladling out tribute money to the Selcuks, Mongols and Ottomans when words failed. Like the Habsburgs, Comnenes were always careful to marry well; contemporary accounts suggest that the dynasty's greatest resource was cute princesses, much desired by neighbouring potentates. This allowed the Grand Comneni to keep their web of alliances intact at all times.

By the middle of the 15th century, unfortunately, the only neighbour Trebizond had left was the voracious Ottoman sultan, who already had enough wives. After Mehmet Fatih captured Constantinople, Trebizond, the last free Greek state, was obviously next on the menu. Mehmet appeared in 1461, with the greatest army and fleet ever seen in the Black Sea before or since. It made the desired impression on David Comnenus, the last emperor, who surrendered the city without a shot. The Turks treated Trabzon (as they came to call it) very well; the 17th-century Turkish traveller Evliya Celebi praised its well-educated, poetry-loving populace. But, faced with endemic attacks from Russians and pirates, as well as constant local feudal quarrels, the city inevitably declined. The Russians did considerable damage when they captured the city in 1916, but Trabzon has been recovering. Today, it's a friendly, peaceful, rather conservative place. Its port is busy, its suburbs expanding and, best of all, its Trabzonspor is the best soccer side outside Istanbul; they've won the national title six times.

The Modern Town

Don't be discouraged by the entrance to the town. The neglect and squalor of the port area and coastal highway, with their vistas of rubbish and broken concrete, leads directly into a shambolic red-light district, populated by 'natashas' from the sizeable Russian community that has appeared here since 1990. You have to climb the hill to get into the city, going up İskele Caddesi to the **Meydan** (also known as **Atatürk Alanı**), the main square of the modern city; once up there, you'll be relieved to see that Trabzon is quite an agreeable town after all. The square, with its shady park, city hall and fire station, with shiny red engines out on display for all to admire, is not only the centre of the business district; almost all the hotels and restaurants congregate here as well. Next to the fire station, the 16th-century **İskender Paşa Camii** commemorates a popular Ottoman governor; its shallow dome, curved like an upside-down soup plate, shows Byzantine influence.

Along Kahramanmaraş Caddesi

Either of the two big streets leading west from the square, Kahramanmaraş Caddesi or Hükümet Caddesi (which also appears as Uzun Sokak or Uzun Yol on maps), will take you to the old Greek city, but Kahramanmaraş Caddesi is by far the more interesting. It skirts Trabzon's **bazaar**, a large and colourful district of narrow

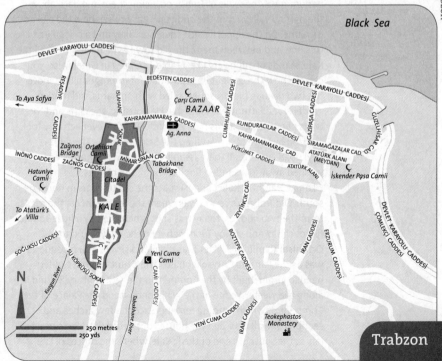

Trabzon

streets where many of the crafts that once brought Trabzon fame – all manner of work in copper, silver and gold – are still going strong. As is common in Muslim cities, Trabzon sees no need to separate religion and commerce. The attractive 1839 **Çarşı Camii**, right at the heart of the market district, is directly connected to the 16th-century *bedesten*. All around, the maze of blind alleys and old *hanlar* with a talent for somehow looking even older than they really are give the place a rare air of mystery and impenetrability.

Further along Kahramanmaraş Caddesi, peering out from a tiny square, stands the oldest Byzantine church left in Trabzon, **Ag. Anna (Küçük Ayvasıl Kilisesi)**, built in the 7th century and restored in the 9th. There is something endearing about this plain, forlorn, padlocked little church. The basilica form is unusual in Byzantine buildings – except in Trabzon, a town strictly orthodox in doctrine (St Athanasius himself is said to be buried here), but heretical in architecture. Trabzon's churches eschew the centralized pattern of their counterparts in Constantinople and elsewhere. The plan of Ag. Anna has three parallel naves, the one in the centre raised to form a clerestory with a few small windows.

The Old Town and Walls

To get into the old town, find your way back to Hükümet Caddesi. You soon come to the high **Tabakhane Bridge**, and, beyond it, a panorama of the walls of Trebizond, rising sheer and hard above the narrow valley. From the bridge it's easy to see how the city got its name. On the opposite side there's a valley and a bridge just like this one, and between them, the old town, which the Turks call the **Kale**, stands up high very like a table – *trapeza* in Greek. Also, you can see how the city got its reputation for impregnability; above the two ravines, picturesquely filled with orchards and market gardens and latterly with ramshackle housing, the cliffs and the walls above them rise as high as 150ft. No army ever actually took Trabzon by force of arms; when the Selcuks under Alâeddin Keykubad tried to, all their assaults failed and their army was washed away in a sudden flood through the ravines.

Long, straight **İç Kale Caddesi** splits the old town from north to south. Old Trabzon's centre was where the İç Kale meets the roads from the two bridges; today this spot is occupied by a little square full of chairs and sleepy Turks, between the Vilayet and the **Ortahisar Camii**. This latter is as plain and severe as a mosque as it was as the Panayia Chrysokephalos, the 'Church of the Golden-headed Virgin', built by the Comneni in the 13th century. Behind it, along the western edge of the walls, once stood the Palace of the Comneni, of which nothing remains except a few arches and sections of wall between the houses of the district. Nor is much left at the southern end of the İç Kale, where the offices of the

Trebizond state and army had their quarters, at the highest and least vulnerable end of the 'table'.

Byzantine Monuments

If you follow İç Kale Caddesi beyond the walls to the south, you will enjoy the best view of the city and its extensions up the surrounding hillsides. From out here, you can pick out three other Byzantine monuments in the steep neighbourhoods south of Atatürk Alanı – they will thus be easier to find if you wish to visit them. Following Boztepe Caddesi south takes you to two of them. Ag. Eugenios was one of the first works of the Comneni after their arrival, built on the site of an older church and dedicated to Trebizond's patron saint. Mehmet Fatih converted it into a mosque on the first Friday after his conquest of the city, and it has been called **Yeni Cuma Cami** (New Friday Mosque) ever since. On the other side of the hill called **Boztepe** stands the **Teokephastos Monastery** of the same period. One of the last churches to be built, the 14th-century Ag. Philipi, is now the **Kudrettin Mosque**. Further out, on a dirt track on the back slope of Boztepe, the little-known Kaymaklı Monastery contains fascinating Armenian frescoes. Some, like the Last Judgement and scenes from the Apocalypse, date back to the 15th century.

Kaymaklı Monastery
for entrance ask at the tourist office

Leaving the Kale over the western **Zağnos Bridge**, you soon find yourself in another pleasant square, with mighty plane trees surrounding Trabzon's finest Islamic work, the **Hatuniye Camii**, built by Sultan Selim I in honour of his mother; her tomb stands just outside the entrance.

Aya Sofya and Atatürk's Villa

If Trabzon's most famous building must be mentioned last, it is only because it's the furthest from the centre, a good mile's walk or dolmuş ride from the Kale. Set on a little hill planted with roses, above the fortunately invisible coastal highway, stands the Aya Sofya. This church had been neglected for centuries, and was on the verge of collapse when a team of archaeologists went to work on it in the 1950s. Many parts, including the soaring cylindrical dome, have been almost completely reconstructed, but, more importantly, the original **frescoes** have been recovered from beneath the plaster and restored. These are Trabzon's greatest tourist attraction, the finest late Byzantine art east of Istanbul.

⭐ Aya Sofya

Emperor Manuel Comnenus had the church built in 1245, one of the last great buildings the Greeks made when time was running out for them in Anatolia. Between the Romanesque arches, the Western-style naves with their barrel-vaulted ceilings and the sculptural frieze of Adam and Eve on the south porch, there are almost as many Western European and Armenian elements in the design as Byzantine. What the builders lacked, the artists more than made up for; Aya Sofya's vivid 13th-century frescoes, with their perfection of line and colour, have a special place in the story of the last Byzantine renaissance, the efflorescence of painting in the Greek twilight whose influence helped make possible Western Europe's own Renaissance. Almost half of all the original paintings survived sufficiently to be restored. The best, perhaps, are those in the narthex, various scenes of miracles from the life of Jesus. There are many other familiar themes: the Annunciation, and the four Evangelists with their attributes. The Virgin Mary in the Ascension takes her place in the central apse, while a huge, half-effaced figure of the Christ Pantocrator looms over all from the dome. Most unfortunately, another scene in the porch, a Last Judgement in the manner of Bosch or Brueghel, is almost completely lost; among the remnants a lone wolf devouring souls can be made out. In the grounds of the church, a quaint **tea garden** operates around a traditional Black Sea farmhouse with a raised granary.

Atatürk Köşkü
take a city bus, dolmuş or taxi; open daily 9–5; adm

Atatürk's villa, the **Atatürk Köşkü**, presides over a wooded slope of pines, 5km southwest of Trabzon. This moulded white concoction was constructed between 1890 and 1903 and presented to Kemal in 1931 after he expressed an interest on one of his three visits here. After his death in 1938, the municipality appropriated the villa and subsequently turned it into a museum, with endless Atatürk memorabilia throughout. The gardens are a peaceful spot, with a pleasant tea garden set in the pines and a restaurant next door.

South of Trabzon

Even if you intend to push on to the end of the coast, the temptation to turn inland will be strong here; the Trabzon–Erzurum road, the last stretch of the Silk Route in the days of the Comneni, is today one of the few good roads over the steep eastern Black Sea Mountains between Samsun and Artvin. Over **Zigana Pass**, climbing up to 6,300ft, the road ascends more sharply, contorts along more hairpin turns and looks down over more bottomless cliffs than any mountain road you've ever seen. For your trouble, the views will be reward enough; all around, the slopes and crags are covered with forests and banks of wild flowers, at least until the treeline is crossed, shortly before the eternal snows of the pass. (The rest of this route is described under 'Erzurum', see p.466.)

From the wilderness of Judea to the cloudy heights of Mount Athos, the Greek Orthodox Church always likes its monasteries perched high and precariously: fortresses in the sky that freed the monks from unnecessary exposure to the world below. Nowhere in Turkey is this better exemplified than at the **Sumela Monastery**, 43km east of Trabzon near the pretty village of **Maçka**. It's a

Sumela Monastery

Getting to Sumela

To get to Sumela from Trabzon in summer, **buses** leave from the offices on Taksim Caddesi, to the southeast of the main square. **Dolmuşes** run from the southwest corner of Atatürk Alanı. Or you could try getting a few people together to share a **taxi**: the tourist office should be able to help out here.

remarkable sight, 1,000ft above a deep valley kept verdant by a bubbling river, the white walls of its façade standing out sharply from the sheer grey cliff in which it is embedded. Sumela was founded in the 4th century when a monk, having received divine instruction in a dream, brought to the cliff's caves an icon of the Virgin painted by the Apostle Luke. As increasing numbers of monks came to pray before the icon and to invoke miracles, the complex was extended, often with the assistance of the Byzantine emperors. By the 14th century its power and influence was second only to that of Mount Athos. Yet this eminence collapsed within the space of a year, after the fiasco of the Greek invasion and the subsequent population exchange of 1923 resulted in its monks being expelled *en masse*. The holy icon was spirited away to Athens and gradually, inexorably, Sumela began to crumble.

Today, despite the restoration attempts, the actual complex may prove a little disappointing, but it is still worth a visit – and the views are spectacular. The steep climb up to the monastery ends in a series of gutted shells, defaced by the scrawl of graffiti. Only the cave in which Luke's icon was stored has been spared, and that merely in part; sealed off by an iron grille, some of the frescoes that once beautified its interior can still be discerned.

This region was once rich in convents and monasteries, but today only two are left, both in appalling condition – **Peristera**, 35km from Trabzon, and **Vazelon**, south of Maçka. Both are very difficult to reach and of interest only to serious Byzantine monastery buffs.

East of Trabzon

East of Trabzon, the Empire of Tea truly begins. By now, even if you've spent only a little time in Turkey, you'll have had countless glasses of tea thrust in front of you; it all comes from these green mountain slopes. Demand is high, and this far corner of the nation has become quite prosperous in a modest way. Around Rize you will notice that the women wear a very distinctive costume consisting of the *keşan*, a vertically striped black and purple or black and tan apron worn over a skirt; and the *peştemal*, a very attractive multicoloured shawl. Both these garments can be tied up to form a pouch for harvesting hazelnuts. Many of the people are Laz, a largely Muslim folk, culturally related to the Georgians, who have been here a long time; before and after Roman rule they briefly had an independent kingdom along the coast. Once renowned as fighters, the Laz made up Atatürk's bodyguard. Today you'll see the old men in the cafés and buses, with their berets, big moustaches and long watch-chains, jolly and easygoing; the Turks secretly envy them. Also present are Georgians; the Republic of Georgia is just across the border at Hopa.

Rize, the capital of the tea region, barely squeezes in between the mountains and the sea. Here, behind the tea slopes, mountains comprising the **Kaçkar** chain rise as high as 12,500ft. Approximately 45km to the east of Rize is **Ardeşen** and a turning to **Çamlıhemşin** and **Ayder**. Both these villages are set in magnificent mountain scenery and are starting points for walks. Near Çamlıhemşin are the **Valley of Storms** (**Fırtına Vadisi**), and **Zil Castle** (**Kale-i Zir**).

It is possible to visit to one of the many **tea factories** lining the main road round Rize and Hopa. But beware: the strong smell of the fermenting leaves may well turn your stomach, and if you are offered a cup of tea, ask for it *açık* ('open', i.e. weak): the tea workers favour tea so strong it can be an emetic for those unused to it.

Once you have reached **Hopa**, there is nowhere to go apart from the Georgian border, some 30km away. In the days of the Soviet Union the border was closed and this part of Turkey seemed a dead end. Today, with the border wide open, prosperity is growing.

Where to Stay in and around Trabzon

ⓘ Trabzon >
behind the İskender Paşa Camii, next to the Hotel Benli,
t 0462 326 4760

ⓘ Rize >>
on the 5th floor of the Valilik, to the west of town, t 0464 213 0407

Trabzon

With the opening up of the former Soviet Union to trade and travel, Trabzon has metamorphosed from a neglected provincial backwater to a vital stepping stone to the east. Most hotels are around the main square, making them convenient but noisy.

*****Zorlu Grand Hotel, Kahramanmaraş Caddesi 9, t 0462 326 8400, *www.zorlugrand.com* (€€€€€–€€€€). It's stylish and impressive, with a sweeping marble double staircase leading up to a luxurious reception area the size of a small aircraft hangar. Rooms are similarly airy and well-upholstered.

***Horon Otel, just north of Atatürk Alanı at Sıramağazalar 125, t 0462 326 6455 *www.hotelhoron.com* (€€€–€€). The façade has been recently restored and there is a pleasant lobby, with two modern oil paintings showing what the management claims was Trabzon in 1880 and 1940, although

the romanticized depictions look more like Trebizond *c.* 1400. Bedrooms are faded, though those facing north are probably the quietest in the city.

Nur, Cami Sokak 4, t 0462 323 0445 (€€). Next to the İskenderpaşa Camii. The staff are very friendly, the en suite rooms compact but bright. Rooms on the top floor have good Black Sea views, but are also exactly level with the nearby minaret's loudspeakers, so much so that you can hear the muezzin swallow before starting his call to prayer.

Rize

**Keleş Oteli, Palandöken Caddesi 2, t 0404 217 4612, *www.kelesotel.com.tr* (€€€). A very good stopover option.

****Peronti, Turgay Ciner Cad. 78, t 0466 351 7663, *www.peronti-otel. com* (€€€). Corner rooms overlook the sea. Popular with tourist groups, but it has more of a business hotel feel.

Hopa

**Cihan, in Hopa, t 0466 351 2333, *www.hotelcihan.com* (€€–€). Simple but pleasant.

Eating Out in Trabzon

Trabzon

Özgür Restaurant, t 0462 321 2370, *www.ozgurrestaurant.com* (€). With set menus from 7 YTL, this attracts most of the tour groups. The food is standard bistro snacks and kebabs.

Kıbrıs, on the main square (€). A good, cheap restaurant (5 YTL). The décor is much nicer upstairs and you can also enjoy the view of the square.

Çınar Restaurant, on the southeast corner of the square (€). Sells freshly cooked dishes made from local meat and produce; for now at least it's as busy and as cheap as the McDonald's next door.

Şişman Restaurant, Kahramanmaraş Caddesi 5 (€). The never-ending climb upstairs to the rooftop will be rewarded with excellent inexpensive food (10 YTL for a kebab, salad and a beer).

Tao-Georgia

 Georgian villages

Up in the mountains above the coast, the far northeastern corner of Turkey is wild and inaccessible territory. These lands are the former marches of the ancient kingdom of Georgia. The former principalities of **Tao** and **Klarjeti** today lie in Turkey, and make up the area known as Tao-Georgia.

All that remains of the Georgians is their churches, beautiful both in themselves and in their settings. Built in the 9th to 11th centuries, many of the churches are nevertheless in a quite remarkable state of preservation. The architecture is similar to Armenian, but less sombre; typical features are tall naves, usually crowned with a drum and dome, and carvings of animals inspired by the Persian bestiary. The churches lie off the beaten track, some of them in *yaylalar* (summer villages) and accessible only after a strenuous walk of an hour or so. However, take heart; you can be toiling up an inhospitable mountainside, with the sound of the river below echoing up the valley, when you'll round a corner and

---

The Georgians

One of the most ancient Christian nations, Georgia was converted to the new faith in the 4th century by St Nino, a female missionary from Cappadocia who, fleeing from the Great Persecution of Diocletian, had earlier converted the Armenians. Georgia was fought over by the Byzantines and the Persians and even came under the control of Arab caliphs before settling down to be a relatively stable feudal state, ruled over by a branch of the Armenian Bagratid family, who claimed descent from King David of Israel. During the reign of King David the Great of Taik (a southern province, with its capital at Oltu), the kingdom of Georgia extended as far as Van. David, who died in 1001, was also a great church-builder, and his work was carried on by his descendants, particularly David the Restorer, who subjugated the feudal lords and defeated the Selcuks, regaining control of Tiflis (now in the Republic of Georgia). He died in 1125, after which there was relative stability for the rest of the century.

Under the leadership of Queen Tamara (who reigned from 1144 to 1212), Georgia waxed into its golden age and became influential as well as stable. Tamara was an able diplomat with an expansionist foreign policy. She captured Kars and harassed northern Persia. But the Mongols arrived early in the 13th century and the Tao-Georgians gradually converted to Islam; by the end of the 17th century, Christianity had almost died out in the area, leaving the churches to the elements.

Given how isolated the villages are, you might expect still to find speakers of Georgian (*Gürcü* in Turkish); but no, they are always in a village 'over there'.

Getting to and around Tao-Georgia

Artvin can be reached by **bus** from Trabzon (via Hopa), Erzurum and Kars. Yusufeli is connected to Artvin by regular **minibuses**, although the last one from Yusufeli often leaves at lunchtime. Less regular services connect Yusufeli to Erzurum and Trabzon.

The Georgian churches are scattered over the area and it is difficult to see more than two or three in one day, even if you have your own car. A taxi can be hired for the day from Artvin; agree on a price before setting out. Buses from Artvin travel regularly along all the main roads, so a cheaper alternative would be to catch a bus to Yusufeli or Ardanuç and get a taxi there.

come across the church sitting in a green oasis of fruit trees with a little stream running next to the path.

The Unfortunate River Çoruh

The region is dominated by river valleys that provide the key to its charm, isolation and history. The river Çoruh and its tributaries such as the Tortum, Berta and Oltu are fast-flowing mountain rivers that have sliced steep-sided gorges through the rocks. Just as the Çoruh was becoming known as a destination for rafting and hiking, the busy beavers of the state Directorate of State Hydraulic Works (DSI) swooped in to turn it into a miniature version of the Southeast Anatolia Project (see p.494). No less than eleven hydro-electric dams are built or planned on the river and its tributaries, and they will create a chain of lakes that will submerge large parts of the valleys. With all the construction, the area will be torn up for years to come.

The valleys are littered with castles perched high on rocky outcrops, bearing testimony that times here have not always been as peaceful as they are now. Two of the largest castles, at Artvin and Ardahan, were built by Selim the Grim in the 16th century, when the Ottomans were consolidating their power in the northeast. Other castles can be seen at Ardanuç and near Şavşat.

Look out for the picturesque wooden footbridges and for 'basket'-type bridges, where people haul themselves along a rope or wire while standing on a platform. Stone bridges are few and far between; there is an attractive one across the Berta.

Artvin and Around

Artvin is a charming little provincial capital perched high on a mountainside, with a pleasant, relaxed atmosphere despite the narrow streets coughing with traffic for much of the day. One of the new dams is being built close by, and soon Artvin will be practically on the shore of a lake. Many of the women here walk freely in European dress with heads uncovered – surprising in a town so far east and so small (just over 22,000 inhabitants). It is impossible to confuse these women with the 'natashas', heavily

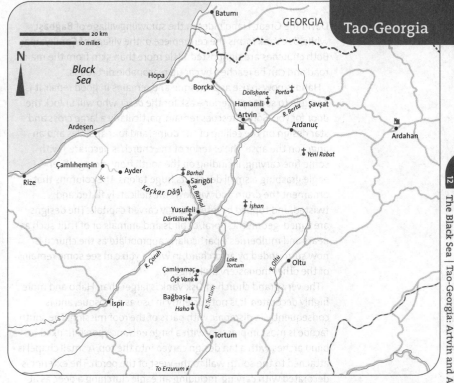

dolled-up Russian prostitutes who have been drawn westwards since 1991 by the honeypot of Turkey's (relatively) buoyant economy. By the mid-1990s, their presence had reached epidemic proportions, but now, though they are still evident in Artvin and nearby towns such as Rize, their numbers are on the wane. Artvin is also famous for its pastry shops, and for the annual bull-fighting festival at **Kafkasor** in late June.

The alternative base is **Yusufeli**, a village on the lovely Barhal river that is threatened with total immersion by another controversial, 700ft-high dam. The NGOs are on the case, and European companies have already been forced to drop out of the project. Right now, though, this welcoming and relaxing village remains a base for many outdoor activities: rafting down 'plus five' rapids in May–August, or hiking in the Kaçkar mountains, including four-day treks to the 3,937m summit of **Mount Kaçkar** itself. Experienced canoeists and rock-climbers will have no lack of rivers deep and mountains high to keep them busy.

Haho and Öşk Vank

These are the two largest churches in the area, both monastery churches of cruciform plan, with a circular drum surmounted by the typical conical roof, and both built in the late 10th century by

David the Great. Haho hides in the sprawling village of **Bağbaşı**, while Öşk Vank forms the centrepiece of the village of **Çamlıyamaç**. Both churches are signposted, little more than 5km from the main road and can be reached by car up reasonable dirt roads.

Haho is now in use as a mosque and remains in good repair. It is possible to see the interior – ask for the *bekçi*, who will unlock the door for you. Some frescoes remain, particularly a large cross and star design on the ceiling of the dome, and four apostles and an angel on the apse. The exterior of the church is decorated with some fine carving, including on the south front a magnificent eagle grasping a small deer in its huge talons. The columns that ornament the drum and windows are delicately fluted and twisted, and topped by interestingly carved capitals. The designs are varied: geometric, floral, of birds and animals or of fruit such as pears and mulberries – particularly appropriate as the church is now surrounded by an orchard, in which you can see some remains of the other monastery buildings.

The very grand church of **Öşk Vank** is larger than Haho and more highly decorated. It is not currently in use as a mosque, and is consequently in disrepair, with parts of the roof missing. The south façade is most impressive, with a large entrance porch flanked by blind arches with a fan design carved into the top. A small chapel is attached to the south wall to the west of the porch. The exterior is decorated with carving, including an eagle clutching a deer, as at Haho, and two angels – both headless – on the south wall, another headless angel on the west wall of the chapel, and a bull and a lion on the north wall. Again, as at Haho, the capitals of the columns that decorate the windows and drum are worth inspecting – the drum has a charming pair of kissing rabbits. The interior also contains fragments of frescoes showing biblical scenes.

Barhal, Dörtkilise and İşhan

Further north, in the Çoruh valley, these churches provide an architectural contrast to Öşk Vank and Haho. Instead of a dome, they have tall, steeply roofed naves, flanked by two aisles. The exterior of both churches is decorated by blind arcades and some carving. Barhal also has some exterior terracotta decoration. Both these churches were built in the 10th century. Barhal is now used as a mosque, Dörtkilise as a barn. To get to **Barhal**, drive first to Yusufeli, then up into the mountains to Sarıgöl and continue along the Barhal stream to the church. **Dörtkilise** can be reached after a drive of about 5km along the Yusufeli–Bayburt road, followed by a two-hour walk.

İşhan lies just off the Yusufeli–Oltu road, a little after the turning to Erzurum. A new asphalt road (stabilized for the last few kilometres) goes direct to İşhan, winding up a mountainside so bare, you wonder how people can possibly live up here. Then, after about 5km of desert, suddenly round a corner is the green village of İşhan, full of children, shade and fruit. İşhan is a cathedral church, very elegant and similar in type and size to Haho. It was founded in the 7th century, rebuilt at the beginning of the 9th and converted in the 11th to a domed church with a lengthened west wing. The roof has gone but the walls and drum are intact. The oldest part of the church is the apse, which has an unusual arcaded ambulatory. The arches are horseshoe-shaped and are supported on capitals carved with rosette and floral reliefs. Some frescoes remain, including one in an alcove above a window, showing a black-faced man carrying a church that could be either Barhal or Dörtkilise.

Yeni Rabat

The chief charm of this little church is its setting, in a cabbage patch on a lush green alpine mountainside reminiscent of Switzerland. Yeni Rabat can be reached by taking the road to **Ardanuç** across the Berta Bridge. The road passes along a steep-sided gorge known locally as Cehennem Deresi (Hell Valley). After Ardanuç – formerly the capital of Tao-Georgia, but now a pleasant village guarded by a ruined castle – take the road to Ardahan. Some 12km from Ardanuç is a yellow sign to Yeni Rabat, pointing to a field of flowers. After a stiff climb of a quarter of an hour, you get your first glimpse of the church and the summer village of four houses. The 9th-century monastic church is in relatively good condition, with the drum and dome and much of the roof still intact. Although the exterior has lost many of its dressing stones, some very worn decorative carving remains, including some curiously looking like mushrooms or bundles of corn.

Dolişhane and Porta

Both these churches lie just off the Artvin–Şavşat road, above the valley of the river Berta. **Dolişhane** is in the village of **Hamamlı** and can be reached by car; the turning is on the right bank of the river, opposite Berta Bridge. The little church was built in the early 10th century and remains in good condition. Fragments of frescoes remain in the apse; these show figures labelled in Georgian. Outside, on the south wall is a sundial, a common feature of Georgian and Armenian churches. Some of the windows are decorated with carving; one has an inscription, a Star of David and two angels.

Only the fit and strong should attempt to visit **Porta**. About 45km along the Artvin–Şavşat road, a small yellow sign points to a pretty little waterfall. The path to Porta starts by the waterfall, then winds up the mountainside, past dwarf oaks and pomegranate trees. After a strenuous climb of about an hour, just when you feel you can go no further, you will be rewarded by the sight of the church in the middle of a charming summer village of wooden houses. The village, inhabited only in August, appears untouched since the 19th century. The electric cables visible are for the winter village, a further two-mile climb away, but which can be reached by car from Şavşat. The church itself, although more ruined than some of the others, is picturesque none the less; the drum is unusual, being connected to the dome in a zigzag pattern. To the west is a small drum and dome, now used as a store for hay.

Where to Stay in Tao-Georgia

Apart from in Artvin, accommodation in the far northeastern corner of Turkey is sparse and simple.

(i) Artvin >
Cami Meydanı,
t 0466 212 3071

Artvin

**Karahan, İnönü Caddesi, t 0466 212 1800 (€€). On the main road, and the most comfortable hotel in Artvin. Most rooms have baths. The hotel, which occupies the top four floors of a shopping centre, has splendid views of the town and valley; it is owned by two brothers, one of whom is a keen photographer and local historian. Unfortunately, even this is not immune to the allure of the income provided by the 'natasha' trade.

Kaçkar, on Hamam Sokak, just behind İnönü Caddesi, t 0466 212 9009 (€€). Double rooms with TV and few frills; ask for one of the rooms on the top floor, which have excellent views.

Yusufeli (Barhal Village)

Accommodation here is cheap, cheerful and natasha-free. Owners will be able to assist with trekking and rafting also.

Marsis Otel, Altiparmak (Barhal) Köyü, t 0466 826 2002, *www.marsisotel.com* (€€). A village house and trekker's favourite in the beautiful village of Barhal, with panoramic views of the mountains from its dining terrace; if you're lucky, you may even spot a bear.

Karahan Pansiyon, Altiparmak (Barhal) Köyü, t 0466 826 2071 *www.karahan pension.com* (€€–€). Simple mountain lodge also popular with trekkers, who use it as a base for various routes including the two-day trek to Çamlıhemşin. Not to be confused with the hotel in Artvin town.

Across Yusufeli's bridge and a short walk along the river are two basic campsites. **Greenpeace Camping**, t 0466 811 3620, has the edge over **Akın Camping**.

Eating Out in Tao-Georgia

Artvin

Restaurants in Artvin are few and simple; the pastry shops are excellent. **Karahan Hotel Restaurant** (€). Serves good 'real' food and not just the wretched grills that most hotels think they can get away with. A meal will cost about 15 YTL per person.

Hanedan Restaurant, opposite the hotel (€). Similarly priced and worth a stop if you can get one of the tables at the window with panoramic views of the mountains and valley.

Yusufeli

Mahzen Restaurant, t 0466 811 2008 (€). Opposite the Hotel Bahal by the suspension bridge, with tables overlooking the river. Alcohol is also served, but the steps leading into the river are for white-water rafters who pit stop here; they are not there to fish out drunks from the river. Basic meals 15 YTL.

Saray, t 0466 811 2816 (€). The favoured spot for a good 'workers' lunch, with traditional home-type foods from 5–10 YTL.

Ardanuç

For a good, cheap lunch while visiting the Georgian churches, plan your trip so that you are in Ardanuç around lunchtime. The village, despite having a population of fewer than 3,500, has an excellent *lokanta*.

Northwestern Anatolia

This is the real Anatolia: a stark, rough-edged, land, where bleak and empty vastnesses change in a twinkling to little green paradises and spectacular mountain scenery. Parts of the Anatolian interior can still seem like a country for explorers. Everywhere, you will see the fine caravanserais built for merchants by the medieval Selcuk sultans. This is the Turkey of sheep and shepherds and donkey carts, carpet weavers and whirling dervishes, an ageless and endlessly fascinating place. It was the homeland of Anatolia's first historical nation, the Hittite Empire, with the tremendous ruins of its capital. And now it is the home of Ankara, with all its skyscrapers and shiny shopping malls, dragging the rest of Anatolia into the 21st century along with it.

13

Don't miss

1 Turkey's city of ceramics
Kütahya **p.386**

2 Ancient Phrygia and Midas' temples
Near Afyon **p.390**

3 The best of Turkey's past
Museum of Anatolian Civilizations, Ankara **p.401**

4 The lost capital of the Hittite empire
Hattusas **p.407**

5 A gracious town on a green river
Amasya **p.416**

See map overleaf

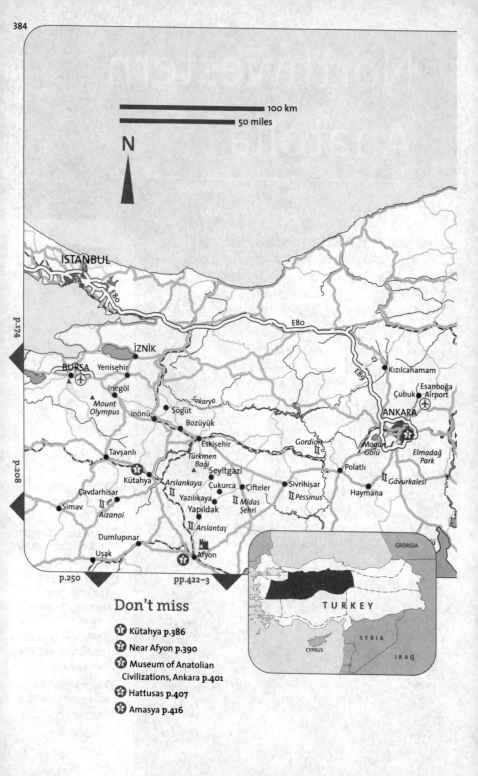

100 km
50 miles

N

ISTANBUL

p.174

İZNİK

BURSA Yenişehir

Mount Olympus İnegöl

İnönü Söğüt

Sakarya

Bozüyük

Eskişehir

Türkmen Baği

Tavşanlı

Kütahya

Arslankaya Çukurca

Yazılıkaya Çifteler

Yapıldak Midaş Şehri

Arslantaş

Seyitgazi

Sivrihisar

Pessinus

Gordion

Polatlı

Mogan Gölü

ANKARA

Çubuk Esanboğa Airport

Kızılcahamam

E89

E80

E80

Elmadağ Park

Gâvurkalesi

Haymana

p.208

Çavdarhisar

Simav

Aizanoi

Dumlupınar

Uşak

Afyon

p.250

pp.422–3

GEORGIA

TURKEY

SYRIA

CYPRUS

IRAQ

Don't miss

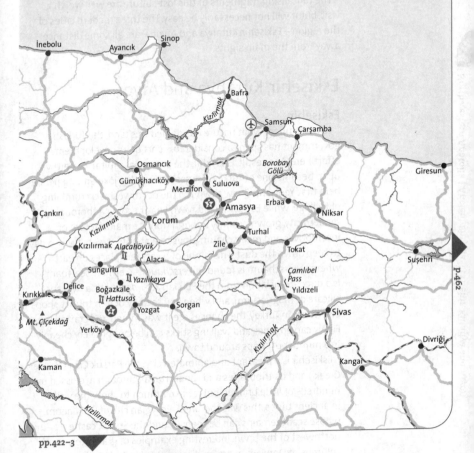

Black Sea

İnebolu
Ayancık
Sinop
Bafra
Kızılırmak
Samsun
Çarşamba
Osmancık
Borobay
Gölü
Giresun
Gümüşhacıköy
Merzifon
Suluova
Çankırı
Amasya
Erbaa
Niksar
Kızılırmak
Çorum
Zile
Turhal
Tokat
Kızılırmak
Alacahöyük
Alaca
Suşehri
Sungurlu
Yazılıkaya
Çamlıbel
Pass
Kırıkkale
Delice
Boğazkale
Hattusas
Yıldızeli
Mt. Çiçekdağ
Yozgat
Sorgan
Sivas
Divriği
Yerköy
Kaman
Kangal

pp.422–3

p.462

Ancient Phrygia:
Eskişehir to Gordion

Once you get to know the Phrygians, you'll wish they were still around. They had style. Just enough of their art survives to make us wish we could see more – the way they dressed and decorated their houses. And we would love to hear some of their famous music, played on lyres, cymbals and flutes in the weird, wailing

'Phrygian mode'. Musicologists would give anything for a chance; it was the foundation of the music of the classical Greeks. The Greeks may even have learned their alphabet from these talented people. Besides music, the Phrygians were famous for their roses (Midas, like King Cyrus of Persia, was one of the legendary gardeners of antiquity), for embroidery and for woven wool carpets.

The tantalising fragments of this lost culture are well worth a visit, but it will not necessarily be easy. The three modern cities of the region – Eskişehir, Kütahya and Afyon – are all some distance away from the main sights.

Eskişehir, Kütahya and Afyon

Eskişehir

To make up for what nature has denied this land, the Turkish government has spent a considerable part of its development effort here. As a result, Eskişehir, the provincial capital, has grown up to become one of Turkey's largest cities. It's a joke among people here that **Yenişehir** ('new town') to the northwest is a crumbling old village, while Eskişehir ('old town') has become a thoroughly modern city, grown wealthy enough from its manufacture of locomotives and **meerschaum pipes** to water its streets twice a day to keep down the dust. This is one of a very few places on earth where meerschaum is found (*meerschaum* – German 'sea-foam' – is a direct translation from the Persian *kef-i-daryâ*; it's a hydrous silicate of magnesium), and when you see any of it in tourist shops elsewhere in Turkey, the chances are it was mined and crafted here. Finely carved pipes and walking sticks can be bought very cheaply in a number of shops around town.

Eskişehir is a pleasant and animated city; the **Porsuk Çayı** ('Beaver Creek') and its tributaries and canals run all through it, crossed by hundreds of little bridges, but it hasn't much to show the visitor. In ancient times, this was the Greek-Phrygian city of Dorylaeum, whose scant remains can be seen around the Selcuk **castle** northwest of the town. Interesting examples of grave steles and columns of Dorylaeum are on display at Eskişehir's **Archaeological Museum**. On the eastern edge of the city is the 16th-century **Kurşunlu Mosque**, a complex attributed to Mimar Sinan.

Kütahya

⭐ Kütahya

Kütahya, a prosperous and amiable city that spreads under an Ottoman castle, would be unremarkable but for its **ceramics**, one of the great craft traditions of Turkey. You'll notice it as soon as you arrive; the bus station is the prettiest in Turkey, with pillars tiled from floor to ceiling. Hotels, shops and even bars in the modern town have façades covered in Kütahya tiles, and all the main

Getting to Eskişehir, Afyon and Kütahya

Eskişehir, Kütahya and Afyon are all connected by **rail** and **bus** to Istanbul and İzmir. Train stations in these cities are within easy walking distance of the centres. As always though, buses are the better deal. The *otogar* in Eskişehir is 3km from the town centre, in Afyon just over a kilometre out, and in Kütahya only half a kilometre.

streets are lined with showrooms for the scores of workshops in and around the city. The first to practise the art here were Persians, brought as captives by Selim the Grim in 1514. While the art of ceramics declined in İznik in the 18th century, Kütahya seized the opportunity to fill the gap, and now makes fine china and faïence in classic Ottoman patterns, as well as architectural tiles, used in the restorations of all the old mosques. If you are looking for something besides carpets to take home, Kütahya is well worth a stop. You can window-shop conveniently or go in and have a cup of tea; quality is high and prices relatively low, in everything from simple vases and plates to urns the size of refrigerators for your favourite pasha's seraglio. Once you have ogled at a few *çiniler*, you will see that there is a vast range of quality and price, from low-grade souvenir trinkets right up to hand-painted masterpieces.

Altın Çini
Belediye Meydanı,
t 0274 212 2975

Güven Çini, along Atatürk Bulvarı, has a reasonable selection of factory-printed tiles and ceramics, as well as some handmade pieces. But the best quality and range of factory tiles are to be had at **Altın Çini**; ask at their boutique to see their nearby workshop and warehouse, which also houses a fine collection of hand-painted ceramics. If you are interested in seeing masterworks, visit the affable Mehmet Gürsoy at his **İznik Çini**, Atatürk Bulvarı; much of his work is covered in especially beautiful tulip motifs (his symbol, and also a stylised form of 'Allah' in traditional script).

Kütahya was ancient Cotiaeum, a town several times destroyed and rebuilt, most recently by Mehmet the Conqueror; he captured it from another, more obscure Turkish tribe called the Germaniyids, for whom Kütahya served as capital. It has a few Ottoman mosques of its own, notably the 15th-century **Ulu Cami**, in a pretty garden at the end of **Cumhuriyet Caddesi**, the street that leads from the centre through Kütahya's **bazaar** district. The extensive *külliye* of the mosque, built by the Germaniyids, now houses Kütahya's two museums. First is the **Tile Art Museum**, with a collection of fine ceramics from as far back as the 14th century. The adjacent **Archaeology Museum** is a reminder that one should never pass up a provincial museum in any Turkish town, no matter how obscure. The best, like Kütahya's, can offer some genuine treasures of ancient art: surprises here include some painted geometric pots from Hacılar (some of the oldest in the world), fine grave steles with the death's door motif common on the southern coast, a big flashy Hellenistic sarcophagus with a Battle of the

Tile Art Museum
open Tues–Sun 8–12
and 1.30–5.30; adm

Archaeology Museum
open Tues–Sun 8–12
and 1.30–5.30; adm

13

Northwestern Anatolia | Ancient Phrygia: Eskişehir, Kütahya and Afyon

Amazons, and some unique terracotta ex votos: a weird triple-formed Hecate with torches (she was the underworld patroness of witches who was worshipped at Colophon and in Caria), and another, unidentified, goddess fondling her flowing tresses, with a bird in her other hand, a small boy by her side, and a snake emerging from her genitals. There are several versions of her; the later ones, from Roman times, are at least decently covered.

In the older neighbourhoods, on the slopes around the Ulu Cami, are many lovely Ottoman wooden houses, some of which have been restored. One of them can be visited, the **Kossuth Evi**, where Lajos Kossuth, romantic leader of Hungary's 1848 fight for independence, spent part of his subsequent exile (the Hungarians, like the Poles, were natural friends of Ottoman Turkey, having common enemies in Austria and Russia). Today the interior has been recreated as it was at the time Kossuth lived there. From nearby a track leads up to the ruined castle, begun under the Byzantines.

From Kütahya, the first slopes of a broad massif called **Türkmen Dağı** rise up over the horizon, stretching off to the east. On its opposite slope, in difficult hill country, is the source of the Sakarya river. There you will find **Midas City** and nearly a dozen temple façades and tombs in the heartland of ancient Phrygia. There is no way over the mountain; adventurous souls desiring to explore Phrygia must start from Eskişehir or Afyon to the south. Paved roads from either city will carry you 60 or 70km into the area, but then, if you're not driving, you will be at the mercy of whatever taxis you can find in the villages of **Seyitgazi** or **İhsaniye**.

Aizanoi's Temple of Zeus

Aizanoi (Aezani in Turkish), an important town in Greek and Roman times, stood 36km southwest of Kütahya, near the present-day village of **Çavdarhisar** (the 'rye castle'). Almost nothing remains of it – nothing except the best-preserved ancient temple in Turkey. The **Temple of Zeus** is also one of the largest, almost 100ft across the bottom of its podium, and one of the last to be built – in the 2nd century, during the reign of Hadrian. Despite the fashion of the day for the Corinthian order, the temple is Ionian, showing the age's preference for tall elevations and narrow columns.

Most of these columns and half the walls of the cella still stand. Parts of the frieze connecting the tops of the columns are present as well, though the pediment and roof are long gone. This pediment had been decorated at its peaks and corners with huge *acroteria*, carved stone acanthus leaves, and bits of these lie on the ground. Hadrian's reign was one of the better times for Asia Minor and the rest of the empire, when both prosperity and building talent were still undiminished. The style of the temple may have been thought old-fashioned when it was built, and less charitable

Getting to Aizanoi

Çavdarhisar, with the ruins of Aizanoi, is easy to reach from Kütahya. There are village **minibuses**, and most Uşak- or İzmir-bound **buses** stop in the village's *otogar* (make sure you ask beforehand where they stop so you don't get left on the highway, 4km from the village).

critics today may find it lacking in inspiration. The temple's form, which the scholars call 'pseudodipteral' (having open corridors behind the columns instead of a second row of columns), is a copy of the admired Temple of Zeus Sosipolis at Magnesia (Manisa).

One Roman innovation, made possible by the temple's great height, is the **cellar**, with its barrel-vaulted roof. Zeus had to share his temple with the goddess Cybele, which is not unusual in a town so near Phrygia, although in Phrygia proper Cybele's orgiastic rites were conducted in the open air; it's difficult to say what went on in her subterranean sanctuary here. It may have been an oracle. The arrangement captures wonderfully the state of mind of the ancient world. Zeus, representing reason, order, and light, rules the upper world, while just below the surface lies mystery and the unconscious bound up in the formidable personality of the great goddess. The huge acroterion from the east front, now on the ground, was a bust of Zeus, while that on the west depicted Cybele.

Little remains of the rest of Aizanoi; if you have time you can trace the outlines of the **stadium**, with a unique architectural trick: the town's theatre does double duty, closing its open end. The Temple of Zeus faced an **agora** fronting on the now intermittent stream that the Greeks called Rhyndakos, where there are still remnants of bridges and quays, and a market inscribed with Diocletian's famous AD 301 edict on wages and prices – the catastrophic 'reform' that wrecked the Roman economy.

Afyon: City of Opium

Afyon's official name is Afyon Karahisar, which means 'opium-black fortress'. That little product has been the city's name and its fame for centuries. Today, the poppies have largely been replaced by sunflowers; nevertheless, you'll still see vast expanses of poppy fields all around the city – the trade is strictly controlled, but Afyon is still famous for its poppy-seed pastries, and it celebrates its ancient speciality with a big **poppy-head fountain** in the middle of town. The **black fortress** remains, on top of an enormous black rock, thrusting 741ft into the sky. The original castle was probably Hittite, *c*. 1500 BC; it has been rebuilt many times since then and was used as a treasury by both the Selcuks and the Ottomans.

In the old town, which is clustered round the foot of the rock, is the **Ulu Cami**, a fine Selcuk mosque built in 1273. It has a flat roof supported by 40 wooden columns with stalactite-carved capitals. Near the mosque are some well-preserved **Ottoman houses** with typical overhanging upper storeys. Also in the area is a **Mevlevi Museum**, housed in a converted mosque; Afyon is not far from Konya (*see* p.435), and the Mevlâna's teachings found favour here.

In the new town, one building dominates all others, the **Gedik Ahmet Paşa Külliyesi**, built by a grand vezir of Mehmet the Conqueror. The mosque, the **İmaret Camii**, has a minaret decorated with İznik tiles, but the adjoining medrese and hamam (currently closed) are squat and functional.

The area round Afyon is famous for its **hot springs**. Some not-so-hot springs near the Gazlıgöl ('Gassy Lake'), north of Afyon, supply the mineral water you find in little green bottles all over Turkey.

The Phrygian Heartland

2 Temples near Afyon

Anyone interested in the fascinating world of pre-Hellenic Anatolia should not be discouraged from pushing into this little-visited region. The Phrygian monuments are well preserved and quite impressive in their lonely settings, and you'll have a chance for some real exploration. No archaeological area in western Anatolia is less documented; many of the sites are known only to the locals. Though Bursa's Uludağ and Murat Dağı, west of Afyon, are both taller, **Turkmen Dağı** and its surrounding peaks between Afyon and Eskişehir make the rooftop of northwestern Anatolia; many important rivers, including the Sakarya and the Menderes, have their sources here. If this area was not the most populous part of Phrygia, it was at least the holiest place. The evidence suggests that the Phrygians' religion had much to do with water; each of the great temple façades was located near a spring.

Midas Şehri

If there's only time for one site, head for Midas Şehri, the so-called 'Midas City', 25km southeast of Seyitgazi. Here, bordering the modern village of **Yazılıkaya**, the acropolis of a 6th-century BC Phrygian city, whose true name we do not know, rises up from the surrounding plains. There's little left on top, but a wealth of detail carved into its steep sides.

It was named Midas City by Captain Leake, a British traveller who discovered it in the early 1800s. At the end of the acropolis facing Yazılıkaya stands its largest and most striking monument, a **temple façade** some 70ft high; at its top, Leake thought he could discern the letters 'MIDAI' in a long Phrygian inscription, and reported back to the world that he had found the grave of King Midas. In truth, the Phrygian language still remains something of a mystery. Most of the letters were adapted from the Greek, however, and more likely than not, some 'Midas' had something to do with it. This is no tomb, however; the experts think of it as a kind of stage for the

Getting around the Phrygian Heartland

You have a choice of **bases** for seeing Midas Şehri and nearby sites, all of them inconvenient. Afyon is perhaps the best, since it is closest to the ruins and there are a number of village **dolmuş** lines running at least close to the sites. The village of Seyitgazi is even closer, though there is only the most rudimentary and unreliable accommodation there, and the same chance of a dolmuş that takes you more or less near the sites, and maybe, just maybe, another one to bring you back. In other words, hire a **car** if you're serious, or initiate some serious bargaining with **taxi** drivers. It will help if you can find a driver who actually knows where the sites are and doesn't have to stop for directions every few minutes.

It's much easier visiting Gordion. From Eskişehir or Afyon, any **bus** for Ankara can leave you in the village of Polatlı; **dolmuş** service from there to the village of Yassıhöyük is regular, and you can walk from there.

outdoor rites of Cybele. Her cult statue would be placed in the niche at the bottom of the monument during the festivities.

Around the niche, the precise, symmetrical maze-like pattern that covers most of the monument's face shows the odd degree of abstraction the Phrygians had reached in their religious art. The pediment suggests roof beams resting on a central ridge-pole, and it may be that the cliff façades are representations of wooden temples that no longer exist. A second, somewhat smaller façade was carved into the north face of the hill, roughly the same in form, with a frieze along the top decorated with acanthus leaf designs. All around the other hillsides, both above and below the bits of the original defence wall, a day's exploration will reveal any number of other niches and altars, inscriptions, underground chambers, and other features whose uses can only be guessed at.

Sites near Midas Şehri

A third temple façade, smaller and somewhat eroded, can be seen near Yazılıkaya at **Arezastis**. You can compare all three with the whole temples in the same area, one cut out of the **Gerdek Rock** near the village of **Çukurca**, and another at **Hisar Kale**, 9km to the southwest at Yapıldak village. Another site near Çukurca, perhaps the most unusual of all, is the **Doğanlı Kale**, an outlandishly eroded crag of limestone, honeycombed with chambers and niches, with hollows that seem to have held wooden beams and stairways at one time. Some of the work is said to date from Byzantine times, and like the similar oddities in Cappadocia may have been used as a monastery.

The road going west from Yazılıkaya passes a **Phrygian tumulus** on its way to the village of **Kümbetköy**, which takes its name from a Roman-era tomb guarded by two lions in low relief, a recurring symbol in Phrygian art just as it was for the Hittites. South of here, on the way to Afyon, other Phrygian lions have given the villages of **Arslantaş** and **Arslankaya** their names. The temple façade at Arslankaya is a remarkable sight, carved out of a thin, twisted pinnacle of rock; two lions keep watch from its pediment while two other huge figures as high as the façade itself, though badly eroded, flank the monument. Both this and the smaller façade at Arslantaş are done in the same angular patterns as at Midas Şehri.

North of the Phrygian sites, **Seyitgazi** is worth a stop for the **Mosque and Tomb of Seyit Battal Gazi**, the semi-legendary Arab warrior who died in battle here in AD 740, when the town was much more important than it is now. The tomb at the centre of this large complex was constructed around 1200 by the mother of the Selcuk sultan Alâeddin Keykubad; Seyit Gazi lies inside a sarcophagus a full 20ft long, next to his Greek wife Eleonora. The mosque and medrese were added in the 16th century by Selim I.

Pessinus

Pessinus, 16km south of where the Eskişehir–Ankara highway passes Sivrihisar, was the religious and geographic centre of Phrygia. Almost nothing can be seen on the site, but archaeologists have found a 1st-century AD temple at the top of a broad ceremonial stair. A college of priests ruled the city; an inscription records that half were Phrygian and half Galatian. Even during the two centuries when Pessinus was under the sovereignty of the kings of Pergamon, these priests, or *galli*, ruled the city and its hinterlands as a theocratic state, and their influence spread far beyond Phrygia's borders. The Romans put a stop to this in their usual ingenious fashion. In 204 BC, they instructed their Pergamene allies to send them the cult figure, a *baetyl* from Pessinus. King Attalos was glad to comply; the respected Sibylline Oracle had commanded it, and the *baetyl* (probably a meteorite, like the Kaaba in Mecca) was conveyed to Rome with all proper observances and placed in a temple specially built for it. The Romans expanded their power as much through this talent for taking over other people's religions as by triumph of arms; no one knows what happened to all the statues, relics and cult objects they collected. Does the Pope have them up in his attic?

In Phrygia, the worship of Cybele had much to do with **bees**; Greek mythographers always associated her with Aphrodite Ericyna and her golden honeycomb, the aspect worshipped at Mount Eryx in Sicily. Today, the site of Pessinus is known to the Turks as Ballıhisar – the Honey Castle.

Gordion

Gordion, like Pessinus, is a site only an archaeologist could really love. The early Phrygian capital contains no well-preserved buildings or fine reliefs; and only parts of it have been fully excavated, though enough has been done for specialists to have drawn up a ground plan of the major palace buildings. Much more interesting is the Great Tumulus on the edge of the city, which

Gordius and Midas

Arrian, in his *Life of Alexander*, relates the two great myths of ancient Phrygia. Gordius, the king who left us the famous Knot, started out as a poor farmer. One day an eagle perched on his wagon tongue, and Gordius, taking it as an omen, decided to visit an oracle at Phrygian Telmessus to ask its meaning. On the way, the eagle still riding along with him, he met a local priestess who instructed him in the proper sacrifices for the oracle. He married her, and she bore him a son named Midas. In the meantime, the Phrygian king had died and the country was drifting into factional strife. The oracle announced that a man in an ox-cart would come to bring peace to the land, and when the unsuspecting Gordius rode into the city one day, he found himself proclaimed king. He founded the city of Gordion, and laid up his wagon there. Over the years, a prophecy gained currency that whoever could solve the cornel-bark knot that bound the yoke to the wagon tongue would become 'master of Asia'. Much speculation has gone into the nature of this knot, although its presence here is historical fact. When Alexander passed this way – Gordion lay on the Persian Royal Road – he felt obliged to fulfil the prophecy, since becoming master of Asia was exactly what he had in mind. Most commentators claim he cut the knot with his sword. Robert Graves believes the knot was an alphabetic cipher, expressing the secret name of a god (Incas and ancient Britons had such devices, so why not the Phrygians?); he sees Alexander's sword stroke as a historical turning point, at which the power of blind ambition and main force broke the last barrier to the destruction of the ancient authority of religion.

Of Midas, we learn that he planted famous rose gardens and was a great musician, taught by Orpheus himself. As well as the tale of the golden touch, Midas is said to have had a pair of ass's ears planted on him by Apollo; Midas unwisely voted against the god when the latter competed in a musical contest with Midas's countryman Marsyas. His barber was supposed to keep the secret (which Midas hid from others with a conical Phrygian cap, of the kind that was the fashion during the French Revolution) but simply couldn't bear to keep quiet. He dug a hole in the ground near a river and whispered, 'Midas has ass's ears!' into it; most unfortunately for him, the reeds that grew on the spot immediately spread the message to everyone within earshot: 'Midas has ass's ears!'

Midas's name, like Gordius's, probably has a basis in history. He, or one of the kings with that name, appears in Assyrian records as 'Mita of Mushki'. This Mushki, most likely, was the Phrygians' own name for their nation. 'Phrygian' is a Greek word meaning 'free men'. As a pastoral people without a strong state, they might have been just that.

Despite the wealth that lay behind the legend of Midas's golden touch, his capital was not to endure. The Great Tumulus was built around 720 BC, and the Cimmerians came to sack Gordion a mere couple of decades later. Though it revived in the 6th century, by Roman times writers were already sadly remarking that the once-great city was dwindling into little more than a village.

everyone calls 'Midas's Tomb'. Gordion is reached from the same Eskişehir–Ankara road, 20km northeast of the town of **Polatlı**, with yellow signs marking the route from there. Approaching the site, you see mounds of all sizes, gradually increasing in number. The largest, most likely, were for the kings, though even mere nobles apparently had the resources to build them. Few of the smaller tumuli have been excavated; the burials in them were cleverly placed off-centre to discourage grave robbers and archaeologists. One they did find yielded the remains of a five-year-old boy, with some charming toys that are now in the Ankara Museum.

The Great Tumulus

The Great Tumulus, now worn down to about 160ft in height, must originally have been close to 250ft. In Turkey the only bigger example of a mound is the one near Sardis called King Alyattes's

Tomb, and it's difficult to say if a taller one could be found anywhere in the world. Whether or not the king inside was a Midas or a Gordius is unknown – they alternated these names the way Danish kings used to do with Christian and Frederick – but he was a small man, no more than 5ft 2in, and close to 60 years of age. The tomb at the centre of the mound has been thoroughly excavated, and you can reach it through the long, lighted tunnel.

To build this mound, the Phrygians started with a double-walled wooden house set into the ground, covered it with stones and clay, and then piled up the earth above it. The wood – great logs of cedar that must have come from Lebanon, still sound after 2,600 years under the earth – is mortised at the corners like a frontier cabin. Inside, interestingly, no gold or silver was found; there were dozens of pots, many with inscriptions in the Phrygian alphabet, some very well-crafted furniture, now in Ankara, and, inexplicably, 145 brass fibulae – the archaeologists' word for safety-pins.

The current excavations of the city are surrounded by a fence. Having been nearly completely covered with centuries of silt from the Sakarya's floods, the site is now exposed and you can look down into the diggings and make out, at the southeastern end, the monumental gateway, and behind it the palace buildings and a long row that belonged to the palace household. The palaces themselves consisted of a row of megaron-style structures, with a central hearth surrounded by rooms and one large hall in front serving as the entrance; it is quite likely these had façades in wood similar to the temple façades mentioned above.

Whatever finds the government hasn't carried off to Ankara are on display in the small **museum**. Small bits of red, white and black architectural ceramics give some idea of how the palaces originally looked. On your way back to Polatlı, take time to notice the **Atatürk Monument** on the crest of the most prominent hill north of town. This could well be the only really successful modern memorial anywhere in Turkey, an attempt, perhaps, at recapturing the ancient Anatolians' talent for monumental sculpture. It's as abstract and as memorable as any work of the Phrygians.

ⓘ Eskişehir >>
*Vilayet Binası
(provincial government
office),* **t** *0222 230 1752*

Where to Stay in Ancient Phrygia

Eskişehir, Kütahya and Afyon are all towns where you will have trouble spending a lot of money on hotel rooms. In interior towns like this there are no pretensions – you can almost always judge a place from its façade. Most of the moderately priced hotels are clean and comfortable, even if English-speaking staff are a rarity.

Eskişehir

Two modest hotels next to each other have thermal baths, which you may appreciate after visiting the Phrygian sites.

Has Termal Oteli, Hamamyolu Caddesi 7, **t 0222 231 9191, *www.hashotel.com* (€€–€). The better of the two. Rates average 50 YTL per double.

*Sultan Termal Otel, Hamamyolu Caddesi 1, **t** 0222 230 3051 (€). Worth trying if the Has Termal Oteli is full.

ⓘ Kütahya ›
*Fuatpaşa Caddesi, in
the centre, t 0274 223
6213; there is also a
booth in the central
Azerbaijan Park (open
summer only)*

ⓘ Afyon ›
*2nd floor, Hükümet
Konaği, t 0272 213 5447*

Kütahya

Gül Palas, Belediye Meydanı, t 0274 216 1759, *www.gulpalas.com* (€€). With its lovely tile-covered façade on the central street, this is the best hotel in town. Tiles cover much of the interior too, although the tile paintings of earth-movers and quarry trucks in the stairwell may be taking the art a little too far. Bedrooms are well furnished with good en suite bathrooms; 70 YTL including a big buffet breakfast. The basement sauna is just a little extra.

Otel Köşk, nearby, t 0274 216 2024 (€). Has bigger but plain double rooms; traffic noise could be a problem.

Afyon

*****Termal Resort Oruçoğlu**, 15km outside Afyon, is on the Kütahya road, t 0272 251 5050, *www.orucoglu.com.tr* (€€€€). A good place to take in the hot springs. It's an apparition in these empty landscapes, a weird futuristic concrete spa hotel next to a big water slide in the middle of nowhere. All rooms have satellite TV, sauna and hamam. Half board.

Cakmak Marble Hotel, Süleyman Gönçer Cad. 2, t 0272 214 3300, *www. cakmakmarblehotel.com* (€€€). A large, comfortable and modern hotel offering well appointed doubles with breakfast for 132 YTL. There is a nicely laid out hamam and sauna to boot.

Lale, opposite the İmaret Camii, t 0272 215 1580 (€). One of the several rudimentary places in Afyon.

Eating Out in Ancient Phrygia

Eskişehir

Kazan, İstasyon Cad. 37/A, t 0222 233 5253. Serving up authentic local dishes in a relatively modern setting where you can even watch the activity in the kitchen on monitors in the diner. Don't miss the baklava, all 44 delicately thin pastry layers of it.

Kütahya

All the restaurants are near the central Belediye Meydanı.

Gül Palas, Belediye Meydanı (€). The best place for a gastronomic splurge, where a smorgasbord buffet of salads, stews and meats costs 10 YTL in the bright top-floor restaurant.

Meşhur ('Famous') **İskender Salonu**, on Azerbaycan Parkı, t 0312 348 7888, next to Belediye Meydanı (€). Lays on a quite nice bowl of *mercimek* (red lentil) soup and *iskender kebap*.

Bursa İskender, Atatürk Bulvarı (€). A simple kebab salon that tries hard; good cooking.

İnci Pastaneleri, just off Belediye Meydanı. If your tooth is sweeter, join Kütahya's younger crowd, where off-duty teenage army conscripts glance longingly across at the local girls as they tuck into sticky cakes and profiteroles, washed down with a deliciously gloopy distant relative of the cappuccino.

Afyon

Land of *sucuk*! Turkey's spicy hooped sausage is at its best here.

İkbal Lokantası, Uzun Çarşi (€). Close to the Oruçoğlu Oteli, this is the place to go. It's an excellent, old-style restaurant, so popular with the locals at lunchtime that the waiters have to run while they serve the food. Finish your meal with *ekmek kadayıf* (bread soaked in syrup) or *vişneli ekmek tatlısı* (bread soaked in cherry juice); both come topped with a slab of the rich cream for which Afyon is renowned.

13 Northwestern Anatolia | Ankara

Ankara

Most people have the impression that Ankara, the capital of the Turkish Republic since 1923, is absolutely new, a modern toadstool of a city conjured up out of bleakest Anatolia by Atatürk as a symbol of his country's pride and aspirations. Modern it is of course, and toadstool beyond question, but underneath all the clutter of ministries, highways, and apartment blocks there is a

Getting to and around Ankara

Ankara is one of the cities where **taxis** not only have meters but usually use them. You'll probably need one if you arrive by bus or train. The **train station** is on Hipodrom Caddesi, 2½km from Kızılay, the centre of the city. The huge **bus station**, known variously as the AŞTİ (Ankara Şehirlerarası Terminale İşletmesi), Yeni Terminal or Yeni Otogar, is in the Soğütözü district, 5km west of the city centre. From Esenboğa Airport, 33km northeast of the city, you have a choice of a taxi (about 50 YTL) or the usual THY Havaş bus to the city centre and *otogar*.

Ankara isn't encouraging for those who like to explore cities on foot. As well as having dirty air, it is a typical Turkish strip-city blown out of all proportion; almost any destination will be on or near the 5km length of Atatürk Bulvarı. There's an **underground** system with two lines: the Ankaray runs from the AŞTİ *otogar* via Kızılay to Dikimevi in the east. The second line, the Metro, starts at Kızılay (where it connects to the Ankaray line) and heads northwest past Ulus to the suburb of Batıkent. **Buses** (buy tickets in the booths at the major stops, as in Istanbul) and **dolmuşes** are crowded but frequent; look at the destination signs to see if they're going in the direction you want.

If you're not ready to climb up to the Hisar, take one of the **minibuses** from the broad open space that serves as a terminal just east of Ulus Meydanı. The Anıt Kabir, on its hill, and the Atatürk Orman Çifliği are best reached by taxi, but all the recreation areas in the vicinity of the city can be reached easily by bus.

---

genuine old city too, as old as the Hittites, and layered with memories of all the nations that have come and gone since then. Atatürk chose his capital more cleverly than at first appears. Above all, Ankara is an entirely Turkish city, and has been for eight centuries, even though the traces of the Phrygians, Greeks and Romans are still out in the open for all to see.

History

A relief map shows why the spot has always attracted so much attention. Just to the east, a gap between the Köroğlu Mountains and the bare plateau south of them forms a natural corridor called the Halys Gates. The Persian Royal Road and the Via Regalis of the Romans passed through here, as did conquerors from Alexander to Tamerlane. The Hittites were the first to build on Ankara's lofty citadel, and the Phrygians after them made it one of their most important cities. Dozens of Phrygian tumuli once covered the plain, but almost all have vanished. The Celtic Galatians succeeded them – there is still plenty of red hair and freckles in this part of Turkey – and Augustus annexed their lands for Rome in 25 BC. By then, the city had assumed a variant of its modern name, Ancyra. Europe knew it for a long period as Angora and it gave its name to the soft wool produced by the region's goats.

Although continuously occupied through all the centuries since, Ankara was never a great city but, as Atatürk realized, it is a natural capital of Anatolia. Also, it's a good distance from the intrigue synonymous with the old capital – a clean break with the past.

Museum of the National Assembly

The **Ulus Meydanı** (National Square) is where modern Ankara and modern Turkey began. Most visitors don't stop at the little grey building just off the square, but you wouldn't go to Philadelphia

Ankara Today

Around four million people live in Ankara now. Those who have jobs work for the government or businesses attracted by proximity to the government; those who haven't get by as best they can while looking. Much of the city's phenomenal growth, like Istanbul's, has been due to the unplanned and unwanted migration of hundreds of thousands of villagers from every corner of Turkey. For all Turks, Ankara is just the symbol Atatürk wanted it to be, the nation's pre-eminent city of opportunity.

In no way can Ankara be called a well-planned city. Turkey's first town planners were civil engineers, not artists. Ankara has more gratuitous highway interchanges than the rest of the country put together, some in the centre of the town where everyone can enjoy them. The exact centre, between Gençlik Parkı and the business district, is occupied by a railway yard. The highways and the railways combine to give the city the worst air pollution in Turkey. Don't imagine for a minute that any native of Ankara minds discussing these problems. Quite the contrary; as in many busy and thriving big cities, Ankara seems almost to get a perverse joy from them. The city has skyscrapers, fine parks and residential districts, trendy stores, a good university, and nothing to envy in any other town save Istanbul. And if they must sacrifice other amenities to gain these, what of it? Ankara is on top, and it knows it.

One thing the planners didn't do was to try to integrate the new Ankara with the old. As a result, the two exist uneasily side by side, with that freightyard for a border. As the newer, southern districts grow and prosper, the old town suffers. Some parts still retain the village atmosphere of old Ankara; some have deteriorated to nothing more than poor shops and junkyards, while still others have had new streets of modern buildings smashed carelessly through them. The planners seem to hope that one day the old town will just disappear.

without seeing Independence Hall and you should take a few minutes to visit the Museum of the National Assembly. After the Erzurum and Sivas Congresses decided in 1919 to co-ordinate and extend the efforts of the local defence committees across Anatolia, elections were held wherever possible for the new Grand National Assembly; it met here for the first time on 23 April 1920. Atatürk, elected chairman on the first day, was at the time under death sentence from the Istanbul government. Greek troops were occupying the Aegean coast, and French, Italian, British and Russian forces were also present on Turkish soil, and advancing.

In this hall, with its school desks jammed together and the chairman within spitting distance of nearly every deputy, the Turks did the last thing anyone expected: they roused themselves as a nation for the first time, and prevailed against a host of enemies. Not having attended a Turkish grammar school, you will not know all the serious-looking men in the photos that cover the walls, or be familiar with the significance of the letters and declarations on display in the glass case, but you will come away with the impression that some great work was done here.

Old Ancyra

The Temple of Augustus and the Roman Baths

From here, you can walk six blocks north and 1,600 years back to the **Hükümet Meydanı**, and the tall, worn **Column of Julian**, currently crowned by a stork's nest. The Galatians of Ancyra, who

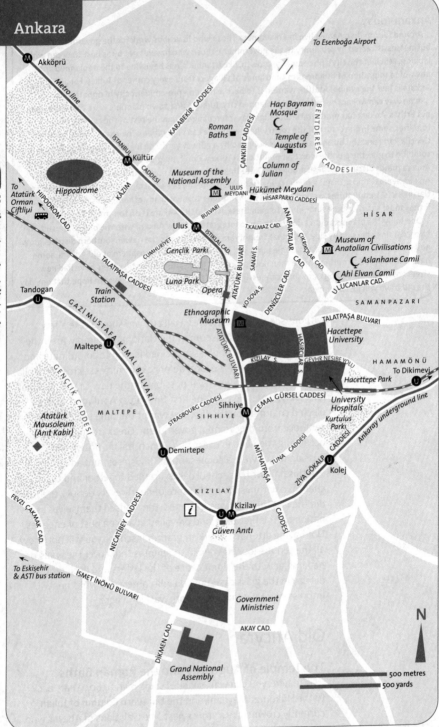

To Esenboğa Airport

Akköprü

Metro line

İSTANBUL CADDESİ

KARABEKİR CADDESİ

Kültür

KÄZIM CADDESİ

Hippodrome

To
Atatürk
Orman
Çiftliği

HİPODROM CAD.

Haçı Bayram
Mosque

Roman
Baths

ÇANKIRI CADDESİ

Temple of
Augustus

BENDERESİ CADDESİ

Museum of the
National Assembly

Column of
Julian

ULUS
MEYDANI

Hükümet Meydani

HİSAR PARKI CADDESİ

HİSAR

Ulus

BULVARI

İSTİKLAL CAD.

CUMHURİYET

Gençlik Parkı

Luna Park

Opera

T.KALMAZ CAD.

ANAFARTALAR

ÇIKRIKÇILAR CAD.

SANAYİ S.

Museum of
Anatolian Civilisations

Aslanhane Camii

Ahi Elvan Camii

U LUCANLAR CAD.

SAMANPAZARI

ATATÜRK BULVARI

KO-SOVA S.

DENİZCİLER CAD.

Tandogan

TALATPAŞA CADDESİ

Train
Station

GAZİ MUSTAFA KEMAL BULVARI

Maltepe

GENÇLİK CADDESİ

Atatürk
Mausoleum
(Anıt Kabir)

MALTEPE

Ethnographic
Museum

ATATÜRK BULVARI

TALATPAŞA BULVARI

Hacettepe
University

HAŞIRCILAR S.

KIZILAY S.

GEVHR NESİBE YOLU

HAMAMÖNÜ

To Dikimevi

Hacettepe Park

University
Hospitals

Sihhiye

CEMAL GÜRSEL CADDESİ

STRASBOURG CADDESİ

SIHHIYE

Ankaray underground line

Kurtulus
Parkı

Demirtepe

MİTHATPAŞA

TUNA CADDESİ

ZİYA GÖKALP CADDESİ

Kolej

FEVZİ ÇAKMAK CAD.

NECATİBEY CADDESİ

KIZILAY

Kizilay

Güven Anıtı

To Eskişehir
& ASTI bus station

İSMET İNÖNÜ BULVARI

Government
Ministries

AKAY CAD.

DİKMEN CAD.

Grand National
Assembly

CADDESİ

N

500 metres

500 yards

made up most of the population in the 3rd century AD, had a reputation among their neighbours for devotion to their cults of Cybele and the moon goddess Men; it's not all that surprising that they erected this monument in honour of the apostate emperor. Julian was a good general, and one of the last Roman emperors to make a serious effort to hold the eastern borders. He passed through Ancyra in AD 362 on his way to campaign against the resurgent Persians, and after a series of frustratingly indecisive encounters he fell ill and died the next year, derided by the Christians but mourned by the poets and the soldiers.

History has had its little joke with the Galatians. Their temple of Cybele, converted after the conquest to the worship of Augustus and of Rome, was to end its career as a Christian church; if the Christians had not maintained it for so many centuries, the Temple of Augustus would not have survived at all. As it is, the pediment and all the columns have fallen, but enough remains to prove that this, like the temple of Aizanoi, was, in its plan, a copy of the Zeus Sosipolis temple in Magnesia. The walls of the cella, the inner sanctuary, are inscribed with a text in Latin and Greek, the 'Deeds of the Deified Augustus', the longest Latin inscription found any-where. Little of it is legible, effaced less by time than by modern Ankara's exhaust fumes; fortunately a scholarly 16th-century Spanish ambassador took the trouble to write down the full text.

Unlike some of the decadent later emperors, Augustus, a good Roman, was mildly disgusted by the idea of being worshipped. He insisted that such worship should be deferred until after his death: his advisers convinced him that the people of Syria and Asia Minor, grown accustomed to divine rulers from Persian days, would expect it. Even then, he decreed that a divine personification of Rome should take precedence in the temples. What meant more to him was effective and just government, and he took pains to ensure that his biography and political testament, including a report on the state of the empire he was leaving his successors, would be carved into the walls of all his temples. Oddly, this is the only complete text anywhere.

Adjacent to the temple, the 15th-century **Hacı Bayram Mosque** is always full of worshippers at Fridays. Hacı Bayram was a dervish whose virtues and deeds for him almost the character of a saint. His memory is especially revered here in his home town, and his tomb is a place of pilgrimage.

Ankara's other Roman major thoroughfare, on the 3rd-century **Roman Baths**, stands just a bit on Çankırı Caddesi, the northern extension by Emperor Caracalla, Atatürk Bulvarı. Of the and caldarium (cold and hot rooms) to work out direct ancestor of the Turkish hamam, and oth and the adjacent cloistered quadrangle that served as the palaestra, or exercise yard. These aren't as big as Caracalla's famous baths in Rome, but in a provincial city like Ancyra they are a remarkable monument to the perverted soul who spent whatever time he could spare from murdering his countrymen on improving the hygiene of the survivors.

The Hisar

Everything else built by the Greeks, Romans, or Byzantines in Ankara still exists – but the last Byzantines, and the Turks who followed them, carried it all up the hill to the Hisar, the citadel. And a most remarkable citadel it is; it's common in sites in Turkey for ancient stones to be reused in fortress walls, but only here do you find a castle built of little else. Some parts of the walls are all marble and good sandstone, carved with pieces of a hundred different inscriptions and architectural trimmings. Whole courses consist of drums of ancient columns, lined up on their sides like rows of portholes on a ship. The Hisar is a huge jigsaw puzzle; if there were time and archaeologists enough, most of old Ancyra could be reassembled from the pieces.

It's a stiff climb up, as many would-be invaders have found. Today, the formal entrance runs from Hisarparkı Caddesi through a road lined with gardens to the top. At the entrance to the Hisar, a 1522 caravanserai called the Çengelhan has been restored to house the **Rahmi Koç Industrial Museum**, a smaller branch of the museum in Istanbul. Generations ago the Koç family, now Turkey's biggest industrialists, got their start here. Now there are classic cars, appliances, innumerable gadgets, and a pleasant café with an outdoor terrace.

Inside the walls you find a tranquil old Turkish town, unchanged and utterly remote from the city of skyscrapers down below. Though still a relatively poor area, it has seen some restoration in recent years, and a few restaurants have opened. Cars can hardly get through the narrow bumpy streets, which keeps them relatively clean and quiet. The views from the walls are superb; to [th]e south and west the modern city stretches to the horizon.

Rahmi Koç Industrial Museum
open Tues–Fri 10–5, Sat and Sun 10–7, closed Mon; adm

The Battle of Ank[ara]

To the northeast of the [...] hordes overcame Sultan Y[...] e direction of the airport, are the plains on which Tamerlane's disaster, the first serious def[...] it in the Battle of Ankara in 1402. The Turks attribute this siege of Constantinople and [...] tomans, to a point of honour. Beyazıt, abandoning the first completely by surprise. To take[...] y east to meet the advancing Tamerlane, caught him however, and he gave his enem[...] e of a noble foe seemed shameful to the young sultan, exhausted troops proved no mat[...] itself and meet him in proper battle array. Beyazıt's rout that followed the sultan hims[...] horsemen and Tamerlane's elephants, and in the captured potentates. After this blow[...] r inmate of Tamerlane's sad menagerie of [...] fore the Ottomans recovered their strength.

Gecekondu

Looking from the east wall, you will see how Ankara's other half lives. If you imagined the shanty town districts, the *gecekondu* (*see* p.154), as dreary expanses of grim hovels, you haven't given Turkey's urban migrants, raised in their village traditions of self-sufficiency, the credit they deserve. *Gecekondu*, in time, have a way of metamorphosing into decent little cottages, and the areas they create, though unplanned, become real neighbourhoods. The view from the walls is startling; the *gecekondu* begin at the slopes of the citadel, fill the valleys around it and climb the next hills, descending and climbing again and again, as far as the eye can see: hundreds of thousands of homes, unbroken by a single landmark. Some areas have utilities and schools, others are still waiting; the worst look full of despair (though even here there is hardly any crime), while the best seem almost garden suburbs. From all of them, Ankara's poor make the long trip each day to the city centre on foot or in the minibuses that swarm around the Ulus district.

Museum of Anatolian Civilizations (Anadolu Medeniyetleri Müzesi)

⭐ Museum of Anatolian Civilizations
open Tues–Sun 8.30–5; closed Mon; adm

You have to climb halfway up the citadel hill to find it. Many visitors to Ankara come only to see this surprisingly small museum, in a beautifully restored *bedesten* of the 15th century that was once the heart of the city's bazaar. Though it's small, there are few museums anywhere in the world that can offer so many treasures from the distant past. Like Paris, Ankara is a cultural imperialist, and all the best Hittite reliefs, Phrygian pottery and Urartian metalwork have been brought here. It was Atatürk who first had the idea for such a collection. It was originally known as the Hittite Museum in an attempt to call the world's attention to the newly discovered works of the first great Anatolian nation, and at the same time to be an inspiration to the new nation he was trying to build. As other sites came to light in the explosion of archaeological activity here, explorations that have reshaped our knowledge of the ancient Middle East, other fine artefacts have been brought to the museum. Unlike so many other museums, this one does not overwhelm with endless cases of broken pots: every item is significant.

From the Neolithic Period, the prize exhibits come from Çatal Höyük, the 8,000-year-old town whose recent excavation changed all our ideas of ancient history. One entire temple from the site has been reconstructed, with its bull's-head idols and sophisticated frescoes, and a host of figurines of the chubby mother goddess in both her forms, as fertility symbol and as mistress of wild animals. The Hittites, not surprisingly, occupy a lion's share of the exhibit space, with plenty of their curly-maned lions in attendance too.

The large number of well-preserved reliefs in the museum's great hall come both from sites of the Hittite Empire, such as Boğazkale and Karatepe, and from the weaker kingdoms that rose up following its collapse. The Hittites used sculpture not only for serious religious and state subjects, but to depict scenes from everyday life and from pure fancy; as a result, their artistic themes range from gods and kings astride their sacred mountains to sphinxes, hunting scenes and domestic tableaux – children, musicians, and a master of animals leading them in procession like a Pied Piper.

With all the attention given to the Hittites, it can be easy to overlook the works of the Hatti and other early Bronze Age peoples who preceded them. This collection remedies that. Some of their cast bronze works here must surely rank among the greatest ancient art; their style bears a striking resemblance to the celebrated bronzes of the *nuraghe* culture of Sardinia, whose ancestors may have been migrants from Anatolia. Most of these bronzes, found at Alacahöyük and other sites, seem to have been mounted on the tops of standards or sceptres. Some are stylized bulls and stags, but the most memorable are the circular or elliptical shapes, covered with geometric lattice designs, many with stags, bulls or asses in the act of passing through the circle. The scholars call them cosmological symbols, and throw up their hands in despair of ever understanding them completely. These compelling symbols fascinate the modern Turks. On Ankara's Atatürk Bulvarı a gigantic copy of one has been erected right in the middle of the city.

Two later nations with a marvellous artistic talent, the Phrygians and Urartians, round out the museum's collection with rooms of their own. The Urartian finds come from a wide area; their empire, at its height, reached from Sivas to western Iran, from Trabzon to Aleppo. Like the Phrygians, they loved detail and geometric patterns; these can be seen adorning a bronze warrior's shield, several inscribed bronze belts worn by Urartian kings and priests, and in a beautiful soapstone carving of the winged god Haldi, standing on the back of a lion under the towers and gables of a many-storeyed fortified palace.

A room on a lower level has cabinets full of coins, jewellery, glass, tilework and votive steles, giving a whistlestop tour of Turkey since the Greeks. One cabinet is given over to works by modern ceramics masters from Kütahya, including Mehmet Gürsoy (*see* p.387).

Samanpazarı

Southeast of the citadel, the quarter called the 'haymarket' contains, as well as the ramshackle bazaar, three of the oldest mosques: the 13th-century **Aslanhane Camii** built by the Selcuks during the brief period they held Ankara, the **Yeni Cami**, and the **Ahi Elvan Camii**, built by the Ahi Brotherhood in the early 1400s.

New Ankara

A broad highway, **Talat Paşa Bulvarı**, cuts off the old town, and all the land on the other side has been cleared for the huge campus of modern Turkey's educational showpiece, **Hacettepe University**. Where Talat Paşa crosses Atatürk Bulvarı stands the **Ethnographic Museum** (Etnografya Müzesi), the first important building created by the Turkish Republic, started by Atatürk in 1925 to further the study and appreciation of native Turkish folklore and crafts. Atatürk himself lay in state here from 1938 to 1955 when his mausoleum was finished. Today the museum is the largest of its kind in the country, with rooms devoted to costumes and embroidery, metal-crafts, calligraphy, and objects collected from the dervish *tekkeler* after their dissolution. There is a 17th-century room from an Ankara home, furnished to recreate a picture of life in that era, and, best of all, some excellent wood-carving from the Selcuk period.

Ethnographic Museum
open Tues–Sun 8.30–12.30 and 1.30–5.30; adm

As well as museums, Atatürk thought his city should have formal European-style parks. The first of these lies catercorner to the Ethnographic Museum and behind the city Opera. **Gençlik Parkı** ('youth park'), like Kültür Parkı in Bursa, has lagoons and island cafés, an open-air theatre and a Luna (amusement) Park.

The Modern Districts

Like most Turkish cities, Ankara is long and thin, growing up along the main streets and the bus and dolmuş lines that traverse it. Consequently it's almost a kilometre from here to the centre of the modern city, the intersection called **Kızılay** ('crescent') where a curving avenue crosses Atatürk Bulvarı. The 20-storey inter-national-style skyscraper here was Turkey's first, a big deal 20 years ago, although no one gives it a second look today. Across the street, the small park around the **Güven Anıtı** ('Confidence Monument') is a little oasis in the middle of the crowds and ferocious traffic of this district, which has most of Ankara's shops, offices and hotels. The monument itself, with its glowering Atatürk and Turks gazing hopefully into the future, will make a fine exhibit in someone's archaeology museum in a millennium or two.

Another half-kilometre south takes you to the corner of **Gülhane Caddesi** and the centre of Ankara's government district. The office blocks go on and on, stretching towards infinity. In the middle, in a very tired style of government architecture, stands the **Grand National Assembly**, known to the Turks as the TBMM, the parliament building. Still further south, Atatürk Çaddesi becomes Embassy Row, leading to the fashionable suburbs of Kavaklıdere and Çankaya. Here is another of Atatürk's parks, **Kuğulu Parkı** ('swan park'), with plenty of the birds , and also Ankara's tallest building, the **Atakule Tower**, with a revolving restaurant on top.

Tomb of Atatürk

Anıt Kabir
*open daily 9–4.30; free;
a sound and light show
on summer evenings*

Not far from the Kızılay, on a hilltop above the suburb of Maltepe, the Tomb of Atatürk or **Anıt Kabir**, 'monumental tomb', rises like an ancient temple on an acropolis over Ankara. It means a lot to the Turks; the building is shown when Turkish television signs off every night, accompanied by the national anthem. At night the illuminated monument becomes the city's most conspicuous landmark. It took nearly ten years to build, and in it the Turks made a serious attempt to recapture some of the massive monumentality of the ancient civilizations, while establishing a new style of their own. From Anıt Caddesi, you go down a long promenade lined with Hittite-style lions, leading up to a square of low stone buildings that contain a **Museum of Atatürk** and his works.

**Museum of
Atatürk**
*open Mon 1.30–5,
Tues–Sun 9–5; free*

The entire complex is packed with soldiers, an honour guard from each of the services, all enormously tall and decked out in American-style military pomp. The monument, a plain box with a decorated cornice and surrounding colonnade of square pillars, is reached by a long flight of steps. On the walls are lengthy quotes from Atatürk and İsmet İnönü, who is also buried here. Inside, the great building is empty save for Atatürk's huge sarcophagus, with glass walls affording views over the city he built.

Around Ankara

There are a number of recreation areas around the capital. Perhaps the favourite picnic-spot is the **Atatürk Orman Çiftliği**, a kilometre west of town. Late in his career, Atatürk started this as a model farm to introduce new agricultural methods into Turkey. Other pleasant resorts are around **Mogan Gölü** to the south, **Kızılcahamam**, 80km to the north up in the mountains, and the skiing centre of **Elmadağ** just southeast of the city. At **Gâvurkalesi** ('infidel's castle'), 60km to the southwest, you can visit a religious site of the Hittites.

Where to Stay in Ankara

ⓘ **Ankara** ›
*Gazi Mustafa Kemal
Bulvarı 121, next to
the Maltepe stop on
the Ankaray line,
t 0312 231 5572*

Ankara

Ankara's fanciest hotels are mostly around busy Atatürk Bulvarı, between Kızılay and Kavaklıdere.

*****Ankara Sheraton**, Noktalı Sokak, t 0312 457 6000, *www.sheratonankara. com* (€€€€€). The most opulent place in town, constructed in the shape of a giant tube. A double room costs €270, but if you've come up on the pools and intend to blow all your winnings

on a luxury holiday in Ankara, do it properly and reserve the presidential suite at well over €523.

*****Hilton Oteli**, Tahran Caddesi, t 0312 468 2888, *www.ankara.hilton. com* (€€€€). Almost as sumptuous.

First Apart Hotel, İnkılap Sokak 29 t 0312 425 7575, *www.firstapart.com.tr* (€€€). On a quiet pedestrian street in Kızılay, this is the best in this category. The staff are courteous and knowledgeable about the area. Standard rooms are on the small side; it's worth paying extra for a larger deluxe room. Bigger still are the corner rooms.

Ogultürk, Rüzgarlı Esdost Sokak No.6, t 0312 309 29 00, *www.ogulturk.com* (€€€–€€). In Ulus off Çankırı Caddesi, and a step up from the other hotels in the area, with anonymous rooms with minibar, TV and small bathtubs.

***Elit, Olgunlar Sokak 10, a few hundred yards to the south, t 0312 417 5001 (€€). With a double-doored elevator you could fit a camel in. The bedrooms themselves are unexciting, albeit equipped with minibars and TV.

**Spor, Rüzgarlı Plevne Sokak 6, t 0312 324 2165, *www.hotelspor.com* (€€). Bright, well-run and packed with businessmen; the rooms are on the small side, but en suite.

Opera Meydanı, a frantic square in the Ulus district that's within walking distance of most of the museums, is the area to find Ankara's cheaper abodes and the places listed below are either on or off that square. All have rooms with en suite facilities.

Otel Mithat, Tavus Sokak 2, t 312 311 5410, *www.otelmithat.com.tr* (€€). Far and away the best inexpensive place.

**Klasman, Rüzgarlı Plevne Sokak 4, t 0312 310 9797 (€€). Brightly painted reception decked out with chat-show sofas. The large bedrooms have TV, minibar and small en suite baths.

Otel Sipahi, Kosova Sokak 1, t 0312 324 0235 (€€). Big and airy rooms that are tatty but tolerable. Avoid the top floors which have water-pressure problems; there's no lift, either.

Eating Out in Ankara

If money is no object, try the superb restaurants at the five-star hotels.

Yakamoz Restaurant, Koroğlu Caddesi in the fashionable suburb of Gaziosmanpaşa, t 0312 491 5504 (€€€). Well known for its fresh fish, a precious commodity in Ankara.

Yeşil Vadi Lokantası, just off Arjantin Sokak further up the hill on Kırlangıç Sokak next to a small park of the same name (€€€–€€). Packed with Ankarites, it is alive with chatter and filled with smoke. A wide array of kebabbery is on offer, as well as a small selection of fish.

Kınacılar Evi, Kalekapısı Sokak 28, t 0312 312 56 00 (€€). In a restored mansion in the citadel, with a very intimate, homely feel, with wooden ceilings and only one or two tables per room. As well as *à la carte* dishes, there's a 30 YTL fixed menu. Bizarrely for such a beautiful old house, it has a disco bar in the cellar pumping out a mix of Turkish and Western pop and rock until 4am.

Turkish Daily News Café and Restaurant, Arjantin Caddesi (€€). Strategically located along with a dozen or more bars and restaurants on this street, close to the big money of the five-star hotels. It proves its journalistic credentials with an extensive alcohol list and a free TDN at the door. The menu casts its net widely, including a vegetarian section, albeit with a beef dish plonked in among the aubergine and spinach. The cherry cheesecake is fine.

Behind the northeast quadrant of the Kızılay intersection, some streets have been closed off to traffic: these are a good bet for kebab houses.

Mülkiyeliler Birligi Lokalı, Konur 1 Sokak, No 1 Kızılay, t 0312 418 0020 (€€). Has a café on the ground floor and a restaurant above. With more Turkish traditional dishes and some world cuisine oddments, it's neither flashy nor pretentious.

Kösk Restaurant, Plaz Sokak, No 2 Kızılay, t 0312 432 1300 (€). At the sophisticated end of the kebab house scene; all plate glass and mirrors, with a pleasant terrace. It's very popular at lunchtimes, with all the traditional favourites on offer: *şiş kebap*, *köfte* in the region of 8–10 YTL.

Zenger Pasa Konagı, t 0312 311 7070, at Dış Hisar Doyuran Sokak No 13 Ulus (€). Within the citadel walls are several Ottoman houses that have been converted into restaurants; this is the original, a charming establishment with its very own small and dusty ethnographic museum as well as the 'Salon of the Republic', covered in ludicrously lurid murals of an inspirational nature. The restaurant on the top floor has panoramic views over the city. Although you could make do with a filling *gözleme* for 4–7 YTL, other Ottoman treats such as *köfte* or *mantı* may prove too tempting to resist.

Land of the Hittites

Towards the east, just beyond Ankara, lies the **Kızılırmak**, the Crescent River, curving in a broad loop from its mouth near Samsun around past Ankara and through Cappadocia, back to its sources in the east near Sivas. To the Greeks this was the Halys, a name famous from the campaigns of Alexander and Xenophon, but before that its arc enclosed the home counties of the Hittite Empire, a fertile and defensible country with the Hittite capital of Hattusas, near modern Boğazkale, at its centre.

Boğazkale and Hattusas

Boğazkale itself is a small pretty village of prosperous farmers. All around it, in an area of roughly two square kilometres, lie the scattered remains of the capital of the Hittites, Hattusas (also spelt Hattusa, Hattuşa or even Hattuşaş). Most travellers' first great surprise on coming here is that all the excavated buildings, temples and fortifications they visit among the farms and fields of Boğazkale were in fact parts of one city, a metropolis whose 7km of walls contained nearly 200 towers.

The earliest traces of habitation at Hattusas go back as far as 3000 BC. By about 2000 BC, there was a settlement around the citadel (**Büyükkale**). This would be a town of the people of Hatti, from whom Hattusas took its name, but it's uncertain whether it was their capital. From the many natural advantages of the site, we can guess that it might have been; besides the fertility and beauty of the area, its strategic location for trade and its suitability for defence, there are natural springs everywhere. These ensured a source of water within the walls, and may conceivably have had some importance to the religion of the place.

The first written record mentioning Hattusas is unsettling. Anitta, king of Kushar, a city of unknown location, is the subject of the oldest tablet in the Hittite State Archive. The inscription recalls his total destruction of the city, and the curse he put upon it, which was that it never again be inhabited. This was in about 1720 BC. We also learn from the archive, however, that by the late 17th century BC another king of Kushar had moved his capital to Hattusas, and styled himself 'the man from Hattusas' or Hattusilis. A capital it remained throughout the Hittite old kingdom and empire (c. 1600–1200 BC), with one brief interruption when King Muwatalli moved his court to the southeastern city of Dattassa for what must have been reasons of temporary political distress. Shortly after it was restored, the great palace on Büyükkale burned down, again perhaps as a result of civil strife, but both the city and its fortifications reached their highest stage of development under

Getting to Boğazkale

Tours of the site are organized through travel agents in Ankara, and occasionally in Çorum. If you prefer travelling on your own, the best base for the expedition is Sungurlu, the closest town to the ruins, which can be reached by any Ankara–Samsun or Ankara–Amasya **bus**. From there, about 100 YTL is the going rate for a complete trip by **taxi** (extra if you want to take in Alacahöyük too), taking half a day or more.

You can avoid this by taking the Sungurlu–Boğazkale village bus and walking to the sites, but be warned it's a good 13km walk if you want to see everything.

King Tudhaliya IV (*c*. 1250 BC), shortly before the catastrophe that ended the Hittite kingdom forever.

Symptoms of the coming end do not turn up clearly from the archaeological record. Reports of wars with the frontier tribes are common enough, and according to Dr Kurt Bittel, the archaeologist who devoted much of his life to the excavations, there was a decline in building standards in the city's last period. In any case, unknown invaders annihilated city and empire around 1200 BC.

Afterwards, the city seems to have been abandoned until the 9th century BC, when a Phrygian or Phrygian-influenced community grew up over the ruins of the Hittite palace, a well-built, important town that unfortunately isn't mentioned in a single ancient record. Most of its works have been cleared away by archaeologists to expose the Hittite levels underneath. The famous smiling Cybele in Ankara's archaeological museum was found in the Phrygian town.

Hattusas

 Hattusas

The Great Temple (Büyük Mabet)

Arriving in Hattusas, you'll be greeted with a startling sight, a 200ft reconstructed section of the formidable **city wall**, complete with two defence towers. This was finished by the German archaeologists in 2005, as an experiment in using ancient techniques to build in mud brick. The pattern came from a clay model of the fortifications found in the ruins. This part of the wall abuts the ruins of the **Great Temple**, at the modern entrance to the complex. Even though this temple, with the narrow store rooms surrounding it, was built in the last century of the Hittite Empire, about 1250 BC, its site is one of the oldest parts of the city, on the slopes just below the Büyükkale fortress. Nearby, excavations have revealed older buildings that belonged to an Assyrian trading colony, or *karum*, that flourished within the city during the Hittite old kingdom. Here, as everywhere else in Hattusas that has been excavated, are neatly squared stone **foundations** all rising to a single level, with nothing above. The Hittites used sun-baked brick, covered with plaster and probably painted, in their building; consequently, the actual walls disintegrated long ago.

Near the entrance of the temple complex are the remains of an enormous **ceremonial basin**, carved with lions. Though broken now, it was originally almost 15ft long, carved from a single piece of limestone. The entrance itself, the once-imposing **gateway** through which the Hittite king entered with his retinue on formal occasions, leads to a paved street where there is another basin. Here the street curves, and completely surrounds the actual temple, which is recognizable by the larger and more carefully cut stones used for its foundation. In the temple, it's easy to distinguish the central courtyard and the most important chambers, which are to the northeast: two large rooms of equal size that contained statues of the weather god and sun goddess, illuminated by windows to the outside. It is most likely that the temple, as well as the surrounding store rooms, were two or three storeys high, but there is no evidence as to how the outside of the temple looked.

The temple store rooms must have contained the treasury, although nothing of this survived the sack of the city. Many of the cuneiform tablets that have contributed so much to our knowledge of the Hittites were found here, including one that contains a list of 208 members of the temple household, including:

...18 priests, 29 women musicians, 19 scribes for clay tablets, 33 scribes for wood tablets, 35 soothsayers, 10 Hurrian singers...

The remainder is lost. Also in these store rooms are the huge jars for wine or oil, some of which bear inscriptions.

The rooms in this part of the temple were long and narrow, and opened out only onto each other at the points where there are the huge, U-shaped marble thresholds, with doorposts sunk into them. Archaeologists never mention the great green stone, found in a room at the southern end of the street leading from the gateway. It is carved into an irregular shape and polished as smooth as glass, and its purpose is unknown. To the southwest, across an ancient street, which incidentally carries the storm drains underneath it as do other streets in Hattusas, is another complex of rooms built around a courtyard; it is believed that this too was part of the temple complex. At its southern edge, a subterranean **fountain** was discovered in a small room with a corbelled roof.

As you follow the modern road up to Büyükkale, you pass **Ambarlıkaya** and **Büyükkaya**, other natural rock-heights to the left that the Hittites were forced to include in their defensive works. The walls that ran between these were among the most impressive achievements of the Hittite architects, with gigantic earthen dykes supporting walls that in some places climbed slopes at an angle of 45°. Castles once perched on top of both these rocks.

Büyükkale

Büyükkale, the citadel and original centre of Hattusas, served in late Hittite times as the capital of the state and the residence of the kings. The stairs at the entrance are near the site of the original

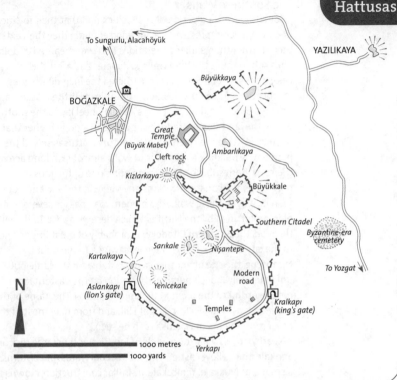

main gate, and lead to the lowest of three ascending courtyards, this one the so-called **state agora**. The complex to the west, consisting of four long rooms, was the **state archive**, perhaps the oldest library building in the world. Among the thousands of records found here was the famous Treaty of Kadesh, signed with the Egyptians in 1259 BC. We owe its preservation, ironically, to Hattusas's anonymous invaders. When they put Büyükkale to the torch, the clay tablets were fired as if in a kiln; otherwise they would have disintegrated long ago. It is believed that the middle courtyard was a kind of 'buffer zone' separating the bureaucracy from the royal residences in the upper courtyard, of which little remains but two large cisterns. On the southern edge of the citadel is a line of temples and state buildings; here some of the original brick still survives.

Looking out from here, two large rock formations rise up from the nearby heights to the south. The cleft parting them is partly man-made; apparently there was a well or spring inside. This area, which stretches from the limits of modern Boğazkale in an arc across to Büyükkale, marked the southern edge of the city wall; its foundations, as well as some of the postern gates in it, are still present.

The Southern Walls

Sometimes after a period of crisis, cities find that their fortifications, however impressive, are not good enough; they then extend them farther than earlier generations had ever dreamed of doing. Thus Athens built the long walls to Piraeus, and after the Peloponnesian War Syracuse constructed the incredible series of fortifications up to Euryalos. Some episode in Hittite history caused its kings to realize that their city's Achilles' heel lay to the south, where the land slopes gradually upwards to a ridge higher than Büyükkale itself. The rulers of 14th-century Hattusas solved the problem by building a broad arc of walls almost 5km long across their southern suburbs, thus completing one of the most magnificent urban fortifications anywhere in the ancient world.

On its way to these walls, the modern road passes several natural heights, fortified by the Hittites, which deserve a visit. To the left of the road, the **Southern Citadel** was probably of great importance to the city, but little has yet been excavated. To the right is **Nişantepe**, the site of another castle notable for the large but unfortunately indecipherable inscription on the eastern face of the rock, referring to the great King Suppiluliumas I. The name of the castle means 'Mark Hill' or 'Target Hill', and from here most of the other monuments of Hattusas can be seen.

Nearby, across a narrow saddle of land, is another large rock and **Sarıkale**, the 'yellow castle', with rooms, courtyards and cisterns like a smaller Büyükkale. **Yenicekale**, a similar construction, crowns the mount furthest south. The foundations of four important temples have been discovered near the southeast corner of the walls.

The southern walls themselves are a symmetrical configuration, with the great gateway **Yerkapı** at their centre. Even in its ruined state, Yerkapı is perhaps the most memorable sight in Hattusas. Only the foundations of the double wall and towers remain, but these were built on a man-made ridge some 30ft high, and here the slopes are paved to further disconcert attackers. Two long stairways, one on either side, lead down from the outer wall. The gate was decorated, or guarded, by finely carved sphinxes, one now in the museum of İstanbul, the other in Berlin. There is a surprise directly underneath Yerkapı, a strange, sloping 200ft **tunnel** through the mound, built of rough Cyclopean masonry corbelled inwards, altogether unlike anything else in Hattusas. Archaeologists call it a **sally port**, a gate from which the defenders could sneak out and harry their attackers from behind, but this is a poor explanation; the tunnel is too noticeable and too carefully sited (lying directly north–south, on the central axis of the city). It is more likely it held some religious or ceremonial significance.

A kilometre away, two other important gates, **Kralkapı** and **Aslankapı**, can be seen on either side of Yerkapı. These are well known for the reliefs that give them their names, meaning King's Gate and Lion's Gate, although like most of Hattusas's sculptures they have been removed to the Ankara museum and replaced with concrete casts. The king carved on Kralkapı is probably really a god protecting the gate. Whichever, he looks remarkably placid and confident, and the axe he carries looks very serious. So do the lions of Aslankapı, although they're not nearly as well preserved. The unusual architectural feature of these gates is their well-executed parabolic arches, a form probably unique to the Hittites.

Boğazkale Museum

open daily 8–5.30; adm with the same ticket as for Hattusas

Many of the finds of Hattusas not in the Ankara museum are in the small **Boğazkale Museum**. These include some intricately carved seal rings, pithoi and other ceramics, Byzantine steles, and an unimaginative reconstruction of the Great Temple of Hattusas.

Yazılıkaya

Most visitors try to plan their trip so that they are in Hattusas at about noon, when the reliefs carved into the rocks at Yazılıkaya are best seen. Yazılıkaya is the national shrine of the deified Hittite kings, on the heights 2km northeast of the city.

The early Hittites seem to have conducted their rituals out of doors, not surprisingly for a people whose chief deities were gods of sun and storms. The two chambers in the natural rock formation at Yazılıkaya were thus open to the sky, even after the monumental gateway and complex of buildings (of which only the foundations remain) were constructed at the entrance to the chambers.

Bittel believes that the **small gallery** to the right served for the funeral rites of departed kings. Certainly the reliefs carved in this shadowy, narrow chamber support this. Menacing lion-headed figures guard the entrance, and once inside you are confronted with the bizarre and mysterious 'sword god', the head of a god (perhaps Nergal, lord of the underworld) over a body which is a composite made up of four lions symmetrically arranged, and which terminates in a tapering sword blade, pointing downwards.

Another relief in this chamber shows **King Tudhaliya** – one of the four Hittite kings of that name – in the protective embrace of the god **Sharruma**, both of whom are in the conventional Hittite pose: standing in profile, with the left hand pulled back and the right extended. This is a particularly fine and well-preserved work, as is the famous **frieze of the 'twelve gods'** on the opposite wall. These fellows, in a row like a Bronze Age chorus line, carry curved swords or sickles and wear the conical hats allowed to Hittite deities.

In the small gallery, there are niches cut into the walls that may have held burial urns of the kings. At the corner near the entrance is a statue base that once supported a figure of the god Sharruma; it's worth noting that the eyes of all the figures in the reliefs are turned towards this spot.

Conventions of Hittite Art

Although much of the meaning of Hittite art and writing remains to be deciphered, erudite scholars such as Dr Bittel have sorted out the basics, comparing the reliefs with the extensive texts found in the state archives here. You recognize a Hittite king, such as Tudhaliya, by his rounded skull cap and earring, and by his *Kalmush*, the curving Hittite sceptre that resembles a monkey's tail. Note the Turkish slippers with the upturned toes, sported by both kings and gods. Among the ideograms that accompany the king will be a winged sun-disc, almost the same as that found in the art of the Assyrians and other ancient peoples. Beneath it, there is often a pair of what look like columns topped with Ionic capitals; these are taken to mean 'great king'. The other ideograms declare the king's name.

Gods are recognized by the pointed caps, and their standing in the divine hierarchy is indicated by the number of horns on the caps. Goddesses wear long pleated skirts and tall hats like those called *polos* by the Greeks, seemingly simulating the walls and towers of a city. Both are often portrayed with animal attributes; some stand on the backs of leopards or on eagles' wings, while the greatest gods often bestride sacred mountains. The ideogram for 'god' is an ellipse, divided vertically in half.

To the left of the small gallery, a cleft in the rocks covers what seems to have been a well or spring. The large irregularly shaped gallery to the left of this contains reliefs of 63 Hittite gods and goddesses: 42 gods marching from the left to meet 21 goddesses coming from the right. It is believed this chamber was important in the New Year celebrations that took place in the spring. It's difficult to ascribe names or functions to most of these images. From left to right, the first twelve are the same chorus line of gods represented in the small chamber, in the same pose. The other gods on this panel are unknown. In the next section, the badly worn part that seems to be a kind of house is really, on closer inspection, two bull-headed gods supporting the sky. The four figures on the far right represent **Shaushga**, local name of Ishtar, her two handmaidens, and the Mesopotamian water-god Ea.

The next, and largest, section portrays the **chief deities of the Hittite pantheon**. The first two are unnamed gods of agriculture and weather; the next, the one with the most horns, is the Weather God of Heaven, **Teshub**, facing his consort **Hepatu** depicted astride a leopard. Her son **Sharruma**, also on a leopard, is directly behind. None of the goddesses that follow have been clearly identified.

Most of the names of these deities are from the **Hurrians**, the people to the southeast who strongly influenced Hittite art and culture. It is interesting to speculate on the cultural sources of this complicated pantheon. If the Hittite religion followed the usual pattern of that era, it may have worked like this: the northern invaders, the Hittites from the Balkans, brought down a Zeus-like storm god and grafted him and his companions on to a matriarchial system of the indigenous Hatti folk, represented by Hepatu. Her son Sharruma is a typical Tammuz-Adonis-Osiris figure of death and rebirth; his importance as mentor and exemplar of the sacred kings betrays a strong conservative instinct in the religion. In the frieze in the large gallery, he stands among the goddesses, as one of the original deities of the country, while the imported goddess Shaushga-Ishtar keeps company with the males.

One mortal has elbowed his way into this divine congregation: **King Tudhaliya IV**, whose image is carved into the opposite wall, larger than any of the gods, with his sacred mountains and his symbols exactly as in the portrait in the small gallery. It's ironic that the last known Hittite king should be the only one to receive this treatment – apotheosis, just before *Götterdämmerung*. As in so many other cases – the Romans, the kingdom of Commagene, the Incas or Aztecs or old Ozymandias – an excess of king-worship seems to be the sign of an overripe nation that has lost its mental balance. When Tudhaliya had himself immortalized on this rock, his civilization had not 50 more years to live; his apotheosis speaks as clearly of the coming end as anything in the state archive.

Alacahöyük

A possible afternoon detour from Hattusas is to Alacahöyük, on a side road going back towards Sungurlu. Long before the Hittites ever entered Anatolia, as far back as 4000 BC, there was a settlement here of the indigenous Hatti people. In their best days, about 2500–2000 BC, the Hatti had one of the most advanced cultures anywhere outside Mesopotamia. Later occupations have covered up the Hatti at sites like Alacahöyük, and it's hard to tell what kind of talent they had for town-building; apart from the later Hittite reliefs, there's really little left to see. Their wonderful metal cosmological discs and figurines have already been mentioned. Most of these are in Ankara, though copies are in the small **museum** here.

The Hittite reliefs, contemporary with those at Hattusas (and like them, concrete casts of the originals), are a puzzle. Two musicians play outlandish instruments, while two other men climb a ladder to nowhere. Archaeologists have named one figure the 'sword-swallower'. There is a procession of animals, a seated female goddess, and a king and queen standing before an odd T-shaped object and what appears to be an altar with a bull on it.

13 Northwestern Anatolia | Land of the Hittites: Boğazkale and Hattusas

---

ⓘ **Çorum** ››
fourth floor, Valilik Binası (provincial government headquarters), Yeni Hükümet Konağı 8, t 0364 213 8502

Where to Stay and Eat around Boğazkale

There are simple *lokantas* in Çorum and Sungurlu, as well as at Boğazkale. The restaurant at the **Hitit motel** in Sungurlu is quite good (€€).

Boğazkale

Aşıkoğlu Motel, t 0364 452 2004 (€€–€). The best accommodation here.

Hattusas Restaurant and Pansiyon, in the centre of the village, t 0364 452 2013, *www.hattusha.com* (€).

Çorum

This is the nearest large town, and a place to look for a room in summer when Boğazkale gets crowded. Çorum also has several cheap *pensions* (about 15 YTL per person).

Anitta Otel, İnönü Caddesi, t 0364 213 8515, *www.anittahotel.com* (€€). Not the cheapest option, but rooms are comfortable and the amenities good.

**Kolağası, 97 İnönü Caddesi 97, t 0364 213 3545 (€). Çorum's old standard, with doubles for 40 YTL.

Sivas to Amasya

East of the turn-off for Sungurlu and Çorum, the Ankara–Sivas road follows the green and pretty valley of the river Delice before reaching **Yozgat**, an agricultural centre distinguished only by its Ottoman clock tower. After Yozgat, the road passes through one of Anatolia's emptier quarters for 210km before rejoining the valley of the Kızılırmak at Sivas, a peaceful city of 300,000 people, founded during Roman times as Sebasteia.

Sivas

Sivas first gained importance during the Middle Ages as capital of the Selcuks and other Turkish emirs. Its golden age lasted until Tamerlane sacked it in 1395. Today, Sivas is most proud of its role at the beginning of the War of Independence; during the summer of 1919, when much of the country was under foreign occupation, Mustafa Kemal (Atatürk) called together the first National Congress in this safe, remote city. On 4 September, the decision was made to ignore the Istanbul government and work for the liberation of Turkey. Today, the place where the congress met, the old boys' high school on Konak Meydanı in the centre of Sivas, is the **September Fourth Museum**, with the congress hall and Atatürk's apartments just as they were during that eventful hour.

To the south, Konak Meydanı extends into a park that contains four of medieval Sivas's finest monuments: the **Kale Cami** of 1580, the **Şifa'iye Medrese** and **Çifte Minare Camii** (twin minarets), these two facing each other across an ancient street, and the **Buruciye Medrese**. These last three structures were begun in 1271. Although by then the Selcuks had moved their capital to Konya, they still took great interest in the eastern marches. This complex, despite its ruined state, is as fine as anything they built in the west. All three have beautifully carved gateways, the Şifa'iye adorned with stern Selcuk lions, the Çifte Minare with acanthus-leaf capitals, probably borrowed from an earlier Byzantine structure. The two minarets, made from brick and blue İznik tiles, and the exterior walls are all that remain of the mosque. Already they list as much as the Tower of Pisa, so see them while you still can.

The park containing these was the heart of Selcuk Sivas. Above it rises the old **Kale** (citadel) on the hill: although it was occupied from the time of the Hittites, nothing remains today, and the old fort has been converted to parkland. The neighbourhoods around it, to the south and west, are the oldest in Sivas, with quiet and pretty streets where the appearance of a foreigner is a rare event. Here stands the 12th-century **Ulu Cami**, and yet another Selcuk theological school, the **Gök Medrese**, also built in that great year of 1271. Although derelict, this is one of the most famous works of

Getting around between Sivas and Amasya

You can get to the Amasya region by **train** from Ankara, but it is served by the slow, infrequent Samsun–Amasya–Sivas line, with good scenery through the mountains.

There are no difficulties with **bus** connections anywhere, but trips through the mountains will take longer than you'd expect – although the network of paved roads is better than in most parts of Turkey. Both in Tokat and Amasya you can get a **taxi** to take you up to the high castles for about 25 YTL.

Selcuk architecture for its gateway, with fanciful sculptured patterns that include styles from every corner of Anatolia, with some old Byzantine carved thistles and angels thrown in.

Outside Sivas, two long and graceful **Ottoman bridges** span the Kızılırmak, lying parallel to the roads to Ankara and Amasya.

Divriği

To see the greatest of all medieval Turkish mosques in this corner of Anatolia, you must make the long and difficult trip to Divriği, 150km southeast of Sivas. It is actually easier to reach by train than by the long and roundabout routes on unpaved roads. In the 13th century, Divriği was the capital of the short-lived Mengüçeh Turkish emirate. The **Ulu Cami**, near the town citadel, is similar in form to the Selcuk mosques of Sivas or Erzurum, with its short minaret, low sloping roof, and conical *türbeler* protruding from the top. Its carved portals are judged among the best work of the age. Divriği was flourishing then, as a stop along the important trade route from Sivas down to the Euphrates valley; the sources of that legendary river are in the surrounding mountains and a number of caravanserais, in various states of preservation, dot the Sivas road, most notably at **Kangal**, a village midway between the two towns.

Besides the road to Divriği there are three other routes from Sivas: the main highway east to Erzurum, the bad road over the Tahtalı Mountains to Malatya, or a slight backtrack along the valley of the Yeşilırmak ('Green River') to the northwest. Of the three, this last is by far the most scenic, crossing the Yıldız ('star') Mountains at the pass of Çamlıbel and then continuing through forest and mountains that become increasingly more rugged and green the closer you come to the Black Sea.

A Dog's Life

The kangal is the Turkish sheep dog, bred in the mountains around Sivas, and if you venture out into the rocky wastes of eastern Anatolia you may see one. If you do, stay in your vehicle or, if you're on foot, keep calm and back away very, very slowly. Don't run and don't do anything daft such as hurling stones at it. You don't mess with a kangal. They lead a hard life; the viciously spiked collar about its neck is there to protect it from bears and wolves. As dogs go, they are hard to describe – some sort of vague cross between a St Bernard and an Alsatian. Turks, not normally a nation of animal-lovers, speak fondly of the kangal; some keep them as pets. In a way, the beast represents how they like to see themselves: loyal, tough, and hard-working yet a terrible foe when provoked. They are held in such high esteem that in the solitary sheep farms up in the mountains, where babysitters are hard to find, parents will happily leave young children in the care of the family kangal.

Tokat

The farmers of the Yeşilırmak grow a lot of tobacco and one of the Turkish monopoly's most popular brands is named after Tokat, a lovely town on the river that has been occupied for thousands of years. Recorded history first mentions Tokat under the name of 'Comana Pontica', the religious centre of Mithridates' Pontic Kingdom. Orestes, son of Agamemnon, is said to have visited here on his wanderings, introducing the rites of Artemis and leaving a famous image of the goddess that Persian king Xerxes later stole.

Up on the slender peak that guards the town, the picture-book **castle** was built by the Byzantines and restored by the Turks. The Byzantines only interested themselves in holding this strategic position; under them the city dwindled, reviving under the Selcuks and other Turkish emirates who contested the town in the Middle Ages. Among Tokat's Selcuk legacy is the **Gök Medrese** of 1270, a medical college that is now the **Tokat Museum**, with the usual grave steles and Turk's attic of folk arts and crafts. One tomb in the medrese belongs to Mu'in al-Din, the Selcuk vezir who built the complex. Alongside the museum is the **Taş Han**, a 17th-century caravanserai lined with artisan's cells; sitting among all manner of bric-a-brac within the glassed-in cloisters are numerous old men, endlessly discussing life over endless glasses of tea.

Tokat Museum
open daily 8.30–12 and 1–4.30; adm

Other Ottoman contributions to Tokat include the 16th-century **Ali Paşa Camii**, centre of a group that includes a tomb and baths; the **Hatuniye Camii**, built by Beyazıt II; a fine stone **bridge** at the northern end of the town; and the **clock tower**, across from the Ali Paşa Camii in the town square. If all these clock towers, seen from İzmir to Yozgat, look alike, they should; all were built during the 19th-century reign of Abdülhamid. He may have earned his reputation as a black-hearted reactionary in a thousand ways, but he did want the Turks to know what time it was.

Amasya

⭐ **Amasya**

The great citadel of Tokat closes off one end of the valley of the Yeşilırmak, and its counterpart at Amasya seals the other. In between, the Yeşilırmak lives up to its name, for, although the river itself is muddy brown with the soil of Anatolia, the land it waters between these two high citadels is one of the greenest and most fertile corners of the nation.

Amasya itself is small, but offers some of Turkey's best travel poster shots. Squeezed into a steep valley, under cliffs carved with rock tombs of the ancient Pontic kings, and with its old Ottoman houses overhanging the Yeşilırmak, it is one of the loveliest cities in Anatolia. Its strategic position gained it the attention of kings and sultans, and they endowed it with many fine buildings.

The Kingdom of Pontus

In antiquity, the Yeşilırmak was called the Iris, the messenger of the dawn, for to the Greeks this was one of the borders of the known world, beyond which lay only Amazons, Scythians and other barbarians. As some-time capital of the various kings named Mithridates and their obstreperous Pontic kingdom, Amaseia gave the Romans a big headache. Rome captured the city in 70 BC, but with the revolt of Phanarces, she was forced to send Julius Caesar to finish the job. After the battle at nearby Zile in 47 BC and the destruction of the Pontic army, Caesar came up with the tag *Veni, vidi, vici*, a political slogan that was to carry him a long way.

Along the River

The centre of Amasya is a broad square on the river's edge, with one of the better equestrian Atatürks; the conqueror in his beaver hat, surrounded by resolute soldiers and anxious women, gazes fiercely at the police station across the river. From here, a pretty shaded promenade follows the river; the main street, Atatürk Caddesi, runs parallel towards the south. Between them, the shopping district surrounds a 16th-century *bedesten*, still in use.

Amasya Museum
open Tues–Sun 8.30–12 and 1.30–5; closed Mon; adm

A few blocks further, past the twin domes of the **Sultan Beyazıt II Mosque** complex, the city's most impressive, is the **Amasya Museum**. This museum contains, in its large new building, a fair collection of artefacts from the various chapters of the past. There is a good-as-new Roman bathtub and two curious cylindrical sarcophagi, as well as local arts and crafts. Some of the most beautiful objects made in the medieval Islamic world were astronomical instruments, and there are fine examples here. The undeniable attraction of the museum, however, is the Mongol mummies in the adjacent Selcuk **Türbe of Sultan Mesut**. Mesut sleeps peacefully in the crypt, but the Mongols, Cumodar and Oshuga Nuyin, two governors of the 14th century who served under the renegade Khan Hülâgü and his successors, are displayed in glass cases, along with the members of an important Selcuk family and their children. The museum's sculpture garden surrounds the *türbe*: the columns with Latin inscriptions served as milestones and were found along the Roman road that traversed the valley of the Yeşilırmak. Just around the corner from the museum is another *türbe*, the **Türbe of Halifat Gazi**, the best of the many tombs in this city. The asymmetrical decoration, with delicate geometric patterns inside small circles randomly arranged over the tomb, is a peculiarity of local architecture.

Markets, Mosques and a Madhouse

Two other mosques can be seen in the district above Atatürk Caddesi. Near to the old *bedesten* stands a tumbledown *han*, constructed in 1758 by order of the local *paşa* and used today by metalworkers and hardware sellers. On the hill behind it stands the 13th-century mosque of **Burmalı Minare**, taking its name from the spirals of its beautifully hewn 17th-century 'twisted' minaret. A few blocks further uphill, the **Fethiye Camii** was originally a Byzantine church of the 7th century.

Beyond the main square, the Yeşilırmak twists northwards. Following it along the main road, you'll find more of Amasya's medieval landmarks; first, the **Bimarhane** of 1309, an insane asylum founded during the period of Mongol rule. Despite its function, the Bimarhane has been blessed with an intricately carved gate as fine as that of any mosque. In contrast to this, the interior is starkly simple and remains unfinished, reflecting the uncertainty of the times after the collapse of the Selcuk state. A block further on lies the **Mehmet Paşa Camii** (late 15th century), and, beyond that, the early 15th-century **Beyazıt Camii**. Through much of early Ottoman history, the sons of sultans were shuffled off to Amasya as governors to keep them out of trouble until their turn on the throne. These two mosques, as well as many others in the town, are a result of the royal attention, as is the **Büyük Ağa Medrese**, just across the bridge from the Beyazıt Camii. This beautiful octagonal complex, with its interior arcade and court-yard, was founded by Beyazıt's Chief White Eunuch. The medrese is still in use today, and is home to 40 boys from all over Anatolia. Although the front door may be locked, if you knock and express an interest in looking around inside, you may well end up being shown around by a clutch of eager young students.

Maiden's Palace and Citadel

On the northern shore of the river, where the old wooden houses crowd against the banks in varying states of dilapidation, the huge rock crowned by the citadel rises straight up above them, with royal tombs burrowed out of its cliffs. According to the geographer Strabo, a native of Amasya who knew the city under both Roman and Pontic rule, the ledge above this narrow bank was the site of the Pontic royal palace, known locally as the **Maiden's Palace**, with walls that extended down to the river. Parts of these still exist, built into the walls of the old houses of the quarter, although they're only visible once you climb the stairs of the palace proper. Here the walls have been restored in recent years, and amid the gardens you can see remains of painted arches and domes, part of the baths built by Mithridates. The strategically placed **café** here also offers fine views of the town.

From the **rock gardens**, stairs lead up to the **tombs of the Pontic kings**. Marvellous as these seem from down below (the city illuminates them at night), little of colour or interest has survived the centuries, and it's impossible to tell which kings were buried there. Sockets cut into the stone indicate there must have been imposing stone façades and balustrades, but nothing of these or any other artwork or grave goods exist today. Still, the effect is royal and grand enough. Visitors are usually surprised that the tombs are not merely façades themselves but entire buildings chiselled out of the dark basalt cliffs; you can walk completely around two of them, into the mountain and out again. Altogether there are four tombs here, but the surrounding region has ten more, all overlooking the Yeşilırmak and comprising the national pantheon of this forgotten kingdom.

In ancient times, Amasya's **citadel**, high above the tombs, was reputed to be impregnable, and from below it does in fact seem utterly inaccessible. However, there's a way around the back (yellow signs indicate the way from the vicinity of the Büyük Ağa Medrese) and the summit can be reached by car. Here, in a kind of museum of masonry, the building styles of the ages betray the various reworkings of the fortress, and its continuous importance over 2,000 years; first, there is ancient rough stone, then good square ashlar from the Hellenistic era, then Roman brick, and finally the characteristic Ottoman sandstone that comprises the greater part of the ruins. Flowers and some of the prettiest butterflies in Anatolia currently occupy the site, and, if the terrain is difficult, the panorama over Amasya's valley and surrounding mountains makes it all worthwhile.

At the entrance, a marble lintel with a Greek inscription has been built into walls of a later era. In the derelict lower citadel, a cistern remains that provided the fortress with its water. The upper citadel is better preserved, and here you can find the famous secret passage: look for a large surviving stretch of wall, high but not broad, with an opening in it that looks, from a distance, like a keyhole. Near its base is a spot where the wall has crumbled away to form a set of steps on its jagged edge. Climb up, and you'll see an arched brick tunnel with slippery descending steps. Supposedly it leads down to the tombs, but no one in Amasya, it seems, has ever tried it. Bring a torch and half a mile of rope.

Around Amasya

Today, as in the days of Mithridates, the area around Amasya is one of the most productive and densely populated farming regions of Turkey. The valleys of the Yeşilırmak and its tributaries, between the peaks and crags, are dotted with towns, each with its castle hovering over it and some well-built foundations of the medieval Turks at its heart. **Zile**, where Caesar conquered, is one of these, also **Merzifon**, the ancient Phazemon. **Niksar**, further east in the valley of the Kelkut Çayı, has kept its name since Roman times, or almost. The Romans called it Neocaesarea, but time has eroded the name just as it has the old fortress, one of Mithridates' strongholds. Niksar received some fine buildings from the Selcuks, notably the 12th-century **Yağıbaşan Medrese**.

It's out of the way, some 60km along mountainous roads from Amasya, but a trip to **Borabay Gölü**, a volcanic crater lake surrounded by forests, will reward you with some of the best scenery these mountains have to offer.

Where to Stay between Sivas and Amasya

Everywhere in this region, accommodation will be clean but modest; it's a pleasant part of Turkey, but hardly overwhelmed with tourists.

(i) Sivas >
Vilayet Konağı,
t 0346 221 3135

Sivas

Hotel Köşk, Atatürk Caddesi 7, t 0346 225 1724, *www.koskotel.com* (€€). This modern beast boasts colourful furnishings, flat screen TVs and contemporary bathrooms.

(i) Tokat >
first floor of the Taş
Han, t 0356 211 8252

Tokat

****Büyük Otel**, Demirköprü Mevkii, t 0356 228 1661 (€€€–€€). Inconveniently situated in the new suburbs to the northwest of the central sights. It has the standard four-star lofty glass-roofed lobby, swimming pool and rooms with mini-bar and satellite TV.

Çamlıca, Gazi Osman Paşa Bulvarı 86, t 0356 214 1269 (€€–€). The best of the cheapies. The carpets may be threadbare, but the rooms at the back are quiet and sunny.

(i) Amasya >
Mustafa Kemal
Bulvarı 27,
t 0358 218 7427

Amasya

This is a gem of a town, so its accommodation is correspondingly more expensive than average.

Emin Efendi Pansiyon, Hazeranlar Sokak 73, t 0358 212 0852, *www.eminefendi.com.tr* (€€). In a 200-year-old house overlooking the river. Double rooms for 70 YTL are smaller and less atmospheric than the Ilk, below, and all but one have shared bathroom facilities, but the views are the best in town.

İlk Pansiyon, Hittit Sokak 1, t 0358 218 1689 (€€–€). The town's most atmospheric offering; a lovingly restored Ottoman mansion. Bedrooms are carpet-bedecked, with high ceilings and wooden fittings. 40–100 YTL, depending on the size of the room and plumbing.

****Harşena Otel**, opposite the post office, t 0358 218 3979, *www.harsena. com* (€€–€). Spacious rooms, comfortable accommodation in an historic building which has good views of the river.

Konfor Palas, Ziyapaşa Blv. 2/B, t 0358 218 1260, *www.konforpalas.com.tr* (€). Has been in business since the 1950s and has a wonderful location directly opposite the rock tombs and river.

Eating Out in Amasya

Nothing either special or unpleasant is likely to come your way. Amasya has a strip of riverside cafés from which to gaze up at the tombs, serving *pide* and kebab variations.

Gamasuk Çay Bahçesı, in front of the Taş Han (€€–€). A good people-watching platform in a creeper-festooned building.

İşçimen, t 0358 233 8854 (€€–€). Has a huge garden and an even bigger selection of specials including seafood.

Bahçeli Bahar Lokantası, down a small street at Sadıkesen Sokak 3, t 0358 218 1316 (€). Amasya's best place to eat; it's unprepossessing and serves huge portions of Tokat kebap (skewered lamb, aubergine and potatoes) for 15 YTL – usually enough for two people.

Çiçek Lokanta, t 0358 218 1337 (€). Good and moderately priced.

Southwestern Anatolia

A 600-mile wall of mountains cuts
the playgrounds of the southern coast
off from the Anatolian interior. Over
on the other side is a broad slab of
Turkish exotica at its best. Tourists
come here too, not to lounge in the sun
but to soak up a little culture.

The names of many of the towns here
will be familiar only from the Bible;
St Paul and his followers spent a lot
of time on these plains looking for
converts. Centuries later, Anatolia's
biggest monastic community grew
up in the fairytale landscapes of
Cappadocia. A few more centuries, and
the same population, now mostly good
Muslims, were making pilgrimages to
the tomb of a Sufi mystic called the
Mevlâna, in the holy city of Konya.

There's more to it than religion; as in
most of Turkey, this region has no
shortage of ruins and lost cities. It also
has a surprise: the unique landscapes
and friendly people of Turkey's own
Lake District.

14

Don't miss

⭐ **A cosy
hideaway in
Turkey's lake
district**
Eğirdir **p.424**

⭐ **City of the
Selcuks and
whirling
dervishes**
Konya **p.430**

⭐ **Rock churches
and fairy
chimneys**
Göreme, Cappadocia
pp.445/6

⭐ **Mysterious
undergound
cities**
Cappadocia **p.449**

See map overleaf

Southwestern Anatolia

Afyon

Eber Gölü

Çay

Akşehir Gölü

Cihanbeyli

Hoyran Gölü

Yalvaç

Akşehir

Ilgiri

Gelendost

Şarkıkaraağaç

Dinar

Eğirdir Gölü

Eğirdir

Kizildağ Milli Parkı

Eflatun-pınarı

Sille

Konya

Çatal Höyük

Burdur Gölü

Isparta

Kovada Milli Parkı

Zindan Cave

Beyşehir Gölü

Beyşehir

Burdur

Insuyu Cave

Sagalassos

Kovada Gölü

Alaca Daği

Çumra

Bucak

Kovada

Sütçüler

Seydişehir

Suğla Gölü

Cremna

Gölhisar

Tefenni

Karabük

Bozkur

Kibyra

Çavdar

Köprü

Manavgat

Akseki

T o r o s
(T a u r u s)

Antalya

Manavgat

Ermenek

Akçali Dağları

Alanya

Gulf

of

Antalya

Mediterranean Sea

GEORGIA

TURKEY

SYRIA

CYPRUS

IRAQ

Don't miss

⭐ Eğirdir p.424

⭐ Konya p.430

⭐ Göreme, Cappadocia pp.445/6

⭐ Cappadocia p.449

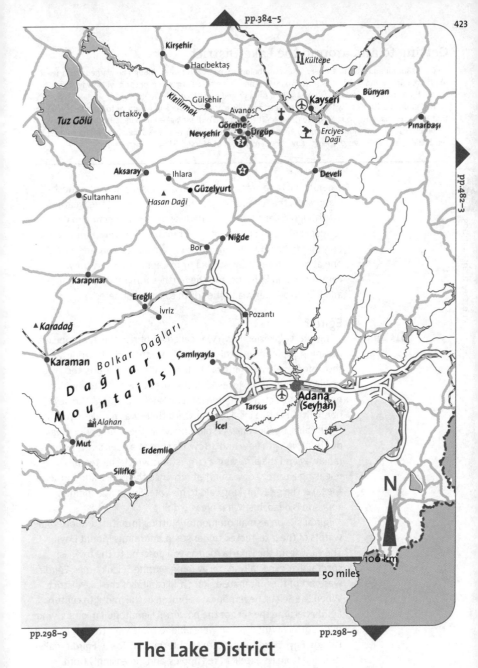

The Lake District

For a change from the endless blue sky and sea, seafood and
trinkets of the Mediterranean coasts, there's either the gloomy
grey Marmara and the Black Sea, or this seldom-visited corner of
the country, which has quite a personality. There's nothing in
Europe or anywhere around the Mediterranean quite like it: sparse

Getting to and around the Lake District

Eğirdir, Burdur and Isparta are very accessible, being on major **bus** routes, though be warned that the roads are narrow and wind all over the map; whether you're travelling by bus or car it will always take longer than you expect (2½hrs from Eğirdir to Antalya and more than 4hrs to Konya).

The Eğirdir tourist office will help to arrange **taxi** trips to Zindan Cave and Adada, or to Kovada; if you can find some companions, you can share the 120 YTL for a car to either place – lunch included.

There are regular **minibus** services to Ağlasun, Bucak and Gölhisar, but in each case you will need a car to reach the sites. Minibuses to Insuyu leave frequently from Burdur.

emerald hills and craggy mountains, enclosing enormous freshwater lakes that change colour with every mood of the weather.

Although it lies at the crossroads of routes connecting major tourist centres, the region of lakes remains relatively undiscovered; only Eğirdir has any pretensions to be a tourist town, and a modest one at that. The east–west road from Cappadocia and Konya to Pamukkale and Ephesus, and the north–south road from İstanbul and Bursa to Antalya and the south coast, meet here.

Eğirdir

 Eğirdir

This pretty lakeside town was called Acrotiri in the Byzantine era, meaning 'promontory'; this changed into the Turkish Eğridir, with the unfortunate meaning of 'it's bent'. In the mid-1980s, the residents, tired of the jokes, changed the name to Eğirdir, which has the more satisfactory meaning of 'she is spinning'. The new name fits in with a local legend. Once there was no lake. Up in the mountains, the queen was spinning while the young prince was out hunting with bow and arrow. He shot at a deer, but the animal ran away and the arrow hit a large stone, which shattered, releasing a torrent of water that drowned the prince and formed the lake. The grieving king said to his wife, 'Spinning! Spinning! Your son is dead. Just what are you doing?'

Eğirdir sits on a small promontory jutting into the turquoise-blue waters of the lake, tucked under steep, enormous Mount Davras. The view from the Isparta road as you descend to the town is spectacular, especially in the evening. During Selcuk times, Eğirdir was part of the Sultanate of Rum and capital of the lake district. When the Selcuk hegemony was broken in the mid-13th century, Eğirdir became the seat of the powerful Hamitoğulları emirs, who had control of Antalya and were able to trade with the Aegean islands, Egypt and the eastern Mediterranean. Today, Eğirdir makes its living from its excellent red apples, and increasingly from tourism. It is a humble, almost too friendly and entirely too relaxing resort where people seem absolutely delighted you've come so far to visit their town. Its nightlife consists of watching the kids play football on the lighted pitch facing the harbour. Boat tours, offered around the harbour or arranged through hotels, are nothing like as lavish as the ones on the sea coast – just a pleasant outing around the lake in a motorboat. Market day is Thursday, when you can sample the apples and other specialities of the area, such as rosewater soap from Isparta.

One of the Hamitoğulları emirs, Felekeddin Dündar, changed the name of the town to Felekabad, and built the attractive **Dündarbey Medrese**, which has been restored and converted to a shopping bazaar. The magnificent stalactite gateway formerly belonged to a ruined caravanserai 5km from Eğirdir. Other reused stones from the caravanserai can be seen in the wall which bars the entrance to the peninsula and connects the medrese to the earlier **Hızarbey Camii**. The minaret is unusual in that it is not free-standing, but sits on top of this wall. Below the minaret is an arch that allows passage between the religious complex and the inner town; on the lake side of the wall you can see doors that lead to a tunnel in the wall, for use in times of trouble. The mosque has an ornate door with a wooden porch. An unusual floral pattern is carved into the stone above the door. Inside is an İznik-tiled mihrab and a forest of wooden pillars, painted blue, which support the roof. A causeway, built in the early 1980s, joins the promontory to a small island, **Yeşilada** (Green Island). A sizeable Greek community lived here before the exchange of populations, and it is possible to see old Greek buildings on the island and on the promontory, within the town's dilapidated fortress. Today the island is full of *pansiyonlar*.

The water in Eğirdir Lake is sweet and full of good fish, the hot item in the town's restaurants. It is possible to swim at the town beach, a 10min walk from the centre, though you may prefer the bigger and nicer **Altınkum** (Golden Sand) beach, less than 3km from the centre of town in the direction of Isparta, or **Bedre** beach, the best of all, nearly 11km on the road to Barla.

Kovada National Park and Zindan Cave

About 30km south of Eğirdir Lake is the small **Kovada Lake**. The road from Eğirdir runs beside a canal connecting the two lakes and is lined by the apple orchards that form the basis of the town's economy. In the summer, as you near Kovada, you can see the goat's-hair tents of nomads who have migrated to their *yaylalar* (summer pastures). The area round the lake is a national park, **Kovada Milli Parkı**, reputedly with 70 species each of trees and animals, including wild boar. In winter, hunting is possible.

If you get excited by bats, and the stench of bat guano, and slithering snake-like through narrow, mud-lined passages, you will enjoy a visit to **Zindan Cave**, about 27km southeast of Eğirdir. Old clothing, stout shoes and a torch are essential. The cave is 2.4km long and it is possible to 'walk' to the end. By the entrance is a pretty stone bridge across a little stream – very convenient for washing off the mud. On this bridge, an ancient relief can be made out; it's said to be the Titan Eurymedon, father of Prometheus. Apparently the cave was a holy place in antiquity; the bridge leads to a nearby necropolis. The road passes a turning to **Adada**, where there are three almost completely preserved Roman temples, a forum and some Hellenistic buildings. After **Aksu**, the road passes through a magnificent gorge. Beehives dot the surrounding hills.

Another possible excursion from Eğirdir is to **Yalvaç**, 65km to the north. About 2km from this village are the ruins of Pisidian Antioch, a city founded in Hellenistic times that was the capital of the province under the Romans; both St Paul and St Philip passed through. The ruins include the first church anywhere dedicated to Paul, the theatre where his convert St Thecla was martyred, and various foundations of temples and public buildings. Yalvaç has a small museum of finds from the site.

Isparta and Burdur

Famous for attar of roses and carpets, **Isparta** is an attractive city of modern boulevards with lots of trees and little else; its old town was devastated by an earthquake at the end of the 19th century. The rose fields lie in the plains north of the town; out of them Isparta makes rose oil, rosewater soap and shampoo, rose cologne, rose-flavoured *lokum* (Turkish delight) and rose everything else. The carpets are for domestic consumption; you will find them not in tourist carpet shops, but on the floors of Turkish houses or in the town **museum** on Kenan Evren Caddesi. Another speciality of Isparta is *Isparta kebap*, made of lean roast meat in *pide* bread.

Unlike Eğirdir, **Burdur** is not directly on the lake. There is little to see in the town, apart from the **Ulu Cami**, built in the 14th century by Dündar Bey, the Hamitoğulları emir. South from the main street and across a little river is a charming residential area. Here, through the open doors of the houses, you can see carpet looms being worked. Women sit on the pavements, chatting and doing their knitting, tatting, needlework and crochet-work. The **museum** is just off the main street and houses finds from **Hacılar**, a Neolithic settlement 24km southwest of Burdur that was one of the successors (*c*. 6600 BC) to the more sophisticated culture of Çatal Höyük. Hacılar itself is not worth a visit.

The water of Lake Burdur is saline, containing about 21 grams of dissolved salts per litre, and it supports only very small fish. There are beaches near **Çendik**, on its southeastern side, where it is possible to swim. **İnsuyu Cave** is a popular recreation spot about 14km east of Burdur. The cave is clean and well lit, and its 600m series of grottoes with stalagmites and stalactites can be walked in comfort. Its nine lakes contain mineral water so clear it might not be there; this water is thought to be therapeutic for diabetics.

Sagalassos

The largest towns in Pisidia were Sagalassos, Termessos and Selge; recent research shows that Sagalassos was both the wealthiest and the most populous. Like the other Pisidian cities, Sagalassos lies high in the mountains between Burdur and Isparta, in a spectacular setting some 7km from the village of Ağlasun. Alexander the Great came to Sagalassos in 334 BC and captured the city. At that time there were no city walls; to the south of the main path through the city is a small flat hill, which slopes steeply to the south and from which the Sagalassians believed they could defend themselves. However, Alexander and his army managed to scale the hillside and thus took the city. Some walls were built much later, but Sagalassos was never enclosed by real city walls; the walls just connected the public areas. The city was finally abandoned in the 13th century; at that time it was little more than a fortified monastery.

Sagalassos remains
open Sun–Thurs 7.30–6; adm

The **remains** are extensive and still under excavation.The older part of the city lies to the north of the main path. Among a few late Hellenistic buildings, the best-preserved is a 1st-century BC Doric **temple** with two standing walls but fallen columns. Southeast of the temple are benches indicating a **bouleuterion**; to the northeast is a terrace supporting a heroon. The beautiful frieze from this heroon can be seen in the fire station in Ağlasun, though there are plans for a permanent museum (other carvings currently adorn a tea garden in Ağlasun). Also in the upper city is a large, well-preserved **theatre**, approximately the same size as those at Perge and Side. The **agora** lies between the theatre and the temple.

The lower city dates from Roman times. **Baths** flank the lower agora, and it is near here that a colossal **statue of the emperor Hadrian** (AD 117–138) was found in 2007, including the now-famous 27-inch head that formed the heart of an exhibition in London's British Museum in 2008. To the north of the baths is a large 2nd-century AD **nymphaeum**, currently being restored to its original state. Two temples have been identified here: the **temple of Apollo Clarius**, which was transformed into a Christian basilica, and the **temple of Antoninus Pius** (AD 138–161). To the southwest of this can be seen the sarcophagi of a Hellenistic and Roman **necropolis**. At the far west is a Christian **basilica** made of the remains of two Roman monuments. The cliff face to the west of the city is full of small **rock tombs** for cremated bodies, from the 2nd and 3rd centuries AD; some are decoratively carved with animal heads and garlands. A third **necropolis** lies southeast of the theatre.

Cremna (Kremna) and Kibyra

If you have time for another ruined city in an isolated, picturesque setting, there's **Cremna**, an Augustan colony just over 15km from the village of Bucak, just east of the Antalya highway. Cremna is situated on top of a steep hill; there is much climbing to do. The **city walls** to the west are well preserved; outside them lies a **necropolis**. As you approach the city from the southwest, you will come across the two arches of a **gate**, probably Hellenistic. Within the city, the public **agora** can be identified by the 20 steps which form its north side. A very large triple gateway, whose façade was a close copy of that of the library of Celsus at Ephesus, once stood at the top of these steps; although the steps remain, the gateway is scattered in ruins at the bottom. Behind where the archway should be are great **cisterns**. East of the public agora, the **Forum of Longus** contains the remains of a **basilica**, with some arches still standing, as well as a large inscribed pillar; this is a dice oracle, used in fortune-telling. There's little else to see: a small **theatre** in the middle of the town, the excavated remains of a **bath** to the west, and scanty remains of a few temples.

Kibyra is a wonderful windswept site, high on a hilltop over-looking a broad plain. The ruins are neglected save for the goat-herds who bring their goats to graze on the wild thyme, producing very tasty meat ideal for *Isparta kebap*. Graves tumble down the hillside, which is littered with fluted columns and carved blocks of stone, some inscribed, including one on which the letters KIBYR can clearly be seen. The remains of several public buildings can be identified, including, on the eastern side of the hill, a **theatre** and a less-well-preserved **stadium**. Next to the theatre is a large building with arches, now half-submerged in the soil.

Kibyra is about 100km from Burdur and can be reached by heading southwest via the villages of **Tefenni** and **Çavdar** ('barley') to **Gölhisar** ('lake castle'), the nearest village to Kibyra. The lake in question has, as a result of canalization, shrunk to a tiny size, leaving a broad, fertile plain between Çavdar and Gölhisar; crops grown here include sugar beet and aniseed, used to make *rakı*.

Where to Stay between Eğirdir and Burdur

ⓘ Eğirdir ›
2 Sahil Yolu 13 A,
t 0246 311 4388

Eğirdir

Eğirdir has a wide choice of *pans-iyonlar*, sweet family-run places of a very good standard that can make the trip here worthwhile.

***Eğirdir, Kuzey Sahil Yolu 2, t 0246 311 3961, *www.hotelegirdir.com* (€€). On the lakefront. There are only a few places with any pretensions, and they include this old reliable.

Atabey, on Yeşilada, t 0246 311 5006 (€€–€). Standard rooms, with none of the charm of the nearby *pensions*.

Choo Choo, on Yeşilada, t 0246 311 4926 (€€–€). Newer and slightly more luxurious than the other *pensions*, though not as cosy and welcoming. Thre rooms are named after Utrillo, Toulouse-Lautrec and Rembrandt, with appropriate prints on the walls.

Lale Hostel, near the castle, t 0246 312 2406, *www.lalehostel.com* (€). En suite rooms with a view of the lake. A delightful family who do everything to make you happy; and very cheap dinners (mom's an excellent cook). It's popular with backpackers.

ADAC, one of the first *pensions* you see as you cross over to Yeşilada, t 0246 312 3074 (€). Run by a friendly lady who indulges in good-natured back-slapping to compensate for the language barrier; bright rooms with showers and views east or west.

Akdeniz, tip of Yeşilada island, t 0246 312 3432 (€). Another good choice.

Isparta

****Büyük Isparta Oteli**, Atatürk Caddesi 8, t 0246 232 4423 (€€€€–€€€). The most comfortable hotel is this modern place; doubles 200 YTL, but discounts are usually available.

***Bolat**, Demirel Bulvarž 71, t 0246 223 9001 (€€). Boasts a tennis court and central heating; it is very relaxing.

Yeni Gulistan, Mimar Caddesi 31, t 0246 218 4085 (€). Isparta has a handful of cheap hotels and *pensions*, mostly around Mimar Caddesi, the main street. This is a pleasing place to stay; a double room with phone and private shower will cost just 30 YTL.

Burdur

Hotel Özeren, Gazi Caddesi 51, t 0248 234 1600, *www.hotelozeren1.com* (€€–€). Doubles with showers 50 YTL.

Eating Out between Eğirdir and Burdur

The star attraction here is fish from the lake, which is inexpensive and delicious – much more delicate than most salt-water fish, a lot like perch from the Great Lakes in America. There are also lake crayfish. There's nothing out of the ordinary in Isparta or Burdur – but try a goat-meat *Isparta kebap*, available anywhere.

Eğirdir

Home cooking at the *pensions* is universally cheap and tasty.

Deyra Restoran, on the waterfront, near the Eğirdir Oteli, t 0246 311 4047. Offers a large selection of cold *mezes* and excellent fish in batter, served by waiters dressed in picturesque orange Adana *şalvar*. A meal costs about 20 YTL, only slightly more than the many other fish restaurants around the lake and on Yeşilada island.

ADAC, where the owner jokes that if you don't like her food you don't have to pay; if you love it you should pay double.

West towards Konya

To get to Konya, it's a long and roundabout trip up the west side of Lake Eğirdir and then down the back side of the biggest of the region's lakes, **Beyşehir Gölü**, passing on the way the most unspellable, unpronounceable village in Turkey, ramshackle **Şarkıkaraağaç**. Just south of here a national park has been established, the **Kızıldağ Milli Parkı**. To the north, **Akşehir** claims to be the home of the legendary Nasreddin Hoca; you can visit his tomb in a little pavilion on the town green. On the gate is a big heavy lock, though it's wide open on the other three sides.

Down the eastern shore of Beyşehir Gölü, some 4km off the main road at **Eflatunpınarı** is a Hittite relief, with figures of four kings

Nasreddin Hoca

This fellow, the clever-foolish country priest (*hoca*) who goes under the name of Goha in the *Arabian Nights*, is the classic comic figure of Turkish folklore. Outwitting himself as often as Emperor Tamerlane, at whose court he is supposed to have lived, the Hoca's adventures are still current among all Turks; you'll see souvenir pictures of him everywhere, seated backwards on his donkey. The Hoca is very much a creation of the Sufis, the mystics of Islam who condense volumes of theology into such tales. One famous story has the Hoca walking with a friend discussing the completeness of creation. The Hoca considers that it would have been better if horses had wings; thus, they would be much more helpful to mankind. Just then some pigeon droppings fall on the Hoca's turban. He reflects, 'Allah knows best!'

and some mythological beasts, set by a small lagoon. **Beyşehir**, at the southeast corner of the lake, is a bedraggled town that could be much nicer. It's a poor, out-of-the-way place, a reminder of what most Turkish provincial towns were like 20 years ago. Nevertheless, it's worth a stop for the **Eşrefoğlu Camii** and its *külliye*, built by the Eşrefoğlu emirs, who installed themselves here after the breakup of Selcuk power. The mosque has a beautiful interior of painted tiles and carved wood; adjacent is the *türbe* of the emirs, with more fine tiles, a medrese and a hamam.

Neither Beyşehir nor its lake get many visitors. This is a corner still open to exploration. In Beyşehir or any of the little fishing hamlets around the lake you may find someone with a boat to take you around the lake's many islands. None seems to be inhabited now, though a few have traces of Byzantine monasteries. West of Beyşehir on the lakeshore are the ruins of **Kubadabad Palace**, the summer retreat of the Selcuk sultans. There isn't much to see, but if the finds now in Konya's Karatay Medrese are any indication it must have been a marvel. It would have been impious to build a palace to last, so in medieval times Muslim rulers always made their pleasure domes of perishable materials: mud brick covered with painted tiles, and wood. As far as we know, the only medieval Muslim palace surviving anywhere is the Alhambra in Granada. Imagine what the others must have been like.

East of Beyşehir, on the way to Konya, the bleak scenery is interrupted by a rather incredible sight, the **Atatürk 100 Yıl Ormanı** (Atatürk Centennial Forest): several million young trees, all recently planted in a wonderfully mad project to make a wasteland into a forest. In a century it will be truly impressive, even if now it looks like the world's biggest Christmas tree farm.

Konya

 Konya

Some cities, such as Istanbul, are forced by their location to play a large role in the world's affairs; others may survive for millennia without contributing anything. Most fortunate of all, however, are the towns that at one time in their lives have a little empire of their own, and then move off history's stage into a long golden twilight. Bursa is one such Turkish city; Konya, the old Selcuk capital, is another. These two have other things in common: both have wonderful heritages of Turkish art and architecture, and both are trying hard to manage the difficult process of becoming modern and prosperous on their own terms. Turkey often advertises itself as the 'Land of Civilizations', and, with the many peoples and cultural influences that have drifted through over the centuries, it is hard to isolate anything as specifically 'Turkish', until you come to Bursa or Konya, the most Turkish of the nation's cities.

Konya has a reputation for being the most conservative and devout corner of Turkey; in truth, there are plenty of other candidates for that honour. This is nothing to be alarmed about; Konya is a city where culture and tolerance have always been accounted virtues. If it has a living faith to sustain it, so much the better. The spirit of the Mevlâna still protects this city, and ensures that religion shows us only its most benign face.

History

The first we hear of Konya is as a Phrygian town called Kawania; later, under the Greeks and Romans, it became Iconium, capital of the province of Lycaonia. The **Selcuks**, with whom medieval Konya is usually associated, were not the first Turks in the neighbourhood; other warrior bands were around as early as the 9th century, and the Arabs of the Abbasid Caliphate had arrived before them, twice capturing the city from the Byzantines though they could not keep it. When the Selcuks came in 1076, after the Battle of Manzikert gave them control of Anatolia, **Sultan Süleyman Ibn Kutulmuş** made Konya his capital. Not that the city had much to commend it; its only real advantage was equal distance from all possible enemies. Perhaps the broad, treeless Plain of Konya reminded the Selcuks of their ancestral home on the Asian steppe.

For a time the Selcuks, strong as they were, had a hard time holding Konya. During the first Crusade, Godfrey of Bouillon occupied the city for a short while, and Barbarossa passed through in 1190 on his way to the Holy Land. Neither of these harmed either the city or the Selcuks. Like any of the early Turkish principalities, the Selcuks' **Empire of Rum** was hardly a modern, centralized state; the real 'capital' was the sultan's throne, and that moved with him wherever his whims or campaigns took him. Konya, however, was the major beneficiary of their building work and philanthropy.

Under the Selcuks' intelligent and tolerant regime, Konya in the 12th and 13th centuries became a refuge for artists and men of learning, fleeing the depredations of the Mongols and Crusaders from all over the Middle East and Muslim Asia. Rulers such as **Alâeddin Keykubad**, who liked to surround himself with poets and erudite dervishes, endowed a collection of mosques and schools that has made the city the equal of Istanbul and Bursa as a showplace of Turkish architecture. They had hardly begun when the **Mongols** came in 1243 to spoil the party; they never sacked Konya, but they did put an end to the Selcuk state, which survived for a few decades afterwards only as a much-reduced, tribute-paying vassal of the Great Khan. After the fall of the Empire of Rum, the **Karamanoğulları**, the Turks from Karaman, filled the vacuum but moved the capital to their own town of Ermenek. Konya declined and did not recover until the coming of the republic.

Getting to and around Konya

Konya has an **airport**, with daily flights to Istanbul and İzmir. **Trains** from Istanbul pass through Akşehir, Konya and Karaman on their slow way to Adana. Your best bet is the **bus**: as usual, there will be no problem making connections to anywhere. The **train station** is on Ferit Paşa Caddesi, about a kilometre southwest of the Alâeddin Hill. The **bus depot** is equally far, but towards the northwest on Ankara Caddesi; **dolmuşes** to the centre are infrequent, and you might as well take a **cab**.
Konya is a compact city, and you can easily go everywhere **on foot**.

Celâleddin Rumi, the **Mevlâna** (*see* p.50), one of the great mystics of Islam and founder of the 'Whirling' Mevlevi dervishes, was the most famous of all the figures of Konya's golden age and his spirit continues to animate the city today. Throughout the Ottoman period, Mevlevi sheikhs were often close advisers to the sultan. Even in 1919, Konya elected the sheikh (the head of the order) to represent it at the first Turkish National Assembly.

Around the Alâeddin Hill

Today the dervishes may be less conspicuous, but the people of Konya like to joke that they're still going around in circles; any trip through the town is likely to lead through the **Alâeddin Bulvarı**, the circular road around the **Alâeddin Hill** in the centre of the city. This little mound, like the scores of others in the broad plain of Konya, is a 'tell', the sort of hill that grows up wherever a small town or village occupies a site continuously for thousands of years. Later cultures, including the Selcuks, simply built over the top. The **Alâeddin Köşkü**, the palace of the Selcuk sultans, or rather the last little bit of it, still stands, lovingly preserved under a modern arched pavilion; interestingly, they built all their schools and religious buildings in stone and good brick, but, as at Kubatabad, expended only cheap mud brick and conglomerate on themselves.

Their **Alâeddin Camii**, begun by Sultan Rukaeddin Mesut in 1130 and finally completed by Alâeddin Keykubad in 1221, has therefore fared somewhat better. Though well built, its position on the northern slope of the unstable mound has made almost constant restoration work a necessity. The changes and additions of various sultans over those 91 years explain the unusual form of the mosque; together with its courtyard behind the great façade, it has the shape of an open book, with a large pillared hall in one corner. The plan of this hall is that of the Selcuk 'great mosques' all over Turkey, but here the neat rows of columns are marble, reused from Greek and Byzantine buildings. There are more old columns on the façade; the Selcuks apparently found them in different sizes, and cleverly arranged them in a series of arches, slanted to match the slope of the hill. At the centre of the structure are two large *türbeler*. The largest, with a conical roof, contains the bodies of eight Selcuk sultans, including Alâeddin Keykubad, all in tiled sarcophagi; the adjacent *türbe* stands empty.

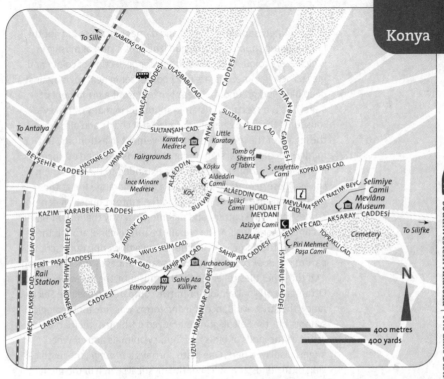

The rest of Alâeddin Hill, once all part of the Sultan of Rum's palace grounds, has been rehabilitated and planted with pine trees and flower-beds among shady cafés. Just across Alâeddin Bulvarı from the mosque stands another Selcuk masterpiece, the **Karatay Medrese**. Once famous for its dome of coloured tiles, this former theological school has now, fittingly, become a museum of Selcuk and Ottoman ceramics. Its founder, Celâleddin Karatay, was vezir to the Selcuk sultans for 40 years; he is buried under the smaller dome of the medrese's mosque. Much of this building complex, like so much else the Selcuks built, has disappeared, but fortunately the portal still stands, echoing the Alâeddin Mosque across the way, with its geometric patterns in white and blue-grey stone. Nothing symbolizes the synthesis of cultures the Selcuks tried to create better than this gate. Influences of the Arab and Persian are obvious, and the Greek declares itself in two Corinthian columns flanking the entrances. Even the ancient Phrygians seem to be recalled in the geometric lattices of the lower section; the great Phrygian temple façades aren't very far from Konya, and they must have been known at the time.

Few museum buildings are their own prize exhibit; nothing in the collection of this one, in fact nothing in Turkey, can compare with the Karatay's domed mosque, completely covered in miniature tiles of unsurpassed precision and intensity of colour (though

Karatay Medrese
open Tues–Sun 9–12 and 1.30–5.30; closed Mon; adm

unfortunately somewhat faded and damaged). These are not the large painted squares of Ottoman İznik, but a kind of mosaic in which every colour is fired separately for perfection of colour and glaze. These geometric stars of 24 points, set in neat rows against a deep blue background, are meant to represent a firmament of stars. This is a specifically Islamic approach; in many of Turkey's museums there are carefully detailed star charts and almanacs, the legacy of the great Muslim achievement in astronomy, but hardly ever are actual stars or constellations depicted on them, as if the Islamic prohibition of images extended to the stars themselves. These geometric stars, with a hint of orange fire at the centre, shine like the real thing, and their interconnection demonstrates the divine pattern and meaning in a way that might never occur to a non-Muslim. The equally beautiful panel around the bottom of the dome is an inscription, in a flowering Kufic script, of part of the *Book of the Cow*, the first and longest *sura* of the Koran.

Of the other tiles collected for the museum, the examples of later Ottoman work look almost primitive compared to the fine Selcuk fancy; the strict avoidance of living forms was fine for theological schools, but the Selcuk princes enjoyed nothing in their art so much as the kinds of birds and fantasy animals and crowned angels displayed here. One plate portrays a *simurgh*, the mythical king of the birds, the object of the mystical search in the great Persian poem *Parliament of the Birds*, which was a favourite among princes and dervishes alike in Selcuk times (and the source of Chaucer's *The Parliament of Fowles*). Among the later work are plenty of fine ceramics from Kütahya, from 17th-century tiles to a lovely sign for a printer's shop, made in the 1920s.

Across the street, sheltered under a pavilion like the Alâeddin Köşkü, you can see the portal and sparse remains of another Selcuk school, the **Little Karatay Medrese**.

İnce Minare Medrese

If any film director ever needed a backdrop for the palace of a science-fiction Emperor of Mars, he might copy the unique and thoroughly bizarre portal of the İnce Minare Medrese, three blocks down Alâeddin Bulvarı. But give credit to the architect Keluk, and to Fahreddin Ali, the Selcuk vezir who paid for it; besides the skilful carved calligraphy of the portal, this remarkable building has a lot to say about the Selcuks and their architecture. A *medrese*, or *madrasa*, was originally only the house of a teacher; it was only under the Selcuks that it became a monumental public building dedicated to education. This is one of the first, and its centralized plan built around a dome would influence the architecture of the Ottomans as well as other nations. The complex has suffered much during centuries of neglect; most of the outbuildings are gone, and the 'slender minaret' that gave the place its name was swatted down to stubbiness by a lightning bolt in 1901. The remains are now the **Museum of Selcuk Stone and Woodcarving**. As with the ceramics, many of the artefacts are from the Selcuk palace on Alâeddin Hill, and the same fantastical forms are represented.

Continuing your whirl around Alâeddin Bulvarı, you pass a 19th-century French church and then, one block later, come to Alâeddin Caddesi (also called Hükümet Caddesi), the business street of the modern town and the way to the Mevlâna's tomb. Here, the many reconstructions of the 13th-century **İplikçi Camii** have left only a plain brick barn, but this is the mosque in which the Mevlâna did much of his teaching and practised his meditations. The tomb of his spiritual guide, Shems ed-Din of Tabriz, a dervish from Persia, can be seen on a side street two blocks north. The Mevlâna's own disciples murdered Shems in strange circumstances.

Further down, Hükümet Caddesi skirts the market district, passing through the large Hükümet Meydanı with its 16th-century **Şerafettin Mosque**, a distinguished Ottoman-style work that replaced a Selcuk original destroyed by fire; around the back is the city's best hamam. The square has been redone, with an underground shopping mall, the **Şaraflar Yeraltı Çarşisi**, full of glittering jewellery. Beyond that, the street changes its name to Mevlâna Caddesi, and the green tiled dome of Rumi's tomb comes into view.

Mevlâna Museum

Mevlâna Museum
*open Tues–Sun
9.30–5.30, Mon
10–5.30; adm*

It is believed the site of the Mevlâna Museum, formerly the central *tekke* (dervish house) of the Mevlevi order and burial place of Celâleddin Rumi, was a garden belonging to the Selcuk sultans, presented as a gift to the Mevlâna's father, Bahaeddin Veled. He was buried here in 1232, and, when the Mevlâna joined him in 1273, work was immediately begun on a cylindrical *türbe*. Over the years, the buildings adjacent to the *tekke* were enlarged and expanded; the whole seems to have been reconstructed in the 15th century under the patronage of the Ottoman sultans, particularly Beyazıt II. Over the nearly 700 years of the *tekke*'s existence, the *çelebiler* ('inheritors'), the descendants of the Mevlâna who assumed the hereditary leadership of the order, were men influential not only in Konya and among the dervishes but in affairs of the empire too.

By the 20th century, it seemed to many that such influence, and such easy living, had staled the original spiritual impulse, and the Mevlevi sheikhs were known to be among the most reactionary and self-serving upholders of the old order. Atatürk's inability to prevent them from interfering in the politics of his new republic was the main reason for his decree dissolving the dervish orders. In 1925, a year later, the Konya *tekke* became the first of Atatürk's new museums, with the title of 'Konya Museum of Ancient Works'.

Dervishes of the Mevlevi and other orders do still practise semi-openly in modern Turkey: as long as religion stays out of politics, the authorities are content. Even though this *tekke*, along with the others, has been secularized, good Muslims come to pray at the tomb of a man they regard almost as a saint. Over the last 15 years, large numbers of pilgrims have again started coming from the former Soviet republics of central Asia.

Through the entrance, incongruously embellished with a ticket window, you pass into a small courtyard. The fountain on the left is the *şadırvan*, where ablutions are performed before prayer; the one on the right is the **Şeb'i Arus** (wedding night pool), a gift of Yavuz Selim; the Mevlâna, in his later years, always spoke of his coming death as a 'wedding', an event to be celebrated not mourned, and on its anniversary every 17 December (a modern adjustment from the Muslim calendar) the dervishes perform their whirling dance, the *sema*, around this fountain in remembrance. Three small *türbeler* nearby with shallow domes were contributed by governors of the 16th century, when Konya was subject to the Karamanoğulları emirs, themselves also patrons of the Mevlevis.

Inside the main building, beyond a hall containing exhibits of Islamic calligraphy, lie the Mevlâna, his father, his son Sultan Veled, and other notables of the order, all in elaborate **sarcophagi** covered with richly embroidered cloths, with the turbans of the deceased placed at the top; six of the sarcophagi belong to the 'men of Horosan' who accompanied the Mevlâna and his father in their flight to Konya. The famous **green dome**, Konya's most conspicuous landmark, rises over the Mevlâna's sarcophagus. On the outside, the blue band of tiles around the dome has the words of the *bismele*, the formula 'In the name of Allah, the compassionate, the merciful' that begins each book of the Koran. Inside, the dome is covered with a pattern of geometric stars; the Mevlevis called it the 'Dome of the Pole'. The vast array of sumptuous carpets, cloths and other works of art show the favour the Mevlevis always enjoyed with the powerful, for almost everything here came as gifts from sultans and princes. One of the exceptions to this is the **Mevlâna's sarcophagus**, a triumph of Turkish woodcarving, done by an artist named Abdulvahid solely as a labour of love. Built entirely without nails, the sarcophagus is completely covered with the Mevlâna's poetry, carved in different styles and patterns of calligraphy. The inscription begins: 'Here lies Mevlâna, sultan of scholars...'

The Mevlâna's prayer carpet, said to be a wedding gift from Alâeddin Keykubad, is a work of art in its own right, but it cannot compare with another on display, a 500-year-old silk carpet from Persia, said to be the finest ever woven; it has 144 knots to the square centimetre, 2,197,000 in all – it isn't surprising it took five years to complete. Other treasures include hairs from the beard of

Mohammed, in a mother-of-pearl box; huge carved rosaries that look like wooden ropes; musical instruments; books, among them the illuminated first edition of Mevlâna's great poetical work, the *Mathnawi*; and the April Cup, a huge carved crater of gold, silver and bronze, made in Baghdad and presented to the Mevlevis by Elen Said Bahadır, the last İlhanlı Mongol ruler of Mesopotamia.

The **Semahane**, a grand vaulted hall adjacent to the mosque and tombs, was the site of the *sema*, the whirling dance, still performed here every year in December. With its carpets and delicate chandeliers, it is as opulent as the tombs. The great chain suspended from the ceiling to balance the chandeliers was carved from a single piece of marble, link by link. Note also the separate galleries for women spectators at the *sema*; although the Mevlâna himself had little use for such foolishness, later dervishes have been notoriously afraid of women, and prefer to keep them out of sight.

Other parts of the museum that may be viewed are outside the complex of tomb and *semahane*. The **dervishes' cells** line parts of the compound's walls; some have been restored to their original appearance, as has the **soup kitchen** where would-be dervishes served an apprenticeship of 1,001 days while learning the manners and precepts of the order. Next to the sheikh's quarters, now the museum office, stands the famous **library** of 5,000 old works on the Mevlevis and Islamic mysticism. The southern gate of the outer wall leads to a dervish cemetery, the **Garden of Souls**.

Other Sights in Konya

Sultan Selim I, Yavuz Selim, of all the Ottoman rulers perhaps the most devoted to the work of Mevlâna, left behind the large **Selimiye Mosque** next to the Mevlevi House. With little of the architectural sophistication Selim could get in Istanbul, where the Selimiye is one of the finest imperial mosques, this ungainly work, in elevation a simple cube, is domed and surrounded by domed arcades. From here, a walk down Selimiye Caddesi through the **bazaar** and Konya's southern districts will reveal some of the city's other monuments. The **market district**, while large and colourful, is not the same sort of attraction as Istanbul's or Bursa's. Konya is not a wealthy city, and what you'll see is mostly everyday clothing and housewares. Still, there are some traditional craftsmen and tailors.

Selim's reign also saw the construction of the **Piri Mehmet Paşa Camii**, built around the *türbe* of its founder. Another, more endearing mosque, right at the centre of the market district, is the **Aziziye Camii**, a 17th-century structure rebuilt by Sultan Abdülaziz in 1867 in the gaudiest style of Turkish rococo. Continuing on west from Selimiye Caddesi, you pass another of the great Selcuk works, the 1258 **Sahip Ata Külliye**, founded by the famous vezir Fahreddin Ali. Its half-ruined state and out-of-the-way location have

Archaeological Museum

open Tues–Sun 9–12 and 1.30–5.30; closed Mon; adm

conspired to keep this complex obscure, but its brick and stone entrance portal is as fine as any in Konya. Konya's **Archaeological Museum**, nearby, has an unremarkable collection, except for three well-preserved Roman sarcophagi from Pamphylia. The best known, the Hercules Sarcophagus (*c.* AD 260), depicts the hero gliding through all twelve of his Labours.

Just outside Konya, on a side road off the main route for Beyşehir and Isparta, you can take a brief excursion (by city bus) to the pretty, bucolic village of **Sille**; here, the **Aya Eleni** church may be as old as the 5th century, but was rebuilt in the 19th. There are paintings to see inside, if the key can be found.

Information and Festivals in Konya

In the museum there is a small bookstore with books in English about the city and the Mevlevis, as well as tapes of Mevlevi music.

Mevlâna festival takes place on 10–17 December each year. Hotel rooms are hard to come by, and performances of the *sema* can be sold out months in advance. The tourist office can help with arrangements.

Where to Stay in Konya

Konya

Konya's accommodation is mediocre: even four-star hotels can be a let-down. Most of the more expensive places are located on Mevlâna Caddesi or adjacent Hükümet Meydanı.

***Balıkçılar Hotel, Mevlâna Karşısı, t 0332 350 9470, *www.balikcilar.com* (€€€). Great location opposite the Mevlâna museum, and popular with tour groups. Rooms are air-conditioned, with satellite TV.

Hotel Rumi, Mevlâna Karşışı, t 0332 353 1121, *www.rumihotel.com* (€€€). Also popular with tour groups and near the main attractions. The hotel is a recent addition to the town and offers comfortable modern facilities including a sauna and hamam, though with little overall charm.

***Selçuk, Alâeddin Caddesi, t 0332 353 2525, *www. otelselcuk.com.tr* (€€€). The reception has an impressive inlaid marble floor; the quiet rooms have baths, balconies and air-conditioning.

(i) **Konya >**
Mevlâna Caddesi 21, near the Mevlâna museum, t 0332 351 1074

**Sema, Mevlâna Karşısı, t 0332 350 4623 (€€). Modern, with TV and refrigerator in the rooms, and plenty of brown carpet. Still, it is a good bargain at around 70 YTL.

Konya does have inexpensive hotels and *pensions*, serving the many Muslims who come to Konya on pilgrimages, but on the whole the situation is not encouraging; you might be happier splurging on a (bargained-down) room in one of the places listed above. To find the cheapest places, just look in the side streets off Mevlâna Caddesi, or around the Aziziye Mosque.

*Başak Palas, t 0332 351 1338 (€). Pleasant; 40 YTL for a double with shower; rooms with balconies have a view over the car park, but the quieter rooms are at the back.

Azizye Otel, just beyond the Azizye Cami, t 0332 352 2287 (€). The Tardis of Konya, seemingly tiny from the outside but massive within, with dozens of relatively clean, well-maintained rooms along endless corridors illuminated by coloured lightbulbs. For what you get, it's terrific value; some 30 YTL rooms even have baths. The toilets are down the hall and are cleaned several times a day.

Eating Out in Konya

Most of the tolerable restaurants (and the only ones where you can get a glass of beer) will be found along Mevlâna Caddesi, around the hotels.

Mevlevi Sofrası, Nazimbey Caddesi (€€). Good traditional soups, *kebaps* and desserts on its large terrace with great views of the Mevlâna museum. 25 YTL will buy a good set menu; your best bet in Konya for flavour and ambience. Inside, the restaurant shows off its historical heritage, a restored Ottoman house.

Sema, Mevlâna Caddesi (€). That Turkish rarity, a restaurant that advertises vegetarian food (mostly the usual aubergine stews and such); tasty, though, and costing only around 10 YTL.

The Plain of Konya

Konya province, the largest in Turkey, is also one of its most important agricultural regions. One would hardly guess this from looking at a map: the region appears a strangely empty space, stretching over 240km from the lake district to Cappadocia. It looks even emptier when you're in it, but this is the breadbasket of Turkey. The roads east from Konya are all lined with grain elevators and flour mills. Its farmers have serious faces, rosy children, shiny tractors, and do a lot to keep Turkey self-sufficient in food.

They were at it with much the same vigour 8,000 years ago, with enough leisure left over to create one of the world's first urban cultures, at least until archaeologists find an even older one. History used to begin with Sumer. Now with the great discoveries by James Mellaart at **Çatal Höyük**, we say it begins here on the Plain of Konya where, long before nation-states, sky-gods or warrior castes, this town, and probably dozens like it, enjoyed what seems an easy and blessedly peaceful existence in trade and agriculture, making the beautiful works of art on display in the Ankara museum. Don't bother to visit the site – all you will get there is a lesson in the archaeologist's talent for recreating a culture from the tiniest of clues. If you are travelling this way you'll see plenty more tells (*see* p.432, 'Alâeddin Hill'); the areas west and south of Konya, as far as Karaman, have Turkey's greatest concentration of them. None has been excavated.

The road passing Çatal Höyük continues on to the Mediterranean coast at Silifke, crossing the beautiful Taurus (Toros) Mountains after **Karaman**, the Larende of ancient times and capital of the Karamanoğulları Turks after the fall of the Empire of Rum. Karaman's landmark, set in a big park in the centre, is its castle, most noteworthy for being the only one in Turkey with its name in an electric sign on top. There's also a 14th-century Mevlevi house called **Ak Tekke**, where members of the Mevlana's family are buried, and a number of other mosques built by the Karamanoğulları.

North of Karaman, in and around the huge caldera of an extinct, 7,400ft volcano called **Karadağ**, you can explore the forgotten relic that the Turks, with some exaggeration, call **Binbir Kilise** (1,001 churches). This was once a thriving, Cappadocian-style network of religious communities. It isn't the easiest spot to reach, around the villages of **Madenşehir** and **Değre**, on a dead-end dirt road some

45km north of Karaman. Spread around are the ruins of at least 50 churches, some of them quite substantial ruins with stone walls and vaulting intact. Karadağ was a holy mountain for the Hittites too, and, if you can find someone in the village to guide you, they might know of the caves and cliffs with Hittite hieroglyphic inscriptions. Also on Karadağ's slopes was the once-thriving city of **Derbe**, 30km north of Karaman, one of the places St Paul visited on his trip through Asia Minor; almost nothing of the city remains.

South of Karaman, on the road to the coast, lies one of the most remarkable early Christian monuments in Turkey. The once-great 5th-century Byzantine monastery at **Alahan** is built on a mountain-side terrace, with two churches and other buildings, some in a fine state of preservation. It must have been one of the most important centres of its day, but no one knows anything about it today.

North of Konya, the roads to Ankara and Kayseri pass on either side of Turkey's biggest lake, **Tuz Gölü**, the Salt Lake, a truly dismal corner of the republic. These roads were important in Selcuk times, and the Sultans of Rum built many elegant *hanlar* (caravanserais) along them, free to merchants and travellers. You see them on the route to Kayseri, mostly in ruins, every 15km, the distance a caravan covered in a day. The best preserved is at **Sultanhanı**, about 100km northeast of Konya. Alâeddin Keykubad built it in 1229; lately it has been restored with modern stonework as good as the Selcuks'.

Sultanhanı
open daily 9–7; adm

Cappadocia (Kapadokya)

Although never a distinct nation like Lydia or Phrygia, Cappadocia was known as a kingdom as early as 600 BC – it was probably really a loose confederacy of towns or tribes united to keep the Persians out, which didn't always work. Usually reduced to a tributary state of the Persian Empire, Cappadocia's rough terrain helped it survive with a modicum of independence into Roman times. Under the

The Cappadocian Landscape

The real history of Cappadocia begins some 30 million years ago. In the Cenozoic era, Erciyes Dağı, Hasan Dağı and Melendiz Dağı, the three tall peaks that dominate the region, were still active volcanoes. Over millions of years, their eruptions covered the land between them with thick layers of volcanic tufa, a stone made of compressed volcanic ash that is soft and easily worked. A few million more years of erosion turned Cappadocia into the dream landscape that attracted the hermits and monks, and now entertains over 100,000 visitors each year.

Words fail the honest writer attempting to do justice to the Cappadocian landscape; landscape, in fact, does not even seem the right word, for no other corner of the earth can have anything like the twisted, billowing forms found in the rocks of Göreme or Ortahisar. What makes Cappadocia so exceedingly strange is the very domesticity of the place. When wandering through the valley of Göreme, you may run across a stack of tufa shaped like a banana sticking out of the ground, white as sugar, with a door and window cut at the base, hollowed out long ago by a hermit or just a local farmer. On the window is a potted geranium, and on the doormat a sleeping cat.

Getting to and around Cappadocia

Wherever you're coming from, chances are you'll find a **bus** to Nevşehir, and then make a connection to Ürgüp, Göreme or the other villages from there. The **bus station** is on Lâle Caddesi at the northern end of town; almost all buses pass through the centre first, so if you mean to stay in Nevşehir, be alert and ask them to let you off there. Besides Nevşehir, Niğde, and less frequently Ürgüp, have regular coach services in all directions.

Compactness is definitely one of Cappadocia's charms. The greatest part of its attractions is contained in an area about 15km square, marked by the triangle of villages Nevşehir–Avanos–Ürgüp, with Göreme at its centre. It's not really difficult to see a lot without a **car**. The tourist office in Ürgüp prints a timetable of the regular Ürgüp–Nevşehir and Ürgüp–Ortahisar **bus services**; there's a bus every half-hour or so in season on these lines. Less frequent services take you to the underground cities, though **minibuses** (and big buses) are very frequent between Nevşehir or Ürgüp and Derinkuyu, the easiest of the underground cities to visit. But be careful planning return trips – the last ones on most lines run at 5pm, or 6 in summer.

You can **hire a car, moped or even a taxi** for the day (around 100 YTL). But no doubt about it, Cappadocia is Turkey's perfect spot for hiking or **biking**; the sights are suitably close together, and there are few tiring hills to climb. You'll find rental agencies in Nevşehir, Ürgüp and Göreme. **Horses** are another popular way of sightseeing here. Several of the many travel agencies offer days in the saddle, or you can rent one in Göreme, Ürgüp or Avanos: travel agencies all over Cappadocia can arrange this.

Romans it was still a client state, with kings named either Ariarathres or Ariobarzanes, ruling first at Nyssa (the modern Nevşehir), and later at Mazaca (today's Kayseri).

In AD 17, Emperor Tiberius's legions invited themselves in, and Cappadocia became a Roman province. Still a backwater, it never did receive its share of theatres or aqueducts; in fact its only discernible benefit from joining the Mediterranean community was a visit from St Paul, who corralled the inhabitants for Christianity with ease. Paul never had to rebuke the Cappadocians as he did the Galatians; so fervently did they take to the new creed that Cappadocia replaced Africa as the great stronghold of Christian monasticism. St Basil, the 4th-century prelate who laid down the rules for Orthodox monks, as St Benedict was later to do for the Christians of the West, was bishop of Caesarea (Kayseri's

Ballooning in Cappadocia

With its gentle winds and dramatic scenery, it is easy to see why Cappadocia is so often billed as the best place in the world to fly in a hot air balloon. Experienced balloonists Lars-Eric Möre and Kaili Kidner established the industry here and, together with their team at Kapadokya Balloons in Göreme (t 0384 271 2442, *www.kapadokyaballoons.com*), start trips in the early morning. Subject to weather conditions, you could spend on average 90 minutes in the air. But what a 90 minutes!

The take-off area is carefully selected to make the most of the conditions. You will be involved in the preparation of the balloon before slowly ascending and floating over the awe-inspiring landscape. Descend slowly into the canyons; drift over tree tops and past isolated fairy chimneys. Old irrigation channels and ancient agricultural terracing suddenly become visible from the balloon's basket. It's the best way to view the region's bird and animal life; time it right and you could be picking apricots from the tops of the trees. A 4x4 vehicle follows the balloon throughout the trip; when it is finally time to come down, the wind is often gentle enough for the skilled pilots to actually land on the trailer towed by the vehicle. After a celebratory glass of sparkling wine, a certificate is presented and passengers are transferred to their hotels in time for a late breakfast. At €230 per person, the price compares favourably to flights in the world's other great ballooning destinations such as Kenya. A shorter flight of one hour is available for €165, in slightly larger baskets.

The Cappadocian Picture Show

Some 200 of Cappadocia's rock churches are decorated, though it must be said that their artistic merit is limited at best. Whether any of the works were exceptional to begin with, we will never know – many have been repainted over and over through the centuries whenever they began to fade, on up to the expulsion of the Greeks in 1923. Nevertheless, these paintings are a landmark; during the Iconoclastic troubles of the 8th century, the Cappadocian monks kept the tradition of Greek painting alive, just barely, in this inaccessible spot, scrawling red and white crosses and arabesques until the whim of Empress Irene made images permissible once again.

You'll see nothing of the sophistication of the frescoes in Istanbul's Kariye here, but Cappadocia's styles, symbols and motifs provide a useful handbook to decipher a thousand years of Greek art. For example, look out for the often-repeated image of two symmetrical **angels in flight**, holding a crown or a cross between them. Originally these were two allegorical spirits holding a laurel crown – the seal and symbol of the Roman Empire, invented in the time of Augustus and common in all the propagandist artworks of the age; the Christians took it over later to remind people how their Church was taking the place of the dying Roman state. In works from the 6th century onward, you will see important figures, such as **Jesus** or **Constantine**, dressed in stylish tunics with a design of small rectangular plaques and white dots. These represented golden plates and jewels; such costumes were nothing but precise pictures of the Byzantine court dress in fashion since the time of Justinian – if they were good enough for the Emperor and Empress, they would do for God and the saints also.

Even as simple a symbol as the **cross** is worked for its historical resonance; in many scenes on the arches before the main altars, the familiar chi-rho monogram of Christ turns into an **eight-pointed star**, like an asterisk. That's another old political logo, the one adopted by Alexander the Great for his short-lived empire, and maintained by his Seleucid and Commagene successors. Keep an eye out for trivial details like the fall of draperies, the kinky folds in the clothing of figures from the 10th and 11th centuries. This very strange and stylized kind of art is unmistakable – especially to us Westerners, since it is exactly the same as in the reliefs on Romanesque churches of the early Middle Ages, heavily influenced by the Greeks. One frequently recurring motif from that time is **Daniel in the lion's den**, another Byzantine obsession, as common in the churches of Cappadocia as it is in the churches of England and France (no one really knows why it was so important). Another is **St George and the dragon**, this one not surprisingly, since George was a native Cappadocian. In domes and apses, the common figure is **Christ Pantocrator** ('ruler of all'), sending a blessing down from heaven.

Some churches have no great pretensions, like the one near Çavuşin that shows **Emperor Nicephoras Phocas** on his triumphal tour through Cappadocia in the 10th century. Others are intensely spiritual, like the scene of the **Ascension** on celestial blue in a Göreme church. As always, it's those big, staring Byzantine **eyes**, eyes that look straight into your soul. No better artistic trick was ever invented for expressing the outlook of early Christianity and its transcendent God. They are eyes that ask the big questions, eyes not content with the pageantry of earthly rulers – not even the Byzantine emperors'.

name in Roman times); monks following his rule made the region's peculiar landscapes the biggest monastic centre of the east, a role Cappadocia was to retain for over a millennium. Generation after generation, they hollowed out the easily worked tufa of Cappadocia's cliffs and canyons to make cave sanctuaries, and often entire churches complete with columns and domes – in all, Cappadocia has over a thousand rock-cut churches and chapels. In the 7th and 8th centuries, the monks survived the recurring attacks of Arab armies by squirrelling themselves deeper away in their mountain fastnesses. The monasteries, though much reduced, survived for over eight centuries under Turkish rule, up until the exchange of populations of 1923.

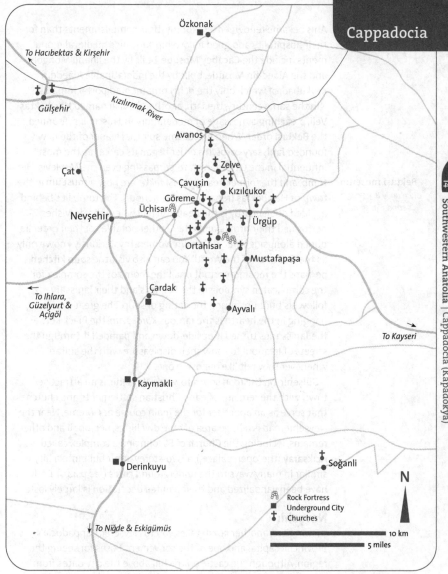

Özkonak

To Hacıbektas & Kırşehir

Gülşehir

Kızılırmak River

Avanos

Çat

Zelve

Çavuşin

Kızılçukor

Göreme

Üçhisar

Nevşehir

Ürgüp

Ortahisar

Mustafapaşa

To Ihlara,
Güzelyurt &
Açigöl

Çardak

Ayvalı

To Kayseri

Kaymakli

Derinkuyu

Soğanli

N

To Niğde & Eskigümüs

Rock Fortress
Underground City
Churches

10 km
5 miles

Kırşehir and Hacıbektaş

If you are travelling from Ankara, to reach Cappadocia you pass
through towns that have nothing to do with the Greek-Christian
air of the cave cities, but add an Islamic angle to the ambient piety;
both were the homes of mystic Muslim sects that gained great
popularity in the late Middle Ages. **Kırşehir** was the headquarters
of the **Ahi brotherhood**, a sensible, plain-living society, widespread
among the artisan guilds and workmen of central Anatolia. Following the precepts of their leader, Ahi Evran, who is buried here, the

Ahis became renowned less for mystic accomplishments than for their hospitality and good fellowship. Kırşehir's medieval monuments include the **Cacabey Mosque**, built by the İlhanli Mongols, and the **Alâeddin Mosque**, built by the indefatigable Alâeddin Keykubad, of which only the richly ornamented portal remains.

In the same century, the 13th, another dervish named **Hacıbektaş Veli**, preaching a message of moderation and discipline, founded the **Bektaşi order**. When he became spiritual leader of the newly founded **Janissary corps**, his order began its career as the most influential in the Ottoman state, surpassing even the Mevlevis. His **tomb**, and the former head Bektaşi *tekke*, are now a **museum** in the town of Hacıbektaş (renamed in his honour). The tomb lies behind a gilded door; nearby is the beautiful hall where the dervishes performed their rituals, and where other notables of their order lie buried alongside three unknown women, mysteriously known only as the 'Beauties of the World'. You can also visit the **soup kitchen**, perhaps the most important of all the rooms of the complex for the complicated symbolism the Bektaşis and their Janissary followers built up around the eating of soup. The great cauldron hanging in the hearth is the famous *Karakazan*, the Black Kettle; the Janissaries turned it upside-down and paraded it through the streets of Istanbul to show their displeasure with the sultan whenever they felt like deposing one.

Bektaşi museum
open daily 8.30–12.30 and 1.30–5; adm

Gülşehir, on the road south towards Nevşehir, is an attractive town with the remains of early Christian settlements and churches that serve as an appetiser for the main course at Göreme. Near the Nevşehir road is a huge area of cave dwellings, necropoli and other remains, including the **Church of St John** and a complex called **Açıksaray** (the 'open palace'), a two-storey affair built into a hill, similar in many ways to the underground cities (*see* p.449). Both have been vandalized and their painted decoration is largely lost.

Nevşehir

From here, another 50km takes you to Nevşehir, Cappadocia's provincial capital and one of the convenient bases for seeing the region. Although the castle on the hill above the city dates from the Crusaders, Nevşehir is not an old city. Damad İbrahim Paşa (born 1678), an Ottoman vezir of the Tulip Period, famous for attempts at reform and for introducing European art and culture into Turkey, was born in the tiny village of Muscara. His efforts earned him assassination in Istanbul, but not before he had refounded his home village as a city (Nevşehir means 'new town'), and built mosques, schools, libraries and an aqueduct; his statue stands in the centre of the town.

Nevşehir is tidily chopped into quarters by **Lâle Caddesi**, leading north to the *otogar*, and east–west **Atatürk Caddesi/Yeni Kayseri**

Caddesi, the road to Ürgüp. The benefactor's main complex of buildings stands south of the bazaar district off Lâle Caddesi, around the **Damad İbrahim Paşa Mosque**, with a lovely Turkish Baroque interior much more subtle than Konya's Aziziye. The complex includes a medrese and library, and also a hamam, still in operation and little changed since it was built. Behind the mosque, the narrow streets of old Nevşehir climb up to the ruined Selcuk castle. Nevşehir's **museum**, on Yeni Kayseri Caddesi, offers the typical mix of archaeological finds and old carpets and bric-a-brac.

Nevşehir museum
*open Tues–Sun 8–12
and 1–5; closed
Mon; adm*

Market day is Sunday, usually carrying on through Monday. West of Nevşehir, another underground city (*see* p.449) has been found at **Tatlarin** (from the city turn left at Acıgöl, 22km out; it's signposted), not as impressive or as large as the ones at Derinkuyu and Kaymaklı. Tatlarin also has a very fine painted church.

Üçhisar and the Fairy Chimneys

Halfway along the route between Nevşehir and Ürgüp, the triple rock of Üçhisar introduces you to the oddities of the region. Although the villagers of Üçhisar have long ago moved down into more modern lodgings, the peak, the largest in the area, remains laced with the tunnels and chambers they used when it served as their giant apartment house. From the top – a road leads most of the way up – there is a panoramic view of the Göreme valley, just to the east, with Mount Erciyes in the distance. Come past at night, if you can; the entire rock is illuminated, appearing like some post-modernist skyscraper. If you mean to do any exploring in Üçhisar, be careful; some of the floors are weak and could collapse. Keep this caveat in mind for the rest of Cappadocia, too, though there is little danger in seeing the main attractions.

From Üçhisar to Göreme, the road passes more curiosities, including some of the famous **fairy chimneys**, tall needles of stone, often with large rocks balanced on top. Their volcanic origin is not hard to detect. As well as vast quantities of ash, Mount Erciyes would occasionally toss out some boulders of hard basalt. During the periods of erosion, these boulders protected the ash, now hardened into tufa beneath, resulting in a column that grows taller as the land around it is scoured away.

✪ Fairy chimneys

Also on this road, there is a **viewpoint** (unmarked) to the right, from which you can see one of the most remarkable corners of Göreme. By now you will certainly have been surprised at the greenness and fertility of this part of Cappadocia; if you saw pictures, you will have come expecting desert rockpiles, only to find instead rolling hills of pretty farms and vineyards (the region is famous for its wine). Beneath the good volcanic soil are the rocks, and the narrow valleys where they have been eroded away are low-set and easy to overlook. Here, masses of glistening white tufa, blown into shapes of futuristic World's Fair pavilions, fill the valley, dotted here and there with doors and windows, with little gardens and apricot orchards in between.

Göreme

 Göreme

Göreme is the real centre of Cappadocia, the village closest to the heart of the area. It's commercialized out of all recognition, boiling with *pansiyonlar* and carpet shops – yet somehow it's still fun; you can still walk a few minutes outside town and be lost among the marvels and jests of nature.

The attractions are a short walk away in the **Valley of Göreme**, which goes on and on, the scenes changing continuously; many visitors become entranced and spend days wandering along its quiet paths. If you haven't the time, at least visit the **Göreme Open-air Museum**, where over two dozen churches, some with beautifully painted frescoes, make up the largest monastic complex in the region, all hewn out of the cliffs and crags and joined by stairs, paths and tunnels. Two very distinct styles of Byzantine painting explain between them something of the Iconoclastic conflict of the 8th and 9th centuries, the bitter struggle over images (and church politics) that sent so many refugees into Cappadocia. Those painted just after the downfall of the Iconoclasts are awkward, almost primitive geometric patterns and symbols – the Greeks had forgotten how to draw. By the 10th century, however, in the surprisingly quick renaissance of art that followed, the monks of Cappadocia contributed some fine work.

Göreme Open-air Museum

open summer daily 8.30–7; winter daily 8.30–5; adm

Most of the churches are called after some feature of the paintings; the **Church with the Apple** (Elmalı Kilise), for example. Many of these small churches are carved with arches, pillars, vaults and domes, distinguishable from an ordinary church only by a lack of windows. In the Church with the Apple, many of the frescoes have peeled away, revealing the simple post-Iconoclastic decoration underneath. Like many others, this one has been defaced by graffiti, the oldest in Greek, the most recent in Turkish, as high up as an adolescent can reach. Only recently has the government, along with private foundations and UNESCO, spent money to protect and restore them (the area is a World Heritage Site).

Among the other noteworthy churches nearby are the **Church with the Buckle** (Tokalı Kilise), with painted scenes from the life of St Basil; the **Church of the Sandal** (Çarıklı Kilise), where an imprint on the floor is said to be a cast of Jesus's own footstep, brought from Jerusalem; and the **Dark Church** (Karanlık Kilise) with familiar New Testament scenes, some of the best work in Cappadocia, restored by UNESCO. The **Church with the Snake** (Yılanlı Kilise) shows St George with his dragon, and large figures of Helen and Constantine holding the True Cross. There's more fine work at the

Hidden Church (Saklı Kilise) – if you can find it. Further inside the complex, the **Jerphanion Church** was discovered only in 1965 and named after Guillaume de Jerphanion, the French art historian who spent his life uncovering and cataloguing the Göreme paintings; it has some of the most interesting primitive frescoes, sun symbols and interlaced crosses.

Two large, self-contained monasteries can be seen near the valley, the **Firkatan** for men, and the **Girls' Monastery**, accommodating some 300 nuns, a network of tunnels, cells, and churches on three floors, carved from a large crag (the Turks call it the 'Virgins' Castle'). From here, several other attractions of the Göreme valley can be reached on foot, notably the village of **Çavuşin**, a rock-fortress similar to Üçhisar. Here though, half the original rock collapsed long ago, leaving the walls and corridors of the ancient rock town open to the sky; in places, the crag is so thin you can see through it. A stairway off the Avanos road, just north of the village, leads up into the **Çavuşin Church**, guarded by frescoes of the angels Michael and Gabriel which were exposed by the collapse; inside are more fine paintings, scenes from the life of Christ. Up in the hills nearby is another exceptional painted church, the **Church of St John the Baptist**, with works from the 6th to 8th centuries.

Kızılçukor and Ortahisar

Kızılçukor, a village just to the east of the Nevşehir–Ürgüp road, has been a wine-making centre since antiquity, and its **Church of the Grapes** (Üzümlü Kilise) has frescoes of scenes of the harvest and wine-making, as well as the usual saints. Five kilometres to the south, the crumbling crag of **Ortahisar** is perhaps the only rock in the world with sash windows; there's an electric sign on top, too, and an underground tunnel (now collapsed) to a similar complex on the village's edge. Enough of Ortahisar has been repaired so that you can climb to the top for a view of further religious complexes, fairy chimneys and strange rock formations. Several churches in the area worth visiting include the **Church with the Hare** (Tavşanlı Kilise) and the **Church of the Beet** (Pancarlık Kilisesi), both with 11th-century frescoes of New Testament scenes. West of the village are the ruins of an Armenian monastic complex called **Halaşdere**, with an underground basilica.

Zelve

There is yet another canyon full of churches, 6km northeast of the Göreme museum at Zelve – a district where, in some spots, the fairy chimneys grow as thick as a forest. Two old valleys converge at the site of the complex, eroded from the warm, tan rock with an outcrop like a steamship between them. It is believed that St Basil himself founded one of the first important Greek seminaries here.

Among the many churches is another **Church with the Grape** (Üzümli Kilise), which has some primitive paintings. Here, too, parts of the cliffs have collapsed, exposing, in one spot, a wall lined with neatly cut compartments in rows, like pigeonholes in a post office.

At the far end of the left-hand valley, you can pick your way through a narrow natural tunnel in the rocks and come out into a beautiful isolated **canyon**, full of wild flowers around a running stream. Cappadocia is full of surprises like this, both natural and man-made. As times grew worse in the later days of the Byzantine Empire, when the monastic communities began to suffer from raids of marauding Turkish and Arab tribes, defence became a prime consideration. The best defence for the peaceful monks was concealment, and many of the monastic buildings are cleverly hidden in crevices in the cliff faces; undoubtedly some exist that are as yet undiscovered.

Avanos

At its northern fringes, Cappadocia touches the southernmost bend of the **Kızılırmak** ('red river'), the major river of central Anatolia. The red clay along its banks has kept the potters of Avanos in business for thousands of years. Avanos is an attractive town, reached from Göreme or Nevşehir by an elaborate old bridge over the Kızılırmak. At the centre, a statue of a working potter testifies to the fame that Avanos work has always had in Anatolia. Traditionally painted red with a minimum of decoration, the pottery of the modern artisans is enjoying something of a revival.

Just east of Avanos, on the old road to Nevşehir, stands another of the caravanserais built by the Selcuk Sultan Alâeddin Keykubad, the **Sarıhan**, with an elaborate entrance portal.

Ürgüp

Even more than Avanos, Ürgüp is an exceptionally lovely town, unlike any other in Turkey, with its Belgian-block paved streets and unusual designs carved into the stone of the older buildings. Like Üçhisar and Ortahisar, it has come down from the cliffs in recent decades, and today it is the main base for Cappadocian tourism. Here, however, a few of the cave houses are still occupied; one troglodyte on the edge of the town has added a cave-garage for his new car. Ürgüp has most of the region's hotels and restaurants, and also a small **museum** in the city park. Most of the region's vineyards are on the roads just outside Ürgüp, and you can visit the **Tursan winery** just outside town and have a few samples.

Ürgüp museum
open Tues–Sun 8–5.30;
closed Mon; adm

Up until the exchange of populations in the 1920s, Ürgüp and its neighbouring villages had sizeable Greek communities. If you approach Ürgüp from Nevşehir, the new one-way system takes you down into town past some fine old houses, many with wooden balconies; the exit road back up the hill passes more of the same. These are the old Greek houses, several restored and converted into hotels. When the Greeks left, they were replaced by Muslims from Thessalonika who spoke a Macedonian dialect. You can still hear this language spoken, especially in nearby Mustafapaşa, by the original settlers and their children; grandchildren understand but are not fluent, and the language will soon die out here.

South of the town, the road to Yeşilhisar passes through other towns with cave churches: **Mustafapaşa**, with irregular dolmuş service from Ürgüp, is the first. This village wants its cut of Cappadocian tourism, and a few *pansiyonlar*, carpet shops and restaurants have appeared. There is little to see, though, save the restored church of **SS. Constantine and Helen** in the centre, and the 18th-century **St Basil's Church** on the northern outskirts, with some of its original frescoes. South of Mustafapaşa the landscape changes completely, into a Wild West backdrop of mesas and buttes. You can swim here, at the **Damsa Reservoir**, created by a dam on a tributary of the Kızılırmak.

There is little public transport in this part of Cappadocia, and you'll need a car or a horse or some determination on your bike to push on the next 21km to one of the grandest and least-known sights the region has to offer: the **valleys of Soğanlı**. Here, unlike the other sites in which churches are merely cut into the rocks, is a crag that has been sculpted into a church, with even a typical Byzantine cylindrical dome; there are frescoes inside. The locals call it the **Church with the Beret** (Kubbeli Kilise). Some other rock-cut churches are nearby, including the **Church of the Snake** (Yılanlı Kilise), named for a painting of St George and the dragon. There are more churches further up the valley, some of them painted.

Another spot you'll need transport for is **Sultan Sazlığı** (Sultan Marshes), on the southern slopes of Mount Erciyes, centre of a beautiful area of lakes, of which the largest is **Yay Gölü** (south of Yeşilhisar on the road to Niğde, turn left for Yahyalı and look for the signs). The government has recently declared the area a nature reserve; it is one of the country's major nesting areas for waterfowl, as well as a major migration stopover for flamingos, herons, cranes and dozens of other species on their way to and from Africa. The centre of the reserve is the village of **Ovaçiftlik**, a short distance from the edge of the Yay Gölü marshes; it has a small museum and observation tower, as well as the only accommodation in the area.

Underground Cities

After all this, the most outlandish feature of the Cappadocian fun-house has not yet even been mentioned: the underground cities. Thirty-six have been discovered so far, and eight have been excavated and lit for visitors, at least for a small part of their total extent. Each of them was capable of accommodating as many as 60,000 inhabitants, supplied with water by underground springs and air through elaborate ventilation systems.

None has been completely explored – they haven't even found the bottom of one yet. The best known, at Derinkuyu, goes down at least 15 floors, with air shafts as deep as 400ft. At Özkonak, the top levels cover some five square kilometres. Strangest of all, these cities are all interconnected by a network of tunnels, some as much as 9.5km long—in truth, it's a single underground city, one of the biggest man-made works on planet Earth. No one knows who built it. Medieval Christians certainly occupied the cities, but a Roman tomb has also been found on the seventh level of one, and a Hittite-style grain mill and Hittite seals deep in another. Except for one brief mention in Xenophon, ancient and medieval authors ignore them entirely. It's likely that the cities were never continuously occupied, but served the inhabitants of the region as refuges in times of trouble. They are invulnerable fortresses. Storming them would be quite impossible; at all the entrances, and even at many points within the cities, great round 'blocking stones' were set that could seal off the passages in a minute, with no room for the enemy to work at moving them, and with plenty of slits in the walls through which the defenders could thrust their spears. Secret entrances and hundreds of airshaft openings are scattered over kilometres of difficult terrain; it would be impossible for an enemy to find them all, and wonderfully easy for the people inside to send out forces to harry the attackers, or restock their supplies.

Of the underground cities that have been excavated, the most extensive are at **Özkonak**, on a dirt road 21km north of Avanos; and **Kaymaklı** and **Derinkuyu**, 20km and 30km south of Nevşehir respectively. None of the three has any special features peculiar to itself; the cities are strictly utilitarian, with no embellishment. All have 'blocking stones' and other defensive features, and churches, common dining halls and even tombs marked out in them. All three will wear you out as you climb back up from the lower levels, but the air is surprisingly fresh, and the temperature always cool.

At Derinkuyu, a fascinating separate underground city has been discovered. It's connected to the main one by a 1.5km tunnel, now collapsed; at its centre is a kind of 'temple' with a grand hall supported by 16 columns. You can also visit the unusual **Greek Church** of the 19th century, with blind arcades and lovely carvings of birds, vines and floral crosses that hint at an Armenian influence. Inside are frescoes and carved wood details (if the guardian is not around, try asking at the village hall for the keys).

Among the other underground cities that are open are those at **Tatlarin**, west of Nevşehir (*see* p.444), at **Çardak**, south of Nevşehir (ask at the village hall for a tour), at **Acıgöl**, near the village of

Kaymaklı and Derinkuyu
both open summer daily 8–7; winter daily 8–5; adm

Karacören, east of Ürgüp, and at **Gülşehir**; the latter two are not open to visitors. The latest to be discovered, at **Gaziemir**, near Güzelyurt, is a particularly interesting one, with baths, kitchens, churches and room for camels inside. Open since 2007, it is believed to have been a kind of hotel for travelling merchants.

South and West of Göreme

Ihlara

For those not sated with the rupestrian excess of the Göreme area, little bits have spilled over into the lands west and south. On the lowest slopes of **Hasan Dağı**, one of the region's extinct volcanoes, the **Valley of Ihlara** has another entire complex of churches, many with excellent frescoes, in a steep and picturesque valley. No public transport runs here (except minibuses from **Aksaray**, the nearest city), and it's 52km west of Derinkuyu on a back road, the most distant and hardest to reach of all the sights of Cappadocia. Nevertheless, it's worth a visit for the natural beauty of its red clay cliffs, and its relative isolation.

The sights lie in a 10km stretch of the Melendiz river valley, in a rugged canyon between the villages of **Ihlara** and **Belisırma** (from Peristrema, the old Greek name for the valley); exploring them will be a day's work, but a day you won't regret. Really, you can walk in from anywhere, but the main entrance is off the road between the villages, at the centre of the old monastic community. Near this entrance are a number of churches, including the **Snake Church** (Yılanlı Kilise), where the paintings show the Last Judgement and some interesting tortures of the damned. To the north, towards Belisırma, you will find the **Church of St George** (also called Kırk Damalı Kilise, the 'church with 40 roofs'), with familiar scenes of the dragon-killer, and Greek inscriptions to the glory of the medieval Selcuk emirs; and the **Columned Church** (Direkli Kilise), one of the prettiest in the valley, with more frescoes of St George, and the Virgin and Child. South of the entrance, the **Church under the Tree** (Ağaçaltı Kilise) has scenes of the Three Kings, and Daniel in the lions' den, while more well-preserved New Testament vignettes can be seen in the **Fragrant Church** (Kokar Kilise), halfway to Ihlara.

Near Ihlara, a side road leads off to the town of **Güzelyurt**, built over and below a cliff full of caves. North of Belisırma, **Selime** is one of the most charming and totally unspoiled villages of Cappadocia, surrounded by fairy chimneys and other weird formations; many of its people still live in houses partially cut out of the rock, or in old monastic cells.

Eskigümüş

To the south of Göreme, the road through Derinkuyu continues on to Eskigümüş ('old silver'), a former troglodyte colony with yet another Byzantine monastery cut into the cliffs; especially interesting here is the large, open courtyard carved out of the rock, completely hidden from view from the outside. Cells and corridors are carved into the sides on several levels, with sockets for beams and posts that suggest the entire space was once filled with a building of several storeys encased in solid rock. Frescoes in the church within, from the 7th to the 11th centuries, include some particularly well-executed figures of Christ, Mary and the saints.

Niğde

Niğde, a quiet provincial capital west of Hasan Dağı, marks the southern limits of the land of fairy chimneys and caves. Quiet is the word, for somehow, between Selcuks and Karamanoğulları, Mongols and Ottomans, Niğde has avoided having much history. All the same, it managed to get a good building or two from most of its medieval rulers, and while none of them is exceptional on its own, together they make a lovely, unified cityscape. Unfortunately, it doesn't seem as if anyone cares about the place; the centre is shot to hell, while folks get on in the outlying districts manufacturing cement and breeze blocks. Sultan Alâeddin Keykubad is represented here up in the deserted **citadel**, in the **Alâeddin Mosque** (1223), decorated in unusual geometric flowers and wave designs; its three domes are Niğde's landmark, together with an odd minaret that looks more like a lighthouse. In the town below, the **Sungurbey Mosque** of 1335, built by and named after an İlhanlı Mongol emir, has a much more graceful, spirally fluted minaret, but the decoration of its portal and roofline, as in most works begun by the Mongols, are incomplete.

Just off Bor Caddesi, the main street, the **Akmedrese** of 1409 is the Karamanoğulları contribution, with the uncommon feature of a loggia built into its façade. Other medieval mosques, as well as schools and fountains, two lovely *türbeler* and a 16th-century *bedesten* in the bazaar under the citadel walls, combine to make Niğde one of the most architecturally distinguished cities of Anatolia. On the west side of town, the province keeps a small **museum** with a grave stele and handicrafts (but of course everyone really comes to see the Byzantine mummy).

Tours of Cappadocia

Various tour companies offer local excursions, adventures and more. This is a convenient and cost-effective way to get an insight into the area. These are just a few of the many good ones. **Middle Earth Travel**, t 0384 271 2559, *www.middleearthtravel.com*. An adventure specialist based in Göreme.

Heritage Travel, t 0384 271 2687, *www.goreme.com*. Operates out of Kelebek Hotel and has long experience organizing local tours and treks.

Journey Anatolia, *www.journeyanatolia.com*. Reliable company that organizes boutique hotels, tours and hot air ballooning packages in the area.

Yuki Travel, t 0384 341 6125, *www.yukitour.com*. Your best bet in Ürgüp.

Where to Stay in Cappadocia

It's hard to choose between the Cappadocian villages for a base. Although they're close together, the atmosphere in each is very different. Göreme, from where the open-air museum is but a stroll, is a vibrant, laid-back place. Mustafapaşa is a quiet backwater, ramshackle and old-fashioned. If you have longer, Ürgüp is better, being the biggest town, with the best choice in accommodation and restaurants. Avanos has a few too, but it's a bit out of the way.

Nevşehir may seem the obvious choice with its good bus connections and fancy hotels, but there are no dreamy landscapes in its immediate vicinity, and staying over among the fairy chimneys is half the fun.

ⓘ Nevşehir >
*Atatürk Bulvarı,
Hastane Önü,
t 0384 213 3659*

Nevşehir

Recent years have seen a boom in hotel-building in Nevşehir, waiting for a tourist boom that so far hasn't happened. They take what they can get, so always bargain.

*****Dedeman Oteli**, 1km out of Nevşehir on the Ürgüp road, t 0384 213 9900, *www.dedeman.com/ kapadokya.aspx* (€€€). The best for the time being. It looks like a state mental hospital but has all the appropriate trimmings: rooms with minibars, satellite TV, air-conditioning, hamam, disco, etc.

****Lykia Lodge**, 300 yards further along, t 0384 213 9945, *www. lykialodge.com* (€€€). Much more inviting. Although the hotel's idiosyncratic design was supposedly inspired by the shape of the region's *kale*, it looks more like a cross between a Moroccan casbah and Breughel's tower of Babel. Comfortable, low-key rooms at 240 YTL include dinner.

Şems, right in the centre on Atatürk Bulvarı, t 0384 213 3597 (€€). Probably the best bargain. Once a hotel of some pretensions, with a star or two, it's deteriorated at a modest pace, but in the meantime you can have an acceptable room with bath for 70 YTL.

Üçhisar

A favourite with French tourists, Üçhisar has a load of *pansiyonlar*,

ⓘ Göreme >>
*municipality office at
the bus station*

most of which are quite nice, and go for about 70 YTL. Some of them are built into the rock, or at least have underground breakfast rooms. Streets here are not likely to have names, but proprietors put up little signs everywhere to direct you in.

Jardin des 1,001 Nuits, t 0384 219 2293 (€€). As over-the-top as its name would suggest. Rooms with panoramic views are set among the fairy chimneys; some beds are on raised stone plinths. There's a restaurant. Ring ahead, since some rooms are dear, others cheaper.

Les Terrasses d'Uçhisar, t 0384 219 2792, *www.terrassespension.com* (€€). Has some well-restored cave rooms on the ground floor; upstairs the rooms are bright and have splendid views. Guides for a valley walk.

Anatolia Pension, t 0384 219 2339, *www.anatoliapension.com* (€€). One of the best *pansiyonlar*, simple but clean and very well run.

Kaya, t 0384 219 2441, *www.kaya pension.com* (€€). A friendly place with views to the north. Some of the en suite rooms open out onto a terrace.

Göreme

Göreme House Hotel, t 0384 271 2060, *www.goremehouse.com* (€€€–€€). A stone building with large terraces and some rooms with barrel vaulting. Very reasonable, and atmospheric; doubles are 120 YTL, suites with Jacuzzi cost 190 YTL including breakfast.

Ottoman House Hotel, Orta Mahalle 36, t 0384 271 2616, *www.ottoman house.com.tr* (€€). A modern, well-run establishment, grander than the Göreme House but less atmospheric. It's good value at around 100 YTL and is decorated with Turkish handicrafts.

Elif Star Caves, t 0384 271 2479, *www. elifstar.com* (€€). Well located a short walk to the southwest of the *otogar*. Run by Jacky, a professional chef, and her husband Mustafa, assisted by their daughter Elif. 64–76 YTL lands you a spectacular and unique double cave room in this small gem. Ask for the omelette at breakfast!

Göreme is where the backpackers go, and this is the place to find dozens of *pansiyonlar*, many of them with rooms cut out of the rock, so that you can live like a Byzantine ascetic, with or without bath. Almost all are modern, purpose-built and family-run, and rates are 40–60 YTL for a double room. To choose one, go to the information office at the bus station (*open 5am–11pm daily*), where you will find, pinned to the walls, photographs of a great many of the *pensions*, information on their facilities, and directions on how to get to them.

Kelebek, in the southwestern corner of the village, t 0384 271 2531, *www. kelebekhotel.com* (€€–€). One of the best and very welcoming. Some of its rooms are set in fairy chimneys and Kelebek includes 'hotel' and 'pension' options, for a range of budgets.

Paradise, on the road to the open air museum, t 0384 271 2248, *www. paradisepension.com* (€€–€). Rooms carved into the rock. Well kept and also with a range of options.

Peri, nearby, t 0384 271 2136, *www. pericavehotel.com* (€€–€). Has rooms right in the fairy chimneys. Very well kept; rooms with baths are available.

Köse Pension, on a back street near the PTT, t 0384 271 2294, *www. kosepension.com* (€€–€). Deservedly popular with backpackers, and always a hive of activity. Dawn and her family can never do enough to help and make you feel welcome. The swimming pool is renowned and Spot, the dog, is always on hand to guide your walking adventures!

Ortahisar

You may find Ortahisar a welcome alternative to Göreme or Ürgüp; it's smaller and less overloaded with tourists, although that's because there's less to do and see.

Burcu Kaya Hotel, t 0384 343 3200, *www.burcukayaotel.com* (€€€). A motel-style place built from native tufa. Money has been spent here in recent years and organized travel is the target market. The main strength is a beautiful location close to the weird rocks. A double room will set you back 160 YTL including breakfast and dinner, more in high season.

Avanos

Pansiyonlar are spread pretty much all over the village. The quietest ones

will be found further in, up the hillside behind the town square.

(M) Sofa, Orta Mahalle, t 0384 511 5186, *www.sofa-hotel.com* (€€). A charmingly furnished stone-built motel with an accommodating, English-speaking proprietor.

Duru, Cumhuriyet Meydanı 15, t 0384 511 4005 (€€). The stiff walk up cobbled lanes is well worth it for the views it offers of Avanos and the Kızılırmak. The management are jovial, the en suite doubles plain but clean and the vine-covered terrace the perfect place to unwind.

Ada Camping, just outside the town, t 0384 511 2429 (€). A modern facility with everything you would ask for in a campground, including a pool.

Ürgüp

Ürgüp, like Nevşehir, has seen its share of hotel-building in recent years; most of them are nearly empty much of the time, and big discounts are more the rule than the exception.

Esbelli Evi, Esbelli Sokak 8, t 0384 341 3395, *www.esbelli.com* (€€€). Perched on a hill on the edge of town. The Esbelli is an oasis of tranquillity, due in part to the location, but also to the warm personality of the owner, Süha Ersöz. Over the past 20 years, he has painstakingly converted a row of old stone houses, with many rooms incorporating caves that date back to the 5th or 6th centuries. Süha has gone further than anyone else to make guests feel at home: free use of the kitchen, washing machine, unlimited free beer and soft drinks in the fridge, Internet, mountain bikes, a hi-fi and definitive classical CD collection in the barrel-vaulted living room, two spacious sun terraces... If you're going to spoil yourself once in Turkey, this is the place to do it: rooms can be booked up months in advance.

*****Perissia Hotel, t 0384 341 2930, *www.perissiahotels.com.tr* (€€€). Has the best pool, plus air-conditioned rooms with balconies, minibar and satellite TV, and all the facilities you would expect in what has recently become a five-star hotel.

Ürgüp Evi, a short walk further up the hill, t 0384 341 3173, *www.urgupevi. com.tr* (€€€). Its distinct similarity to

ⓘ **Ürgüp >>**
behind the pleasant tea garden in the Kültür Parkı, t 0384 341 4059

ⓘ **Avanos >**
Açık Pazar Yeri (marketplace), over the bridge from the central square, t 0384 511 4360

the Esbelli is not surprising, since it is owned by the stonemason who spent years working on Süha's place. Open all winter.

(S) Alfina, İstiklâl Caddesi, **t** 0384 341 4822, *www.hotelalfina.com* (€€€). Like so many of the old houses here, this is built into the side of a cliff: a series of terraces of tufa-built rooms with balconies.

Cappadocia Hotel, opposite hamam, **t** 0384 341 3314, *bahce@altavista.net* (€€). A ramshackle but cheery backpacker sleepery, but at 50 YTL a double you'd be better off in Göreme.

Mustafapaşa

(i) Mustafapaşa ›
on the central square, open irregularly in summer

Old Greek House, **t** 0384 353 5306, *www.oldgreekhouse.com* (€€). A delight – the paint may be peeling and the wooden embellishments worn, but the faded grandeur of this 250-year-old mansion is all part of its charm. It's run by the Öztürk family, who take great pride in showing guests around. There's a small marble-clad hamam from 1879, still in use, and an old kitchen: a living museum piece with a sooty fireplace the size of a small bus where bread is still made. The double bedrooms are very bright and airy, kitted out with orthopaedic beds. Good inexpensive home cooking, which non-residents can also enjoy if they ring a few hours ahead.

Manastır Pansiyon, nearby, **t** 0384 353 5005 (€€). A cheaper alternative, carved into the rock; a pleasant evening can be spent listening to the owner playing his *saz* in the cave bar. It's friendly; €30/60 YTL per double with a traditional Turkish breakfast.

Ayvalı

(i) Niğde
Belediye Binası (town hall), **t** 0388 232 3392

This village is even more rustic and tranquil than Mustafapaşa. To get there from Ürgüp, turn right down a side road just before Mustafapaşa.

Gamirasu Hotel, **t** 0384 354 5815, *www.gamirasu.com* (€€€€€–€€€). More retreat than hotel, set into the rock at the beginning of a 7km-long valley filled with caves and pigeon houses; As well as rose gardens and comfortable bedrooms with Ottoman cushions at the windows, there's also a hamam and massage room (the hotel is part-owned by a group of German therapists); doubles range

from €90 to €300 including breakfast. The honey, yoghurt, cheese and eggs that appear at breakfast are all produced on the site's organic farm.

Ihlara and Belisırma

In this last frontier of Cappadocian tourism, choices are few, but such accommodation as there is will inevitably be cheap and amiable.

Akar Pansiyon, on the road to Aksaray, **t** 0382 453 7018 (€). Basic but clean en suite doubles for 40 YTL. There are other *pansiyonlar* in Ihlara, and also some rudimentary campgrounds.

Belisırma Pansiyon, in the neighbouring village of Belisırma (€). Unpaved lanes and cowpats drying in the sun – a rudimentary place with showers in wooden cupboards and basic beds; ideal for those wanting to experience rural Turkish life.

Eating Out in Cappadocia

Üçhisar

Les Terrasses d'Üçhisar (€€; *see* p.453). The cooking is a blend of French and Turkish styles, with predictably mouthwatering results; a range of set menu options, good value for money.

Göreme

There is something for everyone here. Hang out with backpackers in the many small restaurants, offering similar examples of local cuisine and clearly keen for your business. Or dine in a little more style at the accomplished **Local Restaurant** on the way out towards the museum. The centrally located **Fat Boys Bar** offers an excellent bar menu.

Alaturca, **t** 0384 271 2882 (€€). Dominates the area off the main street in the centre of town and has built up a good reputation among locals and tourists alike. The food is authentic, well presented and the atmosphere pleasant. Certainly at the upper end of what is available in the region.

Orient Restaurant (€€). Long established with a good reputation, particularly for its carefully selected steak dishes. Enjoyable dining either in its sensitively decorated restaurant, or in more open surroundings.

Kardeşler >>

Üçhisar

Elai Restaurant, t 0384 219 3181, www.elairestaurant.com (€€). Winning fans across the country, the upmarket style, setting and content do not disappoint here; with main courses at around 25 YTL, it's not the cheapest in town, but certainly worth the extra.

Avanos

Tuvanna Restaurant, on the main square (€). One of the best in the area: home-made *pide*, tasty kebabs, even omelettes and other breaks from the usual, for an average 8 YTL. Not to be confused with the popular **Tafanna**, on main street Kenan Evren Caddesi.
Köşk Restaurant, just down the street (€). Good for a filling plate of *mantı*.

Ürgüp

Şömine, in the centre of town (€€). Large terrace for summertime eating, as well as an indoor dining room with a carved fireplace for winter. The *testi kebap* is particularly good. Lamb, or sometimes beef or turkey, is sealed in an earthenware pot and cooked for six hours, after which the pot is ceremoniously sliced open at your table.

Kardeşler, in the centre near the Hitit Otel. The best of the simple *lokantas*, with *pide*, kebabs and just about everything else for small change. The *tandır kebap* and *tandır* soup are a house speciality, a dish prepared in a clay pot, covered with bread dough and baked in the wood oven. It arrives with its own freshly baked bread serving as the lid, under which the flavoursome stew stays hot till the last mouthful. It may not look like much, but do not miss this place.

Hanedan, further out, built into the rocks on the Nevşehir road (€€). It's a refined place, despite the stuffed foxes and pelicans glowering down from the ceiling, with perhaps the biggest choices of *mezes* you'll see outside Istanbul and a changing menu of surprising main courses; 30 YTL, cheaper for the lunch buffet.

Ziggy's (€€). Full of character, this beautifully restored cave restaurant with appealing terrace dining offers mostly pasta dishes. Conveniently located if you find yourself in the Esbelli region on the hill overlooking the town of Ürgüp, but worth travelling for, as well.

Kayseri

Cappadocia's last capital, Kayseri, has something of a reputation. As you stroll the ancient streets around the centre of town, looking at the wealth of medieval buildings left by the Selcuks, before long a well-dressed young man will turn up, exchanging pleasantries with you in fluent English or French or German. Expressing a heartfelt interest in your wellbeing, he will offer many interesting sidelights on the city and its people to entertain you. Three minutes into the conversation, you will hear: 'You know, many (Americans, English, Germans etc.) who come to Kayseri are interested in the fine carpets and kilims made here...' You have met your first commission agent, and the further you walk, the more you'll encounter. An old Turkish proverb expresses it best: 'He can't read or write, but he's from Kayseri.' Turkish folklore abounds with tales of the Kayseri Man, the clever fellow who outwits the *kadi*, or the Jewish merchants, or the devil. He doesn't only sell carpets; Hrozny, the great Czech linguist who deciphered the Hittite hieroglyphics in 1912, found this out to his cost when the Kayseri Man sold him an inscribed tablet from the Hittite city of Kaneş and turned up again regularly over the next few months, each time

Getting to and around Kayseri

Kayseri has an **airport** with daily flights from Istanbul. It has a **railway station** too, part of the long, slow route from Ankara to Malatya or Adana. The station is in the Devlet Yolu, half a kilometre north of the centre, and the **bus station** is on the state road half a kilometre west, both on central **dolmuş** routes.

Buses run hourly to Nevşehir, the capital of Cappadocia. A modern **tram** system is under construction, and parts should be finished in 2009; meanwhile, any dolmuş or city bus along Talas Caddesi can take you out to the archaeological museum.

with another newly 'discovered' tablet to sell; he'd bought them all for a pittance from a farmer, and dangled them before the poor scholar one at a time to get the best price.

Kayseri, originally called Mazaca, started out as a Hittite town. It served as capital of the Kingdom of Cappadocia and then prospered under the Romans, who renamed it **Caesarea**, in honour of Augustus. In the 7th century the first bands of Muslim Arab raiders appeared, wrecking its economy, putting it to the sack on several occasions, and mangling its name into Kaisariyeh. Under that name, the city found itself playing a role in one of the stories of the *Arabian Nights*. The background to the long, sad 'Tale of King Umar al-Numan' is the king's struggle for the city with Afridun, the 'Sultan of Constantinople'. Despite the endless treachery of the Christians, aided by the redoubtable witch 'Mother of Calamity', the soldiers of Allah prevailed. Whatever really happened, the story relates that Kaisariyeh's defenders converted to Islam to a man and invited the Arabs in for tea.

Nowadays Kayseri's businessmen are keeping their old reputation alive, and not just with their famous carpets. Along with Bursa, Gaziantep, Denizli and some others, they've made their city of 900,000 one of the sharpest of the 'Anatolian Tigers', the go-ahead cities renowned for economic innovation and spawning new businesses. Turkey's first aeroplane was built here in the 1940s, and it is the home town of one of Turkey's two big business dynasties, the Sabancı family.

Getting to Kayseri from fairy-chimney-land takes about an hour by road, a journey dominated by **Erciyes Dağı**, a formidable snow-clad volcano; at 12,727ft it is Turkey's highest peak west of Ararat. It has one of the nation's busier ski resorts, open 150 days a year. The mountain was well known in classical times as Mount Argaeus, a word meaning 'bright' or 'white', and on certain days, when the sun is behind it (the mountain lies south of Kayseri), Erciyes does seem to glow, a wonderful sight wreathed in its entourage of clouds.

Around the Citadel

Kayseri boasts two **Atatürk monuments**, one beside the other, in the chaotic **Cumhuriyet Meydanı**, where the Sivas and Istanbul roads meet at the heart of town. Most of Kayseri's fine medieval

14

Southwestern Anatolia | Cappadocia (Kapadokya): Kayseri

monuments are very near, but the old city around them has been bulldozed to make way for new apartment blocks and boulevards. Kayseri wants to be up to date, unlike traditional Konya, and all its old districts have suffered except the bazaar.

Right on the square, the black basalt **walls** of the citadel still watch over Kayseri. Built by the Byzantines, expanded and rebuilt first by the Selcuks and again by Mehmet II, the walls explain at a glance the city's long history of unsuccessful defence. There's no height on which to build a proper fortress here. Some stretches of the city's outer walls remain, in the old quarter south of the square.

Around the square, the **Kurşunlu Camii** of 1584, sometimes attributed to Mimar Sinan, faces a grim medical school, the **Sahabiye Medrese**, and Kayseri's most important medieval structure, the **Hunat Hatun Külliye**. Across the road from the latter is the Gürgüpoğlu Konağı, an 18th-century stone mansion, now housing the city's **Ethnographic Museum**. Some interesting rooms contain Selcuk artefacts, ceramic tiles and coins.

Ethnographic Museum
open Tues–Sun 8–5; closed Mon; adm

Despite all the attention the Selcuk sultans lavished on Kayseri, the loveliest and best-proportioned structure in the town is not one of theirs. It is a building few tourists or even residents ever notice. The **Zeymel Abidin Türbesi** is a mausoleum built in 1886. Its elegant dome, betraying influence from the city's Christian community, is very similar to that of the 1835 Meryem Ana Church of the Armenians; this church, near Talas Caddesi, on the east end of the old town, is worth a visit even in its present state, as a much-neglected home for a sports club. Almost all of the huge slabs of which it is built reveal strange carvings of what appear to be tools – scissors, knives, carpenter's squares, saws – and other inexplicable symbols.

The Bazaar Area

In the old town just behind the citadel, a fine Ottoman house – perhaps the only one left in Kayseri – has been restored as an **Atatürk Museum**. A little further to the west, if you can avoid the carpet sellers, a walk through the exotic bazaar area will reveal the 12th-century **Ulu Cami**; a 15th-century theological school, the **Hatuniye Medrese**; and the **Vezir Han** and **Bedesten**, built by the Ottomans. In the Ulu Cami you'll find most of the townspeople who aren't out selling carpets; with its recycled Corinthian columns, colourful carved mimber and wooden ceiling, it is a lovely spot, and as with many of the huge 'Great Mosques' of central Anatolia, people use it as a kind of park in which to sit and reflect.

For whatever reason, Kayseri has by far the most mausolea of any Turkish city. The classical conical-roofed *türbeler* are everywhere along the outskirts of town. The famous **Döner Kümbet** ('revolving tomb'), carved with tree-of-life motifs, was built for Shah Cihan of

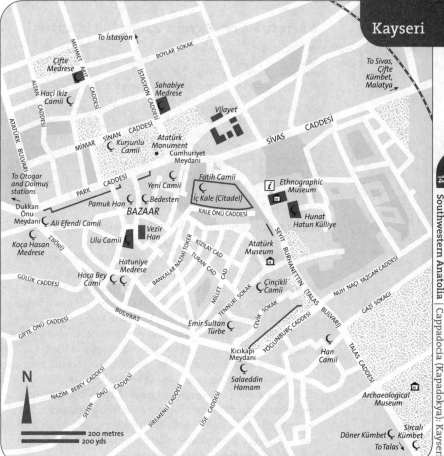

the Danişmend Turks, an emirate that held Kayseri through most of the 12th century, and also constructed the Ulu Cami. It stands just off Talas Caddesi south of the old town, with two other mausolea nearby: the **Emir Ali Kümbeti** and the **Sırçalı** ('crystal') **Kümbet**. To the west, the austere and dignified **Ali Cafer Kümbet** is lost among the apartment buildings of the new town; here the main street is **Sivas Caddesi**, broad and dismal, a perfect setting for postwar Italian *cinema verité*. If you follow it long enough, just as anomie sets in you'll run into the 13th-century **Çifte Kümbet**.

Near the Sırçalı Kümbet, in a large park on the southern edge of the city, the **Archaeological Museum** shows off its interesting accumulation of finds: a sympathetic-looking Neolithic goddess from nearby Sarayak, some good geometric-style pots, a Roman sphinx, baby mummies, Hittite reliefs with King Tudhalya's mark, inscribed steles of bragging potentates, cow-shaped pitchers, the best pair of Hittite lions, and the silliest pair of Roman eagles.

ⓘ **Kayseri >**
*next to the Hunat
Hatun Külliye,
t 0352 222 3903*

Where to Stay in Kayseri

***Hotel Almer**, Osman Kavuncu Caddesi 15, **t** 0352 320 7970, *http://almer.com.tr* (€€). Kayseri's finest, although you may find the good-luck cow's skull that is nailed above the entrance a trifle disconcerting. The hotel is bright and friendly.

Hunat Oteli, behind Hunat mosque at Zengin Sokak 5, **t** 0352 232 4319 (€). Good value. There are several other cheap hotels here, and a few near the bus station, although then you will require a dolmuş to get into town.

Eating Out in Kayseri

There are some excellent restaurants serving good local and inexpensive menus.

Kösk Kebab Solonu, Serçeönü Mahalle, No.9/E, **t** 0352 231 5456 (€). Specializes in *pide* and kebabs for around 6 YTL.

Iskender Kebab Salonu, Millet Caddesi No.5, **t** 0352 231 2769 (€). Slightly more upmarket; here you will be able to experience the real Kayseri speciality, the *Iskender kebap*, named after Alexander the Great. Expect to pay around 10 YTL.

Around Kayseri: Hittite Ruins and Selcuk Hanlar

Outside Kayseri, the road to Sivas will take you to an important Hittite site: **Kültepe**, the 'hill of ashes', near **Karahöyük**. Even before the Hittites, this city was a flourishing commercial centre, and it lasted well into Roman times. The inscribed tablets found here – those Dr Hrozny bought so dearly – have contributed much to our knowledge of the Hittites and their language. Kaneş was its name, and, besides the city upon its mound, where the foundations of the palaces may be seen, there was a lower city just down the hill, a *karum*, or trading colony of the Assyrians. In about 1800 BC, long before the Assyrians became a vicious empire, they were a prosperous trading people who established a network of trading centres across Anatolia and Mesopotamia. Though subject to the local rulers, they lived as closed, self-governing towns; Kaneş, itself overseen directly from Nineveh, was the head town in the system. Both the city and colony were destroyed by fire, and the wealth of objects the fleeing residents left behind constitute one of the greatest Hittite treasures; most are now in Ankara, but a few remain in the small **museum** on the site.

Two Selcuk caravanserais in this area are in good shape: **Sultan Hanı**, built in 1236, some 30km past Kültepe on the Sivas road; and **Karatay Hanı** 50km outside Kayseri on the road to Malatya. Celâleddin Karatay, Alâeddin Keykubad's grand vezir who also endowed the Karatay Medrese in Konya, is responsible for both.

On the road to Malatya you pass the town of **Pınarbaşı**, unremarkable save that most of its inhabitants are Circassians (or Adygei as they call themselves), part of a great wave of refugees from enforced Christianization at the hands of the Russians, who seized their home north of the Black Sea in 1829. Centuries ago, the Circassians were famous for the beauty of their women and the fierceness of their soldiers. The early Ottoman sultans, treating them as a favourite nation, made good use of both. There are about two million Circassians spread around Turkey today.

Northeastern Anatolia

*You may have seen the Dakotas
or Saskatchewan, Yakutsk or the
endless Gobi; you may have
travelled the world in search of the
bleakest and emptiest landscapes,
but you can't say you've seen it all
until you've been on the lonesome
Plain of Erzurum or traversed the
featureless black mountains
around it.*

*On the other hand, you might like
it. There's a kind of poetry in such
a landscape, so grim and still, it
shames its people and towns to
silence. Every spot of colour – a
peasant woman's bright costume,
a green irrigated farm, the blue
tiles of an ancient minaret –
becomes meaningful.*

15

Don't miss

⭐ **City on the
high plains**
Erzurum **p.463**

⭐ **The lost capital
of medieval
Armenia**
Ani **p.471**

⭐ **The Palace of
Ishak Paşa**
Doğubayazit **p.477**

⭐ **Noah's landing
place**
Mount Ararat **p.479**

See map overleaf

pp.358–9

GEORGIA

100 km
50 miles

N

Hopa • Veliköy
Artvin • Ardahan • Çıldır
Lake Çıldır

Trabzon • Rize • Yusufeli
Zigana Pass • Çaykara
Uzungöl • Lake Tortum • Selim • Kars
Gümüşhane • Sarıkamış • Ani

ARMENIA

Kağizman

Kale
Bayburt • Pasinler • Tuzluca • Iğdır • Aralık
Kelkit • Aşkale • Horasan
Cobandede (Köprüköy) • Mt. Ararat ▲
Erzincan • Altıntepe • Palandöken • Erzurum • Ağrı • Taşlıçay • Doğubayazıt
To Van

GEORGIA

TURKEY

SYRIA

CYPRUS

IRAQ

pp.482–3

Don't miss

⭐ Erzurum p.463
⭐ Ani p.471
⭐ Doğubayazit p.477
⭐ Mount Ararat p.479

The road through Erzurum has been a route for would-be conquerors, marching in either direction, as far back as the chronicles go; at present, no foreign army has camped here for 80 years, perhaps a record in modern times. In the very stillness of this land, however, there is a sense of danger. Sudden, fierce blizzards rule this country's winters, and tremendous earthquakes shake its towns to dust with a regularity known in few corners of the earth.

People here respond to the precariousness of life as they do everywhere. When earthquakes wreck their hopes, they rebuild; when invaders come, they resist, and in their lives the bleakness is tranformed to dignity of bearing and a quiet friendliness that matches the landscape perfectly.

Erzurum and Around

To get there, just take the little trip east from Sivas to **Erzincan**. It's 150 miles (240km), and the road passes only four villages along the way. Erzincan, called 'Aziris' in ancient times, was once renowned as one of the most beautiful cities in Anatolia. A series of earthquakes, the worst in 1939 killing 40,000 people, and the most recent in 1991 killing 4,000, have left all the Selcuk mosques and medreses in ruins, although the town once again has been rebuilt. The Turks have invented a fancy etymology for the name, from 'Ezercan' meaning 'life-crusher'. Once known for metalwork, carpets and (according to Marco Polo, who travelled here) buckram, Erzincan today is famous only for its earthquakes. So many of them have shattered the Urartian fortress of **Altıntepe**, 10 miles (16km) east, that little remains to be seen; the best objects, including two great lions, have been removed to Ankara.

Don't give up at Erzincan; it's only 112 more miles (180km) to **Erzurum**. Once in the town, you'll forget some of your misgivings about this trip. Erzurum, if you come from the west, may be the first Turkish city you find as exotic as you expected; it is good and grey, clean and quiet, and, apart from the modern centre, its streetscapes have not changed for centuries. In winter you can go skiing just five miles southwest of the city at **Palandöken**, Turkey's best ski resort. It also has the country's longest ski run, almost four thigh-busting miles long.

Erzurum

 Erzurum

Over 300,000 people live in Erzurum, but it's a mystery how they support themselves. The city itself seems still to be living in an age of handicrafts and small shops. A few factories and agricultural installations lie on the outskirts, and there is also a major military base and large university, but the surrounding Plain of Erzurum, between the Çoruh Mountains to the north and the Palandöken to the south, seems utterly empty.

History

Erzurum guards the approaches to Anatolia, and consequently has always been an important military prize. As Theodosiopolis, it marked the eastern frontiers of the Romans and Byzantines; the waves of Turks who began battering its ramparts in the 9th century called it Arz-er-Rum, 'land of Rome', and the name stuck when the Selcuks conquered it in 1071. The Selcuks, on their westward path, never looked back, and cared little when the Saltuk Turks took it away from them. İlhanlı Mongol and Ottoman occupations were to follow; after the 1700s, control of Erzurum became a major goal of the Russian Empire. Battles took place on the plain in most of the Russo-Turkish conflicts, the last in 1916, when the Czar's troops captured it in one of their few successes in the First World War. The Turks soon reasserted themselves, however, and one of the congresses that led to Turkish independence took place here in July 1919.

Getting to and around Erzurum

There are two **flights** daily to Erzurum, from Ankara, and Istanbul. **Bus** connections to Erzurum are regular from Sivas, Malatya, Kars and Trabzon, the latter a spectacular route over the eastern Black Sea Mountains. The **railway** from Ankara passes through on the way to Kars, though trains are not frequent (one a day). Erzurum's **bus station** lies a mile out of town, and the **rail station** half a mile out.

You probably won't require public transport for anything within the city. As in other cities where the bus station is far from the centre, it may be worthwhile to check at the bus company offices in town for times, and for the possibility of a connecting **minibus** (some companies provide this service).

Minibuses regularly ply the winding route between Erzurum and Palandöken during the ski season (Nov–April).

Streets, Mosques and a Castle

It's pleasant strolling around Erzurum, but don't be surprised if you find yourself tiring easily. This is Turkey's highest provincial capital, some 6,400ft above sea level. All the way from the Aegean coast, the Anatolian plateau has been gradually rising: the eastern end of it, from Erzurum to Mount Ararat, may not be as high as the Himalayas, but the peoples of the Middle East have always thought of it as the 'roof of the world'. Many of the great rivers have their sources here: the Tigris and Euphrates, flowing down to the Persian Gulf; the Aras (ancient Araxes), heading for the Caspian; and the rivers of the eastern Black Sea, the Çoruh and the Yeşilırmak. Thanks to its height, Erzurum and all the lands east of it stay in the deep freeze all winter; the snow piles up and transit becomes difficult.

Cumhuriyet Caddesi, the modern main street of Erzurum, chops its way right through the old town. Huddled behind its glass and concrete banks and shops are fine, narrow cobbled streets full of children and cats, lined with the city's typical grey stone houses. Cumhuriyet Caddesi, though broad and straight, roughly follows the course of an older thoroughfare, and most of Erzurum's sights are located on or near it. Near the town hall, at the corner of Mumcu Caddesi, a small park contains the **Yakutiye Mosque and Medrese**, built by the Mongols in the 14th century. The stumpy remnant of its minaret is covered by an attractive latticework of delicate bricks and blue tiles, making the medrese an ideal location for the **Turkish and Islamic Arts and Ethnography Museum** (Türk İslam Eserleri ve Etnografya Müzesi). Wide-ranging exhibits fill the former student cells: everything from dervish wear to *oltu taşı* – black amber mined in the local mountains, which can also be found for sale in city shops.

Turkish and Islamic Arts and Ethnography Museum
open Tues–Sun 8.30–5; closed Mon; adm

To the east, the next mosque down is the **Ulu Cami**, built in 1179 by the Saltuk emir Abdül Muhammad. Like most of the 'Great Mosques' in Turkish cities, this one is huge and plain. Until the conquest of Istanbul, the Turkish idea of architecture was, in respect to where the artistic effort should be made, just the opposite of Christian Europe. The biggest central mosques, submitting to the puritanical streak Islam has always had, are usually little more than utilitarian prayer-halls. Islam has no cathedrals. Adornments, in stone and glazed tile, were saved for the smaller mosques and above all the schools, most of them endowed by a single patron anxious to be remembered.

Çifte Minare Medrese
open daily 8.30–5

A 13th-century Mongol princess named Huant was one of these patrons, and her gift to Erzurum, the **Çifte Minare Medrese**, is one of the masterpieces of Turkish architecture. Behind the massive portal, one of the best examples of the style begun by the Selcuks, the gateway arches open to a spacious courtyard, enclosed by a two-storey gallery with a free-standing arch at its centre. From the opposite end, a vaulted hall leads to a very large and beautiful unoccupied *türbe*, with a shallow dome under the usual conical roof. The strange device on the entrance of the medrese is a symbol seen in various forms on the religious buildings of eastern Anatolia. It's a palm tree, representing the tree of life; its roots have become snakes, and an eagle perches on its topmost branch. This is an İlhanli symbol, adapted from the eagle and tree the Selcuks used before them.

Just two blocks behind the Çifte Minare, in one of the most picturesque corners of old Erzurum, a fenced garden encloses the **Üç Kümbet**, literally 'three tombs'. *Kümbet* is just another name for *türbe* – a round or octagonal mausoleum with a conical roof; these three, with the remains of Saltuk emirs of the 13th century inside them, are especially splendid examples. More than most *türbeler*, they show the Armenian influence; under Roman and Byzantine rule, Erzurum had been a predominantly Armenian town.

Castle
open daily 8.30–5.30

On the other side of Cumhuriyet Caddesi, the old lanes wander crazily upwards to the **castle**, well preserved since its last, Ottoman, rebuilding. The **clock tower**, looking out over the city from inside the castle, began life as a minaret. You can fumble your way up the precipitous spiral staircase like the muezzins of old, blinking in the sunlight as you reach the top. Directly below, nestling in the lee of the castle walls, are some of Erzurum's oldest dwellings, a surprising number of which are still covered by roofs of earth and grass. Although they look primitive, earthen roofs are ideally suited to the climate, keeping the rooms below cool in summer and cosy in winter. Elsewhere in the castle there is little to see save Turks sneaking off the job for a snooze, and little boys pretending to be Kılıç Aslan (the legendary Selcuk emir).

In the area surrounding the castle, young males coax their throbbing discomobiles down narrow lanes, squeezing past horse-drawn carts and old women enveloped in *ihram*. These traditional shawls are unique to the Erzurum region and are made from roughly woven, undyed sheep's wool embroidered with blue or green patterns. Vintage examples of this work can be bought in

the carpet shops near the castle. New *ihram* can be found in the
market district that occupies many of the streets north of here.
With more donkeys and fewer plastic buckets than most, it's one of
the most old-fashioned and interesting bazaars in Turkey. The old
bedesten at its heart, the **Rüstem Paşa Çarşısı**, bristles with a host
of pyramidal chimneys, creating the impression of a strange city's
skyline in miniature.

West of Erzurum: the Çoruh Mountains

The black mountains that surround the Plain of Erzurum seem to
close it off like a castle wall, and in fact getting out by any road
except the main east–west highway can be difficult three seasons
of the year. The road to Artvin and the Black Sea is decent, but a
wilder and more interesting route would be to retrace your steps
to Aşkale and take the route through the Çoruh Mountains to
Trabzon, passing two Turkish castles that would put the imagination of a Hollywood director to shame.

Bayburt has been the main stronghold along this route since the
days of the Kingdom of Trebizond; its castle, with dozens of towers,
dwarfs the little village in its shadow. Stouter souls may climb up
to the one at **Kale**, perched like a beret atop a needle-thin peak.
From here, the road passes through **Gümüşhane**; the name, 'silver
house', denotes a mint, a reminder of the ancient mines between
here and Bayburt. The town is another new creation, rebuilt from
the ruins of an earthquake. This is the route Xenophon and his Ten
Thousand took at the end of their epic journey across eastern
Anatolia. Before they could reach Trebizond and the sea, they had
to cross over Turkey's highest pass, the **Zigana Geçiti**, where snow
may be blowing across the road any month of the year.

East of Erzurum

If you proceed east from Erzurum, the route is equally scenic,
following the boisterously rushing Aras River, through green
meadows and steep canyons on its way to the Armenian border.
At **Pasinler**, you see a joke of a castle, a modern restoration, of
which only one side of the walls remains. It looks like a stage prop:
they can't have done it up to impress tourists, and one can only
wonder what the idea was. A better sight, found at **Köprüköy**, also
known as **Çobandede** ('shepherd's valley'), is the well-preserved
Ottoman bridge, one of the best remaining, with six graceful
arches over the stream. It's attributed to Mimar Sinan, but then so
is every other old bridge in Turkey.

Towards Kars

Heading east of Erzurum, the villages become rougher and poorer, the amenities fewer and the stares directed at tourists longer. **Horasan** and **Sarıkamış**, built around army bases, are two of these villages. The former is named for the great city of Turkish Central Asia, Khorasan, and probably got its start with the waves of Turkish migration that followed the Mongol destruction in that region. Near Sarıkamış, the government has constructed a small **ski resort**, and why not? The chief distinction of Sarıkamış is its mean annual temperature of 35°F, the lowest in Turkey and equal to that of the northernmost town in Norway. At 8,600ft, the highest peak is the **Cıbıtepe**. At present, the resort is equipped with only two chairlifts, one T-bar and a limited number of runs. Until Sarıkamış develops further, other resorts such as Palandöken offer much more of a challenge for skiers.

Where to Stay in Erzurum

(i) Erzurum >
Cemal Gürsel Caddesi 9,
t 0442 235 0925

Erzurum

For Erzurum's priciest accommodation, you'll have to head for the hills, where the excellent Palandöken ski resort sits in splendid isolation. In Erzurum proper, most of the mid-range and cheap lodgings (there is nothing very expensive) can be found in an area between the train station and city centre, around the busy traffic roundabout known as the Gürcü Kapı. Budget-conscious skiers could save liras by staying in town and taking a taxi the 8km to the runs.

****Dedeman, five miles southwest of Erzurum at Palandöken, **t** 0442 316 2414, *www.dedeman.com* (€€€€). An overgrown pseudo-chalet with all the luxuries, including satellite TV. It is situated at well over 7,000ft by the main ski runs in ski season there is a good hire shop and a few instructors. You may be able to negotiate on price.

***Dilaver, Aşağı Mumcu Caddesi Pelit Meydanı, **t** 0442 235 0068, *www.dilaverhotel.com.tr* (€€). The best city-centre hotel. Its big bright lobby makes a good first impression, and the well-appointed bedrooms don't disappoint either.

Polat Otel, Kazım Karabekir Caddesi 4, **t** 0442 235 0363, *www.otelpolat.com* (€€). Snaps at the heels of the Dilaver in terms of comfort. With en suite rooms from only €28/55 YTL, it's the best deal in town. The Polat's one drawback is its location near the noisy Gürcü Kapı roundabout.

*Kral, on a side street off the main Cumhuriyet Caddesi at Erzincankapı 18, **t** 0442 234 6400 (€€). Closer to the action. Once you've braved the dingy staircase, you'll be relieved to see that the beds upstairs are pleasantly clean.

Oral Hotel, Terminal Caddesi 6, **t** 0442 235 2500 (€€). Inconveniently located on the road leading out to the bus station, its grey façade is drab to an almost Soviet degree, although the décor improves once you're inside. Doubles have bathtubs rather than showers. Rooms at the back escape the worst of the traffic noise.

Yeni Çınar, Ayazpaşa Caddesi 18, **t** 0442 213 6690 (€). The best budget option in town, on a quiet lane off the Gürcü Kapı. The beds are very clean indeed, with sheets so starched you can barely fold them back.

Grand Hitit, Kazım Karabekir Caddesi 26, **t** 0442 283 5001 (€€). Through the haze of cigarette smoke in the lobby you may be able to make out a TV set flickering dimly in the corner. But with its volume turned to eleven when the football's on, there'll be no mistaking the TV's presence even when you're in your room upstairs. This aside, the Hitit makes an excellent choice, setting you back only €33/65 YTL for a room with shower; the embroidered bedcovers featuring exotic peacocks picked out in gold thread come as an unexpected bonus.

Eating Out in Erzurum

Güzelyurt, Cumhuriyet Caddesi 54, **t** 0442 234 5001 (€€). Perhaps the best restaurant in eastern Turkey. Its high-ceilinged dining room, with walls panelled in light and dark wood, has a distinct Art Deco feel to it. The solicitous waiters recite an extensive menu of Turkish regional specialities; better still, ask to see the kitchens, where you can nose around as many pots and trays as you wish before selecting your food. Although you may be forced to eat your meal to the strains of easy listening piano, the restaurant serves alcohol to help you come to terms with this. About 18 YTL for a meal.

Erzurum Evleri, Cumhuriyet Caddesi, Yüzbaşı Sokak, **t** 0442 213 8372 (€€). Set inside a cluster of delicately restored

18th-century houses; this is the best restaurant for atmosphere with its authentic Ottoman and nomadic décor. Antique lanterns, doorknockers and old weapons rub up against more 'modern' items like the collection of 1960s radios and 1970s folk LPs. But do not let the overdose of paraphernalia distract you from the edible classics, the *kesme* and *ayran* soups (4 YTL), are excellent, the mains are few but well prepared, but the *pièce de résistance* is dessert: *pestil çullama*, also known as a '25', will have you merrily bouncing home, even at bitterly cold temperatures. Full meal 15 YTL; alcohol is not served.

Koç Cağ Kebap Salonu, out near the minibus station at Kongre Caddesi Nazik Çarşısı 8 (€). The skewers of kebab are cooked over wood fires, turning on a horizontal axis just like the good ol' days when kebabs were in their infancy: men camping out in the desert pressed slabs of meat onto their swords, resting them over open fires until they were cooked.

 Erzurum Evleri >

Kars and Ani

Kars

Sarıkamış may be a little colder, but Kars gets more snow. The word itself means 'snow' in Turkish, and here it means about 40ft in the worst winters. Most people come here only because it's the nearest town to the ruined city of Ani. Few writers have had anything good to say about it; they come by bus or train, see the shacks and mud, and bolt. It's a pity, for outside the squalid market area Kars is one of the prettier towns in the east. Its secret is that it's really a Russian town, most of it built between 1878 and 1921 when the region was part of the Russian Empire; most citizens of Kars don't know this, nor are they aware that their town was founded by the Armenians. As capital of the Bagratuni dynasty before Ani, it flourished in the 9th and 10th centuries. Tourism here has picked up in recent years, thanks in part to the novel *Snow* by Orhan Pamuk, Turkey's Nobel prize-winning novelist, and in part to the lifting of travel restrictions to Ani.

The Russian Occupation

The Selcuks destroyed Kars in the 11th century, and attempts at rebuilding were foiled by the Mongols and later Tamerlane, both of

Getting to Kars and Ani

There is currently one **flight** a day from Istanbul and Ankara. The Turkish Airlines office can be found on Faik Bey Caddesi, t 0474 212 4747. The daily **train** from Istanbul passes through Erzincan and Erzurum on its way to Kars. At some point in the future, the town will become the jumping-off point for travellers heading into Armenia, whose border with Turkey is currently subject to the vagaries of international politics. **Bus** connections into the region from Sivas, Trabzon or the major cities of the southeast are no problem, but all routes are long and usually dreary. The new **bus station** is three miles outside Kars, but the bus companies all have ticket offices in the town centre; a free **minibus** service shuttles between these offices and the main bus station.

If you're **driving**, keep in mind that distances in this area are often very great, with few services and no accommodation along the way. If you're not driving, a **taxi** is the only way to see Ani (27 miles/43km of good road, about 100 YTL for a half-day trip). The tourist office in Kars can arrange it.

whom massively damaged the town in their invasions. Just as Erzurum protects Anatolia, Kars protects Erzurum, and until very recently there has always been a garrison up in Kars castle. Like Erzurum, Kars was a prize the Russians wanted badly, and they spent much of the 19th century trying to get it; in 1807, their siege failed, but in both 1828 and 1855, during the Crimean War, they wrested it from the sultan only to find the European powers forcing them to give it back. On the latter occasion, Kars was defended by a Turkish force led by British officers under General Williams. Their heroic defence against great odds was one of the famous events of the Crimean War: the English public held its breath for weeks as reports and rumours dribbled in over the telegraph line. In 1877 the Russians took Kars again and got to keep it, by the goodwill of Bismarck at the Treaty of Berlin.

Lenin and Trotsky, in a rare lapse of judgement, gave it back with the rest of the province in 1921. Atatürk and the Turkish assembly had been playing a little game with the Bolsheviks, issuing communiqués about the evils of capitalism and the eternal solidarity of the Russian and Turkish workers. The Soviets fell for it, and gave up their border claims to earn Turkey's friendship. They probably couldn't have held Kars in any case, with the Red Army busy elsewhere and General Kazim Karabakir's Turkish nationalist army knocking on the door.

New Town

During their 40-year occupation, the Russians laid out the new town south of the citadel with broad, tree-lined streets. On the business streets, Atatürk Caddesi and Karadağ Caddesi, you'll see blocks of attractive neoclassical façades. Some, like the old government buildings on Ordu Caddesi, and one semi-ruined palace that may once have served as an opera house, are wonderfully grandiose, and seem even more so in this incongruous setting. On one old Russian house, you can admire what must be the best Art Nouveau balcony in all Anatolia. Near the river, the little Kars Çayı, a few Russian cottages with nicely carved porches and window frames moulder away under the plane trees.

The Kars Çayı marks the boundary between the Russian town and the older village under the walls of the **castle**. Sultan Murat III built this fortress over the ruined Armenian foundation in the 1590s. The Turkish army used it until recently; now the grounds inside are the town park. Murat also built the stone bridge over the stream.

The city's solid-fuel storage facilities are a feature at which most visitors turn up their noses. Expertly constructed 15ft beehives of dried dung are dotted all over Kars, which fights off strong local competition for the title of cowpat capital of Turkey. It's an ideal fuel for domestic use: odourless (the smell evaporates as the pats dry), slow-burning, and free.

Cathedral of the Apostles

All that remains from the days when Kars was home to the kings of Armenia is its Cathedral of the Apostles, built by King Abbas in 937. The church has led a hard life. Only a century after its construction, Alp Arslan's Selcuks converted it into a mosque, but the Russians made it a church once again in 1878. After the recapture of the town and the dispersal of the Armenian community, the city made it a museum for a while; now it stands empty. The cathedral has managed to survive somehow in reasonably good repair; impressive in its own right, it provides a good introduction to the wealth of Armenian architecture you see at Ani.

Few builders ever piled up so much stone to cover so little space as the Armenians did. Like the Cathedral of the Apostles, most of their religious buildings are quite small, with centralized plans and a space under the dome, usually no more than 30ft in diameter, surrounded by three apses and the entrance where the fourth would be, in the form of a cross. The tip of the dome, however, may be as much as 150ft high. We don't know whether the medieval Armenians stayed at home on Sundays or squeezed themselves into their churches like sardines, but buildings like this are a kind of 'pure architecture', in which function is subordinated to form for the glory of God. The familiar outline of Armenian churches, a cylinder carved with blind arcades – pillars and arches sculpted in relief – covered with a cone-shaped dome, is a style you've probably seen in enough places already; the Selcuks and other Turkish states copied it for their mausolea.

Here, the cylinder is really a 12-sided figure, carved with mysterious figures, lions and whorls in high relief, somewhat like the decoration of the famous Armenian church on Akhtamar Island in Lake Van. Eight semi-domes, the roof of the body of the church, support the central dome and drum, and inside some of the sculpture on the pendentives can still be seen, though most has fallen victim to time or the Iconoclasts. Note also the altar screen, carved from a single block of marble; here, and elsewhere in the cathedral, geometric patterns are used in a way that seems Islamic in inspiration.

The cathedral doors, with a bell and other artefacts sent as a gift from Tsar Nicholas II, can be seen at the **Kars Museum** on Cumhuriyet Caddesi, on the outskirts of the town, along with the usual ethnographic exhibits.

Ani

 Ani

**Private guide
Celil Ersoğlu**
*t 0474 212 6543, mobile
t 0532 226 3966; runs
private tours, arranges
transport if you have
none, and speaks
good English*

Ani is one of the most impressive sites in Turkey and is best visited with a knowledgeable guide; the tourist office can help you here, or you can contact a **private guide**.

En route to Ani, you pass through the garrison village of **Subatan**. If the place seems to have a heavy military presence now, consider that before 1991 there were three times as many soldiers stationed in these parts. In Soviet times tourists had to trade in their passports and cameras at the garrison for a sulky conscript under orders to escort them around Ani. Strictly no dawdling, taking notes or defecting to the enemy. Ani itself lies 28 miles (45km) west of Kars, right on the Armenian border where two streams meet – the usually dry Alaca Çay and the Arpa, a tributary of the Aras.

The Armenian Kingdom

Ani's citadel, on the steep peninsula between the two streams, owes its beginnings to a 5th-century AD prince named Karisarkan, although the site had been occupied for centuries. The name came from Anahit, an ancient Persian goddess whom the Greek mythographers identified with Aphrodite; before the time of Gregory the Illuminator, she was one of the chief deities of the Armenians. Located on a major east–west caravan route, the town grew steadily through the following centuries. At the height of Armenia's golden age in the mid-10th century, King Ashot III transferred the capital here from Kars and, in the century that followed, Ashot and his successors endowed the city with the lavish array of sumptuous churches that attracts visitors today.

At that time, according to the chroniclers, Ani was a metropolis of some 100,000 people. Nothing in Europe at the time could rival it, and in the Middle East only Constantinople, Cairo and Baghdad were as large and well built. The great wealth of the Bagratuni kings that made it all possible, unfortunately, was soon dissipated in increasing warfare against the Byzantines, their old enemies, and the Selcuk Turks, newly arrived out of Asia. The Byzantines held the independent-minded Armenians to be schismatics, and therefore thought nothing of breaking a treaty and attacking them just at the moment when their resources were concentrated against the Selcuks. Greek subversion had been undermining Armenia for a century, and Emperor Constantine IX was finally able to annexe most of Armenia in 1040. By doing this, the Byzantines foolishly destroyed their own best ally, and, when Ani fell to the Turks in 1064, the disaster at Manzikert that lost Anatolia to the empire forever was only seven years away.

As the Selcuks continued west, Armenian nobles were able to reassert their independence, though as isolated feudal lords, not as a united nation. Ani prospered nevertheless, until an earthquake in 1319 completely levelled the city. Now, with the eastern trade routes circumvented by the merchant adventurers of Italy, and the royal patronage gone, there was nothing to stop Ani's slide into a long decline. Today the city is a ruin, abandoned save for the tiny shepherd village outside its walls. The walls still stand, along with the citadel and the churches; together they make up the greatest achievement of medieval architecture to be seen anywhere in Turkey, the inspiration for Selcuk architecture and everything else in this corner of the world that is well made.

The Walls

In spite of the best efforts of the men at the ministry, Ani still makes an overwhelming impression on the visitor. It is situated amid rolling grassland on the very eastern edge of Turkey and, when you get to the end of the long, narrow road connecting it to the present day, your imagination soon gets the better of you. If you are lucky enough to have the site to yourself, you become an honoured guest of the past: illusory buildings spring up from mossed-over foundations; paths winding through the rubble become peopled with obscure processions of old. Even before you see the churches, the attention given to even the defence walls gives an indication of the talent of the Armenian builders. The rounded, covered towers are unusual, more reminiscent of bunkers on the Maginot Line than anything from the Middle Ages. The Armenians took the time to beautify them, laying the sandstone blocks of two colours in simple designs.

Unfortunately, the Ministry of Culture, in its effort to preserve the walls, has seen fit to 'improve' upon them as well. At great expense to the state, a team of master masons has been brought in not just to strengthen the existing defences but to encase whole towers with a new stone fascia; in places, whole sections of crumbling wall have been replaced. It's like improving one of Rodin's bronzes by polishing it up with Brasso.

Near the car park, the **Lion Gate** provides an entrance to the town; the sculpted lion that occasioned the name is said to have been added by Alp Arslan. Once inside, you will find two paths through the weeds that roughly follow the route of two of Ani's principal streets. The path to the left leads to the cathedral and citadel; the right-hand path to the most conspicuous monument near the gate, the Church of Our Saviour.

On the way to the church you can look out for the remains of a **linseed oil press**, excavated at the end of the 1990s. The lower section of this large square room still survives, with a huge millstone in the centre which was powered by man or horse. Of more interest is the carefully constructed stone oil press in one corner. The milled linseed would be pounded and pressed in its square recess, producing oil which would trickle down into a container below. This was measured against a calibrated stone slab which remains in position today.

Church of Our Saviour and Surp Gregor

Trdat, architect of the cathedral, rebuilt the **Church of Our Saviour** (Prkitch Kilisesi) in the 12th century after an earthquake; it had been originally constructed in 1036 by the Pahvaluni family. The location must be bad for building, for today exactly half of the church remains, as if the rest had been sheared off by a monstrous axe. Don't go in: there's concern that the rest may follow.

Many visitors overlook the **Church of Surp Gregor** (Tigran Honents Kilisesi), which is a pity since it's one of the highlights of the complex. It is hidden on the cliffs above the Arpa but below the level of the city. This is only one of three churches of St Gregory in Ani, and it's easy to get confused. A prominent noble, Tigran Honents, built this one in 1215; it's the most complex of Ani's surviving churches both in design and in ornamentation. Though some 300 years younger than the church at Akhtamar (*see* p.518), which it resembles, this one shows the same love of naturalistic detail in the finely carved animal motifs around the blind arcades.

Inside, well-preserved frescoes depict some of the oddest scenes in Christendom. For those of us accustomed to the Western European or Greek tradition of religious art, these subjects are difficult to identify. The old Armenians kept a number of books from the Apocrypha in their Bible, which may explain some of them. The twelve apostles are easy enough, and a series of pictures from the life of St Anne, mother of the Virgin Mary – a popular saint here, perhaps simply the spiritual descendant of old Anahit. Some of the others, scenes from the story of Gregory and other early Armenian saints, defy description. In two places on the walls, you see a man suspended upside down from a tree with his legs crossed – the very picture of the Hanged Man from Tarot cards. One series of paintings has an urban background of arches and gables; medieval Ani must have looked like this.

Cathedral of the Apostles

Surp Gregor Church stands at the easternmost corner of Ani, where a dry stream bed is lined with man-made caves, like those of Cappadocia. Nearby, there's another of the **city gates**, with a relief, crucifix and long inscription in Armenian. From here, you can either retrace your steps back along the path or cut through the jumble of mounds and ruined foundations westwards to the largest of Ani's buildings, the Cathedral of the Apostles, which Trdat built for Gagik I in 1010. Here, to accommodate large crowds, the centralized plan has grown into a broad rectangular nave where the dome, now collapsed, covered only the centre. Unlike European churches, with their monumental west entrances, this cathedral is oriented north–south, with the entrance at the centre of the nave; on the southern wall a tall slit of a window along the meridian was designed to flood the church with light only at high noon.

Some frescoes still exist, but under Allah's whitewash, awaiting a restoration that may never come. Beyond these, the cathedral's modest decorative scheme hints at the same pious simplicity of a Turkish Ulu Cami; of all Ani's churches, it's the most austere. A single whimsical adornment is allowed in a kind of crypt entrance at the rear, built at a later date and half-hidden by weeds. In the same two-tone sandstone of the city walls, this addition is built of great stones masterfully cut into pentagons and five-pointed stars.

Menucehr Mosque

Back towards the palisade of the Arpa Çay, a lonely minaret protrudes from a ruined structure on the edge of the cliff. This building that the sign calls Menucehr Mosque (Ebul Menucehr Camii) is actually something of a mystery. Believed to date from the year 1072, eight years after the Selcuk conquest, it seems nevertheless to have originally been an Armenian work – not a church, but perhaps – with its colonnaded terraces and wonderful view over the Arpa – a palace. The slopes of the valley below are full of sculptural fragments that are obviously Armenian in style, but the small domes in the colonnades, with their inlaid stonework in geometric and stalactite patterns, suggest a Muslim hand. Whether mosque or palace, here Armenian and Islamic styles harmonize nicely, and suggest that the Selcuk conquest may not have been such a disaster as historians make it out to be. The minaret has been closed since a German tourist committed suicide by leaping from its top; like many others in the Islamic world, it has 99 steps, one for each of the Names of God.

Perhaps the German suffered an attack of melancholy. This part of Ani is certainly conducive to it. Look down into the river to see the ruins of an exquisite bridge with stone towers, and another, unreachable chapel poised gracefully on a little hill on the

Armenian side. You find yourself imagining colourful royal processions, columns of victorious soldiers or caravans from Persia climbing the road from the bridge up to the city gates. Turn around, and see the city's skyline of churches still intact, with only the houses between them missing. As corpses of cities go, Ani is still warm. If it were not so beautiful, it would not be so sad.

Along the Alaca Çay

Crossing over to the Alaca Çay side of town, another bridge, more troglodyte caves and a gate and several surviving towers of the fortifications become visible. The narrow strip of land you stand on connects the city proper with the **citadel**, which is off-limits. Instead, follow the cliffs to the next St Gregory, **Little St Gregory of Abighaurentz** (Polatoğlu Abughamrents Kilisesi), an especially tall church with an exceptionally small floor space. Built during the reign of Gagik I in 994, it features six domed apses forming a circle around the central drum and dome, all supported by columns bearing the distinctive Armenian style of capital, a variant on the Ionic form but with three scrolls instead of two. The ruin nearby, called the caravanserai, was really a church rebuilt as a mosque by the Selcuks, with the same coalescence of two styles as that seen in the Menucehr Mosque. Another mosque, the **Ebul Muammeran Camii** with its fallen minaret, stands as the only monument to the short-lived Ani-Shehhad Kingdom, a state formed in the confusion of the Selcuks' move westward. Below ground level nearby are the excavated remains of what archaeologists think is a Zoroastrian fire temple from the 6th century BC. The four remaining columns are plain and wonderfully squat, a case of function over form.

The first King Gagik also gets the credit for the final **St Gregory Church** (Gagik Kilisesi), built in 1001 near the northwestern edge of the city. The church has been a victim of earthquakes, but even in its derelict state it is clear that it was one of the grandest of all, comparable in size to the cathedral. The circular form, with an interior circle of columns and four mighty piers that must have carried a great dome, is probably unique in Armenian architecture. The crater in the floor you almost fell into is not a baptismal font, but a well, cut right through the centre of the church and now filled with rubble. The original religion of the Armenians had much to do with sacred trees and springs, and Gregory the Illuminator made many concessions to the old order in this conversion of the nation; he kept the old hereditary caste of priests, for example, and it would be interesting to learn what else survived as well.

Returning to the Lion Gate, you pass a single wall remaining from the oldest church in Ani, a relic of the family that founded the city; the three-tiered arches of the 7th-century **Karisarkan Church** are carved with a scene of the Annunciation.

(i) **Kars >**
Lise Caddesi,
t *0474 212 6817*

Where to Stay in Kars

Kars

With the exception of Kar's Otel (*see below*) the town has a terrible dearth of decent hotels. It's as if all the town's hotel owners met up one night and agreed to throw the hoteliers' rulebook out of a top-floor window. Hotels here are less friendly than anywhere else in eastern Turkey, and surprisingly expensive too.

Kar's Otel, Halitpaşa Caddesi 79, **t** *0474 212 1616, www.karsotel.com* (€€€€). Finally a boutique hotel in Kars, and a pretty impressive one at that – could this be a dream? Contemporary interiors within a charismatic old Russian mansion, comfortable, clean and with a good restaurant to boot. It's not cheap, but it's the nicest option in town by far if you can afford it.

***Karabağ, Faik Bey Caddesi 184, **t** *0474 212 3480, www.hotel-karabag. com* (€€€–€€). Rooms at the front are prey to street noise; those at the sides have windows so close to the buildings next door that you're in a permanent twilight zone. Only the rooms at the back are bright and quiet. The saving grace of the hotel is its en suite toilet and showers: the lashings of hot water are just what you need after clambering over Ani.

Güngören, Halit Paşa Caddesi, Millet Sokak 4, **t *0474 212 5630* (€€). Well-run. Unusually for Kars, staff are friendly and the rooms spacious and clean, with private bathtubs as well as showers. For more intense aqua-therapy, head down to the hotel's

sauna and hamam. The Güngören is also good value.

Temel, Yeni Pazar Caddesi 9, **t *0474 223 1376* (€€). The only one of the other hotels in a similar price range not to smell too bad, though the décor is pure 1970s. The beds are clean and most rooms are equipped with showers and toilets.

Eating Out in Kars

Hukukçular Lokalı ('Lawyer's Club') (€€). The best dining spot in Kars is hidden away above a stationery shop on the corner of Faik Bey Caddesi and Ordu Caddesi. An inconspicuous sign by a side entrance points you up to it. The owner, Ali Özkiran, has gone to great lengths to banish Kars' rough-and-ready atmosphere from his establishment: the waiters are discreet, the crockery is crested and the tablecloths and napkins are linen. Not surprisingly, the club is a fixture in the diaries of the town's tie-wearing types. A wide selection of *mezes* and hot dishes are on offer, with a different special each day. A full meal may cost only 10 YTL, more if you order beer or wine.

Ocakbaşı, Atatürk Caddesi (€€). The place to go for good grilled food in cavelike surroundings.

Sema Tatlı Pastanesi, Atatürk Caddesi (€). A good place to stop for a relaxing afternoon pastry. Its cheap chandeliers and white walls with gilded embellishments give it the air of a down-at-heel imperial Russian salon. It is also a good place to stock up on snacks for a trip to Ani.

Mount Ararat

If you think you've reached the end of the world at Ani, you haven't yet been to Mount Ararat. From Kars, or for that matter from anywhere else, there's no easy way to get there; whether you drive or take the untamed mountain buses, you will have to pick your way slowly between the peaks, sometimes on long stretches of unpaved road, before you eventually arrive. The short cut to Kağızman will spare you another trip to Sarıkamış, and the red, tan and green Arizona landscape between Mount Aladağ and its shorter cousin Yağlıca Dağ may or may not be worth the damage the road does to your nerves. Among the dirty and disorganized villages of this region, **Kağızman** stands out; the government has put a lot of money into agriculture here, and it shows.

Don't bother with the next short cut – to **Ağrı**, Turkey's most woebegone provincial capital. The east road for Iğdir follows a narrow plain and, with no little mountains crowding it, affords a view of the big ones, mostly far off across the border, their iridescent peaks catching the sun. Clouds cling to the slopes, but the winds hardly ever permit them to stay still, and the swirling mountain panorama changes by the minute. In many places along this road, the Armenian border is only a mile or so to the north, across the Aras. From this road, it looks more like Tolkien's land of Mordor, with grey cliffs wreathed in smoke, squat factories, and even a nuclear power plant belching steam. On the Turkish side, you'll see more troglodyte caves at **Tuzluca**. At **Iğdır**, an awful place, take the right turn for Doğubayazıt; the entire 34 miles (55km) of this road follows the western flank of Ararat.

Doğubayazıt

🏰 Doğubayazıt   Doğubayazıt is definitely a frontier town of the Wild East; disconcertingly deep potholes often fill with water on the paved roads, which peter out into mud or dust without warning. The streets are full of tractors and sheep; there are few amenities and plenty of bad smells. Being on one of the main roads from Iran, it's usually full of Iranian tourists exchanging currency.

Palace of İshak Paşa

Nothing in the town is very old. A century ago, this was all a lake bordered with marshes; travellers since ancient times have remarked on how the tremendous flow off Ararat turns all the surrounding country to a bog in the spring, though many parts have lately been drained for farming. The original settlement, **Beyazıt**, was up in the hills three miles (5km) east, near one of the most unusual attractions in eastern Turkey, the half-ruined Palace of İshak Paşa. The Turks like putting this pleasure dome on their travel posters. With its pointed dome and striped minaret, made in two shades of sandstone, Armenia-style, it matches its romantic setting under Ararat, and whispers to the gaping tourist of caravans laden with spices and silk, eunuchs with scimitars and dark-eyed houris in pointed slippers, with djinns and *afrits* and the rest of the *Arabian Nights* paraphernalia just offstage.

The joke is, it's no older than the 1700s. İshak Paşa, like his father before him and his son afterwards, were give the title of governor in these parts by the sultan, but the sultan was a thousand miles away; conferring the office was only a polite oriental gesture

Getting to Doğubayazıt

Getting to Doğubayazıt on the **bus** can be difficult. Buses from Kars that claim to be going all the way may leave you stranded in Iğdır. There are direct **minibuses** from Van to Doğubayazıt, but some only go to Ağrı. Connecting minibuses do exist, but the connections sometimes aren't made.

However you travel in this area, long detours around big patches of mountains will be the rule. Large sections around Ağrı are unpaved, and there's no easy route across the mountains to Van or Diyarbakır. Fortunately, the government tourist office's map is quite accurate for this region.

You can take a **taxi** to the İshak Paşa palace, but the three-mile (5km) walk, passing nomad encampments and a military base full of gloomy soldiers, is very pleasant, albeit tough on your calf muscles.

---

acknowledging the power these feudal lords held over the area. According to who you ask, you will hear that İshak was an Armenian, a Kurd or a Jew, and no doubt a man of refinement, too. He built his barely fortified *saray* in the eclectic style, just at the time his counterparts in Europe were beginning to construct Greek or Gothic hotels and railway stations.

Almost two centuries of exposure to the unforgiving climate of eastern Turkey has taken its toll on the palace; several sections of the complex have been re-roofed and some of the interior walls have been reinforced by ungainly steel girders. Don't let that detract from your enjoyment of this lovely place. The sculpture of the entrance, like an old-fashioned **medrese gate**, and the tree-of-life motifs on the **fountain** in the inner courtyard, are fine works, as is the **mosque**, built over the parapets of the castle. Inside, note the odd mimber hidden inside the wall, where the imam would have to climb up and reappear in a little window like a character in a puppet show. The upper galleries are, of course, for the ladies. İshak Paşa always had plenty on hand – the **harem apartment** makes up half of his palace. Each of the harem rooms is fitted with a conical stone fireplace, a reminder to fair-weather visitors that ferocious winds lash out at the beleaguered pleasure palace each winter.

The ruins of the **palace garden** and an early 16th-century mosque can be seen on the opposite hillside. Your eyes may take a little longer to focus on the **fortress**, which in some weather may be difficult to distinguish from the jagged outcrops of the mountain range behind it. A fortress has guarded this mountain pass since Urartian times, although the walls have been rebuilt many times since then; the ruins lower down belong to old Beyazıt.

Where to Stay in Doğubayazıt

***Sim-er Hotel**, 2 miles (3km) out of town at İran Transit Yolu 3, t 0472 312 4842, *www.simerhotel.com* (€€). Also with a hotel in Kars.

***İsfahan**, İsa Geçit Caddesi 26, t 0472 312 4363 (€€–€). Looks good from the outside, brightly painted in blue and white and set back from the road. Inspiration ran out before they considered the interior; the rooms are run-of-the-mill.

Tahran, Büyük Ağrı Caddesi 124, t 0472 312 0195, *www.oteltahran.com* (€). There are lots of good-value cheap hotels on or off the main street; this is the most welcoming. Downstairs the lobby is bright and the staff friendly. Upstairs the metal beds have solid mattresses for a healthy night's sleep, and you can have a private toilet and shower. The sheets are spotlessly clean, the carpets filthy.

İshakpaşa, Büyük Ağrı Caddesi Emniyet Karşısı 10, **t 0472 312 7644 (€). Has en suite rooms with TV, phone and a balcony. It overlooks a busy traffic junction (although 'busy' is a relative term in Doğubayazıt).

There are two basic camp grounds just outside town: the **İshakpaşa** just above the palace of the same name, and **Murat Camping**, just below.

Eating Out in Doğubayazıt

Doğuş Restaurant, Belediye Saray Cad., **t** 0472 312 7348 (€). Near the bus station, this is one of the best; Turkish staple dishes from stews to the *lahmacun* and *pide* for 4 YTL.

Evin Restaurant, Abdullah Baydar Caddesi 92, **t** 0472 312 6073 (€). *Kebap, pide* and trout.

Ararat Itself

 Mount Ararat

When you see Ararat (Ağrı Dağı), you won't be surprised that so many stories have grown up around it, or that so many peoples thought of it as the centre of the world. From the plain of Doğubayazıt, it rears itself startlingly heavenwards, as if out of

Arks and Archaeologists

You may find the streets of Doğubayazıt full of lost Americans, as well as Iranians. Since the latest book about a sighting of Noah's Ark on Mount Ararat, hosts of divinity professors and evangelists have descended on the unsuspecting town. Medieval travellers like Mandeville report that the remains of the Ark were there for all to see, and we can guess that the business of peddling old planks to Christians sprang up here at an early date.

It is no disgrace if these seekers go home empty-handed. Even with aircraft and satellites to help, 600 square miles of mountain make for quite a job. Somewhere on Ararat, a holy place the Armenians called Jacob's Well has been lost for centuries. If there were any literal truth in the story of Noah, it would be a disappointment; finding the original impulse for the myth would be much more significant.

Battalions of scholars have already spent careers tracking down and sorting out stories of the flood: those of Noah, of the Sumerian Utnapishtim, the Deucalion and Pyrrha myth of the Greeks and dozen of other variants from Uganda to Wales. Innumerable theories have been propounded. The school of thought that believes that myths often stem from misrepresentations of pictures in ancient religious icons, for example, sees the story of Noah deriving from a painted scene in which a ship, representing the sun in its passage through the year, carries a sacred king and animals representing the signs of the zodiac. Other scholars find in the tale a confusion of myth with real floods; tidal waves from the disaster that overtook Minoan Crete, perhaps, or a great flood in the valleys of the Tigris and Euphrates in Mesopotamia. The Utnapishtim story, from that part of the world, describes the ark as a perfect cube – intriguing, though highly unseaworthy. The Knights Templars, who knew all these old stories, used a cubic 'ark' as the altar for their secret observances.

For the moment, the last word must go to Hertha von Dechend, a renowned and remarkable scholar who has spent her life reinterpreting ancient stories as a kind of scientific shorthand for astronomical events. To her, all flood stories denote the passing of a World Age, in a vast cosmic clock measured by the procession of the equinoxes. Briefly, just as the North Pole moves around the sky every 26,000 years, so does the equinoctial colure, the point the sun occupies at the spring equinox. When it passes from one constellation of the zodiac to another (say, from Pisces to Aquarius), a new age begins and the old one, with the old constellation, is 'drowned' beneath the celestial equator. The ancients did love to water their heavens with constellations of rivers and seas, and in the astronomy of the Mesopotamians there is not only a boat (now called *Argo*), but even a star they call Mount Ararat.

Activities on Ararat

Climbing tours of Ararat can be arranged from Doğubayazıt. You will need to check carefully on the security situation prior to departure.

Mefser Tur, Belediye Caddesi, Doğubayazıt, **t** 0472 312 6772. This reputable agency charges a rather steep €650/1,300 YTL for an all-inclusive four-day climb.

the sea. An extinct volcano, its mass rises as neatly symmetrical as Etna or Mount Fuji. The summit, now visible, now hidden in clouds, is 3½ miles up; of its entourage of smaller peaks, those on the right are all Iranian, those to the left in Armenia.

Southeastern Anatolia

This quarter of Turkey lies just outside the boundary of the known and familiar, where mere geography evaporates into myth along the banks of the Tigris and Euphrates and the mile-high shores of Lake Van, and the ghosts of numberless dead civilizations rise up to spook you from their ruins. It isn't a part of the world that calls to mind any particular associations, unless you are a scholar familiar with names like Edessa, Harran and Carchemish, and few people ever think of it as a place in which to spend their holidays. Approach it in the right frame of mind, however, and it could be a trip to remember.

16

Don't miss

⭐ **Holy city of mystery**
Şanlıurfa **p.487**

⭐ **Astral temple of the last pagans**
Soğmatar **p.492**

⭐ **Massive mountaintop egomania**
Nemrut Dağı **p.498**

⭐ **A city of striped minarets**
Diyarbakır **p.504**

⭐ **An artistic marvel on a bottle-green sea**
Akhtamar Island **p.517**

See map overleaf

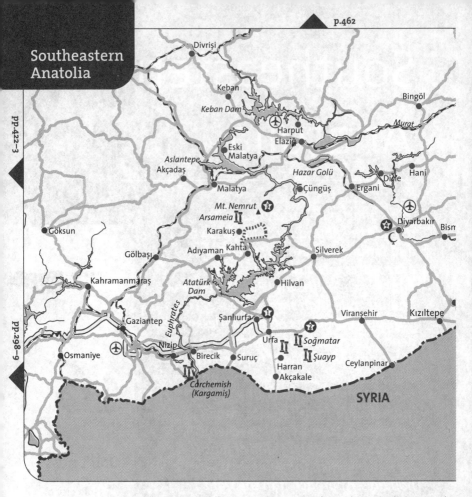

This is the Middle East, make no mistake, with parched plains and barren hills, where sheep outnumber people. Long ago, the climate was much less dry, and the plains of the southeast marked the north edge of the Fertile Crescent, fought over by the Egyptians, Assyrians and Hittites and many others. Biblical sites and early Christian centres abound, and the present population of Kurds, Turks and Arabs each have stories of their own about the region.

Right now, two big facts dominate life in the southeast. The first is GAP, the Greater Anatolia Project (*see* p.494), which is not only bringing water and electricity to a land of ancient poverty, but transforming it from the bottom up. The second is the resurgence – so far, at least, a limited one – of the PKK. With the rise of a *de facto* autonomous Kurdistan in northern Iraq, and the flooding of arms and money into it by the Americans, the PKK has been able to mount a comeback after years of decline. Since 2007, ambushes of Turkish soldiers and police have become regular occurrences, and Turkish troops and planes are staging heavy raids on PKK bases

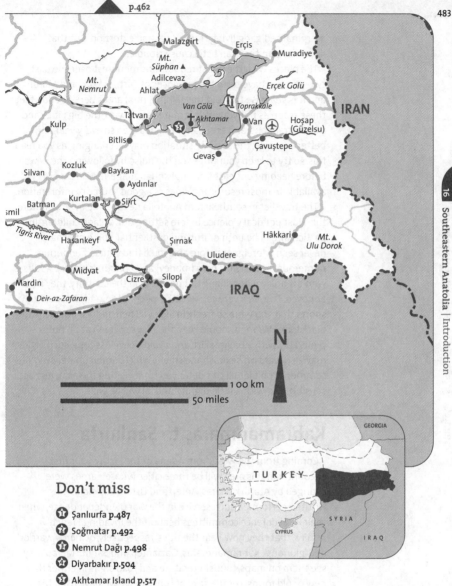

Don't miss

over the border in Iraq. Although you won't find many people who back the PKK (or who will admit it), you will undoubtedly encounter strong separatist feelings in some of the people you meet in this region. In cities such as Diyarbakır and Mardin, the Atatürk statue is under 24-hour armed guard to protect it from desecration. Overwhelmingly, Kurds today hope to achieve greater cultural freedoms and local autonomy through political means; the PKK, like the ETA in Spain, has been reduced to a politically marginalized gang living from drugs and extortion. But that doesn't mean they can't still cause trouble.

The places with the worst reputations for unrest over the past two decades have been the provinces of Siirt, Hakkâri and Mardin, and it is still wise to avoid travelling in rural areas here. Yet don't let these troubles put you off. It is quite safe to visit the big cities and their attractions, and thousands of people do so every year. For better or worse, the security situation may be changing as you read this, so try to keep your finger on the pulse by following the news before heading out east; the English-language *Turkish Daily News*, available in most resorts and cities, is a good source of information.

The traveller in southeastern Anatolia needs to be aware of more than just political violence before setting out. Village children, in particular, can be both pitiful and pestilential; some may have never seen a foreigner before and you'll find yourself enduring numerous requests for *para* (money) and *bonbon* (sweets). Adults won't thank you for doling out goodies; on the contrary, they'll be annoyed. They're a very conservative people, too, and those skimpy shorts that you wore so freely in Side will here induce nothing but black looks. Women should keep their legs covered at all times, preferably with a baggy skirt, and avoid sleeveless tops; such attire may also ward off sexual harassment which, unfortunately, is quite common. Don't let all this deter you from visiting the east; just act sensibly, and with a little dignity, and all will be well.

Kahramanmaraş to Şanlıurfa

Coming from the west, from Adana or the Hatay, your first encounter in this area will be three cities whose names were changed by Atatürk. Maraş, Antep and Urfa, all as old as the Hittites, performed such service in the War of Independence, when their local defence committees beat off the invading French armies, that they now bear the titles, respectively, of 'hero', 'warrior' and 'glorious': Kahramanmaraş, Gaziantep and Şanlıurfa. You may see them on maps, tourist literature and road signs in either their new or old forms. For the sake of consistency we have used the new forms throughout.

Kahramanmaraş and Gaziantep

Kahramanmaraş was once the capital of the 12th-century BC Hittite state of Gürgüm, but there's not much to the city today. If you like Hittite sculptures, the archaeological museum is good for a brief browse, and there are two 15th-century mosques. Otherwise, it's a town one can bypass without guilt – unless you're crazy about ice cream; Kahramanmaraş is famous for it throughout Turkey and beyond.

Getting to and around Kahramanmaraş and Şanlıurfa

Gaziantep and Şanlıurfa are connected by direct THY **flights** from Ankara and Istanbul. Gaziantep is linked with Sivas and Malatya by rail.Be advised that **buses** in the region, and indeed in all of eastern Anatolia, are not always up to the standard that obtains in the rest of the country – lots of cracked windscreens are the rule, and they travel at hair-raising speeds when they have a mind to. Still, there's no problem getting anywhere you want to go.

If **driving**, you need take no special precautions except to make sure that you've got plenty of extra water and a good spare – and be especially careful on the bizarre E24 speedway around Şanlıurfa. You'll have to rely on the locals for directions quite often if you're trying to find the sights in the countryside – they aren't well signposted.

Don't take your car to Soğmatar or Şuayp, especially in the summer: it won't be worth the risk, and you probably won't find the sites anyway. Instead, employ the services of **Harran Dolmuş**, behind the Şanmed hospital in Şanlıurfa, t 0414 215 1575. In summer, subject to numbers, they run minibuses to all the sites in the area, and Harran too, with prices averaging around 70 YTL per person; the more who sign up for the trip, the cheaper it becomes. If you'd prefer to see the sites alone or with your own small group, the company can organize this too, with a taxi for a long day costing around 200 YTL. **Taxi** hire can also be arranged via the local tourist information office, although they tend to be less particular about which drivers they choose. For a round trip to Harran only by taxi you should expect to pay 90 YTL.

Gaziantep, Turkey's sixth city, with 850,000 people, bestrides the two roads into the southeast, and it will probably either introduce you to the region or help you rest at the end of the trip. It's a good place for that, with nice hotels and a reputation for tasty food. Kebab houses all over Turkey proclaim 'Gaziantep style' on their signs. Despite its venerable history, Gaziantep is a thoroughly up-to-date town and its air of youthful vigour also brings with it more chewing gum on the pavements than anywhere else in Turkey. And today, it offers a first-rate reason for visiting: the newly discovered Roman mosaics from **Zeugma**, now in the city's museum.

Like Kayseri, Gaziantep is one of the rapidly modernizing 'Anatolian Tigers'. It owes much of its impressive growth to a burgeoning textile industry, including machine-made carpets; along with prosperity, this has brought the city an expanse of *gecekondu* neighbourhoods spreading over the surrounding hills. The city's ancient fame, the pistachio nut, is still in evidence; any sweet shop in the town will sell you a box at astoundingly cheap prices. Like any busy, lively city, Gaziantep has its share of peculiarities: the motorcycles with sidecars like big wagons, used as informal taxis and delivery trucks in the poorer sections; and the traffic lights in the centre fitted with digital displays to count down the seconds until the lights change. From the past, the city retains an unusual fashion in minarets, some with spiral fluting and others topped with ornate wooden crow's-nests for the muezzin. In the older, eastern parts of the town, these stand side by side with asymmetrical grey stone houses whose interior stairways project over the sidewalk to form a kind of bay window, a style unique to Gaziantep.

The town's major thoroughfare begins at the central square as **Suburcu Caddesi** and changes its name several times on its way through the old town and the **bazaar**. No amount of modernity

The Lucky Mosaics of Zeugma

Zeugma, on the Euphrates 45km southeast of Gaziantep, was founded by Alexander's general Seleucus Nicator. It became an important city when the Romans built a floating bridge across the Euphrates there, and then installed a military headquarters. Destroyed by the Sassanid Persians in the 250s, and then again by the Arabs, the city completely vanished from sight.

Excavations began in the 1990s, just at the time that GAP, the Southeast Anatolia Project, was beginning its Birecik Dam, which would flood most of the site. Surprise... The archaeologists started digging up one first-rate Roman mosaic after another, in one of the greatest finds of the century. Zeugma, it turned out, had been a wealthier town than anyone suspected. The Turks, as usual, were rather unfairly criticized from some quarters for not delaying the project to excavate all of Zeugma. But isn't easy to stop a billion-euro dam after all the contracts are signed, and the frustration of the engineers was perhaps understandable, in this land where a dog can't bury a bone without uncovering a lost city. A compromise was reached. GAP co-operated with a dramatic, last-minute international effort to save as much of Zeugma as possible, and the results are here to see in the museum: a collection of mosaics almost as good as Antakya's, including scenes of Achilles and Odysseus, Pasiphae and the Minotaur, Gods of the Sea, the Birth of Aphrodite, the river god of the Euphrates, Perseus and Andromeda, Daedalus and Icarus, and a haunting face called the 'Gypsy Girl' that captivates the people of Gaziantep; you'll see her reproduced all over town. Besides mosaics, the site produced statues, bronzes and frescoed walls. Not all of Zeugma has been drowned by the dam, and the site will be yielding new discoveries for years to come.

can kill off a Turkish market, and Gaziantep's is as colourful as any; there are a number of historic *hans* and *bedestens*, and you'll still find some traditional copper wares here, another longstanding tradition. North of Suburcu, the Selcuk-era **castle** is usually locked up. The castle stands on a hill – a tell like Konya's.

Archaeology Museum
open Tues–Sun 8.30–12 and 1.30–5; closed Mon; adm

Enough of these tells have been excavated for the **Archaeology Museum** to be worth a detour. It lies on the north fringe of the town on İstasyon Caddesi, past the stadium and the garden cafés of the city park, where *nargile*-smoking is still very much the thing. The museum, in its modern building, claims the largest collection in the southeast, with Hittite reliefs, some fine Roman sculpture on grave steles from as far away as Palmyra in Syria, mosaics and cylinder seals, even some recently unearthed mastodon bones to remind you that these hot plains were cool pine forests during the last Ice Age. One finely carved relief has an odd deity brandishing an axe and a thunderbolt. This is Jupiter Dolichenos, a local boy who made it big. Doliche is an ancient city 10km from Gaziantep, currently being excavated; its warrior version of Zeus, or Jupiter, became a favourite cult of the Roman legions as far as Britain and Spain. Another relief shows a smiling Hellenistic-era king shaking hands with the god Apollo. This is Antiochus I, king of Commagene, and, if both the pose and subject seem presumptuous, just wait until you've seen the rest of this man's work up on Nemrut Dağı.

Carchemish and Birecik

Like Gaziantep itself, most of the ancient cities in its province have little to show for their long histories. Carchemish, or **Kargamış** in Turkish, a city straddling major trade routes between Mesopotamia and the Mediterranean that first flourished under the Hittites but only really took off when that empire was extinguished. It was sacked around the same time as Troy and Hattusas, c. 1180 BC, but it soon recovered and, as an independent Hittite kingdom surviving on trade and clever diplomacy, it lasted until the Assyrians razed it in 717 BC. British excavations, beginning in the 1880s, contributed some of the first clues to the identity of the Hittites; the finds, now mostly in London or Ankara, attracted a lot of attention at the time, and many of the grand Edwardian dilettantes (T.E. Lawrence among them) spent time helping with the dig. Nowadays, Carchemish lies in a minefield right on the Syrian border, and can't be visited.

Turkey doesn't have many oil deposits, but the oil isn't far away. The road from the east into Gaziantep seems a sort of pipeline in itself; more often than not, its narrow two lanes are packed solid with tank trucks going in both directions, making the ride east a thrill you'll remember, especially if you take the bus. The road crosses the Euphrates (Fırat Nehri in Turkish) at **Birecik**, a sorry little town on white cliffs, but well liked by the bald ibis, an almost extinct crane, now a project of the World Wide Fund for Nature.

Birecik's ruined castle was built or rebuilt by the Franks of the First Crusade as a border outpost for their County of Edessa. Whatever made Count Baldwin and his merry men try to set up a state so far east – the furthest penetration into the Islamic world that the Crusaders ever made – is not clear. Founded in 1092, the County of Edessa was hardly defensible, and the Selcuks destroyed it less than 50 years later. In the First Crusade, at least, we can give the knights some credit for pious motivation: the ancient city of Edessa, now known as Şanlıurfa, is holy ground for Christians as well as Muslims.

Şanlıurfa (Edessa)

⭐ Şanlıurfa   Abraham, according to both Christian and the Muslim traditions, received his summons to prophecy while living in the city. The Şanlıurfans will show you Job's cave as well, and the belief is widely current among them that Adam and Eve lived here, and that these parched hills were once the Garden of Eden. Şanlıurfa, a city like none other, has been a holy place for millennia upon millennia. No ground could store up spiritual energy for so long without becoming at least a bit strange and otherworldly, but Şanlıurfa and its hinterlands go too far. It is the vortex of Turkey, not a Canterbury but a Salisbury Plain, full of mystery. The city, with its scholarly legacies and its air of distinction, will seem reasonable enough, but, once outside it, anything can happen.

The name Urfa may be a very ancient corruption of Hurri; archaeologists speculate that it was an important town of the Hurri-Mitanni confederation, the state that pushed the Hittites around until the successful reign of Hittite King Suppiluliumas I ended the Hurri ascendancy in c. 1400 BC. Every power in the Middle East ruled here at least once. As Orhoe, or Orhai, the town continued quietly until Alexander the Great's Seleucid successors renamed it Edessa and helped it grow into its new role as clearing house of goods, gods and ideas between the Greek world and the East. In the Hellenistic period Urfa finally managed to run a state of its own, called the Osrhoene Kingdom and ruled by an Arab dynasty called the Abgarids. The Romans first made a client king-dom of it, and finally gobbled it up altogether. Roman Osrhoene was a permanent military province, on the busy border with Persia.

Under the Byzantines, Urfa found itself attacked repeatedly by the first waves of the expanding Muslim Arabs in the 7th century, changing hands back and forth as of old. While the soldiers were out banging their swords, Christian and Muslim scholars inside the walls and in the nearby city of Harran were beginning the great work of translation and teaching that made Greek science and philosophy available to the Muslim world. In 1098, at the beginning of the Crusades, Baldwin of Boulogne stumbled into the city on his way to becoming King of Jerusalem. The Crusaders made the city capital of their County of Edessa, and under their rule the learned men of Islam were to return the favour. Books that had long been lost to the West, including important works of Aristotle, were regained by contacts made here and in the other Crusader states. Along with them came the fruits of the golden era of Arabic science, works of mathematics and astronomy that were to have an incalculable influence on the West.

Zengi, the Turkish Atabeğ of Mosul, retook the city for Islam after a bloody siege in 1144. Since then it has been a sleepy place. Today the GAP is waking it up. As HQ for the project, Şanlıurfa and its hinterlands are at the heart of GAP's modernization efforts, and the countryside is looking considerably greener now that it is being served by the biggest irrigation tunnels on earth. The difference from the Şanlıurfa of even 20 years ago is striking; nowhere in Turkey, perhaps, are the contrasts of old and new more pronounced.

The Pool of Abraham

Striving to maintain something of its old distinction, Şanlıurfa is a surprisingly lovely city. Its economy is still based more on pilgrimages and religious institutions than commerce, and, although it seems as prosperous as Gaziantep, its air of pleasant tranquillity has not suffered. Şanlıurfa has a compact centre, strung out along the 2.5km length of **Atatürk Caddesi** (part of which is called Sarayönü Caddesi). Most of its sights can be seen in a day, but before you go out walking in this ferocious climate – Şanlıurfa is on the edge of the Syrian desert – take note of the best place in town for a cold drink and a spot of shade. In **Gölbaşı** (literally 'at the lakeside'), a park around the **Pool of Ayn-ı Zeliha** on the southern edge of town, are cafés, pavilions, garden paths and the biggest concentration of trees in Şanlıurfa province. Take a seat by the water and almost instantly sleek grey fish will poke their noses out expectantly. Next, a small boy will appear with a plate of seeds or chickpeas to sell; you will earn a little grace for contributing to the upkeep of Şanlıurfa's sacred carp, who have inhabited this pool for thousands of years. No one knows exactly how long: local stories associate the fish with the story of Abraham. Ancient religions from Ireland to China have had the like, often carp or salmon at holy springs, but few examples have survived. The carp may not be caught or even disturbed – in Şanlıurfa they will tell you about the drunken soldier who went fishing one night and ended up with a stiff prison sentence. Everyone feeds them; with such a soft life, it's no wonder there are so many of them, and that they look so fat and serene as they glide through the cool waters. They say if you see a white one you're sure to go to heaven.

This pond actually serves only for the carp to make little excursions; their true abode is the nearby **Pool of Abraham**, joined by a small canal. No one knows exactly how long this has been here, or to whom it was originally sacred, although it has been associated with the goddess Astarte. The Greeks called the spring that fills the two pools 'Callirhoe', 'fair-flowing'. In the Muslim tradition, Abraham began his career as the first prophet of monotheism in Şanlıurfa. His refusal of idolatry so outraged Nimrod, the legendary Assyrian king associated with so many places in Anatolia, that he determined to have the troublesome prophet burned. An immense pyre was constructed under the walls of Şanlıurfa's citadel, but just as Abraham was being tossed onto it, God, or rather Allah, turned the fire into a flowing spring and landed him safely on his feet. On the edge of the Pool of Abraham, reflected in its waters, is an exceptionally lovely mosque, the **Halil Rahman Camii**, its three pointed domes built in 1775 while the square minaret survives from the medieval original.

The Citadel

An Assyrian chronicler, writing of a siege here almost 3,000 years ago, described the citadel as like 'a cloud hung from heaven'. Romans and Byzantines would later occupy this dramatic rock, but the castle you see today was built by the Frankish Crusaders, who built the towers and bastions, the *donjon* inside and the ditch around, cut in some places out of bare rock. The prominent landmark on top, two lone Corinthian columns, has acquired the name the **Throne of Nimrod**; no one knows who actually erected them. The spur on which the citadel rises is a part of a long cliff that bounds Şanlıurfa on its southern and eastern edges. Of the dozens of man-made and natural caves along the cliff, two are of great importance to Muslims: the **Cave of Abraham** (İbrahim Halilullah Dergâhı) and the **Cave of Job** (Eyyüp Peygamber Makamı). Both of these are religious sites of immeasurable antiquity, and were associated with the two biblical figures before Muslims ever came here, but now they have become one of the most important places of pilgrimage in the Islamic world. Devout Turks rub shoulders with Iranian and Syrian pilgrims, who carry off holy water from the site in recycled Coke bottles. Non-Muslims may also visit, except during the month of Ramazan.

Beneath the cliffs, adjoining the gardens and two pools, a complex of mosques and schools has grown up that is worthy of this holy city. Most of it is Ottoman work or later – at the very base of the cliff, one mosque with a huge dome was completed to receive pilgrims in the late 1980s – but all are in the elegant style of the Halil Rahman Camii. **Hasan Paşa Camii**, near Abraham's Cave, and the **Mevlid-i Halil Camii** make the greatest impression, along with the waterside **Rizvaniye Mosque and Madrasa** (1736); taken all together, this complex, with its arches, colonnades and cloisters, gardens and fountains, is a masterpiece of urban design.

Old Neighbourhoods

In the old neighbourhoods, along twisting, narrow, unusually clean streets, fine old homes with stone balconies harmonize well with the design of the mosques. One early Islamic motif you see everywhere, the zigzag line, always appears as if it were a symbol – on the balustrades of the Halil Rahman, on the arches above private doors, and in the metal grillework. Like the homes in many Middle Eastern cities, Şanlıurfa's face inwards, turning their backs on the street. Beside the balconies, the doorways are the only decoration, but the citizens have made it a point of pride to beautify them; many have miniatures of the Ka'aba or other religious subjects painted over the arch. If you can find the way through this maze of streets to the east, you'll see the last remaining section of the old city wall, the **Mahmutoğlu Tower** (Mahmutoğlu Kulesi) and the gate for the Mardin road beside it.

Şanlıurfa's **bazaar** seems to have selected the very narrowest streets in which to ply its trades, just to the north of the religious complex. This is Turkey's most timeless bazaar. Carts drawn by tired donkeys push their way through the throng; knife-grinders sharpen blades in a fiery shower of sparks in the musty holes in the walls that pass as workshops; women, veiled even across their eyes, glide by ethereally. You wouldn't be surprised to see Abraham himself come around the corner. One of the historic *hans*, the **Millet Han**, is currently being restored for a new archaeological museum that promises to be one of Turkey's most interesting.

Atatürk Caddesi skirts the bazaar's edge, and continues north from there into the modern town, passing several mosques with squat Persian-style minarets. One, the **Hüseyin Cami**, stands right in the middle of the avenue. Its three-domed porch gives it away as an early Ottoman work. The **Ulu Cami**, a bit further north, dates from the 12th century; the Selcuks built it immediately after their conquest of the city in commemoration of the event. Unique among the mosques of Turkey, its minaret has a clock on top. The back streets here have some of the best of Şanlıurfa's old houses.

Archaeological Museum

open Tues–Sun 8.30–12 and 1.30–5; closed Mon; adm

In the modern end of Şanlıurfa, the **Archaeological Museum** has increased its collections greatly in recent years, waiting for the new building to be finished, with exhibits from the new excavations at Göbekli Tepe. Plenty of peculiar stone carvings may be seen in the sculpture garden outside. There aren't any of the customary stone lions here – just several stone pussycats.

Around Şanlıurfa

One biblical site this area doesn't claim, surprisingly, is the Valley of Dry Bones. Don't go lightly into any trip into the empty spaces

History's New Beginning

If the recent discoveries around Şanlıurfa are all that they seem to be, they'll be rewriting all the textbooks on ancient history soon. Most people haven't heard the news yet, but Professor Klaus Schmidt and the German Archaeological Institute have hit upon the archaeological find of the century, the biggest thing since Arthur Evans dug up the lost civilization of Crete.

The sophisticated temple complex they have discovered at Göbekli Tepe, 15km northeast of the city, is a remarkable sight. Everything is circular: sinuous, curving banks and stone walls, and inside them rings of T-shaped columns, some over 20ft tall. The columns are often decorated with elegant carved reliefs of animals, stylized humans and abstract symbols. Professor Schmidt quite rightly calls it the 'Anatolian Stonehenge'. Even more remarkably, Göbekli Tepe dates to 9100 BC – in other words, it is more than twice as old as Stonehenge, millennia older than the Giza pyramids or the ziggurats of Sumer – nothing less than the oldest monumental architecture on earth.

Such a unique and exceptional find makes the archaeologists wonder what else might be hiding under the tells of southern Turkey. Until they get a chance to explore, they can only speculate. Professor Schmidt believes that Göbekli Tepe might mark the beginning of the Neolithic revolution, the transition from hunter-gatherer cultures to settled agriculture, and that wheat may have first been domesticated here. Intriguingly, the site seems never to have been permanently inhabited; it was a ritual centre, not a town. And stranger still, it was purposely, carefully buried for unknown reasons, *c.* 8000 BC.

Several related sites have been discovered in the area, including a temple complex at Nevali Çori, now drowned by the Atatürk Dam, and another at Mezraa Taleilat, 5km south of Birecik. This one, and Göbekli Tepe, aren't really open to the public yet. But the Germans are already organizing tour groups (*www.dr-koch-reisen.de*); occultists are already writing books about it. You'll be hearing a lot more about Göbekli Tepe in the future.

around Şanlıurfa. In winter and early spring it can be green, thanks to GAP's irrigation tunnels, but during the hot months daytime temperatures of 110°F/43°C are common, and shade and water are rare. Without a drop of humidity, the air scorches the soil with arid blasts, and the sparse grass left over from spring crackles underfoot like broken glass. If you've always wanted to see a genuine mirage, come in July or August, though after a few hours on the plains you may not be able to distinguish them from the hallucinations.

It isn't the heat that bewilders, nor the uncanny landscape, wrinkled and ugly and covered with rocks. Both of these add much to the ambience, but the unfathomable strangeness of the place comes from the works of man. All around Şanlıurfa, the country-side is littered with caves and mounds, standing stones and cairns, ruins and inscriptions, along with such exotica as the little city, dug down several levels, around a square subterranean courtyard, visible along the road from Şanlıurfa to Gaziantep. Most of the curiosities here remain unexplained.

The Tek Tek Mountains: Soğmatar and Şuayp

The best places to see lie among the awful Tek Tek Mountains east of the town. With proper directions from the Şanlıurfa tourist office, you will know where to leave the Mardin road. Along the passable dirt track south, the first sight to greet your eyes is a blue man painted on a cliff next to a small cave. It's somewhat disconcerting; it can't be too old. Every height in the Tek Tek bears some sort of marker on its summit, such as a large stone or cairn. They stand like sentinels, overlooking the valleys with their dry stream beds that once ran down to the Euphrates. The villages are hard to see, low on the ground or buried in it, with mud-walled huts and stables the same colour as the earth. The semi-nomadic, largely Arab inhabitants are just as invisible; not even they can stay out in the summer oven for long.

Some 20km south of the highway, you reach the ruins of **Soğmatar**. The origin of this religious centre has evaporated in history, but a star- and planet-worshipping cult called the Sabians occupied it well into the Middle Ages. This unusual group, the origins of which are unknown, was the heir of all the astrological mysticism of the ancient Chaldeans, to which they added a good dose of Neoplatonic philosophy. Because they believed in a single God, the Muslims at first tolerated them. Sabian scholars and mathematicians played an important role at the great university at Harran, even after the sect was outlawed in the 9th century – the Muslims claimed they were performing human sacrifices.

The site has never been thoroughly examined or explained, but enough remains to suggest a little of what went on. At the centre of the modern Soğmatar village, the largest of several natural and

🟡 **Soğmatar**

artificial hills bears a large ruin believed to be the Temple of the Sun. Around it, the other heights have caves or buildings dedicated to the planetary deities, all orientated towards the sun temple; this is arranged, oddly enough, as if it were an up-to-date model of our heliocentric system. One of the hilltops, for instance, contains a cave decorated with trident shapes or pitchforks, and the hole bored through its front wall is sighted directly on the sun temple. On the cliffs above, an apparently Greek- or Roman-era relief depicts a man and a woman – the villagers claim they are Adam and Eve – and a long inscription in Syriac. Another summit has a well-preserved round tower; other remains are difficult to identify.

Someone from the village will be around to let you into the former stable where another shrine can be seen. When your eyes become used to the darkness, a procession of eleven figures, badly eroded, and other Syriac inscriptions come into view, carved into the rock around which the stable is built. Around a central altar are two relief bulls with crescent-moon horns.

15km further on, the same road finds the once-lost city of **Şuayp**. Prosperous under the Assyrians and Romans, Şuayp was abandoned in the Middle Ages. The largest structure still standing amid its extensive ruins is a three-storey building of uncertain age; crosses are carved into the walls in some places. Much of Şuayp seems to have been built underground, or into the hillsides. The present village occupies many of these holes. Many of these caves and warrens were carved out of the soft rock with care, adorned with arches and pilasters, niches and decorative entrances.

Harran

The next stop, only 15km from the Syrian border, is Harran, more easily accessible by a paved track off the Şanlıurfa–Syria road for those who wish to avoid the Tek Tek. Harran has been a city for perhaps 6,000 years, at times reaching prominence in trade and culture. Today, its ruins shelter a small village of semi-nomadic Arabs in beehive-shaped desert-style houses; these domes, oddly enough, are structurally identical to those of the famous *trullo* houses of Puglia in southern Italy. These Arabs may be the most colourful community in Turkey, with unusually pretty children and women who wear all their jewellery all the time.

To guess at the founding of Harran is impossible – it's been there since at least 6000 BC – but only after the 9th century BC does it take its place among the big towns of the Near East. Somehow, Harran managed the neat trick of prospering under the Assyrians without being annihilated in a revolt or during the series of wars that followed the Assyrian decline. According to the *Book of Genesis*, Abraham and his family lived here for several years on their way from Ur to Canaan. In Roman times, the town had come to be known as Carrhae, and its one appearance in history was a disaster the Romans would long remember. The first Roman triumvirate consisted of Julius Caesar, Pompey and a useless fool named Crassus whom the two great generals kept around to appease the Senate. To prove his mettle while Caesar worked over the Gauls and Pompey cleared up the Cilician pirates, Crassus led an army against the Parthian (Persian) Empire. At Carrhae, in 53 BC, he walked right into a trap; his men were surrounded and cut

GAP: The Southeast Anatolia Project

The Middle East usually makes the headlines for other reasons, but its biggest story is happening right here. Turkish engineers are currently hard at work on the most ambitious development project ever attempted in the region. Atatürk Dam is only a part, though the most conspicuous one, of the Southeast Anatolia Project (Güneydoğu Anadolu Projesi, or GAP), designed to make this wasteland into the breadbasket of the Middle East, and at the same time produce enough electricity to make Turkey self-sufficient, and end a dangerous addiction to Russian amperage.

In its scope, GAP rivals its model, America's Tennessee Valley Authority of the 1930s. When it's finished, there will be 22 dams, 19 power plants, and irrigation schemes covering 1.7 million hectares over nine provinces. GAP already runs the biggest cargo airport in Turkey, and it wants to use the power it generates to bring new business into the region. But there is much more to it; GAP is an attempt at nothing less than a complete transformation of the lives of all the people in Turkey's poorest region. Land reforms are turning the area from an anachronistic bastion of feudalism into a region of independent small farmers, and GAP wants to bring electricity and clean water to every home in it. The sophistication of the project is impressive. GAP planners use progressive phrases like 'sustainable development', 'institution building' and 'popular participation', and, unlike so many other development projects around the world, they seem to mean what they say. Other aspects include aid to local entrepreneurs for small businesses, farmers' training and extension services, health clinics and schools, programmes to preserve the region's cultural heritage, locally managed irrigation co-ops, and 'eco-city' and 'eco-village' pilot projects. Women, who have been kept back here more than anywhere in the country, are getting special attention, with greater access to education and 'women's community centres' to be built in every village.

But it's not all good news. There is a great deal of controversy over the planned construction of the Ilisu Dam, the reservoir of which would flood many Kurdish towns, including the ancient settlement of Hasankeyf, and necessitate the forced relocation of many inhabitants. Independent reports have been strongly critical of the negative impact the dam would have on the area and its people.

At present, the physical side of GAP is nearing completion. Its total cost is estimated at $32 billion, nearly all of which the Turks are supplying themselves; the World Bank at first refused assistance because of the objections Turkey's neighbours had to the project.

Whenever events in the Middle East begin to seem mysterious, think of the issue of water. Nothing is more important in this dry region, not even oil, and the water issues are usually hiding somewhere behind the turmoil of the newspaper headlines (as in the negotiations over the water-rich Golan Heights). It is no coincidence that Syria and Iraq began their heavy support for the Kurdish guerrillas of the PKK in the 1980s when the planning for GAP was under way; both countries stand to lose some of their share of the Euphrates' water (and the water they get will be more saline after it irrigates Turkish fields). In January 1990, the Turks began filling the Atatürk Dam; they announced they would cut off the river's flow almost completely for a month, intending to send a message to the Syrians and Iraqis about their aid to the PKK. Both countries threatened war, and the Turks put the tap back on after three weeks. Turkey claims that its water policy is not political – but with neighbours like Syria and Iraq even the best intentions in the world would cause troubles. But negotiations do go on, and there is talk of a major water pipeline that could carry fresh water as far as Israel. With a little goodwill on all sides, GAP could be the first step in helping all of the ancient Fertile Crescent live up to its name once again.

down by the Parthians' Scythian allies – the first serious Roman defeat since Hannibal. Later, under the Romans and Byzantines, the city became renowned as a centre of learning, and its reputation continued after the Arab conquest, as the home of the first great Islamic university. When the Mongols wrecked it in the 13th century, it stayed wrecked, though it has harboured intermittent Arab settlements ever since.

If you look at Harran on Google Earth, you can plainly make out where the **walls** ran, and even part of the street plan. It isn't so clear on the ground. At the centre stood the **Great Mosque**; its one surviving arch and stunted square minaret are the oldest Islamic architecture in Turkey (*c.* 750). Harran's fortress, with unusual 12-sided towers, still remains partially intact, as do sections of the walls, including the **Aleppo Gate** on the southern edge. Of the rest, little survives. Most of the space within the walls serves as the Arabs' vegetable gardens and grazing lands. As for the famous university, they are not even sure where it was.

Atatürk Dam

The ancient city of **Samosata**, 60km north of Şanlıurfa, now lies submerged under the artificial lake bordered to the south by the Atatürk Dam, the sixth largest in the world. At a height of over 600ft, it curves like some enormous amphitheatre for more than a mile between two hills, and holds back a lake covering hundreds of square kilometres. In front of the dam, a tunnel over 20 feet in diameter has been drilled under 26km of the Şanlıurfa Yaylası (highlands) to bring this water into the south. Not surprisingly, the landscape and economy of the Şanlıurfa and Harran regions has been radically altered. Infertile plains have been supplanted by vegetable and cotton fields that spill out into the emptiness. The most diligent farmers can now squeeze three harvests a year from their lands. Such opportunity has brought unprecedented wealth to one of Turkey's poorest backwaters. The ferro-concrete houses that have sprouted up in consequence may not be as picturesque as the traditional mud homes, but, as any resident will soon tell you, mud is not actually the best of building materials.

Where to Stay in Gaziantep and Şanlıurfa

ⓘ Gaziantep >
100 Yıl Kültür Parkı içi,
Vilayet Konağı Arkası,
t 0342 230 5969

★ Anadolu Evleri >

Gaziantep

Anadolu Evleri, Üekeroglu Mahallesi, Köroglu Sokak 6, t 0342 220 9525, *www.anadoluevleri.com* (€€€€–€€€). A truly lovely hotel worth every lira of its 200 YTL price tag. Drenched in traditional motifs and boasting stunning architecture, this is one of the nicest places in the country to while away a few days.

*******Tuğcan Hotel**, Atatürk Bulvarı 34, t 0342 220 43 23, *www.tugcanhotel. com.tr* (€€€). Strategically situated away from the bustling city centre, this is nevertheless within walking distance of all the sights. Its lofty reception area and indoor pool more than make up for the plain bedrooms.

***GAP Hotel**, Atatürk Bulvarı 10, t 0342 220 3974, *www.gaphotel.com.tr* (€€). Whimsically named after the dam project. The hair-rinse-purple carpets and five-foot bronze dog statue standing guard at reception lift this establishment out of the ordinary. Ask for rooms on the top floors so as to escape any errant vibes from the basement disco.

***Kaleli**, Hürriyet Caddesi, t 0342 230 9690, *www.kaleliotel.com.tr* (€€). A long-standing hotel right in the thick of it on the noisy main street. As if to compensate for this, the staff are unusually courteous. The large rooms come with balconies and bathtubs.

Bulvar Palas, İstasyon Caddesi 11, Üahinbey, t 0342 231 3238 (€). There are very few savoury places to sleep cheap in Gaziantep. This is a labyrinthine place. Its rooms are dingy, but if you can find your way through the maze of corridors to the back of the hotel, these rooms are quiet.

Şanlıurfa

Cevahir Konuk Evi, Vali Fuat Bey Caddesi 3, t 0414 215 9377, *www. cevahirkonukevi.com* (€€€). In a quiet street near the Selahaddin Eyyubi Mosque, this is by far the best deal in town. This converted Ottoman mansion, with its improbably delicate stone staircase and heavy wooden armoires in the hallway, oozes with charm. The six en suite bedrooms filled with modern furniture jar in comparison. The courtyard outside is a postcard-writing haven and the balustraded terrace offers views of the castle. At only €64/128 YTL, the rooms are booked far in advance.

****Edessa**, Balıklıgöl Mevkii, t 0414 215 9911, *www.hoteledessa.com* (€€). A stone's throw from the sacred pools. Its reception area has a low-key elegance and the spacious rooms are decorated in subtle shades of beige. Minimalist sophistication.

****Harran**, Atatürk Bulvarı, t 0414 313 2860, *www.hotelharran.com* (€€). The big draw here is its pool – the only one in Şanlıurfa, a major consideration if you're here in midsummer.

Gülizar Konuk Evi, Karameydanı Camii Yanı, İrfaniye Sokak 22, t 0414 215 0505 (€€). Tucked away down a cobbled lane, this offers an authentic retro experience. You sleep as in Ottoman days of old on silk futons, which are rolled up and stored during the daytime. The wood-panelled bedrooms are part of a painstakingly restored stone house, with vaulted dining rooms and a secluded courtyard. Rooms have air-conditioning, which is just as well since there is only one shower (and just two toilets).

Hotel Güven, Sarayönü Caddesi 78, t 0414 215 1700, *www.hotelguven.com* (€€). Modern. It may lack charm, but it has an elevator and air-conditioning.

İpek Palas, behind the Dünya Hospital at Köprübaşı Mevkii 4, t 0414 215 1546 (€). Small and friendly and the best of the cheaper bunch; en suite doubles.

Uğur, Köprübaşı Caddesi 3, t 0414 313 1340 (€). If money is tight you can sweat it out at this unashamedly old-style cheapie where waterless doubles cost 30 YTL without breakfast.

Harran

One or two of the famous beehive houses have converted into guest houses in recent years and offer an accommodation experience that is certainly out of the ordinary;

Harran House, İbni Teymiye Mah., t 0414 441 2020 (€). Perfect for a bit of authentic Bedouin ambience. Harran is a scorching desert in the summer, but the unbaked clay-domed structures here are said to have a cooling effect that betters air-conditioning; 30 YTL per person, half board.

Eating Out in Gaziantep and Şanlıurfa

Gaziantep

This is a good town for a baklava binge. Kebab restaurants are good too.

İmam Çağdaş Et Lokantası, Kale Civarı Uzun Çarşı, t 0342 220 4545 (€). Combines great kebabs with even better pistachio baklava offerings. It is firmly on tour itineraries but don't let a group of camera-swinging coach-dwellers put you off this one!

Çavuşoğlu, Eski Saray Caddesi, t 0342 338 1828 (€). Cheap and cheerful for kebab, *pide* and of course – baklava.

(i) **Şanlıurfa >**
Harran-Nemrut Tours,
t 0414 215 1575;
information and
local tours

Ekim 29 Café-Restaurant, t 0342 230 2766 at Gaziler Caddesi. Çekemoğlu Çıkmaz 4, Şahinbey, www.ekim29.com (€). In a narrow lane leading off from the pedestrianised Gaziler Caddesi. Not only is the restaurant named after the date on which the Turkish Republic was declared (October 29), but instead of the usual picture of Atatürk on the wall it has gone one better and sports a mosaic of the great man. Its walled courtyard is a pleasant place to relax with a drink. The usual array of kebabs are on offer, with a meal costing about 8 YTL.

Şanlıurfa

The area around the sacred pools is dotted with shady tea gardens, although the waiters there show about as much energy as the carp. The beautiful surroundings ensure that the kebabs and drinks are on the expensive side. Şanlıurfa's restaurants, though modest, are good and inexpensive but rarely serve alcohol. In the hotter summer months ensure your meat is freshly cooked.

You'll see things sold on the streets here that aren't found elsewhere in Turkey. Some are utterly mysterious and beyond the range of adventurousness of most travel writers, but if you come across a dangerous-looking black liquid in Şanlıurfa, it will be either *murra*, a kind of over-boiled fermented coffee, or else home-brewed Turkish root beer. Drinking either one could change your life.

Cevahir Konuk Evi (*see* 'Where to Stay', €) has a courtyard that is one of the most pleasant dining spots in town, particularly in the evening.

Halil İbrahim Sofrası, on the Atatürk Bulvarı opposite the stadium (€). A good 15-minute walk from the town centre; a regular fixture for the locals.

Şurkan İş Merkezi No 5, t 0414 216 8444 (€). Try the regional speciality of *içli köfte*, although the kebabs here are some of the most succulent you'll find, with a meal costing 12 YTL.

Urfa Ev Sofrasi, t 0414 315 3535 (€). Another good option for kebab, in particular the *tandir* lamb and the aubergine kebab at 6 YTL.

Çardaklı Köşk, Vali Fuat Caddesi, t 0414 217 1080 (€). Great views and decent fodder, from 12 YTL, in this restored old house overlooking Gölbaşı.

Commagene

In the upheavals and confusions that attended the collapse of Alexander's short-lived empire, adventurers among his generals and their successors were able to seize the main chance and carve out little tax farms to keep them in spending money. Some of the larger ones, like the Ptolemaic kingdom in Egypt and the Seleucid Kingdom in Persia and Anatolia, survived as well-organized states for a long time; others have been gathering dust in history's curiosity shop ever since. To take the prize of most curious, we offer Mithradates Kallinikos and his son Antiochus I, kings of Commagene, a small mountain country famous for flowers, one of the last garden spots of the once-Fertile Crescent. Commagene only appeared as an independent state in 162 BC, as the Seleucid Kingdom was breaking up. For all the monuments those two left behind, you might think they ruled over a vast empire instead of a kingdom hardly more than 100 kilometres wide.

By the time of Mithradates and Antiochus, Commagene seems to have come upon some mysterious windfall (mining was long-established there). Whatever its source, the kings spent the money partly on a tough little army, and partly on self-glorification. From

Getting to and around Adıyaman Province (Commagene)

Tours to Nemrut Dağı and the Commagene sites are big business in these parts. From as far afield as Cappadocia, hotels, travel agencies and dolmuş drivers all run tours at (mostly) affordable prices. If you're entering the region from the northwest, Malatya is the most logical place to tour from, which is fine. The Malatya tourist office organizes trips to Nemrut Dağı, as do local agencies such as **Cem Tours** at Galeria İş Merkezi No.1/11, **t** 0422 322 6666, *www.cemtour.com*.

Adıyaman and Kahta may seem like the most obvious bases, both being close to the mountain, but there are problems attached to going from either, not least the fact that both towns are dismal places with nothing to see and everything to avoid. The second problem is that, for decades, the tour operators of both towns have had the reputation of being the most rapacious, avaricious specimens of Turkish manhood to be found between Edirne and Kars. Although the touristic downturn has forced them to clean up their act in recent years, old habits die hard and you still hear horror stories about their wheeling and dealing. There again, if you're dead set on seeing the summit at sunrise, these are the towns to go from. Just remember that you'll share the experience with countless others.

You can visit all the Commagene sites by **car**, but it's a long, petrol-gobbling trip with few road signs and no service stations along the backroads. You might wait until the tour buses go and follow them.

their largely Armenian subjects, these Greco-Persian Zoroastrian potentates asked only that they treat them as gods, and spend most of their free time carrying rocks up mountains to build them tombs. But even in their heyday, it was obvious that Commagene would eventually be swallowed up by Rome. Mark Antony himself tried to grab it in the Roman civil wars, but Antiochus's army forced him to abandon a siege of the capital, Samosata. After that unpleasantness, the Romans gradually took in the Commagene kings as clients, and they led the people in constant prayers to their ancestors until Vespasian finally deposed them in AD 72.

Nemrut Dağı

⭐ Nemrut Dağı

Nemrut Dağı, the mountain where Antiochus I is buried, has become one of the most popular tourist sights of Turkey, and the high seriousness of the deified Commagenes has at last got its just deserts. In **Adıyaman** or the dismal village of **Kahta**, at two in the morning, tourists are dragged out of bed and tossed into mini-buses for the long drive to Nemrut. Just as the first signs of dawn appear in the east, the long procession of headlights begins to snake up the mountain, and when the sun finally peeks over the horizon it finds the assemblage huddled together for warmth atop the stepped altar where Commagene hierophants once made dawn sacrifices to their defunct despot; blinking and mumbling, they gasp like people who have never seen a sunrise before.

In Kahta, they don't mention the stiff 20-minute walk from the car park and refreshment stand up to the summit. When you come to the end of the path, it joins the **Processional Way**, leading to the **East Terrace**, where five colossal statues face the dawn. The heads have toppled to the ground, although as Nemrut's popularity increases the Turks are starting to replace them. It's quite a job; they weigh several tons and the ground is extremely unstable.

Explaining just who these five were is difficult. The Commagene kings traced their lineage back to Alexander the Great on one side and the Persian king Darius on the other. In their little cosmopolitan state, halfway between Greece and Persia, they tried to keep up the Alexandrian principle of syncretism – combining similar gods from different cultures into a single figure, and creating out of the synthesis a new, heavily astrological cult, with room in its pantheon for the likes of Antiochus and Mithradates. Thus the aesthetic-looking fellow on the left is not only Apollo, but Mithra and Helios at the same time. Tyche, the only lady present, is the 'good spirit' of the Greeks, magnified into a figure that includes all the region's myriad goddesses. Zeus, or Ahuramazda, takes pride of place in the centre, with a pointed cap and bushy whiskers. Next comes Antiochus, and finally Heracles, or Artagnes or Ares. These five are flanked by pairs of equally colossal staring eagles and lions, looking perhaps for an empire to symbolize. The altar, a massive square of stone, is now occasionally used as a helicopter platform. All around, and on the backs of the statues, the Commagenes have left us the longest Greek inscription ever found, detailing their royal descent, their births, careers, and the rites with which they desired to be worshipped.

With all this to take in, it may escape your notice that the neat symmetrical peak of this mountain is a fake. Though the highest in the area, Nemrut isn't much of a mountain, and Antiochus found it necessary to add another 150ft of loose stones to get the desired silhouette. On the ground, it would make a fair-sized pyramid. Somewhere underneath, Antiochus lies buried, but the team of archaeologists who are cleaning up Nemrut have so far been unable to find his tomb; they fear any attempt at tunnelling will bring down the entire tumulus. An organization called the 'International Nemrut Foundation' is overseeing the effort.

Another path leads around the north side of the summit to the **West Terrace**. But for the lack of an altar, this is a carbon copy of the East Terrace, where the same five gods enjoy the sunset. Here, however, the statues are in better shape, and some of the sculptural reliefs have survived. Three of these portray Antiochus shaking hands with gods – Apollo, Zeus and Heracles. Another relief shows the constellation Leo with a carefully plotted backdrop of a crescent moon and a planetary conjunction; from this and the inscriptions, it has been calculated that Antiochus's coronation took place within 10 minutes of 7.30pm on 14 July 109 BC.

Not only is the sculptural work here of high artistic merit, but something about these thoughtful, expressive faces seems eerily modern. The Commagenes, for all their nonsense, were sophisticated rulers living at the height of the Greek world's achievements. We give the Greeks credit for the invention of the free man, the individual, but if these reliefs of Commagene symbolize anything it is the decay of that man, and his submission to the statist mysticisms of the East, a process that would later reach its culmination in the palaces of Constantinople.

You may mourn for this countryside, once celebrated for its beauty and fertility; something here has gone very wrong. Twenty years ago the poverty and depression of the people and the land was shocking. Although the GAP and the new, nearby oil fields have gone some way towards eradicating the worst, Commagene is still a rough place. Most of the hills have eroded into slag heaps, but here and there, in a cared-for field or lonely grove of trees, you can see how the grandeur of the mountain scenery was once complemented by greenery. No doubt Commagene had more rain in ancient times, but that doesn't account for all the change. Ambitious kings often lay their lands waste, and perhaps what we see around us is Antiochus's true memorial.

Arsameia and Karakuş

The other Commagene sites are in the valleys of the **Cendere** and **Nymphaion**, tributaries of the Euphrates, and can be seen, along with Nemrut, in a day. You won't see its capital Samosata; the scanty ruins of which now lie mostly under the waters of Atatürk Dam. **Arsameia**, higher up on the Nymphaion river, served as a summer capital; whatever endured of it into medieval times was incorporated into the Turkish castle called **Yeni Kale**. On the opposite hillside, the **Eski Kale**, despite its name, isn't really a castle at all, but the *hierothesion*, or temple tomb Antiochus built for his father Mithradates, not quite as grand as his own. At the entrance, a large upright slab bears a relief of Mithra, looking towards a large cave in the side of the mountain. It may be the only image of this god you will see in Turkey, in spite of the widespread popularity of this Persian cult, which as late as the 3rd century AD could claim more followers than Christianity. It seldom penetrated the Greek upper classes deeply enough to be expressed in art.

Where Mithra directs, in the cave, is another relief which depicts King Mithradates with Helios-Apollo. There is a large cistern opening out from the cave. From here, another path leads across the mountainside to the centrepiece of the *hierothesion*, where an even larger relief has Mithradates shaking hands with a clumsily sculpted Heracles. The king, portrayed as the taller and more impressive of the two, wears a tunic decorated with eight-pointed stars, the dynastic emblem of the Commagenes, who adopted it from Alexander. Next to this, a Greek inscription, similar to those on Nemrut, was carved over the entrance to a tunnel, leading over 300ft down stairs through the bare rock. What the purpose of this was, and where Mithradates may be buried, no one knows.

Where to Stay and Eat in Commagene

Adıyaman

★★★Bozdoğan, Atatürk Bulvarı, **t** 0416 216 3999, *www.otelbozdogan.com* (€€). At the western edge of town, and very much tour group territory. En suite doubles are comfortable but bland.

Unal, Harıkçı Caddesi 14, **t** 0416 216 1508, *www.unalhotel.com* (€). Amidst the hubbub of the town centre, this is rather basic but friendly and its staff try hard to keep customers happy.

Kahta

Pansiyon Kommagene, on the Girne Mah. Eski Kahta Yolu at the junction with the Nemrut Dağı road, **t** 0416 715 1092 (€€–€). Welcoming place that has doubles with toilet for €25/50 YTL, and also a campsite.

★★Hotel Bardakçı, Mustafa Kemal Caddesi, **t** 0416 725 8060, *www.bardakcihotel.com* (€). Across the way from the tourist office, newish with plain en suite rooms.

The road to Nemrut Dağı has a number of places to stay:

Karadut Pansiyon, in the tiny village of the same name, **t** 0416 737 2169, *www.karadutpansiyon.net* (€€). The most pleasant budget option; 40 YTL.

Kervansaray, on the right-hand side of the old road to the summit, several km beyond Karadut Köyü, **t** 0416 737 2190, *www.nemrutkervansaray.com* (€). Better for those who prefer a bit more comfort. The garden has a pool, and rooms cost €11/22 YTL per person, which includes dinner – not that you'd be eating anywhere else up here.

Akropolian restaurant, at the nearby lake. Good if you have your own transport and it's fish you're after; serves up freshwater fare on a pleasant terrace overlooking the water for under 10 YTL.

Leaving Arsameia for the third Commagene *hierothesion*, on a hill called **Karakuş**, you pass an **Ottoman bridge** over the Nymphaion; at the point where that stream, now called Kahta Çayı, empties into the Cendere stands a **Roman bridge**. Septimus Severus, who had it built, added two columns at each end, honouring himself and his family. Karakuş, a tumulus of small stones similar to Nemrut but smaller, holds the remains of Antiochus's wife. The tumulus was surrounded by tall columns surmounted by the Commagene familiars – eagles, lions and hand-shaking kings, of which only three remain erect. The eagle may have contributed the modern Turkish name: '*karakuş*' means 'black bird'.

Malatya and Elazığ

Malatya

Just north of ancient Commagene, a long chain of mountains, the Anti-Taurus, stretches the length of southeastern Anatolia from the Hatay to Lake Van. On the opposite northern slopes, the central highway from Kayseri to Van passes through difficult mountain terrain into the valley of the Murat River, climbing gradually upwards through *yaylalar* (highland pastures) crowded during the summer with nomadic herdsmen and their flocks.

Malatya, the first and most interesting of the towns along this route, cannot stand still. Although its history has been continuous

Getting to and around Malatya and Elazığ

THY **flights** connect Istanbul and Ankara with Malatya and Elazığ. The major east–west **rail** line to Lake Van passes through Elazığ and Malatya, and the only north–south line through the eastern provinces connects Sivas with Malatya.

Harput can be reached by **bus** from Elazığ. **Minibuses** go to Keban and Sivrice, a village on Hazar Gölü. Sivrice is also on the railway, but not on the same line as Elazığ; trains branch off for Elazığ in the north, on the way to Lake Van, and Diyarbakır to the south, a dead-end line that terminates near Siirt.

since the Hittites, it has occupied three different sites. The modern city, founded only in the early 19th century, has already grown to a population of almost 300,000, supporting themselves by modern industry and ancient crafts; the city has had a reputation for its copper works since the Middle Ages. Today you can see these for sale in the boisterous **bazaar area** north of the PTT Caddesi. While seeking out the copperware, you'll no doubt stumble across stalls heaving with dried apricots, for which the city is renowned.

Eski Malatya, the town gradually abandoned since the new foundation was begun, flourished in the 13th century as an eastern outpost of the Selcuk sultanate. Parts of the walls remain, along with some of the **Ulu Cami**, built in 1247 by the famous Selcuk architect Hüsrev: its outstanding entrance portal is a unique work with tiny faïence tiles set into the stone almost like mosaics.

If Malatya has not stayed on one site, it does have the distinction of holding on to its name as long as any city in Turkey. Records of both the Hittites and Assyrians speak of a city-state of Milid, or Milidia, that made a name for itself after the Hittite collapse and lasted until the Cimmerians sacked it in the 8th century BC, only to reappear in Roman times as Melitene. The site of ancient Malatya, where ruins of the palace can be seen, are at a spot the Turks call **Aslantepe** because of the reliefs of lions that once guarded its gate and now adorn the Ankara Museum. Aslantepe lies 11km north of modern Malatya, and Eski Malatya, the original site, a further 14km north along the same road.

Elazığ and Harput

Some 100km to the northeast of Malatya is another prospering modern town that tells much the same story. **Elazığ** too began in the last century. Named after its founder Abdül el-Aziz, it has gradually replaced the ancient city of **Harput**, 6km to the north, where there is less water, though Harput remains a sizeable town. Both once had large Armenian populations, decimated in the pogrom of 1895, and again in 1915. There is still an enchantment in the air of Harput, high on its hilltop. The people who have lived and fought here through the millennia – starting with the Hurri around 2000 BC, then Hittites, Urartians, Romans, Sassanids, Byzantines, Arabs, Byzantines again, Selcuks and Ottomans – have left behind tangible evidence, and also part of their spirit. The Turks feel this too; the area is full of legend and folklore.

In the centre of Harput, opposite the post office, is the 18th-century **Kurşunlu Mosque**. Walking up the main street, you pass, on your right, the **Cimşit Baths** and the **Sara Hatun Mosque**, both 16th-century, and, on your left, the heavily restored octagonal tomb of **Mansur Baba**, built in the 12th century during the time of the Artukoğulları emirs and destroyed by the Selcuks. Opposite this tomb is the **Ulu Cami**, also dating from the 12th century. Attached to the mosque is a medrese; together they form a rectangular building with a lovely open courtyard, surrounded by brick arcades. The minaret, broken off halfway down during an earthquake, leans jauntily and is decorated with brickwork flowers.

The **castle**, originally Urartian, is visible from the mosque, and was restored in 1997. Near the castle are the ruined **Hoca Hasan baths**. Back in the centre of town, the 13th-century **tomb and shrine of Arab Baba** shelters a disgusting mummy, complete with its skin. The original head has been broken off, and this is a replacement. The story goes that, in a year of drought, a woman had a dream, instructing her to take the head off Arab Baba and put it in water. This proved successful: it poured with rain and the whole town was flooded. In a second dream she was told to take the head out of the water and replace it on the body. The rain stopped, but the head didn't fit. So now Arab Baba is invested with magical qualities and people visit the shrine to pray for good fortune.

Elazığ owes its modern good fortune to the giant **Keban Dam**, built in the 1970s as the first stage of the Southeast Anatolia Project. Keban is a prohibited area, but tourists are welcome at the dam providing they produce a passport, stick with the guide and take no photographs. The approach to Keban is lovely; the road passes along a steep-sided rocky valley with the occasional waterfall. The first glimpse of the dam takes your breath away; surrounded by mountains, with the Euphrates emerging at the bottom in a beautiful mixture of blue, green and turquoise, it is a most impressive feat of engineering. Eight vast pipes, each 17ft in diameter, lead to the turbines. The dam backs up a huge **lake**, 400 square kilometres in area.

About 30km south of Elazığ is **Hazar Gölü**, a crater lake where camping and swimming are possible. However, as the lake is about 4,000ft above sea level, the season is very short – by late August, only the hardiest will feel like swimming. Beyond Elazığ, the country becomes steeper and less populated. **Bingöl** means 'a thousand lakes', and if 'thousand' in Turkish may really mean 'quite a few', the mountain scenery is still nice. Glaciers gouged out the lake beds two ice ages ago. The area and the town of Bingöl itself are still recovering from a bad earthquake in 2003.

Where to Stay and Eat in Malatya and Elazığ

(i) **Malatya >**
Valilik Binası (in a booth behind the Vilayet, the provincial government building on the main square), t 0422 323 2942

(i) **Elazığ >>**
Hükümet Konağı, 2nd floor, inside the Vilayet on Zübeyale Hanım Bulvarı, t 0424 212 2159

Malatya

**Malatya Büyük,Zafer İşhanı 1, t 0422 325 2828, *www.malatyabuyukhotel. com* (€€). Opposite the Yeni Cami and the best on offer. The rooms are bright and clean with small bathtubs en suite, and are keenly priced at 60 YTL when things are quiet. Although not prey to traffic noise, the Büyük's front rooms do get the full blast of the Yeni Cami's calls to prayer; the rooms at the back, on the other hand, overlook the lively bazaar area and are the perfect place to enjoy the sound of metal shop grilles being rolled up first thing in the morning.

Huzur, on a back street at Nasuhi Caddesi 6, t 0422 323 5928, *www. otelgrandhuzur.com* (€). Adequate if street noise is of paramount concern. Its rough and ready rooms are not as comfortable as the Büyük's, and those with shower and TV cost more.

Yeni Otel, Zafer İşhanı, t 0422 321 1090, *www.malatyayenihotel.com* (€€). Nestling in a back street directly behind the Malatya Büyük is the best cheaper choice in town, where

doubles with minuscule shower and toilet cost €30/55 YTL. With bedroom windows positioned just a few feet above the bazaar, this could make for unexpectedly early starts to the day.

Much of Malatya's city centre is given over to pleasant tea gardens, which can be found both in front of and behind the Vilayet.

Beyaz Saray, Kırgöz Mevkii, Battalgazi, t 0422 846 1246 (€). A dependable establishment. A full meal can be had for around 12 YTL.

Kaşık Restaurant, Hamit Feboglu Caddesi, Kanal Boyu, t 0422 323 6292 (€). Specializing in meat cooked in clay dishes, served sizzling hot from around 6 YTL.

Elazığ

Turistik Otel, Hürriyet Caddesi 41, t 0424 218 1772 (€). On a noisy street but more reasonably priced. Bright rooms with TV and shower.

Varran, İcadiye Mah. Sarı Saltuk Cad, t 0424 218 5770 (€). For relative peace and quiet, head for this friendly place off the busy main street.

Kilis Kebab Salonu, İşbankası Yanı, t 0424 236 7572 (€). A simple restaurant with some 50 years in the business of grilling meat.

Diyarbakır

 Diyarbakır

From Kahramanmaraş to Bitlis and beyond, the Anti-Taurus mark the southern limits of the Anatolian plateau. To the south of it, the land descends in a broad, broken plain towards the deserts of Syria. The Tigris and the Euphrates flow here, and by the time they reach this plain they've gathered enough tributaries to rank as important rivers, sufficiently impressive in their spring floods; by June they slow down to trickles. The country is fertile, and these tan and treeless plains have supported large populations for millennia.

The natural capital of this region is now and always has been Diyarbakır, the informal 'Kurdish capital' on the banks of the Tigris (*Dicle Nehri*). Few cities in the world are older. Though its beginnings are so ancient that not even legends survive, Diyarbakır has been a town at least since the time of the Hurrians, some 5,000 years ago. A record from Assyria's archives from a later age makes the first mention of the city by its ancient name of **Amida**.

Since antiquity, its citizens have brought dark, heavy basalt from the northern hills to build and rebuild its **walls**. Even today, these

Getting to Diyarbakır

There are direct **flights** every day from both Ankara and Istanbul to Diyarbakır. Otherwise, **buses** are the only way to get around this region. In the city, all the sights are within walking distance in the old town. The **bus and train stations** are some distance out, however. Buy your bus ticket in town; most companies have a free **minibus** service to the station. For sights outside the city, see p.511.

walls are the city's pride and its symbol: over the centuries they have made such an impression on the succession of travellers and conquerors who have passed beneath them that the city is renowned as 'Amid the Black'.

Like all these surprisingly large cities of southeastern Anatolia, Diyarbakır is modern, pleasant and booming, with a population nearing a million. However, although the recent political troubles seem to be on the wane, the city still has an almost tangible edge to it. Whilst its centre is colourful and lively by day and night, you should still follow your intuition and temper curiosity with caution.

History

Whoever built here first, the town plan shows Diyarbakır in its present form to be a child of the Romans. The city, like so many from Britain to Iraq, is a classic Roman *castrum*, roughly rectangular with two broad streets connecting the four gates at the cardinal points. The Romans under Constantius II built the oldest surviving sections of Diyarbakır's walls; beneath the later façades of black basalt arches and vaults, the characteristic thin Roman brick can be seen in many places. For the Romans, the city was a crucial bastion in the defence against the Sassanid Persians; later Roman emperors mounted campaigns here whenever they could, among them Julian the Apostate in 362–3.

For the next 300 years, Amida was a Christian town, often brimming with refugees from the surrounding settlements that fell to the Persians. Amida's own turn came in 639, when the new Muslim Arab army made the city its first important conquest within the present-day borders of Turkey; from this, Diyarbakır today likes to claim Turkey's oldest mosque, the Ulu Cami, and its oldest Arabic inscriptions. Curiously, despite its formidable walls, Diyarbakır was never especially successful at keeping out conquerors. The centuries that followed the decline of the Abbasid caliphate saw dozens of them check their turbans at Diyarbakır's gate. Nearly every warrior clan, great or obscure, that clutters the pages of Turkish history came to rule Amid the Black for a time: Marvanids, Selcuks, Damascus Selcuks, Nishanli, Artukid, Turkmen clans of White Sheep and Black, and more. Ottoman control, in the person of Selim the Grim, came in the 16th century.

Today, besides its walls, Diyarbakır is most proud of **watermelons**. They say their farmers grow the world's biggest, weighing up to

160lbs when the rains are good. The best-selling postcards in the town show hollowed-out melons with grinning children peeking out from inside. Diyarbakır also plays host to a commercial fair each year at the end of September, the **Ticaret ve Sanayi Fuarı**. One highlight of the festivities is a watermelon competition, in which the heaviest rather than the prettiest melon wins the cash prize.

Old Diyarbakır

Old Diyarbakır can be entered through two gates in the northern walls. In this area, some of the walls were demolished in favour of automobile traffic, while other parts have been included in the **50 Yıl Parkı** (Fiftieth Anniversary Park), which separates the new city from the old. Near the park's centre, **Çifte Kapı**, the 'twin gates', are a more modern incision in the walls, and near them stands a small 13th-century tomb, the **Sarı Saltık Türbe**, that can serve as an introduction to the city's unique and excellent vernacular architecture. Besides basalt, the region also yields a fine pale sandstone. In all their mosques, tombs and *hanlar*, Diyarbakır's medieval architects acquired the habit of using the two together, in alternating layers, so that within its walls Amid the Black becomes, less formidably, Amid the Striped. This practice has been continued in more recent times by city planners. who have surfaced Diyarbakır's pavements in alternate bands of black and white stone. The effect is very attractive, and few cities anywhere have managed the trick of evolving such a simple and lovely style to give themselves a sense of place. On many of the buildings, like the Sarı Saltık Türbe, what appear at first to be decorative plaques of the same black and white stone turn out to be Arabic inscriptions in the rectangular Kufic script, adding to the charm of the design.

The second entrance to the old town, only a few blocks east along İnönü Caddesi, was the **Harput Gate** in ancient times. This has become the busiest corner of the modern city. Every day these streets fill up with every manner of man: peasants from the countryside, street hawkers, soldiers, porters with their packs, smug-looking businessmen in expensive suits. As a backdrop, new hotels and office blocks of seven or eight floors push their way up through the chaos of the older buildings. Modern Diyarbakır makes its big splash outside the walls, where the biggest buildings and new shopping malls rise. But there's an increasing amount of modernity in the old city too, co-existing with the markets, the primeval alleys and the mosques. Of these, closest to the Harput Gate is the **Nebi** ('prophet') **Camii**, at the corner of Gazi Caddesi. This lovely and thoroughly striped mosque was built by the White Sheep clan (a Turkmen tribal federation) around 1530. Its typical minaret, striped also, like a giant ice-cream parfait, is tall and square, like the ancient ones in Harran and Şanlıurfa.

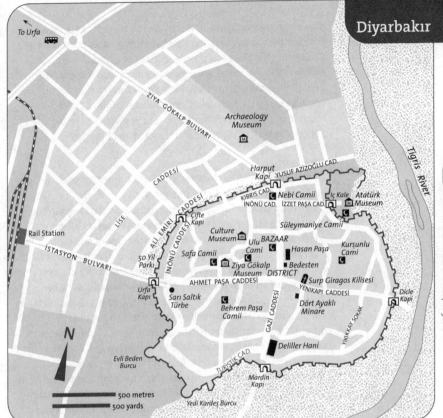

İç Kale

From this corner, **Gazi Caddesi**, one of two wide cross-streets of the Roman city, leads south towards the centre, while **İzzet Paşa** heads towards the Tigris and the İç Kale, or Inner Fortress, the oldest part of Diyarbakır. The grand pointed arch at the entrance is said to be all that remains from the palace of the Artukid Turks who once ruled here; on it can be seen their symbol, a lion attacking a bull. The bull represents worldly riches, and the lion those strong enough to seize them.

In the citadel, under venerable trees, there's room enough only for the provincial courts, the inevitable **Atatürk Museum**, one of two in the city, the late Roman church of **St George**, built into the walls, and the **Süleymaniye Camii** (or İç Kale Camii) begun in the 12th century. Of the city's landmarks, this mosque, with its tall minaret, is famous for the deep underground spring that supplies the water to its şadırvan in the courtyard. The water stays cold all year, which makes this a popular spot during the brutal summer days; it is probably the original spring that has supplied this citadel for 5,000 years. Outside the citadel walls, you can hire a horse-drawn carriage for a ride in the city, or else try to find your way through the narrow twisting streets of this quarter back to Gazi Caddesi. It won't be easy; the old sections of Diyarbakır are as exasperating a maze as any medieval town. If you're lucky, you may find another fine mosque, the **Fatih Paşa Camii** of 1520, better known here as the **Kurşunlu Cami** ('bullet mosque'). These ancient residential quarters are charming, though given over to the city's poor, in the modern fad for concrete apartment blocks.

Ulu Cami

Back on Gazi Caddesi, look for the Ulu Cami, just off the avenue behind a shady square that was the town's centre. This, perhaps the first mosque in Turkey, was reconstructed out of a Byzantine church called the Martoma. Most of what you see, however, was constructed by the Selcuks in the late 11th century, and many other rulers have had a hand in the reconstructions. The Artukids added parts of the courtyard, as evidenced by the lions and bulls over the main gate. This **courtyard** is the main attraction of this rather austere mosque. Almost everything in this area was quarried from older buildings. There are colonnades where each capital is different, columns stacked on larger columns, beautiful friezes of Greek designs next to Arabic Kufic script, intertwined with grapevines. Greek inscriptions look out from the walls.

While in this courtyard, you may hear a banging and clattering in the distance, as if a whole army of tinkers were nearby. They are – in their street in the crowded and colourful **market district** just outside these walls. As usual, every trade has its own part of the market; the ancient *bedesten* may be full of butchers now, but the street called 'Gold Alley' still glitters with scores of shops, and deals are still made in the **Hasan Paşa Hanı** of 1572, an excellent striped building that once was a great caravanserai terminal. It stands just across Gazi Caddesi from the Ulu Cami.

There are two museums within a short distance of each other in the streets just behind Ulu Cami. The **Ziya Gökalp Museum** was the home of that very influential turn-of-the century Turkish sociologist and writer, the father of secular Turkish nationalism and a great influence on Atatürk (ironically, many say he was really a Kurd). The home of one of his near contemporaries, the poet Cahit Sıtkı Tarancı, has become a **Culture Museum** in his honour, with exhibits of local arts and crafts. The house itself, with a typical courtyard decorated with patterns stencilled in whitewash, is a lovely example of the local fashion, and the poet's sitting room, with its stone fountain and elegant old radio, gives an insight into the heights of gracious living in the Diyarbakır of the 1930s. In this area, too, is the **Safa Camii**, with its striped porticos and one of the most unusual minarets in Diyarbakır.

South of Melek Ahmet Paşa Caddesi, the long east–west axis of the city (its name becomes Yenikapı Caddesi as it crosses Gazi Caddesi), stand two other interesting mosques. The **Behrem Paşa Camii** (1572) is claimed by some to be the jewel of Diyarbakır's mosques, and the **Kasim Padişah Camii**, just off Yenikapı Caddesi, is best known for its minaret, the **Dört Ayaklı Minare**, which is very lofty, but mysteriously separated from its mosque; indeed, the minaret is set up right in the middle of the street, hoisted in the air by four broad basalt columns. The locals claim that your wish will come true if you pass between the columns seven times. Near this mosque is one of Diyarbakır's two surviving Christian churches still in use, the Armenian **Surp Giragos Kilisesi**.

Another fine *han*, the **Deliller Hanı**, stands at the south end of Gazi Caddesi, at the Mardin Gate. An Ottoman work completed in 1527, it was built especially for travellers to Mecca. The city has recently restored this *han* from the ground up, and it has resumed its old function in a new way – as a modern hotel (*see* p.510).

The Walls

Mardin Gate, next to an odd, square *türbe* of uncertain origin, is a good place to begin a tour of Diyarbakır's walls. Few city walls have so much of interest chiselled into them. Inscriptions in every language, some as old as the Abbasid caliphs of the early 10th century, can be found anywhere – in decorative friezes around the towers, over the gates, in corners where no one looks. Almost every gun port has an inscription. In addition, there are several examples of medieval stonework. You can inspect the outside of the wall, walk over the top of it, and, in many places, even walk through it; numerous corridors inside the walls connect the inner chambers of the towers. The most impressive section is in the southwest, at a naturally weak point in the defences, where in 1208 the Artukids constructed two mighty bastions expanding out from earlier works of the Selcuks. The two round towers, the **Evli Beden Burcu** and the **Yedi Kardeş Burcu**, are almost identical, and are elaborately decorated. Yedi Kardeş ('Seven Brothers') probably takes its name from the seven chambers that radiate from the central hall inside.

From these walls, you can see a long and graceful **bridge** over the Tigris, built probably by the Ottomans; 'Ten Eyes' the locals call it, from its ten arches. According to another story, the *paşa* who built it caused a large sum of gold to be hidden under one of its piers.

Diyarbakır's **Archaeological Museum** includes items from as far back as Hittite times. It is located to the north of the city walls, next to the unmistakable pink Dedeman Hotel.

South of the walls by the Tigris, the **Gazi Köşkü** is a prettily striped 16th-century country house, built by a local bey and now housing a small museum, café and gardens.

Archaeological Museum

open Tues–Sun 8.30–12 and 1.30–5; closed Mon; adm

16 Southeastern Anatolia | Diyarbakır

(i) **Diyarbakır >**
*Dağkapı Burcu Giriş
Bolümü (inside the
Mountain Gate),*
t 0412 228 1706

⭐ **Güneydoğu
Gazeteciler
Cemiyeti >>**

Where to Stay in Diyarbakır

Diyarbakır

****Dedeman**, Elazığ Caddesi, t 0412 299 0000, *www.dedemanhotels.com* (€€€€). An apparition in pink outside the city walls, next to the archaeological museum. With its pastel décor and lifestyle floor full of boutiques and beauty parlours, you may be forgiven for thinking you've stumbled into the latest shopping mall. It does have a full checklist of amenities, though, including a pool and parking.

****Otel Büyük Kervansaray**, Gazi Caddesi, t 0412 228 9606 (€€€). Near Mardin Gate, the only hotel in town that is truly excellent, and better than those at much higher prices. It's a converted caravanserai, the Deliller Hani (*see* p.509) with elegance and peace, not to mention satellite TV, hard liquor and a large pool.

***Balkar**, Kıbrıs Caddesi 38, t 0412 228 1233 (€€). Clean, nondescript rooms with TV and air-conditioning.

Kaplan, off İnönü Caddesi at Sütçü Sokak 14, t 0412 224 9606, *www.hotelkaplan.com* (€). The pick of the cheaper hotels. All the rooms have air-conditioning and TV and some have en suites. Secure parking.

Kristal, off Kıbrıs Caddesi at Yoğurtçu Sokak 10, t 0412 224 0297 (€). Under the same management, equally good and identically priced.

Hotel Van Palas, İnönü Caddesi 3, t 0412 221 1218 (€). Where backpackers all seem to end up at and seem happy enough paying 12 YTL for a double.

Aslan Palas, Kıbrıs Caddesi 21, t 0412 223 6810 (€). Reasonable at 30 YTL, full of cigarette-sucking businessmen.

Eating Out in Diyarbakır

Otel Büyük Kervansaray, Gazi Caddesi, t 0412 228 9606 (€€€€). A conventional dining experience, offering meals in its relaxing courtyard for 40 YTL including wine.

Güneydoğu Gazeteciler Cemiyeti, or Journalists' Club of Southeast Anatolia, on the Ali Emiri Caddesi to the west of the Mountain Gate (Dağ Kapısı), t 0412 226 5717 (€€). Diyarbakır is not blessed with an abundance of good eating places, which is why its one hidden gem shines all the more if you can find it. An inconspicuous sign points you to a large, shady garden where the great and the good of Diyarbakır congregate for the city's best food – and cheapest beer. *Tava* is a house favourite, a sizzling platter of spicy lamb, mushrooms and tomatoes topped with cheese. Specialities of the region on offer include *haydari*, a mild yoghurt mixed with local herbs. But beware the mighty *kibe-mumbar*, a potent ribbed sausage filled with mixed meats. You could finish by ordering watermelon, which arrives at your table hollowed out with a candle inside. A blow-out meal may cost 25 YTL, but you can eat well for half that.

Around Diyarbakır

Most of the countryside of this region is given over to sheep and cattle, though nowadays GAP irrigation is making the dry hills blossom with cotton. If you look carefully, on many hillsides you can make out the traces of ancient agricultural terraces. More common, however, are the networks of faint lines winding around the lower slopes: the trails left by columns of sheep.

The landscape may be uninviting, especially in the summer, but it contains a good number of religious and antiquarian sites that foreign visitors seldom see. At **Ergani**, for instance, on the road to Elazığ, a very ancient mosque on the mountain called **Zülkifil Dağı** is dedicated as a shrine to Zülkifil (Ezekiel). This decidedly non-

Getting around Diyarbakır

In 2008, this is no place to be fooling around looking for ancient sites in the countryside. If the security situation improves, rural sights such as Deir az-Zafaran near Mardin can be seen by **taxi** or local **minibus** services; just check to make sure that there will be a way to get back. For motorists, the same caveats mentioned previously (p.XXX), regarding water and difficulties in finding your way to the sights, apply here. This area may also be your introduction to military checkpoints, which become more common the further east you travel. Although passing through one may initially feel disconcerting, the young conscripts who check your passport and car documents are usually polite and friendly.

Islamic prophet is honoured by Muslims and Christians alike. They say he is buried here, and people of both faiths make pilgrimages here from all over southern Anatolia. Another such site, at **Çüngüş**, is an 11th-century dervish retreat still in use. To the east, in **Hani**, pilgrims come to wash in the five-sided holy **Pool of Ayn Kebir**, reputed to have great healing powers. Ruins of the Greek city of **Dakyanos** lie near the town of **Lice**. Finally, in this region near the village of **Birklin** are caves near which is carved a relief of that most insufferable rooster of an Assyrian, King Tiglath-Pileser III, together with the usual cuneiform inscription boasting of his conquests.

Mardin

South of Diyarbakır, in the baking plains near the Syrian border, the highway for Mosul and Baghdad reaches a kind of world's end at Mardin, perched on the edge of the Syrian desert. Due south from here, the next towns of any size are Mecca and Medina, far off in Arabia. Mardin's reason for existence is its strong **citadel**; the name itself means 'fortress'. Though probably as old as Diyarbakır, Mardin has never been more than a distant outpost of any state that ruled it, with the exception of the Artukid Turks, who made it their capital in the 12th century. Mardin is often called the 'White City', in counterpoint to black Diyarbakır. The pale sandstone used, as in Şanlıurfa, for its homes and monuments gives the city a striking appearance when seen from a distance. Mardin speaks four languages, transacting its business in Turkish, Kurdish, Arabic and sometimes Aramaic (Syriac), the ancient language of the Holy Land, spoken by the population of Jacobite (Syrian Orthodox) Christians who have coexisted peacefully with their Muslim neighbours ever since the Arab conquest, barring a few nasty skirmishes that followed the Greek invasion in 1920.

The White City may be poor and primeval, but it is a place you won't forget; a stunning cityscape of terraces and houses, stacked up a steep mountainside and laced with shady passages under the houses like some Italian hill town. The houses come with ornate and charming stonecarving, and many have elegant courtyards. The Artukids built the city's two fine mosques, the **Ulu Cami**, with its distinctive ribbed dome and minaret, and the **İsa Bey Medrese** near the citadel, an unusual building with beautifully carved friezes and medallions on its gate. The new **museum**, in a building at Cumhuriyet Alani, has finds from 4000 BC to Ottoman times.

The region of the Jacobite or Syrian Christians is east of Mardin, around the attractive village of **Midyat**. Several Christian churches and monasteries here and in the surrounding villages are still occupied, including the recently restored **Mor Gabriel**, 20km east of Midyat, one of the oldest monasteries in the world (397).

Deir az-Zafaran

The greatest of the monasteries, the former home of the Syrian patriarchate, is Deir az-Zafaran. It is sparsely populated today, its days of massive wealth and influence never to return. Founded in 762, the monastery acquired the seat of the once-proud Patriarch of Antioch in 1293, retaining it for over 600 years until the anti-Christian riots that followed the Greek invasion led to the Patriarchate being shifted to Damascus. The monastery is only 8km from Mardin although it seems much further away, standing alone in the scorching Mesopotamian plain, its tawny stones barely distinguishable from the featureless desert.

One of the monks speaks English and acts as a tour guide for visitors, of whom there are few. He will point out the inscription above the doorway as you enter, inscribed in Aramaic, the language of Christ and the first tongue of this small monastic community. You will see the underground vault, reputedly used as a site of ritual sacrifice by sun-worshippers some 4,000 years before. The ceiling of the vault is astounding; an interlocking network of huge, flat stone slabs that support each other without the aid of mortar. Adjacent to the vault is a mausoleum, the last resting place of past patriarchs. The chapel is unspectacular – its riches were rushed to Damascus along with the patriarch in 1922. Around the chapel and in the courtyard outside are several rooms, each one containing a curio or two. You won't be shown the collection plate in the chapel, but you may like to know it's there.

Towards Lake Van

To go any further eastwards, you will have to retrace your steps to Diyarbakır. From there, the road to Lake Van passes through **Silvan**, a dusty farm town built in and around the ruins of a 6th-century Byzantine fortress. Some 24km further on, you cross the Batman, a tributary of the Tigris, on a modern bridge built parallel to the majestic single-arched **Malabadi Bridge**, a famous work of the Artukid Turks. Somewhere in this region, no one is sure where, one of the peculiar historical events that followed the collapse of the Seleucid Empire took place: the founding of the now completely vanished city of Tigranocerta.

Just beyond the Malabadi Bridge, the highway begins climbing into the lovely **Bitlis Mountains**, an eastern extension of the Taurus that serves to seal off Lake Van and the hidden valleys of Siirt and Hakkâri provinces from the rest of Anatolia. **Siirt**, a city of 300,000, is certainly one of the more out-of-the-way corners of Turkey; until the railway came in in 1944, it was lost in its own world, barely part of Turkey at all. Apart from the mountain scenery, the sole reason to head this way would be to visit the **Mausoleum and Museum of İbrahim Hakkı**, a complex from Ottoman times in the town of **Aydınlar**, 6km from Siirt. İbrahim Hakkı was a famous Muslim astronomer, and his observatory and instruments are here. Nobody – nobody – ever takes the road south to **Cizre**, at the point where Iraq, Syria and Turkey come together, but if you make it this far, they can show you the **tomb of Noah**; Muslims honour him as a prophet, and a mosque has been built around it.

On the map you'll notice that the railway line from Diyarbakır ignominiously fades out in the little village of **Kurtalan**, some 45km short of Siirt. This deserves an explanation. It's an obscure chapter in history now, but at the turn of the century, the Germans' plan for a Berlin–Baghdad railway was at the heart of the Kaiser's vast geopolitical scheme; he aimed to create a single economic sphere comprising all of Central Europe and the Middle East, dominated by Germany. The First World War, of course, intervened, and afterwards Kurtalan was as far as the line ever got.

Bitlis, deep in the mountains, is a town that sticks in the memory for the distinctive cool grey stone and rounded windows of the old buildings, which climb up steep streets to a well-preserved citadel built by the Ottomans. The **Ulu Cami** here, though restored several times, was originally a 12th-century Selcuk work. From here, it's only 22km to **Tatvan** on Lake Van, the terminal of the T.C. Denizyolları ferry that transfers rail users over the lake to Van.

Lake Van

Out here in Turkey's southeastern marches, on the shores of the bottle-green sea, it's quite simply another world. The superbly queer lake itself, the mighty volcanoes that add so much to the scenery along its shores and the exotic landmarks of the Armenians, Urartians and Kurds all coalesce to make this unique and fascinating country.

Take the lake for starters. Lake Van is old, even as geological time is measured; since the volcanic upthrusts that isolated this basin, water has been able to flow in, down from the mountains, but not out. With no circulation, the lake is left to stew in its own juice, a thick broth of sulphides and mineral salts; consequently, except in

Getting to and around Lake Van

Planes connect Van to Ankara twice daily and to Istanbul once per day. Istanbul Airlines, probably the cheapest, have flights three times a week to Istanbul.

In happier days the daily **train** from Istanbul ended at Tatvan, where the T.C. Denizyolları **steamer** awaited to carry its passengers and freight across to Van. In recent years this service has become less reliable. Trains now frequently terminate at Elazığ and there are no set times for the ferry. If you are planning to take it, check in advance that you're not going to be marooned in Tatvan for days on end.

Because of the rugged mountain terrain in this district, the **road** network is sparse. To travel from Van to **Akhtamar Island**, you may be able to find a **minibus** which goes from the centre of Van to the boat dock 8km beyond the village of Gevaş. Most probably you will have to change at Gevaş, or pay the driver another 10 YTL to take you the final stretch to the jetty. Another option is to get on one of the **intercity buses** en route to Diyarbakır and other western destinations; these can drop you off right next to the dock. The ferry goes when it fills up and costs whatever the boatman feels like asking, usually around 15 YTL per person, round trip. It's in your interest to go when others do, to avoid a long wait. If you find anyone in Van going on a group tour, ask when they're leaving and get there first.

If you're without a car, a trip to **Hoşap** can be made by bus or minibus, leaving from Cumhuriyet Caddesi near Van's tourist information office, but the return is chancy, especially if you want to stop at Çavuştepe.

The farther you get from Van, the more difficult getting around becomes. In some areas the army stops people from travelling after 3.30pm in summer, earlier in winter. Be advised that there is, as usual, a security problem in the mountain fastnesses where the paved roads don't go. In Siirt and Hakkâri provinces, and the southern fringes of Van, the PKK has lately been stepping up its ambushes of army and police patrols, and the security forces are very busy.

---

the fresher water at the mouths of the feeder streams, it has always been biologically dead. One wonders what the large gull population finds to eat; apart from the *darekh*, known as the poor man's herring, there are no fish, no molluscs, and no seaweed – but no pollution. The water, though the foulest-tasting stuff anywhere, is said to be good for your skin and you can swim in it without harm, although its high mineral content makes it sting if you have any cuts. The water is almost supernaturally luminescent, as if some as yet undiscovered light source lurks deep below. Though not unusually buoyant, it has a peculiar viscous appearance. It rises in billows and wrinkles, never in ripples or waves. Then there are the Van cats. This rare breed is supposedly fond of swimming; the cats have short legs, long white hair and one yellow and one blue eye. Their breeding and export is strictly controlled. One of the first sights to greet you as you arrive in Van from the west is a hideously cute pair of eight-foot-high concrete cats, erected in the middle of a busy traffic roundabout. The same Commissariat of Kitsch is no doubt responsible for the city's statue of the Lake Van Monster, a Loch Ness-style misplaced ichthyosaur who has been sighted a surprising number of times, for a country where alcohol is scarce.

The mountains circling Lake Van are full of **cave paintings**, some of them 15,000 years old. The Hurrians, the shadowy late Neolithic people who provided the indigenous stock of so much of Anatolia, arrived some time around the third millennium BC, and the population increased markedly in the second millennium BC, when a prolonged drought in the plains to the southwest caused many of the semi-nomadic tribes of that area to migrate into the mountains. In the 9th century, the lake's shores were the heartland of the new state of the Urartians. Today the ancient migrations are echoed in the annual spring wanderings of the shepherds, sometimes covering great distances, to their *yaylalar* or summer pastures in these highlands. From late May onwards their tents blossom everywhere in the mountains of eastern Anatolia, although today, more often than not, the shepherds and sheep make the trip by truck.

History

The Hurrian-Mitanni state that developed *c.* 1500 BC, lasting until the Assyrians exterminated it in the 9th century, marks the beginning of recorded history in the region. The Assyrians provide most of the records, mostly detailing the looting and carnage caused by their forays. To them, Lake Van was the 'Upper Sea', a strategic spot on the borders of their Hittite or Hurrian enemies. In their records of the 10th century BC, King Shalmaneser I claims victories over a new nation, the Uratri, or Urartu, the first mention of that name in history, at a time when the Urartians were probably nothing more than a feudal confederation for defence against the Assyrians (Urartu was an Assyrian name, the same as 'Ararat'; this people really called themselves Biainili, from which comes the name of Lake Van). The two centuries of Assyrian weakness that followed gave the Urartians the chance to build a nation and a culture for themselves, with its heartland around Lake Van but extending at times as far as the Black Sea and the Caspian; once they even sacked Babylon. The Assyrians were always Urartu's arch-enemy. The two nations fought until they both disappeared in the 7th century, to be replaced first by the short-lived Babylonian Empire, and soon after by the Persian Empire.

Even if the refined culture of the Urartians can be better seen in the museums of Ankara and Van than at the sites themselves, you can exercise your imagination in trying to recreate this lost culture on its own grounds. The accounts of the Assyrian King Sargon II describe the hills around Van as thickly forested with pines, beech and oaks; so dense, in fact, that Sargon's chronicles noted that his soldiers could only march through them two abreast (there are still some of these oak groves in the mountains near Bitlis). Rising up out of the forests on natural eminences were fortified palaces with whitewashed and, most likely, elaborately decorated walls, crowned with stepped crenellations like the gables of Dutch houses. Such scenes are portrayed on Urartian metalwork, which also shows kings in their chariots hunting wild game in the forests, and the priests in their rich costumes, trimmed with gold sashes and jewellery. Ordinary people, not surprisingly, do not appear

The Armenians

You don't hear much about Turkey's Armenians these days, but they're there. They keep to themselves, quietly going about their business and maintaining their churches. Their numbers are tiny, yet it was not so long ago that they lived here in their millions, in cities such as Van which, up to 1915, was almost exclusively Armenian. Yet the fact that Armenians still live in Turkey at all is surprising.

As the Urartian kingdom crumbled in eastern Anatolia in around 600 BC, the Armenians arose in their place, the new taking its name from the old, 'Armina' being 'Urartu' in the language of the most powerful nation of the day, the Persians. Some scholars believe the Armenians had been there all along, a subject people of the Urartians. Now they became loyal vassals of the Persians and in 331 BC, when Alexander's Macedonians met King Darius's Persians at Issus, the Armenian King Orontes II supplied 40,000 foot soldiers and 7,000 cavalry to comprise the Persian right flank. In the ensuing battle, Alexander swept the field. Orontes was killed, Darius fled to die from the knives of his courtiers, and the long Armenian tradition of backing the wrong horse was born.

The Armenian kingdom, after Alexander's death a Seleucid province, stumbled on for a century or so, occasionally doing battle with its overlords, always losing, except during the brief, glorious career of Tigranes the Great. Throughout the years that followed, Armenia enjoyed an independence that depended largely on the goodwill of whoever was powerful in the area at the time, be they Byzantine, Selcuk, Georgian or Ottoman. Most of the time, the big powers left them alone, despite their stubborn Christianity in a largely Islamic region. Indeed, Armenia was the first nation to accept Christianity as its state religion, in 301, 36 years before Constantine's deathbed conversion.

The early Middle Ages saw a brief Armenian renaissance. Ani (see pp.471–5) boomed, art and architecture flourished, and small Armenian provinces were established on the southern coast of Anatolia; but by the 13th century continuous raids by Mongols from the east were exerting a heavy toll on the kingdom's wealth and strength. In 1463 the Ottomans stepped in with ease. For over 400 years, Turks and Armenians enjoyed a mostly peaceful coexistence, despite their differing faiths. In many ways, the Armenians became vital to the Ottoman regime; they were literate when most of the Ottoman populace was not, they had good business sense, and they held top positions in the civil service and in finance. None of this endeared them to the Ottoman peasant, particularly towards the end of the 19th century when the empire was in terminal decline and the people getting poorer by the day. It was a time when blame for the empire's ills had to be apportioned somewhere and the infidel, prosperous Armenians fitted the bill perfectly. Anti-Armenian riots occurred, the biggest coming in 1895; Armenian villages were sacked and their inhabitants murdered and the sultans, eager for a scapegoat for their own woeful shortcomings, were happy to nod approvingly. The situation worsened when the Great War began. Turkey was fighting Christian Russia, and to the Young Turks of Enver Paşa the Armenians were nothing more than the country's fifth column. To an extent, this was true. Many Armenians did see the Tsarist army as a liberating force from Turkish oppression and offered assistance accordingly. It must also be said that the Armenians would respond in kind to the brutalities meted out to them, and the sight of burning Turkish villages within the Armenian provinces became common.

Yet no one could have foreseen the solution the Young Turks had to the 'Armenian problem'. In April 1915, orders were given for the round-up and deportation of the entire Armenian population. Whether or not the Young Turk leaders also actually planned their wholesale massacre may never be known – but that is what happened. Whole towns and cities were emptied of Armenians, who were then marched south into the Mesopotamian desert, without food or water. Those who survived these forced marches were then either shot or simply left to die. Armenians working in the civil service or serving with the Turkish army were taken from their offices or barracks and shot. The Armenians claim that over a million of their countrymen were murdered; the Turkish government estimates some 250,000. Whichever, the issue will probably go on poisoning international relations indefinitely. Not so long ago, the new Armenian government shot itself in the foot, blowing a crucial trade and communications deal with Turkey by insisting the Turks publicly agree to their side of the story. Because of this issue, the Turkish-Armenian border has been closed for over ten years. Holding the modern Turkish republic responsible for the crimes of its decadent, defunct predecessor is blatantly unfair. The Turks, for their part, continue to be incredibly touchy and defensive about such affairs – Turkish politicians, especially, don't seem to have noticed that their nation is mature enough to stand a little more openness.

anywhere in Urartian art; some evidence from the inscriptions has led scholars to believe the Urartians were a slave society as brutal as that of their Assyrian neighbours. Their art makes us wish to disbelieve it, but probably, in that nest of snakes that was the early Middle East, it could hardly have been otherwise.

Süphan Dağı and Nemrut Dağı

Two mighty volcanoes crowd the north shore of Lake Van, creating a centrepiece for the region's postcard scenery. At 13,188ft, **Süphan Dağı** is the third-highest peak in Turkey, its summit snow-covered most of the year. Like Ararat, Süphan Dağı towers alone over the low hills, and provides a landmark for the entire region.

The second peak, **Nemrut Dağı**, barely pokes its head above the lofty mountains behind Tatvan. Not to be confused with the Nemrut Dağı of Commagene, this Nemrut, instead of having colossi on top, boasts a lake, **Nemrut Gölü**, rather like the famous Crater Lake in Oregon but without the trees. There are actually several lakes, some hot and some cold, and the odd volcanic formations create a genuine scenic wonder. Only part of the road up is asphalted and no organized transport exists. You have to climb it yourself, or find someone in Tatvan with a jeep.

Ahlat and Adilcevaz

Ahlat, on the lake shore under Nemrut, was an Armenian principality that flourished under the Selcuks, becoming so famous for stone-carving that its artists were in demand throughout Anatolia. Over the centuries, the city was gradually abandoned, and today, in this grave of a town, only the graves remain; there are several fine *türbeler* of the 13th–15th centuries, and a famous graveyard of distinctive Selcuk tombstones. Strangely, these heavy, rectangular, upright stones of volcanic rock, most taller than a man, have been more painstakingly carved with more elaborate designs than any of the mausolea, each with a kind of window at its centre, surrounded by calligraphy and geometric designs so densely packed that they resemble some Mayan relief. No others exist outside the Van region. Near the town of **Adilcevaz**, some 25km further along the shore, are the remains of an unnamed Urartian town built by King Rusa II; the Turks call it **Kefkalesi**. As the fine stone reliefs discovered here have been removed to the Van museum, little remains to be seen.

Akhtamar Island and its Church

 Akhtamar Island

Along the southern edge of the lake, mountains prevent the road from hugging the shore for over half the distance to Van. When the road finally winds down from the hills, it affords a wonderful prospect of the lake, its surrounding mountains, and its several islands, the largest of which is **Akhtamar**.

During the 10th and 11th centuries, the same period when the Armenian kingdom at Ani was in full flower, a separate Armenian state called Vaspurakan flourished on the shores of Lake Van. The greatest of the Vaspurakan kings, named Gagik like his contemporary in Ani, constructed a palace for himself on this lovely island c. 920, and raised next to it the **Church of the Holy Cross**, a sight no one should miss if they're anywhere near Lake Van.

It is perhaps the obscurity of these Armenian kingdoms that has denied their sacred structures their rightful place in the history of art. But 200 years before anything resembling them was produced in Europe, and 300 years before the best Selcuk work, this nation, with no greater cultural influence than its tenuous link to Byzantium, created a masterpiece like Akhtamar. In those rough times, it is as if the Armenians had pulled it out of a hat. The government restored the church in 2007, and now runs it as a 'museum', like the Aya Sofia.

In form, Akhtamar differs very little from the churches of Ani. Its central plan supports the usual drum and conical dome; here, strangely, the drum is 14-sided and irregular. What makes the church such a jewel is the wealth of sculpture, in an unusual squarish style of high relief possibly unique to this building. Later additions have defaced the structure somewhat – a low, clumsy porch and what might be either a bell tower or a minaret. The tower has a sundial, like some of the churches at Ani, but on the other hand, it also has Islamic-style stalactite decoration.

The reliefs of the original church nearly cover it from top to bottom. So rich and varied are its subjects, it seems the artists' intention was not just to tell the whole story of the Bible, but to weave in the fabric of life itself. With infinite care for detail, Akhtamar exhausts the eye before it exhausts the interest: one could gaze upon it for days on end and still find new scenes.

The foundations of Gagik's **palace** surround the church. The only other building lies on a small islet nearby, the romantic ruin of a **chapel** that greets you near the pier on your arrival from the mainland. Akhtamar Island is uninhabited, but it's a beautiful spot, a bare cliff rising straight out of the lake and sloping gently down to the east. There's a beach and a picnic grove, and most visitors spend the whole morning or afternoon on the island. When you're through with the church, take time to observe the equally fascinating variety of the island's natural life; besides the many birds and flowers, some of which you'll never see on the mainland, there are innumerable secret kingdoms of insects among the ruins and rocks, droning away in a hundred different voices, displaying a hundred exotic shapes and colours. Separated by a mile of poisonous water from the rest of the world, the wildlife of Akhtamar Island has evolved into a world of its own.

The quay for ferries to the island lies off the Van–Tatvan road, near **Gevaş**, 30km from the city of Van. In Gevaş, a 14th-century Turkish princess lies in an elegant 12-sided *türbe*, and nearby there's a graveyard with some of the same curious stones as at Ahlat. In the mountains above the town, the village of **Çatak** is located in a wooded corner of the region; near it the waterfalls of **Gahnisipi** carry a distant tributary of the Tigris.

Van

The city goes back to the 9th century BC and the Urartian King Sarduri I, its founder. His capital, originally called Tushpa, was erected on a great rock on the lake shore that has been the heart of the city throughout its existence; or at least until the First World War, when old Van was completely destroyed in battles first with the Armenians and later with the Russians. Instead of rebuilding on the spot, the new population of Van instead relocated their town to a higher and healthier spot, just over a kilometre from the lake. It was hardly under way when a big 1950 earthquake levelled the place. Modern Van, not surprisingly, has little of interest, but is making a credible start toward becoming a pleasant town.

Very little remains of old Van apart from the **citadel** (Van Kalesi) on the rock 5km from the centre. Here, above the serious, neatly cut 30-ton blocks of the Urartian master masons, a succession of Armenian and Turkish rulers built Van's castle in rubble wall and mud brick, now just eroded enough to give the whole an outlandish appearance, like an outsized sandcastle after the tide has turned. The foundations of the Urartian castle, called **Sardurburcu** today, yielded numerous inscriptions that have contributed much to our knowledge of the Urartians. Most concern relations with Assyria, and the older ones are written in Assyrian cuneiform, the first script used by the Urartians, while later writings appear in their own hieroglyphs. The best examples of cuneiform can be seen in a series of tombs cut into the south side of the rock. The path to them is sealed off by a gate but a caretaker is normally on hand to show visitors around.

From the citadel, the ruins of Armenian Van can be seen, as well as the second Urartian capital of Toprakkale, built in the last century of the kingdom's existence. Just why, no one knows; Tushpa, though often besieged, was never taken. The foundations of a temple and palace remain, but as the site is located in a military zone, it cannot now be visited.

Van Museum
*open Tues–Sun 8–12
and 1.30–5.30;
closed Mon; adm*

However, you can see the best of both Urartian sites and many others at the **Van Museum**, one block north of Cumhuriyet Caddesi, with one of the best archaeological collections of any provincial museum. Here, the outdoor sculpture garden competes with the works inside for one's attention. The star of the collection is an exquisitely carved relief of the god Teshup, for whom the Urartian capital was named. Teshup stands on the back of a bull, Hittite-fashion, and near him are what appear to be two tridents with their tines shaped like leaves, an unusual attribute for a god of storms. Inside, the museum offers the best collection of Urartian art works, surpassing even Ankara's. There are many examples of intricately carved jewellery and cylinder seals, and the well-known bronze and gold plates and belts, engraved with lions, bulls, sphinxes, hunting scenes and religious processions. One intriguing subject is a seated god with a head that resembles the famous Hatti cosmos symbols in the Ankara museum. The Urartians were also skilled in casting bronze, shown here by brooches and bells, and standards in the form of antlers. Finally, there's an Urartian gameboard, for which you'll have to imagine the rules.

To remind us that even the Urartians were really mere latecomers in this ancient land, the museum also contains some of the pictographs archaeologists found carved on rocks on the **Trişin Kaya Plateau**, 120km south of Van. Some go as far back as 9000 BC, depicting animals such as bison and reindeer that have long since died out in this region. One theory as to why these ancient pictographs look so similar to the primitive motifs appearing on some of this region's carpets and kilims is that the local women who wove them spent their summers in tents high on the plateau, surrounded by a vast outdoor gallery of neglected Stone Age art.

Turkey's Southeast Corner

Lake Van isn't the only lake around. The topography from Ararat down to the Mesopotamian plain was formed by volcanic action, and instead of neatly folded linear mountain ranges, patches and circlets of extinct volcanoes and lava plateaus surround a series of isolated basins, some low enough to be lakes. Other large lakes are nearby in the Republic of Armenia, and Lake Orumiyeh in Iran is even bigger than Lake Van. Sheep thrive here; difficulty of access makes this corner of Turkey one of the quietest and least known parts of the nation.

These mountain fortresses are the heart of Kurdistan, and depending on your outlook you may see them as the last strongholds of the traditional Kurdish mountain culture, or merely as backward and poor. Either way, the setting, in the streams and woods of Hakkâri province, is one of the most scenic in all Turkey. Only one road leads into this province, following the lovely valley of the River Zap as it negotiates its way through the mountains.

Some 36km southeast from Van, this road passes the ruins called **Çavuştepe**, the 8th-century BC Urartian palace-city of **Sardurihinili**. Sarduri II founded it and named it after himself, and here many of the finest art works of the Urartians have been found. At first glance, the long narrow ridge at the centre of a mountain basin seems much too thin for any sort of a city to fit on it. It is – only the fortress and palace stood here – but look closely down at the fields and faint traces of ancient streets and foundations will become visible, though they've been tilled over for centuries.

Sarduri's palace must have been a work of some architectural sophistication, strung out along an arrow-straight axis from the castle at the highest point of the ridge, down through the upper and lower terraces of the palace. You can follow the long corridor along this axis, past the royal apartments and offices, the cisterns and storerooms with their huge *pithoi*. As always, only the foundations (of finely worked masonry) remain; in the lower terrace a cuneiform inscription states that Sarduri built the palace and city in honour of 'Haldi, the War God'. Sarduri goes on to speak of 'cities and gardens where nothing was before', and if you look down at the southern flank of the ridge you'll see the famous work that made it possible. The **Semiramis Canal**, associated with that legendary queen but actually a project of the Urartian King Menua, is a 52km irrigation canal still in use after 2,700 years. During the extensive excavations of Çavuştepe, tens of thousands of arrowheads (Scythian in origin) were found scattered in and around the fortress and stuck in Sardurihinili's walls, testimony to the violent and sudden end of Urartian civilization.

Hoşap

When the great states falter, isolated regions like this naturally revert to the feudal rule of the local strongman. As evidence from another age, take in the wonderfully evocative **Castle of Hoşap**, gripping the summit of a tall crag along the main road some 23km beyond Çavuştepe. Hoşap appears on Turkish maps as **Güzelsu**; both names mean 'sweet waters', referring to the springs in the village below, but Hoşap is a Kurdish word and this is a Kurdish castle, built in 1643 by a local despot named Sarı Süleyman in the days when Ottoman control over these parts was slipping.

Hoşap could easily be a castle on the Rhine; certainly it's the only substantial fortification in this corner of Turkey since the days of the Urartians. However he came by it, Sarı Süleyman had the money to do the job right; his great gate with its carved lions and

Where to Stay on Lake Van

ⓘ Van ›

Cumhuriyet Caddesi 19, t 0432 216 2530/2018

Van

***Büyük Urartu Hotel, Cumhuriyet Caddesi 60, **t** 0432 212 0660 (€€). Van's nicest, with a lobby adorned in Urartian Art Deco, spoiled only by a location in one of the dingier parts of town.

Büyük Asur, Cumhuriyet Caddesi, Turizm Sokak 5, next to the tourist information office, **t 0432 216 8792, *www.buyukasur.com* (€€). Its faded charms may not appeal to everyone, but it has a welcoming air.

***Yakut, Posta Caddesi 8, **t** 0432 214 2832 (€€–€). On a quiet street and offering a far better deal. Posted prices for en suite doubles with TV and mini bar are a notional €39/78 YTL, but the receptionist quotes only half that.

Ada Palas, off Cumhuriyet Caddesi, near HSBC Bank, **t** 0432 216 2234 (€). There's no shower, and your roommates may well be grizzled Iranian truckies who'll hawk and spit in the morning with a gusto you would never believe possible.

Eating Out on Lake Van

Van has several good *lokantas*, all serving meals for around 10 YTL.

Merkez, İskele Caddesi Karayolları Kavşağı, **t** 0432 216 9701 (€). On the edge of town, sharing the same premises and management as a petrol station, this is an unlikely venue for excellent cuisine. It's a ten-minute taxi ride from the centre. Don't be put off by the mirrored glass façade, as inside they serve excellent traditional food, including *tandır* kebab and lamb which falls off the bone.

Besse Restaurant, Sanat Sokak, parallel to Cumhuriyet Caddesi, **t** 0432 215 0050 (€). A great selection of meat and freshwater fish, and by Van standards it is also relatively stylish.

Çınar Restaurant, attached to the Bayram Hotel, Cumhuriyet Caddesi 1/A (€). Clean, bright and conveniently central, with a relaxed family atmosphere.

Büryancı Azmi Usta'nın Yeri, Balıkçılar Sok. No.17, **t** 0434 226 1370 (€). One of several *lokantas* in the area specializing in the local *büryan* kebab: lamb cooked in an underground earth oven which normally begins its roasting process at around 6am, so it is ready in time for lunch. Often accompanied by *büryan* soup. Get in there quick; these places close by 3pm.

Sütçü Fevzi, Cumhuriyet Caddesi, Eski Sümerbank Sokak 11 (€). A good bet for a cheap breakfast, open from 4am: bread, butter, Van honey and cheese, olives and all the tea you can drink for 8 YTL. You could ask to try *otlu peynir*, a tangy Kurdish cheese that looks more like bread dough. If they don't have any that day, you'll be able to find some in the shops along Cumhuriyet Caddesi.

Akdamar Adası Restaurant and Camping (€). The basic Akhtamar *lokanta*, frequented by tour groups, serves grilled lake fish for 6 YTL. Elsewhere in the province, don't expect anything special and remember to eat early; most places are closed by early evening.

teardrop arabesques is both impressive and beautiful. From the castle, it's easy to make out the wall that once enclosed the town of Hoşap, now a mere village. Also from the castle, you can look over to the mountains of Iran and Iraq. This is about the end of the line; beyond Hoşap, you can take the scenic route as far as **Hakkâri**, a dull, small provincial capital set among exquisite mountains, lately swarming with troops.

Language

Linguists say Turkish is a member of the Ural-Altaic group, which makes it related to Finnish, Hungarian and little else. Dialects are spoken by perhaps as many as 100 million Turcomans, Kirghiz, Uzbeks and others in Central Asia, as well as the 50 million Turks in Turkey; a Turk from Istanbul could make himself understood as far east as Manchuria. He couldn't get far, though, in Helsinki or Budapest. This is one of the truly grey areas in linguistics, but what strongly suggests these languages have a common origin is their use of agglutination. Turkish has no prepositions, and most of the difficulties of the language are caused by the subtleties of the infinite number of suffixes that are tacked onto words or replace them. In this book, for instance, words may often be disguised by their endings: Yeşil Cami – Green Mosque, but Rüstem Paşa Camii – Mosque of Rüstem Pasha.

The Turks are very proud of their language, with its long and distinguished list of poets and writers, its melodious vowel harmony, and its wealth of expressive colloquialisms. There is even a slang dictionary for Turkish. The Turks love playing word games; there are palindromes like 'Traş niçin şart?' or 'Why get a haircut?', and nightmares of agglutination.

Like the French, the Turks have a semi-official body concerned with maintaining the purity of the language. In the 1930s, this was a hot political issue; reforming the language was one of Atatürk's pet ideas, and he replaced thousands of Arabic, Persian and Greek words with 'Turkish' equivalents, either invented or found in use in obscure corners of the nation. The drive for reform slowed down when parents began to have trouble understanding their children – and Atatürk's speeches. The 1930s was also the decade of the great **Alphabet Reform**. Previously, Turkish, with its eight vowels, had been shoe-horned into Arabic characters, which have only three, with results such as the words for 'great' and 'dead' being written the same (*ulu*, *ölü*). In part for this reason, but also to make European languages accessible to the Turks, Atatürk decreed that the change must be made. Throughout the decade, he travelled to almost every large town in Turkey with chalk and a blackboard. While the people crowded around in thousands to see their nation's hero, they got their first lesson in Roman letters. Amazingly, it all worked, far better, in fact, than Atatürk ever dreamed. The changeover that was supposed to take fifteen years was accomplished in five.

Learning Turkish

If you want to learn some Turkish before you go, try either *Teach Yourself Turkish* by Asuman Celen Pollard and David Pollard

---

Language Quiz!

You may well know more Turkish than you think. Try and puzzle out these common words:
şoför küaför şantöz komplo şofben org otogar fayton şanjman pardesü
Partly thanks to the Lise (*lycée*) of Galatasaray, where the late Ottoman Empire's élite was trained, French cultural influence has always been strong here, and hundreds of French words insinuated themselves into the language, mostly for modern inventions and innovations. After Atatürk's revolution all of these were spelled out phonetically in Turkish, so they may not look familiar at first glance. The answers: *chauffeur, coiffeur, chanteuse, complot* (a conspiracy), *chauffe-bain* (a water heater), *orgue* (organ), *autogare* (the bus station), *phaeton* (the horse-drawn carriages they still use on the Princes' Islands), *changement* (gearshift), *par-dessus* (those ugly overcoats pious Muslim women have to wear).

(Teach Yourself, 2004), or *Colloquial Turkish* by Ad Backus, Sinan Bayraktaroğlus *et al* (Routledge, 2000), both of which come with audio CDs. Failing that, if you can learn the numbers and some of the words listed below, you can communicate almost all your wishes. Literature from the Turkish Travel Office tends to overestimate the number of people you'll find who speak English or German (which does come in handy, though). Knowing just a few words will endear you to the Turks and probably prevent you from getting ripped off.

Yok is an essential word to know. Its meaning approximates to 'There is none', but it's used much more commonly than 'no' (*hayır*). It is a sentence from which there is no appeal. If a Turk is at all inclined to help you out he will exhaust all possibilities before intoning the fatal *yok*. Its positive counterpart is *var* ('There is'), always a cheering note in Turkey, although when you do get it, it may not be what you expected.

Turkish **plural** forms are *-ler* or *-lar* added to the end of the word, for example *adam* (man), *adamlar* (men), or *kalem* (pen), *kalemler* (pens).

Pronunciation

This is regular and logical, since the alphabet was designed to fit the language.

The **vowels** are pronounced as follows, not always as they would be in English:

a	between *u* in 'fuss' and *a* in 'flat'
â	faint *y* sound in preceding consonant; *lâleli* is lyaah-leh-lee
ay	*i* in 'bike'
e	*e* in 'pet'
i / İ	between *i* in 'hit' and *ee* in 'meet'
ı / I	the half-swallowed vowel sound of *a* in 'about' or *e* in unstressed 'the'
o	*o* in 'pot'
ö	the *er* sound in the middle of 'word'
u	the *oo* in 'moo'
ü	the *u* in French '*tu*' or German *ü*

These **consonants** are significantly different from English:

ç	*ch* as in 'chin'
c	pronounced like the English *j*
g	always hard, as in 'goat'
ğ	silent, as the *gh* in 'eight'; it sometimes lengthens the preceding vowel
j	*zh* as in 'measure'
ş	*sh* as in 'ship'
v	more like the English *w*

Something that could cause confusion is **vowel harmony**. There are two sorts of vowel: the 'back' vowels (**a**, undotted **ı**, **o** and **u**) and the 'front' vowels (**e**, **i**, **ö** and **ü**). Genuine Turkish words contain one of these sorts of vowel only, and suffixes have their vowels changed, if necessary, to comply with the rules of vowel harmony. Words of foreign origin, like *şoför* (chauffeur) often contain a mixture of the two types of vowel.

Note: Turkish **syllables** almost always carry equal weight. If there is any **stress**, it will usually be at the end. Besides forgetting that **c** is sounded like English *j*, the most common mistake foreigners make is to put stresses where they don't belong. We do it naturally, but it makes Turkish words unintelligible.

Verbs

If you want to try a few sentences, here are some verbs and how to use them.

The verbs 'to be' and 'to have' don't really exist in Turkish. 'To be' appears as a suffix, as in, for example:

İngilizim English – I am
Türküm Turk – you are

Var, 'there is', and *yok* 'there is not' are used in place of 'to have'. For example:

Su var There is water
Su yok There is no water

Common Verbs

anlamak	ahn-lah-mahk	to understand
bakmak	bahk-mahk	to look
beğenmek	beh-ehn-mehk	to like
beklemek	behk-leh-mehk	to wait
bilmek	bihl-mehk	to know
çalışmak	chahl-ush-mahk	to work
dinlemek	dihn-leh-mehk	to listen
dinlenmek	dihn-lehn-mehk	to rest
duymak	dooy-mahk	to hear
gelmek	gehl-mehk	to come
gezmek	gehz-mekh	to walk
gitmek	giht-mehk	to go
görmek	geur-mehk	to see

içmek	ihch-mehk	to drink
istemek	ihs-teh-mehk	to want
konuşmak	koh-noosh-mahk	to speak
öğrenmek	er-ehn-mehk	to learn
okumak	oh-kool-mahk	to read
sevmek	sehv-mehk	to love
uyanmak	oo-yahn-mahk	to wake up
uyumak	oo-yoo-mahk	to sleep
yazmak	yahz-mahk	to write
yemek	yeh-mehk	to eat
yüzmek	yeuz-mehk	to swim

To form the present continuous, future and past definite tenses, a tense marker is added to the verb root, followed by the suffix indicating person. Vowel harmony is obeyed.

-yor- is the present continuous tense marker. After consonants, an **i** is inserted. Thus, using *gezmek*, we have:

geziyorum I am walking
geziyorsun you are walking
geziyor he/she/it is walking
geziyoruz we are walking
geziyorsunuz you are walking
geziyorlar they are walking

-ecek- is the future tense marker. Before a vowel, the **k** turns into a **ğ**:

gezeceğim I will talk
gezeceksin you will walk
gezecek he/she/it will walk
gezeceğiz we will walk
gezeceksiniz you will walk
gezecekler they will walk

-d- is the past definite tense marker:

gezdim I walked
gezdin you walked
gezdi he/she/it walked
gezdik we walked
gezdiniz you walked
gezdiler they walked

A verb is turned into the negative form by inserting *-mi-* between the root and the tense marker. For example:

geziyorum I'm walking
gezmiyorum I'm not walking

A question is formed by inserting *-mi-* after the tense marker, or in the case of the past definite tense, after the whole word:

geziyorsun you are walking
geziyor musun? are you walking?
gezdin you walked
gezdin mi? did you walk?

There is no need to use **personal pronouns**, except for emphasis, or if you are worried that you have got it wrong. They are:

ben I
siz you
o he/she/it
biz we
sen you
onlar they

Vocabulary

We have represented the sounds of the Turkish **ü** as *eu* and **ö** as *er*. The sound of **ı** is represented by *uh* and that of **ay** as *iy*. See above for the pronunciation of these vowels.

Signs

dikkat (dee-kat) caution
dur (doohr) stop
girilmez (gee-reel-mez) no entry
şehir merkezi (sheh-heer mer-keh-zee) city centre
sigara içilmez (sih-gah-rah itch-il-mez) no smoking
tehlike (teh-lee-keh) danger
tekistikamet (tek-ee-stee-kah-met) one way
yasak bölge (yah-sak berl-geh) forbidden area
askeri bölge (as-ker-ee berl-geh) military area (i.e. no photographs)
yavaş (yah-vash) slow

Places

ada (ah-dah) island
bekçi (bek-chee) caretaker
çay (chiy) stream
cadde/caddesi (jah-deh/ jah-deh-sih) street
cami (jah-mee) mosque
çarşı (chahr-shuh) market, bazaar
çeşme (chesh-meh) fountain
çiftlik (chihft-lihk) farm
deniz (deh-nihz) sea
dere (deh-reh) valley
geçit (geh-chit) pass
göl (gerhl) lake
hamam (hah-mahm) Turkish bath
han (hahn) inn
hisar (hih-sahr) castle
höyük (her-yeuk) mound
ırmak (uhr-mahk) river
kale (kah-leh) castle
kapı (kah-puh) gate

kilise (kih-lih-seh) church
köy (keuy) village
kümbet (keum-beht) mausoleum
kuyu (koo-yoo) well
mahalle (ma-hal-leh) city ward or district
mevki (mev-kee) place, site
meydan (may-dahn) square
nehir (neh-hihr) river
orman (ohr-mahn) forest
pınar (puh-nahr) spring
saray (sahr-iy) palace
şehir (sheh-hihr) city
sokak (soh-kahk) street
su (soo) stream
tepe (teh-peh) hill
yayla (yiy-lah) mountain pastureland
yol (yohl) road
Akdeniz (ahk-deh-nihz) Mediterranean ('white sea')
Karadeniz (kah-rah-deh-nihz) Black Sea
Ege Deniz (eg-eh deh-nihz) Aegean Sea
Trakya (trahk-yah) Thrace
Anadolu (ah-nah-doh-loo) Anatolia
Yunanistan (yoo-nan-ih-stan) Greece
Kıbrıs (kuh-bruhs) Cyprus

Directions

where is? *nerede?* (neh-reh-deh)
where is the police station? *karakol nerede?* (kah-rah-kol neh-reh-deh?)
where is the toilet? *tuvalet nerede?* (too-vah-let neh-reh-deh?)
north *kuzey* (koo-zay)
south *güney* (geu-nay)
west *batı* (bah-tuh)
east *doğu* (doh-oo)
left *sol* (sohl)
right *sağ* (sah)
short *kısa* (kuh-sah)
long *uzun* (oo-zoon)
near *yakın* (yah-kuhn)
far *uzak* (oo-zahk)
here *burada* (boo-rah-dah)
there *şurada* (shoo-rah-dah)
over there *orada* (o-rah-dah)
stop (noun) *durak* (doo-rahk)
stop! (imperative) *dur!* (door)
I want to get off *inecek var* (in-eh-jek vahr)
airport *hava alanı* (hah-vah ah-lah-nuh)
bus station *otogar* (oh-toh-gahr)
train station *gar, istasyon* (gahr, ihs-tas-yohn)
post office *postane* (pos-tah-neh)

petrol station *benzin istasyonu* (ben-zihn ihs-tahs-yohn-oo)
restaurant *lokanta* (loh-kahn-tah)
customs *gümrük* (geum-reuk)
port *liman* (lih-mahn)
quay *iskele* (ihs-keh-leh)
bridge *köprü* (ker-preu)

Time

morning *sabah* (sah-bah)
evening *akşam* (ahk-shahm)
night *gece* (geh-jeh)
week *hafta* (hahf-tah)
month *ay* (iy)
season *mevsim* (mev-sihm)
year *yil* (yihl)
this *bu* (boo)
next *gelecek* (gel-eh-jek)
now *şimdi* (shihm-dee)
today *bugün* (boo-geun)
tomorrow *yarın* (yahr-uhn)
yesterday *dün* (deun)
What time is it? *Kaç saat?* (kahtch saaht?)
At what time? *Kaçta?* (kahch-tah?)
When? *Ne zaman?* (neh zah-mahn?)

Days and Months

Monday *Pazartesi* (pah-zahr-teh-sih)
Tuesday *Salı* (sah-luh)
Wednesday *Çarşamba* (chahr-shahm-bah)
Thursday *Perşembe* (pehr-shem-beh)
Friday *Cuma* (joo-mah)
Saturday *Cumartesi* (joo-mar-teh-sih)
Sunday *Pazar* (pah-zahr)
January *Ocak* (o-jahk)
February *Şubat* (shoo-baht)
March *Mart* (mahrt)
April *Nisan* (nih-sahn)
May *Mayıs* (miy-uhs)
June *Haziran* (hah-zih-rahn)
July *Temmuz* (tem-mooz)
August *Ağustos* (ah-oos-tohs)
September *Eylül* (ai-leul)
October *Ekim* (eh-kihm)
November *Kasım* (kah-suhm)
December *Aralık* (ah-rah-luhk)

Numbers

one *bir* (bihr)
two *iki* (ih-kih)
three *üç* (eutch)
four *dört* (deurt)

five *beş* (besh)
six *altı* (ahl-tuh))
seven *yedi* (yeh-dih)
eight *sekiz* (seh-kihz)
nine *dokuz* (doh-kooz)
ten *on* (ohn)
eleven *onbir* (ohn-bihr)
twelve *oniki* (ohn-ih-kih)
twenty *yirmi* (yihr-mih)
twenty-one *yirmibir* (yihr-mihbihr)
thirty *otuz* (oh-tooz)
forty *kırk* (kuhrk)
fifty *elli* (el-lih)
sixty *altmış* (ahlt-muhsh)
seventy *yetmiş* (yet-mish)
eighty *seksen* (sek-sehn)
ninety *doksan* (dohk-sahn)
hundred *yüz* (yeuz)
two hundred *iki yüz* (ihk-yeuz)
564 *beş yüz altmış dört* (besh-yeuz-ahlt-muhsh-deurt)
thousand *bin* (bihn)
a thousand and one *bin bir* (bihn-bihr)
million *milyon* (mil-yoan)
billion *milyar* (mil-yahr)
2000 *iki bin* (ih-kih bihn)
2009 *iki bin dokuz* (ih-kih bihn doh-kooz)
half *yarım, buçuk* (yahr-uhm, boo-chook) (*buçuk* is used after numerals)
quarter *çeyrek* (chay-rehk)
...per cent *yüzde ...* (yeuz-deh)
first *ilk, birinci* (ihlk, bihr-ihn-jih)
tenth *onuncu* (ohn-oon-joo)
hundredth *yüzüncü* (yeuz-eun-jeu)

For a **number of objects**, use the word *tane* (tah-neh) (piece, unit, bit) after the number e.g. *iki tane bilet*, two tickets (not *iki biletler*).

Conversation

welcome *hoş geldiniz* (hohsh gehl-dihn-ihz)
reply to welcome *hoş bulduk* (hohsh bool-dook – we have found well)
I don't understand *anlamadım* (ahn-LAH-mah-duhm – stress second syllable)
I understand *anlıyorum* (ahn-luh-yohr-oom)
do you understand? *anlıyor musunuz?* (ahn-luh-yohr moo-soon-ooz)
yes *evet* (eh-veht)
no *hayır* (hiy-uhr)
there is *var* (vahr)
there's none *yok* (yohk)
perhaps *belki* (behl-kih)
I know *biliyorum* (bihl-ih-yohr-oom)

I don't know *bilmiyorum* (bihl-mih-yohr-oom – stress first syllable)
Do you speak English? *İngilizce biliyor musunuz?* (Ihng-ih-leez-jeh bihl-ih-yohr moo-soon-ooz?)
I don't speak Turkish *Türkçe bilmiyorum* (teurk-cheh bihl-mih-yohrum)
Do you speak Turkish? *Türkçe biliyor musunuz?* (Teurk-cheh bihl-ih-yohr moo-soon-ooz?)
a little *bir as* (bihr ahs)
like Tarzan *Tarzanca* (tahr-zahn-jah – i.e. 'broken' Turkish)
please *lütfen* (leut-fehn)
thank you **(very much)** *(Çok) teşekkür ederım* ((Chohk) tesh-eh-keur eh-deh-ruhm)
you're welcome *bir şey değil* (bihr shay dayl)
pardon, excuse me *affedersiniz* (ahf-feh-dehr-sih-niz)
goodbye *Allahaısmarladık* (ahl-ahuhs-mahr-lah-duhk – 'Allah go with you' – said by the person leaving)
goodbye *güle güle* (geu-leh geu-leh – 'smiling, smiling' – said by the person staying behind)
hello *merhaba* (mehr-hah-bah)
hello *selamaleyküm* (sehl-ahm-ahl-ay-keum)
hello (reply) *aleykümselam* (ahl-ay-keum-seh-lahm – 'peace be with you')
good day *günaydın* (geun-ahy-duhn)
good evening *iyi akşamlar* (eey ahk-shahm-lahr)
goodnight *iyi geceler* (eey geh-jeh-lehr)
slow, wait! *yavaş yavaş* (yah-vahsh yah-vahsh)
beautiful *güzel!* (geu-zehl – all-purpose compliment)
very good *çok iyi* (chohk eey)
How are you? *Nasılsınız?* (nah-suhl-suhn-uhz)
What is this/that? *Nu nedir? O nedir?* (noo/o neh-dihr)
How much is it? *Ne kadar?* (neh kah-dahr)
I want... *...istiyorum* (ihs-tih-yohr-um)
how? *niçin?* (nih-chihn)
wait a minute *bir dakika* (bihr dah-kih-kah)
useless! *yaramaz* (yahr-ah-mahz)
cheap *ucuz* (oo-jooz)
expensive *pahalı* (pah-hah-luh)
money *para* (pah-rah)
sick, ill *hasta* (hahs-tah)
hot *sıcak* (suh-jahk)
cold *soğuk* (so-ook)
old *eski* (es-kih)
new *yeni* (yeh-nih)

Glossary of Terms

acroterion acanthus-leaf decoration on the roofline of a Greek temple

acropolis citadel; usually the original habitation of a Greek city

agora market-place, public forum

ashlar masonry with squared stones laid in even courses

basilica a rectangular building of three aisles divided by columns: originally a Roman government building, later a form for Byzantine churches

bedesten an inner chamber of a Turkish market, built to keep safe the merchant's most valuable goods

bouleuterion council chamber of a Greek city

cami mosque

caravanserai inn for caravans and merchants

çarşı bazaar

cavea semicircle of seats in a Greek theatre

cella inner sanctum of a Greek temple

exedra semi-circular recess – space contained under a semi-dome

eyvan in early Ottoman mosques, a chamber to the side of the main prayer hall

Geometric style of early Greek pottery, roughly 900–700 BC, so called for its abstract geometric designs

gymnasium Greek or Roman school

hamam Turkish bath

han inn for merchants

heroon shrine of a hero – demigod or mortal

heykel statue

hisar a Turkish citadel or castle

kale a hisar

kapı a gate

kilim woven wool mat

kilise Turkish for church

külliye complex of pious foundations (educational or charitable) around a mosque

kümbet a *türbe* (*q.v.*)

medrese old school of theology

megaron large house from Mycenaean period

mescid/mescit a place set aside for Muslim prayer; it may be anything from a small mosque in a palace or *han* to a simple room in a bus station

mihrab niche in a mosque indicating the direction of Mecca

mimber mosque pulpit

naos the inner chamber of a temple, containing the cult image

narthex outer porch of a church

nave central aisle of a basilica-form church

nymphaion sanctuary of nymphs, or public fountain

oculus a circular opening at the top of a dome

odeion concert hall

orchestra the circular space at the centre of an ancient theatre; originally the dancing ground, later the centre of the action in early Greek drama

palaestra exercise ground of a gymnasium

pendentives (also known as squinches) spherical sections that support a dome over a square space

prytaneion committee room of a bouleuterion (*see* above), locale of a city's sacred fire

şadirvan mosque fountain

stele an upright stone, decorated with inscriptions or a relief, often a gravestone

stoa large colonnaded porch attached to another building

tekke dervish lodge

temenos sacred enclosure of a temple

türbe a mausoleum for a ruler, political dignitary or holy man. In Turkey they are usually free-standing structures with six or eight sides, and a round or prismatic dome

Further Reading

History

Ancient History

Akurgal, Ekrem, *Ancient Civilizations and Ruins of Turkey* (Türk Tarih Kurumu, Ankara, 1983). The indispensable guide for anyone interested in exploring Turkey's innumerable archaeological sites in detail (though weak on eastern Anatolia).

Apollonius of Rhodes, *The Voyage of Argo*, translated by E. V. Rieu (Penguin, 1971). Jason's journey along the Black Sea coast.

Arrian, *The Campaigns of Alexander*, translated by Aubrey de Sélincourt (Penguin, 1971).

Bean, George, *Aegean Turkey*, 1966; *Turkey's Southern Shore*, 1968; *Turkey Beyond the Maeander*, 1971; *Lycia*, 1978 (Ernest Benn). Fine, anecdotal accounts and detailed guides to Turkey's Greek and Roman sites, by a scholar who discovered not a few of them himself.

Bittel, Kurt, *Guide to Boğazköy* (Ankara, 1972). A must for all Hittite fans, by the archaeologists who excavated their capital.

Erzen, Prof. Dr. Afif, *Eastern Anatolia and the Urartians* (Türk Tarih Kurumu, Ankara, 1984).

Mellaart, James, *Earliest Civilizations of the Near East* (Thames and Hudson, 1965) and *Çatal Höyük* (Thames and Hudson, 1967). Two fascinating books by the archaeologist who uncovered the most important site in the Middle East since Schliemann.

Sandars, N.K., *The Sea Peoples: Warriors of the Ancient Mediterranean* (Thames and Hudson, 1978). The true story of the dark age that brought down the curtain on Troy and the Hittites.

Sinclair, T.A., *Eastern Turkey: An Architectural and Archaeological Survey* (Pindar Press, 1987). The three volumes of this work contain all you could possibly want to know, but, at £135 per volume, are beyond the means of the average pocket.

Wood, Michael, *In Search of the Trojan War* (BBC, 1985). A good compilation of current thought on Troy, from the popular TV series.

Young, Rodney S., *Gordion* (Ankara, 1975). More about the Phrygians.

Byzantines and Ottomans

Barber, Noel, *The Sultans* (Simon and Schuster, 1973). The inside story.

Billings, Malcolm, *The Cross and the Crescent* (BBC Publications, 1987). A history of the Crusades.

Goodwin, Godfrey, *A History of Ottoman Architecture* (Thames and Hudson, 1971). The best book on the subject.

Goodwin, Jason, *Lords of the Horizons* (Vintage, 1999). A very readable history of the Ottoman sultans and their culture.

Finkel, Caroline, *Osman's Dream: The History of the Ottoman Empire* (Basic Books, 2007). A revisionist history, and a welcome attempt to overcome some of the old Western prejudices and misconceptions of a state that lasted six centuries.

Lord Kinross, *The Ottoman Centuries* (Morrow, NY/Jonathan Cape, London, 1977). A well-known popular history.

Mansel, Philip, *Constantinople, City of the World's Desire 1453–1924* (St Martin's Griffin, 1998). It's Istanbul, not Constantinople, but this is still a fine biography of the city in Ottoman times, full of fascinating detail.

Norwich, John Julius, *Byzantium: The Early Centuries* (1990), *Byzantium: The Apogee* (1993), *Byzantium: Decline and Fall* (1996), *A Short History of Byzantium* (1998), all Penguin. A marvellously readable and entertaining history of the Byzantine empire. The

Short History is a one-volume abridgement of the previous three.

Rodley, Lyn, *Cave Monasteries of Byzantine Cappadocia* (Cambridge, 1986).

Runciman, Steven, *Byzantine Civilization* (Edward Arnold, London, 1933), and *The Fall of Constantinople, 1453* (Cambridge University Press, 1965). Excellent accounts by the foremost scholar in the field, coloured by a dislike of both Muslims and Turks.

Shaw, Stanford and Ezel, Kual, *History of the Ottoman Empire and Modern Turkey*, 2 vols (Cambridge University Press, 1976).

Modern Turkey

Garnett, Lucy M. J., *The Turkish People: their social life, religious beliefs, institutions and domestic life* (Methuen, London AMS Press NY, 1909). Hard to find but very interesting account by a turn-of-the-century traveller.

Hotham, David, *The Turks* (Murray, London, 1972). One of the best books about modern Turkey.

Kazancagil, Ali and Özbudun, Ergun, eds, *Atatürk, founder of a modern state* (Anchor Hambden, Conn, 1981).

Kinzer, Stephen, *Crescent and Star* (Farrar, Strauss and Giroux, 2008). A *New York Times* reporter's take on the nation and its prospects. Kinzer recommends more democracy.

Lewis, Bernard, *The Emergence of Modern Turkey* (Oxford Library Press, 1968).

Michaud, Roland and Sabrina, *Turkey* (Thames and Hudson, 1986). Magnificent photographs.

Morris, Chris, *The New Turkey: Quiet Revolution on the Edge of Europe* (Granta, 2006). A good guide to the country's

convoluted politics and the eternal Kurdish question.

Pamuk, Orhan, *Istanbul: Memories and the City* (Faber, 2005). The Nobel-winning novelist (*see* p.531) recounts his life-long love affair with his native city and its ineffable quality of *hüzün*, or melancholy. A better evocation of modern Istanbul couldn't be done.

Volkan, Vamik D., Itzkowitz, Norman, *The Immortal Atatürk, A Psychobiography*. Unintentionally hilarious ('Little Mustafa's grandiose self was his basic character trait').

Religion and Folklore

And, Metin, *Karagoz: Turkish Shadow Theatre* (Dost, İstanbul, 1979). An excellent account of a dying art, readily available in Turkey.

Nicholson, Reynold A., trans., *Rumi: Poet and Mystic* (George Allen & Unwin, 1950). An introduction to the great Sufi teacher, the Mevlâna.

Önder, Mehmed, *Mevlâna and Mevlâna Museum* (Istanbul, 1985). Story of the Mevlâna's life in Konya.

Walker, Warren S. & Uysal, Ahmet E., *Tales Alive in Turkey* (Harvard University Press, 1966). An absorbing collection of Turkish folk tales and lore.

Travel Writing

Burnaby, Frederick, *On Horseback Through Asia Minor* (Alan Sutton, 1985). A fascinating account of a journey undertaken in the winter of 1876/7.

Freely, John, *Istanbul: the Imperial City* (Penguin, 1998). A sort of travel guide through time, explaining İstanbul's history and development. Very readable.

Turkey on Film

Photographer and film-maker **Nuri Bilge Ceylan** has received international acclaim for his stunning cinematography and starkly poetic studies of relationships and the human condition. Ceylan's slow-moving pace and minimal use of dialogue is not to everyone's taste but, like classical music, his films have an international resonance. Whilst his place in world cinema is assured, in Turkey few people attend his movies, preferring instead the slapstick, caricature nonsense served up by soap opera directors. *Uzak* and *Climates* are his best features to date, and his latest film *Kül* is in the pipeline at the time of writing. See *www.nuribilgeceylan.com*.

Other contemporary directors of note include **Fatih Akın**, with his impressive features *Head On* and *The Edge of Heaven*, and **Özer Kızıltan** with *Takva*, offering a rare insight into an Islamic sect.

Orhan Pamuk

Turkey's first Nobel Prize-winning novelist, born in 1952 to a wealthy family and raised in the Nişantasi district of Istanbul, where he still lives today, Pamuk is Turkey's best selling author by far. His novels are typically set amidst a backdrop of the East and West cultural clash, or explore the volatile relationship between religion and the secular state. Pamuk's outspoken nature on politically sensitive issues such as the Kurdish problem has seen him in trouble with the authorities on more than one occasion; in 2005 he was charged with 'insulting Turkishness' when he commented on the nation's reluctance to discuss openly the alleged killing of Armenians in 1915; the case was later dropped. See *www.orhanpamuk.net*.

Among the Nobel Prize winner's many works in translation are:

My Name is Red (Vintage, 2002). Art, intrigue and murder in 16th-century Istanbul.

Snow (Vintage, 2005). A political exile returns home, and experiences the existential tangles of modern Turkey in the frozen and forlorn eastern town of Kars.

The White Castle (Vintage, 1998). Intricate psychological tale of an Italian who becomes a slave at the Ottoman court.

Glazebrook, Philip, *Journey to Kars* (Penguin, 1985).

Pereira, Michael, *East of Trebizond* (Geoffrey Bles, 1971). For those interested in Tao-Georgia.

Stark, Freya, *Alexander's Path* (Century, 1984); and *Ionia* (Century, 1988). Two beautiful, evocative accounts that bring Turkey's ancient cities to life.

Literature

Cleary, Jon, *The Fall of an Eagle* (1964). Romantic thriller set in Cappadocia.

De Bernières, Louis, *Birds Without Wings* (Vintage, 2005). From the author of *Captain Corelli's Mandolin*, a novel on an epic scale set against the grisly end of the Ottoman Empire and the establishment of modern Turkey.

Dunnett, Dorothy, *Pawn in Frankincense* (Cassell, 1969, also available as an Arrow paperback). An historical adventure story featuring Süleyman, Roxelana, Dragut and others mentioned in this guide.

Kemal, Yaşar, *Mehmed, My Hawk*, 1961; The Lords of Akchasaz, 1979; and *The Sea-Crossed Fisherman* (1985, Collins and Harvill). Novelist from the back of the Anatolian beyond, Kemal draws on rural stories and folklore in his internationally popular works. More of his books are available in English translation.

Macauley, Rose, *The Towers of Trebizond* (Futura, 1981). A classic and very funny novel about a journey in Turkey with the wonderful eccentrics Aunt Dot and Father Chantry-Pigg.

Chronology

BC

c. 50,000	Neanderthal man inhabiting southwestern Anatolia
c. 8500	Oldest known urban society flourishes at Çatal Höyük
c. 5000	Neolithic cultures in southern Anatolia
c. 2500	Hatti people reach the height of their culture in the Kızılırmak valley region
c. 2000	Arrival of Hittites in Anatolia
c. 1720	Hattusas becomes Hittite capital
c. 1600	*Mursilis I (Hittite)*
c. 1450–1400	Series of long wars, between Egypt (19th dynasty) and the Hurri-Mitanni kingdom of east Anatolia
c. 1400	Extension of literacy to Anatolia
1380–1346	*Suppiluliumas (Hittite)*
1259	Treaty of Kadesh between Hittites and Egyptians – earliest recorded peace treaty
1260–1240	*Tudhalyas IV (Hittite)*
c. 1200	Destruction of the Hittite Empire
c. 1180	Fall of Troy
c. 1000	Greeks begin to colonize Aegean coast
c. 900	Anatolian wool and timber begin to enter main Mediterranean trade routes
c. 760	*Sarduri I (Urartian)*
c. 750	Sinope, first Greek town on Black Sea, colonized by Miletus
c. 700	*'King Midas' (Phrygia)*
717	Sack of Carchemish by Assyrians
690	Cimmerians raid throughout Anatolia
612	Medes conquer Urartians, Assyria
c. 600	Kingdom of Cappadocia begins
550–530	*King Cyrus (Persia)*

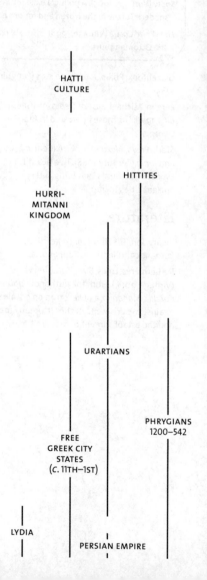

HATTI CULTURE

HITTITES

HURRI-MITANNI KINGDOM

URARTIANS

PHRYGIANS 1200–542

FREE GREEK CITY STATES (C. 11TH–1ST)

LYDIA

PERSIAN EMPIRE

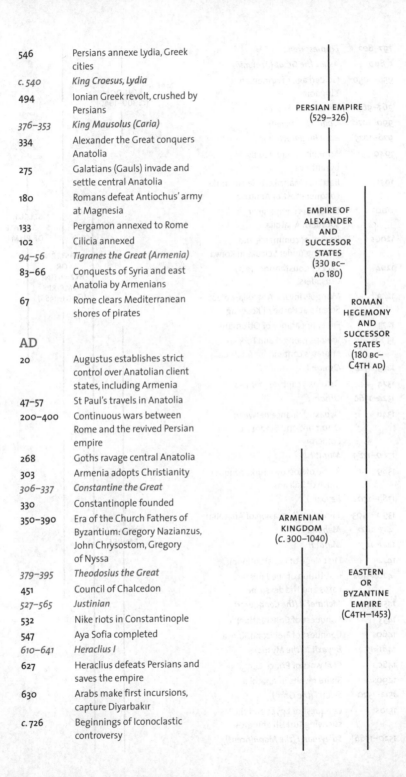

20 Chronology

546	Persians annexe Lydia, Greek cities	
c. 540	*King Croesus, Lydia*	
494	Ionian Greek revolt, crushed by Persians	**PERSIAN EMPIRE** (529–326)
376–353	*King Mausolus (Caria)*	
334	Alexander the Great conquers Anatolia	
275	Galatians (Gauls) invade and settle central Anatolia	
180	Romans defeat Antiochus' army at Magnesia	**EMPIRE OF ALEXANDER AND SUCCESSOR STATES** (330 BC–AD 180)
133	Pergamon annexed to Rome	
102	Cilicia annexed	
94–56	*Tigranes the Great (Armenia)*	
83–66	Conquests of Syria and east Anatolia by Armenians	
67	Rome clears Mediterranean shores of pirates	**ROMAN HEGEMONY AND SUCCESSOR STATES** (180 BC–C4TH AD)

AD

20	Augustus establishes strict control over Anatolian client states, including Armenia	
47–57	St Paul's travels in Anatolia	
200–400	Continuous wars between Rome and the revived Persian empire	
268	Goths ravage central Anatolia	
303	Armenia adopts Christianity	
306–337	*Constantine the Great*	
330	Constantinople founded	
350–390	Era of the Church Fathers of Byzantium: Gregory Nazianzus, John Chrysostom, Gregory of Nyssa	**ARMENIAN KINGDOM** (c. 300–1040)
379–395	*Theodosius the Great*	
451	Council of Chalcedon	**EASTERN OR BYZANTINE EMPIRE** (C4TH–1453)
527–565	*Justinian*	
532	Nike riots in Constantinople	
547	Aya Sofia completed	
610–641	*Heraclius I*	
627	Heraclius defeats Persians and saves the empire	
630	Arabs make first incursions, capture Diyarbakır	
c. 726	Beginnings of Iconoclastic controversy	

797–802	*Empress Irene*	
c. 860	*Ashot the Great (Armenia)*	
950–1050	Golden age of Armenian Kingdom	ARMENIAN KINGDOM (c. 300–1040)
963–969	*Nicephorus Phocas*	
990–1020	*Gagik I (Armenia)*	
976–1025	*Basil Bulgaroctonus*	
1040	Armenia conquered by Byzantines	
1071	Battle of Manzikert; Selcuk Turks conquer most of Anatolia	
1100s	Crusaders campaign in southern Anatolia	SELCUK SULTANATE OF RUM
1200s	Revival of commerce and learning under Selcuks in Konya	EASTERN OR BYZANTINE EMPIRE (C4TH–1453)
1204	Sack of Constantinople by Crusaders	
1243	Mongols invade Anatolia; defeat Selcuks at Battle of Kösedağ	
1273	First appearance of Ottomans	
1300s	Various Mongol and Turkish emirates contend for Anatolia	
1293–1324	*Osman I*	
1324	Ottoman capture of Bursa	
1324–1360	*Orhan*	
1346	Dynastic alliance between Ottomans and Byzantine Emperor	CRUSADERS
1360–1389	*Murat I*	
1389	Battle of Kossovo: Turks conquer much of Balkans	
1389–1402	*Beyazit I*	
1390–1403	Tamerlane's invasion of Anatolia	
1413–1421	*Mehmet I*	OTTOMAN EMPIRE
1421–1451	*Murat II*	
1422	First siege of Constantinople	
1420s–30s	Institution of the Janissary corps and the devşirme	
1451–1481	*Mehmet II (the Conqueror)*	
1453	Conquest of Constantinople	
1460s	Conquest of Trebizond, Konya	
1481–1512	*Beyazit II (the Mystic)*	
1480s	Civil wars of Prince Cem	
1490s	Shiite revolts in Anatolia	
1512–1520	*Selim I (the Grim)*	
1510s	Conquest of Egypt and the last surviving Turkish emirates	
1520–1566	*Süleyman I (the Magnificent)*	

20 Chronology

Index

Main page references are in **bold**. Page references to maps are in *italics*.

About the Updater

Ever since leaving Turkey at the age of seven, **Serkan Çetin** had a yearning to return, so much so that he put aside his career as a sound engineer and documentary film maker to set up his own specialist travel company, **Journey Anatolia**, partly as an excuse to enjoy more time in his native land, and partly to fulfil his passion for sharing its wonders.

Updater's Acknowledgements

Serkan would like to thank İlke Durmay and the excellent team at Geo Tourism for opening the doors we knocked on; Esra Çıtlak for additional hotel research; Pelin Turgut for her assistance with current affairs; Ömer and Sarah Çalık, Evrim Tüfekcioğlu, Mike Miners and Jo Grimwood for their assistance in Patara, İzmir, Cappadocia and Marmaris respectively; and Phil Buckley for his help in Kaş.

First American edition published in 2009 by

CADOGAN GUIDES USA
An imprint of Interlink Publishing Group, Inc.
46 Crosby Street, Northampton, Massachusetts 01060
www.interlinkbooks.com
www.interlinkbooks.com/cadoganguides

Text Copyright © Dana Facaros and Michael Pauls 1986, 1988, 1993, 2000, 2009
Copyright © New Holland Publishers (UK) Ltd., 2009

Cover and photo essay photographs: © Serkan Çetin
Maps © Cadogan Guides, drawn by Maidenhead Cartographic Services Ltd
Cover design: Jason Hopper
Photo essay design: Sarah Rianhard-Gardner
Editor: Linda McQueen
Proofreading: Dominique Shead
Indexing: Isobel McLean

Printed and bound in Italy by Legoprint
Library of Congress Cataloging-in-Publication Data available

ISBN: 978-1-56656-762-6

To request our complete full-color catalog, please call us toll free at 1-800-238-LINK, visit our website at www.interlinkbooks.com, or send us an e-mail: info@interlinkbooks.com